I0047623

CRIMINAL INVESTIGATION:

HANDBOOK FOR SPECIAL AGENTS

INTERNAL REVENUE SERVICE

INTELLIGENCE DIVISION

Books for Business
New York - Hong Kong

Criminal Investigation: Handbook for Special Agents

by

Internal Revenue Service
Intelligence Division

ISBN: 0-89499-220-1

Reprinted from the original edition

Books for Business
New York - Hong Kong
http://www.BusinessBooksInternational.com

Table of Contents

Table of Contents

(Next page is 9781-2.1)

Table of Contents

Table of Contents

Table of Contents

Table of Contents

Table of Contents

400
Tax Cases (Evidence and Procedure)

Table of Contents

Table of Contents

500
Procedures and Techniques in Other Investigations

600
Reports

Table of Contents

700
Federal Court Procedures and Related Matters

Table of Contents

EXHIBITS

Table of Contents

(Next page is 9781–3)

210 *(1-18-80)* 9781
Introduction

This chapter contains the complete text of the sections of Title 18, United States Code, that may be involved in criminal investigations; the more frequently used penal and civil penalties of the Internal Revenue Code of 1954 (Title 26, United States Code); and the sections of Title 18 and the Internal Revenue Code of 1954 relating to limitations on criminal prosecution. The less frequently used penalties of the internal revenue codes and the sections concerning periods of limitation for assessment and collection of tax are set forth in outline form.

220 *(1-18-80)* 9781
Criminal Penalties Applicable to Fraud and Miscellaneous Investigations

221 *(1-18-80)* 9781
Internal Revenue Code of 1954

221.1 *(1-18-80)* 9781
Effective Date and Application

Chapter 75 of the Internal Revenue Code of 1954, entitled Crimes, Other Offenses, and Forfeitures, is effective for offenses committed after August 16, 1954. The following penal sections of chapter 75 apply to all taxes imposed by Title 26, United States Code (Internal Revenue Code of 1954) unless the particular section states that it applies to a specific tax.

221.2 *(1-18-80)* 9781
IRC 7201. Attempt to Evade or Defeat Tax

"Any person who willfully attempts in any manner to evade or defeat any tax imposed by this title or the payment thereof shall, in addition to other penalties provided by law, be guilty of a felony and, upon conviction thereof, shall be fined not more than $10,000, or imprisoned not more than 5 years, or both, together with the costs of prosecution." See text 413 and IRM 9212.

221.3 *(1-18-80)* 9781
IRC 7202. Willful Failure to Collect or Pay Over Tax

"Any person required under this title to collect, account for, and pay over any tax imposed by this title who willfully fails to collect or truthfully account for and pay over such tax shall, in addition to other penalties provided by law, be guilty of a felony and, upon conviction thereof, shall be fined not more than $10,000, or imprisoned not more than 5 years, or both, together with the costs of prosecution." See text 414 and IRM 9212.

221.4 *(1-18-80)* 9781
IRC 7203. Willful Failure to File Return, Supply Information, or Pay Tax

"Any person required under this title to pay any estimated tax or tax, or required by this title or by regulations made under authority thereof to make a return (other than a return required under authority of section 6015), keep any records, or supply any information, who willfully fails to pay such estimated tax or tax, make such return, keep such records, or supply such information, shall, in addition to other penalties provide by law, be guilty of a misdemeanor and, upon conviction thereof, shall be fined not more than $10,000, or imprisoned not more than 1 year, or both, together with the costs of prosecution." See text 415 and IRM 9212.

221.5 *(1-18-80)* 9781
IRC 7204. Fraudulent Statement or Failure to Make Statement to Employees

[Applies to withholding statements required of employers.]

"In lieu of any other penalty provided by law (except the penalty provided by section 6674) any person required under the provisions of section 6051 to furnish a statement who willfully furnishes a false or fraudulent statement or who willfully fails to furnish a statement in the manner, at the time, and showing the information required under section 6051, or regulations prescribed thereunder, shall, for each such offense, upon conviction thereof, be fined not more than $1,000, or imprisoned not more than 1 year, or both." See text 416 and IRM 9212.

221.6 *(12-7-81)* 9781
IRC 7205. Fraudulent Withholding Exemption Certificate or Failure to Supply Information

"Any individual required to supply information to his employer under section 3402 who willfully supplies false or fraudulent information, or who willfully fails to supply information thereunder which would require an increase in the tax to be withheld under section 3402, shall, in lieu of any other penalty provided by law (except the penalty provided by section 6682), upon conviction thereof, be fined not more than $500, or imprisoned not more than 1 year, or both." See text 417 and IRM 9212. The Economic Recovery Act of 1981 raised the fine from $500 to $1,000 for acts and failures to act after December 31, 1981.

221.7 *(5-9-80)* 9781

IRC 7206. Fraud and False Statements

"Any person who—

"(1) *Declaration Under Penalties of Perjury.*—Willfully makes and subscribes any return, statement, or other document, which contains or is verified by a written declaration that it is made under the penalties of perjury, and which he does not believe to be true and correct as to every material matter; or

"(2) *Aid or Assistance.*—Willfully aids or assists in, or procures, counsels, or advises the preparation or presentation under, or in connection with any matter arising under, the internal revenue laws, of a return, affidavit, claim, or other document, which is fraudulent or is false as to any material matter, whether or not such falsity or fraud is with the knowledge or consent of the person authorized or required to present such return, affidavit, claim, or document; or

"(3) *Fraudulent Bonds, Permits, and Entries.*—Simulates or falsely or fraudulently executes or signs any bond, permit, entry, or other document required by the provisions of the internal revenue laws, or by any regulation made in pursuance thereof, or procures the same to be falsely or fraudulently executed, or advises, aids in, or connives at such execution thereof; or

"(4) *Removal or Concealment With Intent to Defraud.*—Removes, deposits, or conceals, or is concerned in removing, depositing, or concealing, any goods or commodities for or in respect whereof any tax is or shall be imposed, or any property upon which levy is authorized by section 6331, with intent to evade or defeat the assessment or collection of any tax imposed by this title; or

"(5) *Compromises and Closing Agreements.*—In connection with any compromise under section 7122, or offer of such compromise, or in connection with any closing agreement under section 7121, or offer to enter into any such agreement, willfully—

"(A) *Concealment of Property.*—Conceals from any officer or employee of the United States any property belonging to the estate of a taxpayer or other person liable in respect of the tax, or

"(B) *Withholding, Falsifying, and Destroying Records.*—Receives, withholds, destroys, mutilates, or falsifies any book, document or record, or makes any false statement, relating to the estate or financial condition of the taxpayer or other person liable in respect of the tax; shall be guilty of a felony and, upon conviction thereof, shall be fined not more than $5,000, or imprisoned not more than 3 years, or both, together with the costs of prosecution." See text 418.1 and 418.2 and IRM 9212.

221.8 *(5-9-80)* 9781

IRC 7207. Fraudulent Returns, Statements, or Other Documents

"Any person who willfully delivers or discloses to the Secretary or his delegate any list, return, account, statement, or other document, known by him to be fraudulent or to be false as to any material matter, shall be fined not more than $1,000, or imprisoned not more than 1 year, or both." See text 418.3 and IRM 9212.

221.9 *(5-9-80)* 9781

IRC 7210. Failure to Obey Summons

"Any person who, being duly summoned to appear to testify, or to appear and produce books, accounts, records, memoranda, or other papers, as required under sections 7602, 7603, and 7604(b), neglects to appear or to produce such books, accounts, records, memoranda, or other papers, shall, upon conviction thereof, be fined not more than $1,000, or imprisoned not more than 1 year, or both, together with costs of prosecution." See text 36(10).4 and IRM 9212.

221.(10) *(5-9-80)* 9781

IRC 7212. Attempts to Interfere With Administration of Internal Revenue Laws

"(a) *Corrupt or Forcible Interference.*—Whoever corruptly or by force or threats of force (including any threatening letter or communication) endeavors to intimidate or impede any officer or employee of the United States acting in an official capacity under this title, or in any other way corruptly or by force or threats of force (including any threatening letter or communication) obstructs or impedes, or endeavors to obstruct or impede, the due administration of this title, shall, upon conviction thereof, be fined not more than $5,000, or imprisoned not more than 3 years, or both, except that if the offense is committed only by threats of force, the person convicted thereof shall be fined not more than $3,000, or imprisoned not more than 1 year, or both. The term "threats of force," as used in this subsection, means threats of bodily harm to the officer or employee of the United States or to a member of his family. See text 511 and IRM 9212.

"(b) *Forcible Rescue of Seized Property.*—Any person who forcibly rescues or causes to be rescued any property after it shall have been seized under this title, or shall attempt or endeavor so to do, shall, excepting in cases otherwise provided for, for every such offense, be fined not more than $500, or not more than double the value of the property so rescued, whichever is the greater, or be imprisoned not more than 2 years." See text 512.

221.(11) *(1-18-80)* 9781
Other Criminal Penalties

See Exhibit 200-1 for a listing of other criminal penalties.

221.(12) *(5-9-80)* 9781
IRC 7215. Offenses With Respect to Collected Taxes

"(a) *Penalty.*—Any person who fails to comply with any provision of section 7512(b) shall, in addition to any other penalties provided by law, be guilty of a misdemeanor, and, upon conviction thereof, shall be fined not more than $5,000, or imprisoned not more than one year; or both, together with the costs of prosecution.

"(b) *Exceptions.*—This section shall not apply—

"(1) to any person, if such person shows that there was reasonable doubt as to (A) whether the law required collection of tax, or (B) who was required by law to collect tax, and

"(2) to any person, if such person shows that the failure to comply with the provisions of section 7512(b) was due to circumstances beyond his control.

"For purposes of paragraph (2), a lack of funds existing immediately after the payment of wages (whether or not created by the payment of such wages) shall not be considered to be circumstances beyond the control of a person." See text 414.2 and IRM 9212.

221.(13) *(1-18-80)* 9781
IRC 7512. Separate Accounting for Certain Collected Taxes, Etc.

"(a) *General Rule.*—Whenever any person who is required to collect, account for, and pay over any tax imposed by subtitle C or by chapter 33—

"(1) at the time and in the manner prescribed by law or regulations (A) fails to collect, truthfully account for, or pay over such tax, or (B) fails to make deposits, payments, or returns of such tax, and

"(2) is notified, by notice delivered in hand to such person of any such failure, "then all the requirements of subsection (b) shall be complied with. In the case of a corporation, partnership, or trust notice delivered in hand to an officer, partner, or trustee, shall, for the purposes of this section, be deemed to be notice delivered in hand to such corporation, partnership, or trust to all officers, partners, trustees, and employees thereof.

"(b) *Requirements.*—Any person who is required to collect, account for, and pay over any tax imposed by subtitle C or by chapter 33, if notice has been delivered to such person in accordance with subsection (a), shall collect the taxes imposed by subtitle C or chapter 33 which become collectible after delivery of such notice, shall (not later than the end of the second banking day after any amount of such taxes is collected) deposit such amount in a separate account in a bank (as defined in section 581), and shall keep the amount of such taxes in such account until payment over to the United States. Any such account shall be designated as a special fund in trust for the United States, payable to the United States by such person as trustee.

"(c) *Relief From Further Compliance With Subsection (b).*—Whenever the Secretary or his delegate is satisfied, with respect to any notification made under subsection (a), that all requirements of law and regulations with respect to the taxes imposed by subtitle C or chapter 33, as the case may be, will henceforth be complied with, he may cancel such notification. Such cancellation shall take effect at such time as is specified in the notice of such cancellation."

222 *(1-18-80)* 9781
Title 18, United States Code

222.1 *(1-18-80)* 9781
Introduction

The following penal sections of Title 18 apply to violations that may be encountered in connection with Criminal Investigation Division investigations.

222.2 *(1-18-80)* 9781
Section 2. Principals

"(a) Whoever commits an offense against the United States, or aids, abets, counsels, commands, induces or procures its commission, is punishable as a principal.

"(b) Whoever willfully causes an act to be done, which if directly performed by him or another would be an offense against the United States, is punishable as a principal." See IRM 9213.

222.3 *(1-18-80)* 9781
Section 3. Accessory After the Fact

"Whoever, knowing that an offense against the United States has been committed, receives, relieves, comforts or assists the offender in order to hinder or prevent his apprehension, trial or punishment, is an accessory after the fact.

"Except as otherwise expressly provided by any Act of Congress, an accessory after the fact shall be imprisoned not more than one-half the maximum term of imprisonment or fined not more than one-half the maximum fine prescribed for the punishment of the principal, or both; or if the principal is punishable by death, the accessory shall be imprisoned not more than ten years." See IRM 9213.

222.4 *(1-18-80)* 9781
Section 4. Misprison of Felony

"Whoever, having knowledge of the actual commission of a felony cognizable by a court of the United States, conceals and does not as soon as possible make known the same to some judge or other person in civil or military authority under the United States, shall be fined not more than $500 or imprisoned not more than three years, or both." See IRM 9213.

222.5 *(1-18-80)* 9781
Section 111. Assaulting, Resisting, or Impeding Certain Officers or Employees

[The provisions of IRC 7212 relating to Attempts to interfere with Administration of Internal Revenue Laws are set forth in 221.(10).]

"Whoever forcibly assaults, resists, opposes, impedes, intimidates, or interferes with any person designated in section 1114 of this title while engaged in or on account of the performance of his official duties, shall be fined not more than $5,000 or imprisoned not more than three years, or both.

"Whoever, in the commission of any such acts uses a deadly or dangerous weapon, shall be fined not more than $10,000 or imprisoned not more than ten years, or both." See text 411.2 and IRM 9213.

222.6 *(1-18-80)* 9781
Section 201. Offer to Officer or Other Person

"Whoever promises, offers, or gives any money or thing of value, or makes or tenders any check, order, contract, undertaking, obligation, gratuity, or security for the payment of money or for the delivery or conveyance of anything of value, to any officer or employee or person acting for or on behalf of the United States, or any department or agency thereof, in any official function, under or by authority of any such department or agency or to any officer or person acting for or on behalf of either House of Congress, or of any committee of either House, or both Houses thereof, with intent to influence his decision or action on any question, matter, cause, or proceeding which may at any time be pending, or which may by law be brought before him in his official capacity, or in his place of trust or profit, or with intent to influence him to commit or aid in committing, or to collude in, or allow, any fraud, or make opportunity for the commission of any fraud, on the United States, or to induce him to do or omit to do any act in violation of his lawful duty, shall be fined not more than three times the amount of such money or value of such thing or imprisoned not more than three years, or both."

"This section shall not apply to violations of section 212 of this title." (Section 212 relates to an offer or threat to a customs officer or employee.) See text 420 and IRM 9213.

222.7 *(5-9-80)* 9781
(Reserved)

222.8 *(1-18-80)* 9781
Section 285. Taking or Using Papers Relating to Claims

"Whoever, without authority, takes and carries away from the place where it was filed, deposited, or kept by authority of the United States, any certificate, affidavit, deposition, statement of facts, power of attorney, receipt, voucher, assignment, or other document, record, file, or paper prepared, fitted, or intended to be used or presented to procure the payment of money from or by the United States or any officer, employee, or agent thereof, or the allowance or payment of the whole or any part of any claim, account, or demand against the United States, whether the same has or has not already been so used or presented, and whether such claim, account, or demand, or any part thereof has or has not already been allowed or paid; or

"Whoever presents, uses, or attempts to use any such document, record, file, or paper so taken and carried away, to procure the payment of any money from or by the United States, or any officer, employee, or agent thereof, or the allowance or payment of the whole or any part of any claim, account, or demand against the United States—

"Shall be fined not more than $5,000 or imprisoned not more than five years, or both." See IRM 9213.

222.9 *(1-18-80)* 9781

Section 286. Conspiracy to Defraud the Government With Respect to Claims

"Whoever enters into any agreement, combination, or conspiracy to defraud the United States, or any department or agency thereof, by obtaining or aiding to obtain the payment or allowance of any false, fictitious or fraudulent claim, shall be fined not more than $10,000 or imprisoned not more than ten years, or both." See IRM 9213

222.(10) *(1-18-80)* 9781

Section 287. False, Fictitous or Fraudulent Claims

"Whoever makes or presents to any person or officer in the civil, military, or naval service of the United States, or to any department or agency thereof, any claim upon or against the United States, or any department or agency thereof, knowing such claim to be false, fictitous, or fraudulent, shall be fined not more than $10,000 or imprisoned not more than five years, or both." See Text 318.5 and IRM 9213.

222.(11) *(1-18-80)* 9781

Section 371. Conspiracy to Commit Offense or to Defraud United States

"If two or more persons conspire either to commit any offense against the United States, or to defraud the United States, or any agency thereof in any manner or for any purpose, and one or more of such persons do any act to effect the object of the conspiracy, each shall be fined not more than $10,000 or imprisoned not more than five years, or both.

"If, however, the offense, the commission of which is the object of the conspiracy, is a misdemeanor only, the punishment for such conspiracy shall not exceed the maximum punishment provided for such misdemeanor." See Text 31(10) and IRM 9213.

222.(12) *(1-18-80)* 9781

Section 372. Conspiracy to Impede or Injure Officer

"If two or more persons in any State, Territory, Possession, or District conspire to prevent, by force, intimidation, or threat, any person from accepting or holding any office, trust, or place of confidence under the United States, or from discharging any duties thereof, or to induce by like means any officer of the United States to leave the place, where his duties as an officer are required to be performed, or to injure him in his person or property on account of his lawful discharge of the duties of his office, or while engaged in the lawful discharge thereof, or to injure his property so as to molest, interrupt, hinder, or impede him in the discharge of his official duties, each of such persons shall be fined not more than $5,000 or imprisoned not more than six years, or both." See IRM 9213.

222.(13) *(1-18-80)* 9781

Section 494. Contractors' Bonds, Bids, and Public Records

"Whoever falsely makes, alters, forges, or counterfeits any bond, bid, proposal, contract, guarantee, security, official bond, public record, affidavit, or other writing for the purpose of defrauding the United States; or

"Whoever utters or publishes as true or possesses with intent to utter or publish as true, any such false, forged, altered, or counterfeited writing, knowing the same to be false, forged, altered, or counterfeited; or

"Whoever transmits to, or presents at any office or to any officer of the United States, any such false, forged, altered or counterfeited writing, knowing the same to be false, forged, altered, or counterfeited—

"Shall be fined not more than $1,000 or imprisoned not more than ten years, or both." See IRM 9213.

222.(14) *(1-18-80)* 9781

Section 495. Contracts, Deeds, and Powers of Attorney

"Whoever falsely makes, alters, forges, or counterfeits any deed, power of attorney, order, certificate, receipt, contract, or other writing, for the purpose of obtaining or receiving, or of enabling any other person, either directly or indirectly, to obtain or receive from the United States or any officers or agents thereof, any sum of money; or

"Whoever utters or publishes as true any such false, forged, altered, or counterfeited writing, with intent to defraud the United States, knowing the same to be false, altered, forged, or counterfeited; or

"Whoever transmits to, or presents at any office or officer of the United States, any such writing in support of, or in relation to, any account or claim, with intent to defraud the United

States, knowing the same to be false, altered, forged, or counterfeited—

"Shall be fined not more than $1,000 or imprisoned not more than ten years, or both." See IRM 9213.

222.(15) *(1-18-80)* 9781
Section 1001. Statements or Entries Generally

"Whoever, in any matter within the jurisdiction of any department or agency of the United States knowingly and willfully falsifies, conceals or covers up by any trick, scheme, or device a material fact, or makes any false, fictitious or fraudulent statements or representations, or makes or uses any false writing or document knowing the same to contain any false, fictitious or fraudulent statement or entry, shall be fined not more than $10,000 or imprisoned not more than five years, or both." See Text 318.4 and IRM 9213.

222.(16) *(1-18-80)* 9781
Section 1002. Possession of False Papers to Defraud United States

"Whoever, knowingly and with intent to defraud the United States, or any agency thereof, possesses any false, altered, forged, or counterfeited writing or document for the purpose of enabling another to obtain from the United States, or from any agency, officer or agent thereof, any sum of money, shall be fined not more than $10,000 or imprisoned not more than five years, or both." See IRM 9213.

222.(17) *(5-9-80)* 9781
(Reserved)

222.(18) *(1-18-80)* 9781
Section 1114. Protection of Officers and Employees of the United States

[Sections 1111 and 1112 provide the penalties for murder and manslaughter.]

"Whoever kills . . . any officer, employee or agent of the Customs or of the Internal Revenue or any person assisting him in the execution of his duties . . . while engaged in the performance of his official duties, or on account of the performance of his official duties, shall be punished as provided under sections 1111 and 1112 of this title." See IRM 9213.

222.(19) *(1-18-80)* 9781
Section 1501. Assault on Process Server

"Whoever knowingly and willfully obstructs, resists, or opposes any officer of the United States, or other person duly authorized, in serving, or attempting to serve or execute, any legal or judicial writ or process of any court of the United States, or United States magistrate; or

"Whoever assaults, beats, or wounds any officer or other person duly authorized, knowing him to be such officer, or other person so duly authorized, in serving or executing any such writ, rule, order, process, warrant, or other legal or judicial writ or process—

"Shall except as otherwise provided by law, be fined not more than $300 or imprisoned not more than one year, or both." See Text 411.5 and IRM 9213.

222.(20) *(1-18-80)* 9781
Section 1503. Influencing or Injuring Officer, Juror or Witness Generally

"Whoever corruptly, or by threats of force, or by any threatening letter or communication, endeavors to influence, intimidate, or impede any witness, in any court of the United States or before any United States magistrate or other committing magistrate, or any grand or petit juror, or officer in or of any court of the United States, or officer who may be serving at any examination or other proceeding before any United States magistrate or other committing magistrate, in the discharge of his duty, or injures any party or witness in his person or property on account of his attending or having attended such court or examination before such officer, magistrate, or other committing magistrate, or on account of his testifying or having testified to any matter pending therein, or injures any such grand or petit juror in his person or property on account of any verdict or indictment assented to by him, or on account of his being or having been such juror, or injures any such officer, magistrate, or other committing magistrate in his person or property on account of the performance of his official duties, or corruptly or by threats or force, or by any threatening letter or communication, influences, obstructs, or impedes, or endeavors to influence, obstruct, or impede, the due administration of justice, shall not be fined more than $5,000 or imprisoned not more than five years, or both."

222.(21) *(1-18-80)* 9781
Section 1510. Obstruction of Criminal Investigations

"(a) Whoever willfully endeavors by means of bribery, misrepresentation, intimidation, or force or threats thereof to obstruct, delay, or prevent the communication of information relating to a violation of any person to a criminal investigator; or

"Whoever injures any person in his person or property on account of giving by such person or by any other person of any such information to any criminal investigator—

"Shall be fined not more than $5,000 or imprisoned not more than five years, or both.

"(b) As used in this section, the term 'criminal investigator' means any individual duly authorized by a department, agency, or armed force of the United States to conduct or engage in investigations of or prosecutions for violations of the criminal laws of the United States." See Text 411.6.

222.(22) *(1-18-80)* 9781
Section 1621. Perjury Generally

"Whoever, having taken an oath before a competent tribunal, officer, or person, in any case in which a law of the United States authorizes an oath to be administered, that he will testify, declare, depose, or certify truly, or that any written testimony, declaration, deposition, or certificate by him subscribed, is true, willfully and contrary to such oath states or subscribes any material matter which he does not believe to be true, is guilty of perjury, and shall, except as otherwise expressly provided by law, be fined not more than $2,000 or imprisoned not more than five years, or both." See IRM 9213.

222.(23) *(1-18-80)* 9781
Section 1622. Subornation of Perjury

"Whoever procures another to commit any perjury is guilty of subornation of perjury, and shall be fined not more than $2,000 or imprisoned not more than five years, or both." See IRM 9213.

222.(24) *(1-18-80)* 9781
Section 1623. False Declarations Before Grand Jury or Court

"(a) Whoever under oath in any proceeding before or ancillary to any court or grand jury of the United States knowingly makes any false material declaration or makes or uses any other information, including any book, paper, document, record, recording, or other material, knowing the same to contain any false material declaration, shall be fined not more than $10,000 or imprisoned not more than five years, or both.

"(b) This section is applicable whether the conduct occurred within or without the United States.

"(c) An indictment or information for violation of this section alleging that, in any proceedings before or ancillary to any court or grand jury of the United States, the defendant under oath has knowingly made two or more declarations, which are inconsistent to the degree that one of them is necessarily false, need not specify which declaration is false if—

"(1) each declaration was material to the point in question, and

"(2) each declaration was made within the period of the statute of limitations for the offense charged under this section.

"In any prosecution under this section, the falsity of a declaration set forth in the indictment or information shall be established sufficient for conviction by proof that the defendant while under oath made irreconcilably contradictory declarations material to the point in question in any proceeding before or ancillary to any court or grand jury. It shall be a defense to an indictment or information made pursuant to the first sentence of this subsection that the defendant at the time he made each declaration believed the declaration was true.

"(d) Where, in the same continuous court or grand jury proceeding in which a declaration is made, the person making the declaration admits such declaration to be false, such admission shall bar prosecution under this section if, at the time the admission is made, the declaration has not substantially affected the proceeding, or it has not become manifest that such falsity has been or will be exposed.

"(e) Proof beyond a reasonable doubt under this section is sufficient for conviction. It shall not be necessary that such proof be made by any particular number of witnesses or by documentary or other type of evidence." See IRM 9213.

222.(25) *(5-9-80)* 9781
(Reserved)

222.(26) *(5-9-80)* 9781
(Reserved)

222.(27) *(1-18-80)* 9781
Section 1955. Prohibition of Illegal Gambling Businesses

"(a) Whoever conducts, finances, manages, supervises, directs, or owns all or part of an illegal gambling business shall be fined not more than $20,000 or imprisoned not more than five years, or both.

"(b) As used in this section—

"(1) 'illegal gambling business' means a gambling business which—

"(i) is a violation of the law of a State or political subdivision in which it is conducted;

"(ii) involves five or more persons who conduct, finance, manage, supervise, direct, or own all or part of such business; and

"(iii) has been or remains in substantially continuous operation for a period in excess of thirty days or has a gross revenue of $2,000 in any single day.

"(2) 'gambling' includes but is not limited to pool-selling, bookmaking, maintaining slot machines, roulette wheels or dice tables, and conducting lotteries, policy, bolita or numbers games, or selling chances therein.

"(3) 'State' means any State of the United States, the District of Columbia, the Commonwealth of Puerto Rico, and any territory or possession of the United States.

"(c) If five or more persons conduct, finance, manage, supervise, direct, or own all or part of a gambling business and such business operates for two or more successive days, then, for the purpose of obtaining warrants for arrests, interceptions, and other searches and seizures, probable cause that the business receives gross revenue in excess of $2,000 in any single day shall be deemed to have been established."

222.(28) *(1-18-80)* 9781
Section 1962. Prohibited Activities of Racketeer Influenced and Corrupt Organizations

"(a) It shall be unlawful for any person who has received any income derived, directly or indirectly, from a pattern of racketeering activity or through collection of an unlawful debt in which such person has participated as a principal within the meaning of section 2, title 18, United States Code, to use or invest, directly or indirectly, any part of such income, or the proceeds of such income, in acquisition of any interest in, or the establishment or operation of, any enterprise which is engaged in, or the activities of which affect, interstate or foreign commerce. A purchase of securities on the open market for purposes of investment, and without the intention of controlling or participating in the control of the issuer, or of assisting another to do so, shall not be unlawful under this subsection if the securities of the issuer held by the purchaser, the members of his immediate family, and his or their accomplices in any pattern or racketeering activity or the collection of an unlawful debt after such purchase do not amount in the aggregate to one percent of the outstanding securities of any one class, and do not confer, either in law or in fact, the power to elect one or more directors of the issuer.

"(b) It shall be unlawful for any person through a pattern of racketeering activity or through collection of an unlawful debt to acquire or maintain, directly or indirectly, any interest in or control of any enterprise which is engaged in, or the activities of which affect, interstate or foreign commerce.

"(c) It shall be unlawful for any person employed by or associated with any enterprise engaged in, or the activities of which affect, interstate or foreign commerce, to conduct or participate, directly or indirectly, in the conduct of such enterprise's affairs through a pattern of racketeering activity or collection of unlawful debt.

"(d) It shall be unlawful for any person to conspire to violate any of the provisions of subsections (a), (b), or (c) of this section.

222.(29) *(1-18-80)* 9781
Section 1963. Criminal Penalties for Racketeer Influenced and Corrupt Organizations

"(a) Whoever violates any provision of section 1962 of this chapter shall be fined not more than $25,000 or imprisoned not more than twenty years, or both, and shall forfeit to the United States (1) any interest he has acquired or maintained in violation of section 1962, and (2) any interest in, security of, claim against, or property or contractual right of any kind affording a source of influence over, any enterprise which he has established, operated, controlled, conducted, or participated in the conduct of, in violation of section 1962.

"(b) In any action brought by the United States under this section, the district courts of the United States shall have jurisdiction to enter such restraining orders or prohibitions, or to take such other actions, including, but not limited to, the acceptance of satisfactory performance bonds, in connection with any property or other interest subject to forfeiture under this section, as it shall deem proper.

"(c) Upon conviction of a person under this section, the court shall authorize the Attorney General to seize all property or other interest declared forfeited under this section upon such terms and conditions as the court shall deem proper. If a property right or other interest is not exercisable or transferable for value by the United States, it shall expire, and shall not revert to the convicted person. All provisions of law relating to the disposition of property, or the proceeds from the sale thereof, or the remission or mitigation of forfeitures for violation of the customs laws, and compromise of claims and the award of compensation to informers in respect of such forfeitures shall apply to forfeitures incurred, or alleged to have been incurred, under the provisions of this section insofar as applicable and not inconsistent with the provisions thereof. Such duties as are imposed upon the collector of customs or any other person with respect to the disposition of property under the customs laws shall be performed under this chapter by the Attorney General. The United States shall dispose of all such property as soon as commercially feasible, making due provision for the rights of innocent persons."

222.(30) *(1-18-80)* 9781

Section 2071. Concealment, Removal or Mutilation Generally

"(a) Whoever willfully and unlawfully conceals, removes, mutilates, obliterates, or destroys, or attempts to do so, or, with intent to do so takes and carries away any record, proceeding, map, book, paper, document, or other thing, filed or deposited with any clerk or officer of any court of the United States, or in any public office, or with any judicial or public officer of the United States, shall be fined not more than $2,000 or imprisoned not more than three years, or both.

"(b) Whoever, having the custody of any such record, proceeding, map, book, document, paper, or other thing, willfully and unlawfully conceals, removes, mutilates, obliterates, falsifies, or destroys the same, shall be fined not more than $2,000 or imprisoned not more than three years, or both; and shall forfeit his office and be disqualified from holding any office under the United States." See IRM 9213.

222.(31) *(1-18-80)* 9781

Section 2231. Assault or Resistance

"(a) Whoever forcibly assaults, resists, opposes, prevents, impedes, intimidates, or interferes with any person authorized to serve or execute search warrants or to make searches and seizures while engaged in the performance of his duties with regard hereto or on account of the performance of such duties, shall be fined not more than $5,000 or imprisoned not more than three years, or both; and—

"(b) Whoever, in committing any act in violation of this section, uses any deadly or dangerous weapon, shall be fined not more than $10,000 or imprisoned not more than ten years, or both." See IRM 9213.

222.(32) *(1-18-80)* 9781
Section 2232. Destruction or Removal of Property to Prevent Seizure

"Whoever, before, during, or after seizure of any property by any person authorized to make searches and seizures, in order to prevent the seizure or securing of any goods, wares, or merchandise by such person, staves, breaks, throws overboard, destroys, or removes the same, shall be fined not more than $2,000 or imprisoned not more than one year, or both." See IRM 9213.

222.(33) *(1-18-80)* 9781
Section 2233. Rescue of Seized Property

"Whoever forcibly rescues, dispossesses, or attempts to rescue or dispossess any property, articles, or objects after the same shall have been taken, detained, or seized by any officer or other person under the authority of any revenue law of the United States, or by any person authorized to make searches and seizures, shall be fined not more than $2,000 or imprisoned not more than two years, or both." See Text 412.12 and IRM 9213.

222.(34) *(1-18-80)* 9781
Section 641. Public Money, Property or Records

"Whoever embezzles, steals, purloins, or knowingly converts to his use or the use of another, or without authority, sells, conveys or disposes of any record, voucher, money, or thing of value of the United States or of any department or agency thereof, or any property made or being made under contract for the United States or any department or agency thereof; or

"Whoever receives, conceals, or retains the same with intent to convert it to his use or gain, knowing it to have been embezzled, stolen, purloined or converted—

"Shall be fined not more than $10,000 or imprisoned not more than ten years, or both; but if the value of such property does not exceed the sum of $100, he shall be fined not more than $1,000 or imprisoned not more than one year, or both."

230 *(1-18-80)* 9781
(Reserved)

240 *(1-18-80)* 9781
Periods of Limitation on Criminal Prosecution

241 *(1-18-80)* 9781
IRC 6531. Periods of Limitation

"No person shall be prosecuted, tried, or punished for any of the various offenses arising under the internal revenue laws unless the indictment is found or the information instituted within 3 years next after the commission of the offense, except that the period of limitation shall be 6 years—

"(1) for offenses involving the defrauding or attempting to defraud the United States or any agency thereof, whether by conspiracy or not, and in any manner;

"(2) for the offense of willfully attempting in any manner to evade or defeat any tax or the payment thereof;

"(3) for the offense of willfully aiding or assisting in, or procuring, counseling, or advising, the preparation or presentation under or in connection with any matter arising under, the internal revenue laws, of a false or fraudulent return, affidavit, claim, or document (whether or not such falsity or fraud is with the knowledge or consent of the person authorized or required to present such return, affidavit, claim, or document);

"(4) for the offense of willfully failing to pay any tax, or make any return (other than a return required under authority of part III subchapter A of chapter 61) at the time or times required by law or regulations;

"(5) for offenses described in sections 7206(1) and 7207 (relating to false statements and fraudulent documents);

"(6) for the offense described in section 7212(a) (relating to intimidation of officers and employees of the United States);

"(7) for offenses described in section 7214(a) committed by officers and employees of the United States; and

"(8) for offenses arising under section 371 of Title 18 of the United State Code, where the object of the conspiracy is to attempt in any manner to evade or defeat any tax or the payment thereof.

"The time during which the person committing any of the various offenses arising under the internal revenue laws is outside the United States or is a fugitive from justice within the meaning of section 3290 of Title 18 of the United States Code, shall not be taken as any part of the time limited by law for the commencement of such proceedings. (The preceding sentence shall also be deemed an amendment to section 3748(a) of the Internal Revenue Code of 1939, and shall apply in lieu of the sentence in section 3748(a) which relates to the time during which a person committing an offense is absent from the district wherein the same is committed, except that such amendment shall apply only if the period of limitations under section 3748 would, without the application of such amendment, expire more than 3 years after the date of enactment of this title, and except that such period shall not, with the application of this amendment, expire prior to the date which is 3 years after the date of enactment of this title.) Where a complaint is instituted before a magistrate of the United States within the period above limited, the time shall be extended until the date which is 9 months after the date of the making of the complaint before the magistrate of the United States. For the purpose of determining the periods of limitation on criminal prosecutions, the rules of section 6513 shall be applicable."

242 *(1-18-80)* 9781

IRC 6513. Time Return Deemed Filed and Tax Considered Paid

"(a) *Early Return or Advance Payment of Tax.*—For purposes of section 6511, any return filed before the last day prescribed for the filing thereof shall be considered as filed on such last day. For purposes of section 6511(b)(2) and (c) and section 6512, payment of any portion of the tax made before the last day prescribed for the payment of the tax shall be considered made on such last day. For purposes of this subsection, the last day prescribed for filing the return or paying the tax shall be determined without regard to any extension of time granted the taxpayer and without regard to any election to pay the tax in installments.

"(b) *Prepaid Income Tax.*—For purposes of section 6511 or 6512, any tax actually deducted and withheld at the source during any calendar year under chapter 24 shall, in respect of the recipient of the income, be deemed to have been paid by him on the 15th day of the fourth month following the close of his taxable year with respect to which such tax is allowable as a credit under section 31. For purposes of section 6511 and 6512, any amount paid as estimated income tax for any taxable year shall be deemed to have been paid on the last day prescribed for filing the return under section 6012 for such taxable year (determined without regard to any extension of time for filing such return).

"(c) *Return and Payment of Social Security Taxes and Income Tax Withholding.*—Notwithstanding subsection (a), for purposes of section 6511 with respect to any tax imposed by chapter 21 or 24—

"(1) If a return for any period ending with or within a calendar year is filed before April 15 of the succeeding calendar year, such return shall be considered filed on April 15 of such succeeding calendar year; and

"(2) If a tax with respect to remuneration paid during any period ending with or within a calendar year is paid before April 15 of the succeeding calendar year, such tax shall be considered paid on April 15 of such succeeding calendar year.

"(d) *Overpayment of Income Tax Credited to Estimated Tax.*—If any overpayment of income tax is, in accordance with section 6402(b), claimed as a credit against estimated tax for the succeeding taxable year, such amount shall be considered as a payment of the income tax for the succeeding taxable year (whether or not claimed as a credit in the return of estimated tax for such succeeding taxable year), and no claim or refund of such overpayment shall be allowed for the taxable year in which the overpayment arises."

243 *(1-18-80)* 9781

Title 18, United States Code—General Statute of Limitations—Section 3282. Offenses Not Capital

"Except as otherwise expressly provided by law, no person shall be prosecuted, tried, or punished for any offense, not capital, unless the indictment is found or the information is instituted within five years next after such offense shall have been committed. (June 25, 1948, ch. 645, Sec. 1, 62 Stat. 828 and September 1, 1954, ch. 1214, 2d. session, 68 Stat. 1142.)"

244 *(1-18-80)* 9781
Title 18, United States Code—Fugitives From Justice

244.1 *(1-18-80)* 9781
Section 3290. Fugitives From Justice

"No statute of limitations shall extend to any person fleeing from justice."

244.2 *(1-18-80)* 9781
Section 1073. Flight to Avoid Prosecution or Giving Testimony

"Whoever moves or travels in interstate or foreign commerce with intent either (1)to avoid prosecution, or custody or confinement after conviction, under the laws of the place from which he flees, for a crime, or an attempt to commit a crime, punishable by death or which is a felony under the laws of the place from which the fugitive flees, or which, in the case of New Jersey, is a high misdemeanor under the laws of said States, or (2)to avoid giving testimony in any criminal proceedings in such place in which the commission of an offense punishable by death or which is a felony under the laws of such place, or which in the case of New Jersey, is a high misdemeanor under the laws of said State, is charged, shall be fined not more than $5,000 or imprisoned not more than five years, or both.

"Violations of this section may be prosecuted only in the Federal judicial district in which the original crime was alleged to have been committed, or in which the person was held in custody or confinement and only upon formal approval in writing by the Attorney General or an Assistant Attorney General of the United States, which function of approving prosecutions may not be delegated."

250 *(1-18-80)* 9781
Civil Penalties Applicable to Fraud and Miscellaneous Investigations

251 *(1-18-80)* 9781
Introduction

The complete texts of the civil penalty sections relating to income and miscellaneous taxes are set forth herein.

252 *(1-18-80)* 9781
Internal Revenue Code of 1954, As Amended By Tax Reform Act of 1969

252.1 *(1-18-80)* 9781
IRC 6651. Failure to File Tax Return or to Pay Tax

"(a) *Addition to the Tax.*—In case of failure—

"(1) to file any return required under authority of subchapter A of chapter 61 (other than part III thereof), subchapter A of chapter 51 (relating to distilled spirits, wines, and beer), or of subchapter A of chapter 52 (relating to tobacco, cigars, cigarettes, and cigarette papers and tubes), or of subchapter A of chapter 53 (relating to machine guns and certain other firearms), on the date prescribed therefor (determined with regard to any extension of time for filing), unless it is shown that such failure is due to reasonable cause and not due to willful neglect, there shall be added to the amount required to be shown as tax on such return 5 percent of the amount of such tax if the failure is for not more than 1 month, with an additional 5 percent for each additional month or fraction thereof during which such failure continues, not exceeding 25 percent in the aggregate;

"(2) to pay the amount shown as tax on any return specified in paragraph (1) on or before the date prescribed for payment of such tax (determined with regard to any extension of time for payment), unless it is shown that such failure is due to reasonable cause and not due to willful neglect, there shall be added to the amount shown as tax on such return 0.5 percent of the amount of such tax if the failure is not for more than 1 month, with an additional 0.5 percent for each additional month or fraction thereof during which such failure continues, not exceeding 25 percent in the aggregate; or

"(3) to pay any amount in respect of any tax required to be shown on a return specified in paragraph (1) which is not so shown (including an assessment made pursuant to section 6213(b)) within 10 days of the date of the notice and demand therefor, unless it is shown that such failure is due to reasonable cause and not due to willful neglect, there shall be added to the amount of tax stated in such notice and demand 0.5 percent of the amount of such tax if the failure is for not more than 1 month, with an additional 0.5 percent for each additional month or fraction thereof during which such failure continues, not exceeding 25 percent in the aggregate.

"(b) *Penalty Imposed on Net Amount Due.*—For purposes of—

"(1) subsection (a)(1), the amount of tax required to be shown on the return shall be reduced by the amount of any part of the tax which is paid on or before the date prescribed for payment of the tax and by the amount of any credit against the tax which may be claimed on the return,

"(2) subsection (a)(2), the amount of tax shown on the return shall, for purposes of computing the addition for any month, be reduced by the amount of any part of the tax which is paid on or before the beginning of such month and by the amount of any credit against the tax which may be claimed on the return, and

"(3) subsection (a)(3), the amount of tax stated in the notice and demand shall, for the purpose of computing the addition for any month, be reduced by the amount of any part of the tax which is paid before the beginning of such month.

"(c) *Limitations and Special Rule.*—

"(1) *Additions under more than one paragraph.*—

"(A) With respect to any return, the amount of the addition under paragraph (1) of subsection (a) shall be reduced by the amount of the addition under paragraph (2) of subsection (a) for any month to which an addition to tax applies under both paragraphs(1) and (2).

"(B) With respect to any return, the maximum amount of the addition permitted under paragraph (3) of subsection (a) shall be reduced by the amount of the addition under paragraph (1) of subsection (a) which is attributable to the tax for which the notice and demand is made and which is not paid within 10 days of notice and demand.

"(2) *Amount of tax shown more than amount required to be shown.*—If the amount required to be shown as tax on a return is less than the amount shown as tax on such return, subsections (a)(2) and (b)(2) shall be applied by substituting such lower amount.

"(D) *Exception for Declarations of Estimated Tax.*—This section shall not apply to any failure to file a declaration of estimated tax required by section 6015 or to pay any estimated tax required to be paid by section 6153 or 6154."

252.2 *(1-18-80)* 9781

IRC 6652. Failure to File Certain Information Returns

"(a) *Additional Amount.*—In case of each failure to file a statement of a payment to another person, required under authority of section 6041 (relating to information at source), section 6042 (relating to payments of corporate dividends), section 6044 (relating to patronage dividends), section 6045 (relating to returns of brokers), or section 6051(d) (relating to information returns with respect to income tax withheld), unless it is shown that such failure is due to reasonable cause and not to willful neglect, there shall be paid by the person failing to file the statement, upon notice and demand by the Secretary or his delegate and in the same manner as tax, $1 for each such statement not filed, but the total amount imposed on the delinquent person for all such failures during any calendar year shall not exceed $1,000."

252.3 *(1-18-80)* 9781

IRC 6653. Failure to Pay Tax

"(a) *Negligence or Intentional Disregard of Rules and Regulations With Respect to Income or Gift Taxes.*—If any part of any underpayment (as defined in subsection (c)(1) of any tax imposed by subtitle A or by chapter 12 of subtitle B (relating to income taxes and gift taxes) is due to negligence or intentional disregard of rules and regulations (but without intent to defraud), there shall be added to the tax an amount equal to 5 percent of the underpayment.

"(b) *Fraud.*—If any part of any underpayment (as defined in subsection (c)) of tax required to be shown on a return is due to fraud, there shall be added to the tax an amount equal to 50 percent of the underpayment. In the case of income taxes and gift taxes, this amount shall be in lieu of any amount determined under subsection (a).

"(c) *Definition of Underpayment.*—For purposes of this section, the term 'underpayment' means—

"(1) *Income, Estate, Gift and Chapter 42 Taxes.*—In the case of a tax to which Section 6211 (relating to income, estate, gift and chapter 42 taxes) is applicable, a deficiency as defined in that section (except that, for this purpose, the tax shown on a return referred to in section 6211(a)(1)(A) shall be taken into account only if such return was filed on or before the last day prescribed for the filing of such return, determined with regard to any extension of time for such filing), and

"(2) *Other Taxes.*—In the case of any other tax, the amount by which such tax imposed by this title exceeds the excess of—

"(A) The sum of—

"(i) The amount shown as the tax by the taxpayer upon his return (determined without regard to any credit for an overpayment for any prior period, and without regard to any adjustment under authority of sections 6205(a) and 6413(a)), if a return was made by the taxpayer within the time prescribed for filing such return (determined with regard to any extension of time for such filing) and an amount shown as the tax by the taxpayer thereon, plus

"(ii) Any amount, now shown on the return, paid in respect of such tax over—

"(B) The amount of rebates made.

"For purposes of subparagraph (B), the term 'rebate' means so much of an abatement, credit, refund, or other repayment, as was made on the ground that the tax imposed was less than the excess of the amount specified in subparagraph (A) over the rebates previously made.

"(D) *No Delinquency Penalty if Fraud Assessed.*—If any penalty is assessed under subsection (b) (relating to fraud) for an underpayment of tax which is required to be shown on a return, no penalty under section 6651 (relating to failure to file such return or pay tax) shall be assessed with respect to the same underpayment.

"(e) *Failure to Pay Stamp Tax.*—Any person (as defined in section 6671(b)) who willfully fails to pay any tax imposed by this title which is payable by stamp, coupons, tickets, books, or other devices or methods prescribed by this title or by regulations under authority of this title, or willfully attempts in any manner to evade or defeat any such tax or the payment thereof, shall, in addition to other penalties provided by law, be liable to a penalty of 50 percent of the total amount of the underpayment of the tax."

252.4 *(1-18-80)* 9781

IRC 6211. Definition of a Deficiency

"(a) *In General.*—For purposes of this title in the case of income, estate, gift, and excise taxes, imposed by subtitles A and B, and chapter 42, the term 'deficiency' means the amount by which the tax imposed by *subtitle* A or B or chapter 42 exceeds the excess of—

"(1) the sum of

"(A) the amount shown as the tax by the taxpayer upon his return, if a return was made by the taxpayer and an amount was shown as the tax by the taxpayer thereon, plus

"(B) the amounts previously assessed (or collected without assessment) as a deficiency, over—

"(2) the amount of rebates, as defined in subsection (b)(2), made.

"(b) *Rules for Application of Subsection (a).*—For purposes of this section—

"(1) The tax imposed by chapter 1 and the tax shown on the return shall both be determined without regard to payments on account of estimated tax, without regard to the credit under section 31, and without regard to so much of the credit under section 32 as exceeds 2 percent of the interest on obligations described in section 1451.

"(2) The term 'rebate' means so much of an abatement, credit, refund, or other repayment, as was made on the ground that the imposed by *subtitle A or B or chapter 42* was less than the excess of the amount specified in subsection (a)(1) over the rebates previously made.

"(3) The computation by the Secretary or his delegate, pursuant to section 6014, of the tax imposed by chapter 1 shall be considered as having been made by the taxpayer and the tax so computed considered as shown by the taxpayer upon his return.

252.5 *(1-18-80)* 9781

Other Civil Penalties

See Exhibit 200-2 for a listing of other civil penalties.

(Next page is 9900-29)

Exhibit 200-1

Other Criminal Penalties

Handbook Reference: 221.(11) ◊

Section	Description of offense	Maximum penalty
7208	Offenses relating to stamps— (1) Counterfeiting. (2) Mutilation or removal. (3) Use of mutilated, insufficient, or counterfeited stamps. (4) Reuse of stamps. (5) Disposal and receipt of emptied stamped packages.	$10,000, 5 yrs.
7209	Unauthorized use or sale of stamps.	$1,000, 6 months.
7211	False statements to purchasers or lessees relating to tax.	$1,000, 1 yr.
7231	Failure to obtain license for collection of foreign items.	$5,000, 1 yr.
7232	Failure to register or give bond, or false statement by manufacturers or producer of gasoline or lubricating oil.	$5,000, 5 yrs.
7233	Failure to pay, or attempt to evade payment of, tax on cotton futures, and other violations.	$20,000, 3 yrs.
7241	Failure to furnish certain information regarding windfall profit tax on domestic crude oil	$10,000, 1 yr.
7261	Representation that retailers' excise tax is excluded from price of article.	$1,000 fine.
7270	Failure to affix stamps on foreign insurance policies with intent to evade.	Double amount of tax (fine).

Exhibit 200-2

Other Civil Penalties
Handbook Reference: 252.5

◇

Section	*Description of offense*	*Penalty*
6656	Failure to make deposit of taxes	5% of the amount of the under payment
6657	Bad checks tendered not in good faith.	1% of amount of check; Minimum: $5 or amount of check.
6672	Failure to collect and pay over tax, or attempt to evade or defeat a collected tax	Total amount of tax evaded, not collected, or not accounted for and paid over.
6674	Willfully furnishing fraudulent withholding statement or failing to furnish statement to employee.	$50.
6675	Making an excessive claim with respect to the use of gasoline or lubricating oil	Equal to double the excessive amount claimed.
6676	Failure to supply identifying numbers on returns, statements, or documents, or to other persons, as required.	$5 for each failure.
6677(a)	Failure to file a return required under Section 6048, I R C. (transfers to foreign trusts) or failure to report information required on such return.	5% of the amount transferred, not to exceed $1,000.
6678	Failure to furnish statements to recipients of certain items of income (dividends, interest, certain wage payments, etc.)	$10, each failure.
6679	Failure to file a required return, or to show required information, relating to organization of, or acquisition of stock of, a foreign corporation.	$1,000.
6682	Supplying false information with respect to itemized deductions for withholding tax allowance purposes.	$50. ($500, after 12/31/81)
7265(b)	Oleomargarine or adulterated butter—purchasing when not properly branded or stamped.	$50.
7268	Possession of goods on which taxes are imposed with intent by possessor to sell in fraud of law or to evade tax.	$500, or not less than double the amount of taxes fraudulently attempted to be evaded.
7269	Failure to produce records or property relating to estate tax.	Not exceeding $500.
7271	Penalties relating to stamps—failure to attach or cancel; making, selling, issuing articles or documents without payment of full amount of tax, etc.	$50.
7272	Failure to register.	$50.
7273	Failure to post stamps (not including wagering tax stamp). Not willful.	Equal to special tax but not less than $10.
	Willful.	Double above penalty.
7304	Fraudulently claiming drawback on goods on which no tax was paid, or claiming greater amount than tax paid.	$500, or triple amount of drawback claimed.
31USC231	Liability of persons making false claims.	$2,000 forfeiture for each claim plus double the amount paid out by the United States.

(Next page is 9781-35)

310 *(1-18-80)* 9781
Criminal Investigation Programs

311 *(5-9-80)* 9781
General

(1) General Enforcement Program

(a) This program encompasses all criminal enforcement activities of the Criminal Investigation Division except those included in the special enforcement program. The identification and investigation of income tax evasion cases of substance with prosecution potential is a primary objective. The program also provides for balanced coverage as to types of violations, as well as geographic locations and economic and vocational status of violators as considered necessary to stimulate voluntary compliance. (IRM 9152)

(b) The highest priority of the Criminal Investigation Division is to create maximum positive impact on the compliance attitudes and practices of taxpayers through an effective General Enforcement Program (GEP). Within the GEP Program, priority will be given to high impact coordinated compliance projects. (IRM 9161.1)

(2) Special Enforcement Program

(a) This program encompasses the identification and investigation of that segment of the public who derive substantial income from illegal activities and violate the tax laws or other related statutes in contravention of the Internal Revenue laws. The very nature of their operations requires national coordination of enforcement efforts, close cooperation and liaison with the Department of Justice and other Federal, State and local law enforcement agencies. (See IRM 9400 and IRM 9153).

(b) Criminal Investigation, through the Special Enforcement Program, will continue to participate actively in the Federal effort against persons who derive substantial income from illegal activities and violate the tax laws. (IRM 9161.2)

312 *(1-18-80)* 9781
Definitions (IRM 9390)

(1) A "case" is an accumulation of facts concerning a taxpayer, which are segregated and associated with the taxpayer's name and evaluated for potential assignment to an employee for appropriate action.

(2) An "assigned case" is a case that has been assigned to an employee or group of employees for action, and that is subject to a requirement for a written report or an entry in a log indicating the action taken when the assigned case is completed.

(3) A "case file" is the accumulated notes, documentation and information assembled as a result of Service inquiries of and about a taxpayer which contains the taxpayer's name or identifying number or symbol assigned to the taxpayer.

(4) An "informant's communication" is a communication from anyone outside the Service, written or oral, voluntarily submitted to the Service, identifying one or more taxpayers and providing some information about the taxpayer. The informant may be anonymous.

(5) A "project" is a study, survey or canvassing activity involving a limited number of taxpayers within such categories as an occupation, an industry, a geographic area or those involved in a specific economic activity, undertaken to identify noncompliance with the tax laws.

(6) An "intelligence gathering assignment" is an approved assignment made for the purpose of gathering tax related information concerning a specific individual or entity.

(7) An investigation is the gathering of pertinent evidence to prove or disprove the existence of a violation of the law or regulations within Criminal Investigation Jurisdiction.

313 *(5-9-80)* 9781
Planning (Generally)

(1) The purpose of a special agent's investigation is to obtain facts and evidence. His/her primary aim is to determine whether the person under investigation has committed a criminal violation, and, if the facts disclose violations subject to criminal or civil penalties within the jurisdiction of the Criminal Investigation Division, to obtain whatever evidence is required to sustain criminal proceedings or the assertion of civil penalties.

(2) The special agent should first determine what he/she is attempting to prove. This involves an evaluation and analysis of the allegation to ascertain whether the available facts indicate a violation within Criminal Investigation Division jurisdiction and what evidence must be obtained to establish the elements of the crime. A work chart or other plan of procedure may then be developed. This essentially involves a determination of listing of information and evidence required and the probable source thereof. Planning for fraud investigations is discussed in 3(10)8. See also IRM 9381 and 9382.

(3) All criminal investigations should be commenced and concluded as expeditiously as possible. They should be conducted impartially and thoroughly to obtain all pertinent information and evidence. Duplication in investigations, unnecessary inconveniences to the public and unnecessary embarrassment to the taxpayer should be avoided. Appropriate courtesy should be shown when soliciting information.

(4) Investigations should be terminated when sufficient evidence to convict has been accumulated and there are no reasonable grounds to expect that further investigation may

produce significant results in relation to the available evidence and to the additional investigative time and effort involved. The special agent will seek out all who are implicated in the crime and obtain definitive evidence as to their implication, to the extent reasonable. Investigations with less prosecution potential should be closed when there are insufficient resources in the foreseeable future for completing them and there are others of greater potential for development as substantial or flagrant criminal violations or having a greater deterrent potential.

320 *(1-18-80)* 9781
Knowledge of Law and Evidence

321 *(5-9-80)* 9781
References

Planning and conducting investigations involves the application of knowledge of the criminal and tax laws contained in the Internal Revenue Code (Title 26, United States Code) and the Criminal Code (Title 18, United States Code), together with a working knowledge of the fundamental rules of evidence. Handbook text 322 and 323 concern general information relative to law and evidence. Specific laws encountered in Criminal Investigation Division investigations are set forth in Chapter 200. Trial procedure is discussed in Handbook Chapter 700, and the sections of the Handbook concerning particular investigative devices, techniques, and procedures, such as interviewing witnesses and obtaining documentary evidence, include information regarding related rules of evidence.

322 *(1-18-80)* 9781
Law

322.1 *(1-18-80)* 9781
Definitions of Law

(1) *Laws* are rules of conduct which are prescribed or formally recognized as binding, and are enforced by the governing power.

(2) *Common and Statutory Law*

(a) Common law comprises the body of principles and rules of action relating to government and security of persons and property which derive their authority solely from usages and customs or from judgments and decrees of courts recognizing, affirming, and enforcing such usages and customs.

(b) Statutory law refers to laws enacted and established by a legislative body. All Federal crimes are statutory but common law is frequently resorted to for defining words used in the statutes. For example, statutes provide penalties for attempted evasion of income tax but they do not define the terms "attempt" and "evasion."

(3) *Substantive and Adjective Law*—Substantive law creates, defines, and regulates rights, duties, responsibilities, and obligations, whereas adjective or remedial law provides rules for enforcing rights or obtaining redress for their invasion. Adjective law provides rules of practice concerning proceedings before, during, and after trial, and rules of evidence relating to the admission of evidence at trials and the testing of the credibility and competency of witnesses.

(4) *Criminal and Civil Law*—Criminal law is that branch of law which defines crimes and provides punishments. Civil law relates to the establishment, recovery, or redress of private and civil rights.

322.2 *(1-18-80)* 9781
Definitions of Crimes

An act is a crime against the United States only if committed or omitted in violation of a statute forbidding or commanding it, or in violation of a regulation having legislative authority. Crimes are classified and defined in section 1, Title 18, United States Code, as follows:

> "Notwithstanding any Act of Congress to the contrary:
>
> "(1) Any offense punishable by death or imprisonment for a term exceeding one year is a felony.
>
> "(2) Any other offense is a misdemeanor.
>
> "(3) Any misdemeanor, the penalty for which does not exceed imprisonment for a period of six months or a fine of not more than $500, or both, is a petty offense."

322.3 *(1-18-80)* 9781
Parties to Criminal Offenses

(1) Section 2, Title 18 defines as principal, and punishable as such, one who commits an offense against the United States; aids, abets, counsels, commands, induces or procures its commission; or willfully causes an act to be done which if directly performed by him or another would be an offense against the United States. (See 222.2)

(2) An aider and abettor may be convicted even if the person who commits the offense has not been indicted, tried or convicted. [*Gray v. U.S.; Beauchamp v. U.S.*] One who causes a criminal act may be convicted even if the performer of the act is acquitted. [*U.S. v. Lester*] Acquittal of one mistakenly charged with commission of a crime does not affect the guilt of one proved to have aided and abetted, so long as it is established that the crime was committed by someone. [*Von Patzoll v. U.S.; Legatos v. U.S.*]

(3) To aid and abet, a defendant must associate himself with a venture, whether or not there is a conspiracy, and try to make it succeed. Thus, in United States v. Johnson, where the crime of attempted tax evasion by the main defendant was based on alleged concealment of his interest in, and income from, gambling clubs, his co-defendants were held to be guilty because they consciously were parties to the concealment by pretending to be proprietors even if they did not actually share in the making of false returns. A defendant charged with aiding and abetting in bribery need not have been present when the bribe was paid. [*Daniels v. U.S.*]

(4) A principal is not liable for a *crime committed by an agent* solely because of the relationship. He/she will be liable only if the act of the agent is with his/her knowledge or consent or he/she otherwise comes within the provisions of section 2 of Title 18. The agent, himself/herself, is criminally responsible for his/her own actions.

(5) A person becomes *an accessory after the fact*, if, with knowledge of the commission of a crime, he/she assists in preventing or hindering the apprehension, trial or punishment of the perpetrator. [18 USC 3] Suppressing important evidence also comes within this category. [*Neal v. U.S.*] A person is guilty of *misprision* of felony if he/she has knowledge of the actual commission of a felony, conceals it, and does not make this known to a person in authority as soon as possible. [18 USC 4.]

(6) A *corporation* can be prosecuted for the criminal acts of its officers concerning corporate affairs, but the only possible punishment is by fine. However, the officers themselves are also criminally liable for these same acts. [*Currier Lumber Co. v. U.S.*]

323 *(1-18-80)* 9781
Evidence (General Rules)

323.1 *(1-18-80)* 9781
Definition of Evidence

Evidence is all the means by which any alleged matter or fact, the truth of which is submitted to investigation, is established or disproved. Investigators obtain evidentiary facts which by inference tend to prove or disprove the ultimate, main, or principal fact. The latter is a matter for determination by a court or jury. For example, a special agent obtains, in connection with a net worth case, documents and oral statements showing that a taxpayer's bank balance has increased substantially. That is an evidentiary fact from which an *inference* may be drawn relative to the ultimate or principal fact, namely, that the taxpayer willfully attempted to evade income tax. Legal evidence is such as is admissible in court under the rules of evidence because it tends reasonably and substantially to prove a fact. *Evidence is distinguished from proof* in that the latter is the result or effect of evidence.

323.2 *(1-18-80)* 9781
Classifications of Evidence

(1) *Direct evidence* is that which, if believed, proves the existence of the principal or ultimate fact without any inference or presumption. It is direct when the very facts in dispute are sworn to by those who have actual knowledge of them by means of their senses. It may take the form of admissions or confessions made in or out of court.

(2) *Circumstantial evidence* is that which tends to prove the existence of the principal fact by inference. The use of circumstantial evidence is recognized by the courts as a legitimate means of proof, and involves proving several material facts which, when considered in their relationship to each other, tend to establish the existence of the principal or ultimate fact. In the absence of a confession of a witness to whom the violator has expressed his intent, violations involving willful intent are proved by circumstantial evidence. Indeed, it is the only type of evidence generally available to shown such elements of a crime as malice, intent, or motive, which exist only in the mind of the perpetrator of the deed. The proof of most Internal Revenue violations, therefore, is based on circumstantial evidence. Circumstantial evidence includes direct testimony as to secondary facts which are relied on to establish the main fact in issue. For example, in a tax evasion case, a taxpayer's customer testifies that he/she paid $10,000 for merchandise and a Government agent testifies that the payment does not appear on the taxpayer's books and tax returns. Those facts constitute direct evidence of the ommission of $10,000 in income but not of the main issue, which is, "Did the defendant willfully attempt to evade income tax?"

(a) In addition to proving intent, a subject covered in greater detail in text 41(11).2 on willfulness, circumstantial evidence is also frequently used to prove unreported income as shown by increases in net worth, expenditures, or bank deposits.

(b) Circumstantial evidence may be as cogent and convincing as direct evidence and the jury may properly find that it outweighs conflicting direct evidence. However, the inference must be based on convincing facts and must be a more probable and natural one than other explanations offered. The Supreme Court in the Holland case stated as follows:

> "Circumstantial evidence in this respect is intrinsically no different from testimonial evidence. Admittedly, circumstantial evidence may in some cases point to a wholly incorrect result. Yet this is equally true of testimonial evidence. In both instances, a jury is asked to weigh the chances of the evidence's correctly pointing to guilt against the possibility of inaccuracy or ambiguous inference. In both, the jury must use its experience with people and events in weighing the probabilities. If the jury is convinced beyond a reasonable doubt, we can require no more."

(3) *Evidence may be positive or negative*—Evidence is positive when it relates to proof that a fact did or did not happen or exist. Evidence is negative when a witness states that he does not have knowledge of the happening or existence of a fact or circumstance. Examples of the latter are testimony that the records of a District Director do not show that the taxpayer filed a return and testimony of an agent that he/she examined records relating to real estate, bank accounts, and other assets in a given area and did not find any additional assets at the starting point. Positive evidence is stronger than negative evidence. In the Holland case the Supreme Court held that proof of a likely source of unreported income was sufficient to convict in a net worth case without negating all possible nontaxable sources of the alleged net worth increases. However, certain facts can be shown only be negative evidence. In the Massei case the Supreme Court held that proof of a likely source of unreported income is not necessary where all possible sources of nontaxable income were negated.

(4) *Evidence also may be classified as oral, documentary, and real*—Evidence may be presented orally through witnesses, or by the introduction of records or other physical objects. Oral testimony consists of statements made by living witnesses under oath or affirmation. Documentary evidence consists of writings such as judicial and official records, contracts, deeds, and less formal writings such as letters, memorandums, and books and records of private persons and organizations. Maps, diagrams, and photographs are classed as documentary evidence. Real or physical, sometimes called demonstrative evidence, relates to tangible objects or property which are admitted in court or inspected by a trier of facts. More detailed information regarding oral testimony and documentary evidence is presented in text 737 and 350, respectively.

323.3 *(1-18-80)* 9781

Relevancy, and Competency

(1) To be admissible evidence must be relevant, and competent. If a fact offered in evidence relates in some logical way to the principal fact, it is *relevant.* The word relevant implies a traceable and significant connection. A fact need not bear directly on the principal fact. It is sufficient if it constitutes one link in a chain of evidence or that it relates to facts which would constitute circumstantial evidence that a fact in issue did or did not exist. One fact is logically relevant to another if, taken by itself or in connection with other facts, it proves or tends to prove the existence of the other fact. If the fact is logically relevant, it is also legally relevant unless it is barred by some rule of evidence. The principal question to be resolved in determining relevancy is: "Would the evidence be helpful to the finder of the fact in resolving the issue?" (Rule 401, Federal Rules of Evidence).

(2) The terms relevant and competent are not synonymous. Evidence must not only be logically relevant and sufficiently persuasive but also legally admissible, in other words, *competent.* Relevant evidence may be incompetent and hence inadmissible because it is hearsay, or not the best evidence.

(3) The word "irrelevant" usually refers more particularly to the statement sought to be elicited. Although incompetency may relate to documents, in many cases it may go to the person of the witness in that he/she may be under some disability which prevents him/her from testifying in the particular case. For example, a person is not competent to testify if he/she does not understand the nature of an oath or is unable to narrate with understanding the facts he/she has seen.

(4) As applied to evidence such as documents, evidence is competent if it was obtained in a manner, in a form, and from a source proper under the law. Examples of incompetent evidence are a confession involuntarily obtained or an unsigned carbon copy of a document which is offered without any explanation for the failure to produce the original.

(5) Evidence may have limited admissibility. The fact that certain evidence is not admissible for one purpose, does not preclude its use for another. An evidentiary fact may not be admissible as independent proof of the principal fact, and yet be admitted to corroborate or impeach. To illustrate, tax returns for years prior to those in an indictment may be used to corroborate the starting point for a net worth computation although they would not be admissible as proof of the charge of attempted evasion.

(6) A special agent should obtain and report all facts which logically relate to the subject of his/her investigation. He/she should not omit any significant facts because of *doubt* regarding their relevance. There are no absolute and concrete standards for relevancy because the facts vary in each case. Therefore, judges have broad discretion in determining what evidence is relevant. Likewise, the special agent should not omit evidence because of doubt as to its materiality or competency.

323.4 *(1-18-80)* 9781
Judicial Notice

(1) To save time and expense, a trial judge may accept certain facts without requiring proof, if they are commonly and generally known, or can be easily discovered. [Application of Knapp-Monarch Co ; *Porter v. Sunshine Packing Co.*] Judicial notice of such facts takes the place of proof and is of equal force. This does not prevent a party from introducing evidence to dispute the matter. [App. of Knapp-Monarch Co., 9 Wigmore on Evid. (3rd Ed.) sec. 2567.]

(2) A matter of judicial notice may be said to have three material requisites:

(a) It must be a matter of common and general knowledge (or capable of accurate and ready demonstration). [App. of Knapp-Monarch Co.]

(b) It must be well-settled and not uncertain; and

(c) It must be known to be within the limits of the jurisdiction of the court. [20Am. Jurisprudence, Evidence, p. 81, sec. 59.]

(3) A Federal court must take judicial notice of such matters as the Constitution, statutes of the United States (including legislative history), [*Alaska v. American Can Co.*] treaties, contents of the Federal Register, in which the Internal Revenue and other administrative regulations are published, and the laws of each state. [*Lamar v. Micou;* Application of Dandridge.] Laws of foreign jurisdictions are not judicially noticed.

(4) A Federal court will judicially notice its record in the same case. [*U.S. v. Russell*] It is not required to notice prior litigation in the same court, [*Benetti v. U.S.*] but may do so under certain circumstances where the prior proceedings are closely related, as in a contempt proceeding. [*O'Malley v. U.S.*]

(5) Federal courts may also judicially notice such matters as scientific and statistical facts, well-established commercial usages and customs, and historical and geographical facts.

323.5 *(1-18-80)* 9781
Presumptions

(1) A presumption is a rule of law which permits the drawing of a particular inference as to the existence of one fact not certainly known from the existence of other particular facts. Although it is not evidence, it may be considered as a substitute for evidence. Any inference is a permissible deduction from the evidence and may be accepted or rejected by the trier of fact whether it be the court or a jury. It differs from a presumption in that the latter is a rule of law affecting the duty of proceeding with the evidence. For example, there is a *presumption* in civil cases that the Commissioner's determination of additional income is correct, [Rule 32, Rules of Practice, Tax Court: *Welch v. Helvering, Botany Mills v. U.S.*] although he still has the burden of proving intent to evade tax. However, an *inference* of such intent may arise from certain proved facts.

(2) Presumptions may be conclusive or rebuttable. A *conclusive presumption* is binding upon the court and jury and evidence in rebuttal is not permitted. For example, it is generally recognized that an infant under the age of seven is conclusively presumed to be incapable of committing a felony.

(3) A *rebuttable presumption* is one which prevails until it is overcome by evidence to the contrary. Some rebuttable presumptions are:

(a) In criminal cases, a defendant is presumed to be innocent until he/she is proved guilty beyond a reasonable doubt.

(b) A presumption as to authenticity of signatures on Internal Revenue documents is covered by IRC 6064, which provides: "The fact that an individual's name is signed to a return, statement, or other document shall be prima facie evidence for all purposes that the return, statement or other document was actually signed by him." Presumptions as to the authorization for signing corporation and partnership returns are contained in IRC 6062 and 6063.

(c) It is presumed that public officers perform their duties according to law and do not exceed their authority.

(d) Every person is presumed to know the law, and ignorance of the law is no excuse for its violation. This presumption does not relieve the government from proving willfulness in criminal actions for violation of the Internal Revenue laws. The defendant may show his/her misconception of the Internal Revenue law as evidence of his/her lack of willfulness. [*Haigler v. U.S.*]

(e) A person signing an instrument is presumed to have knowledge of its contents.

(f) A person of ordinary intelligence is presumed to intend the natural and probable consequences of his voluntary acts. Although this presumption in itself will not relieve the burden of proving willfulness, it does operate to permit inferences to be drawn from the acts of the defendant which may constitute the circumstantial proof of willfulness. [*McKenna v. U.S.*]

(g) The deductions and exclusions appearing on an income tax return are presumed to be all that exist. [*U.S. v. Bender*]

(h) Every person is presumed to be sane.

(i) Proof that a letter, properly stamped and addressed, was mailed and not returned to the return address creates a presumption that it was received.

(j) The flight of a person accused of a crime or an attempt to evade arrest *may* create a presumption of guilt.

(k) The destruction, mutilation, or concealment of books and records or other evidence creates a presumption that the production of the records or evidence would be unfavorable to the person destroying them. A fabricator of evidence also creates a presumption against himself/herself. It is proper for a court to charge the jury that it may consider the taxpayer's refusal to produce his/her books and records for Internal Revenue inspection, in determining the question of willfulness. [*Louis C. Smith v. U.S.; Beard v. U.S.; Olson v. U.S.; Myres v. U.S.*]

323.6 *(1-18-80)* 9781
Burden of Proof

(1) Burden of proof is the obligation of the party alleging the affirmative of an issue to prove it. This burden remains on the Government throughout a criminal trial although the burden of going forward with evidence may shift from one side to the other. [*Lisansky v. U.S.*] The doctrine of judicial notice and the operation of presumptions are aids in carrying the burden of proof and in proceeding with evidence. When the party having the burden of proof has produced sufficient evidence for the jury to return a verdict in favor of such party, a *prima facie case* has been established. This does not mean that the jury will render such a verdict, but that they could do so from the standpoint of sufficiency of evidence. At this point the defendant has two choices. He/she may choose to offer no evidence, relying on the court and jury to decide that the Government has not overcome the presumption of innocence, or he/she may offer evidence in his defense. If he/she wishes to introduce new matters by way of denial, explanation, or contradiction, the burden of going forward with evidence is his/her, although the prosecution still has the burden of proof with respect to the entire case. The court pointed this out to a jury in the Littlefield case in the following language:

> "The burden of proof is not upon the defendant to prove that he/she did believe that the way in which he/she computed and returned his/her income was correct, but the burden is upon the Government to prove beyond a reasonable doubt that the defendant intended to commit a crime and intended willfully to defraud the Government. If you have a reasonable doubt arising from the evidence as to whether or not in computing and returning his/her income for the years involved here the defendant acted in good faith according to the best of his/her knowledge and understanding, even though his method of computation might have been entirely wrong, it is your duty to find him not guilty."

(2) Proof beyond a reasonable doubt of every element of the crime charged is necessary for a conviction. In charging a jury as to the meaning of reasonable doubt, the judge in U.S. v. Sunderland stated:

> "A reasonable doubt, is a doubt founded upon a consideration of all the evidence and must be based on reason. Beyond a reasonable doubt does not mean to a moral certainty or beyond a mere possible dount or an imaginary doubt. It is such a doubt as would deter a reasonably prudent man or woman from acting or deciding in the more important matters involved in his or her own affairs. Doubts which are not based upon a reasonable and careful consideration of all the evidence, but are purely imaginary, or born of sympathy alone, should not be considered and should not influence your verdict. It is only necessary that you should have that certainty with which you transact the more important concerns in life. If you have that certainty, then you are convinced beyond a reasonable doubt.
>
> "A defendant may not be convicted upon mere suspicion or conjecture. A defendant should be acquitted if the evidence is equally consistent with innocence as with guilt."

(3) In *civil cases* the burden of proof ordinarily is on the plaintiff to prove his/her case, without any presumption against him/her at the outset. In tax cases, however, the burden is upon the plantiff or petitioner (taxpayer) to overcome the presumption of correctness of the Commissioner's determination of the deficiency. [*Avery v. Comm.*] Rule 32 of the Rules of Practice, Tax Court, provides: "The burden of proof shall be upon the petitioner, except as otherwise provided by statute, and except that in respect of any new matter pleaded in his answer, it shall be upon the respondent." There are four important exceptions to the above rule, namely, fraud cases, [*Paddock v. U.S.*] where assessment is asserted within the six-year limitation on account of alleged omission of more than 25 percent of gross income stated in the return, other new matters pleaded by the Commissioner, and transferee proceedings.

(a) The Internal Revenue Code provides that the burden of proofs is on the Commissioner where fraud is alleged. IRC 7454 states: "In any proceeding involving the issue whether the petitioner has been guilty of fraud with intent to evade tax, the burden of proof in respect of such issue shall be upon the Secretary or his delegate." As a matter of general law it has always been held that one who alleges fraud must prove it. [*Budd v. Comm.*]

(b) Where, under IRC 6501(e), the Commissioner makes an assessment after the three-year limitation period, but within six years after the return is filed, because of omission of more than 25 percent of the amount of gross income shown in the return, the burden of proving the required omission is on him/her. [*Reis v. Comm.*] This is in line with the general rule that one relying on an exception to the statute of limitations must prove the exception. [*Wood v. Comm.*]

(c) Tax Court Rule 32 provides that the Commissioner has the burden of proving new matters pleaded by him/her in answer to the petition. This is an application of the general rule of law regarding evidence which places the burden on the party alleging the fact at issue.

(d) The Commissioner has the burden of proof to establish transferee liability. IRC 6902 provides: "In proceedings before the Tax Court the burden of proof shall be upon the Secretary or his delegate to show that a petitioner is liable as a transferee of property of a taxpayer, but not to show that the taxpayer was liable for the tax." The original tax deficiency is presumed to be correct and the transferee has the burden of establishing its incorrectness.

(4) *The degree of proof required in civil cases* is a "preponderance of evidence," except where fraud is alleged. In the latter case, "clear and convincing evidence" is necessary in order to prevail on the fraud issue. [*Rodd v. Fahs*]

(a) *Preponderance of evidence* is evidence that will incline an impartial mind to one side rather than the other so as to remove the cause from the realm of speculation. It does not relate merely to the quantity of evidence. In the Wissler case the court's instruction concerning preponderance of evidence was as follows:

> "The terms 'preponderance of evidence' and 'greater weight of evidence' as used in these instructions are terms of practically the same meaning, and when it is said that the burden rests upon either party to establish any particular fact or proposition by a preponderance or greater weight of evidence, it is meant that the evidence offered and introduced in support thereof to entitle said party to a verdict, should when fully and fairly considered produce the stronger impression upon the mind and be more convincing when weighed against the evidence introduced in opposition thereto. Such preponderance is not always to be determined by the number of witnesses on the respective sides, although it may be thus determined all other things being equal."

(b) *Clear and convincing evidence* is that which need not be beyond a reasonable doubt as in a criminal case but must be stronger than a mere preponderance of evidence. In the Gladden case the court instructed the jury on this point as follows:

> "A mere preponderance of the evidence, meaning merely the greater weight of the evidence, is not sufficient to prove fraud. This does not mean that you must be convinced of fraud beyond a reasonable doubt, because this is not a criminal case. However, an allegation of fraud does require a greater degree of proof than is required in most civil cases, and a mere preponderance of the evidence, while enough to

incline the mind of an impartial juror to one side of the issue rather than the other, is not enough to prove fraud. Fraud must be established by evidence which is clear, cogent and convincing."

323.7 *(1-18-80)* 9781
Hearsay (Federal Rules of Evidence Article VIII)

(1) A *statement* is an oral or written assertion or nonverbal conduct of a person, if it is intended by a person as an assertion (Rule 801(a)). Hearsay statements are inadmissible at trial unless an exception is applicable (Rule 802). Lack of opportunity for cross-examination and unreliability are the principal reasons for excluding hearsay testimony.

(2) *Hearsay* is a statement, other than one made by the declarant while testifying at the trial of hearing, offered in evidence to prove the truth of the matter asserted (Rule 801(c)). Evidence which does not come from the personal knowledge of the declarant but from the repetition of what the declarant has heard others say is hearsay. For example, testimony of a special agent that third parties made statements to the agent that checks written by a taxpayer were personal in nature is hearsay and inadmissible. The personal nature of the checks would be proved through the taxpayer's admissions and records, and testimony and records of the third parties.

(3) The following statements are not hearsay under the provisions of Rule 801(d):

"(1) *Prior statement by witness.* The declarant testifies at the trial or hearing and is subject to cross-examination concerning the statement, and the statement is (A) inconsistent with his testimony, and was given under oath subject to the penalty of perjury at a trial, hearing, or other proceeding, or in a deposition, or (B) consistent with his testimony and is offered to rebut an express or implied charge against him of recent fabrication or improper influence or motive, or "[This could also include one of identification of a person made after perceiving him/her.]

"(2) *Admission by party-opponent.* The statement is offered against a party and is (A) his own statement, in either his individual or a representative capacity, or (B) a statement of which he has manifested his adoption or belief in its truth, or (C) a statement by a person authorized by him to make a statement concerning the subject, or (D) a statement by his agent or servant concerning a matter within the scope of his agency or employment, made during the existence of the relationship, or (E) a statement by a coconspirator [SIC] of a party during the course and in furtherance of the conspiracy."

(4) Rule 801(d)(1)(A) provides that when a witness testifies at a trial or hearing and is subject to cross-examination concerning a prior statement inconsistent with the witness' present testimony, the prior statement may be admitted for its truth if the witness made it under oath in a previous proceeding (excluding grand jury) or deposition. A proceeding is a formal evidentiary hearing where the witness/declarant is subject to cross-examination. Testimony taken by a special agent in an affidavit or question and answer statement does not qualify.

(5) Admissions of a party-opponent (e.g. taxpayer) which are offered against the party are not hearsay (Rule 801(d)(2)). The admissions include statements:

(a) made by the party, or

(b) shown to have been adopted or believed by the party (adoptive/implied admission), or

(c) made by a person authorized by the party to make a statement concerning the subject of the statement, or

(d) made by an agent or servant of the party concerning a matter within the scope of the agency/employment, and made during the existence of the relationship, or

(e) made by a coconspirator during the course and in furtherance of a conspiracy.

(6) Rules 803 and 804 specify certain exceptions to the hearsay rule. The exceptions are based on the theory that under appropriate circumstances a hearsay statement is of the type that makes its trustworthiness and truthfulness highly probable and the statement is necessary to prove the fact alleged. In these instances the statements can be introduced by other than the declarant even though the declarant is available to testify.

(7) Rule 803, *Hearsay Exceptions; Availability of Declarant Immaterial,* lists twenty-four (24) statements which are not to be excluded by the hearsay rule. Some of the more important exceptions are:

(a) (Rule 803(1)) "*Present sense impression.*—A statement describing or explaining an event or condition made while the declarant was perceiving the event or condition or immediately thereafter."

(b) (Rule 803(2)) "*Excited utterance.*—A statement relating to a startling event or condition made while the declarant was under the stress of excitement caused by the event or condition." This exception refers to spontaneous declarations and acts committed during the event. The trustworthiness of such statements lies in their spontaneity, for the occurrence must be startling enough to produce a spontaneous and unreflective utterance without time to contrive or misrepresent. Once the excitement passes, statements made are not within this exception. They may be made by participants or bystanders, and a person who made or heard such statements may testify about them in court. The trial judge has wide discretion in deciding the admissibility of unsworn statements. The circumstances involved in a raid on a bookmaking establishment may be used to illustrate the application of this rule. One of the persons in the establishment, upon seeing the raiding officers enter the room says: "Burn the betting slips!" Even though the speaker is never identified and is not available as a witness, an agent who heard the statement may be permitted to testify about it in a trial of John Doe, to prove that betting slips existed.

(c) (Rule 803(3)) "*Then existing mental, emotional, or physical condition.*—A statement of the declarant's then existing state of mind, emotion, sensation, or physical condition (such as intent, plan, motive, design, mental feeling, pain and bodily health), but not including a statement of memory or belief to prove the fact remembered or believed, unless it relates to the execution, revocation identification, or terms of declarant's will." Example: Assume that the taxpayer is alleging that the return preparer was in a state of depression when the return was prepared and is responsible for errors on the tax return. A witness (e.g. the return preparer's secretary) who spoke with the return preparer at the time the return was being prepared, could testify that the return preparer expressed a feeling of mental well-being and confidence. The witness could testify, whether or not the return preparer was available.

(d) (Rule 803(4)) "*Statements for purposes of medical diagnosis or treatment.*—Statements made for purposes of medical diagnosis or treatment and describing medical history, or past or present symptoms, pain, or sensations, or the inception or general character of the cause or external source thereof, insofar as reasonably pertinent to diagnosis or treatment." This section does not change the law of privilege (HB 244.6).

(e) (Rule 803(5)) "*Recorded recollection.*—A memorandum or record concerning a matter about which a witness once had knowledge but now has insufficient recollection to enable him to testify fully and accurately, shown to have been made or adopted by the witness when the matter was fresh in his memory and to reflect that knowledge correctly. If admitted, the memorandum or record may be read into evidence but may not itself be received as an exhibit unless offered by an adverse party." Example: A special agent has taken a question and answer statement from a witness. At trial, the witness no longer recollects the facts in the statement. Even if the witness has not initialed the pages and/or signed the statement, the facts of the statement could be read at trial as a record adopted by the witness. In the case of an unsigned affidavit, if it can be shown that the witness indicated that the facts recorded were true, the facts of the unsigned affidavit could be read as a statement adopted by the witness. Similarly, if a witness had in some way indicated the adoption of a memorandum prepared by a special agent, the memorandum could be read as evidence. (See also HB 637.6, Refreshing Memory or Recollection.)

(f) (Rule 803(6)) "*Records of regularly conducted activity.*—A memorandum, report, record, or data compilation, in any form, of acts, events, conditions, opinions, or diagnoses, made at or near the time by, or from information transmitted by, a person with knowledge, if kept in the course of a regularly conducted business activity, and if it was the regular practice of that business activity to make the memorandum, report, record, or data compilation, all as shown by the testimony of the custodian or other qualified witness, unless the source of information or the method or circumstances of preparation indicate lack of trustworthiness. The term 'business' as used in this paragraph includes business, institution, association, profession, occupation, and calling of every kind, whether or not conducted for profit." This rule permits showing that an entry was made in a business record maintained in the ordinary course of business without producing the person who made the entry (HB 253.21). Where there is an indication that the particular record lacks trustworthiness, this rule does not apply. This rule extends the definition of business to include records of institutions and associations like schools, churches, and hospitals. The rule covers data compilations whether stored in a computer or elsewhere.

(g) (Rule 803(8)) "*Public records and reports.*—Records, reports, statements or data compilations, in any form, of public offices or agencies, setting forth (A) the activities of the office or agency, or (B) matters observed pursuant to duty imposed by law as to which matters there was a duty to report, excluding, however, in criminal cases matters observed by police officers and other law enforcement personnel, or (C) in civil actions and proceedings and against the Government in criminal cases, factual findings resulting from an investigation made pursuant to authority granted by law, unless the source of information or other circumstances indicate lack of trustworthiness."

1 The admissibility of official records and copies of transcripts thereof in Federal proceedings is further covered by 28 U.S.C. 1732, *Record made in regular course of business; photographic copies* [HB 253.2]; 28 U.S.C. 1733, *Government records and papers; copies* [HB 253.3]; and *Rule 27, Federal Rules of Criminal Procedure.*

(h) (Rule 803(17)) "*Market reports, commercial publications.*—Market quotations, tabulations, lists, directories, or other published compilations, generally used and relied upon by the public or by persons in particular occupations."

(i) (Rule 803(21)) "*Reputation as to character.*—Reputation of a person's character among his associates or in the community."

1 Rule 803(21) makes admissible the kind of reputation evidence that is provided for in Rule 405(a), *Methods of Proving Character;* and Rule 608(a), *Evidence of Character and Conduct of Witness* (HB 637.4).

(j) (Rule 803(22)) "*Judgment of previous conviction.*—Evidence of a final judgment, entered after a trial or upon a plea of guilty (but not upon a plea of nolo contendere), adjudging a person guilty of a crime punishable by death or imprisonment in excess of one year, to prove any fact essential to sustain the judgment, but not including, when offered by the Government in a criminal prosecution for purposes other than impeachment, judgments against persons other than the accused. The pendency of an appeal may be shown but does not affect admissibility."

(k) (Rule 803(24)) "*Other exceptions.*—A statement not specifically covered by any of the foregoing exceptions but having equivalent circumstantial guarantees of trustworthiness, if the court determines that (A) the statement is offered as evidence of a material fact; (B) the statement is more probative on the point for which it is offered than any other evidence which the proponent can procure through reasonable efforts; and (C) the general purposes of these rules and the interests of justice will best be served by admission of the statement into evidence. However, a statement may not be admitted under this exception unless the proponent of it makes known to the adverse party sufficiently in advance of the trial or hearing to provide the adverse party with a fair opportunity to prepare to meet it, his intention to offer the statement and the particulars of it, including the name and address of the declarant."

1 Rule 803(24) is repeated in Rule 804(b)(5). Under this, the court, having determined that a statement offered as evidence of a material fact is more probative on the point for which it is offered than any other evidence which a proponent can procure by reasonable efforts, may admit the evidence if, by so doing, the general purposes of the Federal Rules of Evidence and the interests of justice will be served. The evidence must demonstrate circumstantial guarantees of trustworthiness and the parties must be advised of its potential use in advance of trial. The use of this exception is rare and should not be relied upon.

(8) Rule 804, *Hearsay Exceptions: Declarant Unavailable.* Rule 804 concerns itself with hearsay exceptions that are limited to situations in which the declarant is unavailable as a witness. Rule 804 is quoted below (except material in brackets):

(a) *Definition of unavailability.*—Unavailability as a witness includes situations in which the declarant—

"(1) is exempted by ruling of the court on the ground of privilege from testifying concerning the subject matter of his statement; or

"(2) persists in refusing to testify concerning the subject matter of his statement despite an order of the court to do so; or

"(3) testifies to a lack of memory of the subject of his statement; or

"(4) is unable to be present or to testify at the hearing because of death or then existing physical or mental illness or infirmity; or

"(5) is absent from the hearing and the proponent of his statement has been unable to procure his attendance (or in the case of a hearsay exception under subdivision (b)(2), (3), or (4), his attendance or testimony) by process or other reasonable means. "A declarant is not unavailable as a witness if his exception, refusal, claim of lack of memory, inability, or absence is due to the procurement or wrongdoing of the proponent of his statement for the purpose of preventing the witness from attending or testifying."

(b) *Hearsay exceptions.*—The following are not excluded by the hearsay rule if the declarant is unavailable as a witness:

"(1) *Former testimony.*—Testimony given as a witness at another hearing of the same or a different proceeding, or in a deposition taken in compliance with law in the course of the same or another proceeding, if the party against whom the testimony is now offered, or, in a civil action or proceeding, a predecessor in interest, had an opportunity and similar motive to develop the testimony by direct, cross, or redirect examination." [Under this section, it does not matter whether the opportunity for examination came in the form of direct or cross-examination, as long as there was adequate opportunity to develop the testimony of the witness in the prior formal hearing.]

"(2) *Statement under belief of impeding death.*—In a prosecution for homicide or in a civil action or proceeding, a statement made by a declarant while believing that his death was imminent, concerning the cause or circumstances of what he believed to be his impending death." [This exception is applicable only in homicide cases or related civil actions. Dying declarations are not normally relevant to tax investigations.]

"(3) *Statement against interest.*—A statement which was at the time of its making so far contrary to the declarant's pecuniary or proprietary interest, or so far tended to subject him to civil or criminal liability, or to render invalid a claim by him against another, that a reasonable man in his position would not have made the statement unless he believed it to be true. A statement tending to expose the declarant to criminal liability and offered to exculpate the accused is not admissible unless corroborating circumstances clearly indicate the trustworthiness of the statement." [The party introducing the statement should be prepared to show that the declarant was aware that the statement was against interest at the time it was made.]

"(4) *Statement of personal or family history.*—(A) A statement concerning the declarant's own birth, adoption, marriage, divorce, legitimacy, relationship by blood, adoption, or marriage, ancestry, or other similar fact of personal or family history, even though declarant had no means of acquiring personal knowledge of the matter stated; or (B) a statement concerning the foregoing matters, and death also, of another person, if the declarant was related to the other by blood, adoption, or marriage or was so intimately associated with the other's family as to be likely to have accurate information concerning the matter declared."

"(5) *Other exceptions.*" [These are the same as those specified in Rule 803(24) (HB 223.7(7)).]

330 *(1-18-80)* 9781
Sources of Information

331 *(1-18-80)* 9781
Introduction

This material concerns sources of investigative information that may be useful to special agents of all districts. Districts offices may prepare an addenda of other sources which are applicable to investigations in the local area. Information regarding any corrections to the material in this section or any additional sources which are of sufficient importance to warrant inclusion in the Handbook may be forwarded to the Director, Criminal Investigation Division, National Office (CP:CI:P).

332 *(1-18-80)* 9781
Confidential Sources of Information

332.1 *(1-18-80)* 9781
Manual References

Procedures for processing information from confidential sources are provided in IRM 9370 through 9373.

332.2 *(1-18-80)* 9781
Informants

332.21 *(1-18-80)* 9781
Definition of Informants

An informant is an individual who furnishes information to the Internal Revenue Service. Such information may be furnished on the informant's own initiative or as a result of being directed to furnish information by a special agent or other Service employee. (See IRM 9373.2)

332.22 *(1-18-80)* 9781
Development of Informants

Many criminal tax cases have originated from information furnished by informants, and many have been successfully completed only because of the use of informants who have supplied information otherwise unavailable. This is especially true with respect to taxpayers engaged in illegal activities.

332.23 *(5-9-80)* 9781
Protection of Informants

(1) *During Investigations*—Communications of confidential informants are based on the informant's trust that his/her identity will not be disclosed and that he/she will not be harmed physically, economically, or otherwise because of his/her action in furnishing information to the Government. The protection of confidential informants, therefore, is absolutely essential in enforcement activities. Special agents will not divulge either the identity of the informant or the existence of a confidential informant in the case to anyone other than authorized persons. To provide maximum security regarding their identity and existence, confidential informants will not be used as witnesses, placed in a position where they might become witnesses, or unnecessarily identified in court without their consent. In order to avoid the conflict between preservation of an informant's anonymity and the possible disclosure of an informant's identity during the investigation and prosecution, the special agent should make a decision early in the investigation about the feasibility of development of other evidence to take the place of the informant as a witness. If this is not feasible, the case should generally be closed. Communications of confidential informants should not be attached to income tax returns, associated with workpapers, or included in the exhibits submitted with a report. Further precautions concerning the treatment of confidential sources of information in reports is set forth in 633.1:(1)(e).

(2) *In the Courts*

(a) It is the duty of every citizen to communicate to his/her Government any information which he/she has of an offense against its laws. To encourage him/her in performing his/her duty, the courts have held such information to be confidential within the discretion of the Government. The courts, on the basis of public policy, will not compel or allow disclosure of an informant's identity without the consent of the Government unless such information is useful evidence to vindicate the accused or lessen the risk of false testimony, or is essential to the proper disposition of the case. [*Rugendorf v. U.S.; Roviaro v. U.S.*] Since the privilege exists in behalf of the Government and not the informant, the Government may waive it, and it is deemed to be waived if the informant is put on the witness stand. [*U.S. v. Schneiderman; Segurola v. U.S.*] Further discussion of the law regarding privileged communications of informants is contained in 344.

(b) If a special agent, who has promised an informant that he/she would keep his/her identity confidential, is asked to disclose such identity on the witness stand and no objection to the question is made or sustained, he/she should not refuse to answer, but should state that he/she cannot disclose the information on the ground that it was a privileged communication to an officer of the Government, [*Scher v. U.S.*] and that he/she is bound by instructions not to disclose such information. He/she should maintain this position pending instructions from his/her superiors and advice from the United States Attorney. The special agent's failure to disclose this information may have several results:

1 The court may, if he/she thinks that no harm is done the defendant, uphold the special agent;

2 The court may dismiss the action;

3 The special agent's superiors may release him/her from his/her obligation; or

4 If he/she persists in his/her refusal to answer, the court may find him/her in contempt.

332.24 *(1-18-80)* 9781
Techniques With Informants

(1) Be fair and truthful with informants. Make no promises that you do not intend to fulfill. Show appreciation for the information furnished but do not let an informant determine the procedure to be used in the investigation or otherwise control it. A Government officer must not condone any violation of law in order to obtain information. Informants may, through ignorance or zeal, induce a violation. If a defendant can show that the informant who induced him/her to commit a violation was acting under some arrangement with Government officers, he/she has a legal defense. Therefore, whenever there appears to be a possibility of entrapment or some other unlawful act by an informant, he should be guided in a manner that will prevent the occurrence of such acts.

(2) Some informants supply only what information they think the officer does not know. The receiver, therefore, should in all instances make every effort to get all facts within the knowledge of the informant. If a telephone call is received from an anonymous source, the receiver should strive to elicit all possible information before the connection is broken because the caller may not offer any further opportunity for communication.

(3) Informants provide information for a variety of reasons. In estimating the reliability of an informant and evaluating the information which he furnished, consideration should be given to his/her motive.

(4) A special agent who receives information about a taxpayer from an informant should check the Criminal Investigation Division files, inasmuch as the informant may have given an incorrect or incomplete name for the taxpayer. If the original file check discloses no record, and the special agent finds during his/her investigation that the taxpayer spells his/her name differently or uses names in addition to the name reported by the informant, the special agent should immediately recheck under the newly discovered name or names.

332.25 *(1-18-80)* 9781

Payments to Informants

(1) Instructions concerning rewards for information submitted to the IRS are contained in IRM 9371. Instructions concerning confidential expenditures and courtesy expenditures which involve payments to or on behalf of informants are contained in IRM 9372 and IRM 9373.3.

(2) Under no circumstances are Internal Revenue employees authorized to assure any person that a reward will be paid in any amount, nor should Internal Revenue personnel indicate to the informant in any manner the amount of the probable tax recovery or whether such recovery is based upon the information submitted by the informant. If inquiry is made as to the amount which may be received, the inquirer should be furnished with a copy of Publication 733, Rewards for Information Given to the Internal Revenue Service, pertaining to rewards for information about violations of the internal revenue laws.

333 *(1-18-80)* 9781

Information From Government Offices In Washington, D.C.

333.1 *(1-18-80)* 9781

General

(1) Requests for tax related information to be obtained from the following governmental offices located in Washington, D.C., shall be sent by the Chief, Criminal Investigation Division, with the concurrence of the District Director to the Director, Criminal Investigation Division, National Office, Attn: Chief, Operations Branch:

(a) national headquarters office of the Federal Bureau of Investigation;

(b) national headquarters office of Selective Service. Records of Selective Service applicants are confidential and the information therein may not be released except in cases where extraordinary circumstances, such as national security consideration, require disclosure;

(c) all congressional committees and subcommittees and their investigatory staffs;

(d) the Securities and Exchange Commission;

(e) National Office of the Internal Revenue Service;

(f) Federal Deposit Insurance Corporation; and

(g) any other requests for information to be obtained from departments and agencies in Washington, D.C. which is not routine in nature. If there is a question as to whether the material is of a routine nature, the request should be sent to the Director, Criminal Investigation Division, who will determine its disposition.

(2) Requests of a routine nature for information from other governmental offices located in Washington, D.C., shall be forwarded to the Chief, Criminal Investigation Division, Baltimore, Maryland, and not to the National Office.

(3) See IRM 9264.2.

333.2 *(9-8-80)* 9781

Social Security Administration Records

(1) Regulations under the Social Security Act authorize the Social Security Administration to disclose information to any officer or employee of the Department of the Treasury lawfully charged with the administration of Titles II, VIII, or IX of the Social Security Act, the Federal Insurance Contributions Act, the Self-Employment Act, or the Federal Unemployment Tax Act, or any Federal income tax law, for the purpose of such administration only. The regu-

lations expressly forbid further disclosure of information thus obtained, or its use for any purpose other than administration of the employment and income tax laws.

(2) The procedures described herein will be followed for all requests (other than those relating to benefit payments) except those made in situations which require a more expeditious response:

(a) Form 2264, Request for Social Security Account Information, shall be used in requesting the name and address of the latest reporting employer of a taxpayer from the records of the Social Security Administration (SSA). Such form shall not be used in requesting other information from the agency. The form should be prepared for each individual involved and care should be exercised to make certain that all applicable items are accurately completed. The space on the form designated "Originating Office" may be left blank or utilized to identify the post of duty of the special agent originating the form request. So that SSA can give priority to IRS criminal cases the form should be labeled as "IRS-CRITICAL CASE" at the top, in such instances. The taxpayer's name should be typed or legibly printed and his/her complete Social Security Number must be shown in order that the Social Security Administration may readily identify the proper account. When the Social Security Number is not known and an inquiry to the Social Security Administration is deemed essential, complete information must be furnished regarding the individual's full name, date and place of birth, and names of both parents including his/her mother's maiden name. IRS district codes, which are set out in text 142.(34):(3) of IRM 4810, Audit Reports Handbook, must be shown in the appropriate space on the form.

(b) When the name and address of the latest recorded employer is requested, the Social Security Administration will return the Form 2264 to the requesting IRS district with the information entered on an electronically prepared form attached to the Form 2264. In completing the space designated "Return To" on the Form 2264, there should be inserted "Attention: Chief, Criminal Investigation Division, and the address of the requesting district. The form will be signed by the Chief in the space provided or by a subordinate supervisory official who has been authorized to sign the form.

(c) Agreement has been reached with the Social Security Administration that its records will be checked only for the calendar year in which the Form 2264 is submitted and, if no employer is found for that calendar year, for the two preceding calendar years.

(d) Requests for itemization of quarterly earnings, which identify employers and amounts of wages taxable under the Federal Insurance Contributions Act, may also be made to the Social Security Administration when such information is needed in the administration of employment and income tax laws. Requests of this type shall be made by memorandum stating that the information is to be used in an official investigation of an employment or income tax matter and identifying the period or periods for which an itemization of quarterly earnings is requested. In addition, the memorandum should show the taxpayer's name and complete Social Security Number, and the name, address, and code of the IRS district originating the request. So that SSA can give priority to IRS criminal cases "IRS-CRITICAL CASE" should be labeled before the body of the memorandum in such instances and should be mailed directly to the Social Security Administration, Division of Adjustment Operations, Receipt and Dispatch Unit, 4–N–7 South Block, Metro West Building, 300 North Greene Street, Baltimore, Maryland 21201. The symbols "Attn: 14:WR:AR" shown on Form 2264 should not be used on memorandum requests. The memorandum should be signed by the Chief, Criminal Investigation Division, of his/her delegate, after the words "For the District Director" in similar signature format to Form 2264. Exhibit 300–20 is an example of a memorandum format which meets the needs of the Social Security Administration for IRS Criminal Cases. If the request to the Social Security Administration should involve a racketeer or any person being investigated under the Special Enforcement Program, extreme care should be exercised not to divulge such information. The Social Security Administration will submit the information on its Form OAR 1009, accompanied by an electronically prepared form giving the names and addresses of the taxpayer's employers for the specified period.

(e) The Social Security Administration will endeavor to process Forms 2264 and requests for itemization of quarterly earnings as expeditiously as possible. Follow-up inquiries should not be made within sixty days from the date of the original request. If, after sixty days, it is found that a follow-up inquiry is necessary, a second request should be prepared in original only and forwarded to the Social Security Administration. However, the second request should not be identified as a follow-up or as a second request, and no reference should be made to the original request.

(f) The Social Security Administration has agreed to give emergency requests from the Director, Criminal Investigation Division, special handling which will lead to prompt responses. The Criminal Investigation Division, National Office, has agreed that such requests will be kept to a minimum. Therefore, expedite action will only be requested in those cases in which a prompt response is essential. The Chief, Criminal Investigation Division, with the concurrence of the District Director or Director of International Operations will telephone the Director, Criminal Investigation Division, National Office (CP:CI:O) and furnish the following information:

1 Sufficient taxpayer identifying and other information to permit the Social Security Administration to search its records.

2 Justification for special handling of the requests.

(g) The Criminal Investigation Division National Office will obtain the requested information and transmit it to the requesting district.

(h) Information regarding the payment of benefits can be obtained by contacting a Social Security Administration Payment Center. The payment center handling a particular account can be determined by reference to the first three digits of the claimant's social security account number. Exhibit 300-21 provides a list of Payment Centers and the numbers each handles.

(i) Special agents will not attempt to obtain information (except information concerning the payment of benefits) from Social Security Administration field establishments. All such requests should be directed to the Baltimore Office of the Social Security Administration or to the Criminal Investigation Division, National Office.

333.3 *(1-18-80)* 9781

Department of Labor Records

(1) Under the Labor-Management Reporting and Disclosure Act of 1959, [29 U.S.C., Ch. 11] every labor organization engaged in an industry affecting commerce must file annually with the Secretary of Labor on Form LM-2 or LM-3, a financial report, including a Statement of Assets and Liabilities, and a Statement of Receipts and Disbursements.

(2) The Act also requires a report (Form LM-10) from every employer who makes or agrees to make any payment or loan, including reimbursed expenses, to any labor organization, labor relations consultant, or any union officer or employee. It requires as well, a report (Form LM-30) from a labor organization officer or employee who receives payments from an employer.

(3) Every labor relations consultant is required to file annually an Agreement and Activities Report (Form LM-20) detailing the specific activities engaged in, and a Receipts and Disbursements Report (Form LM-21), showing receipts from all employers for labor relations advice or services, and all disbursements by the consultant in connection with such activities. Legal fees received by an attorney in connection with labor relations, legal representation, litigation, or advice are excluded from these reporting requirements.

(4) The Welfare and Pension Disclosure Act directs that the administrator of an employee welfare or pension plan file with the Secretary of Labor a plan description (Form D-1) setting forth the plan benefits, other data, and an annual financial report (Form D-2) showing the amounts contributed by each employer and by the employees; the amount of benefits paid; the number of employees covered; and statements of assets, liabilities, receipts, and disbursements.

(5) Copies of reports filed under the Labor-Management Reporting and Disclosure Act ((1)-(3) above) may be inspected at the National Office of the Department of Labor, Office of Labor-Management Welfare Pension Reports, Washington, D.C., or at its area offices covering the geographical localities where the persons or organizations filing the reports have their principal places of business. Copies of reports filed under the Welfare and Pension Disclosure Act ((4) above) are available for inspection only at its National Office.

333.4 *(3-12-81)* 9781
State Department Records

(1) Import and Export Licenses

(2) Foreign Information

(3) Passport Records

(4) Requests for information from the Department of State will be made by collateral request with procedures set forth in IRM 9264.1. Such requests will be forwarded to: Director of International Operations, Attention: Chief, Criminal Investigation Division, CP:OIO:7, for appropriate action. The request should include the taxpayer's Social Security number and the taxpayer's date and place of birth. The Director of International Operations will reply directly to the originating office.

333.5 *(1-18-80)* 9781
Securities and Exchange Commission Records

(1) SEC publications

(a) *Investment Advisor* and *Broker-Dealer Directories* contain current identifications of all investment advisors and broker-dealers registered with the Commission. The identifications include the name and principal mailing address of each of these persons and/or entities; the type of organization it is, where appropriate; and their effective registration date with the Commission. There is also an application or background file available for each of these.

(b) *SEC Daily News Digests* contain daily summaries of civil, criminal and administrative actions initiated by the Commission's Division of Enforcement in addition to other items of interest to the securities industry. The *SEC Weekly Docket* is a weekly summary of items that appeared in the daily Digests.

(c) The Quarterly SEC Securities Violations Bulletin lists all enforcement actions completed by the Commission for the preceding quarter. These include identification of all civil, criminal and administrative proceedings such as suspension and/or revocation of registrations, cease and desist orders, indictments, convictions, and imposition of sentences.

(d) The documents referred to in (1)(b), (c) and (d) are distributed by the National Office to all regional offices of IRS. Copies are also available at any of the SEC regional or branch offices in the following cities: Atlanta, GA; Miami, FL; Boston, MA; Chicago, IL; Cleveland, OH; Detroit, MI; St. Louis, MO; Denver, CO; Salt Lake City, UT; Fort Worth, TX; Los Angeles, CA; San Francisco, CA; New York, NY; Seattle, WA; Washington, DC; and Philadelphia, PA.

(2) Corporate Filings

(a) Form 10-Q. Quarterly corporate financial report.

(b) Form 10-K. Annual corporate financial report.

(c) Form 8-K. Monthly corporate report made upon the occurrence of various key events such as: changes in control of registrant; change in registrant's certifying accountant; and other materially important events.

(d) Form 8. Form used to amend other corporate filings.

(e) Form 13(d). Filed by stockholders who hold 5 percent or more interest. It should identify acquisition, show where money came from and how ownership interest changed.

(f) The documents referred to in (1)(a) and (2) are maintained at SEC's Public Reference Library in Washington, D.C. and can be obtained by written request to the Director, Criminal Investigation Division, Attn: Chief, Operations Branch CP:CI:O.

(3) Enforcement/Investigative files

(a) Corporate documents

(b) Documents from third-party sources

(c) Witness statements

(d) Other appropriate investigatory material

(e) Access to SEC's enforcement files can only be gained through a disclosure grant being conferred on IRS by the Commission (SEC). Request for access to these files must be addressed to the Director, Criminal Investigation Division, National Office, Attn: Chief, Operations Branch as indicated in 333.1:(1).

333.6 *(1-18-80)* 9781
Interstate Commerce Commission Records

(1) Section 20(7)(f) of the Interstate Commerce Commission Act prohibits the divulgence of any facts or information which may come to the knowledge of the Commission agent during the course of his official examination or inspection, except by direction of the Commission or by a court or judge thereof. If, however, it is necessary in connection with the examination of the taxpayer's books and records for a special agent to have access to information or review the files of the Commission, a request for such information in the name of the Commissioner of Internal Revenue may be submitted to the Chairman of the Interstate Commerce Commission.

(2) Requests for information should be submitted by the District Director to the Director, Criminal Investigation Division, National Office, Attention: CP:CI:O. The information desired will be submitted through official channels and when obtained referred promptly to the District Director.

333.7 *(1-18-80)* 9781
Comptroller of Currency (Bank Examiners' Reports)

(1) National bank examinations are made to determine bank financial positions and to evaluate bank assets. Bank examiners' reports contain information about bank records, loans, and operations.

(2) In view of their purpose and the basis on which they are obtained, reports of national bank examinations and related correspondence and papers are deemed to be of a confidential nature. If it is necessary, in an examination of a taxpayer's books and records, that a special agent have access to information contained in a bank examiners' report, the request should be submitted by the District Director to the Collection Division of the National Office, Attention: CP:C:O. The request should set forth the taxpayer's name and address, the information desired, the reason it is needed, and the intended use thereof. The National Office will address the request to the Comptroller of the Currency.

334 *(1-18-80)* 9781
Government Records

334.1 *(1-18-80)* 9781
Internal Revenue Service

334.11 *(1-18-80)* 9781
National Computer Center

The National Computer Center maintains the master file which is a tax record of all known taxpayers. The master file is separated into several categories, some of which are the business master file (BMF), the individual master file (IMF), residual master file (RMF) and the retention register.

334.111 *(1-18-80)* 9781
The Business Master File

(1) The Business Master File (BMF) maintained on magnetic tape is a tax record of business taxpayers required by law and regulations to have Employer Identification Numbers (EIN) as identifying account numbers.

(a) *Design*—The Business Master File is designed to accumulate on tape all data pertaining to the tax liabilities of one taxpayer. The returns filed for each type of tax, the assessments, the debit and credit transactions for each tax account, and a record of all changes made on a tax return are maintained for each taxpayer in the master file.

(b) *Business Taxpayer*—A business taxpayer is a taxpayer conducting a business enterprise, the operations or products of which are subject to Federal taxation.

(c) *BMF Taxes*—The types of taxes processed to the BMF are limited to:

1 Employment Taxes (Return Form 940)

2 Withholding and FICA Taxes (Return Form 941)

3 Corporation Income Taxes (Return Form 1120)

4 Excise Taxes (Return Form 720)

5 Railroad Retirement Taxes (Return Form CT-1)

6 Employment (Household) Taxes (Return Form 942)

7 Employment (Agricultural) Taxes (Return Form 943)

8 Corporation Income (Small Business) Taxes (Return Form 1120S)

9 Fiduciary Income Taxes (Return Form 1041)

10 Partnership Income Taxes (Return Form 1065)

11 Foreign Corporation Income Tax Return (Return Form 1120F)

12 Life Insurance Company Income Tax Return (Return Form 1120L)

13 Mutual Insurance Company Income Tax Return (Return Form 1120M)

(d) In addition, tax returns on exempt organizations which have income from investments are processed on BMF.

(e) *BMF Sections*—Each taxpayer's record on the Business Master File, as on the IMF, contains an entity file and a tax module file.

334.112 *(1-18-80)* 9781
The Individual Master File

(1) The Individual Master File is a magnetic tape record of all individual income tax filers, in Social Security Number sequence, and is maintained at the National Computer Center. All tax

data and related information pertaining to individual income taxpayers are posted to the Individual Master File so that the file reflects a continuously updated and current record of each taxpayer's account. All settlements with taxpayers are effected through computer processing of the Individual Master File account and the data therein is used for accounting records, for issuance of refund checks, bills or notices, answering inquiries, classifying returns for audit, preparing reports and other matters concerned with the processing and enforcement activities of the Internal Revenue Service.

(a) *Design*—The Individual Master File is designed to accumulate in each taxpayer's account all data pertaining to the income taxes for which the taxpayer is liable. The account is further sectionalized into separate tax periods (tax modules) each reflecting the balance, status, and transactions applicable to the specific tax period. This includes the returns filed, assessments, debit and credit transactions, and all changes made to the filed tax returns. The returns filed include Income Tax Forms 1040, 1040A, 1040NR, 1040C, 1040SS, 1040PR, and Estimated Tax Returns 1040ES. (The Form 1040A was not in use January 1, 1970 through December 31, 1972.) Forms 1040C, 1040SS, and 1040PR posted to the Master File beginning January 1, 1971; Form 1040NR beginning January 1, 1973.

(b) *Taxpayer Accounts*—Each taxpayer account has an entity module and one or more tax modules.

(c) *Entity Module*—The entity module contains data which describes the taxpayer as an entity and which applies to all records of the taxpayer. This entity module contains groups of data including name, address, etc.

(d) *Tax Module*—A tax module contains records of tax liability and accounting information pertaining to the income tax for *one* tax period. Each tax module contains groups of data including balance due amounts, refund checks sent, and other accounting information relating to a specific tax period.

334.113 *(1-18-80)* 9781
Residual Master File (RMF)

(1) A magnetic tape containing information on taxpayers filing the following:

(a) Special Taxes (Return Form 11, 11B, 11C)

(b) Wagering Tax (Return Form 730)

(c) Highway Use Taxes (Return Form 2290)

(d) Estate Tax (Return Form 706)

(e) Gift Taxes (Return 709)

(2) The RMF was merged with the Business Master File as of January, 1979.

334.114 *(1-18-80)* 9781
Retention Register

(1) Contains all entity and tax modules removed from the Master File. The basic criteria for removal of a tax module are:

(a) a zero module balance;

(b) no freeze or unsettled conditions present; and

(c) no activity to the module for 27 months.

334.115 *(1-18-80)* 9781
Transcripts of Account

334.1151 *(1-18-80)* 9781
Definitions

(1) *Transcript (Computer Generated)*—A machine printout from the National Computer Center that provides master file information on a particular taxpayer's account.

(2) *Transcript (Manually Prepared)*—A typed transcript from a Regional Service Center of a taxpayer's account which is extracted from microfilm or from non-master file section of the Service Center which maintains manual records relating to controlled situations.

334.116 *(1-18-80)* 9781
Requesting Transcripts of Account

See text 3(10)6 for requesting transcripts.

334.12 *(3-12-82)* 9781
Service Center Records

(1) Each region of the Service has at least one service center. The service centers produce microfilm tapes of tax information, by District, pertaining to the taxpayers for each of the districts which they service. Some of the information which is available is as follows:

(a) IMF and BMF name directories (ALPHA tapes). These directories list the names of the taxpayers in alphabetical order, their SSN or EIN, addresses and; in the case of the IMF directory, the SSN of the spouses. These directories are a quick way to determine the SSN or EIN of a taxpayer.

(b) IMF and BMF reference registers. These registers list the filings of tax returns for many periods, the classes of tax involved and the cycle each return was processed by the service center. The listings are in numerical order by SSN or EIN, as the case may be. These registers are important because they furnish the necessary information concerning the cycles during which returns were processed. This is needed in order to research the IMF and BMF accounts registers.

(c) Accounts Register—A weekly microfilm register of accounts information that lists all postings during a particular cycle to an *active* entity or tax period. It is produced weekly for each district with separate registers for BMF and IMF accounts. Information is in EIN or SSN order. The register is maintained in each District Headquarters Office as well as the Service Center. "Final" cumulative registers are issued every four cycles (weeks) to consolidate transactions occurring in the previous four weeks.

(2) The service centers also produce the master alpha index. This index is the compilation of all information items, open and closed investigations, and other information in which the Criminal Investigation Division may have an interest. The following is a list of "other information":

(a) Referrals to Criminal Investigation Division.

(b) Open investigations.

(c) Currency Transactions Reports (Forms 4789).

(d) Currency or Monetary Instrument Reports (Forms 4790).

(e) U.S. Customs Seizure Reports.

(f) Reports of U.S. Customs Currency Violation Investigations.

(g) Drug Enforcement Administration Class 1 Information Items.

(h) Securities Exchange Commission Project Information Items.

(i) Grand Jury Information Items where there is no 6(e) order.

(j) Referrals from the questionable refund program.

(k) Closed Criminal Investigations.

(3) See also IRM 9311.8.

334.2 *(1-18-80)* 9781
Disbursing Offices of the U.S. Government Records

(1) U.S. Government checks are issued by disbursing offices of the following services and departments:

(a) U.S. Army.
(b) U.S. Air Force.
(c) U.S. Navy.
(d) U.S. Marine Corps.
(e) U.S. Post Office Department.
(f) U.S. Treasury Department.

(2) The military services and the U.S. Post Office Department make disbursements relating to their own activities, and the Regional Disbursing Officers, Bureau of Accounts, U.S. Treasury Department, make disbursements for all other U.S. Government activities. These disbursing offices are located at major military installations and in a number of large metropolitan areas throughout the nation. In general, they maintain copies of paid vouchers and check listings or similar type records which identify each check issued for goods or services. In addition, the Regional Disbursing Officers, Bureau of Accounts, U.S. Treasury, microfilm all checks prior to issuance. All canceled U.S. Government checks, from whatever source issued, are processed by the Office of the Treasurer of the United States (see text 333.3.)

334.3 *(3-12-81)* 9781
Treasurer of the United States Records

334.31 *(3-12-81)* 9781
Introduction

Cancelled checks paid by the U.S. Treasury are processed through the Office of the Treasurer of the United States and may be obtained as described below.

334.32 *(3-12-81)* 9781
Refund Checks

(1) The district requesting a photocopy of a refund check should contact the Chief, Criminal Investigation Branch at the service center which services the requesting district. The request should include the following information:

(a) Name of payee (if the name of the payee is not available, the check may be located by using the payee's Social Security Number or Employer Identification Number);

(b) Social Security Number or Employer Identification Number;

(c) Period and type of tax; and

(d) Amount of check.

(2) The Chief, Criminal Investigation Branch will in turn request a copy of the check through IDRS, in accordance with IRM 3(17)(42)3.(11).

(3) If the check is being considered for use in a trial or a procedure requiring certification, the request for certification should be included in the request.

334.33 *(3-12-81)* 9781
U.S. Treasury Checks Issued for U.S. Government Agencies

(1) Photocopies of U.S. Treasury checks have to be obtained by initiating a request through the U.S. Government agency which authorized the check.

(2) The authorizing U.S. Government agency has to submit a request for the check photocopy to the particular disbursing office that issued the check. The disbursing office verifies the accuracy of the submitted information and forwards the request via a Form 1180, Request for Stop Payment, to the Bureau of Government Financial Operations, Check Claims Division. The Check Claims Division will obtain the requested check photocopy and forward it to the claimant (requesting party) shown on Form 1180.

(3) The initial request submitted by the authorizing agency must contain the following information:

(a) Name of payee;

(b) Date of check;

(c) Amount of check;

(d) Check number;

(e) Disbursing office symbol;

(f) Photocopy is needed (if certification is necessary include this in the request);

(g) Name and address of the claimant (this should be the special agent's name and office address unless the authorizing agency objects; if the authorizing agency does object, then the special agent should make arrangements with the agency to monitor the request); and

(h) The fact that the check photocopy is urgently needed for a criminal investigation.

(4) When the Check Claims Division receives the Form 1180 from the disbursing office, Part C of this form will be sent to the claimant. This should be the special agent (see (3)(g) above). Exhibit 300-1 is an example of a completed Form 1180.

(5) If a response is not received within 45 days of the date of the request, shown in Item 1 of Form 1180, the special agent should submit a memorandum with a photocopy of Part C for each check to:

Bureau of Government Financial Operations
Check Claims Division
401 14th Street S.W., Washington, DC 20227
ATTN: Stop Payment Branch

(6) If a follow-up memorandum is initiated, attach requests for no more than three checks to insure more expeditious handling.

(7) The special agent should not make any request directly to the Bureau of Government Financial Operations, Check Claims Division (unless a follow-up to the initial request becomes necessary). The Check Claims Division will not process any check requests except those which originally came through the disbursing office.

334.34 *(3-12-81)* 9781
Obtaining Original U.S. Treasury Checks

(1) If original U.S. Treasury checks are needed, the following procedure should be followed (original checks will normally take longer to obtain than photocopies since they usually must be retrieved from the Federal Records Center).

(2) Obtain the following information:

(a) Name of payee;

(b) Date of check;

(c) Amount of check;

(d) Check number; and

(e) Disbursing office symbol.

(3) Contact the nearest Secret Service field office or resident agent (see Exhibit 300-4) and complete Secret Service Form (SSF) 1600.

(4) The request should be limited to one original check per SSF 1600, although a number of checks with the same payee may be requested on one SSF 1600.

(5) The Secret Service Special Agent-in-Charge will approve the request and forward it to the Forgery Division.

(6) The original check(s) will be forwarded to the requesting agent through the appropriate Secret Service field office or Resident Agency.

(Next page is 9781-54.1)

(7) When the original check is no longer needed, it will be returned to the appropriate Secret Service field office or Resident Agency.

334.4 *(1-18-80)* 9781
Bureau of the Public Debt Records

(1) Banking institutions generally will handle subscriptions for United States Securities, but only Federal Reserve Banks and Branches and the Treasury Department are authorized to act as official agencies. The Secretary of the Treasury, through the Bureau of the Public Debt, Division of Transactions and Rulings, Washington, D.C. 20225, conducts transactions in securities after issue and answers inquiries concerning such transactions. However, the agent may find it advantageous to make inquiries of the Federal Reserve Bank and Branches, listed in Exhibit 300-3, which are official agencies for the receipt of securities for transactions after issue, and may be authorized to complete such transactions.

(2) Records of U.S. Savings Bonds (registered bonds) purchased and redeemed. This information can be obtained in the following manner:

(a) Request for information must be in the name of the District Director and addressed to:

Bureau of the Public Debt
Division of Transactions and Rulings
200 Third Street
Parkersburg, WV 26101

(b) The request should contain the following information:

1 the complete name that would be shown first on the bonds, including middle name or initial;

2 all addresses, including street and number, city and state which may be shown on the inscription on the bonds and the years the taxpayer lived at each address;

3 the taxpayer's social security account number, if the request is for information about Series H bonds, or Series E bonds issued on January 1, 1974, and later;

4 the years in which the bonds may have been issued as the issue record constitutes the basic reference. Ordinarily the redemption record can be identified only after the issuance is ascertained; and

5 the series of bonds which may have been purchased. The following schedule shows the dates when the sale of each series began and ended:

Series	*Dates*
A	March 1935 through December 1935.
B	January 1936 through December 1936.
C	January 1937 through December 1938.
D	January 1939 through April 1941.
E	May 1941 through present, sales continuing.
F	May 1941 through April 1952.
G	May 1941 through April 1952.
H	June 1952 through present, sales continuing.
J	May 1952 through April 1957.
K	May 1952 through April 1957.

6 A statement that the request has been carefully screened and the information requested is the minimum necessary in the case.

(c) See IRM 937(14) concerning interest earned on savings bonds.

(Next page is 9781-55)

334.5 *(1-18-80)* 9781

Bureau of Government Financial Operations

(1) The Division of Cash Services, Bureau of Government Financial Operations, will notify the Director, Criminal Investigation Division when a person presents $5,000 or more of mutilated currency for redemption. The Director, Criminal Investigation Division will immediately refer the information to the Chief, Criminal Investigation Division, in the district in which the person requesting the currency redemption resides. The Division of Cash Services will withhold payment in such cases for a period of thirty days from date of notification so that the IRS can determine whether further withholding of payment is desired.

(2) A mutilated currency report shall, immediately upon receipt, be classified, as an information item and screened to determine whether preliminary inquiries should be undertaken by a special agent or whether the information should be forwarded to Examination or Collection activity. Care should be taken that the Collection activity is informed of the report immediately upon its receipt, in order that Collection may exercise any right of offset for outstanding assessment against the taxpayer involved. The service center and/or the National Computer Center should be notified if a valid social security number is available.

(3) It is not contemplated that Criminal Investigation will request the Division of Cash Services to withhold payment of mutilated currency beyond the original thirty-day period except in rare or unusual cases. Such cases will generally involve a jeopardy assessment situation where time is an element. Where it is determined that such an unusual situation exists, the Chief, Criminal Investigation Division, with the concurrence of the District Director, will notify the Director, Criminal Investigation Division, National Office, immediately by telegraph or telephone so that the Division of Cash Services may be advised accordingly. If at the time of screening there is no apparent Criminal Investigation, Examination or Collection potential in the matter, it may be closed to file without further action, or disposed of as any information item. No report need be submitted to the Director, Criminal Investigation Division, if it is determined that payment should not be withheld.

(4) When a special agent has information which indicates that a taxpayer has presented mutilated currency for redemption in an amount less than $5,000, the agent should prepare a request for the Division of Cash Services to search their files. The request should be signed by the Chief with the concurrence of the District Director and mailed directly to:

Bureau of Government Financial Operations
DCS/BEPA
Room 126
Treasury Annex #1
Washington, D.C. 20226

(5) The request should contain the following information if it is available:

(a) taxpayer's name and full address;

(b) amount of the redemption;

(c) approximate date the currency was presented for redemption; and

(d) name of the bank where the currency was presented for redemption.

(6) See also IRM 9376.1.

334.6 *(4-15-82)* 9781

Customs Service

334.61 *(4-15-82)* 9781

Customs Records

(1) The United States Customs Service has authorized Directors of Customs at Headquarters Ports to furnish Internal Revenue officials with information from Customs' records, such as owners' declarations, manifests and other documents relating to the importation of taxable articles. Customs officials have been instructed to immediately forward to the Customs Service for consideration all Service requests for information not covered by prior authorizations. Information obtained from Customs will be treated as being of a confidential nature.

(2) The Customs Service has investigative jurisdiction concerning the enforcement of appropriate sections of Title 31, United States code dealing with currency entering or leaving the United States. Sections 103.23(a), 103.23(b) and 103.25(3) state that when any person transporting or causing transportation or more than $5,000 of currency or certain monetary instruments at any one time, into or out of the United States, must file a report with the Customs Service on Customs' Form 4790 Report of International Transportation of Currency or Monetary Instruments (CMIR) at the time of departure, mailing or shipping. (See text 335.22).

334.62 *(4-15-82)* 9781

Verification of Award Payments to Customs Service Informants

(1) In order to protect the identity of informants, it is the policy of the Customs Service to advise such persons that award payments should be reported on income tax returns as "other income", and that, if the source of that income is questioned by the Internal Revenue Service, the informant need state only that the

amount involved was received from the Customs Service for services of a confidential nature and give the name of the Customs officer from whom the award was received.

(2) Upon inquiry from an officer of the Internal Revenue Service, the Customs Service will furnish the name of the informant and the amount of the award. If, during an income tax investigation, a taxpayer should offer that explanation for the source of unidentified income or unreported income, verification should be made only by inquiry of the Supervisory Customs Agent or Customs Agent in Charge by whom the taxpayer claims the payment was made. Whenever practicable, the proper Customs officer should be interviewed personally, without any written communication or other report. Otherwise, the Chief, Criminal Investigation Division, shall prepare a letter to such officer, marked "For Personal Attention Only," requesting verification of the alleged payments.

(3) Special agents shall take all requisite measures to prevent disclosure of any information regarding these award payments. The source of information will not be revealed in reports or otherwise. If necessary, award payments may be identified as "Miscellaneous income (source verified)." Correspondence used to verify such source of income shall be maintained in a secure file under personal control of the Chief.

334.7 *(1-18-80)* 9781

Secret Service Records

(1) Records pertaining to counterfeit and forgery cases.

(2) The Criminal Investigation Division cooperates with the Secret Service in the forgery aspect of criminal tax investigations involving possible forgery of United States Government checks (see IRM 9378). Exhibit 300-4 contains a list of local Secret Service Offices. This listing is furnished so that Criminal Investigation Division field personnel can promptly coordinate any forgery violations with the nearest office.

(3) Records pertaining to anonymous letters and background files on persons who write "crank" letters.

334.8 *(9-8-80)* 9781

Bureau of Alcohol, Tobacco and Firearms Records

(1) Practically every major case perfected by Bureau of Alcohol, Tobacco and Firearms (BATF) investigators involves individuals who, due to the nature of their illicit enterprises, either have not filed income tax returns or have filed false ones. The evidence in many of these cases not only establishes the violation of the laws which BATF is charged to enforce, but frequently makes out a prima facie income tax fraud case or at least furnishes some very definite leads to violation of the income tax laws.

(2) Each case in which it appears to the BATF investigator that a suspect has realized substantial profits from illicit operations or possesses excessive net worth will be referred through the Special Agent in Charge to Criminal Investigation on Form 4314, Enforcement Referral—Non-Bureau Violations, for possible income tax or wagering tax investigation.

(3) Each liquor law violator will be asked if he/she filed a Federal income tax return for the previous tax year, and the Special Agent in Charge will submit periodically to Criminal Investigation, either Form 4314 or lists of the names and addresses of persons who apparently have a tax liability and who stated they had not filed. These names should be processed in Criminal Investigation as information items from a Government source.

(4) BATF records which may be of interest are as follows:

(a) Records of distillers, brewers, and persons or firms who manufacture or handle alcohol as a sideline or main product.

(b) Record of inventory of retail liquor dealers and names of suppliers as well as amounts of liquor purchased by brand.

(c) Names and records of known bootleggers.

(d) Reports of investigations.

(e) Records of firearms registration (alphabetical and numerical).

(5) See also IRM 9378.

334.9 *(1-18-80)* 9781

Federal Bureau of Investigation Records

(1) Criminal records and fingerprints.

(2) National Stolen Property Index—Government property stolen, including military property.

(3) Nonrestricted information pertaining to criminal offenses.

(4) National Fraudulent Check Index.

(5) Anonymous Letter Index.

334.(10) *(1-18-80)* 9781

Drug Enforcement Agency Records

(1) Record of licensed handlers of narcotics.

(2) Criminal records of users, pushers, and suppliers of narcotics.

334.(11) *(1-18-80)* 9781

Immigration and Naturalization Service Records

(1) Records of all immigrants and aliens.

(2) Lists of passengers and crews on vessels from foreign ports.

(3) Passenger manifests and declarations—ship, date, and point of entry required.

(4) Naturalization records—names of witnesses to naturalization proceedings and people who know the suspect.

(5) Deportation proceedings.

(6) Financial statements of aliens and persons sponsoring their entry.

334.(12) *(12-7-81)* 9781
U.S. Postal Service Records

334.(12)1 *(12-7-81)* 9781
Addresses of Post Office Box Holders

U.S. Postal Service regulations authorize disclosure of names, addresses and telephone numbers of post office box holders to a recognized law enforcement agency. Requests for this data must be directed to the Postal Inspector of the area concerned stating that the information is necessary for law enforcement purposes. The requests will be signed by the Chief or Acting Chief, Criminal Investigation Division. Photocopies and originals of applications for post office boxes cannot be obtained from the U.S. Postal Service without a court order.

334.(12)2 *(12-7-81)* 9781
Forwarding Addresses of Taxpayers and Third Parties

(1) U.S. Postal Service regulations authorize disclosure of forwarding addresses. Requests for this data may be directed to the Postal Inspector of the area concerned stating that the change of address is required for law enforcement purposes or that the information is required for official business and all other known sources for obtaining the change of address have been exhausted. When forwarding addresses are requested in writing, they should be signed by the Chief, or Acting Chief, Criminal Investigation Division. Further, personal contact by a special agent is not prohibited when that would be more efficient and practical.

(2) A request for copies of change of address cards filed with numerous Post Offices throughout the country should be coordinated with the Postal Inspector in the key district. He/she will obtain copies of the desired documents and furnish them to the special agent. Originals of the change of address cards cannot be obtained from the U.S. Postal Service without a court order.

334.(12)3 *(12-7-81)* 9781
Photostats of Postal Money Orders

Where it is necessary to obtain information or photostats of postal money orders, where either the IRS or the Department of the Treasury is the payee or purchaser, in connection with a matter being investigated by Criminal Investigation, the request should be addressed directly to Money Order Division, Postal Data Center, P.O. Box 14965, St. Louis, Missouri, 63182 and should bear the signature of the Chief, Criminal Investigation Division; District Director; ARC (Criminal Investigation); or Director, Criminal Investigation Division. Requests for copies of postal money orders which were purchased by and payable to any other entities must be made through the local U.S. Postal Inspection Service office. Ordinarily, a special agent assigned to a District Director's office should prepare the request for signature of the Chief. Those agents assigned or detailed to the office of the ARC (Criminal Investigation) should prepare the request for the signature of the ARC (Criminal Investigation).

334.(12)4 *(12-7-81)* 9781
Mail Covers

(1) U.S. Postal Service regulations which constitute the sole authority and procedure for initiating, processing, placing, and using mail covers are provided in title 39, Code of Federal Regulations, section 233.2; and Part 233.2, *Postal Service Manual.*

(2) The following are U.S. Postal Service definitions relating to mail covers.

(a) "Mail cover" is the process by which a record is made of any data appearing on the outside of any class of mail matter, including checking the contents of any second, third, or fourth class mail matter as now sanctioned by law, in order to obtain information in the interest of protecting the national security, locating a fugitive, or obtaining evidence of commission or attempted commission of a crime.

(b) "Fugitive" is any person who has fled from the United States or any State, territory, the District of Columbia, or possession of the United States, to avoid prosecution for a crime, to avoid punishment for a crime, or to avoid giving testimony in a criminal proceeding.

(c) "Crime," for purposes of these regulations, is any commission of an act or the attempted commission of any act that is punishable by law by imprisonment for a term exceeding one year.

(d) "Law enforcement agent" is any authority of the Federal Government or any authority of a State or local Government one of whose functions is to investigate the commission or attempted commission of acts constituting a crime.

(3) Any data concerning mail covers may at a later time be required to be made available by the U.S. Postal Service to the mail cover subject in a legal proceeding through appropriate discovery procedures.

(4) Regional Commissioners and District Directors are responsible for ensuring that requests for mail covers are made in accordance with established procedures.

(5) All requests by Criminal Investigation Division personnel for mail covers will be signed by the Chief, or Acting Chief, Criminal Investigation Division; addressed to the Postal Inspector in Charge of the postal area involved; and sent directly to the Postal Inspector in Charge, except for the fourth and subsequent renewal requests as provided for in (10) below. A copy of all requests will be forwarded for informational purposes to the ARC (Criminal Investigation.)

(6) Request for mail covers should be made only to locate a fugitive or when there is good reason to believe that a felony has either been committed or attempted. A mail cover should never be requested in a case involving a misdemeanor violation. Whenever such a case has been elevated to a felony, case management records must be updated timely to support any subsequent request for a mail cover.

(7) The requests for mail covers should be made in writing, stating therein which of the purposes specified in (6) above is applicable. It is the policy of the U.S. Postal Service that a separate request will be made for each Post Office which must conduct the mail cover. The mail cover request must also specify, and stipulate:

(a) the identity of each individual or business name to be covered, giving name, address, and ZIP code number;

(b) that an official investigation is in progress;

(c) the Federal statute alleged to have been violated and the criminal penalty, if convicted. Requesters should provide a brief explanation of the statute and the criminal penalty which could be asserted if convicted under that statute. For example; "We are conducting an investigation of Mr. for allegedly attempting to evade his and his wife's personal income tax for calendar years 19 through 19 in violation of Section 7201 of the Internal Revenue Code. Conviction under this statute could result in Mr. being imprisoned for not more than five years and/or fined not more than $10,000 for each of the years for which he is convicted";

(d) the reasonable ground that exists which demonstrates that the mail cover is necessary to locate a fugitive or to obtain information regarding the commission or attempted commission of a felony. This should be detailed enough to enable Postal personnel to form a judgment as to the need for the mail cover (see 334.(12)4:(8)(b)). However, disclosure of return information to the Postal Service must be limited to the extent necesary to obtain the mail cover;

(e) the name and address of any attorney for each person or concern on which a mail cover is requested or that the attorney for each person or concern on which a mail cover is requested is not known (mail cover data excludes matter mailed between the mail cover subject and the known attorney);

(f) that each person or concern on which a mail cover is requested, if not a fugitive, is not under indictment in connection with the matter under investigation;

(g) that if the mail cover is authorized and the subject is indicted for any cause during the mail cover period, the Postal Inspector in Charge will be immediately notified. If the indictment is for an offense that is not part of the CID investigation, the notification should be made in writing and should state that the indictment concerns a matter that is not related to the CID investigation. The notification should request that the mail cover be continued without interruption. If the indictment returned is a sealed indictment in a CID investigation, the Postal Inspector in Charge will be requested to cancel the mail cover. No mention of an indictment will be made to the Postal Inspector in Charge, thus avoiding making an unlawful disclosure by violating the secrecy rules that govern Federal Grand Juries; and

(h) a statement that only first class should be covered, unless it is specifically necessary that other classes of mail be included.

(8) The "reasonable grounds" should be established on each person or concern who is the subject of a mail cover, not only the named subject of the investigation. For instance, a person may be named as the subject of an investigation but a mail cover is necessary on both the subject and his/her spouse (or associate). The request should also explain the necessity for the mail cover on the spouse (or associate).

(a) A request to include a spouse should include specific comment to provide Postal officials with enough information on which to base authorizing the mail cover. This could include mention, for example, that we learned of a spouse's involvement in the evasion scheme being investigated from an informant or other third party witness(es), or through an analysis of bank and other financial records. It is not sufficient to say that "Because the taxpayer is married, we have reason to expect that the spouse may hold assets. . .", or that "Based on our experience in other investigations, we anticipate that the spouse. . .".

(b) The request should stipulate and specify the necessity for the requested mail cover, such as:

1 the taxpayer uses aliases;

2 the taxpayer is known to use nominee ownership in bank accounts or assets;

3 the mail cover is expected to uncover assets, liabilities and/or expenditures; and

4 the mail cover should reveal the taxpayer's contacts or clientele, etc.

(c) Mail covers are usually requested on a stated individual or concern at a given address. Mail arriving for other persons or concerns who also happen to receive mail at the address are not included in the mail cover. In cases where the investigation requires a cover on mail addressed to the known occupant of a particular address and any fictitious names that may be used by the occupant, the following must also be included in the request:

1 a statement establishing the necessity for covering all mail intended for delivery at the particular address.

2 a statement that it is known through investigation that only the subject of the cover resides and receives mail at the address.

3 a statement that all mail received for delivery at the address is intended for the subject of the mail cover. *If persons other than the subject of the mail cover reside at the address, a list of their names must be furnished, and all mail addressed to them is to be excluded from the cover.*

(9) Requests for mail covers should be limited to not more than 30 days and cancelled if the information sought is obtained from other sources prior to the expiration of the period. Cancellations should be sent by the originating office and addressed to the Postal Inspector in Charge of the postal area involved. A request for renewal of a mail cover, when warranted, should be made in accordance with the procedures set forth in (5), (6), and (7) above. In those few cases wherein it may be necessary to extend the mail cover beyond 120 days (three renewals), the fourth renewal request and all subsequent renewals must be submitted to the Director, Criminal Investigation Division, for approval, together with a memorandum giving detailed reasons as to the need to continue the mail cover.

(10) All Forms 2009, reporting mail cover information, received from the Postal Inspection Service must be returned within 60 days to the Postal Inspection Service official from whom received. Mail cover documents are the property of the U.S. Postal Service and are loaned with the understanding they will be treated confidentially. Reproduction of mail cover documents is prohibited.

334.(13) *(11-7-80)* 9781
Federal Aviation Administration (FAA) Records

(1) This agency maintains records reflecting the chain of ownership of all civil aircraft in the United States. These records include documents relative to their manufacture, sale (sales contracts, bills of sale, mortgages, liens) and transfer, inspection and modification.

(2) This information is maintained at:
Federal Aviation Administration
Aeronautical Center-ACC-90
P.O. Box 25082
Oklahoma City, OK 73125

(3) Information can be obtained from FAA as follows:

(a) Request requiring no written response or documentation—When a special agent needs routine information that does not require a copy or extensive research, it can be obtained by a telephone request to the Investigations and Security Division, Oklahoma City, OK, telephone number FTS 749-2522. The special agent should be prepared to furnish the following information:

1 The special agent's identity including name, division and office location.

2 Type of investigation—civil or criminal.

3 The aircraft N-Registration Number if the owner of an airplane is desired.

4 The name, date of birth, and social security number are needed to obtain a listing of aircraft registered in an individual's name.

(b) Request for regular and certified copies of documents—Requests of this nature and requests requiring extensive research should be forwarded by collateral request to the Criminal Investigation Division, Oklahoma City District.

334.(14) *(1-18-80)* 9781
Department of Defense Records

(1) Data concerning the pay, dependents, allotment accounts, soldier's deposits, withholding statements (Forms W-2), and any other financial information relative to military personnel is available at one of the following offices, depending upon the branch of the Armed Forces to which the individual was or is presently attached:

(a) *ARMY:*
United States Army Finance Center
Indianapolis, 46249

Request to include: Complete name and Army serial number.

(b) *AIR FORCE:*
Air Force Finance Center
3800 York Street
Denver, Colorado 80205

(c) *NAVY:*
Director, Bureau of Supplies and Accounts
Department of the Navy
13th and Euclid Streets
Cleveland, Ohio 44115

(2) Requests for information from the sources in (1) above should be forwarded through normal channels to the District Director of Internal Revenue of the area in which the respective finance center is located. It is important that the taxpayer be adequately identified, preferably by name, address, and military serial number. However, if the serial number is unknown or cannot be furnished, the data may be secured if the inquiry includes the serviceman's full name, date of birth, and places of induction and/or discharge from the service.

(3) Addresses of military personnel:

(a) Form 2223, Request for Address of Military Personnel, should be used to obtain from the records of the military services the current or last known address of a taxpayer who is a member of, or who has been recently separated from, the Armed Forces. All Forms 2223 should be carefully prepared. The full name of the taxpayer should be entered accurately, together with his preservice address and serial number, if known. If available, the last known military address of the taxpayer and the latest date such address was known to be current should be furnished. The correct mailing addresses for the military service branches are printed on the face of Form 2223 and the address corresponding to the member's Branch of service *must* be entered in the space provided therefor. Each Form 2223 should be examined prior to mailing to make certain that the return address of the requester has been inserted. Otherwise, even though a current address may be available, the military service Branch will be unable to return the completed Form 2223.

(b) Many of the Forms 2223 will have to be forwarded by the military service branch concerned to various record centers located throughout the United States. Therefore, no followup inquiry should be made within ninety days from the date of the original request. If, after ninety days, it is found that a followup inquiry is necessary, a second Form 2223 should be prepared and mailed to the proper military service branch. However, the second Form 2223 should not be identified as a follow-up request or as a second request, and no reference should be made to the original Form 2223.

(4) Data concerning the personal and medical history of former Army personnel (discharged subsequent to 1912) and former Navy and Marine personnel are located at: Military Personnel Records Center, GSA, 9700 Page Boulevard, St. Louis, Missouri 63132. Requests should include: Complete name, including middle name; Service Serial Number; date and place of birth; dates of service, military organizations or the name of the individual's next of kin.

(5) Records of contracts and all original vouchers covering payments made to persons and firms dealing with the U.S. Air Force are retained at:

U.S. Air Force Accounting and Finance Center.
AFO—Accounts and Mail Branch
3800 York Street
Denver, Colorado 80205

(a) Normally, requests for such information should be made by collateral to the Denver District.

334.(15) *(1-18-80)* 9781

Government Surplus Property Sales

The Director, Directorate of Marketing, Defense Supply Agency, Defense Logistics Services Centers, Federal Center, Battle Creek, Michigan 49061, maintains a master record of all Government surplus items sold through local defense surplus sales offices in the United States. The Center will provide computer printouts from July 1, 1965, forward concerning surplus sales and will identify the local sales office which sold the property and which maintains the original documents relating to the sales.

334.(16) *(12-7-81)* 9781

Defense Investigative Service (DIS)

Their records include case files of individuals who have undergone investigation, both criminal and background, by the Army (Intelligence, CID, etc), Navy (NIS, etc.), Air Force (AFOSI, etc.), and the Department of Defense. Requests for information from DIS files should be forwarded to the Director, Criminal Investigation Division, National Office, Attn: CP:CI:O.

334.(17) *(1-18-80)* 9781

Federal Housing Administration Records

(1) Complete financial information.

(2) Statements of net worth and earnings.

334.(18) *(1-18-80)* 9781

United States Coast Guard Records

(1) Records of persons serving on United States ships in any capacity.

(2) Records of vessels equipped with permanently installed motors.

(3) Records of vessels over 16 feet equipped with detachable motors.

334.(19) *(1-18-80)* 9781

Veterans' Administration Records

(1) Records of loans, tuition payments, insurance payments and nonrestrictive medical data related to disability pensions are available at Veterans' Administration Regional Offices located in a number of large metropolitan areas throughout the country. This information, including photostats, may be obtained by direct mail request to the appropriate regional office or, if necessary, by collateral request.

(2) All requests should include a statement covering the need and intended use of the information. The veteran should be clearly identified and, if available, the following information should be furnished about him:

(a) V.A. claim number.
(b) Date of birth.
(c) Branch of service.
(d) Dates of enlistment and discharge.

334.(20) *(9-4-81)* 9781

Federal Courts Records

(1) Records of civil and criminal cases.

(2) Records of parole and probation officers.

(3) Records of U.S. Marshall, and U.S. Magistrate.

(4) Records of a bankruptcy proceeding except transcripts and summaries of testimony compelled pursuant to a grant of immunity. Effective October 1, 1979, the Bankruptcy Reform Act of 1978 (11 U.S.C. 344) provides that debtors, creditors and other witnesses may be granted immunity under Part V, Title 18. Section 727(a)(6) provides for denial of a discharge in bankruptcy if the debtor refuses to testify after a grant of immunity has been given. A person who testifies without a formal grant of immunity waives his/her Fifth Amendment rights against self-incrimination and the testimony could be used in a subsequent proceeding. Restrictions on the acquisition and use of information obtained under a grant of immunity are contained in IRM 937(17). Bankruptcy cases commenced prior to October 1, 1979 are governed by 11 U.S.C. 25(a)(10) which provides immunity for transcripts and summaries of testimony given by a bankrupt. Under both bankruptcy law provisions the investigating agents may use the public record of the bankruptcy as a starting point for net worth purposes. If 11 U.S.C. 25(a)(10) is applicable, agents must not examine testimony or even transcripts from the referee in order to avoid the burden of proving the absence of tainted evidence.

334.(21) *(1-18-80)* 9781

Federal Records Center

(1) Data concerning former Government employees are on file at:

(a) The Federal Records Center, G.S.A.
(Civilian Personnel Records)
111 Winnebago Street
St. Louis, MO 63118.

(b) Requests for information from such files should be prepared on GSA Standard Form 127, Request for Official Personnel Folder, and mailed direct to the Federal Records Center at St. Louis, Missouri.

334.(22) *(1-18-80)* 9781

Federal Reserve Bank Records

Records of issue of United States Treasury Bonds. See Exhibit 300-3 for a list of these banks.

334.(23) *(1-18-80)* 9781

Railroad Retirement Board Records

No information will be made available by this Agency. (See Sec. 262.16, Title 20, Code of Federal Regulations)

334.(24) *(3-12-82)* 9781
El Paso Intelligence Center (EPIC) Records.

(1) EPIC is a multi-agency operation, basically oriented towards narcotics traffickers, gun smugglers and alien smugglers, that collects, processes and disseminates information in support of ongoing field investigations. EPIC has signed agreements with 48 states, including both state and local agencies, in addition to having representatives from the participating Federal agencies. EPIC has access (terminals) to all major Federal criminal data bases. Inquiries should be limited to Project 21 (narcotics related) cases/files and/or smugglers of funds, other contraband and aliens.

(2) EPIC's "Watch", which is operational 24 hours a day, seven days a week, handles queries from field investigators and provides an immediate response. The "Watch" also handles "Lookout" requests regarding the movements of individuals, aircraft, or vessels in support of ongoing investigations. Lookouts are placed for 90 days, or increments of 1 year. A lookout should be cancelled when it has served its purpose. The "Watch" does not originate lookouts but rather monitors:

(a) INS Lookouts (including Treasury Enforcement Communications (TECS)

(b) TECS Lookouts

(c) Aircraft Lookouts, TECS portion

(d) Aircraft Lookouts, Federal Aviation Administration (FAA) portion

(e) Vessel Lookouts, Coast Guard portion

(f) Vessel Lookouts, TECS portion.

(3) EPIC's Analysis Section studies "Watch" queries, "lookouts", data base information, and other information fed into EPIC, from which it prepares "predictive" intelligence on activities and organizations. This information is subsequently provided to the field through special reports and the weekly brief.

(4) The EPIC Intelligence Terminal (IT) is an internal computer system unique to EPIC and the primary repository for all the "Watch" activity and other investigative and intelligence data fed into EPIC. The information in the data base is comprised of individuals, activities, significant events, associations among individuals and/or activities, aircraft, vessels, observations, and both foreign and domestic movements of individuals, aircraft, and vessels. The EPIC IT system is chronological and provides the name, agency, and telephone number of each investigator having expressed an interest in, or having input data regarding, a subject. EPIC has current Federal Aviation Administration (FAA) aircraft registration information (microfiche) and current United States Coast Guard vessel registration. The IT system allows retrieval of information by an individual's name, a vessel's name or an aircraft N (tail) number. These aircraft and vessel records would not be in an admissible form for use as evidence but would, in most instances, provide leads regarding the ownership, whether foreign or domestic, of that particular asset.

(5) Integrated Combined Systems (ICS) is an Immigration and Naturalization Service (INS) Manual System located at EPIC which consists of three parts, as follows:

(a) *INS Aircraft Arrival Inspection Reports (Form I92A)*. The I92A file is a manual index of private aircraft (U.S. and foreign registered) arriving in the United States from foreign countries. The I92A index overlaps the Treasury Enforcement Communications System's (TECS) private aircraft information (PAIRS), but is a more comprehensive system of records and contains significantly more data. The I92A is indexed and cross-indexed by the aircraft N (tail) number and the pilot's name. The system cannot be queried by passengers, aircraft owners, or points of origin. I92A information is valuable in establishing conspiracies, showing travel patterns and associates, and identifying aircraft ownership. The I92A files are available at EPIC for the current year and the preceding two years. EPIC also has access to an additional two years of I92A information through INS. INS at EPIC can provide certified photocopies of the I92A's and an appropriate witness for evidentiary purposes. The Form I92A includes:

1 Aircraft N (tail) number, make, model and color.

2 Pilot's name, date of birth (DOB), and address.

3 Aircraft owner's name and address.

4 Country and airport (generally the city) of departure.

5 Airport of arrival in the United States, arrival time and date, and the name of the INS/U.S. Customs Inspector.

6 Listing of passengers on the aircraft (sometimes associated with a DOB).

(b) *INS Index of known alien smugglers.*

(c) *INS Index of various schemes involving fraudulent documents and false claims to U.S. citizenship.*

(d) The INS Indexes in (b) and (c) above can be queried by:

1 Name and DOB of smuggler

2 Name on authentic documents used by imposter

3 Imposter's name

4 Supplier of documents

5 Name of user of fraudulent documents

6 Suspect individual or attorney who may have filed fraudulent birth records.

(Next page is 9781—62.1)

(6) All initial inquiries of EPIC should be directed to the "Watch" at FTS 572-2942. Give your title, name and agency. In order to protect the integrity of EPIC information, IRS will provide EPIC an alphabetical listing of Special Agents, updated every six months. Your name must appear on this list before EPIC will respond to your inquiry. No more than five inquiries (names, aircraft, vessels, or combinations thereof) should be directed to the "Watch" at one time. The "Watch" will not provide any written/hard copy reporting. If an agent determines that a written or documented response is needed, he/she should contact the IRS Representative at FTS 572-7255. Agents submitting voluminous requests should have Narcotics and Dangerous Drug (NADDIS) queries from local DEA offices and TECS queries from the local U.S. Customs or IRS Service Center offices completed prior to forwarding their EPIC requests. Voluminous requests should be submitted in writing to the IRS Representative at the following address:

EL PASO INTELLIGENCE CENTER
2211 East Missouri
El Paso, TX 79903
Attn: IRS Representative

(7) In order to place a "lookout" through EPIC, you must furnish the following information to the "Watch".

(a) Your identity
(b) Agency
(c) Case number
(d) Your FTS phone number
(e) Your home phone number
(f) Identity and phone numbers of an alternate agent

(g) On a "hit" of your lookout, EPIC will make every effort to contact the requesting agent, the alternate, or a member of his/her agency immediately.

334.(25) *(1-18-80)* 9781
Import-Export Bank Records

This bank loans funds to foreign countries and businesses to buy goods from U.S. companies. It is located at 811 Vermont Avenue, N.W., Washington, D.C. The borrower can obtain up to 50 percent of the purchase price of the goods being acquired. The selling company must fill out and submit to the bank a supplier certificate. Included in this certificate is a required statement as to commissions paid, especially in the foreign country to foreign sales "representatives" or "agents."

334.(26) *(1-18-80)* 9781
Securities Information Center Records

The Securities Information Center (SIC) is located in Wellesley Hills, Massachusetts. It is operated by Itel Corporation under contract with the Securities and Exchange Commission. All banks and brokerage houses, etc. that receive bad securities are required to report this information to SIC. They are also required to run a check with SIC if they receive $10,000 or more in securities. Information is recorded as of October 1977.

334.(27) *(1-18-80)* 9781
Department of Health Education and Welfare (HEW) Records

HEW records contain information relating to payments made to physicians receiving payments from Medicare and Medicaid programs.

335 *(9-4-81)* 9781
Treasury Enforcement Communications System (TECS)

335.1 *(9-4-81)* 9781
General

The Treasury Enforcement Communications System (TECS) is a computerized information system designed to identify individuals and businesses involved or suspected or involvement in violation of Federal law. It is also an enforcement communications system permitting instantaneous message transmittal between field terminals and between Treasury law enforcement field offices and their National Offices. TECS also provides the capability for direct inquiry to the FBI's National Crime Information Center (NCIC). In addition, the National Law Enforcement Telecommunications System (NLETS) provides the capability of communicating directly with State and local law enforcement agencies through TECS terminals. NLETS also provides direct access to State motor vehicle department files, most of which provide automated response.

335.2 *(9-4-81)* 9781
Information Available from TECS

335.21 *(9-4-81)* 9781
General

(1) Individual records available from the TECS data base include the following:

(a) U.S. Customs Service (General TECS Files):

1 fugitives;

2 known and suspected narcotics traffickers;

3 vehicles, aircraft and vessels known or suspected to be utilized in smuggling activities;

4 known and suspected business entities involved in or related to smuggling activities;

5 individuals known and suspected to be involved in organized crime and racketeering;

(b) U.S. Customs Service (Financial Information Data Base):

1 Since 1977 U.S. Customs and IRS have jointly staffed a Reports Analysis Unit

(RAU) which provides information via TECS as follows:

a Currency Transaction Report (CTR), Form 4789 (see text 338.2);

b Report of International Transportation of Currency or Monetary Instruments (CMIR), Customs Form 4790 (see text 335.22); and

c Report of Foreign Bank and Financial Accounts (FBA), Treasury Form 90-22.1 (see text 335.23).

(c) Bureau of Alcohol, Tobacco and Firearms;

1 fugitives;

2 known and suspected violators of laws falling within the jurisdiction of BATF; and

3 felons and dishonorably discharged veterans who have requested relief to own firearms and/or explosives under the Gun Control Act of 1968.

(d) IRS—Inspection

1 fugitives; and

2 arrested subjects

(e) IRS—Criminal Investigation Division

1 fugitives; and

2 Certain nonresident delinquent taxpayers (see IRM 937(16).2).

335.22 *(9-4-81)* 9781

Report of International Transportation of Currency or Monetary Instruments (CMIR), Customs Form 4790

(1) The Currency and Monetary Instrument Reporting file contains a record of every individual who has filed a Customs Form 4790, Report of International Transportation of Currency or Monetary Instruments (CMIR). This form is required to be filed by each person who physically transports, mails, or ships, or causes to be physically transported, mailed, shipped or received currency or other monetary instruments in an aggregate amount exceeding $5,000 on any one occasion from the United States to any place outside the United States, or into the United States from any place outside the United States. A transfer of funds through normal banking procedures which does not involve the physical transportation of Currency or Monetary Instruments is not required to be reported.

(2) If a TECS query results in a positive response, information contained on the CMIR will be received. If it becomes necessary to obtain a copy of the CMIR, a request which includes the Reports Control Number (RCN), should be directed to the Chief, Criminal Investigation Branch of your service center. The Chief, CIB, utilizing TECS, will request a copy of the CMIR from the U.S. Customs Service.

335.23 *(9-4-81)* 9781

Report of Foreign Bank and Financial Accounts (FBA), Treasury Form 90-22.1

(1) Foreign Bank Account files contain a record of individuals who have submitted Treasury Form 90-22.1, Report of Foreign Bank and Financial Accounts (FBA). Treasury Form 90-22.1 is generally required if an individual has a financial interest in or authority, signatory or otherwise, over one or more bank accounts, securities accounts or other financial accounts in a foreign country, when such account(s) have an aggregate value in excess of $1,000. If a TECS query results in a positive response, the name, address, SSN or EIN of the subject and a microfiche number will be received.

(2) If it becomes necessary to obtain a copy of a Treasury Form 90-22.1, a request should be directed to the Chief, Criminal Investigation Branch of your service center. The request should include the microfiche number of all forms requested. The Chief, CIB, utilizing TECS, will request a copy of the FBA from the U.S. Customs Service.

335.3 *(9-4-81)* 9781

Records Accessible Through TECS

(1) Other records accessible through TECS include the following:

(a) The National Crime Information Center (NCIC), operated by the FBI, contains records on wanted persons, vehicles, license plates, guns, articles, securities and boats which have been stolen, and computerized criminal histories (CCH-Summary police "rap sheets".) TECS has an interface with NCIC permitting entry and instantaneous retrieval of NCIC records.

(b) The National Law Enforcement Telecommunications System (NLETS) links the law enforcement agencies across the U.S. with the TECS system. This automated message switching computer is located in Phoenix, Arizona. From TECS secondary terminals NLETS queries can be made for:

1 Vehicle registration information (RQ)—license plate number, year and vehicle type; or vehicle ID number, vehicle make and vehicle year should be used.

2 Drivers license information (DQ)—name, date of birth (dob), race and sex; or drivers license number must be used.

3 State criminal history record information (CQ).

4 All states will provide driver's license (DQ) and vehicle registration (RQ) information from motor vehicle files; however, the files of all states are not automated. Responses from states with automated files should be received in a matter of seconds after a query. The (RQ) after the state code indicates that only registration checks are automated, e.g., Alaska (AK)

(RQ). The following states (including Alaska (AK) (RQ)) are automated:

Alabama (AL)	Maryland (MD)
Arizona (AZ) (RQ)	Michigan (MI)
Arkansas (AR)	Minnesota (MN)
Colorado (CO)	Mississippi (MS)
Connecticut (CT)	Missouri (MO)
District of Columbia (DC)	Montana (MT)
Georgia (GA)	Nebraska (NB)
Idaho (ID) (DQ)	New Jersey (NJ)
Ilinois (IL)	New York (NY)
Indiana (IN)	North Carolina (NC)
Iowa (IA)	North Dakota (ND)
Kansas (KS)	Ohio (OH)
Kentucky (KY)	Oklahoma (OK)
Pennsylvania (PA)	South Carolina (SC)
South Dakota (SD)	Tennessee (TN)
Texas (TX)	Utah (UT)
Vermont (VT)	Virginia (VA)
West Virginia (WV)	Wisconsin (WI)
Wyoming (WY)	

5 If the need arises, most States will also respond to inquiries for current road and weather information.

335.4 *(9-4-81)* 9781

Types of TECS Queries

(1) The following are types of queries that might be beneficial in IRS enforcement efforts:

(a) *Information Item Evaluation (service centers)*—If a tax-related information item appears to have criminal investigative potential, queries should be made to provide further evaluative information. The response (hard copy printout) will be associated with the Information Item when it is forwarded to the appropriate district office for final evaluation. For this purpose the following queries could be useful:

1 TECS—to determine whether other Treasury agencies have ongoing or closed investigations or other information which might have tax consequences.

2 RAU—Financial information files—To determine whether financial documents have been filed which might have tax consequences.

3 NCIC and State and local criminal history files—To determine criminal history for later use in preparation of prosecution or withdrawal reports.

(b) *Open Investigation (districts)*—TECS may be queried to determine if the subject of an investigation is or may have been, the subject of an investigation by another Treasury agency. TECS may be useful in establishing a contact point within the other agency from whom available tax-related information can be requested. This action will also serve to prevent jeopardizing ongoing investigations and duplication of effort. The financial information files (RAU) should be queried periodically to determine recent filing of financial reports and should be queried each time a new identifier or bank account number is obtained relating to the subject of an investigation.

(c) *Associates*—TECS entries often contain information which may help to identify associates of the subject, and a simple query may produce a number of associates.

(d) *Motor Vehicle Information*—TECS, via NLETS, provides direct access to State motor vehicle departments (see text 335.3). Except where direct telephone access to the State agency is available without charge, motor vehicle or driver's license queries should be made through TECS, especially where State files are automated.

(e) *Aircraft Information*—The Customs Service can routinely check small aircraft traffic coming into the country; therefore, TECS may be queried by the local Customs office to confirm such activity by a taxpayer if tax-related.

335.5 *(9-4-81)* 9781

Requesting TECS Queries

(1) Requests to the Chief, Criminal Investigation Branch, for TECS queries may be made by memorandum; by use of Form 5523, TECS Query Request; or by telephone. The Chief, CIB will not release TECS information requested by telephone until he/she is satisfied as to the identity of the caller (such as by telephone callback).

(2) The Chief, CIB is not required to maintain a log of queries nor retain a copy of the requests.

335.6 *(9-4-81)* 9781

Fugitive Entries

(1) The following procedures will be followed when requesting an entry to be made to TECS or NCIC regarding a fugitive.

(a) All fugitive entries will be made by the CID, National Office. When it is determined that an individual has become a fugitive, a written request should be submitted to the Director, CID, Attention: CP:CI:O, to request an entry be made in TECS and NCIC. If the taxpayer is charged with a felony, the memorandum should also request the issuance of a Wanted Circular per IRM 9377.1:(2). In urgent situations, the memorandum may be faxed to the National Office. The memorandum should contain the following information to the extent available:

1 name and case number;

2 alias;

3 race;

4 sex;

5 height

6 weight;

7 color of hair;

8 color of eyes;

9 description of any identifying scars, marks and tattoos;

10 date of birth;

11 place of birth;

12 Social Security Number;

13 passport number;

14 last known address;

15 nationality;

16 if a naturalized U.S. citizen, date, place, and certificate number;

17 occupation;

18 criminal violation with which subject is charged;

19 date of warrant;

20 warrant number;

21 type of warrant—Bench, Magistrate, etc.;

22 agency holding warrant—U.S. Marshal, IRS—Criminal Investigation, etc.;

23 any information as to whether the subject is considered dangerous, is known to own or currently possess firearms, has suicidal tendencies, or has previously escaped custody;

24 driver's license number, year of expiration and State issued;

25 license number of vehicle, aircraft or vessel subject owns or is known to use, including year and State;

26 description of vehicle, aircraft or vessel subject owns or is known to use;

27 associates of subject;

28 FBI number;

29 name and telephone number of CID personnel to contact when subject is apprehended. If uncertain, the office telephone number and the title—Chief, Criminal Investigation of the requesting district will be used.

(b) The above procedure should also be followed for requesting modifications.

(2) Periodically, the TECS Data Center will mail verification forms to those districts which have generated entries into TECS with regard to fugitives as required in text 335.6:(1). It is very important that the Chief, CID have these forms carefully checked to determine the current validity of the information and make appropriate corrections if necessary. This review is especially important for those items of information which are subject to periodic changes, such as automobile license number. After the form has been reviewed and necessary corrections made, the form will be returned to the Director, Criminal Investigation Division, Attn: CP:CI:O, within five days of receipt (copy to the regional office is optional).

(3) When a fugitive has been apprehended, or for any other reason the Chief, CID, wishes to delete the entry in TECS and NCIC, the National Office, Chief, Operations Branch, sould be contacted immediately at FTS 566-6451 to request cancellation of the entry in TECS and NCIC. This telephonic request should be followed by written confirmation, and if the taxpayer was charged with a felony, the memorandum should also request the cancellation of the Wanted Circular (see IRM 9377.1:(9)).

335.7 *(9-4-81)* 9781

Other TECS Functions

(1) Other functions of TECS are as follows:

(a) Telephone Analysis System (TELAN) is a computerized service available to TECS users for the purpose of analyzing telephone toll data.

1 Requests for the use of Telephone Analysis System (TELAN) should be forwarded by memorandum from the Chief, Criminal Investigation Division, through normal channels to the Director, Criminal Investigation Division, Attn: CP:CI:O.

2 The request should include the following:

a telephone toll information which is to be analyzed by the computer;

b date the telephone data submitted is needed;

c date the case comes before the grand jury or the court; and

d whether the request is priority or urgent.

3 Priority or urgent requests will be expedited and other TELAN requests will be processed in the order in which received, and as resources and time allow.

4 The computer will generate a printout, listing the data in three sequences: Primary phone number, date, receiving phone number; receiving phone number, date, primary phone number; and date, primary phone number, receiving phone number. The computer will also generate a listing, if applicable, of those phone numbers submitted by the Service which have also been submitted by another agency. The listing will indicate the name of the other agency and the case number.

(b) Customs Service terminals located at land-border crossings along the Canadian and Mexican borders, and at key ports of entry at seaports and international airports, provide the capability of querying number plates and names of passengers clearing Customs at such points. These queries are especially helpful in the apprehension of fugitives.

335.8 *(4-15-82)* 9781

New Applications/Uses

While new applications and uses for TECS are encouraged, especially those which would increase effectiveness and efficiency, it must be emphasized that absolutely no entries are authorized beyond those described in the above procedures. Any new uses or applications must first be approved by the Director, Criminal Investigation Division.

336 *(1-18-80)* 9781
State, County, and Municipal Government Records

(1) Sale and transfer of property.

(2) Mortgages and releases.

(3) Judgments, garnishments, chattel mortgages and other liens.

(4) Conditional sales contracts.

(5) Births, deaths, marriages, and divorces.

(6) Change of name.

(7) Auto licenses, transfers, and sales of vehicles.

(8) Drivers' licenses.

(9) Hunting and fishing licenses.

(10) Occupancy and business privilege licenses.

(11) Building and other permits.

(12) Police and sheriff records of arrests and commitments.

(13) Court records of civil and criminal cases.

(14) Parole officers' and probation departments' files.

(15) Registration of corporate entities and annual reports.

(16) Registration of noncorporate business entities.

(17) Fictitious names index.

(18) School and voter registrations.

(19) Professional registrations.

(20) State income tax returns.

(21) Personal property tax returns.

(22) Real estate tax payments.

(23) Inheritance and gift tax returns.

(24) Wills.

(25) Letters of administration.

(26) Inventories of estates.

(27) Welfare agency records.

(28) Workmen's compensation files.

(29) Bids, purchase orders, contracts and warrants for payment.

(30) Civil Service applications.

(31) Minutes of board and agency proceedings.

(32) Public utilities' records.

(33) Health departments' records.

(34) State Unemployment Compensation records.

337 *(1-18-80)* 9781
Records and Information from U.S. Possessions and From Foreign Countries

337.1 *(5-9-80)* 9781
Office Of International Operations

The office of International Operations has the responsibility to make inquiries in foreign countries. If the Taxpayer resides abroad and it is evident that most of the investigation would be conducted abroad, the case should be referred to the Office of International Operations for investigation. If the taxpayer resides within the United States and it is evident that most of the investigation would be conducted within the United States, the case should be referred to the appropriate district office for assignment to a special agent. Where there is a doubt as to the jurisdiction of a particular case because of unknown factors concerning residence or the extent of the investigation to be made abroad, a memorandum setting forth all of the pertinent details should be submitted by the Chief, Criminal Investigation Division, with the concurrence of the District Director, through normal channels to the Director, Criminal Investigation Division, National Office, who will coordinate the matter with the district involved or with the Office of International Operations, as appropriate, and assist in determining jurisdiction. The Office of International Operations has been delegated authority to perform those functions vested in the Secretary or his/her delegate by the Internal Revenue Code of 1954 which may be performed by a District Director in administering the United States internal revenue laws in the Panama Canal Zone, Puerto Rico, and the Virgin Islands. See also IRM 9123:(5).

337.2 *(1-18-80)* 9781
Information From Puerto Rico and the Virgin Islands

Requests for information from Puerto Rico and the Virgin Islands will be handled as collateral requests as provided in IRM 9264.1. Such requests will be forwarded to: Director, Office of International Operations, Attention: Chief, Criminal Investigation Division, CP:OIO:7. See also IRM 9264.3

337.3 *(4-15-82)* 9781
Information from Foreign Countries—General

(1) Tax and related information may be obtained by the Foreign Operations District from sources within foreign countries, embassies or consulates of foreign countries, and United States possessions through:

(a) Collateral or other investigations conducted by:

1 Personnel of the Foreign Operations District permanently stationed or temporarily detailed abroad, or

2 Special Agents and other personnel of the Foreign Operations District in Washington, D.C., or

3 Other Service personnel temporarily detailed to the Foreign Operations District for overseas assignment.

(b) Special investigations conducted for their offices by other Service personnel temporarily detailed abroad either under the supervision of, or with the concurrence of, the Director, Foreign Operations District.

(c) Collateral or special investigations made for the Service by other government agencies such as the Customs Service, the Department of State, or Military Services.

(d) Requests directed through prescribed channels to the tax authorities of certain foreign governments, pursuant to provisions of tax treaties.

(2) Requests for information to be obtained in foreign countries; or from embassies and consulates of foreign governments in the United States outside the Washington, D.C. area; and requests to interview officials located outside the Washington, D.C. area who appear to have diplomatic status will be submitted in triplicate to the Director, Foreign Operations District, Attention: Chief, Foreign Programs Division, by the Chief, Criminal Investigation Division. A copy of each such request will be forwarded to the Assistant Commissioner (CI), Attn. OP:CI:O. The Director, Foreign Operations District will transmit the reply or report direct to the Chief, Criminal Investigation Division requesting the information and furnish a copy to the Assistant Commissioner (CI), Attention: OP:CI:O

(3) Requests for information from embassies and consulates of foreign governments in the Washington, D.C. area, and requests to interview officials in the Washington, D.C. area who have or appear to have diplomatic status will be submitted in triplicate to the Director, Foreign Operations District, Attention: Chief, Criminal Investigation Division, by the Chief, Criminal Investigation Division of the inquiring district. A copy of each such request will be forwarded by the inquiring district to the Assistant Commissioner (CI), Attention: OP:CI:O. The Foreign Operations District will transmit the reply or report direct to the inquiring Chief, Criminal Investigation Division, and furnish a copy to the Assistant Commissioner (CI), Attention: OP:CI:O.

(4) Documents and reports received from foreign countries, or from embassies or consulates of foreign countries, and made available to Criminal Investigation personnel will not be furnished to another government agency, except as required by regulations.

(5) When a foreign government makes direct inquiry of Criminal Investigation personnel or when it is learned that a foreign government is interested in a case, such information should immediately be referred by the Chief, Criminal Investigation Division, to the Director, Foreign Operations District, Attention: Chief, Foreign Programs Division, with a copy of such communication transmitted to the Assistant Commissioner (CI), Attention: OP:CI:O.

337.4 *(1-18-80)* 9781
Information from Canada

(1) National Office approval is not required where travel is to be performed in Canada by personnel of districts or regions contiguous to that country for the sole purpose of obtaining information of a routine nature in the immediate vicinity of and lying adjacent to the United States border. Such travel is limited to nearby points less than 25 miles from the United States border and travel which is not of an extended nature. Personnel in some border districts have developed a close, informal relationship with Canadian tax officials stationed on or in the immediate proximity of the border, and frequently obtain, informally through such tax officials, collateral information from individuals, financial institutions, government officials, and business establishments. It is intended that this type of informal cooperation be continued. However, such personnel are not to make direct requests of the authorities in Ottawa, or for information outside the adjacent border areas. All such requests must be made by the Chief, Criminal Investigation Division, with the concurrence of the District Director to the Director of International Operations, Attention: CP:IO:3, and copy thereof forwarded to the Director, Criminal Investigation Division, Attention: CP:CI:O. Where informal arrangements for inquiries exist in some border districts, such districts should identify in their formal requests those with whom they have been transacting official matters to avoid duplication of effort.

(2) In instances when a United States taxpayer's books and records are maintained in Canada and the taxpayer requests the special agent to inspect such books and records in that country and to be interviewed there, the special agent may be directed by the District Director to proceed to Canada in accordance with the procedure set forth in IRM 9265.4:(2). However, this exception does not apply when inquiries of third parties in Canada are necessary. Except as provided above, no direct inquiry will be made in Canada by special agents without prior approval of the Director of International Operations.

(3) Under normal circumstances in tax evasion cases, information can be obtained more readily by Canadian agents, particularly from such institutions as banks, trust companies and large corporations, than by a United States agent. Therefore, all requests for special agents to travel to Canada will be carefully screened. This does not preclude travel for meetings to exchange information at appropriate times or where the information required is so voluminous or complex that the special agent's presence is desirable. When it is necessary for a special agent to travel to Canada to obtain information from a Canadian citizen or business entity, a request will be prepared in accordance with instructions provided in IRM 9265.4 and forwarded through the Assistant Regional Commissioner to the Director, Criminal Investigation Division, Attention: CP:CI:O, for review and, if travel is believed warranted, for signature and transmittal to the Director of International Operations. It is also essential that the request:

(a) provide adequate background to support a Canadian tax interest, because Canadian tax authorities are authorized to furnish only that information which they can obtain under the revenue laws of Canada;

(b) demonstrate sufficient United States tax interest to justify the request;

(c) not be repetitious of prior request; and

(d) contain an action appropriate in the circumstances.

(4) Upon approval by the Director of International Operations, the International Operations office will obtain the necessary clearances and furnish the originating office with the procedure to be followed and, where appropriate, the name and location of the Canadian tax official who is to be contacted by the special agent. A Canadian agent will usually accompany the special agent when third party contacts are made.

(5) Requests for information from Canada will be prepared, and routed, in the same manner prescribed in IRM 9265.1:(1). The request will contain the information specified in (3)(a) through (3)(d) above as well as the data specified in IRM 9265.3. Except under special circumstances respective procedures should be observed of limiting a request for information to a period not to exceed ten years immediately preceding the request.

(6) In some cases, where the essential information sought is complex, involved and voluminous, it may be desirable to have preliminary discussions with Canadian authorities. The request to hold preliminary discussions in such cases will be prepared and routed in the same manner prescribed in (3) above. Exchange of information resulting from the preliminary discussions will be formalized as early as possible and before any documents are exchanged.

(7) District offices should not refuse to obtain information for Canada if it is requested under the competent authority. However, in situations where it appears that the request from Canada is unreasonable, extremely extensive, or circumstances do not warrant going back beyond ten years, a memorandum reflecting the opinion of the district office will be submitted to the Director, Criminal Investigation Division, Attention: CP:I:O, through the Assistant Regional Commissioner. If the Director, Criminal Investigation Division, concludes that the circumstances justify the opinion expressed by the district office, he/she will forward the memorandum to the Director of International Operations for discussion and explanation with the appropriate Canadian official.

(8) If information received from Canada through regular channels requires further correspondence, the Chief may communicate directly with the Canadian district office which furnished the original information. However, copies of any such communication will be forwarded, one each, to the Director, Criminal Investigation Division, Attention: CP:CI:O, and to the Director of International Operations, Attention: CP:IO:3. Such direct communication applies only in instances where information has been received through regular channels and follow-up communication is necessary. The original communication and any new areas of inquiry must be routed as prescribed in (5) above. Simi-

larly, any Intelligence district office which has provided information to Canadian officials through the usual channels may subsequently communicate directly with those officials with respect to the information so provided. However, copies of any such communication will be forwarded, one each, to the Director, Criminal Investigation Division, Attention: CP:CI:O and to the Director of International Operations, Attention: CP:IO:3.

(9) In accordance with an agreement between United States and Canadian tax officials, where the tax affairs of an individual, partnership or corporation are being investigated by the United States and the same type of investigation is also being currently conducted by Canada, and one country desires to be kept informed of significant developments such as proposal to close case, etc., the authorities of that country will advise the other of this interest so that the desired information may be timely furnished.

(10) See also IRM 9265.2.

337.5 *(1-18-80)* 9781
Summons for Records Outside the United States

Before issuing a summons where the records are outside the United States, a copy of the proposed summons will be submitted, through channels, to District Counsel for review. District Counsel will coordinate their review with Chief Counsel (CC:GL), who in turn will coordinate the matter with the Director, Criminal Investigation Division. The proposed summons will be accompanied by a statement describing the circumstances and efforts that have been made to secure the records and data from the taxpayer and why the taxpayer will not make the requested records available. In no event will the special agent issue the summons until advice has been received from Counsel. See also IRM 9363.4.

337.6 *(1-18-80)* 9781
Specific Data to be Included in Request for Information from Foreign Countries See IRM 9265.3.

337.7 *(1-18-80)* 9781
Interpol

(1) Interpol is the International Criminal Police Organization, better known by its radio designation—Interpol.

(2) The National Central Bureaus of member countries have machinery set up to communicate with member countries. In the United States the National Central Bureau is under the direction and control of the Departments of Justice and Treasury.

(3) The U.S. National Central Bureau can assist when there is a requirement for certain inquiries in any of the Interpol member countries.

(4) Interpol assistance includes but is not limited to the following:

(a) Criminal History check

(b) License plate/drivers license check

(c) Location of suspects/fugitives/witnesses

(d) International Wanted Circulars

(e) Trace weapons/motor vehicles abroad

(5) Requests can be made directly to the U.S. National Central Bureau, Washington, D.C. by calling 202-633-2867 or by mail to: Interpol, Department of Justice, Washington, D.C. 20530.

337.8 *(1-18-80)* 9781

Foreign Intelligence Activities Under Executive Order 12036, Section 2

(1) Executive Order 12036, United States Foreign Intelligence Activities, was issued by the President of the United States on January 24, 1978, to provide for the organization and control of United States foreign intelligence activities.

(2) The Inspector General, Department of the Treasury, has requested that Inspection, Internal Revenue Service, distribute copies of Treasury Order No. 246 (Revision 1) and Executive Order 12036 to, among others, all Special Agents, Criminal Investigations Division.

(3) Although the Internal Revenue Service does not engage in foreign intelligence activities it is required that special agents be familiar with the provisions of these orders.

(4) Treasury Department Order No. 246, (Revision 1). (Exhibit 300-30), requires that any Internal Revenue Service employee shall report to Inspection or to the Inspector General any matters which they feel raise questions of propriety or legality under Section 2 of Executive Order 12036, Restrictions on Intelligence Activities (Exhibit 300-31).

337.9 *(6-13-80)* 9781

U.S.-Swiss Treaty on Mutual Assistance in Criminal Matters

(1) This Treaty provides a vehicle to obtain testimony and tangible evidence from Switzerland. It was designed to deal primarily with the problem of Swiss Bank Secrecy Laws but it offers a wide range of assistance from the judicial and executive authorities of Switzerland. It designates the Attorney General as the Central Authority for the United States who must handle requests under the Treaty and whose approval is necessary for all requests. The Attorney General has delegated these duties and powers to the Assistant Attorney General of the Criminal Division.

(2) Pursuant to a request under the Treaty, Swiss Authorities may:

(a) Execute a search warrant;

(b) Subpoena testimony of persons in Switzerland;

(c) Locate persons in Switzerland;

(d) Subpoena and authenticate documents;

(e) Supply official records;

(f) Provide service of process;

(g) Request persons to appear in United States;

(h) Permit a United States official to take testimony to authenticate documents; and

(i) Transfer prisoners needed in the United States.

(3) The Treaty applies to specified offenses which are mutually criminal, i.e., punishable under the laws of the United States and Switzerland. It generally does not apply to violations with respect to taxes. However, it does apply to offenses relating to tax laws if:

(a) The offense is committed by a person reasonably suspected of being in the upper echelon of an organized crime group or of participating significantly in any important activity of such a group;

(b) Available evidence is insufficient to provide a reasonable prospect of successful prosecution of this person for the illegal activities of such group;

(c) It is reasonably concluded that requested assistance will substantially facilitate the successful prosecution of such person, and should result in his/her imprisonment for a sufficient period of time so as to have a significant adverse effect on the organized criminal group; and

(d) The securing of the information or evidence without the requested assistance is impossible or unreasonably burdensome. Another limitation especially applicable to tax cases relates to requested assistance with respect to two crimes; one to which the Treaty applies and one to which it does not. If, under Swiss Law, the first crime merges into the second, no assistance will be provided.

(4) An "organized criminal group" is defined by the Treaty. The "elements" of such a group, without any one of which the special organized crime provisions will not apply, are:

(a) An association or group of persons combined together;

(b) Association for a substantial or indefinite period;

(c) Purpose of association;

1 monetary or commercial gains for itself or others, and

2 illegal means of obtaining these gains

(d) Carrying out purpose in a methodical and systematic manner, including:

1 acts or threats of violence or other acts which are likely to intimidate and are mutually criminal, and

2 either: striving to obtain influence in politics or commerce, especially in political organizations, public administrations, the judiciary, commercial enterprises, employers' associations, labor unions or other employees' associations, or association with a similar (organized crime) group which strives to obtain such influence.

(5) Requests for assistance must be made via memorandum by the Chief, CID, with the concurrence of the District Director, to the Director, CID, Attn: CP:CI:O. A copy of the request will be sent to the ARC (CI). The Director will coordinate requests with the Government Regulations and Labor Section of the Criminal Division of the Department of Justice. Requests should contain the following elements.

(a) An introductory paragraph naming the authority on whose behalf the request is being made, the offense being investigated, a brief statement of the need for the evidence, identification of the subject of the investigation, and a concise statement of what assistance is requested.

(b) A description of the offense in concise terms. State the code section violated. Include facts of the case, showing that the offense has taken place or your reasons for believing the offense has taken place.

(c) A statement of the need for assistance and how the evidence sought fits into the proof of the case, e.g., to prove one or more of the elements of the crime or to show a motive.

(d) A statement of the full name, place and date of birth, address, and any other information which may aid in the identification of the persons who are at the time of the request the subject of the investigation. Also include the person's citizenship.

(e) A statement naming witnesses or other persons who may be affected by the request, e.g., joint bank account holders.

(f) The statement as to any particular procedure that is requested, e.g., the use of compulsory process for documents before notice to a witness.

(g) A statement as to whether the testimony to be taken (if any) should be done under oath or not.

(h) A description of the information, statement or testimony sought.

(i) A description of documents, records or articles of evidence to be produced or preserved, the persons on whom they are to be obtained, and the desired method of reproducing or authenticating them. This description must be as specific as possible.

(j) Information as to the allowance and expenses to which a person appearing in the United States will be entitled. The dollar amount for attendance fees and per diem can be ascertained from 28 U.S.C. 1871.

(k) Information which provides reasonable suspicion under the organized crime provisions. Reasonable suspicion is less than reasonable cause.

338 *(1-18-80)* 9781
Business Records

338.1 *(1-18-80)* 9781
Banks

338.11 *(1-18-80)* 9781
Function and Organization

(1) A bank is fundamentally an establishment for the custody, loan or exchange of money, and for facilitating the transmission of funds by checks, drafts, and bills of exchange and the like. Its services to customers may include administering estates; storing valuables; purchasing and selling securities; rendering advice concerning business transactions; lending money; collecting notes, drafts, bills, and coupons; furnishing business credit references; preparing tax returns; and many other services.

(Next page is 9781-68.1)

(2) The principles of bank accounting are basically the same in all parts of the United States. If a special agent understands these principles, he/she should be able to locate whatever available evidence there is in a bank and be able to trace transactions from one account or bank to another account or bank.

(3) The principal officers of a bank are the president, vice president, secretary, and cashier or treasurer. In many banks, vice presidents act as senior department executives or as loaning officers. The cashier ordinarily is the business manager of the bank and is the one to whom requests for information are usually made. However, there frequently is one other officer or employee of the bank who is most familiar with the accounting system, or who has been designated by the management to handle requests from the Internal Revenue Service for information. The special agent should learn the identity of that person, and should consult him/her when making official requests for information, rather than make indiscriminate inquiries of various officers and employees. The special agent should make every attempt to establish a good working relationship with such employees; however, their activities with respect to bank records or information may not be directed as a controlled informant as defined in IRM 9373.2. Chief Counsel expressed the opinion that the Right to Financial Privacy Act of 1978 did not contemplate using bank employees as controlled informants when the exemption provisions applicable to the Service were drafted. Consequently, this may be deemed a violation under the Act.

(4) The main departments of a bank are commercial, savings, trust, loan and discount, consumer credit, and special services. These are divided into subsidiary departments such as receiving, paying, trust, loan and discount, consumer credit, exchange, collection, and safe deposit, bookkeeping, clearing, transit, statistical and data processing.

(5) The receiving department makes the first entry of all items as they enter the channels of the bank. The paying department takes charge of all the cash in the bank, providing an adequate supply for its needs, paying checks, charging currency to customers, settling clearing house balances, and recording and proving the cash of the bank. The loan department is responsible for the granting and collection of loans and has custody of collateral and the credit and files of a confidential nature relating to the customers. The collection department handles items for collection which may, or may not, go through the commercial deposit accounts. For example, an item may be collected by the bank and the funds turned over to the customer in currency, or in the form of a cashier's check, or be applied directly to the credit of the customer's account in the loan department. The safe deposit department handles all business and records in connection with the rental of, and access to, safe deposit boxes.

(6) The bookkeeping department is responsible for posting to subsidiary ledgers of the deposit liability accounts. The clearing and transit departments look after the collection of items drawn on other banks through the clearing house, by mail or messenger, or through the Federal Reserve system, and the computation of exchange charges when necessary. They route items for collection and prepare cash transit letters describing the items sent for collection. The data processing (ADP) department handles some of the above operations, which are performed by computers rather than manually.

338.12 *(1-18-80)* 9781
Bank Records

It is impossible to describe all the bank records which might contain information regarding a customer. However, the principal commercial records which are of interest to special agents are: signature cards; deposit tickets or slips; customer's ledger sheets for checking accounts; savings accounts, special accounts and loan accounts; registers or copies of cashier's checks, bank money orders, bank drafts, letters of credit, and certificates of deposit; teller's proof sheets; copies of settlements with the clearing house; copies of cash transit letters; records of the purchase and sale of securities and Government bonds; collection in and collection out records; customer's unreturned canceled checks; and safe deposit records. Storage considerations have caused many banks to destroy those records not needed for their own use and not required under law to be retained. Therefore, a special agent's success in a bank will depend somewhat on its practice of, and its policy for, retention and destruction of records.

338.13 *(1–18–80)* 9781
Signature Cards

The signature card shows the signature of the person or persons authorized to sign checks, make withdrawals, or initiate transactions through or against the account of the customer. Usually the signature is executed in the presence of an officer of the bank or of a teller or clerk, and by comparison can be used to prove authenticity of the customer's alleged signature on other papers. A bank teller who has frequently handled the customer's checks would be a competent witness to identify his signature not only on documents normally passing through his hands but also on other papers. If the account is in the name of a corporation, partnership, or association, the signature card will be accompanied by copies of resolutions of the board of directors, or partnership and membership agreements, naming the persons who are to draw checks on the account. A signature card may also contain information concerning the name of the person who introduced the customer, prior banking connections of the customer, the names of institutions in which other accounts may be located, and other departments of the bank with which the customer has had transactions. Banks frequently keep in a central file a master signature card containing detailed information about the customer which may indicate the departments of the bank the customer does business with. Each department where the customer has an account also keeps a card bearing only the signature.

(Next page is 9781–69)

338.14 *(1-18-80)* 9781
Bank Deposit Tickets

The deposit tickets or slips of a customer may be found by reference to the dates shown on the ledger sheets, since the tickets for each day are filed separately. Within this group, they are filed alphabetically or in account number order. Inspection of a slip may disclose the nature of the items deposited, classified as currency, checks and coupons. Banks prefer that checks be listed separately on the deposit slip and that they be identified by the name of A.B.A. transit number of the drawee bank. Under a system devised by the American Bankers Association, each bank in the country is identified by a number known as its A.B.A. number (Exhibit 300-2). If the deposit slip does not contain this information, it may be found by examining the proof sheets, the transit letters for foreign (out-of-town) items, and the clearing house settlement for local items. Banks that are members of the Federal Reserve system have another number known as the "routing symbol." If the A.B.A. number cannot be determined (it may be illegible) the routing symbol will indicate the general area in which the bank is located and it is possible to locate the bank by following the amount of the check on cash transit letters. These routing numbers are shown in Exhibit 300-3 and indicate the Federal Reserve District or sub-district in which the bank is located. All banks that are in the area served by a Federal Reserve Bank or Branch carry the routing symbol on their checks right underneath their A.B.A. number as

14-2—A.B.A. number
650—Routing symbol

338.15 *(1-18-80)* 9781
Customer's Account Records

(1) Checking Accounts

(a) The fundamental difference between the bookkeeping records under a manual system and an ADP system is that under the manual system a ledger sheet is maintained for each account carried by the customer.

(b) Under an ADP system the daily information is maintained on magnetic tape, which is updated daily. A printout is made of the transactions on a cyclical basis (usually monthly). Many banks retain a copy of this printout. In some systems the statement printout may be either a detailed ledger statement similar to that used under a manual system or a summary or "bob-tailed" statement which appears as follows:

Opening Balance	01,234.56	Number of Items—00
Deposits	3,248.12	Number of Items—7
Checks	2,222.22	Number of Items—25
Charges	21.00	Number of Items—4
Ending Balance	$2,239.46	Number of Items—00

(c) The banks using an ADP system print-out the balances of all accounts on a daily basis. This printout, which may be referred to as a transaction journal or account balance list, will show the following information: account number, date of last activity, type of activity, previous balance, present balance, uncollected funds, and special instructions. By reference to this daily printout it is usually possible to reconstruct the account, particularly when a "bob-tailed" statement is used. Most banks using this system also microfilm all items daily so further reference can be made to the microfilm for more detailed information. Some banks again microfilm depositor's checks for the statement period before returning them to the customer.

(d) On the detailed statements under either system, all deposits, withdrawals and daily balances are shown. Symbols may appear opposite various items on the statement signifying something more than a simple deposit or withdrawal. Since banks use different symbols, a bank official or employee should be consulted regarding their meaning.

(e) If the customer deposits a check for a substantial amount drawn on a bank in a distant city, the bookkeeper, under a manual system, or the teller under an ADP system, will code the deposit so as to put a "hold" order on the account. This serves as a warning (manually) or reject (ADP) so that the deposit cannot be drawn against until the lapse of a specified period of time within which the check will be paid by the bank of origin.

(2) Savings Accounts

(a) Ledger sheets similar to the manual type used in checking accounts are maintained for savings accounts. In an ADP system, the records will be in periodic statement form (usually quarterly). Some banks keep a copy of this statement. If this is done all that is necessary is to obtain a copy of the statement. If statement copies are not available, then it is necessary to reconstruct the account similar to the method used for "bobtailed" statements.

(b) The deposit tickets and withdrawal slips are maintained in separate files similar to the manner described for checking accounts. These documents may show references to drafts, cashier's checks or other accounts.

(3) Loan Records

(a) Banks maintain ledger sheets for loans and separate sheets for the record of collateral used to secure loans. In those banks which use ADP systems to keep their loan records, the reconstruction problem is similar to that involved with checking accounts unless detailed annual statements are printed out and copies of them retained. The availability of the credit or loan file makes reconstruction easier.

(b) Consumer loan records are usually found in a bank department, which is separate from the commercial and mortgage loans. The credit files may be combined or separate for each department.

338.16 *(1-18-80)* 9781
Certified Check Register

A certified check is a check drawn by a depositor on his account with the bank, across the face of which check a properly authorized bank officer has written the word "Certified," the date, the name of the bank, and his name. The bank has thus contracted to pay the check when presented and has charged the depositor's account. A certified check is not returned to the depositor, but after payment, is retained by the bank in its files. It is recorded in a Certified Check Register which shows at least the amount, the date certified, the depositor who issued it, and the date actually paid. Banks discourage this type of check but perform the service at the insistence of their customers.

338.17 *(1-18-80)* 9781
Bank Exchange Records

(1) Bank exchange may be issued by preparing a single copy check, draft, or other document and then recording it in a register. However, modern practice is to prepare the check, draft, or other document in many copies prepared simultaneously by the use of carbon paper. The original is filed as the bank's copy or register. One copy may be given the customer for his record.

(2) Bank exchange records include cashier's checks, bank drafts (one for each bank on which drawn), and letters of credit, which usually show the purchaser's name. The documents, by endorsement, will show the payees and their locations by the banks where the instruments were cashed or deposited.

338.18 *(1-18-80)* 9781
Bank Teller's Proof Sheets

Each teller prepares daily "teller's proof sheets" on which he/she shows deposits received balanced against items received, divided into currency and coin, checks on "us," checks on clearing house banks, checks on out-of-city banks, and coupons. Unusual or large items in any category may be noted and explained on these sheets. These unusual items are reported daily to the head teller or to the officers. They are frequently retained for some time to facilitate internal audit by the bank.

338.19 *(1-18-80)* 9781
Clearing House Settlement Sheets

Settlement sheets for clearing house items are usually maintained for only a short time. Clearing house items are usually not photographed on microfilm. However, they may be photographed by the bank on which they were drawn.

338.1(10) *(1-18-80)* 9781
Cash Transit Letters

Copies of cash transit letters have information of varying degrees of completeness. Some small banks record the items sent for collection on out-of-town banks on which drawn, last endorser, maker, and other information. Other banks merely list the amounts on the letter and then photograph the entire lot. When information is not available from either of the above sources, the bank or Federal Reserve Bank to which the letter was sent may have photographed the items. The date and total amount of the cash letter and the bank to which it was sent should be secured in order to trace the letter at the other end.

338.1(11) *(1-18-80)* 9781
Securities Buy and Sell Records

In small banks, records of purchases and sales of securities may be in correspondence files, but larger banks may have full departments with detailed records. The record of Government bonds may be in the correspondence files with the Federal Reserve Banks or may consist of copies of the manifold bond, particularly Series "E" bonds. The bank's retained copies of "E" bonds issued may be filed in various ways, such as by dates of issue or alphabetically by customers. Bonds that are cashed by banks are frequently photographed just like any other transit items. The same is true of coupons for interest that are detached from customer's bonds and deposited by them for credit to their accounts, or cashed by the bank. These coupons are usually clipped on quarterly or semiannual dates and appear in bank records at more or less regular periods of time.

338.1(12) *(1-18-80)* 9781
Collection Records

(1) *Collection out*—items that are not cash items are not deposited for immediate credit. They are sometimes recorded in the back of the passbook, if such is used, or they may be entered directly on a manifold form and a copy given the customer as a receipt. These are called collection out items and may include drafts with documents attached, checks with special instructions, matured bonds, acceptances, and a wide variety of commercial documents. Some banks use a collection out register, others a copy of the above described form, and a few use an individual letter, retaining a copy.

(2) *Collection in*—Collection in items are received from other banks and require payment or other action by some customer of the bank. These may likewise be recorded in a register or a manifold form may be prepared and a copy sent as a receipt to the bank from which the item came. The required action is taken and the results mailed to the bank from which the item came. These again may be large checks with special instructions; drafts with documents attached; notes for presentation, collection and payment; acceptances; savings account passbooks; or a wide variety of commercial documents.

338.1(13) *(1-18-80)* 9781
Safe Deposit Box Records

(1) Rental contracts for safe deposit boxes will show who has the right to enter the box, the date of the original renting, various identifying information, and the signature of the renter. Any special instructions will be with the contract, usually on a card.

(2) Access records show date and time of entry and bear the signature of the person entering the box. The frequency of entries may be significant and may correspond in time and date to deposits or withdrawals from other accounts. If the taxpayer agrees to an inspection of the contents of the box, a written inventory showing date of entry, box number, and name of bank, shall be prepared in the presence of taxpayer and, if possible, of another agent. The taxpayer should be requested to initial all pages of the inventory and to sign the last page as acknowledgement of ownership of the contents and of the return of all items. Any currency found should be counted, and the inventory should include the quantity of bills in each denomination; any markings on the tie bands around the bundles of currency or packages of coins; and a notation regarding any bills with unusual features, such as the large size in use before 1929, gold certificates, or National Bank Notes. A record should be made of the serial numbers of large bills, and, when advisable, also of a number of the smaller bills. When a special agent finds deeds or other documents pertaining to land, he should make a record, identifying the type of document, such as "Warranty Deed," and show the names of grantor and grantee; legal description of land showing State, County, Range, Township, Section, dates, consideration, revenue stamps, and book and page number where it is recorded. Sealed matter should be opened only with the consent of the box renter. If consent is not secured, the special agent should not open the package, but should note as full a description of it as possible. The special agent should also make careful note of all comments made by the box renter to him during the inspection of the box and contents.

338.1(14) *(1-18-80)* 9781
Checks Cashed

(1) Banks make a distinction between checks cashed and checks paid. Cashing a check means paying out cash for a check drawn on another bank. The paying teller will mark a check of this type on its face or reverse side. If for any reason the check is returned not paid by the bank on which it was drawn, the teller must know, from the endorsement, who gave it to him in order to get the bank's money back. Paying a check is giving cash for a check on the account of a customer of the bank, or charging a check to his account.

(2) In some areas all checks on which cash is given by the teller are stamped with a code letter or number that indicates which teller and sometimes which bank or branch gave out the cash, regardless of whether the check was on his own bank or some other bank. Also, deposit tickets or withdrawal slips sometimes show denominations of cash deposited or withdrawn.

338.1(15) *(1-18-80)* 9781
Deposits

(1) Deposits may be classified as to their basic sources which are:
(a) Receiving Teller
(b) Mail or Special Messenger
(c) Telegraphic Transfers
(d) Other Bank Departments
(e) Night and Lobby Depositories

(2) Deposits may also be classified according to the terms of withdrawal:
(a) *Demand deposits* which are deposits to a check account subject to withdrawal by check on demand.
(b) *Time deposits*
1 Savings account which may be subject to a 30-day notice of withdrawal.
2 Time certificates of deposit which are made by contract to be left with a bank for definite lengths of time, usually six months, and draw a higher rate of interest than the usual savings account.
3 Open account is used by corporations to put idle money to work during slack seasons where it will earn interest. Corporations cannot use savings accounts as they are prohibited from doing so by the rules of the Federal Reserve System.

(3) The Federal Reserve System forbids banks from paying time deposits before the specified date except in an emergency to prevent great hardships to the depositor. The bank is required before making such payment to obtain from the depositor an application describing fully the circumstances constituting the emergency. The application must be approved by an officer of the bank who certifies that, to the best of his knowledge and belief, the statements in the application are true. These applications are retained in the bank's files.

(4) Special agents making inquiries at Federal Reserve System member banks should be alert for Time Deposit accounts and applications relating to the emergency withdrawal of funds by this nature. These applications could be used to help establish cash on hand, lack of beginning cash and other evidence to resolve net worth claims by taxpayers.

(5) Examination of deposits and tracing of items may reveal the pattern of transactions of prior periods. That is, interviewing the makers of checks deposited may reveal the source of checks in prior periods. For example, an attempt to trace a transaction that occurred three or four years ago may be blocked because the records for the past period have been destroyed. In that event, the source of checks for prior periods might be found by tracing similar current items.

338.1(16) *(1-18-80)* 9781
Microfilm

Microfilm may be used by the bank to photograph various records throughout the bank. These pictures are used to keep a permanent record of transactions in limited storage space. Microfilm has been used for a wide variety of purposes and the extent of such use varies from bank to bank. Some banks photograph everything and others photograph only transit letters. If pertinent, inquiry should be made as to when photographing began and what was photographed. The questions apply to both past and present practices.

338.1(17) *(11-10-81)* 9781
Chase Manhattan Bank

Every direct mail request to Chase Manhattan Bank, One Chase Manhattan Plaza, New York, New York 10081 should contain a statement that a copy of the request has been forwarded to the Chief, Criminal Investigation Division, Manhattan District, for the purpose of having a special agent from that office personally serve a summons and pick up the required data. Upon receipt of such request the bank will immediately begin to assemble the information. When making the request to Chase Manhattan Bank, a copy should be forwarded to the Chief, Criminal Investigation Division, Manhattan District, for necessary action. All other transfer agents in the Manhattan District will comply with direct mail requests for stock transfer information, providing the requests cite IRC 7602 as authority.

338.2 *(9-4-81)* 9781
Currency Transaction Reports, Form 4789

338.21 *(9-4-81)* 9781
General

(1) The Currency and Foreign Transactions Reporting Act, requires that whenever any person engages in a currency transaction involving more than $10,000 with a financial institution, the financial institution must record the identity of the person or persons involved and file a report on Form 4789 containing certain details of the transaction. The reports are filed with the Internal Revenue Service at the Ogden Service Center. The report is made on Form 4789 and must be filed within 15 days of the transaction. (Treasury Regulation 31 CFR Part 103.22, 103.25(a) and 103.26)

(2) Form 4789 contains the following information:
(a) Name, address, identification number, and occupation of person who conducted the transaction with the financial institution.
(b) Person or organization for whom transaction was completed, account number, occupation and social security or taxpayer identification number.

(c) Detailed description of transaction including check data when applicable.

(d) Type of identification presented in the transaction including EIN and business activity.

(e) Financial institution reporting the financial transaction.

(3) All of the information from any form filed can be obtained via a TECS query at any IRS Service Center by requesting a "CTR RCN query".

(4) A copy of each report must be retained by the financial institution for a period of 5 years from the date of the report.

338.22 *(9-4-81)* 9781
Procedures for Obtaining Photocopies of Currency Transaction Reports (CTR's)

(1) Prior to January 1, 1980, CTR's were filed with the Philadelphia Service Center and then forwarded to the various service centers based on the address given in Part II of Form 4789, or if blank, Part I of Form 4789. After processing they became part of the information items files. These CTR's were processed and stored at the appropriate service center. CTR's received on or after January 1, 1980, are processed and filed at the Ogden Service Center. The original CTR is filed with Ogden Service Center Files Unit in the same manner as tax returns.

(2) Initially, a TECS query should be made by your service center to determine if a particular taxpayer has any CTR record. If a CTR relating to the subject has been filed the service center will be able to provide a TECS print-out containing all the information from the document (an abstract copy). If it becomes necessary to obtain a photocopy of a CTR, the following procedures should be followed:

(a) CTR's filed prior to January 1, 1980:

1 If the TECS query reveals a record of a CTR filed prior to January 1, 1980, a photocopy of the CTR may be requested from the Chief, Criminal Investigation Branch of your service center using the Report Control Number (RCN). The Criminal Investigation Branch will also be able to obtain copies of CTR's which were filed with other service centers (based on the address shown on the CTR).

(b) CTR's filed on or after January 1, 1980:

1 If the TECS query reveals a record of a CTR filed on or after January 1, 1980, a photocopy of the CTR may be requested in the same manner as a request for a tax return, using the Report Control Number (RCN).

2 In the event of an extreme emergency, you may call the Chief, Criminal Investigation Branch, Ogden Service Center, FTS 586-3182, and request assistance in obtaining a copy of a CTR. All other requests should be submitted in accordance with 1 above.

3 Since other agencies, including the Department of Treasury, are authorized access to these documents and may have an urgent and immediate need for them only photocopies should be requested for investigative purposes. When needed for evidentiary purposes (actual court appearances) certified photocopies should be requested.

338.3 *(1-18-80)* 9781
Securities

338.31 *(1-18-80)* 9781
Stocks

338.311 *(1-18-80)* 9781
General

(1) When a corporation is formed, capital stock representing the ownership of the corporation is authorized in the corporate charter. There are two principal classes of stock—common and preferred. If only one class of stock is authorized, it will be common stock. The number of shares authorized can only be changed by formal approval of the stockholders.

(2) Shares issued and subsequently reacquired by the corporation through purchase or donation are referred to as treasury stock. The number of shares outstanding will always equal the number of shares issued less the number of shares of treasury stock.

(3) Each stockholder is a part owner of the corporation since each share of stock represents a fractional interest in the corporation. The stockholder is entitled to a stock certificate evidencing ownership of a specified number of shares of stock of the corporation.

(4) If a stockholder desires to buy more stock, it is not necessary to obtain the permission of the company. He/she simply acquires it by purchase in the open market or privately. Conversely, if a stockholder desires to sell shares, he/she cannot demand that the company buy the stock. A stockholder is free, instead, to seek a buyer for the stock either in the market or by private sale.

(5) After the sale terms have been agreed upon, the mechanics of transfer are simple. The seller signs his/her name on the back of the stock certificate and delivers it to the buyer or the buyer's broker. A record of all outstanding certificates is kept by the corporation or by its duly appointed transfer agent, often a bank. The transfer agent has a record of the names and addresses of the stockholders and the number of shares owned by each. After determining that the old certificate is in proper form for transfer, the transfer agent issues a new certificate to the new owner. Also, most companies have a registrar. The duty of the registrar is to double check the actions of the transfer agent to prevent improper issue of stock or fraudulent transfer.

338.312 *(1-18-80)* 9781
Stock Rights

A common stockholder may usually subscribe at a stated discount price to new issues of common stock in proportion to his/her holdings. This privilege, known as a stock right, is usually offered to stockholders for a limited time. During this period, the stockholder may exercise the right to purchase additional shares under the terms of the offer or may choose to sell the rights. If the stockholder allows the time limit to run out without acting, the rights become worthless.

338.313 *(1-18-80)* 9781
Stock Warrants

A stock warrant is a certificate which gives the holder the privilege to purchase common stock at a stated price within a specified time limit or perpetually. Warrants are often issued with bonds or preferred stocks as an added inducement to investors. The stockholder may exercise the right to purchase additional shares or choose to sell the warrants.

338.314 *(1-18-80)* 9781
Stock Splits

When the price of the common stock of a corporation reaches a high market value, the corporation may choose to bring down the price into a more favorable trading range. To do this, the corporation splits its shares, that is, increases the number of shares outstanding without issuing additional stock. If, for example, a stockholder owned 100 shares which had a market value of $150 per share, a 3:1 stock split would increase the stockholder's shares to 300 and decrease the market price to $50 per share. Although the stockholder now owns a greater number of shares than before the split, the value of his/her stock and his/her proportionate interest remains unchanged. Until the new stock is sold, the split has no tax effect.

338.315 *(1-18-80)* 9781
Dividends

(1) A corporation may pay a dividend in cash, in stock, or in property. When cash dividends are paid, the company or its dividend disbursing agent (usually a bank) sends checks to all the stockholders whose names appear on the books of the company on the so-called record date. A dividend is a prorated distribution among stockholders and when cash dividends are paid, they are in terms of so much per share. Cash dividends are usually taxable.

(2) Some companies, in order to conserve cash, pay a dividend in their own stock. A stock dividend has an effect similar to that of a stock split in that the stockholder's proportionate share of the ownership of the company remains unchanged. A stock dividend is usually stated as a percentage of the outstanding shares (up to a maximum of 25 percent, above which it is called a stock split). A stock dividend is not taxable even though cash is paid in lieu of fractional shares—although the cash itself is taxable as a dividend.

(3) When a corporation pays a property dividend, it is usually in the form of stock of another corporation which has been acquired for investment or some other purpose. Property distributions are treated as taxable dividends.

(4) It is common practice for separate financial institutions to serve as transfer agent and dividend disbursing agent. However, a single financial institution can serve both functions.

(5) Names and addresses of institutions providing these services can be found in:

(a) Securities publications such as:

(1) Financial Stock Guide Service. This is the most comprehensive service. It includes name changes, mergers, dissolutions, etc., from 1927 to present. It also includes information about Canadian corporations.

(2) Moody's

(3) Standard and Poor's

(b) Local brokerage houses

(c) Local or main offices of subject corporations.

(6) Information or documentation can be obtained by writing directly to the separate transfer agents and dividend disbursing agents.

338.32 *(1-18-80)* 9781
Bonds

(1) When a corporation or governmental unit wishes to borrow money for some period, usually for more than 5 years, it will sell a bond issue. Each bond, normally of $1,000 denomination, is a certificate of debt of the issuer and serves as evidence of a loan to the corporation or governmental unit. The bondholder is a creditor of the issuer. A bond pays a stated rate of interest and matures on a stated date when a fixed sum of money must be repaid to the bondholder.

(2) Railroad, public utility, and industrial bonds are called corporate bonds. The obligations of States, counties, cities, towns, school districts, and authorities are known as municipal bonds. U.S. Treasury certificates, notes, and bonds are classified as Government securities.

(3) Bonds are issued in two principal forms coupon bonds, and registered bonds. Coupon bonds have interest coupons attached to each bond by the corporation which issues it. Because the corporation keeps no record of the owner of the bonds, they are called bearer bonds. On the due dates for the interest, the owner clips the coupons and presents them to the authorized bank for payment. Also, the principal when due, is payable to the holder or bearer of the bonds.

(4) Registered bonds have the name of the owner written on the face of the bond. The company, or its authorized agent (usually a bank), has a record of the name and address of the owner. When interest is due, it is paid to the bondholder by check.

338.33 *(1-18-80)* 9781
Stock Exchanges

338.331 *(1-18-80)* 9781
General

(1) Securities exchanges or stock exchanges neither buy nor sell securities themselves. An exchange functions as a central marketplace and provides facilities for executing orders. Member brokers representing buyers and sellers carry out these transactions. An exchange provides a continuous market for securities listed on that exchange. The exchanges are auction markets in that prices are determined by the existing supply and demand of the securities.

(2) The two major exchanges are the New York Stock Exchange (NYSE) and the American Stock Exchange (AMEX), both located in New York City. While there are approximately a dozen additional regional exchanges (such as the Midwest, Pacific Coast, and Philadelphia-Baltimore-Washington Exchanges), the NYSE and AMEX together handle more than 90 percent of the trading done through organized exchanges.

338.332 *(1-18-80)* 9781
Listed Securities

If a security is to be traded on an exchange, the issue must be approved for listing by that exchange. The requirements for listing on the NYSE are the most stringent. Although there are only about 1,700 issues traded on the NYSE, these issues are represented by the largest corporations in the country and have an aggregate value of nearly $500 billion (or 95 percent of the value of all listed securities). While the AMEX listing standards are not as restrictive as the NYSE, they are nonetheless designed to insure an adequate market for the securities. Securities traded on the NYSE or AMEX may also be listed and traded on a regional exchange but no security is listed on both the NYSE and the AMEX.

338.34 *(1-18-80)* 9781
The Over-the-Counter Market

(1) The over-the-counter securities market handles most of the securities transactions that take place in the United States. In fact, its operations are so extensive that the easiest way to describe it is to indicate what it does not do in securities transactions. The over-the-counter market does not handle the purchase or sale of securities that actually occur on securities exchanges, but it handles everything else in the way of securities transactions. Thus, securities not "listed" on a securities exchange are "unlisted," that is, traded over-the-counter.

(2) Many different types of securities are traded over-the-counter. These include:

(a) bank stocks
(b) insurance company stocks
(c) U.S. Government securities
(d) municipal bonds
(e) open-end investment company shares (mutual funds)
(f) most corporate bonds
(g) stocks of a very large number of industrial and utility corporations, including nearly all new issues
(h) securities of many foreign corporations

(3) The over-the-counter market is not located in any one central place. Rather, it consists of thousands of securities houses located in hundreds of different cities and towns all over the United States. These securities houses are called broker/dealers and are engaged in buying and selling securities usually for their own account and risk.

(4) The over-the-counter market is a *negotiated market* rather than an auction market. Prices are arrived at by broker/dealers negotiating with other broker/dealers in order to arrive at the best price. They also buy and sell securities for the account and risk of others and may charge a commission for their services. To transact their business, they communicate their buy and sell orders back and forth through a nationwide network of telephones and teletypes.

(5) The exact size of the over-the-counter market cannot be determined since the securities transactions that take place over-the-counter occur in many different places and are not reported to one central agency. However, it is known that in dollar volume, substantially more securities are traded in the over-the-counter market than on all national securities exchanges combined.

338.35 *(1-18-80)* 9781
Transfer Agent

(1) The principal documents available from the transfer agent are:

(a) stockholder ledger card
(b) stock certificate(s)

(2) The transfer agent keeps a record of the name and address of each stockholder and the number of shares owned, and checks that certificates presented for transfer are properly cancelled and that new certificates are issued in the name of the transferee.

(3) In many small firms, the transfer agent is usually an attorney, a bank, or the corporation itself. In most large firms the transfer agent is a bank. The transfer agent can furnish the following information:

(a) stockholder identification
(b) stockholder position
(c) stock certificate numbers
(d) number of shares represented by certificates
(e) dates certificates were issued or surrendered

(f) evidence of returned certificates
(g) name of transferees and transferors

338.36 *(1-18-80)* 9781
Dividend Disbursing Agent

(1) The principal documents available for the dividend disbursing agent are:
(a) cancelled checks
(b) Forms 1099

(2) The dividend disbursing agent is generally a bank and can furnish the following information:

(a) stockholder identification
(b) stockholder position
(c) amount of dividends
(d) form of dividends
(e) dates paid
(f) evidence of payments

338.37 *(1-18-80)* 9781
Broker

(1) The broker is an agent who handles the public's orders to buy and sell securities, usually for a commission. A broker may be a corporation, partnership, or individual and is often a member of a stock exchange, or a member of a stock exchange/over-the-counter securities firm.

(2) A registered representative (also known as a securities salesperson or account executive) personally places customers' orders and maintains their accounts. While commonly referred to as a broker, a registered representative is usually an employee of a brokerage firm, rather than a member.

(3) The broker can furnish virtually all source documents relating to securities account activity. The two most often used accounts are:
(a) cash—an account that requires securities purchases to be paid in full
(b) margin—an account that allows securities to be purchased on credit

(4) Margin is the percentage of the purchase price of a security that the customer must pay. The margin requirement is established by the Federal Reserve Board. To open a margin account, a minimum amount is usually required. Stocks purchased on margin must be registered in the street name while in the account.

(5) There are two principal ways in which securities are held—in the name of the account holder and in street name. In the first instance, the securities owned simply reflect the name of the customer who maintains the account. When securities are held in street name, however, the securities are registered in the name of the broker. This occurs when securities have been bought on margin or when a cash customer wishes the security to be held by the broker, rather than in his/her own name.

(6) The principal documents available from a broker are:
(a) (broker's personal) customer account cards
(b) applications for account
(c) signature cards and margin agreements
(d) securities receipts
(e) cash receipts
(f) confirmation slips
(g) securities delivered receipts
(h) cancelled checks
(i) Forms 1087
(j) monthly account statements.

338.4 *(1-18-80)* 9781
Commodities

(1) Commodity exchanges are similar to stock exchanges except that they deal in futures contracts. A futures contract is a legally binding commitment to deliver or take delivery of a given quantity and quality of commodity, at a price agreed upon in the trading pit or ring of a commodity exchange at the time the contract is executed.

(2) In early futures markets the primary use of the market was that of finding a buyer or seller. Today both commercial and speculative users of the market prefer to offset, or liquidate, the obligation through opposite futures transactions rather than making or taking delivery.

(3) Futures are traded through a commission house which is a firm that transacts commodity business on behalf of commercial users of commodity futures contracts and the investment public. A number of terms are used to describe commission houses such as wire houses, brokerage houses, commodity commission merchants, etc.

(4) Commission houses become registered member firms of given commodity exchanges in order to trade or handle accounts in the markets conducted by those exchanges.

(5) The basic function of the commission house is to represent the interest of those in the market who do not hold seats on commodity exchanges such as placing orders, handling margin monies, providing basic accounting records, and counseling customers in their trading programs in return for a commission.

(6) Most customer operations are handled by a commodity representative who solicits, accepts, or services customer business in commodities traded on the Exchange. The commodity representative is involved in determining prospective customers' financial ability, opening new accounts, and the placement of individual orders.

(7) Standard documents required to open an account include such information as name, address, phone numbers, and banking references. These are usually found on customer signature or agreement forms.

(8) Accounting services usually provided by commission houses include issuance of written confirmation of all futures orders. Most firms also provide weekly purchase and sale statements that show the number of contracts purchased and sold in specific commodity markets and the current margin deposit balances. The customer normally receives a regular monthly statement that shows all trading activity, net position, and margin balance less commissions.

(9) The following is a list of commodities that are usually traded on futures markets:

(a) Grains
(b) Oil and Meal
(c) Livestock
(d) Poultry
(e) Metals and Minerals
(f) Forest Products
(g) Textiles
(h) Foodstuffs
(i) Foreign Currencies and Financial Instruments

338.5 *(1-18-80)* 9781
Abstract and Title Company Records

(1) Maps and tract books.

(2) Escrow index of purchasers and sellers of real estate—primary source of information.

(3) Escrow files—number obtained from index.

(4) Escrow file containing escrow instructions, agreements, and settlements.

(5) Abstracts and title policies.

(6) Special purpose newspapers published for use by attorneys, real estate brokers, insurance companies and financial institutions. These newspapers contain complete reports on transfers of properties, locations of properties transferred, amounts of mortgages, and releases of mortgages.

338.6 *(1-18-80)* 9781
Agriculture Records

(1) County veterinarians.
(2) Commission merchants.
(3) Insurance companies (insure shipments).
(4) Transportation companies.
(5) Storage companies.
(6) Count and state fair bonds.
(7) Country farm agents.
(8) State cattle control boards (some states maintain records of all cattle brought in and taken out of state).

338.7 *(1-18-80)* 9781
Automobile Manufacturer and Agency Records

(1) Franchise agreements.
(2) Financial statements of dealers.
(3) New car sales and deliveries—used car purchases, trade-ins, and sales.
(4) Service department—mileage, order and delivery signature to indicate presence in area.

338.8 *(1-18-80)* 9781
Bonding Company Records

(1) Investigative and other records on persons and firms bonded.
(2) Collateral file.
(3) Financial statements and data.
(4) Address of person on bond.

338.9 *(5-9-80)* 9781
Credit Agency Records

(1) The Fair Credit Reporting Act, an amendment to the Consumer Credit Protection Act, went into effect on April 24, 1971. Certain provisions of this amendment have a restrictive impact on the availability of information involving individuals from consumer reporting agencies to IRS and other Governmental agencies. Consumer reports may be furnished by consumer reporting agencies only in the following situations.

(a) In response to an order of a court having jurisdiction to issue such an order.
(b) Upon written request of the consumer.
(c) To a person who has a legitimate business need for the information in regard to a business transaction involving the consumer.

(2) There is no specific exception provided in the law which will allow Federal law enforcement agencies to obtain credit reports for investigative purposes. As a result, consumer reporting agencies may not furnish credit reports to IRS for use in tax investigations. Further, the Act provides criminal penalties for obtaining information under false pretenses and for unauthorized disclosures by officers or employees of consumer reporting agencies.

(3) The Act provides that consumer reporting agencies may furnish only identifying infor-

mation to a Governmental agency. This identifying information is limited to a consumer's name, address, former addresses, places of employment and former places of employment.

(4) The Fair Credit Reporting Act is directed at consumer credit reporting activities involving individuals and not at commercial credit reporting activities involving business entities.

(5) The provisions of the Fair Credit Reporting Act do not cover commercial credit reports on corporations and similar business entities.

(6) With regard to partnerships, if the report is on the individuals comprising the partnership, the provisions of the Act might apply. Cases of this type should be referred to the District Counsel for advice.

(7) With regard to fiduciaries, the question of whether the provisions of the Act would restrict the furnishing of a report would depend upon the nature of the trust. If it is a business trust, that is, a corporation or similar business entity, the Act does not apply. If the fiduciary is representing an individual, the provisions of the Act might apply. Cases of this type should also be referred to the District Counsel for advice.

(8) When a consumer report is part of the records of an entity which is not a consumer reporting agency, the provisions of the Act do not apply. However, many entities not normally considered to be consumer reporting agencies may be considered such depending on how they receive and share information from other creditors. Therefore, before accepting any consumer report contained in the records of a third party, District Counsel should be consulted.

338.(10) *(1-18-80)* 9781
Department Store Records

(1) Charge accounts.
(2) Credit files.

338.(11) *(1-18-80)* 9781
Detective Agency Records

(1) Investigative files.
(a) Civil.
(b) Criminal.
(c) Commercial.
(d) Industrial.
(2) Character check.
(3) Fraud investigations.
(4) Blackmail investigations.
(5) Divorce evidence.
(6) Missing persons search.
(7) Security patrols.
(8) Guards.
(9) Undercover agents.
(10) Surveillance work.
(11) Lie detector tests.
(12) Employee checking.
(13) Personnel screening.
(14) Fingerprinting.
(15) Service checking.
(a) Restaurants.
(b) Public transportation.
(c) Stores.

338.(12) *(1-18-80)* 9781
Distributors Records

(1) Gambling equipment.

(2) Wire service.

(3) Factory, farm, home office equipment, etc.

(4) Wholesale toiletry—Cash rebates are paid by some toiletry manufacturers. Details of available contracts which pay rebates to wholesale toiletry distributors are contained in publications issued by the Toiletry Merchandisers Association Inc., 230 Park Avenue, New York, New York 10017, and the Druggist Service Council Inc., 1290 Avenue of the Americas, New York, New York 10019.

338.(13) *(1-18-80)* 9781
Drug Store Records

Prescription records.

338.(14) *(1-18-80)* 9781
Fraternal, Veterans, Labor, Social, Political Organization Records

(1) Membership and attendance records.

(2) Dues, contributions, payments.

(3) Location and history of members.

338.(15) *(1-18-80)* 9781
Hospital Records

(1) Entry and release dates.

(2) Payments made.

338.(16) *(1-18-80)* 9781
Hotel Records

(1) Identity of guests.

(2) Telephone calls made to and from room.

(3) Credit record.

(4) Forwarding address.

(5) Reservations for travel—transportation companies and other hotels.

(6) Payments made by guest.

(7) Freight shipments and luggage—in and out.

338.(17) *(1-18-80)* 9781
Laundry and Dry Cleaning Record

(1) Marks and tags.

(2) Files of laundry marks.
(a) New York State Police, White Plains, New York.
(b) Other local or State police departments
(c) National Institute of Dry Cleaning, Inc., Washington, D.C.

338.(18) *(11-10-81)* 9781
Insurance Company Records

338.(18)1 *(11-10-81)* 9781
General

(1) Life, accident, fire, burglary, automobile and annuity policies—net worth data.

(2) Applications—background and financial information as well as insurance carried with other companies.

(3) Fur and jewelry floaters—appraised value and description.

(4) Customer's ledger cards.

(5) Policy and mortgage loan accounts.

(6) Dividend payment record.

(7) Payment records on termination (life), losses (casualty), or refunds on cancellations.

(8) Correspondence files.

(9) Payments to doctors, lawyers, appraisers and photographers hired directly by the insurance company to act for the company or as an independent expert.

338.(18)2 *(11-10-81)* 9781
The Equitable Life Assurance Society of the United States

The Equitable Life Assurance Society of the United States has advised that all inquiries concerning policies issued or its policyholders be made in person or by mail at its home office, 1285 Avenue of the Americas, New York, New York 10019. This company has indicated they would prefer requests be made by mail rather than in person.

338.(18)3 *(11-10-81)* 9781
Prudential Life Insurance Company

Inquiries to Prudential Life Insurance Company are not to be made by mail addressed to its home office, which is in Newark, New Jersey. Special agents with posts of duty outside the Newark District should make inquiry by collateral request together with a summons to the Chief, Criminal Investigation Division, Newark District. For insurance information the collateral request must include the individual's birth date, or the serial number of one of the policies issued to him by the company, or both. A request for mortgage information should include the name of the taxpayer's spouse, the exact location of the property in question, and if possible, other identifying details such as the Prudential mortgage number appearing on the document, or the date of the transaction.

338.(18)4 *(11-10-81)* 9781
Travelers Insurance Company

Whenever information is needed from Travelers Insurance Company, Hartford, Connecticut, special agents outside the Hartford District should prepare a collateral request together with a summons for any information or data desired from the company for transmittal to the Chief, Criminal Investigation Division, Hartford District.

338.(18)5 *(11-10-81)* 9781
Union Central Life Insurance Company

Whenever information is needed from Union Central Life Insurance Company, Cincinnati, Ohio, special agents outside the Cincinnati District should prepare a collateral request together with a summons for any information or data desired from the company for transmittal to the Chief, Criminal Investigation Division, Cincinnati District.

338.(18)6 *(11-10-81)* 9781
Metropolitan Life Insurance Company

Inquiries to the Metropolitan Life Insurance Company may be made in person or by mail. Inquiries should be made at its home office, 1 Madison Avenue, New York, New York 10038, Attn: Policy Services Division, to determine the location of the desired records. For individuals residing in California, Idaho, Montana, Oregon, Utah and Washington, requests should be made to the Pacific Coast Head Office, 600 Stockton Street, San Francisco, California 94120. For individuals residing in Florida, Georgia, North Carolina, Tennessee, Virginia, Kentucky, the District of Columbia and parts of Alabama and South Carolina, inquiries may be made in person or by mail to 4100 Boy Scout Boulevard, Tampa, Florida 33607. Other Records may be available in regional offices in Tulsa, Oklahoma, or Providence, Rhode Island.

338.(18)7 *(11-10-81)* 9781
Pan American Life Insurance Company

Inquiries to the Pan American Life Insurance Company may be made in person or by mail at its home office, 2400 Canal Street, New Orleans, Louisiana. Although personal service of a summons is not required, all mail requests for information should be accompanied by a summons, and addressed to the attention of the Legal Department.

338.(18)8 *(11-10-81)* 9781
CNA Insurance Companies

(1) Inquiries to CNA Insurance Companies are to be made at their headquarters in Chicago, Illinois. Special agents with posts of duty outside the Chicago District should make inquiry by collateral request to the Chief, Criminal Investigation Division, Chicago District.

(a) CNA Insurance Companies are as follows:

1 American Casualty Company of Reading, Pennsylvania

2 CNA Casualty of California

3 CNA Casualty of Puerto Rico

4 Columbia Casualty Company

5 Continental Casualty Company
6 Continental Assurance Company
7 Mid-States Insurance Company
8 National Fire Insurance Company of Hartford
9 Transcontinental Insurance Company
10 Transportation Insurance Company
11 Valley Forge Insurance Company
12 Valley Forge Life Insurance Company

(b) Requests for insurance information on policy holders should include the policy number(s). If the policy number is not available or known, other identifying data should be included, such as Social Security number, Employer Identification Number, etc.

(c) Requests for information concerning employees or agents should be so identified.

(d) Inquiries or summonses for CNA Insurance Companies should be directed to and personally served to:

1 Director, Corporate Security
Controllers Department
CNA Insurance
CNA Plaza—34th Floor
Chicago, IL 60685

2 The exact officer's name will be filled in upon service of the summons.

(e) A special agent from the Chicago District will be assigned to serve summonses and make necessary inquiries for information requested from CNA.

338.(18)9 *(11-10-81)* 9781
Aetna Life and Casualty

(1) Special Agents outside the Hartford District seeking information from Aetna Life and Casualty should request the information through collateral requests to the Chief, Criminal Investigation Division, Hartford District. The summons should be addressed to:

Aetna Life and Casualty
151 Farmington Avenue
Hartford, CT 06156.

(a) The following information should also be supplied with the summons:

1 First, middle and last name, including aliases, or company name in the case of a business.
2 Date and place of birth.
3 Social Security or Employer Identification Number.
4 Address during years under examination.

(b) The following information should also be furnished when possible:

1 Names of spouse, dependents and other persons associated with the taxpayer under investigation.
2 The type of data desired, such as:
a Medical or dental payments to physicians or dentists.
b Insurance policies purchased and premiums paid. Include pertinent dates and policy numbers and specify type of coverage such as Life, Health and Accident, Auto, etc.
c Policy loans and loan repayments. Policy holder's dividends. Include dates and policy numbers.

(c) The following are some of the principal subsidiaries that are commonly involved in requests for information. Summonses involving these companies should be addressed to Aetna Life and Casualty as noted above. Where possible, Criminal Investigation Division personnel should indicate the company involved:

1 Aetna Life Insurance Company
2 The Aetna Casualty and Surety Company
3 The Standard Fire Insurance Company
4 The Automobile Insurance Company of Hartford, Connecticut
5 Aetna Casualty and Surety Company of America
6 Aetna Casualty and Surety Company of Illinois
7 Aetna Life Insurance Company of Illinois
8 Aetna Health Management, Inc.
9 Aetna Premium Plan, Inc.
10 Aetna Variable Annuity Life Insurance Company
11 Aetna Business Credit, Inc.
12 Aetna Income Shares, Inc.

338.(19) *(1-18-80)* 9781
Newspaper Records

Clippings on a given person assembled in one file with photographs, notes, unpublished, data, etc.

338.(20) *(1-18-80)* 9781
Oil Company Records

Various oil companies publish directories of truck stops which may be useful in diesel fuel excise tax cases in providing leads to retail dealers throughout the country.

338.(21) *(1-18-80)* 9781
Photograph Records

(1) Relatives, associates, and friends.

(2) Previous places of employment—employee or company publications.

(3) Police and FBI files.

(4) Schools—yearbooks, school papers, etc.

(5) Nightclub or sidewalk photographers and photography studios.

(6) License bureaus—drivers, chauffeurs, taxis, etc.

(7) Newspaper morgues.

(8) Military departments.

(9) Fraternal organizations.

(10) Church groups.

(11) Race tracks.

(Next page is 9781-80.1)

(12) Photographs made of checks and persons presenting checks for cashing.

338.(22) *(1-18-80)* 9781
Private Business Records

(1) Examination of records for transactions with taxpayer.

(2) Canceled checks and taxpayer's endorsement and disposition.

(3) Discovery of other companies with whom taxpayer transacted business.

338.(23) *(11-10-81)* 9781
Publication Records

(1) Professional, trade, and agriculture directories and magazines.

(2) Who's Who of America and various states.

(3) Tax services.

(4) City directories.

(5) Moody's, Standard and Poor's Corporation Record, Financial Stock Guide Service.

(6) Telephone directories.

(7) Billboard Magazine (weekly)—amusement coin-machine, burlesque, drive-ins, fairs, stage, radio, T.V., magic, music machines, circuses, rinks, vending machines, movies, letter list, obituaries.

(8) Variety (weekly)—literature, radio, T.V., music, stage, movies, obituaries, and the like.

(9) Expenses in Retail Business' shows percentage of profits, costs and expenses for various retail businesses. May be obtained, free of charge, from National Cash Register Company offices.

(10) American Racing Manual—Published by Triangle Publications, Inc., 10 Lake Drive, P.O. Box 1015, Highstown, New Jersey 08520; record showing amounts paid to owners of winning horses by each race track in the United States, Canada, and Mexico. Publishers request that information be obtained in person by a special agent.

338.(24) *(1-18-80)* 9781
Public Utility Company Records

(1) Present and previous address of subscriber.

(2) Payments made for service.

(3) Payments made for "major" purchases.

338.(25) *(1-18-80)* 9781
Real Estate Agency or Savings and Loan Association Records

(1) Property transactions.

(2) Financial statements.

(3) Loan applications.

(4) Payments made and received (settlement sheets).

(5) Credit files.

338.(26) *(1-18-80)* 9781
Telephone Company Records

(1) Local directories—alphabetical and reverse.

(2) Library of "out of city" directories.

(3) Records of toll calls.

(4) Records of payments for service.

(5) Investigative reports on phones used for illegal purposes.

338.(27) *(1-18-80)* 9781
Transportation Company Records

(1) Passenger list.

(2) Reservations.

(3) Destinations.

(4) Fares paid.

(5) Freight carrier—shipper, destination, storage points.

(6) Departure and arrival times.

338.(28) *(1-18-80)* 9781
Consumer Loan Exchange or Lenders Exchange

An organization known as the Consumer Loan Exchange or Lenders Exchange exists in all of the large cities in the United States, as well as in some of the smaller cities. It is a non-profit organization, supported by and for its members. Most of the lending institutions are members of the Exchange. It can supply information concerning open and closed loan accounts with member companies, and other information. These organizations are not listed in directories or telephone books. Their location in a city may be obtained through local ending agencies. Consumer Reports may be obtained from these organizations only by court order or in accordance with written instructions of the consumer to whom the information relates.

338.(29) *(11-10-81)* 9781
Marshall Field and Company

Inquiries shall not be made by mail addressed direct to Marshall Field and Company, Chicago, Illinois. Special agents with posts of duty outside Chicago requiring information from that company shall make inquiry by collateral request together with a summons to the Chief, Criminal Investigation Division, Chicago, for such information. The exact officer to be served should be left blank when forwarding the summons with the collateral request. If a special agent is conducting inquiries in Chicago and it is necessary to obtain information from Marshall Field and Company, he/she shall consult the Chief, Criminal Investigation Division, Chicago, who will make any necessary arrangements with the company so that the agent may obtain the desired information.

338.(30) *(11–10–81)* 9781
Western Union Telegraph Company

Requests for information from Western Union Telegraph Company by special agents with posts of duty outside of St. Louis, Missouri, shall be transmitted via collateral request together with a summons to the Chief, Criminal Investigation Division, St. Louis District. The exact officer to be served should be left blank when forwarding the summons with the collateral request.

338.(31) *(11–10–81)* 9781
Investors Diversified Services, Inc.

Investors Diversified Services, Inc., an investment company, consists of the following subsidiaries and affiliates: Investors Syndicate Life Insurance and Annuity Company, Investors Syndicate of America, Inc., Investors Stock Fund, Inc., Investors Mutual, Inc., Investors Selective Fund, Inc., Investors Group Canadian Fund Ltd. (name changed to Investors Inter-Continental Fund, Ltd. on August 17, 1962), and Investors Variable Payment Fund, Inc. The principal place of business of Investors Diversified Services, Inc. and its various affiliates is located in Minneapolis, Minnesota. All inquiries should be made by collateral request together with a summons to the Chief, Criminal Investigation Division, St. Paul, Minnesota. The exact officer to be served should be left blank when forwarding the summons. All investors are notified by the company that information about their account has been disclosed to a representative of the Internal Revenue Service pursuant to a summons.

338.(32) *(11–10–81)* 9781
National Credit Card Agencies

338.(32)1 *(11–10–81)* 9781
General

National agencies, such as American Express, Diners Club and Carte Blanche, which provide credit cards for use in charging travel, entertainment, goods and services, can determine whether an individual or business concern has an account from their central index files. If details of the account are needed, information requests should indicate whether only copies of the monthly statements or copies of both the statements and charge slips are desired, the time period to be covered, the taxpayer's home address, and the name and address of his/her employer or business.

338.(32)2 *(11–10–81)* 9781
American Express

In order to obtain information from American Express, special agents with posts of duty outside the Manhattan District should make inquiry by collateral request together with a prepared summons to the Chief, Criminal Investigation Division, Manhattan District. American Express will not accept service by mail. The summons should be served in person at 770 Broadway, New York, New York 10003. The Custodian of Records for American Express is Ted Groder. In addition to the taxpayer's name and address, a social security number for the taxpayer should be furnished.

338.(32)3 *(11–10–81)* 9781
Diners Club

In order to obtain information from Diners Club, a summons should be served via mail to 10 Columbus Circle, New York, New York 10019, marked for the attention of the Corporate Legal Department. In addition to the monthly statements and charge slips, copies of the original application and payment check can be made available upon official request. These records are usually maintained by Diners Club for seven years.

338.(32)4 *(11–10–81)* 9781
Carte Blanche

In order to obtain information from Carte Blanche, special agents with posts of duty outside the Los Angeles District should make inquiry by collateral request to the Chief, Criminal Investigation Division, Los Angeles District.

338.(33) *(11–10–81)* 9781
Other Business Records

See 700:(2) through (5) of Law Enforcement Manual IX for additional information concerning business records.

339 *(1–18–80)* 9781
Reporting Threats Against the President and Possible Violations of Other Laws

339.1 *(1-18-80)* 9781
Notification to U.S. Secret Service (IRM 9378)

339.11 *(1-18-80)* 9781
Information Pertaining to Threats Againt the President

(1) The U.S. Secret Service is charged with the responsibility of protecting the President and certain other Government officials and public figures, including: members of the President's immediate family; the President-elect; the Vice President or other officer next in the order of succession to the Office of President; former Presidents; the wife, widow, and minor children of former Presidents; Presidential and Vice Presidential candidates; and visiting heads of foreign states or foreign governments. The Executive Protection Service, under the direction of the Secret Service, is responsible for the protection or the Executive Mansion and foreign diplomatic missions in the District of Columbia metropolitan area.

(2) Any Service employee who receives information either orally or in writing which indicates a potential threat to the health or safety of one of the individuals in (1) above should report the information immediately by telephone to the nearest U.S. Secret Service Office or to the U.S. Secret Service Intelligence Division, Washington, D.C. (Area Code 202-634-5838). If the Secret Service should request information to aid in the prevention of crimes involving a threat to the life of a individual described in (1) above, the employee may, without seeking prior supervisory approval, immediately provide information relevant to the threat. However, if the employee is concerned that the disclosure may involve a protected return, return information or taxpayer return information, see (35)30 of the "new" IRM 1272, Disclosure of Official Information Handbook.

(3) If an employee discloses information as described in (2) above, he/she shall prepare a memorandum setting forth all the facts disclosed, together with any other facts bearing on the matter and full details as to the circumstances under which such information was acquired. The memorandum should be transmitted immediately to the head of the office and a copy should be forwarded to the Director, Disclosure Operations Division, National Office.

(4) When there are Presidential and Vice-Presidential candidates who are not receiving Secret Service protection, any Service employee obtaining information concerning threats against them or other persons in close proximity to them is authorized to disclose this information to the nearest FBI office to the same extent and in accordance with the procedures described in (2) and (3) above.

339.12 *(1-18-80)* 9781
Cases Involving Possible Forgery of U.S. Check

(1) Whenever information is received indicating that forgery concerning a United States Government check is involved in a case within the investigative jurisdiction of Criminal Investigation (including any case involving checks issued to fictitious payees), the nearest office of the U.S. Secret Service shall be notified thereof in writing by the Chief, Criminal Investigation Division. The Secret Service, in turn, will notify the Treasurer of the United States. Cooperation shall be given the Secret Service agents to the extent permissible, within the limitations of IRC 6103 and 7213, in developing the forgery aspect of the case. (See Policy Statement P-9-33.) In order to protect the development by Criminal Investigation of a possible criminal tax case, the Secret Service has informed us that they will make no investigation in the case until such action has been coordinated with Criminal Investigation. The Secret Service officials have stated that they will not consult with the United

(Next page is 9781-81)

States Attorney about the forgery violation until such consultation can be done jointly with representatives of Criminal Investigation, or until such consultation has been coordinated with the Chief, Criminal Investigation Division. Secret Service instructions provide that no action will be taken by the Secret Service on any question of settlement of the forgery case until such action is agreeable with Criminal Investigation. Copies of pertinent affidavits, handwriting exemplars, personal and criminal history, and other items of interest will be made immediately available by each Service to the other investigating agency, and each Service will keep the other informed of the progress of the investigation being made, to avoid unnecessary duplication of effort.

(2) Investigations of this type require the closest coordination between Criminal Investigation and the Secret Service. For this reason the Chief, Criminal Investigation Division, and, where appropriate, the ARC (Criminal Investigation) shall confer with the Secret Service Special Agents in Charge in his/her district or region to work out office procedures for joint handling of these cases which will ensure that the responsibilities of each Service are properly discharged and that all the interests of the Government in these cases are fully safeguarded. They shall keep themselves informed of the development of such cases.

(3) Due to the importance of news coverage in such cases, especially those involving "tax experts" and multiple false returns, the District Director will initiate and control any press releases issued in accordance with IRM 9448.

(4) At the time the Secret Service is notified of possible forgery in a Criminal Investigation case, identification of the check or checks involved, to the extent possible, shall be set out in the notification. The Secret Service office will obtain photostat copies of each such check as requested by Criminal Investigation. Ordinarily, one copy of such check will be sufficient for the Criminal Investigation.

339.13 *(1-18-80)* 9781
Other Information of Interest to the Secret Service

(1) The following are other areas of responsibility of the Secret Service. Procedures in IRM 9378.2 should be followed in reporting information received relating to these activities to the Secret Service:

(a) the use of bodily harm, assassination, or kidnapping as a political weapon. This should include training and teohniques used to carry out the act.

(b) persons who insist upon personally contacting high government officials for redress of imaginary grievances, etc.

(c) any person who makes oral or written statements about high government officials in the following categories:

1 threatening statements

2 irrational statements

3 abusive statements

(d) professional gate crashers.

(e) terrorists (individuals, groups) and their activities (bombing, etc.).

(f) the ownership or concealment by individuals of groups of caches of firearms, explosives, or other implements of war, when it is believed that their intended use is for other than legal purposes.

(g) anti-American or anti—U.S. Government demonstrations in the United States or overseas.

(h) information regarding civil disturbances.

(i) counterfeiting of U.S. or foreign obligations, i.e., currency, coins, stamps, bonds, U.S. Treasurer's checks, Treasury securities, Department of Agriculture Food Stamp coupons, etc.

(j) the forgery, alteration, and fraudulent negotiation of U.S. Treasurer's checks, U.S. Government bonds and Government Travel Requests (GTR's).

(2) In all cases, the person making the referral will prepare and submit a memorandum as provided in IRM 9378.2:(3).

339.2 *(1-18-80)* 9781
Information Concerning Possible Violations of Federal, State and Local Criminal Laws

(1) In the performance of their official duties, special agents should be particularly alert for indications of possible violations of the Internal Revenue Code, as well as violations of other Federal, State, or local criminal laws. Information concerning alleged violations of laws administered by IRS will be reported through

channels in accordance with existing procedures.

(2) Return information (other than taxpayer return information) indicating a possible violation of a Federal criminal law not administered by the Service which is obtained by a special agent during the course of an official investigation, will be reported by memorandum to the Chief, Criminal Investigation Division. Return information (other than taxpayer return information) is information in the possession of the IRS which was not received from the taxpayer, the taxpayer's representative, or the taxpayer's return and supporting schedules. Such information includes the taxpayer's identity, the nature, source or amount of his/her income, payments, receipts, deductions, exemptions, credits, assets, liabilities, net worth, tax liability, tax withheld, deficiencies, overassessments, or tax payments, whether the taxpayer's return was, is being, or will be examined or subject to other investigation or processing, or any other data, received by, recorded by, furnished to, or collected by the Secretary with respect to a return or with respect to the determination of the existence, or possible existence, or liability (or the amount thereof) of any person under the Internal Revenue Code for any tax, penalty, interest, fine, forfeiture, or other imposition, or offense. The memorandum should contain the following information relating to the violation.

(a) Name, social security number, address, and aliases of subject (if known).

(b) Business or occupation of subject (if known).

(c) Facts and circumstances surrounding the nontax violation.

(d) U.S. Code sections believed violated.

(e) Specific source of information, i.e., 3rd party, taxpayer, taxpayer's representative, taxpayer's return and the circumstances under which the information was obtained.

(f) Agency to whom this violation would be of interest, i.e., U.S. Attorney (Judicial District), Strike Force Attorney (location), other agency (specify).

(g) System of Records from which information was obtained.

(3) The Chief, Criminal Investigation Division will furnish such information to the disclosure officer for forwarding to the National Office, Disclosure Operations Division. In cases where the information was obtained during the course of a wagering (IRC Chapter 35) investigation, see IRM 9420 for disclosure procedures as some information may not be disclosed in accordance with IRC 4424. If in doubt as to whether the information may be disclosed, contact your disclosure officer. See IRM 9411.3 for disclosure procedures in Special Enforcement Program (SEP) cases; if the information concerns alleged impersonations of a Federal Officer, see IRM 9123: (4); and, if it indicates that forgery of a United States Government check is involved in a case within the jurisdiction of Criminal Investigation, see IRM 9378.1.

(4) When a special agent either witnesses the commission of any nontax criminal act, or receives information orally or in writing from any source indicating facts that relate to a nontax violation of Federal, State or local criminal laws and such facts are determined to be information not protected from disclosure by IRC 6103, such information may be disclosed to appropriate Federal, State or local law enforcement officials in accordance with procedures in Chapter 100 of "new" IRM 1272, Disclosure of Official Information Handbook.

(5) Information relating to any Federal violation not within the jurisdiction of the Service which the Chief, Criminal Investigation Division believes to be derived from "Taxpayer Return Information" as defined in IRC 6103(b)(3) should be forwarded in the same manner as return information outlined in IRM 9382.4: (3) above. The Service may not voluntarily disclose taxpayer return information but will maintain files in the Disclosure Operations Division, National Office, to assess the impact of the Tax Reform Act of 1976.

(6) In the event that any disclosure described above would impair a criminal tax investigation or any tax administration matter, the Chief, Criminal Investigation Division should weigh the relative significance of this potential impact and the seriousness and significance of the nontax violation in determining whether or not to forward the information. If a determination not to forward the information is made, the Chief, Criminal Investigation Division should immediately advise the District Director of the reasons for that determination. The Chief, Criminal Investigation Division should periodically reevaluate the seriousness and significance of the nontax violation and the impact of disclosure on the criminal tax investigation or tax administration matter to determine if the circumstances causing the decision not to disclose are still valid.

(7) Where an informant's letter contains an allegation of a tax violation and an allegation of some other Federal law violation not within the investigative jurisdiction of the Service, Criminal Investigation may furnish the latter information, in writing, directly to the appropriate agency. However, the informant's letter, or copy thereof, may not be furnished as that would constitute an unauthorized disclosure both of the tax information and of the identity of an informant who furnished information of a tax violation. In such instances, the name of the informant should not be disclosed except when the other agency requests that the source of the information be identified and then only with the permission of the informant after it has been explained to him/her that one or more allegations made by him/her fall within the investigative jurisdiction of another agency.

(8) Information concerning potential diversion of nuclear material should be immediately reported by the special agent to his/her group manager who will transmit the information at once to the nearest FBI field office and, as soon as practicable, to the Assistant Commissioner (Compliance). In all cases, the group manager making the referral will prepare a written report containing all the information furnished to the FBI, the name and title of the person to whom the information was given, and the time and date of the referral. This report should be forwarded through the District Director to the Assistant Commissioner (Compliance), National Office, as confirmation of the telephone referral. If this information is either return information or taxpayer return information, the procedures in IRM 9382.4:(3) and IRM 9382.4:(5) respectively, should be followed. In emergency situations, the Disclosure Officer should be contacted immediately so that he/she may contact the Disclosure Operations Division, National Office for consultation, if necessary.

(9) See also IRM 9382.4

340 *(1-18-80)* 9781

Witnesses and Prospective Defendants

341 *(1-18-80)* 9781

Rights and Obligations of Witnesses and Prospective Defendants

341.1 *(1-18-80)* 9781

General

All persons called as witnesses, whether prospective defendants or otherwise, whether natural persons or corporate entities, and whether they appear as witnesses in response to court or grand jury subpoena, Commissioner's summonses, or simple requests to appear for interview, have rights and obligations defined by the United States Constitution, statutes, and court decisions.

341.2 *(1-18-80)* 9781

Constitutional Law

(1) *Constitutional protections* are provided in the Fourth, Fifth and Sixth Amendments, which read as follows:

(a) Fourth Amendment—

"The right of the people to be secure in their persons, houses, papers, and effects, against unreasonable searches and seizures shall not be violated, and no Warrants shall issue, but upon probable cause, supported by Oath or affirmation, and particularly describing the place to be searched, and the persons or things to be seized."

(b) Fifth Amendment—

"No person shall be held to answer for a capital, or otherwise infamous crime, unless on a presentment or indictment of a Grand Jury, except in cases arising in the land or naval forces, or in the Militia, when in actual service in time of War or public danger; nor shall any person be subject for the same offense to be twice put in jeopardy of life or limb; nor shall be compelled in any criminal case to be a witness against himself, nor be deprived of life, liberty or property, without due process of law; nor shall private property be taken for public use, without just compensation."

(c) Sixth Amendment—

"In all criminal prosecutions, the accused shall enjoy the right to a speedy and public trial, by an impartial jury of the State and district wherein the crime shall have been committed, which district shall have been previously ascertained by law, and to be informed of the nature and cause of the accusation; to be confronted with the witnesses against him; to have compulsory process for obtaining Witnesses in his favor, and to have the Assistance of Counsel for his defense."

341.3 *(1-18-80)* 9781
Legality and Use of Certain Evidence and Equipment

341.31 *(1-18-80)* 9781
Admissibility of Evidence

(1) Evidence obtained by Federal officers in violation of constitutional provisions, at any stage of an investigation or proceeding, will be excluded at the instance of the defendant in the trial of a criminal case. [*Boyd v. U.S.; Weeks v. U.S.; Gouled v. U.S.; U.S. v. Guerrina*] Federal Courts have also excluded such evidence in civil cases, [*Fraternal Order of Eagles v. U.S.*] including those involving collection of wagering taxes, [*Lassoff v. Gray; U.S. v. Four Thousand One Hundred Seventy One Dollars in U.S. Currency*] although it is admissible in a civil wagering case to impeach a person's testimony that he/she has not engaged in the wagering business. [*Walder v. U.S.; Lassoff v. Gray*]

(2) Evidence obtained by state officers under circumstances which would constitute unreasonable search and seizure under the Fourth Amendment if obtained by Federal officers is equally inadmissible in a Federal criminal trial. [*Elkins v. U.S.*] This repudiates the former so-called "silver platter" doctrine which had allowed Federal courts to admit evidence illegally obtained by state officers if there had been no collusion by Federal officials. The Federal court must decide for itself if there has been an unreasonable search and seizure by state officers, even though the state court has already considered the question and irrespective of the state court's findings. [*Elkins v. U.S.; Boyle v. U.S.; U.S. v. Scolnick*]

(3) A person who has thrown records into a trash can, especially if he/she shares it with other building tenants, is considered to have abandoned the records, and cannot claim that agents who later take them from the trash can have violated his/her rights under the Fourth Amendment. [*U.S. v. Minker*]

(4) The rule excluding evidence unlawfully taken does not apply where the unlawful taking was by private persons without participation or collusion of law inforcement officers. [*Burdeau v. McDowell; U.S. v. Morris C. Goldberg*]

(5) The Supreme Court has upheld the use of an informant. [*Hoffa v. U.S.*] or an undercover agent [*Lewis v. U.S.*] to obtain incriminating evidence against a defendant. The Constitution does not protect a wrongdoer's misplaced belief that a person to whom he/she voluntarily confides his/her wrongdoing will not reveal it.

341.32 *(1-18-80)* 9781
Use of Investigative Equipment

Special Agents will at all times conform to the Department of Justice guidelines on monitoring of private conversations. Mechanical, electronic or other devices will be used only in accordance with Policy Statement P-9-35 and the procedures set forth in IRM 9389.

341.33 *(2-8-82)* 9781
Electronic Listening Devices and Other Monitoring Devices

341.331 *(2-8-82)* 9781
General

(1) The legality of evidence obtained through the use of electronic eavesdropping devices depends on whether or not there has been compliance with the Fourth Amendment. [*Katz v. U.S.*] The Government's placing a transmitter above a phone booth in order to electronically listen to and record a suspect's words violated the privacy upon which he/she relied and thus constituted a "search and seizure" within the Fourth Amendment. Failure to obtain a court order prior to the use of the device rendered the evidence obtained inadmissible. [*Katz v. U.S.*]

(2) A court, pursuant to Title III of the Omnibus Crime Control and Safe Streets Act of 1968 (Public Law 90-35), can authorize electronic surveillance to investigate specific criminal offenses. The offenses for which interceptions of such communications can be authorized by court order are listed in 18 U.S.C. 2516. None of the criminal offenses for which the Criminal Investigation Division has jurisdiction are included in this law. The statute does not authorize wiretaps to investigate the tax crimes of Title 26, the Internal Revenue Code (IRC).

(3) Special agents of the Criminal Investigation Division are qualified to receive and use Title III information obtained by other agencies because they qualify as law enforcement officers as defined by 18 U.S.C. 2510 (7). In certain situations they may investigate several of the violations enumerated in 18 U.S.C. 2516. Once having received Title III information, it can be used for any purpose within the scope of their official duties (18 U.S.C. 2517 (1) and (2)).

(4) Electronic or mechanical devices may be used to overhear or record either telephone or non-telephone conversations with express advance consent of all parties to the conversation. Supervisor approval is not required for such use.

341.332 *(2-8-82)* 9781
Consensual Monitoring

(1) The term "Consensual Monitoring" as used herein, means the investigative interception, overhearing, or recording of a private conversation by the use of mechanical, electronic or other devices, with the consent of at least one, but not all the participants, as contrasted to "Non-Consensual Monitoring," where no participant consents.

(2) The monitoring of conversations with the consent of one of the participants is an effective and reliable investigative technique but must be sparingly and carefully used. The Department of Justice has encouraged its use by criminal investigators where it is both appropriate and necessary to establish a criminal offense. While such monitoring is constitutionally and statutorily permissible, this investigative technique is subject to careful regulation in order to avoid any abuse or any unwarranted invasion of privacy.

341.333 *(2-8-82)* 9781
Consensual Monitoring of Telephone Conversations

(1) The monitoring of telephone conversations with the consent of at least one, but not all the participants, requires the authorization of the Chief, Criminal Investigation Division, the Chief, Operations Branch, National Office; or in their absence, the person acting in their place. The Commissioner has designated these officials to authorize consensual monitoring of telephone conversations and this authority may not be redelegated. If these officials cannot be located, their line superiors may grant approval. The line superior for the Chief, Criminal Investigation Division, is the District Director, and the line superior for the Chief, Operations Branch, is the Director, Criminal Investigation Division.

(2) The request for approval will be prepared in accordance with the provisions contained in IRM 9389.2:(2).

(3) Requests for approval should be in writing, or at the discretion of the approving official, may be oral, provided that it is confirmed in writing at the earliest practical time. Approval should not be granted by any designated official until he/she is fully convinced that the investigation warrants the requested monitoring. In any instance where the designated official has some reservation about granting approval, he/she should consult his/her superiors.

(4) Within 10 working days after the completion of the monitoring activities (or attempted monitoring activities) for each specific authorization and each authorization extension, a report will be submitted to the approving authority (Chief, Criminal Investigation Division; or Chief, Operations Branch, National Office), with a copy sent, through channels, including the District Director, to the Director, Criminal Investigation Division. A report will not be submitted if the monitoring occurs with the consent of all parties. The report should complement the information contained in the request for authorization and will be prepared in accordance with the provisions contained in Exhibit 9380-3 of the Internal Revenue Manual.

341.334 *(2-8-82)* 9781
Consensual Monitoring of Non-Telephone Conversations

(1) The monitoring of a non-telephone conversation with the consent of at least one of the parties requires the advance written authorization by the Attorney General of the United States or the Assistant Attorney in charge of the Criminal Division or the Deputy Assistant Attorneys General of that Division, except for emergency situations, when an official designated by the Commissioner (see 341.334:(1)(b)) may grant prior approval (See policy statement P-9-35) as follows:

(a) All requests for approval must be submitted by the Chief, Criminal Investigation Division through channels including the District Director and may only be signed by the Director, Criminal Investigation Division, or, in his/her absence, the Acting Director. These officials have been designated by the Commissioner and the authority cannot be redelegated. Requests will be submitted in writing whenever time and communication facilities allow. If appropriate, consideration should be given to transmittal of written requests via telephone communication facilities. Requests will include the same information set forth in IRM 9389.2:(2), except for the telephone number information required in IRM 9389.2:(2)(e). When time and communication facilities are insufficient to accomplish a written request, the needed information may be orally transmitted to the Director, Criminal Investigation Division, who will be responsible for preparation of a written request which is to be forwarded to the Attorney General. An oral request for approval must be confirmed in writing and submitted within two working days after the oral request is made.

(b) If, in the judgment of the Director, Criminal Investigation Division, the emergency needs of an investigation preclude obtaining such advance approval from the Attorney General, he/she may, without having obtained such approval, authorize consensual monitoring of non-telephone conversations. When the Director, Criminal Investigation Division, cannot be reached to grant such emergency approval, the Assistant Director may grant emergency approval. As a general rule, emergency authorization pursuant to this exception will not be granted where the approving official has in excess of 24 hours to attempt to obtain written advance approval from the Attorney General. The authority to grant emergency approval has been delegated by the Commissioner and cannot be redelegated. Confirmation of emergency approval will be done by memorandum through channels by the Director or Acting Director.

(2) Within 10 working days after the completion of the monitoring activities (or attempted monitoring activities) for each specific authorization and each authorization extension, a report will be submitted to the Chief, Criminal Investigation Division, with a copy sent, through channels, including the District Director to the Director, Criminal Investigation Division. This report should complement the information contained in the request for authorization and will be prepared in accordance with the provisions contained in Exhibit 9380-3.

(3) Under certain circumstances, a special agent may be present with representatives of another Federal agency during the course of consensual monitoring of a non-telephonic conversation when Attorney General approval was initially obtained by such representatives. However, where there is active participation or assistance in the consensual monitoring, and where no emergency situation is involved, the special agent should obtain the approval of both the Criminal Investigation Division and the Department of Justice before actively participating with or rendering assistance to the other agency involved. Reports will be prepared and furnished as provided in 341.334:(2).

(4) See IRM 9267.3:(19) with regard to a request by a Government attorney to monitor non-telephone conversations during a grand jury investigation.

341.335 *(2-8-82)* 9781
Nonconsensual Monitoring

(1) Non-consensual monitoring of telephone conversations is prohibited. The prohibition applies whether or not the information which may be acquired through such monitoring is intended to be used in any way or to be subsequently divulged outside the Service.

(2) Non-consensual monitoring of non-telephone conversations is prohibited.

341.336 *(2-8-82)* 9781
Restrictions on Other Uses of Investigative Techniques and Equipment

(1) The use of transmitters, drip cans or other devices to assist in trailing vehicles is permitted only if the person in lawful possession of the vehicle consents to the installation.

(2) Transmitters or other radio signal sending equipment to facilitate communication between investigators or persons acting under their supervision to coordinate surveillance or raids is permitted without prior supervisory approval.

(3) Investigative devices will not be installed and utilized to intercept, overhear or record conversations in public telephone booths or any type of public telephone installation.

(4) Miniature recorders and radio transmitters will not be used surreptitiously in conducting routine surveys and interviews with third parties.

(5) As provided in IRM 9751:(3), field offices may not procure sensitive-type equipment. Special agents may not use sensitive-type equipment which they have personally procured for investigative purposes.

(6) Permission to employ eavesdropping devices can only be granted to Criminal Investigators (GS-1811 series). The equipment can only be used by them or by personnel acting under their direction. The prohibitions and limitations outlined herein apply equally to non-Service personnel who act at the direction of Criminal Investigators.

(7) Pen registers and other types of telephone number recorders will be used only when authorized by a court order. Unless the Director specifically approves, only IRS owned pen registers and accessory equipment can be used. The procedure for obtaining authorization to use this equipment is contained in IRM 9389.62.

341.337 *(2-8-82)* 9781
Recording the Proceedings of Public Meetings

Recording the proceedings of a public meeting is a permissible means of surveillance. However, one must initially establish that the meeting is indeed public. The court in United States v. Tijerina, without defining the phrase "public meeting" found substantial support in the record that the meeting was public. The meeting was attended by two newspaper reporters and a radio newscaster. The civic auditorium was set up with a television camera and a loud speaker system. Invited guests were admitted to the meeting after paying a $2.00 admittance fee and identifying themselves. Estimates of the number varied from 200 to 600. Based on Tijerina the following criteria should be among those considered in determining whether or not a meeting is public: where was the meeting held, were members of the press present or involved, were there unreasonable restrictions upon entry, how many people were present, and was public notice of the meeting given?

341.4 *(4-15-82)* 9781
Right to Record Interview

(1) An interrogation or conference may be recorded only by a stenographer who is an employee of the Internal Revenue Service. This rule may be waived by the agent's immediate superior. At the request of the Service or witness, which includes a principal, the superior may authorize the use of a stenographer employed by the United States Attorney, a court reporter of the United States District Court, a reporter licensed or certified by any state as a court reporter or to take depositions, or an independent reporter known to the Service to be qualified to take depositions for use in a United States District Court. The use of this procedure is permissible under IRC 6103(k)(6) since it is a disclosure for investigative purposes. When no stenographer is readily available, mechanical recording devices may be used to record statements by advising the witness, in advance, of the use of the device (implied consent). If the witness objects, the interrogator will refrain from mechanically recording the statement. If the witness elects to mechanically record the conversation, the Service will make its own recording.

(2) A witness or principal is not permitted to have his/her own private or public stenographer present to take shorthand notes or transcribe testimony except that he/she may be permitted to engage a qualified reporter as described in (1) above to be present at his/her expense provided that the Service may secure a copy of the transcript at its expense.

(3) Upon request, a copy of an affidavit or transcript of a question and answer statement will be furnished a witness promptly, except in circumstances deemed by the Regional Commissioner to necessitate temporarily withholding a copy. (See Policy Statement P-9-31.)

(4) See also IRM 9353.

342 *(1-18-80)* 9781
Prospective Defendants

342.1 *(1-18-80)* 9781
Individual as a Prospective Defendant

342.11 *(1-18-80)* 9781
Statements of An Individual

(1) The purpose of the Fifth Amendment provision that no person shall be compelled in any criminal case to be a witness against himself/herself is to ensure that no one will be forced in

any manner or at any time to give testimony that may expose him/her to prosecution for a crime. It applies equally whether incrimination be under Federal or state law, and whether the privilege is invoked in the Federal or state courts. [*Murphy v. N.Y. Waterfront Commission;* see also *Malloy v. Hogan.*] If a witness has been compelled to testify in a state court under a grant of immunity, as to matters which could incriminate him/her under Federal law, a Federal court cannot later use that testimony or any fruits of it. [*Murphy v. N.Y. Waterfront Commission*] The grant of immunity applies only to the inability to prosecute the witness based on testimony supplied by him/her. This does not preclude a prosecution of the witness based on the presentation of independent evidence which did not result from his/her own testifying. [*Kastigar v. U.S.*]

(2) A defendant's refusal to testify at the trial for a Federal offense cannot raise any presumption against him/her or be the subject of comment by the prosecution. The right to refuse to answer incriminating questions applies not only to court trials, but to all kinds of criminal or civil proceedings, including administrative investigations. [*George Smith v. U.S.; McCarthy v. Arndstein; Counselman v. Hitchcock; U.S. v. Harold Gross*] The fear of self-incrimination may be with respect to any criminal offense. For example, in the case of Internal Revenue Agent v. Sullivan, a taxpayer was upheld in refusing to produce records in a tax matter on the ground that indictment was pending against him for defrauding the Government on certain contracts.

342.12 *(1-18-80)* 9781
Books and Records of An Individual

(1) An individual taxpayer may refuse to exhibit his/her books and records for examination on the ground that compelling him/her to do so might violate his/her right against self-incrimination under the Fifth Amendment and constitute an illegal search and seizure under the Fourth Amendment. [*Boyd v. U.S.; U.S. v. Vadner*] However, in the absence of such claims, it is not error for a court to charge the jury that it may consider the refusal to produce books and records, in determining willfulness. [*Louis C. Smith v. U.S.; Beard v. U.S.; Olson v. U.S.; Myres v. U.S.*]

(2) The privilege against self-incrimination does not permit a taxpayer to refuse to obey a summons issued under IRC 7602 or a court order directing his/her appearance. He/she is required to appear and cannot use the Fifth Amendment as an excuse for failure to do so, although he/she may exercise it in connection with specific questions. [*Landy v. U.S.*] He/she cannot refuse to bring his/her records, but may decline to submit them for inspection on constitutional grounds. In the Vadner case, the government moved to hold a taxpayer in contempt of court for refusal to obey a court order to produce his/her books and records. He refused to submit them for inspection by the Government, basing his refusal on the Fifth Amendment. The court denied the motion to hold him in contempt, holding that disclosure of his assets would provide a starting point for a tax evasion case.

(3) Where records are required be kept as an aid to enforcement of certain regulatory functions enacted by Congress, such records have been held public records, whose production may be compelled without violating the Fifth Amendment. This reasoning has also been applied in some income tax evasion cases. [*Falsone v. U.S.; Beard v. U.S.*] *Other income tax cases have stated that compulsory production of a taxpayer's books and records for use in a criminal prosecution would violate the constitutional protection against self-incrimination. There has not yet been any Supreme Court decision holding the public records doctrine applicable in income tax cases.*

(4) The decision of the Supreme Court in *Andresen v. Maryland* appears to have resolved conflicting judicial precedents regarding the use of search warrants to seize books and records of financial transactions. In this case the Court held that the search of Andresen's office for business records, their seizure and subsequent introduction into evidence did not offend the Fifth Amendment. Although the seized records contained statements that the accused had committed to writing, he was never required to say anything. The search for and seizure of these records was conducted by law enforcement officers and introduced at trial by prosecution witnesses.

(5) Subject to the restrictions contained in IRM 0735.1, Handbook of Employee Responsibilities and Conduct, books, records, canceled checks, and other documents may be removed from the custody of a principal or witness when he/she voluntarily agrees to such action. When they are obtained by the use of legal process, and it is found that they contain evidence of the crime, it may be desirable to retain custody of such evidence until the case involved is disposed of. Should the witness or defendant desire access to his/her records, he/she is entitled to examine them, but such examination should be made in the presence of the special agent to preclude the possibility of alterations. Where possession of records is not obtained by legal process but is only by sufferance, they should be returned upon request, at the earliest practicable time. (See policy statement P-4-8.) It was held in *Mason v. Pulliam,* that a taxpayer may withdraw an earlier voluntary consent to a taking of possession by the Service of records for examination and copying, the records being immediately returnable upon the withdrawal of that consent. Thus, the Service is effectively prohibited by this decision from making copies of such records following withdrawal of consent. As a practical matter, consideration should be given to copying the records upon receipt.

(6) Records and documents obtained from the principal or a witness which contain information relevant to the apparent issues in the case under investigation should be transcribed or otherwise copied. The transcriptions or copies should be identified and authenticated as outlined in IRM 9383.4 for later use in the event the originals become unavailable to the government for any reason.

(7) The original records of an individual defendant, in his/her possession, cannot be subpoenaed into court for use against him/her in a criminal trial, because to do so would violate his/her constitutional rights against self-incrimination and render his/her records inadmissable. However, authenticated copies of such records are admissible in criminal proceedings.

(8) When records are obtained from a possible defendant, notation should be made of the circumstances to show that they were furnished voluntarily. Notation should also be made of the chain of custody of records and of all other evidence in order that authenticated identification of the evidence may be made. Special agents are not to sign or initial the records of a possible defendant nor to assure him/her in any manner whatsoever that his/her tax liability has been correctly reported as of any certain date. They are not to assure him/her that his/her records will be subject to no further examination.

(9) In all instances when a special agent removes books, records, or other documents from the premises of either a taxpayer under investigation or a third party witness, through legal process or agreement, he/she shall issue a receipt, normally Form 2725, Document Receipt (Exhibit 300-12), identifying the items obtained. The receipt shall be prepared in duplicate and the copy retained for the office file of the case so that the identity of the books, records, or documents obtained may at all times be ascertained. When such books, records, or documents are returned to the taxpayer, third party witness or their representatives, the special agent shall obtain the receipt he/she issued with an endorsement thereon acknowledging the return of the items or obtain such an endorsement on the copy of the receipt. The receipt containing his/her endorsement should be kept in the office file on the case. A special agent assigned to assist a grand jury will not use a Form 2725 when securing documents pursuant to a grand jury subpoena, see 9267.3:(7).

(10) When a taxpayer has voluntarily submitted an altered document and subsequently requests its return, the special agent should consider not complying with the request. Furthermore, it is doubtful that a court will give redress where the party seeking relief is attempting to perpetrate a fraud, and is asking the court to aid in the attempt by forcing the Government to return the altered document. Legible copies may not suffice for requisite examination regarding handwriting (pressure on paper), ink analysis (the composition and dating of the fluid and use of an infrared image converter), typewriter determination (the idiosyncrasies of certain key strikes), paper analysis (watermarks indicating source and availability), etc. Nonetheless, when it becomes known or suspected that a document has been altered, the required expert analysis should be undertaken as soon as possible and the document should then be returned to the taxpayer, provided such return would not foreclose proof of an alteration (See

Text 356.7 for processing questioned documents). However, before suspected originals are actually returned to the person furnishing them, the Government expert should be advised that such return is contemplated and queried as to whether he will be in a position to give effective testimony based upon his past examination of the originals and retention of copies. In the event effective testimony is conditioned on introductions of the originals, such originals should not be voluntarily returned.

(11) See also IRM 9383.3

342.13 *(1-18-80)* 9781
Duty to Inform Individual of His Constitutional Rights

342.131 *(1-18-80)* 9781
General

Special agents *must* abide by the instructions of IRM 9384 and any related Manual Supplements relative to advising individuals of their constitutional rights.

342.132 *(1-18-80)* 9781
Non-custodial Interviews

(1) At the outset of the first official interview with the subject of an investigation, the special agent will properly identify himself/herself as a special agent of the Internal Revenue Service and will produce his/her authorized credentials to the subject for examination. He/she will also state "As a special agent, one of my functions is to investigate the possibility of criminal violations of the Internal Revenue laws, and related offenses."

(2) The special agent will then advise the subject of the investigation substantially as follows:

> "In connection with my investigation of your tax liability (or other matter), I would like to ask you some questions. However, first I advise you that under the Fifth Amendment to the Constitution of the United States I cannot compel you to answer any questions or to submit any information if such answers or information might tend to incriminate you in any way. I also advise you that anything which you say and any documents which you submit may be used against you in any criminal proceeding which may be undertaken. I advise you further that you may, if you wish, seek the assistance of an attorney before responding."

(3) If the subject requests clarification, either as to his/her rights or the purpose of the investigation, the special agent will give such explanation as is necessary to clarify the matter for the subject.

(4) If at any stage of an interview the subject indicates that he/she wishes to exercise his/her rights to withhold his/her testimony or records, or to first consult with an attorney, the special agent will terminate the interview.

(5) In each investigation, the special agent will make a contemporaneous memorandum stating when and where the subject was advised of his/her constitutional rights; what additional explanation, if any, was made; how the subject responded; and who was present at the time.

(6) In dealing with a corporate officer or employee who appears to be implicated in an alleged wrongdoing involving a corporation under investigation, the special agent will advise the person of his/her identity and duties at the outset of the special agent's first official meeting, as required by (a) above. The special agent will also advise the person that under the Fifth Amendment to the United States Constitution, he/she cannot be compelled to answer any questions or to submit any personal information which might tend to incriminate him/her in any way. The person also will be advised that anything he/she says and any personal documents which he/she submits may be used in any criminal action which may be undertaken. The person may, if he/she wishes, seek the assistance of counsel before responding. If the person is the custodian of corporate records which are needed for the investigation, he/she will also be advised that he/she is required to produce such records since rights under the Fifth Amendment do not apply to a corporation and its records.

(7) The special agent will not use trickery, misrepresentation or deception in obtaining any evidence or information, nor will he/she use language which might constitute a promise of immunity of settlement of the principal's case, or which might constitute intimidation or a threat.

(8) A special agent, to avert any attack upon the admissibility of any statement or documentary evidence furnished by a subject under investigation, will inform the subject of his/her constitutional rights at the beginning of a formal question and answer interview, even if the subject was previously advised.

(9) Failure to give taxpayers the constitutional warnings prescribed by Internal Revenue procedures has resulted in the exclusion of evidence obtained from the taxpayers. [*U.S. v. Leahey; U.S. v. Heffner*]

(10) If the subject of a grand jury investigation is interviewed by a special agent acting in the capacity of an assistant to the Attorney for the Government, advice regarding constitutional rights should be governed by those procedures applicable to grand jury investigations rather than by the procedures applicable to investigations of the Criminal Investigation Division. In this regard, the facts that the interview is conducted outside of the actual presence of the grand jury and that there is a related investigation are not relevant. Clarification as to advice appropriate to a particular case should be sought as needed from the Attorney for the Government.

(11) See also IRM 9384.2

342.133 *(5-9-80)* 9781
Custodial Interrogations

(1) The Supreme Court has held that when an individual is taken into custody or otherwise deprived of his/her freedom by the authorities, he/she must be warned prior to any questioning that he/she has the right to remain silent, that anything he/she says can be used against him/her in a court of law, that he/she has the right to the presence of an attorney, and that if he/she cannot afford an attorney one will be appointed for him/her prior to any questioning if he/she so desires. Opportunity to exercise these rights must be afforded to him/her throughout the interrogation. After such warnings have been given, and such opportunity afforded him/her, the individual may knowingly and intelligently waive these rights and agree to make a statement. But unless and until such warnings and waiver are demonstrated by the prosecution at trial, no evidence obtained as a result of interrogation may be used against the individual. [*Miranda v. Arizona; Escobedo v. Illinois*]

(2) Procedures to be followed by special agents in the interview of persons in custody are as follows:

(a) Prior to any questioning the person in custody must be warned in clear and unequivocal terms that he/she has a right to remain silent, that any statements he/she makes may be used as evidence against him/her and that he/she has a right to the presence of an attorney, either retained or appointed.

(b) If the person in custody indicates that he/she does not wish to be interviewed, there can be no questioning.

(c) If the person in custody indicates during questioning that he/she wishes to say no more, the interview must cease.

(d) If the person in custody indicates that he/she wishes to consult with an attorney before speaking, there can be no questioning until that consultation takes place.

(e) If the person in custody indicates during questioning that he/she wants an attorney before speaking further, the interview must cease until an attorney is present and the person in custody has had an opportunity to consult with him/her.

(3) It is mandatory that enforcement personnel comply with the safeguards enumerated in (2) above. However, these safeguards do not apply to the normal administrative processing of an accused after he/she has been taken into custody. He/she may be photographed and fingerprinted, and may still be asked to furnish information necessary for the filling out of administrative forms and the keeping of agency records. Further, these safeguards do not apply: to an interview of one person which develops evidence solely against another; with interviews to secure information for the timely protection of life, property or the national security; or with spontaneous or volunteered statements of any kind.

(4) To secure the admissibility of statements made during in-custody interrogations, certain procedural safeguards are required. Exhibit 300-5 is a copy of Form 5228, Waiver of Right to Remain Silent and of Right to Advice of Counsel. The statement of rights contained therein sets forth the warning which must be given to a person in custody prior to an interrogation. This statement also appears in Document 5661 in card form. If practicable, the waiver form should be signed by the person to be interrogated before the interrogation is initiated. The original Form 5228 is to be attached to and made a part of the case report furnished to the United States Attorney, the first copy given to the person signing the form, the second copy retained by the Chief, Criminal Investigation Division, and the third copy retained by the agent who conducted the interrogation. When it is impossible or impracticable to obtain a signed waiver, an oral waiver may be accepted. In such cases, the warning given and the defendant's waiver should be witnessed by another agent or other credible person, or sound or otherwise recorded. If a written statement is obtained from the person interrogated after he/she has waived his/her right to remain silent, either by execution of the waiver agreement, or otherwise, it should contain an introductory para-

graph which indicates that the person was advised of his/her right to remain silent and of the right to counsel and that he/she waived the rights and voluntarily made the statement.

(5) Spontaneous or volunteered statements of any kind are not barred by the Fifth Amendment and are not affected by the Miranda and Escobedo decisions.

(6) In the Mathis case, the Supreme Court held that statements given by a person, who is in custody or otherwise deprived of his/her freedom, to a revenue agent conducting a tax examination, are inadmissible unless the person has been advised of his/her constitutional rights. This applies though there is no relationship between the tax examination and the reason for custody. [*Mathis v. U.S.*]

(7) See also IRM 9447.3 through 9447.5

342.14 *(9-8-80)* 9781

Voluntary Disclosure

(1) Prior to January 10, 1952, under the so-called "voluntary disclosure policy" then in effect, the Treasury Department refrained from recommending prosecution of persons who made voluntary disclosures of their tax violation before the beginning of investigation. Although this "policy" has been abandoned and a promise of immunity is not enforceable, [*White v. U.S.*] some courts have held that taxpayers' rights under the Fifth Amendment may be violated where testimony has been given or records furnished in reliance upon express or implied promises that prosecution will not be undertaken. [*Daniel Smith v. U.S.*] In the Daniel Smith case, the defendant had objected to admission into evidence of a net worth statement, on the ground that it had been given by his accountant to the Government agent upon the promise that the case would be closed if the statement and a check for the tax deficiency would be submitted. It was held that the court properly instructed the jury to reject the statement and all evidence obtained through it, if it found that trickery, fraud, or deceit were practiced upon the taxpayer or his accountant.

(2) Present Service Policy is found in Policy Statement P-9-2. It provides that although the Service Policy does not necessarily preclude prosecution, IRS will carefully consider and weigh the voluntary disclosure, along with all other facts and circumstances, in deciding whether or not to recommend prosecution.

342.15 *(1-18-80)* 9781

Waiver of Constitutional Rights

(1) The privilege against self-incrimination must be specifically claimed, or it will be considered to have been waived. [*Lisansky v. U.S.*] In Nicola v. U.S. the taxpayer permitted a revenue agent to examine his books and records. The taxpayer was indicted for income tax evasion and invoked his constitutional rights under the Fifth Amendment for the first time at the trial, by objecting to the revenue agent's testimony concerning his findings. The court said, on the question of waiver:

> "But he did not refuse to supply the information required. Did he waive his privilege? The constitutional guarantee is for the benefit of the witness and unless invoked is deemed to be waived. Vajtauer v. Commissioner of Immigration (supra). Was it necessary for the defendant to invoke it in the first place before the revenue agent or could he wait until his trial on indictment for attempting to evade a part of his income tax? (Cases cited) *** it was necessary for him to claim immunity before the Government agent and refuse to produce his books. After the Government had gotten possession of the information with his consent, it was too late for him then to claim constitutional immunity."

(2) A taxpayer who makes verbal statements or gives testimony to agents during an investigation, or at a Tax Court trial, may still rely upon his/her constitutional privilege and refuse to testify at trial of his/her indictment for tax evasion. [*U.S. v. Vadner*] However, any statements inconsistent with his/her innocence may be used against him/her as admissions. [4 Wigmore, *Evidence*, (3d Ed.), Sec. 1048]

(3) If a witness has testified at a trial and voluntarily revealed incriminating facts, he/she cannot in the same proceeding avoid disclosure of the details. [*Rogers v. U.S.; Ballantyne v. U.S.*] However, waiver of constitutional rights will not lightly be inferred, and no specific language is required in asserting them. [*George Smith v. U.S.; Quinn v. U.S.; Emspak v. U.S.*] In the language of the Quinn case:

> "It is agreed by all that a claim of privilege does not require any special combination of words. Plainly a witness need not have the skill of a lawyer to invoke the protection of the Self Incrimination Clause. *** As everyone agrees, no ritualistic formula is necessary in order to invoke the Privilege."

(4) Courts have held in income tax evasion cases that there has been no waiver of constitutional rights where taxpayers have given verbal information or exhibited books and records, during so-called "routine audits," as a result of deception practiced by Government agents. [*U.S. v. Lipshitz; U.S. v. Guerrina*] Neither may the Government use information illegally obtained as a wedge for prying incriminating evidence from the taxpayer, or, as a "lever to spring consent." [*U.S. v. Watson A. Young*]

342.16 *(1-18-80)* 9781
Right to Counsel

(1) A defendant's right to counsel in a criminal prosecution is guaranteed by the Sixth Amendment to the United States Constitution.

(2) The Administrative Procedure Act (Section 6) provides:

> "Any person compelled to appear in person before any agency or representative thereof shall be accorded the right to be accompanied, represented, and advised by counsel or, if permitted by the agency, by other qualified representative. Every party shall be accorded the right to appear in person or by or with counsel or other duly qualified representative in any agency proceeding."

(3) Courts have indicated that under the above section persons summoned to appear before special agents of the Criminal Investigation Division may be represented by counsel. [*Backer v. Commissioner*] However, the courts are in conflict about limitations on the right to counsel. Text 343.3 concerns the right of a third party to counsel, and furnishes guidelines to follow when this right is invoked.

342.17 *(11-7-80)* 9781
Powers of Attorney

(1) The requirements for the filing of a power of attorney or tax information authorization by taxpayer representatives are outlined in IRM 4055 and in Subpart E, Conference and Practice Requirements (26 CFR, Part 601).

(2) Upon receipt, the original of any power of attorney and/or tax authorization will be associated with the case file. A copy will be forwarded to the applicable service center, Taxpayer Relations Branch, Attention: Power of Attorney Unit. This requirement applies to all such documents including those received prior to these instructions. It also applies to all subsequently filed instruments, including revocations, substitutions, etc. This procedure will be followed unless they are clearly intended for one-time use, such as those submitted with Freedom of Information requests or Congressional inquiries. In these instances, no copy should be forwarded to the service center and the original should be associated with the correspondence.

(3) Regulations require submission of sufficient copies of authorizations from representatives for each tax matter involved. Each return for a taxable period represents a separate tax matter. An attorney or certified public accountant, however, is required to file only one declaration for a particular party represented, regardless of the number of tax matters involved (P.L. 89-332 and 26 C.F.R. 601.502(b). Therefore, it may be necessary to make copies of authorizations.

(4) See also IRM 9359.2

342.18 *(1-18-80)* 9781
Representation by Enrolled Persons, Attorneys and Certified Public Accountants and Others

(1) Service employees will recognize persons who are not attorneys nor certified public accountants as representatives of taxpayers only upon presentation of a permanent or temporary enrollment card authorizing practice as an agent, issued under the provisions of Treasury Department Circular 230, provided such enrolled person is not currently under suspension or disbarment from practice before the IRS. Upon a satisfactory showing of proof, Service employees will also recognize the following:

(a) an individual appearing on his/her own behalf;

(b) an individual representing another individual who is his/her regular full-time employer;

(c) an individual representing a partnership of which he/she is a member or a regular full-time employee;

(d) an individual representing without compensation a member of his/her immediate family;

(e) an individual representing a corporation (including parents, subsidiary or affiliated corporations) of which he/she is a bona fide officer or regular full-time employee;

(f) an individual representing a trust, receivership, guardianship or estate of which he/she is its trustee, receiver, guardian, administrator, executor or regular full-time employee;

(g) an individual representing any governmental unit, agency or authority of which he/she is an officer or regular employee acting in the course of his/her official duties; and

(h) individuals participating in rule making as provided by Section 4 of the Administrative Procedure Act (5 U.S.C. 1003).

(2) Service employees will recognize attorneys and certified public accountants as representatives of taxpayers if they file a written declaration containing the following information, provided that the declarant is not currently under suspension or disbarment from practice before the IRS.

(a) A statement that the declarant is currently qualified as a member in good standing of the bar of the highest court, or is a certified public accountant qualified to practice in any State, Possession, Commonwealth, Territory or the District of Columbia, specifying the bar or bars in which he has membership or the Governmental entity or entities in which he is so certified;

(b) The declarant's full name, address, and telephone number;

(c) A statement that the declarant is authorized to represent the particular party on whose behalf he/she purports to represent, and the name and address of that party.

(3) Declarations received from attorneys or certified public accountants will be associated and filed with the tax returns or other matters involved in the same manner as powers of attorney are filed. A declaration once filed with the appropriate tax return(s) or other matter(s) will be presumed to remain valid unless the Service has evidence to the contrary. Thus, a declaration will ordinarily be requested regarding a particular matter only upon the first appearance before the Service of an attorney or certified public accountant.

(4) An alphabetical computer printout listing by districts of agents enrolled to practice before the Service is maintained in the district Examination offices and is available to special agents to verify that a person claiming to be an enrolled agent is currently enrolled to practice before the Service.

(5) See also IRM 9359.1.

342.19 *(1-18-80)* 9781
Dealing with Representatives

(1) When a taxpayer, or his/her representative who has a power of attorney or tax information authorization on file with the Service, and who is not disqualified from practicing before the IRS, requests, orally or in writing, that contacts with the taxpayer by Service personnel be made through the representative, such request will be complied with, except as provided in (2) below.

(2) When repeated attempts to comply with a request that all contacts be made through a taxpayer's representative result in unreasonable delays or hindrances to the investigation, the special agent who is assigned to the matter will discuss the situation with the Chief, Criminal Investigation Division, and request permission to contact the taxpayer direct. The Chief will carefully consider the facts and circumstances concerning the matter and make a determination as to whether or not the request by the taxpayer, or his/her representative, should continue to be honored by the Service. Where the Chief grants permission to deviate from the request of the taxpayer or his/her representative, the case file should contain sufficient facts to show how the investigation or examination was being delayed or hindered by complying with the request of the taxpayer or his/her representative. Except as provided in (3) below, the Chief will provide the taxpayer and the representative with a written notice of the permission to bypass, in advance of direct contact with the taxpayer, briefly stating the reasons for granting such permission.

(3) The sole exception to the requirement for advance notification is the situation of extreme exigency in which immediate, direct contact with the taxpayer must be made, and the time required to issue advance notice of bypass would result in severe prejudice to the taxpayer or the investigation. Under those circumstances, the Chief will consult with District Counsel before granting authority to bypass the representative without advance notification. The case file should contain sufficient facts to support the decision.

(4) Authorization to bypass a representative and to contact the taxpayer direct, with or without advance notice, does not relieve the Service of responsibility for continuing to notify and advise the representative of future appointments with the taxpayer, nor recognizing the representative if the representative makes an appearance.

(5) See also IRM 9359.2.

342.2 *(3-18-81)* 9781
Partnership and Other Unincorporated Association Books and Records

(1) The original rule regarding compulsory production of partnership records was set forth in the Boyd case, [*Boyd v. U.S.*] which held that an invoice for merchandise imported by a partnership was the private paper of a defendant partner, and that its production could not be compelled without violating the Fifth Amendment.

(2) The Supreme Court has ruled that an individual cannot rely upon the privilege to avoid producing the records of a collective entity which are in his/her possession, even if these records might incriminate him/her personally *(Bellis v. U.S.)*. A former partner in a small, three-partner law firm could not invoke Fifth Amendment rights to justify his refusal to produce the partnership's subpoenaed financial records. The firm was an independent entity and not the personal legal practice of the individual partners, and he held the records in a representative capacity. The partnership existed for nearly 15 years, maintained a bank account in its name, and held itself out as a distinct entity.

(3) Similarly, following the principal that an unincorporated labor union with many members was a large, impersonal partnership with the characteristics of a corporation, the Supreme Court held that an officer could be compelled to produce union records in his possession. [*U.S. v. White*] The court stated the rule thus:

> "Whether one can fairly say under all the circumstances that a particular type of organization has a character so impersonal in the scope of its membership and activities that it cannot be said to embody or represent the purely private or personal interests of its constituents, but rather to embody their common or group interests only. If so, the privilege cannot be invoked on behalf of the organization or its representatives in their official capacity."

(4) On the other hand, the Supreme Court indicated in *Bellis v. U.S.* that cases dealing with small, family type partnerships might be treated differently. (In Re Subpoena Duces Tecum; *U.S. v. Slutzky)*

(5) Partnership books and records voluntarily submitted by one partner may be used in evidence against the other partners without violating their constitutional rights.

(6) A trustee can be directed to comply with a summons which calls for the production of certain books and records of the trust. The trust is a separate entity and a taxpayer, the trustee, could not claim the Fifth Amendment privilege since he/she held the books in a representative rather than a personal capacity. *(Mullins v. Angiulo)*

342.3 *(1-18-80)* 9781
Corporations

342.31 *(1-18-80)* 9781
Corporation Books and Records

(1) The privilege against self-incrimination under the Fifth Amendment does not apply to corporations. [*Wilson v. U.S.; Hale v. Henkel*] The theory for this is that the State, having created the corporation, has reserved the power to inquire into its activities, and that an inanimate corporate body should not be afforded the same protection as a natural person in avoiding incrimination. A corporate officer may not refuse to produce corporate records held by him/her in an official capacity, even though their production may incriminate him/her or the corporation. Courts have applied the theory that a corporation is a separate person and have maintained that an individual may not withhold the corporate records nor object to their use against him/her under the self-incrimination doctrine, even if he/she is the only stockholder or the sole director of all the corporate activities. [*Walter B. Grant v. U.S.; Fuller v. U.S.*] Neither may a corporate officer refuse to identify the corporate records under oath on the ground of possible self-incrimination. [*Carolene Products Co. v. U.S.; U.S. v. Austin-Bagley Corporation; U.S. v. Lawn, supra*] A Subchapter S corporation, [*U.S. v. Richardson*] as well as a professional association, [*U.S. v. Theodore Accounting Service, P.A.*] can be required to produce their books and records.

(2) A corporation is protected against illegal searches and seizures under the Fourth Amendment. For example, in Silverthorne Lumber Co. v. U.S., although the corporate officers were in custody, a United States Marshal visited the corporation's office without a search warrant and made a clean sweep of all books, papers, and documents. The court held that this was an illegal search and seizure, prohibited by the Fourth Amendment.

342.32 *(1-18-80)* 9781
Rights of Corporation Officers

The mere fact that a corporate officer may not refuse to produce corporate records does not take away the constitutional protection which is the right way of any individual. He/she may still refuse to give testimony or exhibit personal records which may tend to incriminate him/her as an individual, [*U.S. v. Lawn; Fuller v. U.S.*] or to testify regarding the whereabouts of corporate records not in his/her possession. [*Curcio v. U.S.; U.S. v. Pollock*] The Lawn case, involved the obligations and rights of corporate officers as well. On this point the court made the following comment:

> "The Government, beyond requiring the production and identification of the corporate records, does not have an unbridled right to interrogate the corporate officer, without his constitutional privilege being available to him."

342.4 *(1-18-80)* 9781
District Criminal Investigation Conference

(1) A district Criminal Investigation conference will not be conducted as a matter of course. However, a taxpayer who may be the

subject of a criminal prosecution recommendation will be afforded a district Criminal Investigation conference when he/she requests one or where the Chief, Criminal Investigation Division, determines that such a conference will be in the best interest of the Government. (See policy statement P-9-32.)

(2) No district Criminal Investigation conference will be held if the taxpayer is the subject of a grand jury investigation in which special agents of the Criminal Investigation Division are assisting the Attorney for the Government.

(3) The Chief, Criminal Investigation Division, or his/her designee will offer the conference at the headquarters office of the District Director or at some other location convenient for both the principal, or his/her representative, and the Government.

(4) The conference will be held by the Chief, Criminal Investigation Division, or his/her designee. The Chief may make standing designations or make designations on a case-by-case basis. Where feasible, the Chief's designee should be the Assistant Chief or Staff Assistant, in districts which have such positions. However, the designee may be a group manager or an experienced special agent.

(5) Under no circumstances shall the designee be the special agent who investigated the case, although he/she and any cooperating IRS employee may attend the conference unless their presence is not deemed advisable by the Chief, Criminal Investigation Division, or the designee.

(6) The Chief, Criminal Investigation Division, shall not hold the conference if he/she has participated in the investigation to such an extent that he/she might appear to be a prejudiced party. Should this occur and there is no designee available (see (4) above) the Chief will inform the ARC (Criminal Investigation) of the circumstances and request the ARC to designate someone to hold the conference.

(7) A summary will be prepared of the conference proceeding pursuant to the procedure outlined in IRM 9353 for preparation of a memorandum of information. The conference may be recorded verbatim by an IRS stenographer or other individuals designated in IRM 9353:(3) if deemed advisable because of the importance of the case or for other serious reasons, such as prior refusal of the principal to provide the investigating officer with information relating to the case.

(8) At this conference, which should usually be held before the special agent's report is typed in final form, the IRS representative will inform the taxpayer by a general oral statement of the alleged fraudulent features of the case, to the extent consistent with protecting the Government's interests, and, at the same time, making available to the taxpayer sufficient facts and figures to acquaint him/her with the basis, nature, and other essential elements of the proposed criminal charges against him/her (See Policy Statement P-9-32.) However, extreme care must be exercised to ensure that no information is disclosed to the principal which might reveal or indicate the identity of confidential informants, endanger prospective witnesses, or be detrimental to subsequent prosecution of the case.

(9) When a taxpayer's representative, who has furnished a power of attorney or tax information authorization, attends a district Criminal Investigation conference without the taxpayer, he/she is entitled to receive, to the extent authorized by the taxpayer, the same information that would be furnished if the taxpayer were present.

(10) See Policy Statement P-9-32 regarding persons who may accompany the taxpayer to a district Criminal Investigation conference.

343 *(1-18-80)* 9781

Third Party Witnesses

343.1 *(1-18-80)* 9781

Compelled Testimony or Production of Records of Third Party Witness

IRC 7602 furnishes the authority to compel testimony of third persons and their production of books and records, by issuance of summonses. Restrictions upon that authority as they apply to third parties will be discussed in the remainder of this text and in 344.

343.2 *(1-18-80)* 9781

Rights of Third Party Witness Against Self-Incrimination

(1) A third party witness may not refuse to testify but may decline to give answers that may incriminate him/her [*Hoffman v. U.S.; U.S. v. Benjamin; O'Connell v. U.S.*] under Federal or state law. [*Murphy v. N.Y. Waterfront Commission; Malloy v. Hogan*]

(2) The privilege applies not only to answers or documents which would support a conviction. It extends even to those which provide a link in the chain of evidence which could be incriminatory, and is available if there is a reasonable possibility that an answer might tend to incriminate. [*Blau v. U.S.; Hoffman v. U.S.*] As stated by the Supreme Court in Hoffman v. U.S. "To sustain the privilege, it need only be evident from the implications of the question, in the setting in which it is asked, that a responsive answer to the question or an explanation of why it cannot be answered might be dangerous because injurious disclosure could result." However, a witness is not justified in refusing to answer questions on the ground of possible self-incrimination where the statute of limitations has barred the possibility of prosecution. [*U.S. v. Goodman*]

(3) It is improper for the prosecution to ask a witness in a criminal trial any question calculated to bring out the answer that the witness had refused to incriminate himself/herself in a prior trial or proceeding. [*U.S. v. Merle Long; U.S. v. Harold Gross; Grunewald v. U.S.*]

(4) When a witness appears to be implicated in a criminal violation, he/she should be timely advised of his/her constitutional rights.

343.3 *(5-27-80)* 9781

Right to Counsel of Third Party Witnesses

(1) The Administrative Procedure Act, 5 U.S.C. 555(b) provides, in part, "A person compelled to appear in person before an agency or representative thereof is entitled to be accompanied, represented and advised by counsel or, if permitted by the agency, by other qualified representative . . ." Further, Policy statement P-9-31 provides "A witness in a Criminal Investigation function investigation has the right to have counsel present when questioned, to represent and advise him/her."

(2) A witness who appears in response to a summons must be afforded the opportunity to be represented by an attorney. The right to an attorney of one's own choice is generally an absolute right which may only be modified in the event of obstruction of the orderly inquiry process by improper conduct or tactics by the attorney.

343.4 *(1-18-80)* 9781

Right of Third Party Witness to Refuse Unreasonable Request

(1) Although the restrictions placed upon examination by IRC 7605(b) apply only to the taxpayer under examination, as explained in 367.33, the courts will also prevent arbitrary, unreasonable, irrelevant, and oppressive demands upon third parties for production of their records. [*First National Bank of Mobile v. U.S.; Hubner v. Tucker*]

(2) In the First National Bank of Mobile case, an Internal Revenue agent attempted to have the bank produce any and all books, papers, and records in connection with a tax investigation, *irrespective of whether such records also pertain to similar transactions with other persons or firms during the said years 1940 to 1945, inclusive* (italics by court). The Court of Appeals denied the request, stating:

> "A third party should not be called upon to produce records and give evidence under the statute unless such records and evidence are relevant to, or bear upon, the matter being investigated."

(3) *Hubner v. Tucker* concerned a summons issued by a special agent to a third party in general terms, to produce all books and records relating to transactions with the taxpayer, including miscellaneous records. There was no specification of the particular documents, which precluded a showing, according to the court, that any one of them was relevant to the investigation. The court said:

> ". . . so far as a member of the general public is concerned, not a taxpayer, the privilege against an unreasonable search and seizure should be given great effect. * * * We do not believe that, simply because some taxpayer may have had a grocery account entered upon the books of the grocer, the intention of Congress was to allow the Internal Revenue Service to investigate all the records of the grocer on the theory that some of them might be relevant to the inquiry of the tax status of another person."

343.5 *(1-18-80)* 9781

Witnesses And Records From Foreign Countries

(1) Non-resident aliens physically present in foreign country cannot be compelled to appear as witnesses in a United States Court. Since the Constitution requires confrontation of adverse witnesses in criminal prosecutions, the testimony of such aliens may be used in court only if they agree to appear at the trial. However, certain testimony for the admissibility of documents is allowed without a "live" appearance in the United States under 18 USC 3491. Also, 28 USC 1783 provides a Federal court with sub-

poena powers to compel the appearance before it, or before a person or body designated by it, of a United States citizen or resident physically present in a foreign country.

(2) The following methods may be used to have foreign records authenticated for use in any ensuing criminal proceeding in the United States Courts:

(a) Stipulation—It may be possible to get the defendant in any subsequent litigation to stipulate the authenticity of the records in question.

(b) Voluntary Testimony—It may be possible to have the appropriate witness or official voluntarily appear and testify as to authenticity of the records in question.

(c) 18 U.S.C. § 3491, *et seq.*—These provisions provide a method by which certain foreign documents can be made admissible in a criminal proceeding in the United States. Under the procedures contemplated by these provisions the party wishing to have foreign documents authenticated (*i.e.*, either the United States or the defendant) may, after appropriate notice to the opposite party, apply for the issuance of a commission to an appropriate consular officer. 18 U.S.C. § 3492. The consular official, acting pursuant to the commission, can then take the testimony of the authenticating witness in accordance with the provisions of 18 U.S.C. § 3493. If the consular officer taking the testimony is satisfied, upon all the testimony taken, that the foreign document in question is genuine, he shall certify such document to be genuine under the seal of his office in accordance with 18 U.S.C. § 3494. After the additional requirements of 18 U.S.C. § 3494 relative to the transmittal of the document to the court are satisfied, the document shall be admissible in evidence in any criminal action or proceeding in any court of the United States if the court shall find, from all the testimony taken with respect to such foreign document pursuant to a commission executed under § 3492 of this title that such document (or the original thereof in case such document is a copy satisfies the requirements of § 1732 of Title 28 relating to records maintained in the regular course of business). It is possible that the witness or official will refuse to voluntarily testify. In that event, and providing there is a tax treaty between the foreign government involved and the United States, the foreign government should be requested to compel the witness or official to testify. The foreign agent conducting the interview would then be in a position to ask the necessary questions in the presence of the United States consul (U.S. v. Hav).

(d) Affidavit—In *United States v. Leal,* the court was faced with the question of whether certain documents originating in Hong Kong could be admitted into evidence in a criminal prosecution in the United States. The records in question consisted of the affidavit of the assistant manager of a Hong Kong hotel to which was attached an original hotel registration card and certain telephone booking orders of the defendant and his wife. In this proceeding the Government did not attempt to use the mechanism established by 18 U.S.C. § 3491, *et seq.* Rather, the court allowed the Government to rely solely upon 28 U.S.C. § 1732 (the Federal Business Records Act). Essentially, the procedure which the Government followed was that outlined in Fed. R. Crim. P. 44(a)(2) for authenticating foreign official records. Thus, the assistant manager for the hotel gave a sworn statement before the United States Vice Consul in Hong Kong explaining that he chose not to go to Guam to testify, describing the contents of the attached original hotel records, attesting that he was the official custodian thereof and that the documents had been prepared or witnessed by himself or by persons under his authority and had constantly been in the hotel under his supervisory control, and stating that they constituted records prepared in the normal course of business of the hotel.

(e) Authentication By Testimony From Foreign Government Official—In the case of *United States v. Quong,* the court was faced with questions concerning the admissibility of records obtained from a foreign business. In that case a Canadian law enforcement officer picked up the books and records which had been assembled by an officer of a Canadian company. The officer then transmitted the documents to the United States and testified in the United States District Court as to their authenticity. The court held that the procedure followed was substantially in accordance with the Business Records Act (28 U.S.C. § 1732) and ruled that the records were admissible. The court noted that the officer had taken the records directly from the custodian and that the dates on the records corresponded with dates shown on other records whose admissibility was not in question. Taking this into account the court found that they were kept in the regular course of business and were, therefore, admissible.

(Next page is 9781-98.1)

343.6 *(4-13-81)* 9781
Dual Representation

(1) Treasury Department Circular No. 230 (Rev. 6-79), which covers the practice of attorneys, certified public accountants, enrolled agents, and enrolled actuaries before the Internal Revenue Service, provides the following with respect to dual representation:

§ **10.29 Conflicting Interests**

No attorney, certified public accountant, or enrolled agent shall represent conflicting interests in his practice before the Internal Revenue Service, except by express consent of all directly interested parties after full disclosure has been made.

(2) Dual representation exists when a summoned third-party witness is represented by an attorney, certified public accountant, enrolled agent, or other person who also represents the taxpayer or another interested party. It may also occur where an attorney under investigation represents a third-party witness in that investigation or where an attorney-witness seeks to represent another witness in the same investigation. An interested party is one who has a significant pecuniary interest in the testimony of the witness or who, by virtue of the nature of the investigation and the known facts, may be incriminated by the witness.

(3) Except as provided below, the mere existence of a dual representation situation which may potentially have an adverse impact on the investigation will not, without some action by the attorney to impede or obstruct the investigation, provide a sufficient basis for seeking a disqualification. However, where an attorney's representation has substantially prejudiced the questioning of a third-party witness and, as a result, has significantly impaired the progress of the investigation, the Service will request the Department of Justice to seek a court order, as part of the summons enforcement proceeding, to disqualify that attorney as counsel for that witness.

(4) In view of the well-established principle granting a person the right to counsel of one's choice, this disqualification procedure will only be used in extreme circumstances, such as where an attorney has taken some action to improperly or unlawfully impede or obstruct the investigation. It is essential that the interviewing officer have sufficient facts to support such allegations.

(5) The provisions referring to "attorneys" apply to other representatives (nonattorneys) who represent witnesses or taxpayers.

(6) Interview of Witness

(a) Upon learning that counsel represents both the taxpayer under investigation (or other interested party) as well as the summoned witness, the interviewing officer should give consideration to exploring with the attorney, prior to the interview of the witness whether or not the attorney realizes that his representation of both the subject of the investigation and the witness may occasion a conflict of interest.

(b) If, after discussing the potential conflict of interest situation with the attorney the question is not resolved, at the outset of the interview of the witness, the interviewing officer should ask the following of the witness:

1 Do you wish the attorney to be present during the questioning?

2 Did you hire the attorney for this purpose?

3 Are you paying for the attorney's services, either alone or in conjunction with someone else—if the latter, do you know who?

4 Do you know that the attorney also represents the taxpayer?

5 Do you know that the attorney is being paid by the taxpayer (or some other person)?

(c) In those instances where the interviewing officer becomes aware of the potential conflict of interest during the interview, he/she should explore the issue by asking the questions listed. In some situations it may be appropriate for the interviewing officer to tell the witness that in his/her view, the interest of the taxpayer under investigation conflicts with that of the witness.

(d) After disclosure of the dual or multiple representation has been made, if the witness unequivocally states that he/she wishes the attorney in question to represent him/her and that he/she is utilizing the services of the attorney in this matter, then the interview should proceed.

(e) However, if the witness states that he/she does not wish to retain that attorney because of the possible conflict of interest, then the witness should be given the opportunity of either proceeding with the interview without an attorney present or adjourning the interview to a specific future date in order to afford the witness an opportunity to secure the services of another attorney. If the witness refuses to proceed to obtain the services of another attorney within a reasonable period of time, the witness should be notified that his/her failure to comply with the summons may result in a recommendation to the Department of Justice that a summons enforcement proceeding be initiated.

(7) Obstruction of Interview

(a) If the interviewing officer has reason to anticipate that an attorney will improperly impede or obstruct the questioning of a witness, he/she should consult with District Counsel prior to the interview with respect to the manner of conducting the questioning.

(b) Speculation that the objective of the investigation might be frustrated is insufficient grounds upon which to seek disqualification of an attorney. The fact that the attorney for the summoned witness also represents the taxpayer or other interested party does not provide a basis for concluding that the presence of such attorney would obstruct the investigation.

(c) Thus, the mere potential for obstruction is generally an insufficient basis to justify a recommendation for disqualification of an attorney. There must be active obstruction by an attorney before disqualification will be sought. A suit to disqualify an attorney for obstruction will be undertaken only where the facts clearly indicate that he/she has actively impeded the investigation.

(d) Unjustifiable obstruction by an attorney may take a variety of forms. It is, therefore, impossible to set forth the precise factual circumstances under which the Government would ask a court to disqualify an attorney as counsel for a third-party witness.

(e) The following is an example of a circumstance which may provide the basis for a recommendation for the institution of litigation to seek the disqualification of an attorney:

Taxpayer and third-party witness are both represented by the same attorney. The witness is summoned to testify. The attorney refuses to permit the witness to answer questions for other than legitimate reasons or disrupts the questioning by repeatedly making frivolous objections to the questions, or asserts frivolous claims of privilege or defenses on behalf of the witness to delay the investigation, or so disrupts the interview that the interviewing officer, with due diligence and preseverance, is unable to proceed with the interview. [*Backer* v. *Commissioner*]. This is not intended to suggest that there is anything inherently wrong in claiming the Fifth Amendment privilege.

A careful distinction must be drawn between situations in which the proper remedy is to compel the witness to answer and those in which the attorney may be disqualified because of this conduct. The latter is an extreme remedy which will only be sought in very unusual circumstances, as courts are reluctant to deprive a person of his/her choice of attorney. District Counsel, therefore, will make a considered determination on a case-by-case basis prior to seeking disqualification of an attorney.

(8) Suspension of Interview

(a) If the interview is suspended because of the attorney's actions, the witness should be given the opportunity to secure the services of another attorney within a reasonable period of time or proceed without an attorney. If the witness declines either to proceed without an attorney or retain a new one within a reasonable period of time, the witness should be informed that a summons enforcement proceeding and an action to disqualify the attorney will be recommended.

(b) Upon suspension of an interview, the interviewing officer will consult with his/her manager. If the manager is in accord with the interviewing officer's view that the facts present an appropriate case for litigation, a request will be made to District Counsel that they recommend to the Department of Justice that it seek judicial enforcement of the summons and exclusion of the attorney from representing the witness.

(c) Suspension of an interview should be made judiciously in view of the time delays in the investigation that may be caused by such action.

(d) A record should be made of the circumstances in each instance where an interview is suspended because of dual representation and/or obstruction by an attorney. The interviewing officer should also have a verbatim transcript of the interview (if possible) so that the factual allegations concerning the attorney's conduct at the interview may be proven.

(9) Procedures where an attorney will be excluded prior to interviewing witness are:

(a) Where an individual taxpayer under investigation attempts to appear with a summoned witness as the witness' attorney, the witness should be told that the taxpayer/attorney is the person under investigation and that he/she will not be allowed to be present during the questioning. The witness should be given the opportunity of either proceeding with the interview without the taxpayer present of adjourning the interview to a specific future date in order to afford the witness an opportunity to secure the services of another attorney. If the witness refuses to either proceed with the interview without the attorney's representations or to adjourn for the purpose of obtaining a new representative, the interview will be terminated and a request will be made to District Counsel for judicial enforcement of the summons and exclusion of the taxpayer from representing the witness.

(b) A witness may appear pursuant to a summons accompanied by an attorney who also represents the taxpayer (or other interested party) where the taxpayer (or other interested party) has already made exculpatory statements to the Service alleging that the witness was criminally responsible for circumstances to be discussed during the interview. In this case, the witness will be told that the attorney also represents the taxpayer (or other interested party) and that the agent believes that an irreconcilable conflict of interest exists which could prejudice the investigation. The witness should then be given the opportunity of either proceeding with the interview without the attorney present or adjourning the interview to secure the services of another attorney. If the witness insists upon retaining the same attorney despite the assertion of a conflict of interest, the interviewing officer will terminate the interview and a request will be made to District Counsel for judicial enforcement of the summons and exclusion of the attorney.

(c) Where a witness appears pursuant to a summons and is accompanied by a person (other than the taxpayer) who does not represent the individual witness, such person may be excluded from the interview. An example of a situation in which a person may be excluded from the interview is where a corporate official (witness) is summoned in his/her individual capacity regarding an examination of the corporation and an attorney representing the corporation, who does not also represent the witness, attempts to attend the interview. However, if the witness refuses to be interviewed if that person is excluded and the person is a designee of the taxpayer within the meaning of IRC 6103(c) and its regulations, the interview will proceed unless the interviewing officer makes a determination that continuation of the interview will impede development of the case. If such a determination is made, the interview will be terminated and a request will be made to District Counsel for a recommendation for judicial enforcement of the summons by the Department of Justice and exclusion of the person from any future interviews pursuant to the court's order.

(Next page is 9781–99)

344 *(1-18-80)* 9781
Privileged Communications

344.1 *(1-18-80)* 9781
Conditions for Privileged Communications

(1) There are certain special types of relationships in which information communicated by one person to the other is held confidential and privileged between them. The one to whom the information has been imparted cannot be compelled to divulge it without the consent of the other. There are four fundamental conditions: [Sec. 244—8 Wigmore (3d Ed.) 2285]

(a) The communications must originate in a confidence that they will not be disclosed;

(b) The element of confidentiality must be essential to the full and satisfactory maintenance of the relation between the parties

(c) The relation must be one which in the opinion of the community ought to be diligently fostered;

(d) The injury that would inure to the relationship by the disclosure of the communications must be greater than the benefit thereby gained for the correct disposal of litigation.

344.2 *(1-18-80)* 9781
Attorney and Client Privilege

(1) The attorney-client privilege must be strictly construed. Mere attorney-client relationship does not make every communication by the client to his/her attorney confidential. The communication must have been made to the attorney in his/her capacity as such, employed to give legal advice, represent the client in litigation, or perform some other function strictly as an attorney. When it does apply, the privilege covers corporate as well as individual clients. Basically, attorney-client privilege does not include a right to withhold the name of a client. [*Colton v. U.S.*] However, an attorney's refusal to furnish a client's name has been upheld where it would indirectly amount to disclosure of communications of a confidential nature, as, where the attorney has delivered a check to the Internal Revenue Service in payment of a client's tax but refuses to name the client. [*Tillotson v. Boughner; Baird v. Koerner; Colton v. U.S.*] Dates and amounts of legal fees paid by a client to his/her lawyer do not constitute a privileged communication. [In re Wasserman and Carliner.]

(2) If the attorney is a mere scrivener or a conduit for handling funds, or the transaction involves a simple transfer of title to real estate, without consultation for legal advice, communications from the client to the attorney are not privileged. [*McFee v. U.S.; Polock v. U.S.*] Neither are communications privileged which have been made in the course of seeking business rather than legal advice. [*U.S. v. Vehicular Parking, Ltd.*] The privilege is ordinarily inapplicable to communications made to a person who acts as both attorney and accountant, if they have been made solely to enable him/her to audit the client's books, prepare a Federal income tax return, or otherwise act purely as an accountant. [*Olender v. U.S.*] However, some courts have held that a privileged communication can occur between a client and attorney in the process of preparing a tax return. [*Colton v. U.S.; U.S. v. Kovel*] A person who consults an attorney for help or advice in perpetrating a future crime of fraudulent act is not consulting the attorney for the legitimate purposes intended to be protected, and communications by the client or intended client in connection with such consultation are not privileged. [*Genevieve A. Clark v. U.S.; Pollock v. U.S.*]

(3) A communication by a client to an attorney in the presence of a third person is no longer privileged, unless the third person's presence is indispensable to the communication, e.g., the attorney's secretary. [*Himmelfarb v. U.S.*] Likewise, a client's communication loses its privilege when the attorney relates it to a third person unless that person's services are necessary to furnishing the legal advice. Thus, the records of a bank from which an attorney has bought a cashier's check for an undisclosed client for delivery to the Internal Revenue Service are not covered by the attorney-client privilege, even if the attorney may withhold the client's name. The bank in such case is a third party whose services are not indispensable to communications between client and attorney, and not part of any giving of legal advice. [*Schulze v. Rayunec*] On the same theory, a bank to which an attorney sends a client to work out an estate plan is not essential to communications by the client to the attorney, and information that the client gives the bank is not privileged. Similarly, communications by the client to the attorney are not privileged if the client obviously intended them to be divulged to third persons. [*U.S. v. Thomas G. McDonald; U.S. v. Tellier; Banks v. U.S.*] This includes the contents of closing statements and sales contracts prepared by the attorney, which the client necessarily expected to divulge to other parties at the closing, [*U.S. v. McDonald*] or information

imparted by the client to include in his/her tax return [*Colton v. U.S.*] or to furnish to the Internal Revenue Service in connection with a proposed civil settlement of tax liability. [*Banks v. U.S.*] Likewise, communications between an attorney and a third party not essential to the furnishing of legal advice would not be privileged. [*Schulze v. Rayunec*]

(4) Courts disagree as to an attorney's right to refuse production of a taxpayer-client's records in his/her possession, basing their determination upon whether or not the client could have withheld the records. [*U.S. v. Judson*] Courts which deny the claim of attorney-client privilege point out that every taxpayer is required to keep records for examination by the Commissioner (26 USC 54), [*Falsone v. U.S.; U.S. v. Willis*] or that persons who engage in the business of wagering are required to keep daily records showing gross amounts of wagers (26 USC 3287). [*U.S. v. Willis*] Courts holding the contrary view say that where a taxpayer has already refused to give information on the ground of possible self-incrimination or could have done so, his/her attorney cannot be compelled to produce the taxpayer's records, or workpapers made from them by the taxpayer's accountant at the attorney's request in connection with a pending tax investigation. [*U.S. v. Judson;* In re Fahey.]

344.3 *(2-8-82)* 9781
Accountant and Client Privilege

(1) There is no privilege between an accountant and a client under common law or Federal law. [*Falsone v. U.S.; Lustman v. Commr.; U.S. v. Bowman*] The accountant's workpapers belong to the accountant, are not privileged, and must be produced. [*Deck v. U.S.; Bouschor v. U.S.*] A taxpayer may be required by summons to produce an accountant's workpapers in his/her possession. A Fifth Amendment claim is not appropriate since the privilege protects a person only against being incriminated by his/her own compelled testimonial communications, and the accountant's workpapers are not the taxpayer's nor do they contain the taxpayer's testimonial declarations. (*Fisher v. U.S.*) Neither may an attorney refuse to produce workpapers prepared by the taxpayer's accountant (other than at the attorney's request in connection with a pending investigation).

(2) An accountant employed by an attorney, [*U.S. v. Kovel*] or retained by a taxpayer at the attorney's request to perform services essential to the attorney-client relationship, [*U.S. v. Judson*] may be covered by the attorney-client privilege.

344.4 *(5-9-80)* 9781
Husband and Wife Privilege

(1) Communications between husband and wife, privately made, are generally assumed to have been intended to be of a confidential nature, and are therefore held to be privileged. It is essential, however, that the communications must be, from their nature, fairly intended to be of a confidential nature. If it is obvious from the circumstances or nature of a communication that no confidence was intended, there is no privilege. [*Wolfle v. U.S.; U.S. v. Mitchell; Blau v. U.S.*] For example, communications between husband and wife voluntarily made in the presence of their children old enough to understand them, or other members of the family within the intimacy of the family circle, are not privileged. [*Wolfle v. U.S.*] Likewise, communications made in the presence of a third party are usually regarded as not privileged, and this has been held to be so even though the third party was a stenographer for one of the spouses, where the stenographer was not a person essential to the communication. [*Wolfle v. U.S.*]

(2) Privilege is not extended to communications made outside the marriage relations, as, before marriage, [*U.S. v. Mitchell*] or after divorce. [*Yoder v. U.S.*] Further, the privilege applies only to communications, and not to acts. The mere doing of an act by one spouse in the presence of the other is held not to be a communication. [8 Wigmore (3d Ed.) Sec. 2337] For example, in the Mitchell case where a husband induced his wife to participate in a violation of Federal law and took the proceeds from her, it was held that the taking of money was an act, not a communication, and therefore not privileged. It has been held in an income tax case where the taxpayer's wife voluntarily turned over his business records to a revenue agent without his consent, that the records were not a communication between husband and wife, and not confidential between them. [*U.S. v. Ashby*] It has also been stated that the privilege should not apply to situations where the wife is employed in her husband's business office, and she would learn only what any other secretary would learn. [*U.S. v. Nelson E. Jones*]

(3) Communications remain privileged after termination of the marriage by death of one spouse. [8 Wigmore (3d Ed.) 2341] Likewise, the privilege as to communications made during marriage does not terminate by divorce. [8 Wigmore (3d Ed.) 2341; *Pereira v. U.S.*]

(4) In addition to the privilege of a husband or wife to prevent the other from disclosing confidential communications that occurred during the marriage, there exists an independent privilege of one spouse to refuse to testify adversely against his/her spouse. With respect to this privilege, the testifying spouse alone has the choice of whether or not to refuse to testify adversely against his/her spouse on any act he/she observed before or during the marriage and on any non-confidential communications [*U.S. v. Trammel*]. The spouse may not be compelled to testify nor foreclosed from testifying.

344:5 *(1-18-80)* 9781

Clergyman and Penitent Privilege

Privilege between clergyman and penitent has been recognized in the Federal courts. [*Mullen v. U.S.; Totten v. U.S.*] This privilege has not been extended to financial matters, such as contributions made through a clergyman.

344.6 *(1-18-80)* 9781

Physician and Patient Privilege

As a general rule Federal Courts do not recognize any privilege between physician and patient.

344.7 *(1-18-80)* 9781

Psychotherapist-Patient Privilege

(1) Federal Rule of Evidence 504 specifically provides for a psychotherapist-patient privilege.

(2) Ordinarily a special agent will not need information from a psychotherapist regarding the mental condition of his/her patient. However, such information may be necessary if a taxpayer raises a defense based on his/her mental condition. If a request is made and if the psychotherapist resists, or is expected to resist furnishing the information, the special agent should obtain a waiver of privilege from the taxpayer. The waiver should protect the psychotherapist from any future claim that the privilege was violated. A copy of the waiver should be retained in the case file. A suggested form of waiver is shown in Exhibit 300-18.

344.8 *(1-18-80)* 9781

Informant and Government Privilege

(1) This privilege allows enforcement agencies to withhold from disclosure the identity of persons who furnish information of violations of law to officers charged with inforcement of that law. The purpose of the privilege is the furtherance and protection of the public interest in effective law enforcement. The privilege recognizes the obligation of citizens to communicate their knowledge of the commission of crimes to law enforcement officials and, by preserving their anonymity, encourages them to perform that obligation. [*Roviaro v. U.S.*] The contents of a communication are not privileged unless they tend to reveal the informant's identity. [*Roviaro v. U.S.*]

(2) This privilege differs from all the others in that it is waivable only by the Government whereas the others are for the benefit of, and waivable by, the individual. Where disclosure of an informer's identity or the content of the communication is relevant and helpful to the defense of an accused or is essential to a fair determination, the trial court may order disclosure. [*Rugendorf v. U.S.; Roviaro v. U.S.; Scher v. U.S.*] If the Government then withholds the information, the court may dismiss the indictment. [*Roviaro v. U.S.*]

(3) Generally, if it is shown that the informant participated in the act which is the basis for a criminal prosecution the court will require disclosure of his/her identity. For example, where the informant has been used to buy narcotics or conterfeit money from the defendant, the courts have held that nondisclosure was improper. [*Roviaro v. U.S.; Conforti v. U.S.; Portomene v. U.S.*] On the other hand, where there is sufficient evidence to establish probable cause independent of the information received from the informant, the Government's claim of privilege has been sustained. As an example, in the Scher case, where the defendant's automobile has been searched without a warrant, partly on the basis of an informant's information that bootleg alcohol was being transported, and partly because of the searching officers' own observation that the automobile with its lights out, was being loaded with packages, the court upheld the privilege. [305 U.S. 251] Further discussion relating to protection of informants is contained in 332.23.

344.9 *(5-9-80)* 9781
Claim and Waiver of Privilege

(1) Generally, except in the case of the informant-Government relationship, the privileges are for the benefit of the person making the communication, may be invoked only on his/her behalf, and may be waived only by him/her. [8 Wigmore (3d Ed.) Secs. 2340, 2341, and 2355] With respect to husband and wife, there is some conflict of authority about who may waive the privilege. Some cases state that the privilege belongs to both spouses and must be waived by both. [*Olender v. U.S.; U.S. v. Mitchell;* 8 Wigmore (3d Ed.) Sec. 2343] It has also been held that the privilege is that of the defendant spouse alone, waivable only by him/her. [*Fraser v. U.S.*]

(2) None of the court cases dealing with privileged communications or the privilege against adverse spouse testimony have prohibited the use of such information as investigative leads. A special agent conducting an investigation is not prevented by any rule of evidence from interviewing a spouse, [*U.S. v. Winfree*], attorney, or any other person to whom information has been communicated by a taxpayer. The mere fact that such person's testimony may be inadmissible does not affect the admissibility of the testimony of any other person, not within the privileged relationship, that results from leads obtained by the special agent.

345 *(1-18-80)* 9781
Admissions and Confessions

345.1 *(1-18-80)* 9781
Admissions

345.11 *(1-18-80)* 9781
Definition of Admissions

(1) An admission as applied in criminal cases is the avowal of a fact or of circumstances from which guilt may be inferred but only tending to prove the offense charged and not amounting to a confession of guilt. It is not essential that an admission be contrary to the interest of the party at the time it is made; it is enough if it be inconsistent with the position which the party takes either in pleadings or at the trial.

(2) An admission may be a prior oral or written statement or act of a party. It can be used either as proof of facts or to discredit a party as a witness. An admission can be used only as to facts not as to matters of law, opinion, or hearsay.

345.12 *(1-18-80)* 9781
Judicial Admissions

A judicial admission is one made in the course of any judicial proceeding, by pleadings, stipulations, affidavits, depositions, or statements made in open court. Such admissions may always be used against a party even in subsequent actions where there is a different adversary. A plea of guilty can be used as an admission in a civil action arising out of the same subject matter. Thus, a taxpayer's plea of guilty to tax fraud can be used as an admission concerning fraud in a civil suit involving the same acts. A plea of nolo contendere however, is not an admission. The entry of a judgment against a party is not an admission by him/her, since it may have been due to a failure of proof. (Text 323.7:(3) relates to the admissibility of reported testimony of a previous trial.)

345.13 *(1-18-80)* 9781
Extra-Judicial Admissions

An extra-judicial admission is anything said outside of court by a party to litigation which is inconsistent with facts asserted in the pleadings or testimony in court. It is not limited to facts which are against interest when made, although the weight of an admission is increased if it is against interest at the time.

345.14 *(1-18-80)* 9781
Implied Admissions

(1) There are certain instances where admissions may be implied from conduct. If something is said by a person which naturally calls for a reply, and if it is heard by a second person who understands it and has the opportunity to, but fails to reply, the failure to reply may constitute an implied admission. [4 Wigmore (3d Ed.) Sec. 1071] Thus, if a special agent discusses his/her findings with a taxpayer (especially in the presence of a third party who can testify about the matter) failure to object to such findings may be used as an admission. This would not apply where the taxpayer remains silent, claiming his/her privilege against self-incrimination.

(2) Although there is no question or dispute regarding admissibility of implied admissions as a rule of law, the facts in every case must be individually applied to this rule to determine if those facts show a duty to reply, as for example, the failure to reply to a letter. It was held in Leach & Co. v. Pierson:

> "A man cannot make evidence for himself by writing a letter containing the statements that he wishes to prove. He does not make the letter evidence by sending it to the party against whom he wishes to prove the facts. He can no more impose a duty to answer a charge than he can impose a duty to pay by sending goods. Therefore, a failure to answer such adverse assertions in the absence of further circumstances making an answer requisite or natural has no effect as an admission."

345.15 *(1-18-80)* 9781
Corroboration of Admissions

345.151 *(1-18-80)* 9781
Corroboration of Admissions Before Offense

Competent, material, and relevant statements of fact made by a person prior to his/her alleged commission of a crime are admissible against him/her to prove such facts without need for corroborations. [*Warszower v. U.S.*] Admissions made as part of the act of committing an offense are likewise admissible without corroboration. For example, in a prosecution for income tax evasion based upon understated receipts from business, the cost of goods sold and other deductions shown on the tax return are considered admissions by the taxpayer [*U.S. v. Hornstein; U.S. v. Stayback*] which need not be corroborated.

345.152 *(1-18-80)* 9781
Corroboration of Admissions After Offense

(1) Unlike admissions made before the offense, extra-judicial admissions made by a person after his/her alleged commission of a crime require corroboration. The reason for this rule, which applies to confessions as well as admissions, is to exclude the possibility of having a person convicted of a crime he/she did not commit, as a result of statements after the offense, induced by duress or other improper means.

(2) Evidence corroborating admissions made after the offense need not prove the offense beyond a reasonable doubt, or by a preponderance of the evidence, but there must be substantial evidence and the evidence as a whole must prove the defendant's guilt beyond a reasonable doubt. [*Daniel Smith v. U.S.; U.S. v. Calderon; Olender v. U.S.*] For example, if a taxpayer admits a substantial amount of unreported sales, the taxpayer's admission may be corroborated by evidence that he/she has maintained an unreported business bank account in which he/she has made frequent deposits.

345.16 *(1-18-80)* 9781
Post-Indictment Admissions

In the Massiah case, the defendant, who had retained counsel and was free on bail after being indicted for narcotics violations, made certain admissions to a codefendant, not knowing that the codefendant had agreed to be a government witness and that the conversation was being overheard by federal agents who had installed radio equipment in the codefendant's car. The Supreme Court held that admitting into evidence post-indictment conversations between the accused and the informant which were caused by federal agents and done in the absence of the accused's attorney, violated the defendant's right to counsel under the Sixth Amendment. [*Massiah v. U.S.*] Post-indictment admissions made by the defendant to an informant are admissible in a subsequent trial for an unrelated offense. [*Hoffa v. U.S.*]

345.2 *(1-18-80)* 9781
Confessions

345.21 *(1-18-80)* 9781
Definition of Confessions

A confession is a statement of a person that he/she is guilty of a crime. It may be made verbally or in writing, to a court, officer, or to any other person. It may be merely an acknowledgment of guilt, or it may be a full statement of the circumstances.

345.22 *(1-18-80)* 9781
Judicial and Extra-Judicial Confessions

A judicial confession is one made before a court in the due course of legal proceedings, including preliminary examinations. An extra-judicial confession is one made elsewhere than in court, and may be made to any person, official or otherwise.

345.23 *(1-18-80)* 9781
Admissibility of Confessions

(1) It is essential to the admission of a confession that it be voluntary. An involuntary confession is one which has been obtained by physical or mental coercion, or by threats, or by promises of immunity or reduced sentence made by a person having authority with respect to the prosecution of the accused. The basis for excluding coerced confessions in the Federal courts is that their use violates the due process clause of the Fifth Amendment, which reads:

> ". . . nor be deprived of life, liberty, or property, without due process of law;"

(2) Whether a confession is voluntary depends upon the facts of the case. [22 Corpus Juris Secundum, secs. 817 et seq.] It is not made involuntary and inadmissible because the accused's counsel was not present when it was made, although that fact may be considered. Physical or psychological coercion will invalidate a confession. Falsehood, artifice, or deception may also make it inadmissible. [*Spano v. N.Y.*] The Supreme Court has held that a confession extracted from the defendant by a boyhood friend who falsely represented that his involvement in the case might make him lose his job as police detective and jeopardize the future of his children and his pregnant wife, was an involuntary confession, especially since it came after continuous all-night questioning. An appeal to a person's religious feelings which induces him/her to confess does not invalidate the confession. The fact that a person was intoxicated when he/she confessed does not exclude the confession if he/she had sufficient mental capacity to know what he/she was saying. Expressions such as "you had better tell the truth," "better be frank," and "it will be best for you to tell the truth," could create controversy as to whether they constitute implied threats or promises. [*U.S. v. Abrams*]

(3) Although the Government does not have the burden of proving in the first instance that a confession was voluntarily given, [*Gray v. U.S.; Hartsell v. U.S.*] the trial court must ascertain and determine as a preliminary question of fact whether it was freely and voluntarily made, without any sort of coercion or promise of reward or leniency. The accused, if he/she so indicates, must be permitted to introduce evidence of its involuntary character. The accused may give his/her own testimony on this point, or may call and examine third persons, or he/she may cross-examine the witnesses who are called to testify to the confession or to the circumstances under which it was made. A proper foundation for the admission of a confession is laid where the witness to whom it was made testifies that neither he/she nor anyone in his/her hearing made any promises or threats to the defendant.

(4) Rule 5(a) of the Federal Rules of Criminal Procedure provides that an arrested person must be taken before a magistrate or other committing officer without unnecessary delay. Thus, a confession taken from a person whose arraignment has been delayed unnecessarily so that he/she may be questioned over a period of time is inadmissible. [*McNabb v. U.S.; Upshaw v. U.S.; Mallory v. U.S.*] The reasoning involved in declaring such confessions inadmissible is stated by the Supreme Court in the Mallory case. The defendant, arrested in the early afternoon, was questioned until 9:30 p.m., when he made his confession, at which time an attempt was made by the arresting officers to locate a committing magistrate, before whom the defendant was taken the following morning. The Court held the confession inadmissible and stated:

> "Circumstances may justify a brief delay between arrest and arraignment, as for instance, where the story volunteered by the accused is susceptible of quick verification through third parties. But the delay must not be of a nature to give opportunity for the extraction of a confession."

(5) The mere fact that a confession has been obtained after a person has been arrested does not bar its use at trial. [*U.S. v. James Mitchell; U.S. v. Vita*] It is not made inadmissible unless there has been unnecessary delay. No hard and fast rule can be laid down as to what is unnecessary delay. Each case stands on its own facts. [*Holt v. U.S.; Williams v. U.S.*] Circumstances will vary from case to case, and from metropolitan areas where there may be several available magistrates to other areas where there may be only one magistrate serving on a part time basis. [*Williams v. U.S.*]

(6) It is not unlawful for Federal officers to detain a suspect a short and reasonable time for questioning. A confession obtained during such detention is admissible, providing the purpose of the detention is investigatory and not simply to hold the suspect until he/she confesses, and the officers have good reason to believe he/she should be questioned to determine whether he/she or any other person ought to be arrested. [*U.S. v. Vita; Warren Goldsmith v. U.S.*]

(7) If any part of a confession is given in evidence, the whole must be given if requested by the defendant. A confession made involuntarily is not admissible evidence, and facts discovered in consequence of such confession are also inadmissible. [*Wong Sun v. U.S.*]

(8) A codefendant's extrajudicial confession is inadmissible at a joint trial because of the substantial risks that the jury would look to the statement in determining the defendant's guilt and the defendant is deprived of the right of cross-examination secured by the Confrontation Clause of the Sixth Amendment. [*Bruton v. U.S.*]

(9) The Omnibus Crime Control and Safe Streets Act of 1968 provides:

"18 U.S.C. 3501. Admissibility of Confessions

"(a) In any criminal prosecution brought by the United States or by the District of Columbia, a confession, as defined in subsection (e) hereof, shall be admissible in evidence if it is voluntarily given. Before such confession is received in evidence, the trial judge shall, out of the presence of the jury, determine any issue as to voluntariness. If the trial judge determines that the confession was voluntarily made it shall be admitted in evidence and the trial judge shall permit the jury to hear relevant evidence on the issue of voluntariness and shall instruct the jury to give such weight to the confession as the jury feels it deserves under all the circumstances.

"(b) The trial judge in determining the issue of voluntariness shall take into consideration all the circumstances surrounding the giving of the confession, including (1) the time elapsing between arrest and arraignment of the defendant making the confession, if it was made after arrest and before arraignment, (2) whether such defendant knew the nature of the offense with which he was charged or of which he was suspected at the time of making the confession, (3) whether or not such defendant was advised or knew that he was not required to make any statement and that any such statement could be used against him, (4) whether or not such defendant had been advised prior to questioning of his right to the assistance of counsel; and (5) whether or not such defendant was without the assistance of counsel when questioned and when giving such confession.

"The presence or absence of any of the above-mentioned factors to be taken into consideration by the judge need not be conclusive on the issue of voluntariness of the confession.

"(c) In any criminal prosecution by the United States or by the District of Columbia, a confession made or given by a person who is a defendant therein, while such person was under arrest or other detention in the custody of any law-enforcement officer or law-enforcement agency, shall not be inadmissible solely because of delay in bringing such person before a magistrate or other officer empowered to commit persons charged with offenses against the laws of the United States or of the District of Columbia if such confession is found by the trial judge to have been made voluntarily and if the weight to be given the confession is left to the jury and if such confession was made or given by such person within six hours immediately following his arrest or other detention: Provided, that the time limitation contained in this subsection shall not apply in any case in which the delay in bringing such person before such magistrate or other officer beyond such six-hour period is found by the trial judge to be reasonable considering the means of transportation and the distance to be traveled to the nearest available such magistrate or other officer.

"(d) Nothing contained in this section shall bar the admission in evidence of any confession made or given voluntarily by any person to any other person without interrogation by anyone, or at any time at which the person made or gave such confession was not under arrest or other detention.

"(e) As used in this section, the term 'confession' means any confession of guilt of any criminal offense or any self-incriminating statement made or given orally or in writing."

345.24 *(1–18–80)* 9781
Corroboration of Confessions

As with an admission, and for the same reasons, it is necessary that a confession be corroborated by independent evidence before it may be admitted. [*Daniel Smith v. U.S.*]

346 *(1–18–80)* 9781
Techniques of Interviewing

346.1 *(1–18–80)* 9781
Definition and Purpose of Interviewing

(1) An interview is defined as a meeting between two persons to talk over something special. In investigations it usually includes visiting and holding a formal consultation for the purpose of resolving or exploring issues.

(2) Interviews are used to obtain leads, develop information, and establish evidence. The testimony of witnesses and the confessions or admissions of alleged violators are major factors in resolving tax cases. Cases are presented to a jury through the testimony of witnesses. Therefore, it is the special agent's duty to interview the taxpayer and every witness connected with the case. The record of such interviews will usually take one of the following forms: transcript of interview or question and answer statement, affadavit, memorandum of interview, and recording (tape, wax, etc.).

346.2 *(1–18–80)* 9781
Authority for Interviewing

(1) *IRC 7602.*—Authorizes the Secretary or his delegate to examine books and records and to take testimony under oath.

(2) *Delegation Order No. 4 (as Revised)*—Authorizes the special agent to issue and serve a summons, to examine books and records, to question witnesses, and to take testimony under oath.

(3) *Delegation Order No. 37 (as Revised)*—Authorizes the special agent to administer oaths and to certify such papers as may be

necessary under the internal revenue laws and regulations.

(4) A further discussion of the special agent's authority is contained in text 362.

346.3 *(1-18-80)* 9781
Preparation and Planning for Interviewing

346.31 *(1-18-80)* 9781
Preparation

(1) The special agent must possess the original return or returns involved, if any were filed for the pertinent period, as a prerequisite to independently interviewing a taxpayer, his/her representative, or one of his/her present employees or inspecting the taxpayer's books and records.

(2) Exceptions may be made in cases where an examination is extended to include taxable periods for which the original return is not available and the examination is based on the taxpayer's retained copy, or where such action is approved in writing by the Chief.

(3) The procedure outlined in (1) above is limited to a taxpayer's own tax matters and has no application in an inquiry where an agent is merely securing information from another person, not under tax investigation, but who engaged in transactions with the taxpayer or has data relevant to the tax liability under inquiry.

(4) See also IRM 9323.2.

346.32 *(1-18-80)* 9781
Planning

(1) *Timing*—Proper timing of the interview is essential in obtaining information that is material in resolving a case.

(2) *Review Available Information*—Prior to any interview the agent should review all the information and data he/she possesses relating to the case. Such information may then be divided into three general categories: information which can be documented, and need not be discussed; information which may be documented, but needs to be discussed; information that must be developed by testimony. The interview file should contain only data or information arranged in the order it is to be discussed or covered in the interview. The less data the agent has to cope with during the interview, the easier it will be for him/her to vary the line of questioning. It is very distracting, and may even cause some confusion, for the agent to delay the interrogation to find a document or an item in a voluminous file. However, the files should contain sufficient data to cover all the matters under discussion, provided it isn't unwieldy.

(3) *Prepare Outline*—Before the interview, the agent should determine the goal of, or purpose for, questioning the subject. The topics that will enable the agent to accomplish this goal should be outlined in more or less detail, depending upon his/her experience and the complexity of the case. The outline should contain only information which is relevant and material (including hearsay). Extraneous matter should be excluded because it may be confusing and may adversely affect the end sought. Important topics should be set off or underscored and related topics listed in their proper sequence. A portion of a suggested outline is shown in Exhibit 300-6 (Suggested Outline for Questioning Person Who Prepared Returns, If Other Than Taxpayer). Specific questions should be kept to a minimum, since they tend to reduce the flexibility of the questioner. In addition to the topics to be discussed, the outline should include the following, if applicable:

(a) Identification of the subject.

(b) Information to be given the subject about his/her constitutional rights.

(c) The administration of the oath.

(d) The purpose of the interview.

(e) Questions showing that the subject was not threatened or intimidated in any manner, and that statements were made freely and voluntarily without duress or any promises whatsoever.

(4) *Provide Suitable Surroundings.*

346.4 *(1-18-80)* 9781
Conduct of Interview

(1) *Be Adaptable and Flexible*—The agent should keep an open mind that is receptive to all information regardless of the nature, and be prepared to develop it. If the agent is not flexible, he/she may waste a great deal of time and ask unnecessary questions, resulting in a voluminous statement of little or no value. Although the agent may find it easier to adhere to a fixed pattern of interviewing, or to rely upon a series of questions or topics, rigid adherence to any notes or outline will seriously handicap flexibility. The outline and data should serve only as aids and not as substitutes for original and spontaneous questioning. A carefully planned outline will provide enough leeway to allow the agent to better cope with any situation that may occur and permit development of leads that may arise.

(2) *Follow Through*—Incomplete and irresponsive answers have little or no probative value. Any answer, apparently relative to a pertinent matter, that is not complete and to the point should be followed up by questioning the subject about all knowledge he/she has concerning every facet of the topic. The agent should follow through on every pertinent lead and incomplete answer. The agent should continue asking questions until he/she has all the information he/she can reasonably expect to get.

(3) The following suggestions will help the agent to follow through, and to obtain answers that are complete and accurate:

(a) Use short questions confined to one topic which can be clearly and easily understood.

(b) Ask questions that require narrative answers; avoid "yes" and "no" answers, whenever possible.

(c) Whenever possible avoid questions that suggest part of the answer, i.e., "leading questions."

(d) Question the witness about how he/she learned what he/she states to be fact. The witness should also be required to give the factual basis for any conclusions he/she stated.

(e) Be alert so as to prevent the witness from aimlessly wandering. Where possible, require a direct response.

(f) Prevent the witness from leading the agent far afield. The witness should not be allowed to confuse the issue and leave basic questions unanswered.

(g) Concentrate more on the answers of the witness than on the next question.

(h) To avoid an unrelated and incomplete chronology, the agent should clearly understand each answer and ensure that any lack of clarity is eliminated before continuing.

(i) When all important points have been resolved, terminate the interview; if possible, leave the door open for further meetings with the subject.

(4) The subject should completely answer the following basic questions:

(a) *Who?*—Complete identification should be made of all persons referred to. This includes: description, address, alias, "trading as," "also known as," citizenship, reputation, and associates. If the person cannot be identified by name, a physical description should be requested and should include: age, height, weight, color of eyes, hair, skin, description of build, clothing, unusual markings, scars, mental or physical defects. Questions should also cover any aids worn by the individual, such as glasses, hearing aid, wig or toupee, cane, braces and other items.

(b) *What?*—Complete details as to what happened. Questions should relate to events and methods and systems. A complete answer should be developed. Trace the event from its inception to its ultimate termination. For example, a sale starts with a customer placing an order, either orally or in writing, and terminates when the payment is ultimately placed in some depository. Every detail concerning what happened to that sale and what happened to every book, record, document, or person connected with it should be determined.

(c) *Where?*—Complete details regarding the location of books, records, assets, bank and brokerage accounts, witnesses, clients, customers, safe deposit boxes, safes, and the like. A description of the location should include the general area, as well as the identification of the person who has custody and control of the item. A complete description of the place should include the size, shape, color, and location.

(d) *When?*—The time can be established by direct questioning, by relating the incident to some known event, or by associating the event to some person, place, or thing.

(e) *How?*—Complete details about how the event occurred, or how the operation was conducted. How did the subject acquire knowledge? Was it through seeing, hearing, feeling, or smelling, or performing duties? How were transactions recorded: written, typed, matching entries, others?

(f) *Why?*—Everything is done for a reason. Determine the motive by questioning the witness about his/her actions. What caused him/her to act? Who caused him/her to act? How was he/she motivated? Since these are the most important questions, especially when relating to or reflecting an evil purpose, they should receive special consideration.

(5) *Maintain Control*

(a) The agent should maintain full control of the interview. He/she usually can accomplish this by limiting each participant to the rights, duties, and privileges he/she is entitled to at the interview. Any deviation should be corrected immediately by informing the individual of his/her role and by not allowing him/her to go beyond it. If the agent cannot maintain complete control of the interview, he/she should end it and arrange to continue when the situation is corrected. The record should show all the agent's attempts to correct the individual's improper conduct, as well as the agent's reason for terminating the interview before it is completed.

(b) After all persons are informed of why they are present at the interview, the agent should confine their activities to the roles indicated:

1 *Principal*—The principal is called upon to answer questions, and he/she should be permitted to make any explanations in any reasonable manner he/she may desire. He/she should be encouraged to tell his/her side of the case, without interruption. He/she has a right to refuse to answer any question that he/she feels will incriminate him/her. This is a personal right and can be invoked only by the principal.

2 *Witness*—The witness must comply with every request made by the agent that is both legal and reasonable. However, the witness has a right to refuse the request, if he/she feels that the information may incriminate him/her. This right cannot be invoked on the ground that the information will incriminate the defendant or someone else.

3 *Special agent*—The special agent should question the taxpayer about any matters the agent deems relevant to the tax case, unless the agent feels that it would be to the government's disadvantage to ask questions that would reveal particular information. Since the special agent is responsible for the development of evidence, it is his/her obligation to conduct the interview in any manner he/she deems appropriate. If he/she grants permission to a cooperating officer to question the subject, the agent should instruct the officer in the method and technique to be used.

4 *Cooperating Officer*—The revenue agent or revenue officer may assist the special agent whenever any tax or technical accounting problems occur during the interview. The cooperating officer should not question the witness until the officer has discussed the matter with the special agent.

5 *Accountant representative*—The accountant's duty is to assist his/her client in all bookkeeping and accounting matters.

6 *Legal representative*—The attorney has a duty to furnish legal advice to his/her client relating to any matter discussed. This is the attorney's principal function at an interview.

7 *Recorder*—The recorder's function is to prepare a permanent record of the interview. A mechanical recording device may be used in conjunction with the recorder or in lieu of a recorder, where necessary, provided all parties to the proceeding consent thereto.

(6) The aforementioned rights, duties, and privileges are subject to changes by the courts, legislatures, and the policy of the Service. (See 341 through 345.)

346.5 *(1-18-80)* 9781
Record of Interview

346.51 *(1-18-80)* 9781
Introduction

(1) The principal purpose of an interview is to obtain all the facts helpful in resolving the case. Therefore, it is necessary to prepare a permanent record of every interview to be preserved for future use. It is usually prepared on one of the following forms:

Form	Exhibit No.
(a) Affidavit	300-7
(b) Statement	300-8
(c) Question and answer statement	300-9
(d) Memorandum of interview	300-10
(e) Informal notes or diary entries	300-11

346.52 *(1-18-80)* 9781
Affidavit

An affidavit is a written or printed declaration or statement of facts made voluntarily, and confirmed by the oath or affirmation of the party making it, before an officer having authority to administer such oath. No particular form of affidavit is required at common law. It is customary that affidavits have a caption or title, the judicial district in which given, the signature of the affiant, and the jurat, which properly includes authentication. Exhibit 300-7 is a suggested format containing all these characteristics which add to the dignity and usefulness of the affidavit.

346.53 *(1-18-80)* 9781
Statement

A statement in a general sense is a declaration of matters of fact. Although the term has come to be used for a variety of formal narratives of facts required by law, it is in a limited sense, a formal, exact, detailed presentation of the facts. The statement may be prepared in any form and should be signed and dated by the person preparing it. If possible, the witness should also sign the statement and signify that he/she read and understood it or that it was read to him/her. A statement (Exhibit 300-8) generally contains the comments and remarks of the witness, and is used whenever it is not feasible to place the witness under oath; e.g., a so-called "affidavit," without the affiant's oath is in effect a statement.

346.54 *(1-18-80)* 9781
Question and Answer Statement

346.541 *(1-18-80)* 9781
Elements

(1) A question and answer statement is a complete transcript of the questions, answers, and statements made by each participant at an interview. It may be prepared from the recorder's notes or from a mechanical recording device. A mechanical recording device may be used to record statements when no stenographer is readily available for that purpose, with the express advance consent of all parties to the conversation. The source used to prepare the transcript should be preserved and associated with the case file because it may be needed in court to establish what was said. The transcript (suggested format shown in Exhibit 300-9) should be prepared on standard size (8" × 10½") plain bond paper with each question consecutively numbered and should contain the following:

(a) The time and place where the testimony is obtained.

(b) Name and address of person giving testimony.

(c) The matter the testimony relates to.

(d) Name and title of person asking questions and person giving answers.

(e) The names and titles of all persons present, including attorney or accountant present to assist the witness. Also the reason for each person being present, if not self-evident.

(f) Generally, the purpose for the interview should be stated.

(g) Information given to the witness concerning his rights relating to self-incrimination and counsel, if appropriate.

(h) Administration of oath.

(i) Questions and answers establishing that the statement was made freely and voluntarily, without duress, and that no promises or commitments were made by the agents.

(j) Offer to allow witness to make any statement for the record, and, if advisable, an opportunity to examine and to sign the transcript.

(k) Jurat: The officer who administers the oath should complete the jurat. It is preferable, but not essential, to have the same officer who interviewed the taxpayer complete the jurat.

(l) Signatures of any Government witnesses present.

(m) Signature and certificate of person preparing the statement, showing the source of the original information used to prepare it.

(2) A stenographer's original shorthand notes of statement by a principal or a witness in a case will be filed with the considered part of the workpapers relating to the case. The pages containing such notes will be removed from the notebook, numbered, stapled in order, and sealed in an envelope by the stenographer. The following information will be written on the envelope: the case number, the name of the person whose statements are recorded, the date the statements were made, the number of pages of notes, and the name of the stenographer.

(3) Recordings of statements by a principal or a witness made through the use of stenotype machines or sound recording devices will be labeled and filed in a manner similar to that prescribed in (2) above.

(4) A special agent's notes made substantially contemporaneous to interviews of the taxpayer or prospective witnesses and which are used in the preparation of memorandums of interview, affidavits and other similar reports will be preserved and retained in the case file. Notes should contain the date of the interview and the initials of their maker in the upper right corner.

(5) Stenographers' notes and other verbatim recordings of statements made in connection with a collateral investigation will be packaged and identified in accordance with the procedure prescribed in (2) and (3) above and will be sent,

with the collateral report, to the district that requested the investigation.

(6) See also IRM 9715.

346.542 *(1-18-80)* 9781
Off-Record Discussions

Off-record discussions should not be permitted during a recorded interview of a taxpayer, and kept to a minimum during a recorded interview of a witness.

346.55 *(1-18-80)* 9781
Memorandum of Interview

(1) A memorandum of interview is an informal note or instrument embodying something that the person desires to fix in memory by the aid of written record. It is a record of what occurred at the interview and usually is in the format shown in Exhibit 300-10. The memorandum shows the date, time, place, and persons present as well as what transpired. It should be promptly signed and dated by the agents present. If the witness is advised of his/her constitutional rights during the interview, this fact should be noted in the memorandum.

(2) Since the person interviewed may be a Government witness in a criminal trial, the special agent should bear in mind that 18 USC 3500 provides for defense inspection of any pre-trial statement about whose subject matter the witness has testified on direct examination. Case interpretation of this subsection covers substantially verbatim recitals of witnesses' oral statements which are contemporaneously recorded. This includes memorandums of interview. [*Anthony M. Palermo v. U.S.; U.S. v. Papworth*] Handwritten notes made by an agent during an interview and used as the basis for a more detailed memorandum or report may be subject to inspection by a court and should be preserved and retained in the case file. Trial courts have substantial discretionary authority in interpreting the statute. Special agents, therefore, should confine memorandums to the facts developed in their interviews, and should avoid opinions, conclusions, and other extraneous matters.

(3) Subsection 637.82 contains a discussion of 18 USC 3500 and cases determining when defense inspection of memorandums of interview will be permitted in a criminal trial.

346.56 *(1-18-80)* 9781
Informal Notes or Diary Entries of Interview

Informal notes should contain sufficient details to permit the agent to refresh his memory as to what transpired at the interview. Any method of recording the entries is sufficient, if it shows the time, place, persons present, and what occurred. Details of interviews should not be entered in the diary, but rather a memorandum should be made and kept in the case file (see Exhibit 300-11). A note should be made in the diary of the time, place, and persons interviewed (see Exhibit 300-11).

346.6 *(1-18-80)* 9781
Procedure

(1) *Review and corrections*—Every record of an interview should be carefully reviewed for any typographical errors, and for accuracy of context. If the statement is to be examined by the witness, he/she may be permitted to correct typographical errors or to make minor modifications of his/her testimony. The witness should never be permitted to alter the record, or to delete any of his/her testimony. The witness may, however, submit an affidavit or give testimony modifying his/her original statements.

(2) *Execution*—Every document made under oath should have a simple certificate evidencing the fact that it was properly executed before a duly authorized officer. The usual and proper form, referred to as the "jurat," is "Subscribed and sworn to before me at (*address*)," followed by the date, signature and title of the officer. If the jurat shows an affirmation, the word "affirmed" will be sufficient. The agent administers the oath by having the witness stand, raise his/her right hand, and make a declaration that the document is true and correct.

(3) *Persons entitled to copies*—Upon request, a copy of an affidavit or transcript of a question and answer statement will be furnished a witness promptly, except in circumstances deemed by the Regional Commissioner to necessitate temporarily withholding a copy. (See Policy Statement P-9-31.)

(4) *Subsequent use by special agent*—The record of interview generally is not admissible as evidence at the trial, but may be used to refresh the memory of a witness or to discourage a witness from changing his/her testimony. It may also be used to impeach a witness on the stand when his/her previous statements are inconsistent with his/her testimony, or to furnish a basis for prosecution of a witness who testifies falsely at the trial. If the statement constitutes a confession or an admission against interest, the pertinent parts may be used as such in evidence at the trial. The record also serves as a valuable source of information for subsequent examinations if it contains the personal and financial history of the taxpayer. It may be used to establish a starting point or "cut-off" for a subsequent net worth case, or to provide leads to other violations by the subject or other individuals.

346.7 *(1–18–80)* 9781
Application

All techniques outlined in 346 are subject to IRM 9384 and any related Manual Supplements.

347 *(1–18–80)* 9781
Circular Form Letter

347.1 *(9–8–80)* 9781
General

Mail circularization is a written request to third parties for information where more than ten letters of a similar nature are sent. Mail circularization to obtain third party evidence may be, under certain circumstances, the most practical means of obtaining documentary evidence in an investigation when a large number of persons, widely scattered geographically, need to be reached. If not judiciously used, mail circularization may result in unwarranted embarrassment to the taxpayer or cause unfavorable public reaction, thus subjecting the Service to criticism.

347.2 *(9–8–80)* 9781
Procedure

To ensure proper use of this technique, mail circularization will not be undertaken in any case without the prior approval of the Chief, Criminal Investigation Division, including approval of the letters to be sent out. Care must be exercised in approving mail circularization to ensure that mail inquiries are sent only to those third parties who, in the view of the Chief, Criminal Investigation Division, are a likely source of information; the information sought is important to the investigation; and obtaining the information by other means, if at all possible, would not be practical because of either delays in investigation, costs involved, or similar reasons. Caution must be exercised not be damage the reputation of the taxpayer by making the letter either offensive or suggestive of any wrongdoing by the taxpayer. Appropriate wording could be "The Internal Revenue Service is conducting an investigation of . . .". When mailing circularizations, all such letters will be signed by the special agent with prior approval of the Chief, Criminal Investigation Division, indicated on the file copy. The title "Special Agent" and Criminal Investigation Division will be included in the signature block.

348 *(1–18–80)* 9781
Disclosure

348.1 *(1–18–80)* 9781
General

All returns and return information are confidential and may not be disclosed except as authorized by the Internal Revenue Code. This rule applies to all present and former IRS employees. Civil and criminal sanctions may be imposed upon intentional violators.

348.2 *(1–18–80)* 9781
Definitions

(1) A "return" is any tax return or information return, schedules, and attachments thereto, including any amendment or supplement, which is required or permitted to be filed and is in fact filed by a taxpayer with the Secretary of the Treasury. Examples include:

(a) Forms 1040, Schedules A, B, C and Forms W-2.

(b) A taxpayer has filed an income tax return and subsequently submits a letter to IRS explaining an item on the original return. The letter is within the definition of return.

(2) The statutory definition of "return information" is very broad. It includes any information other than a taxpayer's return itself which IRS has obtained from any source or developed through any means which relates to the potential liability of any person under the Code for any tax, penalty, interest, fine, forfeiture or other imposition or offense. It includes information extracted from a return, e.g., the names of dependents, locations of business interests, bank accounts, etc. Examples include:

(a) The fact that a person has filed a return or is under investigation is recorded in IRS files.

(b) The fact that the Service has copies of public records maintained in its files which were secured from a county clerk's office pursuant to an investigation of a taxpayer.

(3) "Taxpayer return information" is return information which is filed with or furnished to the IRS by or on behalf of the taxpayer to whom the return information relates. This includes, for example, data supplied by a taxpayer's representative (e.g., his accountant) to the IRS in connection with an audit of his return.

(4) Disclosure is the making known of returns or return information in any manner. A disclosure may be either direct or indirect. Discussing specific facts of a case you are working on with your supervisor is a disclosure although clearly a proper one.

(5) Tax Administration includes the enforcement of not only the Internal Revenue Laws, but also the enforcement of other related Federal Statutes where such enforcement is done in connection with the administration of tax laws.

348.3 *(1-18-80)* 9781

Disclosures for Investigative Purposes

Special agents are specifically authorized by IRC 6103(k)(6) to disclose return information to the extent necessary to gather data which may be relevant to a tax investigation. Situations in which special agents may have to make such disclosures in order to perform their duties arise on a daily basis. For example, this occurs whenever they contact third parties believed to have information pertinent to a tax investigation. IRC 6103(k)(6) permits the disclosure of return information in the investigation process but does not authorize the disclosure of returns themselves. They may be disclosed during the investigation process only to their preparer. When soliciting information from a third party other than a return preparer during a tax investigation, a special agent may not show a taxpayer's tax return to the third party. However, pertinent data (e.g., the nature and amount of income, deductions, expenses, etc.) may be extracted from the tax return and used in questions to third parties.

348.4 *(1-18-80)* 9781

Disclosures to Other Treasury Employees

(1) On many occasions, IRS employees have an official need for certain returns or return information in the special agent's case file. Such employees include the special agent's group manager, another special agent, a revenue agent, a revenue officer, etc. The term "official need" is the key to whether disclosure to another IRS employee is proper.

(2) A written request will generally be required before tax information in the possession of the IRS will be disclosed to an employee of another component of the Department of the Treasury whose official duties require the information for tax administration purposes.

348.5 *(1-18-80)* 9781

Disclosures to The Department of Justice for Tax Administration Purposes

Approved special agent reports are referred to the Department of Justice under the authority of IRC 6103(h)(2) and (3). A disclosure may be made to the Department of Justice of relevant returns or return information pertaining to the taxpayer who is or may be a party to a tax administration proceeding or investigation. Returns and return information of third parties gathered in connection with an investigation of a taxpayer may be disclosed to the Department of Justice if such information satisfies the item or transactional relationship test provided in IRC 6103(h)(2). The item test is met if an item on a third party's return may relate to the resolution of an issue in the tax administration proceeding or investigation. The transaction test is met if the third-party's returns or return information may relate to a transaction between the taxpayer and the third party and the third-party information pertaining to the transaction may affect the resolution of an issue in a proceeding or investigation involving tax administration. Agents contacted by a Justice attorney and asked to provide returns or return information in connection with an investigation or prosecution which was not referred by IRS should tell the requesting attorney that the agent will have to seek disclosure advice.

348.6 *(1-18-80)* 9781

Disclosures to a Taxpayer's Representative

(1) Disclosure of returns and return information to the taxpayer's representative will be made only in the following circumstances:

(a) The taxpayer is present at the time of the disclosure; or

(b) If the taxpayer is not present, then a disclosure will be made to the representative only: if the taxpayer has executed a written consent to the disclosure (Form 2848-D, Declaration and Authorization, may be used for this purpose); or if the taxpayer has provided his/her representative with a power of attorney (Form 2848, Power of Attorney, may be used for this purpose).

348.7 *(1-18-80)* 9781

Disclosure of Tax Information for Nontax Criminal Administration Purposes (Federal Only)

Often in the conduct of tax investigations, special agents discover evidence of Federal crimes outside the jurisdiction of IRS. If this information is nontax information, see text 3488. IRC 6103(i) requires IRS in the instance of tax information to make a distinction between taxpayer return information and return information for disclosure purposes. IRC 6103(i) permits disclosure of return information other than taxpayer return information upon the written request of the head of a Federal agency or upon the initiative of the Service. However, IRC 6103(i) permits disclosure of taxpayer return information only upon the issuance of a court order. In both of these instances, the information will be reported by the special agent to the Chief, Criminal Investigation Division. See text 339.2

348.8 *(1-18-80)* 9781

Disclosure of Nontax Criminal Violations

Any Service employee who either witnesses the commission of any nontax criminal act or receives information orally or in writing indicating facts that relate to a nontax violation of Federal, state, or local criminal laws which facts are not directly or indirectly related to a tax return, may disclose this information to appropriate law enforcement officials under the procedures found in Chapter 35(00) of "new" IRM 1272, Disclosure of Information Handbook.

348.9 *(5-9-80)* 9781

Disclosure of Special Agents' Reports and Information Contained in Taxpayer Delinquent Account Files to Probation Officers

(1) U.S. Probation Officers are appointed by and serve under the direction of the United States District Court. 18 U.S.C. §3654. Rule 32(c) of the Federal Rules of Criminal Procedure contemplates that the probation service of the court will make a presentence investigation and report to the court before imposition of sentence, unless the defendant waives, with the permission of the court, a presentence investigation and report, or the court determines that the record contains sufficient information to enable the court to exercise meaningful sentencing discretion. The rule specifically provides that the "report of the presentence investigation shall contain any prior criminal record of the defendant and such information about his/her characteristics, his/her financial condition and the circumstances surrounding his/her behavior as may be helpful in imposing sentence or in granting probation or in the correctional treatment of the defendant, and such other information as may be required by the court." Probation officers are not permitted to submit the presentence report to the court or disclose its contents to anyone, unless the defendant has pleaded guilty or nolo contendere or has been found guilty. The judge may inspect the presentence report at any time, however, with the written consent of the defendant.

(2) It is the view of the Chief Counsel that the special agents' report may be disclosed to a probation officer in cases where a taxpayer has pleaded guilty or nolo contendere or has been found guilty of Federal tax law violations, for the purpose of preparing the report contemplated by Rule 32(c) of the Federal Rules of Criminal Procedure. The disclosure of special agents' reports to probation officers is authorized by IRC §6103(h)(4). However, information contained in the report shall not be disclosed if such disclosure would identify a confidential informant or seriously impair a civil or criminal tax investigation. Inspection of the special agents' report by the probation officer, to the extent material and relevant, should be made at a convenient location, such as the U.S. Attorney's office. Proper care should be exercised to provide adequate security of the report and the information contained therein, to prevent unauthorized disclosure.

(3) Occasionally U.S. Probation Officers will request tax information from the Service as part of a presentence investigation in a non-tax criminal case. Disclosures may be made to probation officers in these circumstances only as provided in IRC §6103(c). Temp. Reg. 404.6103(c)-1 provides the format that must be followed in any taxpayer authorization or waiver that is submitted for the purpose of allowing a probation officer to receive tax information.

(4) Following conviction for criminal tax violations, courts in some instances specify that probation of the sentence imposed is conditioned upon satisfactory settlement and/or payment of civil liability for taxes and penalties. The Director, Criminal Investigation Division, will take whatever steps are necessary to initiate appropriate legal action in any case where the taxpayer has failed to comply with the conditions of the probation. See IRM 9537.2. IRC §6103(h)(4) permits the disclosure of information contained in Taxpayer Delinquent Account files to U.S. Probation Officer in a judicial pro-

ceeding pertaining to tax administration for the purpose of informing the court of any non-compliance with the terms of the taxpayer's probation. See 9537.2 for the rules governing disclosure to probation officers in these circumstances.

350 *(1-18-80)* 9781
Documentary Evidence

351 *(1-18-80)* 9781
Definition of Documentary Evidence

Documentary evidence is evidence consisting of writings and documents as distinguished from parol, that is, oral evidence.

352 *(1-18-80)* 9781
Best Evidence Rule

352.1 *(1-18-80)* 9781
Definition of Best Evidence Rule

(1) The best evidence rule, which applies only to documentary evidence, is that the best proof of the contents of a document is the document itself.

(2) The best evidence rule, requiring production of the original document, is confined to cases where it is sought to prove the contents of the document. Production consists of either making the writing available to the judge and counsel for the adversary, or having it read aloud in open court. Facts about a document other than its contents are provable without its production. [4 Wigmore (3d Ed.) 1248] For example, the fact that a sales contract was made is a fact separate from the actual terms of the contract and may be proved by testimony alone.

(3) Certain documents, such as leases, contracts or even letters, which are executed (signed) in more than one copy are all considered originals and any one of the copies may be produced as an original.

352.2 *(1-18-80)* 9781
Application of Best Evidence Rule

(1) When an original document is not produced, secondary evidence, which could consist of testimony of witnesses or a copy of the writing, will be received to prove its contents if its absence is satisfactorily explained. Unavailability of the original document is a question to be decided by the trial judge, just as he/she decides all questions regarding admissibility of evidence.

(2) The reason for the rule is to prevent fraud, mistake, or error. For example, the testimony of a special agent as to the contents of a sales invoice itself is unavailable. However, in that event, the special agent's testimony is admissible even though the person who prepared the invoice is available to testify. The best evidence rule will not be invoked to exclude oral testimony of one witness merely because another witness could give more conclusive testimony.

352.3 *(1-18-80)* 9781
Secondary Evidence

(1) All evidence falling short of the standard for best evidence is classed as secondary evidence and is a substitute for better evidence. Stated in another way, when it is shown from the face of the evidence itself or by other proof that better evidence was or is available, the evidence is classified as secondary evidence.

(2) Secondary evidence may be either the testimony of witnesses or a copy of the writing. There is no settled Federal rule stating which of these is a higher degree of secondary evidence.

(3) Before secondary evidence of any nature may be admitted, there must be satisfactory evidence of the present or former existence of an original document, [*Fidelity Trust Co. v. Mayhugh; Canister Co. v. U.S.*] properly executed and genuine. [*O'Donnell v. U.S.*] It must be established that the original has been destroyed, lost, stolen, or is otherwise unavailable. In all cases, except destruction provable by an eyewitness, the party proving the document must have used all reasonable means to obtain the original, i.e., he/she must have made such diligent search as was reasonable under the facts. [*Klein v. U.S.*] Some cases have specifically set the rule that search must be made in the place where the document was last known to be, or that inquiry must be made of the person who last had custody of it. In every case, the sufficiency of the search is a matter to be determined by the court. [*Sellmayer Packing Co. v. Commissioner of Int. Rev.; Fogel v. U.S.; O'Donnell v. U.S.*] If a document is offered as secondary evidence it must be shown to be a correct copy of the original.

(Next page is 9781-114.1)

(4) When the original document has been destroyed by the party attempting to prove its contents, secondary evidence of the contents will be admitted, if the destruction was in the ordinary course of business, or by mistake, or even intentionally, provided it was not done for any fraudulent purpose. [*Riggs v. Tayloe*, 9 Wheaton; *McDonald v. U.S.; Granquist v. Harvey*] In the Granquist case the defendant's income tax returns had been destroyed pursuant to Executive Order and statutory authority. At the trial, secondary evidence in the form of oral testimony and state returns was admitted to establish the contents of the missing income tax returns.

(5) In a civil case, secondary evidence of the contents of a document may be introduced if the original is in the possession of the opponent in the case, provided the party attempting to introduce the copy has first served a notice upon his/her opponent to produce the original, and the opponent has failed to do so. In a criminal case not involving corporate records, the Government may introduce secondary evidence of the defendant's records without showing prior notice to produce. [*Lisansky v. U.S.; U.S. v. Reyburn; McKnight v. U.S.*]

(6) The Lisansky case presents a full statement of this rule and illustrates its application. The defendants in the case, on trial for income tax evasion, argued that the court, in allowing Government agents to testify about the contents of the defendant's books and records and permitting photostatic pages of the books to be introduced in evidence, violated the best evidence rule. The Court of Appeals held:

"So far as the best evidence rule is concerned, the government complied with this rule, in that it produced the best proof which could be produced under the circumstances of the case. The books were shown to be in possession of the defendants; and, because of the provisions of the Fourth and Fifth Amendments, the court was without power to require their production at the trial. (Boyd v. U.S. cited). *** But evidence as to the contents of books and papers is not lost to the government because the defendant has them in his possession and their production cannot be ordered or the usual basis laid for the introduction of secondary evidence. In such cases, the rule is that, when they are traced to his possession, the government, without more ado, may offer secondary evidence of their contents."

353 *(1-18-80)* 9781
Admissibility of Specific Forms of Documentary Evidence

353.1 *(1-18-80)* 9781
Statutory Provisions

Admissibility in the Federal courts of various forms of documentary evidence is covered principally in sections 1731 through 1745 of Title 28, United States Code.

353.2 *(1-18-80)* 9781
Business Records

353.21 *(1-18-80)* 9781
Federal Shop Book Rule

(1) Records made in the regular course of business may be admissible under 28 USC 1732(a) which states:

"In any court of the United States and in any court established by Act of Congress, any writing or record, whether in the form of an entry in a book or otherwise, made as a memorandum or record of any act, transaction, occurrence, or event, shall be admissible as evidence of such act, transaction, occurrence, or event, if made in regular course of any business, and if it was the regular course of such business to make such memorandum or record at the time of such act, transaction, occurrence, or event or within a reasonable time thereafter.

(Next page is 9781-115)

"All other circumstances of the making of such writing or record, including lack of personal knowledge by the entrant or maker, may be shown to affect its weight, but such circumstances shall not affect its admissibility.

"The term 'business,' as used in this section, includes business, profession, occupation, and calling of every kind."

(2) The above statute permits showing that an entry was made in a book maintained in the regular course of business without producing the particular person who made the entry and having him/her identify it. [*Hoffman v. Palmer*] For example, in proving a sale, an employee of the customer may appear with the original purchase journal and cash disbursements book of the customer, to testify that these were books of original entry showing purchases by the customer and payments by him/her to a taxpayer for these purchases, even though the witness is not the person who made the entries.

(3) The essence of the "regular course of business" rule is the reliance on records made under circumstances showing no reason or motive to misrepresent the facts. As stated in Clainos v. U.S. "The rule contemplates that certain events are regularly recorded as 'routine reflections of the day to day operations of a business' so that 'the character of the records and their earmarks of reliability' import trustworthiness." For example, the rule is applied to bank records under the theory that the accuracy of the records is essential to the very life of the bank's business. [*U.S. v. Cotter; U.S. Manton*]

(4) The mere fact that a record has been kept in the regular course of business is not of itself enough to make it admissible. The rules of competency and relevancy must still be applied, the same as for any other evidence. [*Schmeller v. U.S.*] If a ledger is offered in evidence to prove entries posted from a journal which is available, the journal itself, as the book of original entry, should be produced.

(5) When in the regular course of business it is the practice to photograph, photostat, or microfilm the business records mentioned above, such reproductions when satisfactorily identified are made as admissible as the originals by statute. [28 USC 1732(b)] Similarly, enlargements of the original reproductions are admissible if the original reproduction is in existence and available for inspection under the direction of the court. This rule is particularly helpful in connection with bank records because of the common practice of microfilming ledger sheets, deposit tickets, and checks.

353.22 *(12-30-80)* 9781
Photographs, Photostats, and Microfilmed Copies

(1) Photographs, photostats, and microfilmed copies of writings not made in the regular course of business are considered secondary evidence of the contents, inadmissible if the original can be produced and no reason is given for failure to produce it. The same rule is usually applied where the original is already in evidence and no reason has been given for offering the copy. The practice has sometimes been followed in income tax cases, of placing the original return in evidence and then substituting a photostat with permission of the court where there has been no defense objection. IRC 7513 as amended provides for reproduction of returns and other documents, and covers use of the reproductions as follows:

"*In General.*—The Secretary or his delegate is authorized to have any Federal agency or person process films or other photo-impressions of any return, document, or other matter, and make reproductions from films or photo-impressions of any return document, or other matter."

"*Use of Reproductions*—Any reproduction of any return, document, or other matter made in accordance with this section shall have the same legal status as the original; and any such reproduction shall, if properly authenticated, be admissible in evidence in any judicial or administrative proceeding, as if it were the original, whether or not the original is in existence."

(2) A photographic or photostatic reproduction of a document may be admitted after evidence has been produced that the original cannot be obtained and that the reproduction is an exact and accurate copy. This principle has been followed where the original was in the hands of the defendant and its production could not be compelled by the Government. [*Zap v. U.S.; Lisanky v. U.S.*] It has further been held that a photograph of a promissory note taken because the writing was becoming faded and illegible was admissible in place of the illegible original. [*Duffin v. People*]

(3) When photostats of documents are obtained during an investigation they shall be initialed on the back, after comparison with the original, by the one who made the photostat or by the agent who obtained the document which was photostated. The date of such comparison shall be noted following the initial. The source of the original document shall be set out on the reverse of the photostat or on an initialed attachment or memorandum relating to each photostat or group of photostats covered by the one memorandum. This procedure will ensure proper authentication at a trial. A MULTI-STAMP Stencil Duplicator or other similar device may be used, on an optional basis, for placing such identifying data with the exception of the agent's initials. The special agent will personally affix his/her initials on such reproductions.

353.23 *(1-18-80)* 9781
Transcripts

Transcripts are copies of writings and are admissible under the same principles governing the admission of photographs or photostatic reproductions (text 353.22). A special agent shall take certain precautions in the preparation of transcripts to ensure proper authentication for their admission at a trial when the original documents are unavailable. The agent shall carefully compare the transcript with the original and certify that it is a correct transcript. The certification shall show the date that the transcript was made, by whom and where it was made, and the source from which it was taken. Each page shall be identified by the special agent to show that it forms part of the whole. A good practice is to show the total number of pages involved, as, page 1 of 5 pages. When a partial transcript is made it should be so indicated, for example, "excerpt from page 5 of the cash receipts book." In the Zacher case [*Zacher v. U.S.*] a Government agent was allowed to identify a transcript of the taxpayer's bank records, which the agent testified had been prepared by fellow agents under his/her direction, control, and supervision.

353.24 *(1-18-80)* 9781
Charts, Summaries and Schedules

(1) Charts and summaries prepared by examining agents may be placed in evidence at the discretion of the court if they are summaries of evidence previously admitted in a case. [*Conford v. U.S.; U.S. v. Doyle*] This is permitted as a matter of convenience to the court and jury. [*Schneck v. U.S.; U.S. v. Dave Beck*] At times such charts and summaries have been permitted in the jury room to aid in the jury's deliberations. [*Beaty v. U.S.; Steele v. U.S.*] Charts are particularly effective in net worth cases to summarize the details of the various items and computations upon which the additional income is based. [*Holland v. U.S.*] Summaries are frequently used to simplify the presentation of a great number of transactions upon which a specific item case is based. For example, in Eggleton v. U.S., involving the purchase and resale of 202 used automobiles, a schedule of those items showing the details of the transactions was admitted into evidence after the introduction of the pertinent records and testimony. However, care should be exercised in the preparation of charts and summaries to avoid prejudicial headings or titles. For example, a chart listing a series of unreported sales should not be entitled "Fraudulently Omitted Sales".

(2) A schedule prepared by the investigating agent from the taxpayer's books and records is admissible as secondary evidence of their contents. It should be properly certified and authenticated in a similar manner to that used for transcripts (text 353.23).

353.25 *(1-18-80)* 9781
Notes, Diaries, Workpapers, and Memorandums

Notes, diaries, workpapers, and memorandums made by examining agents during an investigation ordinarily are not considered evidence. [See text 323.7:(1).] However, they may be used on the witness stand or prior to testifying as an aid to recollection or may be introduced into evidence by the adverse party if they constitute impeaching evidence. Any documents used by a witness while on the stand are subject to inspection by the defense. They should always be carefully prepared to ensure that the whole truth is reflected because of their possible use in court. A further discussion of this subject is contained in Subsection 637.6–637.63.

353.26 *(1-18-80)* 9781
Proving Specific Transactions

(1) In proving specific transactions such as purchases and sales of real and personal property loans, encumbrances, and other commercial events, it is not enough for the special agent to obtain the written record of those transactions. Documents and recorded entries, no matter how honestly made, are not in themselves facts. They are written descriptions of events but are not in themselves proof of the events. Consequently, witnesses should be produced who will testify about the transactions and authenticate the documents. During the investigation, parties to the transactions should be questioned to determine whether the documents or entries truthfully relate all the facts, and that there are no additional facts or circumstances which have not been recorded. The following examples illustrate this principle:

(a) In the case of alleged unreported sales, the vendees should be interviewed to determine whether checks and invoices represent all the transactions with the taxpayer, whether the documents truthfully record the events, whether additional sums might have been paid or refunded, whether there were any other methods of payment or other parties to the transaction, and whether there is other relevant information.

(b) A contract of sale, settlement sheet, closing statement or recorded deed does not necessarily reflect all the facts involved in a real estate transaction. Currency payments over and above those shown in the instrument and nominees or other "straw parties" may be revealed through questioning the parties to the transaction. Mortgages and other encumbrances may not actually exist although recorded documents seem to evidence such facts. Proof of real estate transactions should therefore include the testimony of the parties involved.

(2) No question of admissibility is involved when different items of documentary evidence may be used to prove a fact. The only thing involved in such case is the weight of the evidence, which is determined by the jury in the same way as the weight of any other evidence placed before it. Thus, where the Government is trying to prove that a third party made purchases from the taxpayer, a canceled check of the third party to the order of the taxpayer will not be excluded from evidence merely because purchase invoices, purchase journals, or cash disbursements books of the party, although available, have not been produced. The fact that the check itself may not be the best proof of payment for a purchase is a factual question for the jury. However, complete documentation of every transaction should be obtained whenever possible.

353.3 *(1-18-80)* 9781
Official Records

353.31 *(1-18-80)* 9781
Statutory Provisions Regarding Official Records

The admissibility of official records and copies or transcripts thereof in Federal proceedings is covered by provisions of the United States Code and by rules of criminal and civil procedure.

353.32 *(1-18-80)* 9781
Authentication of Official Records

(1) The admissibility of official records and copies or transcripts thereof is provided for by the United States Code *(28 USC 1733)*, as follows:

> "(a) Books or records of account or minutes of proceedings of any department or agency of the United States shall be admissible to prove the act, transaction or occurence as a memorandum of which the same were made or kept.
>
> "(b) Properly authenticated copies or transcripts of any books, records, papers or documents of any department or agency of the United States shall be admitted in evidence equally with the originals thereof."

(2) The method of authentication of copies of Federal records is set forth in the Federal Rules of Civil Procedure [*28 USC Rule 44*] which is made applicable to criminal cases by Rule 27 of the Federal Rules of Criminal Procedure. Authentication of a copy of a Government record under these rules would consist of a certification by the officer having custody of the records and verification of the official status of the certifying officer by a Federal district judge over the seal of the court. Verification of the official status of District Directors is not required on authenticated copies of Internal Revenue Service documents certified to by District Directors over their seal of office. [*26 USC 7514*]

(3) Tax returns which have been filed, or certified copies of them, are admissible under Title 28, section 1733 as official records of the Internal Revenue Service. [*26 USC 6103*]. Procedures and types of forms for the certification of tax returns or other official records by District Directors are set forth in Chapter 800 of new IRM 1272, Disclosure of Official Information Handbook. Although tax returns or other official records are usually offered in evidence through a Service representative, authenticated copies are generally admissible without a representative.

(4) A Certificate of Assessments and Payments (Form 4340, for non-ADP returns) or a Computer Transcript (Form 4303, for ADP returns) is customarily offered in evidence through a representative of the Internal Revenue Service as a transcript of the records to which it relates. [*Vloutis v. U.S.*] These forms, properly authenticated in accordance with [*28 USC Rule 44*] are admissible without the presence of an Internal Revenue Service representative.

353.33 *(1-18-80)* 9781
Proof of Lack of Record

(1) It is sometimes desirable or necessary to prove that a search of official files has resulted in a finding that there is no record of a certain document. For example, in a prosecution for failure to file an income tax return, the Government, in addition to such oral testimony as it may introduce, may desire some documentary certification that a search had disclosed no record of such return. Rule 44(b) of the Federal Rules of Civil Procedure makes the following provision for this:

> "*Proof of Lack of Record.* A written statement signed by an officer having the custody of an official record or by his deputy that after diligent search no record or entry of a specified tenor is found to exist in the records of his office, accompanied by a certificate as above provided, is admissible as evidence that the records of his office contain no such record or entry."

(2) Procedures and a standard form for the certification of a lack of records by District and Service Center Directors are set forth in Section 850, IRM 1272.

353.34 *(1-18-80)* 9781
State and Territorial Statutes and Procedures

(1) The admissibility of copies of legislative acts of any State, Territory, or Possession of the United States and of court records and judicial proceedings, is provided for in the United States Code [*28 USC 1738*] as follows:

> "Such Acts, records and judicial proceedings or copies thereof, so authenticated, shall have the same full faith and credit in every court within the United States and its Territories and Possessions as they have by law or usage in the courts of such State, Territory or Possession from which they are taken."

(2) The procedures for authentication of the above records are recited in the same section of the Code.

(3) Nonjudicial records or books kept in any public office of any State, Territory, or Possession of the United States, or copies thereof, are made admissible by the United States Code [*28 USC 1739*] and given full faith and credit upon proper authentication.

354 *(9-8-80)* 9781
Receipt for Records and Documents

(1) It is sometimes desirable or necessary to examine a taxpayer's or witness' books, records, canceled checks, and other documents at the Internal Revenue office. The determining factors are the cooperation of the person submitting the records, the volume of documents, the need for photostats or transcripts, and other considerations depending on the individual case.

(2) A receipt must be issued in all instances where a special agent removes records or documents from the premises of a principal or witness by either legal process or agreement. (See IRM 9383.3:(7).) Form 2725 is a document receipt used for this purpose. A specimen document receipt and the general instructions for its preparation are contained in Exhibit 300-12. The hypothetical facts in Exhibit 300-12 coincide with those appearing in a summons illustration (Exhibit 300-14).

(3) The document receipt form assembly consists of two parts. The original, Form 2725, is issued to the person submitting the records, and the copy is retained in the special agent's case file. The substitution of a makeshift receipt may convey an impression of carelessness on the part of the issuing officer. Particularly in dealing with principals, an incomplete or improperly prepared receipt may lead to allegations that records were lost, mishandled, or obtained under improper circumstances. The consistent use and careful preparation of Form 2725 should reduce any possible areas of criticism arising from inadequate receipts. It should also help the issuing officer identify and authenticate records or documents during an investigation and any subsequent court proceedings.

(4) The reverse of the document receipt copy contains a history and custody of documents section. The completion of this section is not required for all documents received by special agents. It need only be prepared when a receipt is issued for records or other documents of a possible defendant.

(5) Many cases call for the circularization of a taxpayer's customers or suppliers by mail. The written requests generally involve a few, easily identified records or documents. Unless required by local instructions or individual circumstances, a receipt need not be issued to a witness who transmits the records or documents through the mail. Since an adequate record of the request for and return of the documents should appear in the correspondence file for each case, it would be impracticable and a duplication of effort to issue a receipt for every document received under circularization procedures. Although a receipt may not be necessary under these circumstances, proper identification and authentication of any photostats or transcripts should not be overlooked by the special agent.

355 *(1-18-80)* 9781
"Chain of Custody"

355.1 *(1-18-80)* 9781
Legal Requirements for "Chain of Custody"

"Chain of custody" is an expression usually applied to the preservation by its successive custodians of the instrument of a crime or any relevant writing in its original condition. Documents or other physical objects may be the instrumentalities used to commit a crime and are generally admissible as such. However, the trial judge must be satisfied that the writing or other physical object is in the same condition as it was when the crime was committed. Consequently, the witness through whom the instrument is sought to be introduced must be able to identify it as being in the same condition as when it was recovered. Special agents must therefore promptly identify and preserve in original condition all evidentiary matter that may be offered into evidence. This would particularly apply to records, documents and other paraphernalia seized in a raid.

355.2 *(1-18-80)* 9781
Identification of Seized Documentary Evidence

(1) In order that a seized document may be admissible as evidence, it is necessary to prove that it is the document that was seized and that it is in same condition as it was when seized. Since several persons may handle it in the interval between the seizure and the trial of the case, it should be adequately marked at the time of seizure for later identification, and its custody must be shown from that time until it is introduced in court.

(2) A special agent who seizes documents should at once identify them by some marking so that he/she can later testify that they are the documents seized, and that they are in the same condition as they were when seized. He/she may, for instance, put his/her initials and the date of seizure on the margin, in a corner or some other inconspicuous place on the front, or on the back of each document. If circumstances indicate that such marking may render the document subject to attack on the ground that it has been defaced or it is not in the same condition as when seized, the special agent may, after making a photostat or other copy for comparison or for use as an exhibit to his/her report, put the document into an envelope and write a description and any other identifying information on the face of the envelope.

356 *(1-18-80)* 9781
Questioned Documents

356.1 *(1-21-81)* 9781
Use and Application of Questioned Documents

(1) Modern crime detection techniques require an extensive use of scientific aids in order to obtain and establish proof of facts not otherwise obtainable. The identification of handwriting and typewriting is frequently of great importance in the investigation of cases. This is especially true when the case involves an anonymous letter, or when a successful solution depends upon determining whether a typewritten document was or was not prepared in a particular office and on a certain machine. Both handwriting and typewriting reflect individual characteristics under the precision instruments of the experts and are susceptible of definite identification and proof.

(2) Questioned document analysis is performed by the Midwest Region Document Laboratory. In addition, the facilities of the National Bureau of Standards and other Government laboratories, whose personnel include outstanding scientists in various fields of investigation are available.

(3) Documents should be forwarded by registered mail to the ARC (Criminal Investigation), Internal Revenue Service, 10th Floor, One N. Wacker Drive, Chicago, Illinois 60606, Attn: QD Laboratory. The requester, before forwarding documents, may wish to contact the document examiners by phone (FTS 886-5713) to determine what is necessary to ensure a complete and satisfactory examination. The accompanying memorandum should describe the documents to be examined, the type of examination required (e.g., handwriting analysis, alterations, ink dating, etc.), and the required completion date. If the Midwest Region Document Laboratory cannot process a request, they will arrange to have the work performed elsewhere.

(4) In some urgent situations an expeditious analysis may be necessary. In these instances, the Chief, CID will call the Special Enforcement Assistant, Midwest Region (who is the immediate supervisor of the Document Laboratory) to ascertain whether technical capabilities or workload will accommodate the urgency of the request. If the Midwest Region Document Laboratory is unable to perform the function for either reason, the Special Enforcement Assistant will grant permission and make arrangements for the analysis to be performed elsewhere. The Chief, CID will confirm approved telephonic request in writing by memorandum to the ARC (Criminal Investigation) Midwest Region.

356.2 *(1-18-80)* 9781

Definition of Questioned Document

A questioned document is one that has been questioned in whole or part with respect to its authenticity, identity, or origin. It may involve handwriting or typewriting comparison, determination of the age of documents and inks, and examination of erasures, obliterations, and overwriting.

356.3 *(1-18-80)* 9781

Standards for Comparison With Questioned Documents

(1) In addition to the questioned document, and in order that its authenticity, identity, origin, or relationship to some matter at issue may be determined, the special agent should secure and submit as many known samples, called exemplars, of the handwriting of the suspected person or the typewriting of the suspected machines, as may be needed for comparison purposes. These are referred to as standards for comparison.

(2) The Federal statutes [*28 USC 1731*] provide for comparison of handwriting standards, as follows:

> "The admitted or proved handwriting of any person shall be admissible, for purposes of comparison, to determine genuineness of other handwriting attributed to such person."

(3) Admissibility of handwriting specimens is determined in the first instance by the trial court, [*U.S. v. Angelo*] although the ultimate comparison is made by the jury. Little or no limitation has been placed by courts upon the nature of documents which may be admitted for this purpose. For instance, the signature of a defendant on a stipulation waiving jury trial was admitted for comparison of the signature with that which appeared on a document offered in evidence, in order to authenticate the document. [*Desimone v. U.S.*] In another case, [*Hardy v. U.S.*] where a defendant was on trial for theft of money and traveler's checks from a bank, the Government was permitted (after concealment of prejudicial portions) to introduce for comparison with his/her alleged endorsements of the traveler's checks, an instrument executed by him/her while an inmate at a Federal penitentiary.

(4) Generally, persons who have seen the defendant write, one or more times, or who are familiar with his/her handwriting from carrying on correspondence with him/her or from handling writings known to have been written by him/her, are competent as nonexperts to give opinions about the genuineness of a writing purported to be that of the defendant. [*Murray v. U.S.; Rinker v. U.S.; Rogers v. Ritter*]

(5) However, in a case where the Government attempted to introduce a bank signature card as a comparison specimen, the court held it to be a properly admissible basis for comparison, even though the witness who identified it was a bank clerk who had not seen the defendant sign the card nor even seen him/her write his name, but testified that the bank referred to the signature card when presented with checks drawn in the defendant's name. [*Woitte v. U.S.*]

(6) Although the statute does not cover comparison of typewriting standards, it would follow logically that any rule respecting handwriting standards would cover typewriting standards as well, and that known specimens would be admissible for such purpose.

356.4 *(1-21-81)* 9781

Handwriting Exemplars

(1) Whenever an agent becomes aware that the authenticity or origin of a document may be questioned, he/she should attempt to obtain handwriting exemplars of the parties involved.

(2) The summonsing of a taxpayer or other witness for the purpose of taking handwriting exemplars is within the authority of IRC 7602 [U.S. v. Euge]. This does not violate any Constitutional rights or policies enuciated by Congress. Compulsion of handwriting exemplars is neither a search or seizure subject to Fourth Amendment protections nor testimonial evidence protected by the Fifth Amendment privilege against self-incrimination. A handwriting exemplar is an identifying physical characteristic.

(3) To provide consistency among special agents in the taking of handwriting or handprinting exemplars, Form 6540, Handwriting or Handprinting Exemplars was developed. It's use is recommended when an agent believes a case will be presented to the Document Laboratory for examination. Ordinarily, all segments of Form 6540 should be utilized. Instructions are provided with the Form.

(4) Following is some general information regarding handwriting exemplars:

(a) The more numerous and lengthy the specimens, the better will be the opportunity for accurate comparison, and the less likely the possibility that the subject will succeed in disguising his/her writing if inclined to do so. It may therefore be advisable to obtain several specimens over a period of days and to have them include some of the more common words and expressions used in the questioned writing.

(b) For the best effect, the exemplars should duplicate the questioned document. It should be made with a similar writing instrument, on similar paper, and should include, as nearly as possible, the full content or text of the questioned writing.

(c) The agent should be alert to the possibility of disguises in handwriting. The most used forms of disguise are: writing unusually large or small; writing extremely fast or with painstaking slowness; backhand or other extreme changes in slant; or complicated embellishments or greatly simplified forms in a disconnected printing style. Requesting the subject to write at normal speed from dictation may be effective for elimination of disguise. If the questioned writing itself is disguised in whole or in part, specimens in a disguised hand may be useful.

(d) Since it may become necessary to establish proof as to whose handwriting, printing, or numerals appear on the books and records, the agent should try to obtain from the appropriate persons samples of writing, printing and numerals which would provide an adequate basis for comparison.

356.5 *(1-18-80)* 9781

Typewriting Exemplars

(1) With respect to typewriting, it is advisable to furnish sets of impressions of all the characters on the keyboard, typed with light, medium, and heavy touch, and at varying rates of speed, to bring out the technical irregularities. The various manufacturers of typewriters have aimed at a certain individuality in their machines and from time to time have made changes in the design, size and proportions of the type and spacing. These serve not only to identify the make of machine used, but to determine that its serial number falls within a certain series. In the ordinary course of use, each machine undergoes deterioration. The type bars lose their vertical and horizontal relationship to each other. Defects and imperfections appear in the type faces of the result of collisions and wear. The spacing mechanism may develop irregularities. These factors impart to each typewriter an individuality which serves to distinguish it from all others and makes positive identification possible.

(2) Exemplars should be made with the ribbon found on the machine and should repeat the complete text of the questioned matter. If the text is extensive, enough of it should be repeated to give all the important letters, figures, and the ribbon adjustment set on stencil, in order to get impressions of type with smallest possible masking. The presence of type scar observed in ribbon specimens should be confirmed by carbon specimens.

356.6 *(1-18-80)* 9781

Other Exemplars

In proving erasures, alterations, overwritings, blotter impressions, or determining the age of a questioned writing or document, exemplars ordinarily are not involved. Through the use of infrared light technique, microscopes, ultraviolet light, and chemicals the laboratory can resolve many questions about a document. However, exemplars have on occasion been used to aid in the determination of the age of documents. Standards for comparison consisted of documents allegedly existing at the time of the questioned document. Comparison of inks, water marks, condition of paper, and other characteristics provides clues to the age of the questioned document. Although pencil notations cannot ordinarily be examined for age, the condition of the material upon which the notations were made might be indicative of the time of writing.

356.7 *(1-18-80)* 9781

Identifying Exemplars and Questioned Documents

(1) Having obtained the necessary numbers and kinds of exemplars, the special agent should initial and date them on the back so that he/she can identify them for use at a trial. He/she must secure the questioned document, care for it properly, transmit it along with the exemplars to the expert, and maintain the chain of custody until it is produced in court.

(2) Questioned document examiners make examinations and analyses of documents to give assurance of genuineness, to detect evidence of erasure, alteration, addition, interpolation, forgery of signature, identity of handwriting and typewriting and to develop information concerning ink, paper, writing instrument and other materials involved in these problems. Examiners prepare reports of their observations and conclusions, as well as, testify in court as expert witnesses.

(3) Whenever possible, a special agent desiring examination and analysis of a document should send the original rather than a photostat. This is to make sure that the examiner can properly analyze all characteristics of the document, including the writing, the instrument used, and the paper upon which the writing was done.

(4) Questioned document analysis is performed by the Midwest Region Document Laboratory. In addition, the facilities of the National Bureau of Standards and other Government laboratories, whose personnel include outstanding scientists in various fields of investigation are available. If the Midwest Region Document Laboratory cannot process a request, they will arrange to have the work performed elsewhere. Documents should be forwarded by registered mail to the ARC (Compliance), Internal Revenue Service, 10th Floor, One N. Wacker Drive, Chicago, Illinois 60606, Attn: QD Laboratory. The requester, before forwarding documents, may wish to contact the document examiners by phone to determine what is necessary to ensure a complete and satisfactory examination. The accompanying memorandum should describe the documents to be examined, the type of examination required (e.g., handwriting analysis, alterations, ink dating, etc.), and the required completion date.

(5) In some urgent situations an expeditious analysis may be necessary. In these instances, the Chief, CID will call the Special Enforcement Assistant, Midwest Region (who is the immediate supervisor of the Document Laboratory) to ascertain whether technical capabilities or workload will accommodate the urgency of the request. If the Midwest Region Document Laboratory is unable to perform the function for either reason, the Special Enforcement Assistant will grant permission and make arrangements for the analysis to be performed elsewhere. The Chief, CID will confirm approved telephonic request in writing by memorandum to the ARC (Compliance) Midwest Region.

357 *(1-18-80)* 9781
Record Retention Requirements

357.1 *(1-18-80)* 9781
General

(1) Except for farmers and wage-earners, any person subject to income tax or required to file an information return of income must keep permanent books of account or records, including inventories, to establish their gross income, deductions, credits or other matters for tax or information return purposes. Farmers and wage-earners whose gross income includes salaries, wages or similar compensation are required to keep records which will enable the District Director to determine the correct amount of such income subject to tax. They need not keep the permanent books of account or records required of others. [*26 USC 6001*]

(2) Required books or records should be available at all times for inspection by authorized internal revenue officers or employees and should be retained as long as the contents may become material in administering any internal revenue law. Employment tax records must be kept for four years after the due date of such tax or the date such tax is paid, whichever is later. [*26 USC 6001*]

357.2 *(1-18-80)* 9781
Record Requirement Guidelines for ADP Systems

(1) Taxpayers who maintain their records on an automated accounting system are required to provide for a program [*Rev. Proc. 64-12 I.R.B. 1964-8.*] which:

(a) writes out general and subsidiary ledger balances (such as accounts receivable, accounts payable, inventories and fixed assets) at regular intervals;

(b) makes supporting documents, including invoices vouchers and general journal vouchers, readily available to the Internal Revenue Service upon request;

(c) makes clear and concise logical procedural directives available for examination, including procedural audit trails, up-to-date operation logs and flow charts and block diagrams of all equipment operations;

(d) provides adequate record retention facilities for storing tapes, print-outs and supporting documents for the time required for record retention in accordance with IRC of 1954 and current regulations. Such facilities also should allow reasonably easy access to listings and records required for examination purposes.

(2) Taxpayers who cannot provide for the above records within their ADP system must provide sufficient records outside the system to meet the Internal Revenue Service requirements.

357.3 *(1-18-80)* 9781
Inadequate Records

(1) If, during a joint investigation relating to an income tax liability, it is determined that the taxpayer has failed to comply substantially with the provisions of the law and regulations in maintaining necessary records, the cooperating internal revenue agent will orally inform the taxpayer thereof. The special agent will determine the appropriate time during the investigation to inform the taxpayer of the inadequacies of his/her records so as not to adversely affect the development of the investigation nor prejudice the criminal potential of the case.

(2) The cooperating revenue agent will include in the transmittal letter of his/her examination report a clear concise statement specifying in what respects the taxpayer's records are inadequate. The statement will be the basis for issuance of an inadequate records letter notice to the taxpayer; however, the time of issuance of the letter notice to the taxpayer must be approved by the special agent so as not to adversely affect the investigation nor prejudice the criminal case.

(3) If prosecution is recommended by the special agent, the special agent will make reference in the final report to the statement in the revenue agent's transmittal letter regarding the inadequacy of records and will indicate whether an inadequate records letter notice was issued to the taxpayer. (See IRM 4297 for Examination Division procedure respecting the issuance of the inadequate records letter notice to the taxpayer.)

(4) See also IRM 9552.

357.4 *(1-18-80)* 9781
Criminal Penalties

See Handbook text 415.24.

360 *(1-18-80)* 9781
Summons

361 *(1-18-80)* 9781
Provisions of Law

(1) The provisions of the law relating to the use and enforcement of a summons are contained in the following sections of the Internal Revenue Code of 1954:

(a) IRC 7602—Examination of Books and Witnesses;

(b) IRC 7603—Service of Summons;

(c) IRC 7604—Enforcement of Summons;

(d) IRC 7605—Time and Place of Examination;

(e) IRC 7609—Special Procedures for Third-Party Summonses;

(f) IRC 7610—Fees and Costs for Witnesses;

(g) IRC 7622—Authority to Administer Oaths and Certify;

(h) IRC 7402—Jurisdiction of District Courts;

(i) IRC 7210—Failure to Obey Summons; and

(j) IRC 6420(e)(2), 6421(f)(2), 6424(d)(2), and 6427(g)(2) (gasoline, lubricating oil, and fuel credits).

(2) The Federal law prevails over state law, statutory or constitutional, and the state law, if in conflict, must yield. [*Falsone v. U.S.*] The words in the statute must be interpreted liberally to fulfill the purpose for which it was enacted. [*U.S. v. Third Northwestern National Bank, 102 F. Supp. 879 D.C. Minn., 52-1 USTC 9302.*] The power granted by the statute is inquisitorial in character and is comparable to that vested in grand juries. [*Falsone v. U.S.*]

362 *(1-18-80)* 9781
Authority To Issue a Summons

(1) The authority to issue a summons, examine records, and take testimony granted to the Secretary or the Secretary's delegate by IRC 7602 has been granted to the Commissioner of Internal Revenue by T.D. 6118, approved December 30, 1954, published in the Federal Register on December 31, 1954 (19 FR 9896), and in turn granted to special agents as well as various other Service employees by Delegation Order No. 4 (As Revised) (Exhibit 300-13). Administrative regulations published in the Federal Register must be judicially noticed. (See 323.4.)

(2) Third party summonses require advanced personal authorization by the issuing officer's case manager, group manager, or any supervisory official above that level. Such authorization shall be indicated either by the signature of the authorizing official on the face of the original and all copies of the summons or by a statement (on the face of the original and all copies of the summons) signed by the issuing officer that he/she had prior authorization to issue the summons. The statement shall include the date of authorization and the name and title of the authorizing official. See Delegation Order No. 4, as revised (Exhibit 300-13).

(3) "John Doe" summonses may be issued by The Chief, Criminal Investigation, only after obtaining pre-issuance legal review by District Counsel and a court order. (See Text 367.591).

(4) The Supreme Court has held that, although the investigation may result in a recommendation that a criminal prosecution be instituted against the taxpayer, an internal revenue summons may be issued under IRC 7602 in aid of an income tax investigation if it is issued in good faith and prior to a recommendation for criminal prosecution. [*Donaldson v. U.S.*]

363 *(1-18-80)* 9781
Considerations Regarding Issuance of Summons

(1) A special agent should use his/her best efforts to obtain information voluntarily from taxpayers and witnesses. If a person is uncertain that he/she should comply with the agent's oral request, his/her consent may often be obtained by acquainting him/her with the provisions of the Internal Revenue Code as printed on the reverse side of Form 2039A.

(2) When a taxpayer or a witness refuses to submit requested information, all surrounding circumstances should be fully considered before a summons is issued. The likely importance of the desired information should be carefully weighed against the time and expense of obtaining it, the probability of having to institute court action, and the adverse effect on voluntary compliance by others if the enforcement efforts are not successful.

(3) No set of specific, all-inclusive guidelines can be prescribed to be followed in all instances. Each situation must be analyzed in the

light of its particular and peculiar facts and circumstances. In this, there is no substitute for good judgment. Consideration must be given to the legal problems of enforcement, the problems of future cooperation of others, and the practical problem of obtaining the desired information and using the person summoned as a witness in subsequent criminal or civil proceedings.

(4) Pertinent law to be considered respecting the issuance of a summons to an individual taxpayer or member of a partnership is covered in 342.1-342.21.

364 *(1-8-80)* 9781
Preparation of Summons (Form 2039)

(1) The Form 2039 summons assembly is the form assembly to be used by all persons authorized to issue a summons under the provisions of IRC 7602.

(2) The Form 2039 summons assembly consists of five parts, as follows:

(a) *Original* (Form 2039)—"Summons," with the "Certificate of Service of Summons and Notice" on the reverse side;

(b) *Part A* (Form 2039-A)—"Summons" (first attested copy), with a reprint of pertinent IRC provisions on the reverse side;

(c) *Part B* (Form 2039-B)—"Notice to Third-party Recipient of IRS Summons";

(d) *Part C* (Form 2039-C)—"Summons" (second attested copy), with a reprint of pertinent IRC provisions on the reverse side; and

(e) *Part D* (Form 2039-D)—notice explaining the rights to stay compliance and intervene, with a reprint of IRC 7609 on the reverse side.

(3) The faces of the first attested copy (Form 2039-A) and the second attested copy (Form 2039-C) shall be exact copies of the face of the original (Form 2039), except for the preprinted annotations and form numbers.

(4) Special care must be exercised to prepare a summons in accordance with the legal requirements. Therefore, the summons will be prepared in compliance with the instructions contained in Exhibit 300-14.

365 *(1-18-80)* 9781
Service of Summons

(1) A summons should be served in accordance with the provisions of IRC 7603, which are set forth in Exhibit 300-14. Briefly, Form 2039A should be handed to the person to whom it is directed, or left at his/her last and usual place of abode in the place where the person summoned will be most likely to find it. Casual "on the spot" preparation and service of the summons should be avoided where possible. The same seriousness and dignity as that attendant to giving information about the constitutional right against self-incrimination should be present. The impact and value would be diluted by casualness and might encourage defiance and noncompliance.

(2) It is preferable to serve the copy of the summons upon the person to whom it is directed. If he/she cannot be readily located, efforts should be made to serve it at his/her last and usual place of abode upon some responsible person who is 16 years of age or older, with instruction that it be given to the person summoned. This procedure will probably result in better compliance than that of merely leaving a copy at the last place of residence.

(3) After completion of the certificate of service, Form 2039 should be placed in the administrative file in the office of the issuing division to be used as the basis for enforcing compliance if such is necessary.

(4) When a witness requests that he/she be served with a summons as evidence of his/her legal duty to produce records or testify and indicates that he/she will voluntarily comply therewith, it should be issued for such purpose (see Policy Statement P-4-2). The summons should be properly prepared and the required notice given, if appropriate (see IRM 9368).

(5) If information requested by a summons is later determined to be unnecessary, compliance with the summons may be waived by the issuing official, provided the summons has not been referred for enforcement. If the summons has been referred for enforcement, concurrence of the Counsel office handling the summons enforcement must be obtained before compliance may be waived.

(6) Witness fees and payments for mileage may be made to all summoned witnesses, whether the witness be a third-party witness, the taxpayer, or the taxpayer's representative (see text 368.2). Reimbursement for search, reproduction, and transportation costs may be made to summoned witnesses other than the taxpayer or an officer, employee, agent, accountant, or attorney of the taxpayer, who, at the time the summons is served, is acting as such. If the person summoned is a third party entitled to reimbursement for search, reproduction, and transportation costs (see text 369), he/she will be given the notice explaining the payment procedures (Form 2039-B). If this information is inapplicable, Form 2039-B should be discarded.

(7) If the summons is served on a third-party recordkeeper and the noticee is entitled to notice of its issuance (see IRM 9368), the second attested copy (Form 2039-C) will be provided to the noticee by the officer serving the summons along with the notice (Form 2039-D) explaining the rights to stay compliance and intervene. If more than one person is entitled to notice of the issuance of summons, the summons and notice may be reproduced to provide such notification. This would occur, for example, in a situation where a bank account is listed in two names even if the two persons reside at the same address.

(8) If the summons is not served on a third-party recordkeeper or notice is not required, the second attested copy (Form 2039-C) and the notice (Form 2039-D) should be discarded.

366 *(1-18-80)* 9781

Time and Place of Examination

(1) The time and place of examination must be reasonable under the circumstances. [26 USC 7605(a)] The date fixed for appearance must be not less than 10 days from the date of a summons issued under the provisions of paragraph (2) of IRC 7602, [26 USC 7605(a)] but the witness may voluntarily comply at an earlier time.

(2) If the prospective witness is cooperative and an affidavit rather than a question and answer statement is desired, the summons should be made returnable, if feasible, at the place that will best suit his/her convenience. The same practice should be followed respecting the examination of records. If a question and answer statement is needed and reference to the witness' records will be essential it may be preferable for the Service stenographer to appear at the office of the witness when interrogated.

(3) If the witness is uncooperative or attempts to hamper the investigation it may be advisable to have him/her produce his/her records at the agent's office. However, this should not be done to penalize the witness. A revenue agent's office, 25 miles away, was held to be a proper place for an estimated 4 months' examination of a corporation's records when its officers and employees interfered with the agent's examination. [*U.S. v. United Distillers Products Corp.*]

367 *(1-18-80)* 9781

Examination of Books and Witnesses

367.1 *(1-18-80)* 9781

Persons Who May Be Summoned

(1) A summons may be issued to:

(a) The person liable for tax or required to perform the act;

(b) Any officer or employee of such person;

(c) Any person having possession, custody, or care of books of account containing entries relating to the business of such person; or

(d) Any other person the issuing officer deems proper. [26 USC 7602]

367.2 *(8-13-81)* 9781

Purpose of Examination

(1) A summons may be issued for the purpose of examining books and records of taxpayers and third parties and obtaining testimony under oath that may be relevant or material in:

(a) Ascertaining the correctness of any return,

(b) Making a return where none has been made,

(c) Determining a tax liability, or

(d) Collecting such liability. [26 USC 7602]

(2) A summons cannot be issued for any other purpose, such as: a grand jury investigation; a personnel examination; an enrollment case; an investigation of perjury or false statements, if not related to tax matters; a current year tax investigation, if a return has not been filed and is not due. However, if a taxpayer's current year is closed on jeopardy, a summons

may be issued if a determination of his/her tax liability is involved.

(3) A summons may properly be issued in aid of internal revenue investigations which have a civil purpose, notwithstanding the fact that the information might also be used in a criminal prosecution. [*Donaldson v. U.S.; Boren v. Tucker; Venn v. U.S.*] A summons may not be issued solely for a criminal purpose. [*U.S. v. LaSalle National Bank*]. Although a summons may be issued after a search warrant has been obtained and executed in a case involving the same taxpayer [*United States v. First National Bank of Atlanta; United States v. Zack*], a summons is not proper after the case is referred for criminal prosecution; if an institutional commitment to make a referral for criminal prosecution has been made; or if the Service has abandoned, in an institutional sense, the pursuit of a civil tax determination or the collection of that tax. [*U.S. v. LaSalle National Bank*].

(4) The right to examine carries with it a right to make photostatic copies, at least where there is a need for a handwriting analysis. [*Boren v. Tucker*]

(5) The purpose of a summons is not limited to obtaining records for what the Government already knows, therefore the Government is permitted to indulge in some "fishing." [*U.S. v. Third Northwestern National Bank*] The inquiry cannot amount to an inquisition or arbitrary inquiry on the part of the tax investigators. A reasonable basis for making the inquiry must exist. What is justifiable "fishing" will be determined from all the facts in each case including the end for which the information is sought. The investigation must not be an unreasonable burden on the third party whose records are sought. [*U.S. v. Third Northwestern National Bank*]

367.3 *(1-18-80)* 9781
Limitations on Authority of Summons

367.31 *(1-18-80)* 9781
Materiality and Relevancy

(1) The examination must bear upon matters required to be included in the returns under examination. [First National Bank of Mobile] The courts have held examinations to be unwarranted when conducted for ulterior purposes, such as to obtain evidence to aid the Government in defense of a suit by a taxpayer for an overpayment of taxes for a year previously examined by the Service, [*Pacific Mills v. Kenefick*] to aid the Department of Justice in the criminal prosecution of a taxpayer under indictment following the completion of a special agent's investigation and the submission of his report, (although indictment brought to prevent bar by statute of limitations after prolonged resistance to summons previously served, does not render the summons unenforceable) and to use in investigating the tax liabilities of unknown and unidentified persons who may have failed to report their income. However, a corporation was required to submit records showing names and addresses of its customers, since inquiring of them should enable the Service to ascertain what they paid the taxpayer corporation for services rendered. [In Re International Corp. Co.; *Miles v. United Founders Corp.*] Having obtained their names and addresses, the Service could then examine their tax liabilities, if it so desired.

(2) The requirement for showing relevancy was not satisfied where the summons was couched in general terms and did not specify the particular documents desired, [*Local 174, etc. v. U.S.*] or where it called for a bank to produce all books, papers and records of whatever nature, irrespective of whether they also pertained to similar transactions with persons other than the named taxpayer, [*First National Bank of Mobile v. U.S.*] and where there was nothing more than the mere declaration of the special agent respecting the relevancy of a particular document. [*Hubner v. Tucker*]

367.32 *(1-18-80)* 9781
Examinations Barred by Statute of Limitations

(1) The statute does not require the Service to show probable cause to suspect fraud. [*U.S. v. Max Powell; Bayard Edward Ryan v. U.S.*] Where a special agent has served a summons covering a closed year, the Government need only show, to obtain enforcement: a legitimate purpose; that the inquiry may be relevant to that purpose; and that it does not already have the information; and that if the records have already been examined, written notice of additional examination has been given the taxpayer.

(2) A taxpayer seeking to prevent enforcement of a summons on the ground that it covers closed years has the burden of showing that it would be an abuse of court process. The taxpayer does not satisfy that burden by merely showing that the statute of limitations has run or that the records have already been examined. [*U.S. v. Max Powell; Bayard Edward Ryan v. U.S.*]

367.33 *(1-18-80)* 9781
Statutory Restriction on Summons

(1) The principal statutory restriction placed on the power to summon and to examine a taxpayer's books of account is found in IRC 7605(b), which provides that no taxpayer shall be subjected to unnecessary examination or investigations and that only one inspection shall be made of his/her books for each taxable year, except upon notice from the Commissioner or upon the taxpayer's request. See Delegation Order 57, as revised.

(2) Authority has been delegated to each District Director to sign the notice to the taxpayer that an additional inspection of his/her books of account is necessary. [IRM 9324.4:(2)]

(3) The limitations imposed by IRC 7605(b) apply only to the taxpayer under investigation and not to a third party. [*Hubner v. Tucker*] The taxpayer may refuse access to his/her records until he/she is given the notice of demand in writing. [*Philip Mangone Co. v. U.S.*] However, after his/her records have been examined respecting his/her own liability, he/she cannot refuse on the ground of an unnecessary examination, to give information from them, concerning another taxpayer. [*Hubner v. Tucker*]

(4) Whether enforcement of summons to examine records will be prohibited as unnecessary is a question to be determined from the facts in each case. A court may refuse enforcement if an agent attempts to examine unrelated transactions or engage in an "irrelevant fishing expedition." [*Zimmerman v. Wilson*] (See Subsections 241.34 and 351.3.)

367.34 *(1-18-80)* 9781
Constitutional Rights of Persons Summoned

Stated generally, the Fifth Amendment to the Constitution provides that no person shall be compelled to be a witness against himself/herself. As regards the privilege against self-incrimination, information or evidence furnished voluntarily by an individual taxpayer or witness who has been summoned may be used even though of an incriminatory nature. The mere fact that a taxpayer or witness would not have appeared before an agent but for the summons does not mean that his/her testimony or evidence was given under compulsion and is therefore inadmissible. Although the individual is required by summons to appear before an agent, the question is whether it can be shown that the individual was not thereafter compelled to testify as to incriminatory matters. While a warning of consitituional privilege against self-incrimination may not be required as a matter of law, such warning may have substantial significance from an evidentiary standpoint in overcoming a contention that the testimony or information was given involuntarily, under compulsion. Accordingly, the procedures outlined in IRM 9384 will be followed to ensure advice to possible subjects of investigation as to their constitutional rights. A witness who contends that the testimony or information was given involuntarily, under compulsion, has the burden of sustaining that contention.

367.35 *(1-18-80)* 9781
Privileged Communications and Summons

In some situations, witnesses, particularly attorneys, may decline to submit information on the ground that it is a privileged communication. This subject is covered in text 344.

367.36 *(1-18-80)* 9781
Destruction of Records Summoned

Witnesses whose records have been summoned by The Service are required to exercise a duty of care to safeguard the records to they will be available when they are required to be produced. (In Re D.I. Operating Co.; U.S. v. Boudreaux; U.S. v. Edmond). If the special agent has reason to believe that destruction is likely, it may be appropriate to draft a letter advising the witness of the requirements of the law regarding the preservation of summoned records.

367.4 *(1-18-80)* 9781
Taxpayer—Records and Testimony

367.41 *(1-18-80)* 9781
General

Inquiries of a taxpayer are "strictly inquisitorial, justifiable because all the facts are in the taxpayer's hands." [*Bolich v. Rubel*] The taxpayer cannot determine which of his/her books and papers are relevant to an investigation of his/her tax liability. That is for the Service to decide, at least initially. [In Re International Corp. Co.] All of a taxpayer's records of financial transactions for the period involved or for the periods which are reasonably relevant are pertinent to a verification of his/her returns. [In Re International Corp. Co.] Accordingly, a taxpayer cannot refuse to submit records on the ground that it is a tax exempt organization [*U.S. v. Stiles*] or that the income earned while residing in a foreign country is not taxable. [Application of Carroll] Neither can he/she refuse, on the grounds of the Fourth or Fifth Amendments, to appear in response to a summons requiring him to testify or produce records. He/she must make the appearance, after which he/she may refuse, on Constitutional grounds, to show records or to answer specific questions. See text 342.12:(1) and (2).

367.42 *(1-18-80)* 9781
Taxpayer's Records in Possession of Others

367.421 *(1-18-80)* 9781
Taxpayer's Records Voluntarily Turned Over to Others

Since the taxpayer's privilege not to surrender his/her books and records is personal, it has been held that an individual taxpayer's records can be obtained by summons when in the independent possession of third parties, including the taxpayer's accountant [*Falsone v. U.S.; Couch v. U.S.*] or attorney, if the latter merely performs clerical or financial service. [*U.S. v. Chin Lim Mow*] Generally, an attorney cannot refuse to produce workpapers prepared and delivered to him/her by the taxpayer's accountant, since they remain the property of the accountant and are not privileged, although one reported case has held to the contrary. [In re House.] However, it has been held that a warehouse in which an individual stored his records was a mere custodian without personal rights in them, and that the individual retained constructive possession and control, entitling him to contest enforcement of a grand jury subpoena for their production on the ground that it violated his constitutional rights. [*Schwimmer v. U.S.*]

367.422 *(1-18-80)* 9781
Taxpayer's Records Involuntarily Turned Over to Others

A person cannot successfully resist the production of his/her records where another obtains possession and control by operation and due proceedings of law. [In re Fuller.] Thus, a taxpayer's records have been obtained from a referee in bankruptcy, [In re Fuller.] a Federal court where they had been impounded, [*Perlman v. U.S.*] a State attorney general, who obtained them by subpoenas, [*Fuller v. U.S.*] a thief, [*Burdeau v. McDowell*] a clerk of a State Court, [*Davis v. U.S.*] a Federal prison official, [*Stroud v. U.S.*] and U.S. Customs agents. [*Nero v. U.S.*]

367.5 *(1-18-80)* 9781
Summons on Third Parties—Records and Testimony

367.51 *(1-18-80)* 9781
General

(1) A third party witness need not produce a summoned document unless it is in his/her possession and relevant to the tax liability of the person named, or material to the inquiry. [*Local 174 etc. v. U.S.*] In addition, the witness may claim his/her individual right against self-incrimination, (text 343.2) and the demand for records must not be unreasonable or oppressive. [*Hubner v. Tucker*] However, after service of summons, deliberately divesting oneself of possession of documents to avoid production will not excuse the noncompliance. In fact, persons summoned to produce records, who conspire to conceal them and falsely state that they have been stolen, may be prosecuted under 18 USC 1001 for making false statements and 18 USC 1503 for obstructing justice. [*U.S. v. Curcio*]

(2) In a fraud case, a test as to whether the examination would impose an unreasonable burden is whether the facts show a reasonable ground of suspicion or probable cause for the examination to ascertain if there has been a fraud. [*U.S. v. Third Northwestern Natl. Bank*] The burden upon the third party must be considered in relation to the expected degree of success in finding documents bearing upon the tax liability of the taxpayer being investigated. If the third party must do considerable work at his/her own expense to supply the requested information, the performance of such a task can be made reasonable and brought within the scope of the statute only if there is some proof of a likelihood that among the many records to be checked will be papers relevant to the tax liability of a particular taxpayer. [*U.S. v. Third Northwestern Natl. Bank*]

(3) Courts have stated that if the Service can meet the foregoing test, a summons will be enforced even though the third party's task of searching and examining may require 10 or 15 days, [*U.S. v. Third Northwestern Natl. Bank*] or may involve several thousand items. [*First Natl. Bank of Mobile v. U.S.*]

(4) The taxpayer cannot prohibit the production of a third party's records, since the privilege is personal to the owner of the records, [*Zimmerman v. Wilson; Grant Foster v. U.S.*] and the third party cannot assert the privilege of self-incrimination on behalf of the taxpayer, since such a defense is personal to the one making the claim. [*Hale v. Henkel*]

(5) The ten-day waiting period provided by IRC 7605(a) is for the benefit of the person to whom the summons is directed. The taxpayer has no standing to object to a waiver of this provision. [*Brunwasser v. Pittsburgh National Bank*]

(6) In Reisman v. Caplin a taxpayer's attorneys attempted on his behalf to restrain enforcement of a summons served by a special agent on accountants retained by the attorneys to assist them in their clients' defense. The Supreme Court stated that a person affected by disclosure (taxpayer), as well as the person summoned, may appear or intervene before the District Court or hearing officer (special agent) to challenge the summons, and that for this reason the injunction suit was improper.

(7) The Supreme Court held that an individual has no right to intervene in a summons proceeding where the summons was directed to a third person and had to do with records in which the taxpayer has no proprietary interest, which are owned and possessed by the third person and which related to the third person's business transactions with the taxpayer. [*Donaldson v. U.S.*]

367.52 *(1-18-80)* 9781
Summons on Banks

367.521 *(1-18-80)* 9781
General

Banks are one of the major groups on which continuous demands for information are made. The depositor has no proprietary interest in the bank's books and records and the bank cannot refuse production of its records on the basis that some of the entries relate to transaction of persons other than the designated taxpayer. [*Cooley v. Bergin*] On the other hand, a bank will not be required to produce all its records so that the Service can determine whether any of them contain information relating to a return under investigation. [*First Nat'l. Bank of Mobile v. U.S.*]

367.522 *(1-18-80)* 9781
Summons on Foreign Branch Banks

A summons on a bank to produce records of one of its foreign branches is enforceable unless compliance would constitute a violation of the laws of the foreign country. [*The First National City Bank of New York v. Internal Revenue Service;* In re Rivera] The basis for compelling production of records is that a bank, like any other corporation, is presumed to be in possession and control of its own books and records. The First National City Bank case states:

> "Any officer or agent of the corporation who has power to cause the branch records to be sent from a branch to the home office for any corporate purpose, surely has sufficient control to cause them to be sent on when desired for a government purpose properly implemented by a subpoena under 26 USC 7602."

367.523 *(1-18-80)* 9781
Summons On Domestic Branches of Foreign Banks

(1) The United States courts have jurisdiction over a domestic branch of a foreign corporation and over its records located in this country (text 367.53). Accordingly, a subpoena issued by an administrative agency was enforced for production of records in the possession of the domestic branch of a foreign nonbanking corporation. [*Securities & Exchange Commission v. Minas De Artemisa*] On the other hand, a court subpoena issued to a New York City branch of a Canadian bank was enforced only for production of records in that branch, but not for records in a branch located in Canada. [*U.S. v. Kyle*] In refusing to compel production of the Canadian branch records, the court held that the records of the Canadian branch were not under the control of the New York branch office.

(2) If the domestic branch sends its records to the foreign bank for storage, the domestic branch may have relinquished control over such records. The question whether summons for such records served on the foreign bank as a corporate entity could be enforced would depend upon whether the foreign bank or a corporation "resides in or can be found in this coun-

try" for the service of a summons and judicial process. This determination requires a close analysis of the relationship between the foreign bank and its domestic branch—a matter which the special agent should refer to his/her group manager.

367.53 *(1-18-80)* 9781
Summons for Records of Foreign Companies

(1) The determination whether a foreign corporation must produce its records for inspection by the Service and other Federal agencies depends in general on whether it is found doing business in this country or has an agent doing business here. [In Re Grand Jury Subpena Duces Tecum.]

(2) A foreign corporation was required to comply with a grand jury subpeona (the summons power of the Internal Revenue Service is comparable to the subpoena power of a Federal grand jury) [*Brownson v. U.S.*] or summons in instances where:

(a) It had a bank account and salaried employees here and shipped newsprint into this country. [In Re Grand Jury Subpena Duces Tecum, *supra*]

(b) It was found to be doing business through wholly owned subsidiaries, in this country. [In Re Electric & Music Industries, Ltd.]

(c) The corporate president, who was served with a subpoena, conducted all of the business of a Mexican corporation, except the actual operation of its mines, from his home in Arizona. The corporate records were in Mexico, but the court pointed out that if the Mexican law forbade their removal to this country the Commission (S.E.C.) could inspect them at the Mexican office or have authenticated copies made and submitted. [*Securities & Exchange Commission v. Minas De Artemisa*]

(3) The president of a nonresident Panamanian corporation was ordered to produce the corporation's records in his possession and control pursuant to a summons served on him in New York, on the theory that it was directed to him as an individual and not to the corporation which might not have been amenable to service of process. [*International Commodities Corp. v. Internal Revenue Serv.*] However, where such records are held in a purely personal capacity, their production may be successfully resisted on the ground of possible self-incrimination. [Application of Daniels]

367.54 *(1-18-80)* 9781
Other Third Parties

(1) The courts have enforced compliance with summonses or subpoenas calling for the production of records by various third parties, [*Falsone v. U.S.*] including accountant's workpapers, attorney's files, involving agency or record keeping matters, [*Pollock v. U.S.*] hospital records, excluding nature of illness, broker's records, [*Zimmerman v. Wilson*] telegraph records, [*Brownson v. U.S.*] records of large impersonal partnerships, relating to a partner's transactions, [*U.S. v. Onassis;* In Re Subpena Duces Tecum.] and records of an unincorporated labor union concerning transactions of its officers. [*U.S. v. White*]

(2) The dissolution of a corporation will not relieve its officers of the duty of producing its existing records within their control. [*Curcio v. U.S.*]

367.55 *(1-18-80)* 9781
Use of Summons—Special Applications

367.551 *(1-18-80)* 9781
Use of Summons to Obtain Information Concerning the Finances of a Political Organization

(1) For purposes of this text, the term "political organization" includes a political party, a National, State, or local committee of a political party, and campaign committees or other organizations that accept contributions or make expenditures for the purpose of influencing the selection, nomination, or election of any individual for elective public office. The term "political organization" does not include an organization to which the taxpayer is the only contributor.

(2) For purposes of this text, information concerning the finances of a political organization includes testimony or documents that disclose the identity of contributors or recipients of expenditures.

(3) Except as provided in (5) below, a summons will not be used to obtain testimony or documents requiring a general disclosure of the finances of a political organization. If the information sought by a summons would generally disclose the finances of a political organization, this restriction applies even though the testimony is to be obtained from, or the documents are owned or possessed by, a source that is not a political organization. For example, a summons to a bank for all of its records of the bank accounts of a political organization is within the coverage of this text.

(4) A summons may be used to obtain testimony or documents concerning the finances of a political organization provided that compliance with the summons would not require a general disclosure of the finances. Such a summons will be restricted to information relating to the tax liability of named taxpayers under examination or investigation. The summons must specifically identify the taxpayer's transactions with the political organization and will be so limited as to require only testimony or documents relating to those transactions or to other transactions of the same type. If, however, the taxpayer's transactions with the political organization are known to have occurred through the use of an intermediary person or organization, the summons may require testimony or documents relating to specifically identified transactions of the intermediary with the political organization.

(5) If an exception to the provisions of (3) above is desired, or if issuance of a summons in conformity with (4) above is desired, a memorandum request, explaining in detail the necessity for the issuance of such a summons, together with a copy of the proposed summons, will be submitted by the Chief, Criminal Investigation Division, with the concurrence of the District Director (for OIO, the Director of International Operations), through channels to the Director, Criminal Investigation Division who may submit the request to the Assistant Commissioner (Compliance) for prior written approval. If time is of the essence, a telephonic request will be made to the Director, Criminal Investigation Division who may submit the request to the Assistant Commissioner (Compliance), for prior approval. A memorandum setting forth the details will be prepared by the Chief, Criminal Investigation Division and forwarded immediately through channels to the Director, Criminal Investigation Division in all situations in which a telephonic request has been made under this procedure.

(6) If there is a question as to the legal sufficiency of the proposed summons, and time permits, it should be referred to District Counsel for a preliminary legal review, prior to referral of the request to the National Office for approval.

367.552 *(1-18-80)* 9781
Summons for Information Pursuant to Tax Treaties

A summons may be issued to obtain information from individuals and entities within the United States, relating to the foreign tax liability of a foreign citizen, in response to formal requests made through the Office of International Operations by foreign tax authorities pursuant to the provisions of the tax treaty between that country and the United States.

367.553 *(1-18-80)* 9781
Restrictions on Examination of Churches

IRC 7605(c) and 26 CFR 301.7605-1(c)(2) impose certain restrictions on the examination of the books of account of a church or convention or association of churches. Before attempting to secure or examine such records, special agents shall ensure that they have complied with the provisions of the IRC and regulations cited above. District Counsel may be consulted, as necessary. (See also Delegation Order No. 137 as revised.)

367.554 *(1-18-80)* 9781
Summons for Records Outside the United States

Before issuing a summons where the records are outside the United States, a copy of the proposed summons will be submitted, through channels, to District Counsel for review. District Counsel will coordinate their review with Chief Counsel (CC:GL:I), who in turn will coordinate the matter with the Director, Criminal Investigation Division. The proposed summons will be accompanied by a statement describing the circumstances and efforts that have been made to secure the records and data from the taxpayer and why the taxpayer will not make the requested records available. In no event will the special agent issue the summons until advice has been received from Counsel.

367.555 *(1-18-80)* 9781
Information from Federal Officials and Employees

No summons will be issued to Federal officials or employees for information they may possess or know in connection with their official responsibilities. Such information may ordinarily be obtained through liaison with the agency involved (for example, see IRM 9264.2, IRM 9375, IRM 937(10), and text 330 of this Handbook. Requests for assistance in situations not covered by existing guidelines should be referred, through channels, to the Director, Criminal Investigation Division (attn: CP:CI:O).

367.556 *(1-18-80)* 9781
Criminal Cases Pending with Justice

No summons shall be issued in connection with a criminal case pending with the Department of Justice either to obtain further information from the taxpayer or a witness or to uncover assets to apply against assessed liabilities unless clearance is first obtained from that Department through the District Counsel, and the Chief Counsel. (See Policy Statement P-4-2.)

367.56 *(1-18-80)* 9781
Special Procedures for Third-Party Recordkeeper Summons

367.561 *(1-18-80)* 9781
Statutory Requirements

(1) IRC 7609 generally provides that:

(a) a taxpayer or other person must be notified if a summons has been served on a third-party recordkeeper to produce records or give testimony relative to records made or kept of the business transactions or affairs of the taxpayer or other person who is identified in the description of the records contained in the summons, except when a summons is used to determine the identity of a person having a numbered account or similar arrangement, to aid in the collection of a tax liability, or to determine the existence of records;

(b) any person who has the right to notice has the right to stay compliance with the summons and to intervene in an enforcement proceeding with respect to the summons;

(c) notice is not required where the Service first obtains a court order based on allegations that there is reasonable cause to believe that notice may lead to material interference with the investigation or examination;

(d) intervention or staying compliance with the summons by the taxpayer or his/her agent suspends the running of the statute of limitations for civil and criminal purposes during the period when a court proceeding and appeals related thereto are pending; and

(e) a "John Doe" summons will be issued pursuant to a court order.

367.562 *(1-18-80)* 9781
Definitions

(1) *Summons*—In this section reference is to an administrative summons which is issued under paragraph (2) of IRC 7602 or under 6420(e)(2), 6421(f)(2), 6424(d)(2), or 6427(f)(2); and is served on a third-party recordkeeper requiring the production of any portion of records made or kept of the business transactions or affairs of any person (other than the person summoned) who is identified in the description of the records contained in the summons. This section does not apply to certain summonses enumerated in IRM 9368.3 below.

(2) *Third-party recordkeeper*—The term applies to any bank, savings and loan institution or credit union; any consumer reporting agency covered by the Fair Credit Reporting Act; anyone extending credit through the issuance of credit cards or similar devices; any broker included in the Securities Exchange Act of 1934; any attorney; and any accountant. The procedures in IRC 7609 apply generally to situations in which the recordkeeper makes or keeps records of the business transactions or affairs of a person identified in the description of the records contained in the summons. All persons who extend "credit through the use of credit cards or similar devices" fall within the scope of these procedures notwithstanding the fact that the principal business of that person may be

something other than the issuing of credit cards. For example, telephone companies and others such as retail stores and oil companies who extend credit through their own credit cards would be considered "third-party recordkeepers." Any retail establishment that does not extend credit through its own credit card or similar device (i.e., some physical object evidencing credit) will not be considered a "third-party recordkeeper." Thus, retail establishments that honor credit cards issued by other parties (e.g., Visa, American Express, Master Charge) will not be considered as extending credit since the issuer of the credit card is actually the lender rather than the retail establishment. If an agent issues a summons to a retail establishment or similar business which has its own credit card, but also honors credit cards such as Visa, American Express or Master Charge, notice will be given under Section 7609. This is due to the fact that it would be unduly burdensome for an agent to issue one summons for records of Visa or American Express transactions and another for records of transactions involving the summoned witness's own credit card. Notice is only required in cases where the Service is summoning records of the extensions of credit "through the use of credit cards or similar devices" and not when it is summoning records of other transactions. For example, if employee X works for credit card company A and also has one of A's credit cards, then no notice would be required in connection with a summons issued to A for X's employment records. However, notice would be required in connection with a summons issued to A for X's credit card records. In addition, if an independent contractor performs services for a retail establishment which issues its own credit card, no notice is required in connection with a summons issued to the retail establishment for the records relating to the services performed by the independent contractor.

(3) *Records*—This term includes books, papers, or other data; and a summons requiring the giving of testimony relative to the contents of records is to be treated as a summons requiring the production of records.

(4) *"John Doe" summons*—This is any summons which does not identify the person with respect to whose liability the summons is issued. Text 367.59 provides procedures required in the use of "John Doe" summons.

(5) *Numbered bank account*—An account with a bank or similar financial institution through which a person may authorize transactions solely through the use of a number, symbol, code name or similar arrangement not involving disclosure of the account owner's identity.

(6) *Stay compliance*—The stopping of compliance with a summons request by giving written notice to the person summoned not to comply and transmitting a copy of this notice to the Service official before whom the person summoned is to appear.

(7) *Intervention*—The act of a person, who is not originally a party to a summons enforcement court proceeding, becoming a party in order to protect his/her interests.

(8) *Noticee*—A person who has the right to notice, stay compliance and intervene when a summons is served on a third-party recordkeeper to produce records or give testimony relative to the contents of records which pertain to that person. For example, if the Service serves a summons on a bank for an account in the name of the taxpayer, the taxpayer is the noticee. If, in the matter of the tax liability of the taxpayer, a summons is served on the bank for the account of a third party, the third party is the noticee. In a summons enforcement action the bank would be the defendant. If the taxpayer (or other party) is clearly identified by name in the description of the records in the body of the summons, that person is entitled to notice of the summons having been issued. For example, when a summons is issued to X Bank for records in Y's account relative to Z, the taxpayer, notice will be given to both Y and Z. If the agent or officer knows prior to service of the summons that an account is styled in the names of more than one person then each person should be named in the body of the summons and should receive notice; for example, if the agent or officer knows that bank accounts are listed in the joint names of husband and wife then both the husband and wife should be identified in the description of the records sought and both should be given separate notice, even if they reside at the same address. In the case where records of a partnership are requested in the body of the summons, notice to one general partner is sufficient.

(9) *Date of service of notice*—The date on which the notice is placed in the mail or delivered personally.

367.563 *(1-18-80)* 9781
Exceptions to Notice Requirement

(1) There is no notice requirement in cases where:

(a) a "John Doe" summons is issued;

(b) the summoned witness is the taxpayer, officer or employee of the taxpayer;

(c) a third-party witness is summoned to give testimony that is unrelated to records; or

(d) the summoned witness is not considered to be a third-party recordkeeper as defined in text 367.562:(2).

(2) Notice is also not required where the stated purpose of the summons is to:

(a) determine whether records of the business transactions or affairs of an identified person have been made or kept; or

(b) determine solely the identity of any person having a numbered account (or similar arrangement) with a bank, savings and loan institution or credit union.

(3) Summonses issued pursuant to a court order:

(a) Notice shall not be required if, upon petition by the Service, prior to the issuance of the summons, the United States district court for the district within which the person to be summoned resides or is found, determines, on the basis of the facts and circumstances alleged, that there is reasonable cause to believe the giving of notice may lead to attempts to conceal, destroy or alter records relevant to the examination, to prevent the communication of information from other persons through intimidation, bribery, or collusion, or to flee to avoid prosecution, testifying or production of records.

(b) in the hearings required under (a) above, as well as those referred to in text 367.59, "John Doe" Summons, the determination shall be made ex parte and shall be made solely upon the petition and supporting affidavits. An order denying the petition is deemed a final order which may be appealed.

(c) except for cases the court considers of greater importance, a proceeding brought for the enforcement of any summons, or a proceeding under this exception, and appeals, take precedence on the docket over all cases and are to be assigned for hearing and decided at the earliest practicable date.

(d) requests for court orders will be forwarded to District Counsel for processing. Included in the memorandum should be a request that the court order the person(s) to be summoned to refrain from notifying the taxpayer, or other person to whom the records or testimony pertain, of the service of the summons.

(e) the third-party recordkeeper will be advised that pursuant to a court order no notification will be given of the summons request and, if appropriate, that notification could subject the person summoned to a contempt citation.

367.57 *(1-18-80)* 9781
General Procedures for Notice, Staying Compliance and Intervention

367.571 *(1-18-80)* 9781
Period in Which Service Is Required To Give Notice

(1) In instances where a summons is served on any person who is a third-party recordkeeper requiring the production of records which relate to the taxpayer, notice shall be given to the taxpayer within 3 days of the date on which service is made and no later than 14 calendar days before the date fixed in the summons as to when the records are to be examined.

(2) Seventeen days generally (but, in no event, more than twenty days) will be allowed from the date of service of the summons to the time for compliance to ensure sufficient time for the notices of issuance of the summons and staying of compliance to be given.

367.572 *(1-18-80)* 9781
Right to Stay Compliance

(1) The taxpayer entitled to notice of the summons has the right to stay compliance with the summons, if not later than 14 days after the date on the notice: notice in writing is given to the person summoned not to comply, and a copy of the notice not to comply is mailed by registered or certified mail to the person before whom the person summoned is to appear at an address appearing on the face of the summons. Where the copy of the notification not to comply has not been received by the Service or the third-party recordkeeper within 3 days after the close of the 14-day period, the Service can presume that the notification has not been timely mailed and compliance should be forthwith. If the dates of serving the summons and the giving or mailing the notice and the copy of the summons are the same, no longer period is necessary.

(2) In instances where a summons is served on a third-party recordkeeper for records relating to a person other than the taxpayer, notice will be given to such person. He/she has the right to stay compliance and intervene in a summons enforcement proceeding.

(3) No examination may be made of any records required to be produced under a summons as to which notice is required before the expiration of the period allowed for the notice not to comply or when the requirements for staying compliance have been met, except with the consent of the person staying compliance or in accordance with an order issued by a court of competent jurisdiction authorizing examination of such records. The waiver must be in writing, prepared in duplicate with copies going to the person issuing the summons as well as the person summoned (see IRM 9368.45).

367.573 *(1-18-80)* 9781
Intervention in Summons Enforcement Proceedings

(1) Upon receipt of the notice to stay compliance, summons enforcement will ordinarily be commenced against the third-party recordkeeper in accordance with IRC 7604. The noticee has the right to intervene in the summons enforcement proceeding.

(2) The running of the statute of limitations for civil and criminal purposes is suspended with respect to the taxpayer if the taxpayer or an agent, nominee, or other person acting under the direction or control of the taxpayer stays compliance or intervenes during the period when a court proceeding and appeals related thereto are pending. The period tolled begins when the summons enforcement case is commenced in court and relates to the years under examination which are identified in the summons.

(3) Staying compliance or intervention by a person other than the taxpayer or his/her agent will not suspend the running of the statutes of limitation.

367.574 *(1-18-80)* 9781
Notice and Instructions to Noticee

(1) Included as part of Form 2039 is a notice which contains instructions concerning the noticee's right to stay compliance and intervene (Form 2039-D). It will be served on the noticee together with a copy of the summons (Form 2039-C) by the person serving the summons. Generally, notice will be given by certified or registered mail to the last known address of the noticee. However, only registered mail should be used when the notice is mailed to persons in foreign countries. The law also permits service of notice by delivering both documents in hand to the noticee, or leaving them at the noticee's residence or, in the absence of a last known address, leaving them with the person summoned.

(2) If the Service has been advised under IRC6903 of the existence of a fiduciary relationship, it is sufficient if the notice of the service of the summons is mailed to the last known address of the fiduciary of the person entitled to notice, even if such a person or fiduciary is now deceased, under a legal disability, or no longer in existence. The filing of a power of attorney or tax information authorization does not qualify as the creation of a fiduciary relationship under this provision and notice would be given to the taxpayer or other person to whom the records pertain.

(3) Certification of serving the summons as well as the certification of giving notice will be completed on the reverse side of the original copy of the summons.

(4) If a summons enforcement is instituted, the third-party recordkeeper, as well as the noticee, is entitled to notice of the enforcement action. Generally, the third-party recordkeeper will be served with process. The noticee will be informed by certified or registered mail. Such third-party notification will be the responsibility of the Department of Justice.

(5) Upon request by the party summoned of proof that notice has been given, the party summoned will be furnished a copy of the back of the original summons which contains certificates of the service of the summons and notice. Since the law requires that the noticee must notify both the summoned party and the Service in order to stay compliance, it is inappropriate for an agent to have to certify that no notice staying compliance has been received by the Service before the summoned party will comply with the summons.

367.575 *(1-18-80)* 9781
Waiver of Right to Notice, Stay of Compliance and Intervention

(1) A person who is entitled to notice, stay compliance and intervene when a summons is issued may waive such rights by executing a

general waiver form. A suggested Pattern Letter (P-549) for waiver purposes is included in Exhibit 300-16. All third-party recordkeepers involved in the waiver should be given a copy of the letter for their records.

(2) Payments for mileage, witness fees and expenses may be made to the third-party recordkeeper in accordance with Subsection 369 if a summons is issued.

367.58 *(1-18-80)* 9781
Coordination of Summons Issuance and Enforcement Actions

To the extent practicable, summonses pertaining to the same person shall be served and be submitted for enforcement action at or near the same time. Likewise, court requests by the Service for exemption from the requirement of notice relative to the same person shall be made at the same time, if possible.

367.59 *(1-18-80)* 9781
"John Doe" Summons

A "John Doe" summons is any summons which does not identify the person with respect to whose liability the summons is issued.

367.591 *(1-18-80)* 9781
Issuance Procedures

(1) A John Doe summons will be issued only by the officials authorized in Delegation Order No. 4 (as revised), and by them only after obtaining pre-issuance legal review by Regional Counsel (or Chief Counsel in the case of OIO). The provisions of the law which require court approval for the serving of the summons are contained in text 367.592.

(2) A statement of the pertinent facts and circumstances and justification for issuing the summons shall be submitted through District Counsel to Regional Counsel, including information to satisfy each of the statutory requirements contained in IRC 7609(f)(1) through (3). The wording to be used in the summons should also be discussed with Counsel.

(3) If Regional Counsel agrees that the summons should be issued, his/her concurrence should be endorsed on the face of the summons and all attested copies by the word "Reviewed" followed by the signature and title of the reviewing official.

(4) If Regional Counsel contemplates not concurring with the issuance of the John Doe summons, the matter should be discussed with the Chief, Criminal Investigation Division.

(5) If agreement cannot be reached, Regional Counsel will prepare and forward a memorandum to the District Director setting forth the reasons for nonconcurrence.

(6) If the District Director does not agree with Regional Counsel's conclusions, the matter will be referred to the ARC (Criminal Investigation) who will explore with Regional Counsel ways of reaching agreement on the action to be taken with regard to the John Doe summons.

(7) If agreement still cannot be reached, the matter will be referred to the Director, Criminal Investigation Division (Attn: CP:CI:O) with the recommendation that Chief Counsel be requested to consider the matter.

367.592 *(1-18-80)* 9781
Service of John Doe Summons

(1) IRC 7609(f) provides that a "John Doe" summons may be served only after a proceeding is held in the United States district court for the district where the person to be summoned resides or is found. The Service must establish that:

(a) the summons relates to the investigation of a particular person or ascertainable group or class of persons;

(b) there is a reasonable basis for believing that such person or group or class of persons may fail or may have failed to comply with any provision of the internal revenue law; and

(c) the information sought to be obtained from the examination of the records (and the identity of the person or persons with respect to whose liability the summons is issued) is not readily available from other sources.

(2) This procedure is inapplicable to summonses issued solely to determine the identity of any person having a numbered account (or similar arrangement) with a bank or similar financial institution.

367.6 *(1-18-80)* 9781
Restrictions on Disclosure of Information Obtained by a Summons

(1) Information obtained through the use of a summons is considered tax return information subject to the disclosure provisions of IRC 6103, IRC 7213, IRC 7217, and 18 USC 1905.

(2) Unless advance approval is obtained from the Assistant Commissioner (Compliance), no commitments will be made to taxpayers or third parties to provide a greater degree of confidentiality or limitation of use than is provided by existing law and regulation; to limit the disclosure of information, such as agreeing that information will not be turned over to other agencies otherwise entitled to disclosure of that information upon proper request; nor to impose other conditions regarding the acceptance and use of information by the IRS, such as agreeing to use tax data for civil purposes only.

368 *(1-18-80)* 9781
Fees and Costs for Witnesses

368.1 *(1-18-80)* 9781
Authority

(1) IRC 7610 provides for the payment of witness fees and mileage to summoned witnesses; and the payment of search, reproduction and transportation costs to certain third-party witnesses. Third parties complying with a summons will be paid under the terms and conditions set forth below.

(2) The search, reproduction, and transportation cost payments discussed in IRM 9369.3 are in addition to and not a substitute for a summoned witness's right to witness fees and travel expenses discussed in IRM 9369.2.

368.2 *(1-18-80)* 9781
Witness Fees and Travel Expenses

(1) Witness fees and travel expenses are amounts which, upon request, are payable to witnesses who for the purpose of giving testimony or producing records are required to appear before Service personnel in compliance with administrative summonses issued under IRC 7602, 6420(e)(2), 6421(f)(2), 6424(d)(2) or 6427(g)(2). Amounts for fees are prescribed in 28 U.S.C. 1821. They include a per diem rate and a rate per mile for associated travel. The procedures and conditions for payment of witness fees and mileage are *not* modified by requirements for reimbursement of third parties for search, transportation, and reproduction cost as provided for in text 369. Witness fees and payments for mileage may be made to all summoned witnesses, whether the witness be a third-party witness, the taxpayer, or the taxpayer's representative. Payment may be made whenever a summons (Form 2039) is issued, regardless of the investigative state of the matter involved.

(2) Procedures for payment of witness fees and expenses are detailed below. Standard Forms 1156, Public Voucher for Fees and Mileage of Witnesses (Original); 1156a (Memorandum copy of SF 1156); 1157, Claim for Fees and Mileage of Witnesses (Original); and 1157a (Memorandum copy of SF 1157); will be used for this purpose.

(a) SF 1157 and 1157a will be prepared, with the assistance of the special agent if necessary, and signed by the payee. In the "Case No." space in the upper right corner, the notation "Form 2039" should be inserted. The special agent before whom the summoned person appears will review the claim and complete the lower portion of the forms to indicate approval for payment of the amount claimed.

(b) The special agent will complete the upper portion of SF 1156 and 1156a, including the "Summary of Payments" section. On the line provided for showing the name of court or board, the special agent will enter "Testimony before . . . (name and title of agent). . . ."

(c) All of the above forms will be forwarded through channels to the Chief, Resources Management Division, for further processing. A check will be issued to the claimant by the Regional Disbursing Office.

(d) When the person summoned demands assurance or guarantee that payment will be made, an additional copy of SF 1157a will be prepared and furnished to the person. The special agent will insert the following statement immediately above the "Approved for $" space in the lower portion of the form: "Payment of witness fees and travel expenses as stated above are guaranteed by the Internal Revenue Service."

(3) When the person summoned cannot comply unless travel expenses are furnished, an advance payment, not to exceed the amount allowable, may be made. The following procedures will be used in those instances:

(a) The special agent will prepare SF 1157 and 1157a in the name of the witness. He/she will also complete the upper portion of SF 1156 and 1156a and enter the date scheduled for testimony on the line provided. All forms will be marked "Advance Payment" and forwarded through channels to the Chief, Resources Management Division.

(b) After processing, the Fiscal Management Branch will forward the check to the claimant by certified mail, noted "For Delivery to the Addressee Only." The certified mail return receipt will be associated with SF 1157a and retained in the Fiscal Management Branch.

(c) When the advance payment covers only a part of the allowable fees and travel expenses, the SF 1157 submitted for the remainder of the allowance will bear a reference of the SF 1157 covering the advance payment.

369 *(1-18-80)* 9781
Payments for Costs in Complying with Summons

369.1 *(1-18-80)* 9781
General

Pursuant to IRC 7610 and implementing procedures, payments may be made to third parties who request reimbursement for costs incurred in complying with a summons. These provisions apply to summonses complied with on or after January 11, 1977. Payments may be made to third parties without the issuance of a summons for records needed in an investigation which are available to the general public, under IRC Section 7801.

369.2 *(1-18-80)* 9781
Definitions

(1) Taxpayer—The person with respect to whose liability the summons is issued.

(2) Third Party—Any person served with a summons other than:

(a) a taxpayer; or

(b) an officer, employee, agent, accountant, or attorney of a taxpayer who, at the time the summons is served, is acting as such.

(3) Third Party Records—Books, papers, records, or other data in which the taxpayer does not have a proprietary interest at the time the summons is served.

(4) Directly Incurred Costs—Costs incurred solely, immediately and necessarily as a consequence of searching for, reproducing or transporting records in order to comply with a summons. Proportionate allocation of fixed costs (overhead, equipment depreciation, etc.) is not considered to be directly incurred. However, where a third party's records are stored at an independent storage facility that charges the third party a fee to search for, reproduce, or transport particular records requested, such fees are considered to be directly incurred by the summoned third party.

(5) Search Costs—Include only:

(a) the total amount of personnel direct time incurred in locating and retrieving records or information; and

(b) direct costs of extracting information stored by computer. Salaries of persons locating and retrieving summoned material are not includible in search costs. Also, search costs *do not* include salaries, fees, or similar expenditures for analysis of material or for managerial or legal advice, expertise or search, nor does it include time spent for such activities.

(6) Reproduction Costs—Costs incurred in making copies or duplicates of summoned documents, transcripts, and other similar material.

369.3 *(1-18-80)* 9781
Delegation of Authority

(1) The Commissioner of Internal Revenue has delegated to the below-named officials the authority to obligate appropriated funds for making payment for search costs, reproduction costs and transportation costs in connection with complying with a third-party summons. See Delegation Order 178.

(a) Regional Commissioners, who will obtain the concurrence of the Assistant Commissioner (Compliance) through the Fiscal Management Officer, National Office, before obligating over $5,000 for payment of such costs associated with any one summons. This authority may not be redelegated.

(b) District Directors and the Director of International Operations to obligate up to $5,000 for payment of such costs associated with any one summons, with authority to redelegate to the Chief, Criminal Investigation Division with respect to any such obligation not exceeding $2,500 except this authority in streamlined districts is limited to the District Director. This authority may also be redelegated to any officer or employee referred to in paragraph 1(d) of Delegation Order No. 4 (as revised) and 4b of Delegation Order No. 178 as having authority to personally authorize the issuance of a summons to a third party witness, with respect to any such obligation not exceeding $1,000.

(2) In accordance with Delegation Order No. 4 (as revised), if a third party summons is issued by a special agent, the prior authorization by group manager or other supervisory official above that level is required as specified in the Order. However, to process the resultant third party invoice for payment as prescribed in text 369.5, certification is required by an official specified above as having obligational authority of the appropriate amount.

(a) In some cases, depending on the dollar amount involved, this could mean that two different individuals might be involved in authorizing issuance of a summons and in certifying its invoice for payment.

(b) To minimize this occurring, and thereby to expedite processing, the procedures described below should be followed.

1 The special agent issuing (or requesting issuance of) a third party summons should first make as reasonable an estimate as possible of the obligational authority level required for payment of the costs of compliance with the summons.

2 The issuing (or requesting) special agent should then initiate the necessary administrative action to have the summons approved, prior to issuance, by an official who has both approval authority under Delegation Order No. 4 (as revised) and the required level of obligational authority under Delegation Order No. 178.

369.4 *(1-18-80)* 9781

Basis for Payment

(1) Payment for search, reproduction and transportation costs will be made only to third parties served with a summons to produce third party records or information and only for material requested by the summons, unless the records are available to the general public.

(2) Payment will be made only for search, reproduction and transportation costs that are both directly incurred and reasonably necessary. In determining whether costs are reasonably necessary, it is essential to consider search, reproduction, and transportation costs separately.

(3) No payment will be made until the third party satisfactorily complies with the summons.

(4) No payment will be made unless the third party submits an itemized bill or invoice showing specific details concerning the search, reproduction and transportation costs.

369.5 *(1-18-80)* 9781

Payment Procedures

(1) Special agents who issue summonses to third parties must obtain prior managerial approval as required by Delegation Order No. 4 (as revised). The agent issuing (or requesting issuance of) a third party summons should first make as reasonable an estimate as possible of the obligational authority level required for payment of the costs of compliance with the summons. The agent should then initiate the necessary administrative action to have that official approve the summons prior to issuance.

(2) Officials considering approval of issuance of a third party summons will take into account the anticipated payable costs of compliance as well as the need for the information sought.

(3) The agent serving the summons on a third party will ensure that Form 2039-B, Notice to Third Party Recipient of IRS Summons, accompanies the summons. Form 2039-B is Part B of the five-part snapset assembly of Form 2039, Summons.

(4) Upon full or satisfactory compliance with a summons, the agent before whom the third party was summoned to appear shall notify the third party that an itemized bill or invoice may be submitted for payment and shall furnish his or her office address for that purpose.

(5) A third party invoice resulting from compliance with a summons and which amount is $25 or less may be paid in cash directly by the issuing employee. This $25 threshold does not include amounts which are claimed separately as witness fees and mileage.

(6) If the summoned third party submits a bill combining search, reproduction and transportation charges with the witness fee, and the total exceeds $25, the direct payment procedures do not apply.

(7) In valid direct payment cases, the agent may claim reimbursement on his/her travel voucher (with the third party invoice attached) under "Miscellaneous Expenses," or may submit the receipted bill to the Small Purchases Imprest Fund Cashier for cash reimbursement. Under either procedure, the expense shall be charged to SOC 2509, Administrative Summons Expense. Amounts for Administrative Summons expenses claimed on an agent's travel voucher under Miscellaneous Expenses

are not to be charged to SOC 2109, Other Reimbursable Travel Expenses.

(8) Bills for more than $25, or $25 or lesser amounts when direct payment procedures will not be used, must be certified and forwarded to the appropriate Fiscal Management office for payment.

(a) The agent receiving the bill for payment should, to the extent that it is practicable for the agent to do so, ensure that the bill does itemize the specific details of search, reproduction and transportation costs as applicable and that charges have been computed at rates which appear to be appropriate and which are not higher than the allowable rates. For allowable rates see Form 2039-B, Notice to Third Party Recipient of IRS Summons, Part B of the five-part snapset assembly of Form 2039, Summons). The agent will next take necessary action to forward the bill through line managers to the official who initially approved the obligation, or the official with obligation authority appropriate to the amount of the bill.

(b) The obligating official, in most instances, the Criminal Investigation Group Manager, will receive the bill, evaluate the charges in terms of accuracy and reasonableness, and certify the bill for payment processing by signing the following statement: "Payment is approved and is within my delegated obligational authority." The approving official will record, along with certification, title and organizational identification. This constitutes that official's verification that the summons has been satisfactorily complied with and that the claim against the Service for reimbursement is valid.

(c) The certified bill will then be forwarded through appropriate channels to the regional Fiscal Management office for payment processing.

(9) A special procedure applies when the summonses are inter-regional or inter-district.

(a) In cases where one district requests a summons to be served by an agent of another district, the official of the initiating or requesting district with authority to obligate at the estimated payment level of the collateral summons, will obligate funds for the payment of that summons. The requesting district will forward to the serving district a completed Form 2039, Summons, with all information provided except for the time and place for appearance and the agent before whom the witness is to appear. The transmittal letter accompanying the summons should indicate the level of obligation authority the approving official has.

(b) If the official of the receiving district determines prior to third party compliance with the summons that the anticipated costs will exceed the obligational amount for which the approving official has authority, he/she will advise the requesting district of the need for the approval of an official with higher obligational authority.

(c) When the agent of the district serving the summons in coordination with the issuing official of the requesting district determines that the summons has been satisfactorily complied with, the summoned materials will be submitted to the requesting district.

(d) The third party will then submit its bill through the serving agent to the official in the requesting district who originally authorized the summons. If the actual bill exceeds the obligational authority of the approving official, it will be that official's responsibility to obtain subsequent approval at the required level.

(e) The issuing official will review the bill for accuracy and reasonableness and then certify the bill for payment. The bill will then be forwarded to Fiscal Management for payment processing.

369.6 *(1-18-80)* 9781
Safeguarding of Documents

To prevent unauthorized disclosure, third party invoices and supporting documents, which result from third party summons, when not being worked on, will be provided with three protection points in accordance with IRM 1(16)41, Physical and Document Security Handbook.

36(10) *(1-18-80)* 9781
Enforcement of Summons

36(10).1 *(1-18-80)* 9781
Appearance, Compliance or Noncompliance with a Summons

(1) In connection with all summonses other than those with which compliance has been stayed or waived, if advance information is received from the summoned witness or from the witness' representative that on the date set for appearance in the summons the witness will not comply with the summons either by not testifying or not producing records, or both, no indication or agreement, express or implied, shall be made on behalf of the Service that it is not necessary or required for the witness to appear and testify or produce summoned records on the date set for appearance. The witness or the witness' representative should be informed that the witness must appear in person with the records to be produced pursuant to the summons and either comply or refuse to comply with the summons, stating reasons for any such refusal. The witness or the witness' representative should also be informed that in the event of refusal or failure to comply with the summons, consideration will be given to resorting to the judicial remedies provided by law. The representative of the witness cannot appear in lieu of the witness on the appearance date set in the summons. In the event the witness for a valid reason (such as illness) cannot appear on the date fixed in the summons, that date may be continued by mutual agreement to another date.

(2) If a taxpayer or witness appears in response to a summons and claims either the self-incrimination privilege of the Fifth Amendment or other privilege, the special agent should continue with the examination even though it is clear that the questions will not be answered. It is important that the special agent ask the summoned person all questions necessary to develop the required information and make requests for production of each of the documents desired so that the person asserting the privilege responds to each inquiry by either answering the question and producing the documents or asserting the claimed privilege. However, if the person summoned refuses to submit to questioning and the requests for documents, the special agent cannot compel the person to remain and continue with the examination. The special agent should not attempt to overcome a blanket claim of privilege or a refusal to submit to specific questioning. A record should be made describing the facts and occurrences at the interview. If it is anticipated or known that the taxpayer or witness summoned intends to assert a privilege, a stenographer should be present to transcribe the interview or another IRS employee should attend the interview as a witness.

(3) The above procedures are important to the enforcement of a summons to establish the facts and circumstances of noncompliance. The procedures respecting claims of privileges are primarily applicable when only the witness and the witness' representative appear in response to the summons. There may be other situations in which the taxpayer or another person attempts to be present when a summoned third-party witness is questioned and the special agent does not desire to disclose in their presence the course of the investigation by requesting the furnishing of each item of information, oral or documentary. In such event other considerations may be involved, and the agent should consult with his superior. District Counsel may also be consulted.

36(10).2 *(7-8-81)* 9781
General

(1) The United States District Court for the district in which the person to whom the summons is directed resides or is found shall have jurisdiction to compel his/her attendance, testimony or the production of books, papers, records or other data, as detailed in IRC 7402(b) and 7604(a). A judge of the district court or a United States Magistrate may by appropriate process compel compliance with the summons. Civil proceedings are utilized to compel the person summoned to furnish information. Criminal enforcement serves "as a deterrent to offenses against the public" and to punish the wrongdoer.

(2) Any summons that has not been complied with within six workdays following the date set for compliance, where enforcement action is appropriate, will be referred to District Counsel for initiation of enforcement proceedings.

36(10).3 *(1-18-80)* 9781
Civil Enforcement of Summons

36(10).31 *(7-8-81)* 9781
General

(1) IRC 7604 provides for the civil enforcement of a summons. The special agent's au-

thority to enforce a summons is granted in the same delegation orders as the agent's authority to issue a summons. [See text 362.]

(2) Under IRC 7604(b), enforcement action may be initiated by applying for an attachment against a person who has failed to obey a summons. The application is made to a district judge or a United States magistrate who will hear the application and, if satisfied with the proof, will issue an attachment for an arrest. When the person is brought before him/her, the judge or magistrate will hear the case. He/she will then issue whatever order he/she deems proper, not inconsistent with the law for the punishment of contempts, to enforce compliance with the summons and to punish such person for default or disobedience. When a petition for attachment is filed the court may choose to proceed by issuing an order to show cause why the summons should not be obeyed. [*Brody v. U.S.*] It may also modify the summons in its order if compliance would be unreasonable or oppressive. [*Brody v. U.S.*] This provision is intended only to cover persons who were summoned and wholly made default or stubbornly refused to comply. [*Reisman v. Caplin*]

(3) Enforcement proceedings are usually commenced by filing a petition for a court order directing compliance with the summons. The summons (or a copy) should be attached to the petition or offered in evidence; otherwise, the court may not enforce it. [*Commissioner v. Schwartz*] Based upon the allegations, the court may issue either an order to show cause, or an ex parte (only one party represented) order directing compliance with the summons. [*Falsone v. U.S.*] The use of procedures other than attachment is authorized by IRC 7604(a), which grants district courts jurisdiction to enforce compliance "by appropriate process."

(4) Requests for civil enforcement of summonses originating in Criminal Investigation will be prepared by the special agent who issued the summons, and will include the following:

(a) The name, full address, and taxpayer identification number of the taxpayer under investigation;

(b) A brief resume of the pertinent facts in the case, showing particularly whether it involves or is related to the Special Enforcement Program;

(c) Exactly what the agent seeks to obtain by the summons;

(d) An explanation of the relevancy of the records sought where the relevancy is not obvious. For example, if records pertaining to years other than those under investigation are sought, the relevancy should be explained. Also, the relevancy of records pertaining to third parties should be explained;

(e) An explanation of the need or importance of such evidence to the success or completion of the investigation;

(f) A statement that IRC 7609(a) notice has been served on persons or entities identified in the description of records or, if not, why it is believed notice is not necessary;

(g) If a corporation is the party summoned, a statement whether service of the summons has been made on a responsible officer and, if not, why not;

(h) The circumstances surrounding contacts with the person summoned showing particularly the defense(s) claimed for refusing to comply with the summons and the circumstances under which the person summoned claimed the defense(s);

(i) A transcript (if recorded) of the questions propounded to the person summoned and the person's answers;

(j) The name of the cooperating IRS agent/officer or, if none, why;

(k) A description of any problems involving the imminent expiration of the statute of limitations with respect to either the criminal or the civil liability; and

(l) A statement as to the existence of any known criminal investigations, by other federal agencies, of the taxpayer and, in the case of a corporate taxpayer, corporate officers or employees.

(m) A statement as to any disclosures made pursuant to IRC 6103(i) concerning possible violations of criminal laws not within Service jurisdiction;

(n) A statement as to any other known requests for summons or subpoena enforcement against the witness or related parties; and

(o) If a pen register was used in the investigation prior to the issuance of the summons, a statement to that effect and the reason the pen register was used.

(5) The Chief, Criminal Investigation Division, if he/she approves, will so indicate by endorsement on the signature page of the requests. The original and four copies together with the original of the summons (Form 2039) will be transmitted, through the District Director or his/her designee, to District Counsel. If the matter relates to a strike force case or a case in which the Department of Justice has expressed an interest, the Chief will forward an extra copy of the special agent's request for transmission through District Counsel and Chief Counsel to the Criminal Division of the Department of Justice.

(6) With respect to a summons issued in connection with a collateral investigation, the replying district will provide to the requesting district, by memorandum, sufficient information regarding noncompliance with the summons, including information about stays of compliance, for the requesting district to prepare a request for civil enforcement of the summons. This request should be directed to and processed by the responsible office of District Counsel servicing the requesting district.

(7) Requests are approved generally by District Counsel and in certain cases by Chief Counsel. Normally, District Counsel will take final action within six workdays from the receipt of a summons case, and Chief Counsel will take final action within three workdays after receipt of a summons case.

(8) After a summons has been referred to the District Counsel for civil enforcement, he/she will be kept informed by memorandum of all situations which have a bearing on the summons enforcement proceeding. In instances where time is of the essence, the District Counsel will be immediately advised by telephone of the facts in the matter, with confirmation by memorandum to follow. Examples of the type of information which will be reported are: the evidence sought is no longer needed; the witness has voluntarily complied with the provisions of the summons; the tax liability is paid or otherwise satisfied; the principal is about to be offered a district Criminal Investigation Division conference; (See IRM 9356.1) or the special agent has submitted a report recommending prosecution of the principal. The memorandum will be prepared as soon as the information is received, with distribution made in the same number of copies and in the same manner as the original referral to Counsel. Copies of any legal documents involved in the action will be forwarded with the memorandum.

(9) Similarly, with regard to any summons referred to the Department of Justice for enforcement, District Counsel will be informed by memorandum if there is either compliance or an initial decision by a federal district court or magistrate that the summons is unenforceable. The memorandum will contain: the names of the taxpayer and witness; the appearance date set in the summons; the date of compliance or the adverse court decision; whether compliance was satisfactory; and whether compliance was pursuant to a court order. The memorandum will be prepared as soon as practicable after compliance or the adverse decision, and distributed in the same manner as the original referral to District Counsel.

(10) Similarly, District Counsel will be informed by memorandum of any ex parte orders under 6103(i) that may be sought and/or granted or head of agency requests received and/or granted after the referral of a summons for enforcement. District Counsel should also be notified if, after a request for summons enforcement, but before its granting, the summonsed information on the witness becomes the subject of a grand jury inquiry.

(11) If there is a pending summons enforcement action related to an investigation when the special agent's report recommending prosecution is forwarded to District Counsel, the memorandum transmitting the report to Counsel (See IRM 9631.2) will include a statement to that effect, with information identifying the party involved in the summons enforcement action and the Counsel office handling it.

36(10).32 *(1-18-80)* 9781
Civil and Criminal Contempt Regarding Summons

(1) A person refusing to obey a court order directing compliance with a summons (civil enforcement) may be held in contempt of court. The contempt proceedings may be civil [*Sauber v. Whetstone*] or criminal, [*Brody v. U.S.; Goldfine v. U.S.*] or both. A defendant may be purged of civil contempt by complying with the court order, but punishment for criminal contempt is usually not conditional. Use of civil or criminal contempt, as with civil or criminal enforcement, depends on whether the purpose is to compel compliance with the summons or to punish disobedience and protect the authority of the court.

(2) A civil contempt proceeding may be commenced by a motion informing the court of the failure to comply with its order and requesting that the person summoned be adjudged in contempt and punished. The recalcitrant party may then be committed to jail until such time as he/she complies with the court order. [*Sauber v. Whetstone*]

(3) A criminal contempt proceeding can be undertaken only on notice given by the judge in open court in the presence of the defendant, by an order to show cause or by an order of arrest, unless the "contempt" was committed in the presence of the court. The notice must state essential facts which constitute criminal contempt and describe the criminal contempt as such. [Rule 42, F.R.C.P.]

(4) In a criminal contempt case, the Government must prove beyond a reasonable doubt that the defendant willfully failed to comply with a lawful court order. To sustain this burden it must show that summoned records are presently within the defendant's power and control [*U.S. v. Patterson; U.S. v. Pollock*] Presumption of continued possession and existence is not enough to shift the burden of proof to the defendant unless the time span is short and there is no outside motivation for destruction of the particular records. [*U.S. v. Goldstein; U.S. v. Pollock*]

36(10).33 *(10–6–81)* 9781
Use of Declarations in Summons Proceedings

(1) To support applications for court orders directing compliance with a summons, the agent will prepare a declaration (Exhibit 300–15 contains a sample) reciting detailed information concerning the nature and purposes of the examination, the testimony and records desired, and their relevancy to the examination. Usually, enforcement proceedings are held solely upon declarations (of the agents and possibly the person summoned) and oral argument. Accordingly, it is highly important that the declaration clearly show that the person summoned has possession, care, or custody of the desired records, and that they are material and relevant to the tax liability of the person being investigated. (*Local 174 v. U.S.*) If the summons pertains to a year previously examined, a copy of the District Director's reopening letter should be attached. Some courts may require that an affidavit, rather than a declaration, be filed. It will contain the same basic information, however, it must be given under oath.

(2) If there is a sharp dispute on the basic question of whether the records are subject to the control of the person served with the summons, the court will usually not resolve the matter on the basis of conflicting declarations, but will have the issue of control and willfulness in failing to comply with the order determined in a contempt proceeding. (In re: Harry J. Reicher.) When a petition for attachment is filed the court may choose to proceed by issuing an order to show cause why the summons should not be obeyed (*Brody v. U.S.*) It may also modify the summons in its order if compliance would be unreasonable or oppressive. (*Brody v. U.S.*) This provision is intended only to cover persons who were summoned and wholly made default or stubbornly refused to comply. (*Reisman v. Caplin*)

36(10).4 *(1–18–80)* 9781
Criminal Enforcement of Summons

(1) If the facts and circumstances warrant penal action, a person who neglects to appear or to produce records pursuant to a summons may be criminally prosecuted under IRC 7210. [Handbook text 221.9] The Government must be able to prove that:

(a) The defendant was duly summoned to appear to testify, or to appear and produce certain records.

(b) He/she did not appear or produce such records.

(c) At least some of the records called for by summons were in existence and in his/her control, and

(d) He/she wilfully and knowingly neglected to appear and produce them.

(2) It has been held that the word "neglect" as used in this Code section means more than mere inadvertence—"To make a criminal offense to neglect in this situation would imply that he must have wilfully failed to comply with the summons with knowledge that a reasonable man should have had that he was failing to do what the summons required him to do." [*U.S. v. Becker*]

(3) Refusal to obey a summons could lead to a prosecution under IRC 7203, for wilful failure to supply information required by the law. [Handbook text 221.4] In such a proceeding, proof that the refusal was intentional and without legal justification is not sufficient. The Government must also establish that the refusal was prompted by bad faith or evil intent; that the defendant did not believe in good faith that refusal was legally justified. [*U.S. v. Murdock*]

370 *(1-18-80)* 9781
Automatic Data Processing (A.D.P.), Scientific Aids And Other Special Equipment

371 *(1-18-80)* 9781
A.D.P.

371.1 *(1-18-80)* 9781
Application

(1) Generally, applications involve the Automatic Data Processing (ADP) tasks of converting source documents into machine sensible forms (keypunch cards, magnetic tape, etc.) to accomplish efficient analysis. This effort is frequently accomplished by indexing or abstracting through sorting, merging, matching or computation of data elements (subparts of a computer record). Outputs are principally in the form of printouts. In addition, applications may involve the analysis, computations and/or retrieval of selected data from machine-sensible files.

(2) By example, the following applications are representative:

(a) Summarization of payments made (or received) by party, dates, periods, types, or amounts, etc. based on some source document; e.g., agency payment logs, corporate disbursements records, physician's daily patient book, municipal warrant ledgers, vouchers, memorandums, W-2s, etc.

(b) Indexing by name, date, address, amount, type, telephone number, or identification number (predetermined or substituted), etc., a significant volume of documents in order to bring together similarities, identify inconsistencies, or develop patterns, etc. that can be easily referenced for later retrieval of either the information or the evidentiary documentation itself.

(c) Merging, matching and sorting of several kinds of information; e.g., checks, receipts, bills of lading, realty records, or mortuary records, etc., into one or more useful listing disclosing items; e.g., name, date, amount, or matches ("hits") of related information in some useful sequence.

(3) Field personnel will identify and explore the possibilities of utilizing ADP to expedite or reduce the cost of investigations, examinations or special projects. Assistance and development of ADP applications is available through Computer Criminal Investigation Specialists, Chiefs, Criminal Investigation Staff, designated regional coordinators and National Office personnel within the Management Information and Services Branch (CP:CI:M).

(4) A completed ADP project request will be approved by the Chief, Criminal Investigation Division and the District Director and forwarded to the ARC (Criminal Investigation). The request should include the project title, brief description of the project, related projects, purpose, description of input (attach copy of input document or tape file layout) and volumes involved, required output (tables, lists, tape file, etc.), required completion schedule, estimated cost if project were handled manually at the district office, and estimated benefit (tangible and/or intangible).

(5) Joint case applications will be controlled through the Criminal Investigation function.

(6) For more details see IRM 938(10).

371.2 *(1-18-80)* 9781
TELAN

(1) Telephone Analysis System (TELAN) is a function of the Treasury Enforcement Communications System (TECS) and is a computerized service provided by Customs to its own personnel and to DEA, BATF and IRS investigators for the purpose of analyzing telephone toll data. Requests for the use of TELAN should be forwarded by the Chief, Criminal Investigation Division through normal channels to the Director, Criminal Investigation Division, Attn.: CP:CI:O. The request should include the telephone toll information which is to be analyzed by the computer. The computer will generate a printout, listing the data in three sequences: primary phone number, date, receiving phone number; receiving phone number; date, primary phone number; and date, primary phone number, receiving phone number. The computer will also generate a listing, if applicable of those phone numbers submitted by the Service which have also been submitted by another agency. The listing will indicate the name of the other agency and the case number.

(2) For details concerning TECS, See Handbook text 335.

372 *(1-18-80)* 9781
Scientific Aids

372.1 *(1-18-80)* 9781
Laboratories

See 356.7 regarding the Midwest Region Questioned Document Laboratory.

372.2 *(1-18-80)* 9781
Chemicals

372.21 *(1-18-80)* 9781
Anthracene

This substance may be obtained in either powder or pencil form from laboratories, drug firms, and chemical houses. It is invisible but gives off a brilliant fluorescence when exposed to ultraviolet light. Identifying marks, initials, dates, etc., can thus be placed on documents, clothes, vehicles, and other objects that a special agent might want to identify later in bookmaking or lottery headquarters.

372.22 *(1-18-80)* 9781
Phenolphthalein

This substance is an almost colorless powder that will turn red in the presence of an alkali or alkaline solution. It is used to determine whether a person has entered a room, picked up an object, opened a parcel, etc. The method employed in its use is to sprinkle a small quantity on a doorknob, package, or other object. Any person touching the object will unknowingly get the powder on his/her hands. Later when he/she washes his/her hands with soap or ammonia the powder will go into solution, turning his/her hands red. Phenolphthalein can be obtained from any drug store.

373 *(1-18-80)* 9781
Special Equipment

373.1 *(1-18-80)* 9781
Proper Use and Limitations on Special Equipment

Special agents must refer to and abide by the restrictions and prohibitions relative to investigative and sensitive equipment contained in Policy Statement P-9-35 and any implementing Internal Revenue Manual issuances.

373.2 *(1-18-80)* 9781
Definitions

(1) The types of technical equipment used by the Criminal Investigation Division are defined as follows:

(a) Document Equipment—Those items of equipment peculiar to and utilized primarily by the Criminal Investigation Division in assisting in the investigation of financial crimes. This classification includes microfilm, portable copying, standard format cameras and portable tape recorders (both reel and standard size cassette) and transcription accessories for these.

(b) Investigative Equipment—Items of equipment specially acquired for and used by the Criminal Investigation Division for carrying out investigative and enforcement functions. This equipment includes surveillance trucks, binoculars and optical equipment, surveillance cameras, firearms and ordnance, electronic surveillance equipment, radio communication equipment, night vision equipment, red lights, sirens, and other enforcement equipment intended for use in surveillance situations. The above definitions do not include equipment normally procured for general office or administrative use such as office furniture and office machines (typewriters, calculators, dictation systems used in centralized operations, etc.).

(c) Sensitive-type Equipment—Any equipment which, in a broad sense, can be used in the interception of telephone communications or non-telephone conversations. This includes any type of relay, transmitter, or microphone for use with a telephone; miniature transmitters; concealed radio transmitters disguised as ordinary objects; wireless and parabolic microphones; and amplified microphones. Pen registers and other similar equipment used to identify telephones called are considered to be sensitive equipment.

(d) Accessories and Supplies—Items of little monetary value ($150 or less) chargeable to contingent funds which are specifically acquired for and used by the Criminal Investigation Division in carrying out investigative and enforcement functions.

373.3 *(1-18-80)* 9781
Document Equipment

373.31 *(1-18-80)* 9781
Microfilm Equipment and Photocopying

Microfilm and photocopying equipment is available at each District Office and obtained through the Chief, Criminal Investigation Division. The use of microfilm equipment is a fast, efficient manner of obtaining copies of documentary evidence required in tax investigations. Considerable special agent time can be saved by the use of this equipment. In situations where only a limited quantity of documents need to be copied, it may be more practical to use photocopying or camera equipment. Some special microfilm equipment is available in selected locations for special purpose application. These include High Speed Microfilm cameras which photograph both sides of the document simultaneously and planetary microfilm cameras. Requests for use of this equipment should be made through your immediate supervisor.

373.4 *(1-18-80)* 9781
Investigative Equipment

373.41 *(1-18-80)* 9781
Radios

(1) Certain Criminal Investigation Divisions investigations require the special agent to maintain surveillances of individuals and localities in order to develop evidence of income and excise tax violations. Under certain circumstances taxpayers under investigation for income or excise tax violations will be placed under surveillance when it is suspected that they are attempting to leave the country prior to indictment, or to dispose of or conceal liquid assets.

(2) Mobile and/or portable two-way radios are essential to surveillance involving the use of vehicles. The special agent should use coded signals or words whenever possible in radio transmitting and should talk "in the clear" only when absolutely necessary. Due to the common use of programmable scanners, a special agent should always assume that someone is listening to his radio conversations. If specific identifying information must be transmitted, a code system should be used. The National Office maintains a supply of code matrix sheets which can be provided upon request. Codes are not easy to use and slow the speed of communication. They also require practice for proficiency. The code matrix system works best when one agent is observing and another is encoding, decoding and transmitting on the radio.

(3) Most district offices have an adequate inventory of radio equipment. Normally the special agent should be able to operate this equipment. If not, another special agent or other officer of the Internal Revenue Service experienced in the use of radio equipment may be assigned to instruct or work with him/her.

(4) Certain types of highly specialized radio equipment are available for use by special agents when authorized in specific investigations. This equipment may be obtained through the Director, Criminal Investigation Division. Prior approval of the Chief, Criminal Investigation Division, should be obtained before requesting or using this equipment.

373.42 *(1-18-80)* 9781
Binoculars and Telescopes

The value of binoculars and telescopes in surveillances is self-evident. However, the special agent should exercise care while using them. Binoculars and telescopes may be obtained from the Chief, Criminal Investigation Division.

373.43 *(1-18-80)* 9781
Camera Equipment

A wide variety of camera equipment, capable of performing many specialized and required tasks is available at each district office and obtained through the Chief, Criminal Investigation Division. This equipment includes 35mm single lens reflex cameras with a wide variety of telephoto and accessory equipment; movie cameras; instant load cameras; cameras with self-developing film; and specialized surveillance cameras. Photographs of defendants, witnesses, residences, automobiles, etc., have often proven valuable in tax cases, especially in Special Enforcement Program investigations.

373.44 *(1-18-80)* 9781
Handcuffs

Handcuffs are available to special agents for use in securing persons arrested. Care and discretion must be exercised in their use.

373.45 *(1-18-80)* 9781
Specialized Investigative Equipment

Specialized investigative equipment is available through the Assistant Regional Commissioner (Criminal Investigation). This equipment includes surveillance trucks, night vision equipment, TV video cameras and recorders, specialized camera equipment, etc. This equipment is valuable as surveillance aides in Special Enforcement Program investigations.

373.46 *(1-18-80)* 9781
Sirens, Warning Lights, and Special Automotive Equipment

Use of sirens and warning lights pose a potential danger to the public; consequently, they should be used only when absolutely necessary. (See Policy Statement P-9-38). In some instances special equipment such as locked hoods and lock-type gasoline filler caps should be installed, since violators have, on occasions, sabotaged Government vehicles by putting emery dust, sugar, and similar substances in the crankcase or gasoline tank. However, special agents must have the prior approval of the Chief, Criminal Investigation Division, or of the Assistant Regional Commissioner (Criminal Investigation) before obtaining this equipment.

373.47 *(1-18-80)* 9781
Security of Investigative/Document Equipment and Other Property

(1) Special agents are responsible for taking adequate precautions to safeguard Criminal Investigation Division investigative/document equipment, as well as other items of Service-owned personal property with which they are entrusted. Chapter 500 of IRM 1(16)41, Physical and Document Security Handbook, contains instructions for safeguarding property of the type frequently utilized by special agents in the course of their duties.

(2) Investigative/document equipment as well as other types of Service-owned personal property, with the exception of permanently installed equipment, i.e., mobile radios, vehicle chargers, amplifiers, red lights and sirens, should generally never be left in an unoccupied automobile. However, under unusual circumstances and if absolutely necessary, these items may be stored for short periods of time in the locked trunk of an automobile provided the doors are also locked. Under no circumstances will equipment be left in an automobile overnight.

373.48 *(1-18-80)* 9781
Firearms and Ammunition

373.481 *(1-18-80)* 9781
Authority to Carry

(1) There is no specific statutory authority for special agents to carry firearms. The General Counsel, Department of the Treasury, has concluded that no specific authority is necessary because "where a Federal Officer has authority to make an arrest, he/she has implied authority to carry firearms." Authority for special agents to make arrests is contained in 26 USC 7608(b).

(2) The authority to carry firearms is limited to the conduct of official duties in enforcing any of the criminal provisions of the Internal Revenue laws or other criminal provisions of laws relating to Internal Revenue where the enforcement is the responsibility of the Secretary or his delegate.

373.482 *(1-18-80)* 9781
Issuance of Firearms to Special Agents

(1) Permission to carry firearms will normally be at the discretion of the special agent's immediate supervisor. The supervisor may authorize special agents to carry firearms both during duty hours and off duty hours, if in the authorizing official's judgement a bona-fide need for firearms exists, related to the performance of official duties.

(2) Before granting permission, the immediate supervisor must be assured each special agent is clearly familiar with the Treasury policy and guidelines for weapons use and has qualified within the past six months. Each agent should be provided with a copy of these Manual provisions and periodically consulted to see they have the most recent issuance.

(3) Firearms may be taken home overnight or during a weekend when the special agent finishes his/her workday which requires the carrying of firearms, or when such firearms will be required for the next work day assignments.

(4) Qualification to carry or use privately owned weapons during off-duty hours is done as a private citizen subject to local, civil and criminal restrictions. Special agents may not use their position or credentials to qualify under state or local laws to purchase, license, carry, or use private weapons; however, credentials may be displayed as occupational identification, upon request, but not to influence the decision.

(5) Special agents will not be allowed to carry a firearm unless they have qualified with that firearm in the past six months. (See IRM 9768.3). All special agents must have their badge and pocket commission on their person, when carrying a firearm, except under unusual circumstances relating to special assignments

approved by the Assistant Regional Commissioner (Criminal Investigation).

373.483 *(1-18-80)* 9781
Firearms Standards

(1) No weapons or ammunition other than that furnished by the Service except as provided in IRM 9756.2:(7) will be carried by any special agent on official business. All handguns furnished for regular assignment to personnel will be American made .38 special caliber revolver type.

(2) Service-issued guns may be modified upon approval of the ARC (Criminal Investigation). Such modifications must be made by qualified personnel or a gunsmith. Installation of grips, and grip adapters are not considered to be modifications to weapons.

(3) Trigger shoes are prohibited on all official weapons.

(4) Criminal Investigation guns must have a minimum of three pound pressure trigger pull.

(5) The .38 special caliber revolver (all steel) with two-inch barrel will be assigned to each special agent at the district office. Firearms may be assigned, one to each special agent, on a permanent basis or they may be retained in a pool in the district or local office and withdrawn as needed. If the weapons are retained in a pool, each special agent should be issued, to the extent possible, the same gun each time to ensure better proficiency in handling the weapon.

(6) The .38 special caliber revolver (all steel) with two-inch barrel will be assigned on a ratio of one for each two special agents or technical personnel at regional offices and the National Office.

(7) The .38 special caliber revolver with four-inch barrel will be assigned, as needed, for special assignments where greater accuracy and reliability may be compelling factors for target practice, training and for competition.

(8) The .38 special caliber revolver with six-inch barrel will be assigned, as needed, for training and competition purposes.

(9) The .22 caliber revolver on a .38 special caliber frame will be assigned, as needed, for training purposes.

(10) Under unusual circumstances relating to special assignments, the ARC (Criminal Investigation) may authorize the use of a Service-owned weapon of any type on a specific assignment basis. The Director may authorize the use of a Treasury-owned weapon of any type for a specific assignment (See IRM 9756.4:(6)).

(11) Holsters of any standard type will be furnished on a basis of one holster for each revolver. The type of holster must be approved by the ARC (Criminal Investigation), except when purchased as accesssory equipment for revolvers by the National Office.

(12) Any firearm which does not meet the prescribed standards shall be forwarded to the district Facilities Management Branch for adjustment or repair.

(13) The Chief, Criminal Investigation Division, shall make provision to ensure that each weapon is in perfect operating condition immediately preceding its issuance and annual inspections thereafter.

(14) Each special agent will be responsible for the weapon in his/her possession and will keep the gun clean and in perfect operating condition at all times.

(15) When a firearm is found to be defective, it will be forwarded immediately to the district Facilities Management Branch for repair.

(16) In accordance with IRM 1(14)49 Personal Property Management Handbook Exhibit 400-1, any acquisition of a firearm must be requested through channels to the Director, Criminal Investigation Division, Attn: CP:CI:M for approval.

373.484 *(1-18-80)* 9781
Ammunition Standards

(1) All Service-furnished ammunition for qualification and Service use will be new and American made. The exclusive use of new ammunition by criminal enforcement personnel has been selected because of quality control.

(2) Experiences of operating personnel indicate that reload ammunition create safety and security hazards, especially if used in line of duty, and may cause accelerated weapon deterioration.

(3) The standard service ammunition for Criminal Investigation will be the .38 special caliber, 110 grain jacketed hollow point available commercially with a copper units of pressure rating (cup) not to exceed 20,000 cup. Law enforcement ammunition with a designation of "+P+" or "++P" should not be used in small frame service owned weapon (i.e., Smith and Wesson Chief, Colt Detective Special, etc.).

(4) The .38 special caliber midrange or wadcutter, 148 grain, lead or lubaloy coated ammunition may be utilized for firearms competition, training, qualification, and requalification purposes.

(5) If the standard service ammunition (110 grain) is not utilized for training, qualification or requalification purposes, personnel should fire 30 rounds of this ammunition for familiarization purposes at each qualification and requalification.

(6) The .22 caliber long rifle pistol match target ammunition (40 grain) may be used for firearms training.

(7) The above ammunition standards and restrictions will not apply when in the judgment of the ARC (Criminal Investigation) the use of different ammunition is necessary or desirable such as in special assignments or situations.

(8) Special agents on dignitary protection under the direction of Secret Service are permitted to utilize ammunition provided them by the Secret Service, however, the Secret Service utilizes only ammunition with a CUP rating of "+P+" or "++P". Special Agents are cautioned not to use this ammunition in small frame weapons (i.e. Smith and Wesson Chief, Colt Detective Special) and to have a larger frame weapon made available to them for these assignments (i.e. Smith and Wesson Model 15, Colt Lawman, etc.)

373.485 *(1-18-80)* 9781
Use of Firearms by Special Agents

(1) Firearms Policy

(a) A firearm may be discharged only as a last resort when in the considered opinion of the officer there is danger of loss of life or serious bodily injury to himself or to another person.

(b) Firing a weapon should be with the intent of rendering the person at whom the weapon is discharged incapable of continuing the activity prompting the agent to shoot.

(c) Warning shots pose a hazard to innocent parties. They should be fired only when the expected effect is to minimize substantially the necessity of firing directly at a person, *AND* there is negligible danger of injury to an innocent party.

(d) Firing at a moving vehicle with the intent of rendering it incapable of being operated poses a formidable danger to innocent parties. The possibility of a richochet is greatly increased when the target is a car body or a spinning tire. Utmost caution must be exercised when considering such action.

(e) Firing at a fleeing person will not be considered justified unless the officer has reasonable cause to believe that the person he/she is considering shooting poses a threat to the life of the officer or others.

(f) As a general rule when in the presence of the public, a handgun should be drawn only when the special agent or his/her superiors have sufficient cause to expect it will be used and the officer is preparing for its use.

(g) When making arrests or searches and seizure, only reasonable and necessary force may be used by the special agent. The special agent should allow the escape of a subject rather than risk inflicting bodily harm by shooting at the subject as stated in P-9-37.

(2) When a handgun is being carried in the conduct of official business, it will be inconspicuously carried upon the person of the agent so as to be away from public view. However, a special agent may display a firearm while in the performance of official business, if the agent feels that by doing so, it will relieve a threat against the agent or another person.

(3) If, while carrying a firearm on official duty, a special agent observes a Federal crime being committed, he/she is expected to respond, depending on the circumstances involved. Ordinarily, the special agent should notify the appropriate Federal or local authority. In life/death situations or incidents in which he/she is inextricably involved, the special agent should respond as a Federal law enforcement officer.

(4) A special agent is also authorized to appropriately respond should a non-Federal crime involving danger of loss of life or serious bodily injury be committed in his/her presence, or where he/she reasonably believes such a crime has occurred; however, the special agent should understand that in non-Federal crime situations, his/her authority is that of a private citizen and the rules of "citizens arrest" apply. If circumstances allow, local authorities should be notified rather than becoming involved. If not, good judgement must prevail in the course of action taken.

(5) In all circumstances involving the use of a firearm to halt a crime involving danger of loss of life or serious bodily injury to themselves or to another person, special agents are to use the Treasury Department guidelines set forth above. They will be followed regardless of the fact that state or local law may be more liberal in allowing their law enforcement officers to use firearms.

(6) Whenever a firearm is discharged by a special agent while in the performance of official duty (except official target practice), the special agent will submit a full explanation of the reasons for such action in a memorandum which will be forwarded through official channels, to the Director, Criminal Investigation Division (CP:CI:M).

373.486 *(3-12-82)* 9781

Carrying Firearms and Armed Escorts on Commercial Airplanes

(1) Federal Aviation Administration Regulations, Sections 108.11 and 108.21 of 14 CFR 108, Airplane Operator Security, provides information and guidance concerning the carriage of weapons and the carriage of passengers under the control of armed law enforcement escort(s). This material is summarized in Federal Aviation Administration (FAA) Advisory Circular 108-2 dated Oct. 16, 1981. These Regulations apply to carriage of weapons and escort of individuals on scheduled passenger and/or charter operations. This definition includes air commuter operations, air taxis and other similar type of air service available to the public.

(2) Carriage of weapons by special agents aboard aircraft should be limited to those instances where the special agent needs the weapon accessible in the performance of official duty during the period from the time it would otherwise be placed in checked baggage until such time as it would have been returned after deplaning.

(3) When a special agent is acting in the capacity of armed escort or other type assignment which requires carrying a weapon onboard commercial aircraft, appropriate airline officials should be notified at least one hour in advance, or in case of emergency as soon as possible, before departure. Special agents will then be guided by instructions from the airline official as to what procedure(s) should be followed.

(4) As a general rule, armed federal law enforcement officers will be in one of the following categories when on travel status:

a) Armed individual traveling alone (occasionally without baggage);

b) Armed, transporting a non-dangerous prisoner;

c) Armed, transporting a dangerous prisoner;

d) Armed escort accompanying a dignitary;

e) Armed, conducting a surveillance on suspect.

f) Armed escort for protection of a witness or information

(5) Your carriage of a weapon and your identity will be made known to airline personnel who need this knowledge.

(6) In the event of a disturbance aboard the aircraft you are not to take any action unless it is specifically requested by the flight captain.

(7) Armed special agents will not consume alcoholic beverages prior to, or during flight.

(8) Instructions pertaining to armed escort of prisoners, are as follows:

(a) The air carrier must be notified at least one hour before departure, or in an emergency, as soon as practicable of the identity of the passenger to be carried and the flight on which it is proposed to carry the passenger.

(b) Whether the passenger is considered to be in a maximum risk category (dangerous) or not.

(c) If the passenger is considered to be in a maximum risk category, the passenger must be under the control of at least two armed special agents.

(d) No more than one passenger in a maximum risk category can be carried on the airplane.

(e) If the passenger is considered to be not in a maximum risk category, the passenger should be under the control of at least one special agent. No more than two of these persons may be carried under the control of any one special agent.

(9) The air carrier should be assured by the special agent, prior to departure, that:

(a) The special agent is equipped with adequate restraining devices to be used in the event restraint of any passenger under control of the special agent becomes necessary. Some aircraft operators do not permit restraining devices to be used while in flight due to perceived safety/liability concerns that might arise in the event of an incident or an accident. The special agent and the aircraft operator should have a clear understanding of this issue prior to initiation of the intended travel.

(b) Each passenger under the control of the special agent has been searched and does not have on or about their person or property anything that could be used as a deadly or dangerous weapon.

(c) Each passenger under the control of the special agent should be boarded before any other passengers at the airport where the flight originates and deplane at the destination after all other passengers have departed.

(d) The special agent and passenger should be seated in the rear most passenger seat when boarding. This seat should be located away from any lounge area and not directly across from any exit. At least one escort should sit between the person in custody and any aisle.

(e) The passenger cannot consume any alcoholic beverages while on board the airplane.

(f) Each special agent, at all times, shall accompany the passenger under their control and keep the passenger under surveillance while aboard the airplane.

(g) This material does not apply to the carriage of passengers under voluntary protective escort.

(10) The following procedures will be utilized in the carriage of firearms and ammunition in checked luggage:

(a) The weapon must be unloaded.

(b) The carrier must be notified prior to checking baggage that a firearm is in checked baggage and that it is unloaded. If requested, the special agent will submit a written declaration that the firearm is stored as specified. It is likely that the carrier will have a preprinted form for this declaration.

(c) The baggage must be locked and the agent in possession of the key or combination. The special agent's name and address should be included inside the baggage. Checked baggage containing weapons will not be carried in the flight crew compartment or any area accessible to passengers.

(d) Small arms ammunition must be packed in pasteboard, or other inside boxes, or in partitions designed to fit snugly into outside wooden, fiberglass, or metal containers, or must be packed in metal ammunition clips. The packaging must be designed to protect the primers from accidental discharge.

(e) Special agents will not carry chemical weapons aboard any aircraft (See IRM 9756.9:(7).

373.487 *(1-18-80)* 9781
Security of Firearms and Ammunition

(1) Due to the dangerous nature of firearms and the potential for accidential injury and damage, the minimum guidelines for storing Government owned firearms and ammunition as contained in 436 of IRM 1(16)41. Physical and Document Security Handbook should be followed.

(2) Provision shall be made by the Chief, Criminal Investigation Division, for at least one safety inspection each year of all Government-owned firearms assigned to the Chief's office. The inspection may be performed by any person competent in the inspection of firearms, including local range officers, gunsmiths, or special agents who have an expert knowledge of firearms.

(3) If it is necessary to store weapons at home, they should be kept under lock and key. Ammunition should be kept locked in a separate location from the weapon. Special agents may wish to insert a padlock through the open cylinder, thereby rendering the revolver harmless.

(4) Firearms and ammunition should never be left in an automobile, even though the automobile is locked. However, if absolutely necessary, these items may be stored for short periods of time in the locked trunk of an automobile, providing the doors are also locked. Weapons will not be left locked in an automobile overnight.

(5) Never handle or point any firearm without first opening the weapon to make absolutely certain it is not loaded.

(6) At the range, do not load or cock your weapon unless you are at the firing line and facing the target. Do not turn around at the firing line with a loaded revolver in your hand without first breaking open the cylinder. Always examine the bore of a weapon before loading it to see that it is free from obstructions.

(7) Never leave an unattended firearm loaded.

373.488 *(1-18-80)* 9781
Chemical Weapons

(1) Chemical weapons may be carried by Criminal Investigation Division personnel when engaged in enforcement activities of such a nature that prudence indicates need for them may arise (i.e., riots, rebellions, arrests, attacks on people or property).

(2) The Director, the Assistant Regional Commissioners and the Chiefs, Criminal Investigation Division or their designees, may authorize special agents in their respective offices (includes posts of duty under the Chief) to carry chemical weapons if in his/her judgment a bona fide need exists, related to the performance of official duties.

(3) The Director, the Assistant Regional Commissioners and the Chiefs, Criminal Investigation Division, or their designees shall ensure that each special agent whose duty requires the handling or use of a chemical weapon thoroughly understands its use and effects, including the proper first-aid treatment for persons affected by its use. Instruction involving the use of and first aid in the treatment of chemical irritants may be incorporated into the firearms refresher training program thereby utilizing the firearms coach concept.

(4) Chemical weapons may be used only when milder forms of persuasion are ineffective and deadly force is not justified. Aerosol-propelled tear gas must be treated as another dangerous weapon, using safety precautions similar to those used with firearms.

(5) Every effort must be made to direct the spray at a person's chest for the minimum time required to incapacitate and at a distance of at least two feet.

(6) It is a misuse of the chemical weapon to deliberately discharge it directly into the face of an incapacitated person or to discharge quantities in excess of the equivalent of five, one-second bursts, or to discharge large quantities of the spray in a confined place such as a small room or a closed automobile.

(7) Special agents will not carry chemical weapons aboard an aircraft. This restriction also covers the placing of these items in checked baggage, inasmuch as the baggage compartment is part of the air circulation system of the aircraft.

(8) Whenever a chemical weapon is discharged by a special agent while in the performance of official duty (except official training or to accomplish disposal at end of shelf life), the special agent will submit a full explanation of the reasons for such action in a memorandum which will be forwarded through official channels to the Director, Criminal Investigation Division, Attention: CP:CI:M. The memorandum should include, where possible, the identity of the person afflicted by the tear gas and any first-aid measures subsequently applied.

373.489 *(1-18-80)* 9781

Security of Chemical Weapons

Due to the potential hazards associated with chemical weapons if indiscriminately used or accidentally misused, the minimum guidelines for storing investigative equipment as contained in Exhibit 500-2 of IRM 1(16)41, Physical and Document Security Handbook will be followed.

373.5 *(1-18-80)* 9781

Sensitive Equipment

(1) With regard to sensitive-type equipment, the following procedures should be followed:

(a) Except for induction coils (as noted below) field offices may not purchase, or obtain in any other way, sensitive-type investigative equipment.

(b) Field offices should not permanently maintain an inventory of induction coils. When consensual telephone monitoring is approved in accordance with IRM 9389.2 field offices may locally purchase an induction coil and retain it for the minimum period of time necessary to conduct the authorized consensual telephone monitoring. The induction coil should then be destroyed in accordance with 650 of IRM 1(14)49, Personal Property Management Handbook.

(2) Only those individuals who have received training in the use, operation, and installation of this equipment will be permitted to install and operate it unless specifically authorized to do so by the Assistant Regional Commissioner (Criminal Investigation). These programs will be conducted with sufficient frequency to assure that operators and installers of this equipment retain their expertise.

373.6 *(1-18-80)* 9781

Electronic Surveillance Equipment

(1) This equipment may only be used for monitoring and recording conversations with the consent of at least one, but not all, the parties to the conversation. The monitoring of telephone conversations with the consent of at least one party can be authorized by the Chief, Criminal Investigation. The monitoring of a non-telephone conversation with the consent of at least one of the parties generally requires the advance written authorization of the Attorney General of the United States. See text 341.33 for additional guidelines.

(2) Consensual electronic surveillance is used when the investigation has progressed to a point where the agent determines that a crucial piece of evidence or corroboration cannot be obtained in any other way.

(3) The only special agents authorized to install and operate electronic surveillance equipment (except induction coils) are those who have attended the Special Electronic Equipment Seminar conducted by the National Office. These agents will be identified by the ARC (Criminal Investigation). In an emergency situation the ARC (Criminal Investigation) may authorize other agents to install this equipment.

373.7 *(1-18-80)* 9781

Tape Recording Equipment

(1) Hand-held cassette recorders are available in most districts to dictate memoranda of meetings, surveillance notes, reports and other documents which will ultimately be transcribed into typed form. They are not recommended for recording question and answer sessions or depositions due to the lack of tape continuity when a cassette must be changed or switched to the other side. Poor quality cassettes or cassettes greater than 90 minutes (45 minutes per side) are not recommended.

(2) Cassette Transcribers are also provided to many offices for secretarial transcription of cassette tapes recorded on hand-held recorders.

(3) Reel-to-reel recorders are available in many offices to record long meetings, question and answer sessions or depositions when tape continuity and increased fidelity are required.

(4) Specialized recording equipment such as mixers for multiple microphones, filters, playback amplifiers and wireless headphone courtroom amplification systems are available for specific situations from the National Office.

380 *(1-18-80)* 9781
Surveillance, Searches and Seizures, Raids and Forfeitures

381 *(1-18-80)* 9781
Surveillance

(1) Surveillance is an investigative technique where an individual or group of individuals are physically observed by special agents in order to obtain information, leads and evidence that have tax significance and would not normally be available through other investigative techniques. Special agents conducting surveillance normally do not have to assume an identity other than their own. However, on some occasions they may need to conceal their identity during the surveillance by assuming a temporary identity.

(2) The following are some of the reasons for conducting a surveillance:

(a) to obtain evidence of a crime;

(b) to locate persons by watching their haunts and associates;

(c) to obtain detailed information about a subject's activities;

(d) to check on the reliability of informants;

(e) to locate hidden property;

(f) to obtain probable cause of obtaining search warrants;

(g) to obtain information for later use in interrogation;

(h) to develop leads and information received from other sources;

(i) to know at all times the whereabouts of an individual; and

(j) to obtain admissible evidence for use in court.

(3) Whenever a special agent perceives a need to conduct surveillance, he/she will submit a memorandum request to his/her group manager setting forth the pertinent details as to the purpose, scope, anticipated duration, probable geographic area, number of agents needed, extra costs involved, need for a temporary identity, etc. The group manager will indicate approval or disapproval on the memorandum request and return it to the special agent with a copy forwarded immediately to the Chief, Criminal Investigation Division.

(4) All authorized surveillance conducted in a high crime area, either on foot or in a vehicle(s), will require at least two agents participating in the surveillance. Whenever possible, surveillance requiring the use of a vehicle should be conducted in government-owned vehicles that have two-way radio equipment.

(5) During the course of a special agent's activities, situations may occasionally arise where immediate surveillance is necessary. In such urgent situations, where the surveillance will last no more than one day, the request may be handled telephonically. If the request is approved, the agent will, as soon as possible, prepare a memorandum setting forth the oral request and submit it to his/her group manager. The group manager will indicate his/her approval on the memorandum and return it to the agent, with a copy forwarded immediately to the Chief. However, in such urgent situations where a telephone request is not practicable, the agent may conduct the necessary surveillance without prior approval of the group manager. The agent will, as soon as possible, prepare a memorandum setting forth the nature of the circumstances which precluded him/her from making a request and submit it to his/her group manager. The group manager will initial the memorandum and return it to the agent and forward a copy immediately to the Chief.

(6) The special agent will prepare surveillance notes daily of all pertinent activity that the person was observed doing. Upon final completion of the surveillance, the special agent will prepare a written summary of his/her notes for the file with a copy to the group manager and a copy as an attachment to any other document that may be prepared, i.e., information item, item for the indexing system, etc.

(7) Surveillance activities at tax protest meetings will be limited to attendance at those meetings for the purpose of obtaining information concerning new techniques being advocated in the so-called tax protest movement. Special agents who attend these meetings will not

identify individuals who attend the meetings unless the individuals openly admit that they:

(a) have committed or intend to commit a tax violation; or

(b) advocate that others commit violations of the tax laws; or

(c) advocate the use of threat and/or assault tactics in dealing with Service personnel.

(8) The information obtained relative to (7)(a) and (7)(b) will be processed in accordance with IRM 9311. The information regarding (7)(c) will be processed in accordance with IRM 9142.4. Special computer applications will not be used for this data.

(9) The attendance at tax protest meetings is to be distinguished from peaceful demonstrations directed towards some sort of tax protest. In this regard, Service personnel will be guided by Treasury Department policy which directs that no information should be collected on peaceful demonstrations which involve the exercise of First Amendment rights without contacting the office of the Assistant Secretary (Enforcement and Operations). In such situations, the Chief, Criminal Investigation Division, with the concurrence of the District Director, and ARC, Criminal Investigation will notify the Director, Criminal Investigation Division, who will contact the Assistant Secretary (Enforcement and Operations).

(10) See also IRM 9383.6

382 *(1-18-80)* 9781

Undercover Work

(1) A penetration-type undercover operation is an investigative technique where an authorized IRS employee assumes an identity and a job or profession other than his/her own for the purpose of legally securing information or evidence necessary in an official inquiry relating to possible tax law violations. In this role, the undercover agent actively attempts to gain the acceptance and the confidence of known or suspected tax law violators and/or their associates.

(2) An undercover operation is a potentially dangerous undertaking and should be limited to those cases or situations that are considered to be particularly significant from a tax administration viewpoint and when other means of securing the desired information or evidence are not feasible.

(3) Requests for undercover operations should specify:

(a) the need for the undercover activity;

(b) the proposed operation objectives;

(c) a cost projection including but not limited to travel, per diem, and confidential expenses;

(d) an estimated completion date for the undercover activity and an estimate of agent-days;

(e) the proposed plan of action including a discussion of any state or federal law violations with which the undercover agent may come in contact, and a proposal for dealing with such situations; and

(f) any other information that is pertinent.

(4) All requests for undercover operations will require the approval of the Director, Criminal Investigation Division. The request must first be approved by the Chief, Criminal Investigation Division, the District Director, the ARC (Criminal Investigation) and then forwarded to the Director. Upon approval by the Director, the request will be forwarded, through normal channels, to the official responsible for approving the confidential expenditures relating to the operation in accordance with IRM 9372.2. The requesting Chief will be notified by memorandum, through normal channels, of the Director's actions. When not approved by the Director, the request will be returned through normal channels to the Chief with an explanation for not approving the operation.

(5) Once the undercover plan for the operation has been approved by the Director, Criminal Investigation Division, no deviation may be made with regard to the stated objectives of the operation without the Director's approval. However, the undercover agent may deviate from the proposed plan of action in order to attain the operation's objective.

(6) The selection, training and cover documents for all agents who will be involved in penetrating-type undercover activities will be provided by the National Office Criminal Investigation Division. All undercover assignments will be on a detail basis. See IRM 0300.4 and Chapter 300, Subchapter 8 of the Federal Personnel Manual with regard to procedures relating to the detailing of employees. The selection of the agent for an undercover assignment must have the concurrence of the Chief in the district where the agent will be working. The agents selected for such assignments will remain assigned to their original districts.

(7) Once the Chief, Criminal Investigation Division, determines that the stated objectives of the undercover operation have been accomplished, or cannot be accomplished, or cannot be accomplished without expending an unreasonable amount of staffpower, he/she should terminate the operation.

(8) Supervision of the undercover special agent will be the responsibility of the Chief in the district in which the undercover agent is working. (See IRM 0300.451 with regard to evaluating an undercover agent when he/she is from another district.)

(9) The Chief will assign a "contact" agent at the district location of the undercover operation to perform on-site liaison with the undercover special agent. The principal duties of the contact special agent are to:

(a) receive daily activity and financial reports of the undercover agent;

(b) provide assistance in the preparation of reimbursement claims and financial earnings;

(c) transmit necessary instructions and information to the undercover agent;

(d) insure that district objectives are being carried out by the undercover agent;

(e) attend to the security and safety of the undercover agent; and

(f) provide immediate assistance in any emergency.

(10) The undercover agent will in all instances report to the Chief or to the contact agent, if the Chief cannot be reached, any illegal activities that come to his/her attention and specify any possible involvement by himself/herself.

(11) Undercover agents will avoid acts of entrapment and will observe the Constitutional rights of those persons whom they come in contact with during their assignments. However, while acting in an undercover capacity, agents are not required to advise a subject of his/her Constitutional rights as contained in IRM 9384.2:(2)(b).

(12) Information obtained as a result of an undercover operation which pertains to violations of laws administered by other law enforcement agencies will be transmitted to the appropriate agencies through regular channels provided the dissemination of the information does not jeopardize the undercover operation or agent. In order to withhold information concerning other violations, the Chief will submit a recommendation, along with justification, through channels to the Director, Criminal Investigation Division. The Director, Criminal Investigation Division will obtain the advice of the Office of Chief Counsel prior to making a final decision. However, in those instances where there is a disagreement between the Director, Criminal Investigation Division and Chief Counsel, the matter will be referred to the Assistant Commissioner (Compliance) for the final decision.

(13) Information items resulting from undercover operations will be handled according to established procedures unless such action might endanger the operation or the undercover agent. In order to withhold action on information which may have tax significance, the Chief, with the District Director's concurrence, will make the final decision. The Chief will notify the ARC (Criminal Investigation) of any such decision.

(14) Information which is withheld in accordance with IRM 9389.(11), (12) and (13) will be processed according to established procedures either at a later point in time during the undercover operation when release of such information would not jeopardize the agent or undercover operation or following the termination of the undercover operation.

(15) The undercover agent will prepare a monthly statement of earnings from all sources associated with the undercover assignment. Arrangements will be made to have the undercover agent submit his/her total earnings to the "contact" agent periodically, but a least on a monthly basis. The undercover agent should use a form of repayment that will not jeopardize his/her cover, such as money order or cash. The "contact" agent will forward the remittance to the Chief, Resources Management Division in the district office, who will follow the standard procedures in 460 of IRM 1717, Administrative Accounting Handbook, in forwarding the remittance to the Chief, Fiscal Management Branch in the regional office.

(16) Expenditures incurred by an undercover agent cannot be offset against his/her cover employment income. Undercover agents will submit monthly reimbursement claims to the specified imprest funds for all expenditures incurred in connection with the undercover assignment in accordance with IRM 9773.3. Each agent will be required to submit documentation of expenses to the extent that obtaining such documentation would not jeopardize his/her security. The agent will also provide explanations as to why no receipts are available for all

those transactions where he/she would be expected to have receipts. Travel and per diem incurred outside of the undercover assignments will be claimed on travel vouchers (see IRM 9773.3:(7)).

(17) Each month, the "contact" agent will prepare a written summary of the results and progress of the undercover operation and forward it together with the daily and monthly reports to the Chief (see IRM 9389.(11):(9)(a)).

(18) Procedures for agents who assume a temporary identity other than their own for non-penetrating type operations such as "shopping" return preparers, surveillance, etc., are provided in IRM 9383.6.

(19) See also IRM 9389.(11).

383 *(1-18-80)* 9781
Searches and Seizures

383.1 *(1-18-80)* 9781
Introduction

This sets forth the procedures governing the applications, issuance, execution, and return of search warrants and the techniques used in making tax related raids.

383.2 *(1-18-80)* 9781
Authority and Procedure

383.21 *(1-18-80)* 9781
Constitutional Authority

The basic authority for making searches and seizures is in the Fourth Amendment to the Constitution of the United States which states:

> "The right of the people to be secure in their persons, houses, papers, and effects against unreasonable searches and seizures shall not be violated, and no warrants shall issue, but upon probable cause, supported by oath or affirmation, and particularly describing the place to be searched and the persons or things to be seized."

383.22 *(1-18-80)* 9781
Statutory Authority

18 USC 3105 and 3109, Rule 41 of the Federal Rules of Criminal Procedure, and 26 USC 7302, 7321, and 7608 contain the statutory authority pertinent to searches and seizures by special agents. Pertinent parts of Rule 41 that a special agent should know before attempting to make a search and seizure are quoted below:

> "(a) Authority to issue warrant.—A search warrant authorized by this rule may be issued by a federal magistrate or a judge of a state court of record within the district wherein the property sought is located, upon request of a federal law enforcement officer or an attorney for the government.
>
> "(b) Property which may be seized with a warrant.—A warrant may be issued under this rule to search for and seize any (1) property that constitutes evidence of the commission of a criminal offense; or (2) contraband, the fruits of crime, or things otherwise criminally possessed; or (3) property designed or intended for use or which is or has been used as the means of committing a criminal offense.
>
> "(c) Issuance and contents.—A warrant shall issue only on an affidavit or affidavits sworn to before the federal magistrate or state judge and establishing the grounds for issuing the warrant. If the federal magistrate or state judge is satisfied that the grounds for the application exist or that there is probable cause to believe that they exist, he shall issue a warrant identifying the property and naming or describing the person or place to be searched. The finding of probable cause may be based upon hearsay evidence in whole or in part. Before ruling on a request for a warrant the federal magistrate or state judge may require the affiant to appear personally and may examine under oath the affiant and any witnesses he may produce, provided that such proceeding shall be taken down by a court reporter or recording equipment and made part of the affidavit. The warrant shall be directed to a civil officer of the United States authorized to enforce or assist in enforcing any law thereof or to a person so authorized by the President of the United States. It shall command the officer to search, within a specified period of time not to exceed 10 days, the person or place named for the property specified. The warrant shall be served in the daytime, unless the issuing authority, by appropriate provision in the warrant, and for reasonable cause shown, authorizes its execution at times other than daytime. It shall designate a federal magistrate to whom it shall be returned.
>
> "(d) Execution and return with inventory.—The officer taking property under the warrant shall give to the person from whom or from whose premises the property was taken a copy of the warrant and a receipt for the property taken or shall leave the copy and receipt at the place from which the property was taken. The return shall be made promptly and shall be accompanied by a written inventory of any property taken. The inventory shall be made in the presence of the applicant for the warrant and the person from whose possession or premises the property was taken, if they are present, or in the presence of at least one credible person other than the applicant for the warrant or the person from whose possession or premises the property was taken, and shall be verified by the officer. The federal magistrate shall upon request deliver a copy of the inventory to the person from whom or from whose premises the property was taken and to the applicant for the warrant.
>
> "(e) Motion for return of property.—A person aggrieved by an unlawful search and seizure may move the district court for the district in which the property was seized for the return of the property on the ground that he is entitled to lawful possession of the property which was illegally seized. The judge shall receive evidence on any issue of fact necessary to the decision of the motion. If the motion is granted the property shall be restored and it shall not be admissible in evidence at any hearing or trial. If a motion for return of property is made or comes for hearing in the district of trial after an indictment or information is filed, it shall be treated also as a motion to suppress under Rule 12.
>
> "(f) Motion to suppress.—A motion to suppress evidence may be made in the court of the district of trial as provided in Rule 12.

"(g) Return of papers to clerk.—The federal magistrate before whom the warrant is returned shall attach to the warrant a copy of the return, inventory and all other papers in connection therewith and shall file them with the clerk of the district court for the district in which the property was seized.

"(h) Scope and definition.—This rule does not modify any act, inconsistent with it, regulating search, seizure and the issuance and execution of search warrants in circumstances for which special provision is made. The term 'property' is used in this rule to include documents, books, papers and any other tangible objects. The term 'daytime' is used in this rule to mean the hours from 6:00 a.m., to 10:00 p.m., according to local time. The phrase 'federal law enforcement officer' is used in this rule to mean any government agent, other than an attorney for the government as defined in Rule 54(c) who is engaged in the enforcement of the criminal laws and is within any category of officers authorized by the Attorney General to request the issuance of a search warrant."

383.3 *(1-18-80)* 9781
Unreasonable Searches and Seizures

(1) The definition of unreasonable searches and seizures as used in the Fourth Amendment has not been expressed in a concrete rule. The various courts have had different opinions of what constitutes the basis for a legal search and seizure. In fact the Supreme Court has varied its opinions so often on this subject there can be but one firm conclusion: namely, that reasonableness is determined in each case based upon the facts and circumstances of the particular case. This is not to say that special agents cannot learn some guidelines to follow and conversely some pitfalls to avoid by studying the court rulings and by learning the procedures that will be discussed in this section. *Essentially any search and seizure without a warrant is automatically unreasonable unless:*

(a) It is made incident to an arrest for a crime committed in the officer's presence, [*Draper v. U.S.*] or

(b) The occupant of the premises who has authority understandingly consents.

(2) Anyone legitimately on premises where a search occurs may challenge its legality, [*Cecil Jones v. U.S.*] It is not necessary for him/her to show ownership, right to possession, or dominion over the premises. Entering a house with permission of the occupant's landlord. [*Elmer S. Chapman v. U.S.*] or a hotel room with consent of the management or a desk clerk [*Stoner v. California; U.S. v. Jeffers; Lustig v. U.S.*] is insufficient, and a search and seizure resulting from such entry is illegal. The Supreme Court has refused to rule specifically on whether a wife may, in her husband's absence, waive his constitutional rights by consenting to a search of their home. [*Amos v. U.S.*] Some lower courts have held that a wife has implied authority to consent to the search. [*Stein v. U.S.; U.S. v. Pugliese; U.S. v Sergio*] Others have declared that she does not have such authority. [*Cofer v. U.S.; U.S. v. Rykowski*] A search has been deemed reasonable where a partner [*U.S. v. Sferas*] or office manager [*U.S. v. Antonelli Fireworks Co.*] consented to it, but not where the consent was that of a handyman in a defendant's store. [*U.S. v. Joseph Harry Block*] One who shares a desk with fellow employees on business premises of their employer may move to suppress evidence against him obtained from a search of the desk without his consent. [*Villano v. U.S.*]

(3) An unreasonable search and seizure, in the sense of the Fourth Amendment, does not necessarily involve the employment of force or coercion, but may be committed when a representative of any branch or sub-division of the Government, by stealth, through social acquaintance, or in the guise of a business call, gains entrance to the house or office of a person suspected of a crime, whether in the presence or absence of the owner, and searches for an abstracts papers without consent. [*Gouled v. U.S.*]

(4) The exclusionary rule suppressing evidence seized in violation of the Fourth Amendment applies to State, as well as Federal, officers in any criminal case. [*Mapp v. Ohio*] Where the State and Federal officers have an understanding that the latter may prosecute in Federal courts offenses which the former discover in the course of their operations, and where the Federal officers adopt a prosecution originated by State officers as a result of a search made by them, the same rule as to the admissibility of evidence obtained in the course of the search should be applied as if it were made by the Federal officers themselves or under their direction. [*Sutherland v. U.S.*] These decisions and others in the same vein are of particular importance since the Criminal Investigation Division, in some instances, may adopt tax-related cases from State officers.

(5) In *Will P. Clay v. U.S.* special agents conducted a two-months' surveillance which indicated that Clay was operating a lottery business involving a pattern requiring him to be at certain places at certain times during the day. He used various automobiles during the period of surveillance and was observed passing and receiving articles common to a lottery business. Based upon this surveillance, Clay was stopped on a highway by special agents and his automobile searched. Clay was arrested after a special agent observed a lottery booklet on his person. The court held that it was an unreasonable search and seizure without the proper search warrant. The "mere act of a known gambler driving an automobile on a public highway will not justify an officer forcing him to stop to be searched or arrested for a suspected violation." Further, "nothing discernable to the senses taught reasonably that crime was then being done until the agent saw, and demanded, the lottery booklet. But this was too late, for the strong arm of the law had peremptorily stopped this traveler and placed him under evident immediate command of Government officers." The court pointed out there was insufficient evidence indicating affirmative acts for the

agents to reasonably believe that a felony had been committed. Therefore, it was essential that the agents discern some evidence by their senses to induce a belief in them that a misdemeanor was being committed in their presence.

(6) Unreasonable search and seizure cases usually result from a lack of understanding of the law and the failure to state in sufficient detail the actual known or available facts, either in applications for warrants or while testifying to the facts. Another cause of illegal searches has been overzealousness on the part of the officers. [*Trupiano v. U.S.*] As a general rule, special agents will find it necessary to secure search warrants in tax cases, since very seldom will a crime be committed in their presence which would give them sufficient probable cause to arrest and then make a search incident to the arrest.

(7) In determining the question of reasonableness, the best rule of procedure is to operate as far away from the dividing line as the available facts of the case will permit and always on the legal side thereof. In addition to learning as much of the law as possible and how to relate the facts in all of their details, the special agent should constantly ask the question, "Are my actions reasonable in the eyes of the courts?"

383.4 *(11-10-81)* 9781

Approval for Search Warrants

(1) Chief Counsel and the Department of Justice will consider requests for search warrants in significant tax cases where a violation of Title 26 can be proved by the evidence allegedly in the possession of the individual, or on the premises to be searched. Search warrants may be authorized in income tax, multiple refund and return preparer cases, however, application for a search warrant should be sought only in connection with significant tax cases in view of the Service's, and the Department's, practice of restraint. The significance of a tax case may be determined by a consideration of such factors as: the amount of taxes due, the nature of fraud, and the impact of the particular case on voluntary compliance with the revenue laws.

(2) The Chief, Criminal Investigation Division may authorize special agents to apply for search warrants in non-income tax cases specifically in the enforcement of the wagering tax & laws. The Chief, Criminal Investigation Division will, upon approval of the District Director, obtain the approval of District Counsel on the legal sufficiency and form of affidavits for warrants prior to contacting the United States Attorney and/or the Federal Magistrate to obtain a search warrant.

(3) All requests for search warrants in income tax investigations must first be cleared with the ARC (Criminal Investigation) and with District Counsel who is responsible for coordinating requests with Chief Counsel and the Department of Justice.

(4) When requesting authorization for a search warrant the request (as well as the accompanying affidavit) must establish the following:

(a) a factual showing that there is current probable cause to believe that a tax crime has been committed, including a factual showing that there is likely to be a significant tax impact.

(b) a factual showing that there is probable cause to believe that evidence sought is seizable by virtue of being connected with the crimes.

(c) a factual showing that there is current probable cause to believe that the evidence sought is on the premises to be searched. The search warrant request should specify the precise location of records on the premises to the extent possible.

(d) The affidavit must contain a particular description of the premises to be searched and of the specific items to be seized.

(e) As is commonly the case, where the affidavit is based on information provided by an informant, it must establish the informant's basis of knowledge and must factually support that the informant is credible and that the information provided is reliable.

(5) Requests for search warrants should be submitted in writing through normal Criminal Investigation channels to District Counsel. District Counsel will coordinate the request with Chief Counsel who will perform a review of the request. Absent extraordinary circumstances, the search warrant request will not be approved by Counsel or the Department of Justice based on an oral presentation of facts establishing that there is probable cause.

(6) To prevent any doubt regarding the origin(s) of information available for civil use, applications for search warrants will not be initiated in administrative cases when a request for a grand jury investigation is in process or it is anticipated that one will be in process during the time the warrant would be executed. See IRM 9267.3:(3) regarding the appropriate indexing of information obtained prior to the receipt of grand jury information. For grand jury investigations in progress, see the special procedures with regard to search warrants contained in IRM 9267.3:(21).

383.5 *(1-18-80)* 9781
Probable Cause and Preparation of Search Warrant

(1) A warrant must be based upon probable cause to be valid. Probable cause consists of facts or circumstances which would lead a reasonably cautious and prudent man to believe that:

(a) the person to be arrested is committing a crime or has committed a felony, or

(b) property subject to seizure is on the premises to be searched and an offense involving it has been or is being committed.

(2) The terms "reasonable search" and "search based upon probable cause" are not synonymous expressions. "Probable Cause" is just one element of reasonableness. Officers may have probable cause to search a house and still conduct an unreasonable search of that house.

(3) In determining what is probable cause we are not called upon to determine whether the offense charged has in fact been committed. We are concerned only with the question of whether the affiant had reasonable grounds at the time of his/her affidavit and the issuance of the warrant for the belief that the law was being violated on the premises to be searched. If the apparent facts set out in the affidavit are such that a reasonably discreet and prudent man would be led to believe that there was a commission of the offense charged, there is probable cause justifying the issuance of the warrant. [*Beal v. U.S.*] Courts are required to interpret the affidavits in a common sense rather than a hypertechnical manner. The Supreme Court has stated:

> "This Court is . . . concerned to uphold the actions of law enforcement officers consistently following the proper constitutional course. . . . It is vital that having done so their actions should be sustained under a system of justice responsive both to the needs of individual liberty and the rights of the community." [*U.S. v. Ventresca*]

(4) The affidavit may be based on hearsay so long as it gives a reason for crediting the source of the information. [*Cecil Jones v. U.S.*] The officer executing the affidavit may rely on information received through an informant if the informant's statement is reasonably corroborated by other matters within the officer's knowledge. [*Cecil Jones v. U.S.; Draper v. U.S.*] The affidavit need not be confined to the direct personal observations of the affiant. [*Aquilar v. Texas*] However, it should at least relate some of the facts from which the officer has concluded the informant was credible or his information was reliable. For example, it may state that the informant has given correct information in the past, and that the present information is confirmed by other sources. [*Acquilar v. Texas*] Observations of fellow officers engaged in a common investigation are also a reliable basis for a warrant. [*U.S. v. Ventresca; Rugendorf v. U.S.; Chin Kay v. U.S.*]

(5) The first thing that a special agent must do is to determine by investigation that one of the three grounds for obtaining a search warrant exists (text 383.22). In applying this to Criminal Investigation Division work, the special agent will usually find that a gaming device violation is involved and that certain paraphernalia and property are being used as the means of committing the criminal offense. The next step is to prepare an affidavit stating facts that will establish grounds for issuing the warrant and convince the issuing authority that such grounds exist, or at least convince him/her that there is probable cause to believe that the facts exist.

(6) Affidavits submitted by special agents to establish grounds for the issuance of a search warrant in a case should include, but not be limited to the following items.

(a) Exact description and location of premises to be searched.

(b) Name of owner or person occupying the premises.

(c) Description of property being used to violate the tax laws.

(d) Internal Revenue Code sections being violated.

(e) If applicable, a chronological detailed statement of facts obtained by surveillance and examination of third party records. In preparation of this part of the affidavit the special agent should make sure that the facts are expressed in clear and unmistakable words, because the validity of the search warrant will stand or fall depending upon what appears within the four corners of the affidavit. The facts set forth need not be sufficient to support a verdict of guilt beyond a reasonable doubt. [*Washington v. U.S.*] They must establish, however, something more than mere suspicion or possibility of criminal activity. It may be said as a general proposition, that mere conclusions of the affiant unsupported by concrete facts, or facts alleged upon bare belief or information, unsupported by other reliable facts affirmatively averred, are inadequate in the eyes of the law to save the affidavit and the warrant based upon it from the condemnation by the courts, if genuine probable cause is not shown. Probable cause must exist at the time of the issuance of the warrant. An affidavit is defective which relates to prior observations and does not allege that there is reason to believe the condition still exists. [*U.S. v. Sawyer*]

(f) Statement of facts obtained from confidential sources, if applicable to the case although this in itself is not sufficient for probable cause.

(7) The special agent should consider obtaining the assistance of district counsel in preparing his/her own affidavit rather than depend upon the issuing authority for search warrants to prepare it for him/her. In a case involving testimony of several special agents to establish probable cause, each agent should prepare a separate affidavit. [*Regina Merrit, et al v. U.S.*] An affidavit is not invalidated if, due to lack of space, material facts are set forth on unsworn attachments stapled to the affidavit at the time it was sworn to. [*Brooks v. U.S.*] However, all pages of the affidavit should be associated by reference, for example, page 1 of 3 pages, and each page should contain the signature of the special agent and the date.

(8) After preparation of the affidavit, the special agent's next step is to make application for a search warrant before one of the issuing authorities. Ordinarily, this person will be a United States Magistrate who will, after review of the affidavit, place the special agent under oath and sign it. (If necessary the special agent should tactfully insist that he/she be sworn.) The Magistrate will then prepare a search warrant based upon information and probable cause contained in the affidavit. Each special agent who submits an affidavit should appear in person before the issuing authority and execute the affidavit. [*Will P. Clay v. U.S.*] The warrant must state the names of persons whose affidavits support it. [*Rule 41(c) F.R.C.P.*] A warrant is invalid if the affidavit is made by a person in a false name. [*King v. U.S.*]

(9) The search warrant should be directed to a special agent or other civil officer of the United States authorized to enforce or assist in enforcing the law. Some courts permit the search warrant to be directed to the Chief, Criminal Investigation Division, or any of the special agents under his/her jurisdiction, while others object to the class identification and require specific persons be named. It is advisable to name more than one person to permit service by any of the named persons in the event of multiple places to be searched, sickness of an agent, etc. It will describe the premises and/or person to be searched, the paraphernalia and property used to violate the tax laws, and a list of the Internal Revenue Code sections being violated. It will make reference to the affidavits attached to support the grounds and probable cause for issuance of the search warrant. Exhibit 600-8 consists of a sample affidavit for search warrant and a sample search warrant.

383.6 *(1-18-80)* 9781
Preparation for the Search

(1) A raid leader should be designed to organize the searching party and to be charged with the responsibility of conducting the search. The leader will determine and secure the number of agents and equipment needed to make the raid; will make specific assignments to each agent; and, decide the appropriate time to start the search. A map and diagram of location and buildings should be prepared.

(2) The leader will brief the searching party on the duties of each agent, acquaint them with the map and diagram, describe the individuals and paraphernalia expected to be in the premises, discuss with the party protective measures for personal safety of agents and alleged violators, tell them the time when the search will start and the methods of communication between members of the party, and furnish the members of the party with necessary equipment to conduct the search.

383.7 *(1-18-80)* 9781
The Approach and Search

(1) Ordinarily, gaming device suspects will not offer resistance to the raiding party. However, to ensure the greatest factor of safety to everyone involved, all raids should be conducted on the assumption that the individuals sought are on the alert and possess the same type of weapons as the raiding party and under the pressure of the search may attempt to use them. Badges should be worn conspicuously when entering the premises.

(2) The exact manner in which the raiding party should approach the premises to be searched will depend upon the type of place and its surroundings. In most tax raids special agents will find it possible to approach the premises in question from different directions so as to cover each exit. In raids on more or less isolated houses which require agents to cover considerable open territory before getting to their posts and where roads lead to the place from only one direction, it is not ordinarily prudent to drive directly to the place with automobiles because this will warn the occupants of the house and enable them to escape from the other side. In such cases automobiles should be left at a distance and the raiding party should proceed on foot to their respective stations. Usually each agent will proceed separately so that suspicion will not be aroused. When the place to be raided is in a city or is a room or apartment, it may be desirable to drive to within a short distance of the place to be raided and to have the agents immediately proceed to their respective posts. In any approach in connection with a tax raid, the main consideration to keep in mind is that entrance should be gained before the occupants have time to destroy the paraphernalia to be seized.

(3) The special agent charged with the responsibility of serving the search warrant and at least one other agent should ordinarily go to the front door of the premises, identify themselves, and ask for admittance. If admitted, they will state their reason for being there, read the search warrant to the person in control of the premises, and serve him/her with a copy of the warrant. If the occupants are attempting to destroy the paraphernalia when the agents gain entrance, steps should immediately be taken to prevent this before the search warrant is read.

(4) Sometimes it is necessary to force entrance if the occupants refuse to answer or open the door. An officer is allowed to break open any door or window of a house to execute a search warrant, if after notice the agent's authority and purpose, he/she is refused admittance, or when necessary, to liberate the agent or any one helping him/her execute the warrant. [*18 USC 3109.*] It may also be advisable to use subterfuge to gain entrance if it is suspected or known that the premises are protected by steel doors or bars that would delay the agent to such an extent that the paraphernalia could be destroyed. Although a special agent has authority to use either force or subterfuge, care should be taken not to give the suspect a basis for claiming an unreasonable search.

(5) After gaining entrance and serving the search warrant, the special agents should assemble all occupants of the premises in one room and place them under control of at least two agents. At this time questioning of suspects, if practicable, should be started by agents assigned to this duty.

(6) A thorough search should be made of the premises to find and seize all gaming device paraphernalia and property used or intended to be used in the commission of the crime. The room should be searched completely and at least two agents should be present at all times. All articles which may be of evidentiary value should be carefully marked for identification. These markings should be of such a character as to not injure the evidence itself, yet not be subject to obliteration. The identification should contain information as to the agent or agents who found the item, date, time, and exact spot where it was located. The identification of documents and chain of custody are discussed in text 355. It may be desirable to take photographs or make diagrams of the entire crime scene and the paraphernalia and property, while it is still at the place where it was discovered. Photographs made in a situation like this are very effective to refresh the memory of the agents.

(7) After proper identification of each item, the best method of maintaining the chain of custody is to appoint one special agent to have continuous control of all evidence until he produces it at the trial of the case.

383.8 *(1-18-80)* 9781
Seizures Under Warrant

383.81 *(1-18-80)* 9781
Gaming Device Seizures Under Warrant

Paraphernalia and property used or intended to be used in violation of tax related and gaming device laws can be seized by special agents. [*26 USC 7302; Handbook Text 383.22.*] When a valid search is made pursuant to a warrant, property related to another crime may be legally seized. [*U.S. v. Eisner*]

383.82 *(1-18-80)* 9781
Inventory of Seized Property Under Warrant

After proper identification; an inventory of all property seized should be made in the presence of the applicant for the warrant and the person in control of the property, if they are present. If the person in control of the premises is not present, the inventory should be made in the presence of at least one credible person besides the applicant for the warrant. Those items named in the search warrant and seized must be listed on the back of the warrant. Those articles seized but not named in the warrant should be listed in a separate inventory. The applicant for the warrant should sign a receipt and deliver it and a copy of the warrant to the person in control of the property, unless there is no one present, in which case he/she will leave a copy of the warrant and receipt in the place where the property was seized. When contraband articles such as counterfeit equipment, non-tax-paid liquor, narcotics, or illegal firearms are seized the special agent should immediately notify the appropriate enforcement agency.

383.83 *(1-18-80)* 9781
Return of Search Warrant

The statute states that the warrant shall be returned within ten days to the issuing authority. Although this provision is directory and failure to comply will not void the warrant, special agents are cautioned to make the return within the ten-day period.

383.9 *(1-18-80)* 9781
Searches and Seizures Without Warrant

383.91 *(9-8-80)* 9781
Searches Incident to Arrest

(1) Special agents should not, in the course of an arrest, conduct a warrantless search of a premises for evidence. Special agents should limit their search to the person of the arrestee. However, no prohibition against warrantless searches for weapons, when necessary, is intended. For example, if during the execution of an arrest warrant, the subject moves towards a desk drawer, that drawer may be searched to determine if it contains a weapon. Nevertheless, in most instances this particular situation can be avoided by requesting the subject to move to a place where he/she will not have access to any weapon. If the subject shows some hesitancy in responding to the arresting officer's request, then he/she may be moved to a place which will insure the safety of our employees.

(2) If, when applying for an arrest warrant, there is probable cause for believing evidence of a crime can be found at a specific location, a search warrant should be sought at the same time. Also, if probable cause as to the presence of evidence on the premises is developed only after the execution of the arrest warrant, the arresting officer may go before a magistrate to secure a search warrant. Other members of the arresting party may remain on the premises in order to prevent destruction of evidence in the interim.

383.92 *(1-18-80)* 9781
Searches Made With Consent

(1) A special agent can make a search at the request or with the consent of the occupant of the premises. [*18 USC 2236 (c).*] However, a search made with permission of the occupant's landlord, and without consent of the occupant, is illegal. [*Chapman, Elmer S. v. U.S.*]

(2) In all cases the person who consents to the search must be the one who has such right or a person authorized to act for him/her. A spouse may not ordinarily waive the rights of the other spouse unless authorized by the other spouse to do so. An employee has no authority to waive the constitutional rights of an employer unless the employee is authorized to act as an agent for the employer.

(3) The following warning should be given when any person is requested to waive service of a search warrant and to voluntarily consent to a search of his/her person or premises: "Before we search your premises (or person) it is my duty to advise you of your rights under the Fourth Amendment to the Constitution. You have the right to refuse to permit us to enter your premises (or search your person). If you voluntarily permit us to enter and search your premises (or to search your person) any incriminating evidence that we find may be used against you in court, or other proceedings. Prior to permitting us to search, you have the right to require us to secure a search warrant."

(4) Giving the above warning does not eliminate the necessity for also giving the *Miranda* statement of rights outlined in Document 5661 when a person in custody is to be questioned on matters other than the request for consent to search. Exhibit 300-5 contains the statement of rights.

(5) Whenever practicable, a written waiver of the Fourth Amendment rights should be obtained from the person granting consent in order to help establish that his/her consent was specific and clear and that he/she made the waiver voluntarily with knowledge and understanding of his/her constitutional rights.

(6) The guidelines contained in (3) to (5) above are not applicable to situations in which consent to search or service of search warrants are not required under existing law, such as searches of persons lawfully arrested, lawful searches of conveyances or frisking for weapons for an officer's protection if the officer has reason to believe that he/she is dealing with an armed and dangerous individual.

383.93 *(1-18-80)* 9781

Searches of Vehicles and Vessels

The right to search conveyances without search warrants arises from their mobile character. Special agents must be able to show probable cause and the impracticability of obtaining a search warrant to search a conveyance without a warrant. [*U.S. v. Stoffey; Clay v. U.S.*]

383.94 *(9-8-80)* 9781

Searches and Seizures of Abandoned Property

A warrantless search and seizure of abandoned property is generally valid unless it intrudes onto premises under the exclusive control of some person who does not consent thereto. This allows special agents to legally conduct a warrantless search and seizure of a taxpayer's trash when it is found in a common area for pick-up by a trash collector or with the trash collector's consent, when it has already been picked up by the trash collector. [U.S. v. Minker].

383.(10) *(1-18-80)* 9781

Seizures of Records

(1) Papers and records, like other forms of property, are subject to seizure and the fact that they possess no pecuniary value is of no significance in determining whether they may be seized. Documents which are the means and instruments or fruits of the crime may be seized in the course of a legal search. [*Gouled v. U.S.*]

(2) Papers and records have been excluded as evidence on the grounds that they were not specifically described in the search warrant or the supporting affidavit failed to show probable cause that they were at the premises to be searched. [*Alioto v. U.S. 216 F. Supp. 48, 63-1 USTC 9552 (E. D. Wis.).*] In other cases, the courts have admitted property not described in the search warrant when it bears a reasonable relationship to the purpose of the search. Because of this relationship, a court approved the seizure of money in a wagering raid even though the search warrant described the property to be seized as "betting slips, rundown sheets, records and other paraphernalia and equipment." [*U.S. v. Joseph*]

(3) The Supreme Court has upheld the use of search warrants to seize books and records of financial transactions. [*Andresen v. Maryland*] In this case the Court ruled that the search of Andresen's office for business records, their seizure and subsequent introduction into evidence did not offend the Fifth Amendment. Although the seized records contained statements that the accused had committed to writing, he was never required to say anything. The search for and seizure of these records was conducted by law enforcement officers and introduced at trial by prosecution witnesses.

383.(11) *(1-18-80)* 9781

Seizure of Contraband

Contraband is subject to seizure at any time, with or without a search warrant. However, if the contraband was seized as the result of an illegal search then the contraband cannot be admitted into evidence. Examples of contraband are counterfeit currency, untaxed liquor, narcotics and illegal firearms.

383.(12) *(1-18-80)* 9781
Duties of Special Agent After Arrest, Search, and Seizure

(1) The prisoners should be escorted without unnecessary delay before the nearest United States magistrate (or other nearby officer empowered to commit Federal prisoners). (See Text 723.)

(2) A Form 1327A, Arrest Report, as required by IRM 9530 will be prepared by the special agent not later than the close of the next business day following the arrest.

(3) Each special agent who participated in an arrest, search, and seizure should prepare a detailed memorandum as soon as possible after the raid setting forth information concerning what was observed, the duties performed, and any statements made by the persons arrested. This memorandum will refresh the agent's memory when he/she has to testify during the trial of the case and will help prevent conflict between the various agents' testimony.

(4) Property seized during a raid should be inventoried, stored, and appraised in accordance with the requirement contained in Text 384 on forfeiture procedures.

(5) A final case report and a seizure report, if applicable, will be prepared by the special agent. Exhibits 600-7 and 600-9 contain sample gaming device and seizure reports.

383.(13) *(1-18-80)* 9781
Seizures By Other Agencies

(1) Special agents have, on occasion, participated in raids conducted by other Federal, State, or local law enforcement agencies. Because of the possibility of legal actions involving special agents for alleged crimes and torts committed by other participants in the raid over whom IRS has no control, and the risk that data obtained by the IRS as a result of the search could be suppressed if the search is deemed to be illegal, the following guidelines should be followed.

(a) Service personnel should refrain from active participation in the execution of a non-IRS search and/or arrest warrant.

(b) When Service personnel accept the fruits of an executed non-IRS search, before they expend manpower investigating a tax case arising from this evidence, they should consult with District Counsel as to the legality of the warrant, the methods used in the search, the objects seized during the search, and any other legal problem that may arise if the evidence were to be subsequently used in a criminal or civil tax case.

(2) See also IRM 9451.2(3)

384 *(1-18-80)* 9781
Forfeiture Procedures

384.1 *(1-18-80)* 9781
Introduction

This covers the internal revenue laws and the Service procedures relating to forfeitures.

384.2 *(1-18-80)* 9781
Authority to Seize Property for Forfeiture

(1) It is unlawful to have or possess any property intended for use or which has been used in violation of the internal revenue laws or regulations prescribed under them, and no property rights exist in any such property. [*26 USC 7302.*] The Secretary or the Secretary's delegate is authorized by statute to seize such property. [*26 USC 7321.*]

(2) Forfeiture is strictly limited to personal property, and is not authorized as to real property. [*U.S. v. One 1953 Glider Trailer; Chief Counsel's Memorandum July 6, 1961, CC:E:E-40.*] A motor vehicle used or intended for use, [*U.S. v. One 1953 Oldsmobile Sedan*] or containing property used or intended for use in connection with operation in violation of the internal revenue laws is subject to seizure for forfeiture. Currency shown to bear a relationship to the offense comes within the definition of property intended for use in violating the internal revenue laws and is likewise subject to forfeiture. [*U.S. v. Leveson; U.S. v. $1,058.00 in currency*]

(3) Failure to pay the special tax on coin-operated gaming devices before they are used in trade or business subjects them to seizure and forfeiture, regardless of the operator's future intent to pay the tax. [*U.S. v. Five Coin-Operated Gaming Devices*]

(4) A search warrant may be issued for seizure of property used or intended for use in violation of internal revenue laws. [*Rule 41(b), F.R.C.P.*] A seizure in violation of the Fourth Amendment will not sustain a forfeiture, [*One 1958 Plymouth Sedan v. Pennsylvania*] unless the property seized is contraband per se. [*U.S. v. Jeffers; Trupiano v. U.S.*]

384.3 *(11-10-81)* 9781
Methods of Forfeiture

(1) Administrative forfeiture procedures, as contained in IRC 7325, are followed when the seized property has an appraised value of $2,500 or less, and no proper claim and cost bond has been filed by a claimant generally within thirty days of the first date notice of seizure is published. The property is forfeited to the United States by the District Director of Internal Revenue, based upon evidence showing that it was used or intended to be used in violating the internal revenue laws. The administrative procedures for both administrative and judicial forfeiture of property seized by the Criminal Investigation Division are set forth in IRM 9454 through 9459.

(2) Judicial forfeiture procedures are employed when the seized property has an appraised value in excess of $2,500 or a claim and cost bond has been timely filed by a claimant concerning property valued at $2,500 or less. A libel petition is filed in the judicial district where the property was seized. The proceedings to enforce such forfeitures shall be in the nature of a proceeding in rem (against the property itself) in the United States District Court for the district where such seizure is made. [*26 USC 7323(a).*]

(3) All necessary documents in all forfeiture cases should be forwarded to the General Legal Services function of the Office of Regional Counsel no later than five weeks after seizure.

384.4 *(1-18-80)* 9781
Essential Element to Effect Forfeiture

384.41 *(1-18-80)* 9781
Burden of Proof in Forfeitures

The Government must establish by the preponderance of the evidence that the seized property was used or intended to be used in violating the internal revenue laws.

384.42 *(1-18-80)* 9781
Evidence to Support Forfeitures

The special agent should submit all available evidence which indicates relationship between the seized property and the violation.

384.5 *(1-18-80)* 9781
Duties of Special Agent in Seizure and Forfeiture Cases

384.51 *(1-18-80)* 9781
Use of Raid Kits

(1) Raid kits have been used in the past with considerable success to aid special agents in completing the documents and reports which are required in gaming device investigations. The necessary forms for use in such kits have been developed to ensure uniformity of reporting and to eliminate confusion and delays which may arise when special agents attempt to improvise forms to meet the circumstances of the raid. The forms are adaptable for use in either income tax or gaming device investigations.

(2) The kits should contain the following as appropriate.

(a) Search warrant, original and one copy.

(b) Arrest warrant original and one copy.

(c) A memorandum setting forth the plan for the raid, responsibilities of each assigned special agent, and description of suspected violators.

(d) A detailed map showing the relative location and interior layout of the place to be raided.

(e) Form 3389, Seized Property Notice and Identification Tag.

(f) Form 181, Inventory Record of Seized Vessel, Vehicle or Aircraft.

(g) Form 141-A, Special Moneys Report.

(h) Form 226-A, Appraisement List (Seized Personal Property).

(i) Form SF 1034, Public Voucher for Purchases and Services Other Than Personal.

(j) Form 4008, Seized Property Report.

(k) Forms 2311 and 2311A, Affidavits.

(l) Forms 2039 and 2039A, Summons.

(m) Masking tape or scotch type tape to seal entry and discharge chambers of gaming devices and for other possible uses.

(n) Pencils, writing pads, paper sacks, and handstapler.

(o) Money wrappers.

(3) Sufficient copies of all forms should be included to meet the anticipated needs of the special agents. Although some forms may not be required on the day of the raid, all materials should be assembled in advance to ensure a more efficient operation.

384.52 *(1-18-80)* 9781
Custody and Storage of Seized Property

(1) All property of any nature seized by a special agent shall remain under the jurisdiction of the United States District Court in the judicial district where seizure was made [*Rush v. U.S.; Gerth v. U.S.*] until such time as forfeiture action has been completed or terminated.

(2) Seized vehicles, coin-operated gaming devices and other personal property (except moneys) of more than nominal value will be stored at the earliest practicable date in the nearest suitable contract garage, or other designated place of storage. The nature of the property to be stored shall be considered in determining whether a garage or other more appropriate storage facility shall be used.

(3) Special moneys seized by a special agent shall be stored in a secure depository at the earliest practicable time after seizure. Special moneys include currency, coins, checks, jewelry, negotiable instruments and other articles of comparatively great value but small in physical size. A separate container or package will be used for the coin content seized from each gaming device, or other tax case and the special moneys seized from each person at each location. Normally, moneys will be placed in a container or package which cannot be opened without obvious break and the container or package will be delivered to the teller of a district area or zone office, if one is located within the judicial district where seizure was made.

(4) When authorized by the District Director as being in the best interest of the Service (because of lack of adequate or secure Service facilities or other good reason), the special agent may rent a safe deposit box in a commercial depository, such as a bank, and store therein moneys seized. The seizing officer and at least one other officer who can identify the moneys shall have access to the box and should be present at each entry into the box.

(5) The seizing officers may store the containers or packages in the common storage facilities consisting of one or more safe deposit boxes which may have been authorized by the District Director. Such boxes are rented in the name, "District Director of Internal Revenue," with only two Criminal Investigation officers (special agent, group supervisor, staff assistant, Assistant Chief, or Chief) having access thereto as custodians. These officers act as safekeepers in the same capacity as the district teller. Constructive custody, however, still remains with the seizing officer as long as he/she is available within the district and he/she is responsible for reporting the disposition of moneys.

(6) As soon as practicable after seizure of a coin-operated gaming device, the seizing officer shall open, or cause to be opened, the coin receptacle or receptacles of the device, and remove and count the money contents of each device separately, in the presence of at least one other special agent who can be a witness. The special agents who conducted the seizure shall deliver the coin-operated gaming device, minus its contents and at the earliest practicable date to the nearest suitable contract garage or other designated place of storage located within the judicial district where the seizure was made. The appraisal of seized coin-operated gaming devices will be made as outlined in Text 384.53. After forfeiture, gaming devices *per se* will be destroyed, or otherwise disposed of according to instructions of the Secretary of the Treasury or the Secretary's delegate. [*26 USC 7326.*] All forms (except Form 181), distributions, and procedures specified in Text 384.53 shall be used to the extent applicable in seizures of coin-operated gaming devices and their contents.

384.53 *(1-18-80)* 9781
Preparation of Seizure Forms

(1) Before or incidental to the storage of property, the special agent will prepare and execute seizure forms in accordance with IRM 9455.

(2) Sample copies of seizure forms are included with the sample seizure report, Exhibit 600-9.

(3) The case number used on the seizure report shall be shown on all copies of the forms and other documents relating to the seizure.

384.54 *(1-18-80)* 9781
Seizure Report

A seizure report, Form 4008, bearing the same number as the related case report, will be prepared as soon as practicable by the special agent in accordance with the procedure outlined in Subsection 634.2. Exhibit 600-9 contains a sample seizure report.

384.55 *(1-18-80)* 9781
Supplemental Investigations and Reports

The seizing special agent will make, as requested, any necessary supplemental investigations and reports relating to the seizure, including investigations relating to the merits of a petition for remission or mitigation of forfeiture or of an offer in compromise. Exhibit 600-10 contains the format and instructions for a report relating to investigations of a petition for remission or mitigation of forfeiture and shall be followed insofar as applicable.

390 *(1-18-80)* 9781
Arrests

391 *(1-18-80)* 9781
Definition of Arrest

An arrest is the taking into custody of a person accused of a crime so as to ensure his/her presence to answer the charges.

392 *(1-18-80)* 9781
Elements of Arrest

392.1 *(1-18-80)* 9781
Authority to Arrest

392.11 *(1-18-80)* 9781
Statutory Authority

(1) A special agent is given authority by statute:

(a) To execute and serve search and arrest warrants;

(b) To make arrests without warrant for any offense against the United States relating to the internal revenue laws committed in his/her presence, or for any felony cognizable under such laws if he/she has reasonable grounds to believe that the person to be arrested has committed or is committing the felony. [26 USC 7608]

392.12 *(1-18-80)* 9781
Non-Statutory Authority

The Supreme Court has stated that in the absence of a controlling federal statute, the law of arrest of the state where the arrest is made is controlling.

392.2 *(1-18-80)* 9781
Arrests Without Warrants

(1) In the absence of a statute authorizing a federal officer to make an arrest without a warrant, that officer has the same powers of arrest as a private citizen.

(2) A special agent's power to make an arrest without warrant as a private citizen, when valid under state law, is not made invalid because the crime is outside the scope of the Internal Revenue laws.

(3) An arrest without warrant is a serious matter and could subject the person making the arrest to criminal and civil liability for false imprisonment or false arrest. Therefore in order for special agents acting as private citizens to be authorized to make a warrantless arrest, it is generally necessary that a violation constituting a felony be committed in their presence or the special agent reasonably believes the person whom he/she arrests has committed a felony.

392.3 *(1-18-80)* 9781
Officer's Intent to Arrest

The officer making an arrest without a warrant should make his/her intent to arrest known to the person arrested. Because intent is subjective in nature and not discernible by one of the five senses, the arresting officer should declare his/her intention to make an arrest and do some physical act to show an intent to restrain the person arrested. Historically arrest has been accomplished by physical laying on of hands but the present concept is that arrest is accomplished when the prisoner complies with the directives of the arresting officer.

392.4 *(1-18-80)* 9781
Offender Must Know He/She Is Being Arrested

It is not enough that the arresting officer should invite the offender to accompany the officer. The offender must know that he/she is under compulsion to go with the arresting officer. This is usually accomplished by the arresting officer's saying "You are under arrest for (here state the offense)" and then doing whatever is necessary to restrain and control the offender.

392.5 *(1-18-80)* 9781
Offender Must Submit

Before arrest is accomplished the offender must submit to the authority and will of the arresting officer. All resistance of the offender must be overcome, however temporary it may be. After the offender submits to the authority of the arresting officer, further resistance or attempt to escape constitutes another offense.

393 *(1-18-80)* 9781
Force in Conducting the Arrest

(1) A special agent may use only that degree of force necessary to ensure compliance with the order of arrest. Use of excessive force may subject the arresting officer to law suits and disciplinary action. (See Policy Statement P-9-37.)

(2) Administrative orders of the Treasury agencies forbid the use of extreme force even in a felony case, except in self-defense or defense of another. Therefore, special agents should use firearms only in self-defense or defense of another.

394 *(1-18-80)* 9781
Proceedings Before the Magistrate

Text 723 covers the preliminary hearing before the United States Magistrate.

395 *(1-18-80)* 9781
Fingerprints

(1) Officers may take an arrested person's fingerprints by force if necessary for the purpose of identifying the individual and for detecting crime. [*Kelly v. U.S.*]

(2) The equipment required for taking fingerprints consists of an inking plate, a cardholder, printer's ink (heavy black paste), a roller and cleansing fluid. A complete fingerprint stand may be obtained from any fingerprinting supply house. Fingerprints should be taken on Department of Justice Form FD-249.

(3) There are two types of impressions involved in the process of taking fingerprints on Form FD-249: Individual fingers and thumbs ("rolled" impressions); and simultaneous prints of all the fingers of each hand and then the thumb, without rolling ("plain" or "fixed" impressions).

(4) In preparing to take a set of fingerprints, a small daub of ink should be placed on the inking plate and thoroughly rolled until a very thin, even film covers the entire surface. The subject should stand in front of and at forearm's length from the inking plate. The operator should stand to the left of the subject when printing the right hand, and to the right of the subject when printing the left hand.

(5) *Rolled Impressions*—Ink and print each finger separately beginning with the right thumb and then, in order, the index, middle, ring, and little fingers. Place the bulb of the finger upon the inking plate and roll the finger from one side to the other. In order to take advantage of the natural movement of the forearm, the hand should be rotated from the awkward to the easy position (rolled away from the center of the subject's body). Care should be exercised so the bulb of each is inked evenly from the tip to below the first joint. By pressing the finger *lightly* on the card and rolling in exactly the same manner, a clear rolled impression of the finger surface may be obtained. The subject should be cautioned to relax and refrain from trying to help the operator by exerting pressure as this prevents the operator from gauging the amount of pressure required.

(6) *Plain Impressions*—Press all the fingers of the right hand lightly upon the inking plate, then press simultaneously upon the lower right corner of the card in the space provided. The left hand should be similarly printed, and the thumbs of both hands should be inked and printed, without rolling, in the spaces provided.

(7) In order to ensure clear impressions, the operator should be aware that:

(a) The use of stamp pads or writing ink is unsatisfactory and will invariably result in illegible prints.

(b) The recommended printer's ink, if unevenly distributed on the inking plate, will result in blotches and blank areas.

(c) Fingers should be wiped clean before inking as moisture or other foreign substance may cause blemishes in the prints.

(d) Incomplete inking or rolling of fingers results in incomplete prints.

(e) Slipping of fingers while being rolled causes blurred and indistinct patterns.

(8) The following precautions should be taken by the operator:

(a) Beware of reversing (printing left fingers or hand in the spaces provided for the right fingers or hand), or double printing (re-rolling finger back over the impression in a mistaken effort to make it more legible).

(b) Be sure impressions are recorded in correct sequence.

(c) Be sure to make a notation in any space left blank because of an amputation.

396 *(1-18-80)* 9781
Juveniles

(1) Sections 5031 to 5037, Title 18, United States Code, set out the limitations concerning the arrest, trial, and punishment of juvenile delinquents. The special agent, as a general rule, will not have occasion to arrest a juvenile for violation of an internal revenue law.

(2) If a special agent does make such an arrest, he/she must comply with the procedure directed by the Code, as follows:

> "Whenever a juvenile is arrested for an alleged violation of any law of the United States, the arresting officer shall immediately notify the Attorney General.
>
> "If the juvenile is not forthwith taken before a committing magistrate, he may be detained in such juvenile home or other suitable place for detention as the Attorney General may designate for such purposes, but shall not be detained in a jail or similar place of detention, unless, in the opinion of the arresting officer, such detention is necessary to secure the custody of the juvenile, or to insure his safety or that of others.
>
> "In no case shall such detention be for a longer period than is necessary to produce the juvenile before a committing magistrate." [18 USC 5035]

(3) The notification required by the above section of the Code should be made through the Chief, Criminal Investigation Division, to the office of the United States Attorney in the judicial district in which proceedings will be held.

397 *(1-18-80)* 9781
Publicity

397.1 *(1-18-80)* 9781
General

(1) The District Director or his/her designated representative is authorized to release information to the public regarding criminal actions, provided the disclosure is not prohibited by law, court rule or order, or Service policy, P-1-185.

(2) For all news releases, the Chief, Criminal Investigation Division or his/her designee will provide the district Public Affairs Officer (PAO) necessary information to be included in a news release.

(3) The PAO is responsible for preparation of draft news releases and their clearance.

(4) All news releases will be prepared for attribution to the U.S. Attorney.

(5) These instructions are not intended to alter the Service policy contained in Policy Statement P-1-183 of endeavoring to obtain optimum news coverage in its enforcement activities by providing general information concerning the work of various divisions, supplying information on a request which is a matter of public record, and cooperating with and furnishing information to U.S. Attorneys for release to the news media.

(6) Under no circumstances will Criminal Investigation personnel release to the public the following types of information:

(a) Observations about a defendant's character.

(b) Statements, admissions, confessions, or alibis attributable to the defendant or the refusal or failure of the accused to make a statement.

(c) References to investigative procedures, such as fingerprints, polygraph examinations, ballistic tests, or laboratory tests, or to the refusal by the defendant to submit to such tests or examinations.

(d) Statements concerning the identity, credibility, or testimony of prospective witnesses.

(e) Statements concerning evidence or argument in a case, whether or not it is anticipated that such evidence or argument will be used at trial.

(f) Any opinion as to the accused's guilt or the possibility of a plea of guilty to the offense charged, or the possibility of a plea to a lesser offense.

397.2 *(1-18-80)* 9781
Raids

(1) At the conclusion of a wagering or other raid, the Service may release to the news media only that information that is contained in the search and/or arrest warrant. The release of such information may be made by the raid leader in response to on-site media inquiries. Other media inquiries should be referred to the district Public Affairs Officer. Consistent with the Department of Justice guidelines, the following may be released to the news media unless there are specific limitations imposed by law or court order:

(a) The defendant's name, age, residence, employment, marital status, and similar background information.

(b) The substance or text of the charge.

(c) The identity of the investigating and/or arresting agency and the length or scope of the investigation.

(d) The circumstances immediately surrounding an arrest, including the time and place of arrest, resistance, pursuit, possession and use of weapons, and a description of physical items seized at the time of arrest.

(2) The information which is released should include only incontrovertible, factual matters, and should not include subjective observations. Also, where such information would be highly prejudicial and where release would serve no law enforcement function, it will not be made public. Information concerning a defendant's prior criminal record will not be made public by Service officials. Media requests for information about a wagering or other raid which go beyond the contents of the warrant will be referred to the U.S. Attorney's office. The information that is in the affidavit for the search and/ or arrest warrant is not to be considered part of the warrant and thus may not be released to the news media by Service officials.

397.3 *(1-18-80)* 9781
Pre-trial Actions

(1) News releases related to pre-trial actions such as indictments and filing of criminal informations will be prepared only upon the specific request of the U.S. Attorney on a case-by-case basis. These news releases must be cleared within the district office in accordance with such procedures as the District Director may establish, and submitted to the U.S. Attorney for approval and distribution to the news media. At the request of the U.S. Attorney, the IRS district office will assist with the distribution of releases to the news media. To avoid any misunderstanding regarding the source of such releases, they will not be prepared on IRS mastheads, or mailed in IRS envelopes.

(2) Media requests for information about a pretrial action which go beyond the contents of issued news releases will be referred to the U.S. Attorney's office.

(3) IRS officials will not participate in press conferences or otherwise serve as a spokesperson in connection with pretrial actions. (See Policy Statements P-1-183.)

398 *(1-18-80)* 9781
Fugitives

(1) In order to assist in the apprehension of fugitives from justice who were the subject of investigation by Criminal Investigation, procedure is provided for issuance of Wanted Circulars (Publication 269) for felony fugitives. For purposes of initiating Wanted Circulars, a fugitive from justice is defined as a person against whom some form of criminal action has been taken, such as the return of an indictment, filing of a complaint or information, or a conviction, and who has fled the jurisdiction to escape prosecution or to avoid serving a sentence.

(2) When it is determined that a taxpayer is a fugitive, the procedures in text 335 of the Handbook will be followed to request an entry be made to the Treasury Enforcement Communications System (TECS) and the National Crime Information Center (NCIC). At the same time a report should be prepared by the Chief, Criminal Investigation Division and immediately forwarded to the Director, Criminal Investigation Division, through the ARC (Criminal Investigation). A Wanted Circular for felony fugitives will be prepared for circulation throughout the country. The report will include the following items and information concerning the wanted person, to the extent they are available.

(a) Name and aliases, last known address, social security number(s), and a complete physical description, including any identifying scars, marks or tattoos.

(b) Date and place of birth, nationality, and information regarding naturalization or foreign citizenship.

(c) Criminal record, fingerprint classification, police and FBI identification numbers, and customary employment or occupation.

(d) Date, place and nature of legal action that is the basis for apprehension, including the applicable criminal statutes.

(e) Name and title of person holding warrant for arrest or commitment papers who is to be notified in the event of apprehension.

(f) Specific comment should be made as to whether the wanted person should be considered dangerous and whether the wanted person is known to carry arms as a matter of practice.

(g) The most recent available photograph, in duplicate. The police type of photograph showing front and profile views is preferred for this purpose. Glossy print photographs, rather than a newsprint photograph, should be submitted.

(h) In lieu of fingerprints or fingerprint classification, clear photographs of the wanted person's customary signature, or, if that is not available, a sample of the wanted person's handwriting, should be submitted in duplicate.

(i) Any other information deemed appropriate that might aid in the wanted person's apprehension.

(3) The report shall be prepared in quadruplicate; the original and two copies forwarded to the ARC (Criminal Investigation) who shall in turn transmit the original and one copy to the Director, Criminal Investigation Division, National Office; one copy shall be retained in the district case file.

(4) Wanted Circulars are prepared and distributed by the National Office direct to law enforcement officials from mailing lists furnished by the ARC (Criminal Investigation).

(5) Such circulars will be distributed from the National Office to appropriate field personnel of Criminal Investigation, Examination and Collection at both regional and district levels. The ARC (Criminal Investigation) of the region originating a request for Wanted Circulars will be furnished a sufficient number of additional unaddressed circulars to enable him/her to intensify the local search for criminals wanted. A file of Wanted Circulars will be maintained on a current basis in all Intelligence field offices as well as in the offices of ARC's (Criminal Investigation).

(6) Distribution of Wanted Circulars should be limited to law enforcement personnel.

(7) When information is received in any Criminal Investigation office that a wanted person has been apprehended, for any reason whatsoever, the arresting authorities should be requested to hold the fugitive for further action by the IRS or the person who is named in (2)(e) above. The Criminal Investigation official who learns that a fugitive has been apprehended shall telephone or telegraph the Chief, Criminal Investigation Division, of the district wherein the fugitive is wanted, *and* the Director, Criminal Investigation Division, National Office, in order that the person holding the warrant or commitment papers can be immediately notified of the detention and steps taken to cancel the Wanted Circular regarding the fugitive. In those instances where the above officials are notified telephonically, the notifying Criminal Investigation official will follow up with a written notification to them. The special agent participating in, verifying, or making the arrest will promptly submit Form 1327, Report of Legal Action. The Chief, Criminal Investigation Division, of the district wherein the fugitive wanted shall follow up to ensure appropriate handling of the fugitive. Thereafter, he/she shall submit a brief report through channels to the Director, Criminal Investigation Division, National Office, detailing the action taken.

(8) When the Chief of a district wherein the fugitive is wanted learns that the fugitive is located in another district he/she will immediately notify the Chief of the other district as to the location of the fugitive, and will furnish all available information necessary to the apprehension of the fugitive. Where such notification is made by telephone with the request that the fugitive be arrested, confirmation should immediately follow by teletype so that the appropriate United States Attorney may have a documented request upon which to act. After the arrest has been made, the procedure in (7) above will be followed.

(9) See also IRM 9376.1 and 9539.(10). For principals who flee or intend to flee the country, see IRM 9376.2.

(10) When a fugitive has been apprehended, TECS and NCIC entries should be canceled.

3(10)0 *(1-18-80)* 9781
Fraud Investigation Assignments

3(10)1 *(1-18-80)* 9781
Nature of Violations

Fraud investigations include all criminal allegations against any person or entity relating to internal revenue taxes (except wagering, narcotics, alcohol, tobacco, and certain firearms taxes) in which defrauding the revenue is a prime factor. Examples are: attempted evasion; willful failure to collect or pay over tax, file required returns, supply information or keep records; conspiracy to commit such acts; and aiding, abetting or counseling such acts. They usually involve fraudulent documents, returns, certificates, lists, offers in compromise, accounts, briefs or claims, false statements, including those made under oath or under penalties or perjury, withholding tax (Forms W-2, 941) or Forms W-4.

3(10)2 *(1-18-80)* 9781
Types of Assignments

(1) The types of assignments, the objectives of the intended investigations, and the conditions under which they are investigated are as follows:

(a) Information Item

1 To assist in evaluation, the Chief, Criminal Investigation Division or his/her designee, who in no event will be below the group manag-

er level, may assign an information item to a special agent for limited inquiries which include:

a Scrutiny of tax returns or IRS files.

b Discussion with the referring officer.

c Interviews with the original informant, if any, in the case.

d Inquiries at Federal, State and local governmental agencies, including, but not limited to: law enforcement bodies; crime commissions; regulatory and licensing branches; motor vehicle registration; and real estate records.

e Inquiries at state and local taxing authorities.

f Contact with the taxpayer by mail to verify his/her filing record. Letter 964(DO), formerly L-210, will be used for this purpose. Publication 876, Privacy Act Notification, should be furnished simultaneously.

2 In making the inquiries enumerated above, the special agent is allowed to disclose the name of the taxpayer for identification purposes in an effort to secure information that is directly tax related and necessary to the administration of the tax laws.

(b) *Investigations*—To gather, through investigation, pertinent evidence to prove or disprove the existence of a violation of the law or regulations within Criminal Investigation jurisdiction. Specific investigative action will be taken to promptly determine whether criminal potential exists. Investigations may be investigated independently or in cooperation with the Examination or Collection Division.

(2) The circumstances determining "joint investigations" and the responsibility of special agents and cooperating officers in such investigations are discussed in 3(10)5.

3(10)3 *(1-18-80)* 9781
Origin of Assignments.

3(10)3.1 *(1-18-80)* 9781
General

(1) Much attention is devoted to allegations before assignments are made to special agents. The Chief, or the Chief's designated representative, evaluates and screens incoming information to determine if assignment to a special agent is warranted. Only those cases warranting the investigative effort of a special agent are assigned. The special agent is assured that the assignment is worthwhile in the judgment of his/her supervisors.

(2) Assignments to special agents generally originate with information items, other information, and referrals for potential fraud cases initiated in other divisions—Examination, Collection, and EP/EO. Information generating assignments are controlled through the centralized evaluation and processing of information items system (CEPIIS) at the Service Centers. The Criminal Investigation function is represented at the Service Centers by the Criminal Investigation Branch.

3(10)3.2 *(1-18-80)* 9781
Information Items and Other Information

3(10)3.21 *(1-18-80)* 9781
Definition

(1) "Information Items" are tax related communications and information received alleging or indicating a violation within the investigative jurisdiction of the Internal Revenue Service.

(2) "Information Items" to be evaluated and processed at the service center include:

(a) letters or other correspondence from informants that are tax related,

(b) memorandums of conversations or interviews with informants that are tax related,

(c) tax information from other government agencies,

(d) mutilated currency reports,

(e) data regarding tax violations developed or received by employees of the Internal Revenue Service,

(f) ADP and service center generated data concerning potential tax violations where a return has been requisitioned, or other investigative steps are taken to obtain further information after receipt of the listing, and

(g) other tax related data as appropriate.

(3) "Other information" in the Master Alpha Index which is a part of this centralized system at the service center includes:

(a) referrals from Examination, Collection, EP/EO and Appellate;

(b) open Criminal Investigation investigations;

(c) Currency Transaction Reports (Forms 4789);

(d) Currency or Monetary Instrument Reports (Forms 4790, U.S. Customs Service Form);

(e) U.S. Customs Seizure Reports;

(f) U.S. Customs Currency Violation Investigations;

(g) information gathering cases and projects;

(h) DEA, Class 1 information items;

(i) SEC Project information items;

(j) referrals from the Questionable Refund Program (QRP); and

(k) closed criminal investigations for the past 10 years.

(4) See IRM 9267.3:(15) concerning the preparation of an information item which contains grand jury information.

3(10)3.22 *(1-18-80)* 9781
Processing of Information Items

(1) The Chief, Criminal Investigation Division, or his/her designate may initially screen information items received in the district to identify items requiring immediate attention and items appearing to have surface potential. However, during this screening process, inquiries as stated in text 3(10)2:(1)(a) may not be made.

(2) If the Chief, Criminal Investigation Division, or his/her designate, wishes to have the item returned to the district for further evaluation, or has local knowledge regarding taxpayers mentioned in information items which would assist the evaluators at the service center, such information may be attached to the appropriate item. For those items which the Chief or designate wishes to have returned to the district, he/she may forward the original information item to the service center for processing and keep a photocopy for immediate assignment to a special agent for him/her to make limited inquiries as provided in text 3(10)2:(1)(a).

3(10)3.23 *(1-18-80)* 9781
Evaluation of Items Having Criminal Potential

(1) The Chief, Criminal Investigation Branch, or his/her designate will perform an initial evaluation of all "Information Items" and appropriate items of "Other Information" to identify those with criminal prosecution potential.

(2) Photocopies of those items evaluated as having criminal prosecution potential will be forwarded to the Chief, Criminal Investigation Division in the district where the taxpayer resides. Appropriate returns, microfilm research and/or transcripts will be forwarded to assist the Chief, Criminal Investigation Division in his/her final evaluation of such items. In addition, queries should be made by the Chief, Criminal Investigation Branch to the Treasury Enforcement Communication system to determine whether other Treasury agencies have ongoing or closed investigations or other information which might have tax consequences and to the National Crime Information Center to determine criminal history for use in preparation of prosecution or withdrawal reports.

(3) The receiving Chief, Criminal Investigation Division will, within sixty (60) workdays from receipt, determine if he/she will select the item for investigation. All information items will be evaluated by the Chief, Criminal Investigation Division or his/her delegate, without regard to available staff power, solely on the basis of possible development of successful prosecution case within Criminal Investigation jurisdiction.

(4) If the Chief, Criminal Investigation Division elects to begin an investigation in the Criminal Investigation Division, he/she will prepare and process Form 4930 in accordance with IRM 9570, Case Management and Time Reporting System Handbook.

(5) If the chief, Criminal Investigation Division, after his/her evaluation elects to reject the item, he/she will return it to the chief, Criminal Investigation Branch.

3(10)3.3 *(1-18-80)* 9781
Potential Criminal Cases Initiated in Audit, Collection, and EP/EO

3(10)3.31 *(1-18-80)* 9781
Indications of Fruad Reported to Criminal Investigation Function

(1) If an examiner during the course of any examination, a revenue officer, or an EP/EO specialist in the performance of his/her duties, discovers firm indications of fraud, he/she will suspend his/her activites at the earliest practicable opportunity without disclosing to the taxpayer, his/her representative, if any, or his/her employees the reason for such suspension.

(2) An examiner who discovers indications of fraud will prepare a report of his/her findings, utilizing Form 2797, Referral Report for Potential Fraud Cases. The report will be forwarded through channels to the district office Chief, Examination Division, who will add his/her comments and will transmit the original and two copies to the Chief, Criminal Investigation Division.

(3) A revenue officer or a Collection Office function representative who discovers indica-

tions of fraud will be responsible for preparation of a report of his/her findings, utilizing Form 3212, Referral Report of Potential Fraud Cases. The report will be forwarded in an original and two copies, through channels, to Chief Criminal Investigation Division.

(4) An EP/EO specialist who discovers indications of fraud will be responsible for a report of his/her findings, utilizing Form 2797. The report will be forwarded through channels to the Chief, EP/EO, who will add his/her comments and will transmit the original and two copies to the Chief, Criminal Investigation Division of the district in which the taxpayer is located.

3(10)3.32 *(1-18-80)* 9781
Action by Criminal Investigation Function

(1) Criminal Investigation shall evaluate the referral from Examination, EP/EO or Collection. If retained, it shall be handled in all respects as an investigation by either assignment to a special agent for appropriate action (including any needed discussions with the referring officer), or by placing it in a pool of unassigned cases. Within 15 workdays after receipt of the referral, the Chief, Criminal Investigation Division, shall inform the appropriate Division Chief, whether the referral has been declined before investigation; and, if so, the reasons therefor; or accepted for investigation.

(3) If no investigation is proposed by Criminal Investigation, Examination or EP/EO may resume its examination or Collection its collection activities. Thereafter, the EP/EO specialist examiner or revenue officer will remain alert for new indications of fraud. Should they develop, the case will again be referred to Criminal Investigation, in accordance with the procedure outlined above.

(4) Upon receipt of the notification from Criminal Investigation that the referral has been accepted and assigned for investigation and request is made for the assignment of a cooperating officer, the Chief of the referring division will assign to the investigation either the referring or another officer, who, in company with the special agent, may continue the examination of the taxpayer's books and records or assist in making other pertinent inquiries relative to the indications of fraud on which the referral is based.

(5) If the evaluator of a referral proposes to decline it, he/she should discuss his/her reasons for the proposed declination with the individual making such a referral or that individual's supervisor prior to writing the closing report. If the referral is declined, a copy of the special agent's closing report will be furnished the referring division. The Criminal Investigation action will also be noted on the original of the referral form.

(6) Delay in the handling of cases in which an allegation of fraud has been made is disadvantage to the Government, especially in matters affecting collections. Speedy determination should be made as to those cases warranting investigation to the end that conclusion of the civil aspects of a case is not unnecessarily delayed.

3(10)4 *(1-18-80)* 9781
Investigations

(1) The Chief, Criminal Investigation Division, or his/her delegate, will select for investigation all information items which, upon evaluation and screening, are deemed to warrant inquiries beyond those enumerated in text 3(10)3.22:(4). It is not necessary that each case be assigned to a special agent for investigation immediately upon selection.

(2) When available resources do not permit an active investigation to be undertaken immediately due to other priorities, consideration should be given to placing the case in a pool of unassigned cases controlled by the Chief's office.

(4) All cases assigned for investigation shall be subject to sufficient investigative inquiry to support the disposition of the case, except when closed for lack of resources.

(5) An investigation may, as appropriate, be conducted as a joint investigation with either the Examination or Collection Activity.

(6) Case numbers will be assigned in accordance with IRM 9570, Case Management and Time Reporting System Handbook.

3(10)5 *(1-18-80)* 9781
Joint Investigations

3(10)5.1 *(1-18-80)* 9781
Circumstances Determining Joint Investigations

Joint investigations are conducted by special agents in cooperation with representatives of other divisions of the Internal Revenue Service (revenue agents and revenue officers). Cases are usually investigated jointly with the Examination Division when false returns are filed or when there is a willful failure to file returns; with Collection when there is a willful failure to pay tax.

3(10)5.2 *(1-18-80)* 9781
Responsibilities of Participants in a Joint Investigation

(1) A joint investigation is to be *jointly* conducted through mutual *cooperation* by representatives of two or more divisions. The special agent is responsible for the development of the case and the ad valorem additions to the tax for civil fraud, negligence, and delinquency (except those concerning tax estimations) unless and until he/she withdraws from the case. The special agent is also responsible for the method of procedure and conduct of the investigation. The cooperating revenue agent is responsible for the audit features, and the revenue officer for the collection features. Because of the varied criminal charges that may attach to taxpayers' actions involving one or more of the other divisions and since these features are commingled in most cases, it is impractical to attempt to separate such features by arbitrary rules applicable to every case. The following guidelines, which are intended to be flexible, define the features of joint investigations:

(a) *Criminal Investigation features* are those activities of developing and presenting admissible evidence required to prove criminal violations and the ad valorem penalties for civil fraud, negligence, and delinquency (except those concerning tax estimations) for all years involved in cases jointly investigated to completion. This includes obtaining testimony of witnesses and the taxpayer; conducting necessary surveillance, undercover work, searches, seizures of property used or intended for use in violating the internal revenue laws, and arrests; and properly documenting pertinent records and transactions.

(b) *Examination features* are those activities of examination and verification of accounts on which such liabilities are based. These include the items required for the audit features in a nonprosecution case, such as reconciliation of the taxpayer's records with tax returns, test checking book entries, inspecting canceled checks, reconciling control accounts with subsidiary accounts, transcribing such accounts or parts of accounts necessary for disclosing bases for adjustments to tax liability, determining and substantiating tax and accounting adjustments having no significant effect on the criminal aspects of the case, and computation of the basis for tax liabilities, including such computations when the taxpayer has no books or records.

(c) *Collection features* are those activities of receiving tax returns and related documents and obtaining payment of taxes. This includes the collection of delinquent accounts through distraint, seizure, levy and other means, canvassing and securing, or preparing delinquent returns.

(2) The special agent is charged with the responsibility for the method of procedure and conduct of joint investigations. This is because of the importance of a criminal case from the deterrent standpoint to buttress voluntary compliance, and the gravity of possible criminal punishment. The criminal aspect is predominant. To prevent prejudice to the criminal features of a case, the special agent, unless and until he/she withdraws from the case, or until the criminal aspects of the case are concluded, will be responsible for the following determinations:

(a) The method to be used for criminal purposes in determining the tax basis, such as the determination of income in an income tax case by the net worth or specific item approach, or by a dual determination where it has a significant effect on the criminal case (the cooperating officer in his/her report may, in addition to the computation for criminal purposes, present an alternative method for computing the civil liability);

(b) The identification of those adjustments upon which a recommendation for criminal prosecution will rest and/or those which will constitute the basis for a recommendation for penalty additions to the tax;

(c) The preparation and issuance of summons (Form 2039); and

(d) The timing and priority of investigative actions in the case.

(3) Since many of the activities performed during joint investigations, particularly with Ex-

amination personnel, are commingled, joint or similar duties and responsibilities exist. To prevent duplication or overlapping of effort in joint investigations, the special agent will determine the nature and extent of participation by the cooperating officer in the following activities:

(a) Assisting in the interview of the principal and witnesses;

(b) Accounting reconstruction of tax bases, including the determination of the starting point for a net worth computation and third-party inquiries, including cases where the taxpayer has no books of account;

(c) Verification of the principal's records by comparison with records of third parties;

(d) Examination or transcription of records, accounts, and other relevant documents, including public records; and

(e) Preparation of inventories of records and/or assets, such as listing the principal's records or the contents of a safe deposit box.

(4) Decisions concerning whether the cooperating officer or the special agent should perform a specific task or part of a joint investigation, or whether they should perform it together, and the extent of participation of either officer must be on the basis of teamwork, mutual cooperation, and the best interests of the Service in the light of the particular circumstances of the case.

3(10)6 *(1-18-80)* 9781
Requesting Returns and Transcripts of Accounts

3(10)6.1 *(1-18-80)* 9781
Returns and Related Tax Information

Form 2275, Records Request, Charge and Recharge, is a two-part form and has two formats (Exhibit 300-24). Form 2275 is to be used by service centers, regional offices, National Office and Office of International Operations; and Form 2275-DO by district offices. Prepare a separate request for each taxpayer's records and for each tax period requested.

3(10)6.2 *(1-18-80)* 9781
Transcripts of Accounts

1 Form 4338, Information or Certified Transcript Request (Exhibit 300-25), and Form 4338-A, IMF Information or Certified Transcript Request (Exhibit 300-25 Cont. (3)) will be used by Criminal Investigation personnel to request both regular and certified transcripts of account and will be forwarded to the service center for the district where the return was filed. Form 4338 will be used for BMF, IRAF, RMF, EPMF and NMF requests, while Form 4338-A will be used for IMF requests only. All requests for transcripts of ADP accounts will be forwarded to the service center servicing the district requesting the transcript. If there is an urgent need for a transcript and there is not enough time for normal processing, telephone or teletype requests may be made directly to the service center.

(2) The service centers will furnish the requested ADP transcripts on Form 4303. Transcript of Account (see Exhibit 300-26). Form 4340, Certificate of Assessments and Payments, will be used by the service centers to answer non-ADP requests (see Exhibit 300-27).

3(10)7 *(1-18-80)* 9781
Commencing Fraud Investigations

(1) When beginning a fraud investigation, the special agent's first action should be to scan the file and determine the objective. For example, is it an investigation of an information item subject to limited inquiries, such as: interview with the informant, if applicable; check of Service files; scrutiny of tax returns; discussions with the referring officer, if applicable; or other inquiries not requiring disclosure of the taxpayer's identity, such as inspection of public records, etc.? In addition, the taxpayer may be contacted by letter to verify his/her filing record. Or, is it an investigation on which the expenditure of extensive and detailed efforts are already authorized? All initial assignments have as their objective the development of a potential criminal case. This involves deciding the specific criminal statute or statutes alleged to have been violated, by whom, when, where, and by what means; and understanding clearly the elements of the offense. The special agent should be continually alert for circumstances such as the death or sudden serious illness of the principal, his/her absence from the jurisdiction of United States courts, inadmissible evidence because of earlier contamination, or other factors which may make the principal immune to criminal prosecution as a practical matter.

(2) The second step normally taken is to begin gathering facts. At this point the special agent commences a file by making a record—whether it be informal notes for his/her own information only or formalized recording of investigative actions. A file should be started by listing the principal's correct full name, address at the time of the alleged offense, present whereabouts, and other information available from the assigned file and from readily available sources, such as telephone directories, city directories, etc. The principal's history and other pertinent information, similar to that tabulated in text 633.3, should be determined insofar as possible from readily available sources. Frequently the Criminal Investigation files contain information about the principal which was accumulated in connection with an entirely different matter, i.e., as an informant, as an enrolled practitioner, CTR reports, newspaper clippings, or other tax related background files such as closed files on prior investigations, collateral inquiries by other districts, and the like. The special agent should ensure that a files check has been made and that he/she is aware of information available from Criminal Investigation files before making inquiries outside the division. This aids the agent in making intelligent inquiries and avoiding embarrassing incidents otherwise likely to occur.

(3) The next effort to gather information will be guided by the particular assignment. Normally the next step is to explore and develop fully the original source of information, e.g., interview the author of a written communication. However, it is sometimes desirable that the special agent possess additional tax related background information before conducting the interview. Such additional data might be available from tax returns involved; the files of other divisions of the Service (such as prior revenue agents' reports possessed by Examination Division), a physical inspection of geographical area, or other sources mentioned in text 330. The decision concerning which source of information should be resorted to, when, and the desired extent of initial efforts are discussed in text 3(10)8.

(4) The initial phase of gathering information is completed when the assigned file is closely examined, appraised, and evaluated; Criminal Investigation files have been searched for correlation purposes; pertinent files possessed by other divisions of the Service have been examined to the extent the particular allegation warrants; the indicated research and consultations with supervisors and employees of the Service who possess pertinent personal knowledge have been completed; and the source of the original information has been fully explored. These actions will constitute the completion of an investigation of an "information item" and may even comprise the entire investigation. In such instances, the special agent should weigh the information gathered, reach a tentative decision, evaluate the decision, and then take action by report (oral or written, as appropriate) to his/her superior.

3(10)8 *(1-18-80)* 9781
Investigations

3(10)8.1 *(1-18-80)* 9781
Planning and Conducting of Investigations

(1) Investigations are detailed criminal inquiries to gather all the pertinent evidence to prove or disprove the existence of a violation within the jurisdiction of the Criminal Investigation Division. Such investigations involving fraud are usually conducted jointly with the Examination or Collection Division (text 3(10)5.2 contains a discussion of joint investigation relationships). They shall be commenced and concluded as soon as possible because of the statute of limitations, the danger of witnesses becoming unavailable or unreliable, the possibility that records and other evidence may become lost or destroyed, and the effect on the civil aspects of the case, especially collection.

(2) Investigations conducted jointly with other divisions are supervised jointly by the group manager of the cooperating agent and the group manager of the special agent (where there is no Criminal Investigation group manager, the Chief, Criminal Investigation Division). Both group managers should exercise sufficient control and follow-up to ensure the prompt completion of the investigation. The District Director, at his/her discretion, may prescribe the use of work plans, investigation

status reports, and joint case review procedures in any joint investigation in his/her district. When the District Director prescribes the use of such work plans, status reports, and supervisory case reviews, he/she will be responsible for providing applicable detailed procedures.

(3) In formulating a plan for a fraud investigation, the special agent should first look to the areas which are most determinative. For example, the special agent should obtain from the referring officer complete information relating to all occurrences in the case from its inception to the date of this interview. Particular attention should be given to statements made by the principal to, or in the presence of, the examining officer. If the principal has made admissions or has given false or misleading statements that can be proved or disproved, the cooperating officer should it make a written memorandum of the details while the facts are still fresh in his/her mind.

(4) The points covered during the special agent's interview with the examining officer will vary depending on the particular type of case and the specific allegations. However, at the conclusion of the interview, the special agent should know the answers to the following representative questions to the extent that they are pertinent and are within the knowledge of the examining officer.

(a) *Origin*—What started the examination? When was initial assignment made? Scope and purpose of initial assignment?

(b) *Records of the Internal Revenue Service*—Are required returns filed? Which original returns are on hand? Are other returns needed? Location and availability of additional returns? (All subsequent returns should be requisitioned.) Which is the better alternative for unavailable returns: retained copies or Certificates of Assessments and Payments? What do the available returns show concerning: who prepared them, what they are based on, who signed them, and the result of analyses made?

(c) *Records of the principal*—What records were initially maintained? Are records in existence? Are these records available? Have available records been reconciled with returns? If no, can the records be reconciled with returns? Has an inventory of available records been made? Who kept the records? Under what circumstances and where were the records maintained? How much detailed information is shown by the records? What supporting records are available, e.g., canceled checks, duplicate deposit tickets, invoices, accounts, shipping tickets, etc.? If available records are incomplete, what is the explanation for missing portions? Have excerpts of records, such as suspected accounts, been transcribed?

(d) *Records of third-party witnesses*—What other records have been determined pertinent? To what extent are they available? What was disclosed by other records examined thus far? Are transcripts or workpapers available and properly identified?

(e) *Allegations or basis of suspicions*—Is there a tax deficiency involved in the allegation? What are the estimated deficiencies and years involved? To what extent are estimated deficiencies made up of technical items? Are the alleged wrongful acts those of commission or omission? Is collection of tax liability in jeopardy? Are there known offsets, such as shifts of income between years, loss carry-forward or carry-back? What methods of determining taxable income have been used by the cooperating officer? What other methods of determining taxable income are feasible?

(f) *Personal contacts*—Has there been any meeting with the principal? What are the exact circumstances under which conversations occurred and records were made available? Is there any reason to anticipate a subsequent defense motion to suppress evidence? What was the principal's attitude with respect to cooperation? Has the principal been asked to explain any apparent discrepancies? What explanations or defenses are indicated? Have there been any discussions regarding settlement of the case? Similar details should be covered with respect to personal contacts with principal's present employees, accountant, and attorney. Is the principal or his/her representatives aware that the case has been referred to the Criminal Investigation Division for consideration? Avoid any deceptions as to the status of the case and the respective roles of the participating agents. After interviewing the examining officer and reappraising the available information accumulated thus far, the special agent should be able to determine whether to terminate the investigation or whether specific issues remain to be resolved before determining disposition.

(5) *Planning*—The "planning" consists of determining what information is needed, the relative importance of the desired data, the sequence believed best in making inquiries, the available sources of information, and which of the various alternative sources is best in the light of all circumstances involved.

(a) *Deciding which inquiries to make first*—The information needed is determined by the particular type of case and the specific allegations. Which inquiry should be made first is guided by the following considerations: Which will have to be made before conclusion? Which are expected to be more incisive with respect to broad areas or general issues? Which will confirm whether or not other contemplated inquiries are necessary? Which will most likely reveal leads?

(b) *Deciding which source of information is best*—Once the desired inquiries are itemized in their respective order of relative importance and planned sequence, the possible sources of information should be studied to decide the alternatives. The perfect source of information seldom, if ever, exists. Most sources will have disadvantages in the quantity and quality of information available, and also in the possible detrimental effect the inquiry may have on the case. Desirable goals to be considered in deciding on alternative sources are:

1 is complete, concise, and accurate information readily available?

2 will the response likely be immediate?

3 is the source proximate geographically?

4 is it economical?

5 is it convenient to the agent?

6 is it convenient to the person to be interviewed?

7 will a minimum of legal compulsion be required?

(c) Detrimental effects to be avoided are:

1 unnecessary embarrassment to the principal.

2 needless disclosure of the Government's affairs or information of a confidential nature.

3 identification of informants.

4 premature disclosure of the course of investigative action to the principal and others.

(6) The question of when the special agent should initially meet the principal should be decided after considering the advantages of both early and delayed interviews.

(7) In any event, whenever the special agent first officially meets with the subject of an investigation, he/she should be introduced as "Special Agent, Internal Revenue Service," and will produce his/her credentials for examination. He/she will state that, as a special agent, one of his/her functions is investigating the possibility of criminal violations of the Internal Revenue laws, and related offenses. There should be no misrepresentation or concealment. The special agent will advise the subject of his/her constitutional rights as required by IRM 9384 and any related Manual Supplements. (See text 342.132) A prerequisite to interviewing the principal, his/her representatives, or his/her current employees is that the investigator possess the original returns involved if any were filed during the pertinent period (exceptions are upon written approval of the Chief, or for cases where investigation is extended to additional years for which no return is available.) Also, all interviews with the principal should be made with at least one other Government representative as a witness.

(8) The special agent's prompt determination in the early stages of the investigation as to what records of the taxpayer are in existence, whether they are available, whether they can be reconciled with returns, etc., will resolve which major kind of possible inquiry are appropriate. In selecting the primary method of proving income for criminal purposes, the special agent should first determine whether the required elements of the basic theory are susceptible to proof before beginning to develop evidence under that method. As an illustration, it should first be determined in a proposed net worth computation that it is possible to establish a firm starting point and cutoff point and that income can be allocated to specific years within the period before gathering documentary evidence to prove known assets, liabilities, and nondeductible expenditures. Before documenting the minor facets of a proposed bank deposits computation, first determine that the basic theory is borne out by records. In short, the special agent should be tentatively satisfied with the whole before refining the parts. In refining the parts, it is essential that the special agent know the relationship and expected use of the product before further development. To copy large segments of records, analyze canceled checks, and the like, without any planned usefulness of the product is wasteful.

(9) The procedure in joint investigations is discussed in text 3(10)5.2, where the respective

functional activities are defined as Criminal Investigation features, Examination features, and Collection features; also the special agent's responsibility for the method of procedure is described and the joint duties and responsibilities of the participating officers are itemized. Determination as to whether the cooperating officer or the special agent should perform a specific task or part of a joint investigation, or whether they should perform it together, and the extent of participation of either officer therein must be on the basis of teamwork, mutual cooperation and the best interests of the Service in the light of the particular circumstances of the case. The following principles should be considered in making such determination:

(a) The special agent should be sufficiently familiar with the Examination or Collection features of the case and the cooperating officer sufficiently familiar with its criminal features to corroborate or complement each other's testimony, if necessary.

(b) Accounting and tax features, or collection activities, are usually the responsibility of the cooperating officer; developing and documenting evidence of intent is usually that of the special agent.

(c) Extensive documentation of adjustments required in a fraud case results in more detailed transcripts or extracts and more extended account verification than is required for the Examination features in an ordinary case.

(d) Often it is inefficient to have the special agent and cooperating officer continually working together on tasks which are normally the responsibility of either one of the officers. Duplication in the preparation of workpapers should be avoided; however, they may be reproduced to the extent necessary.

(e) The special agent is responsible for conserving the cooperating officer's time on a joint investigation and should avoid calling upon him/her unnecessarily for other than normal Examination or Collection functions. If, in making inquiries of third party witnesses, it is necessary to have two officers present, the services of another special agent should be utilized whenever practical. The cooperating officer should not be requested to participate unless his/her presence is required. On the other hand, both officers, i.e., the cooperating officer and the special agent, should usually be present when the taxpayer is interviewed or when the taxpayer's records are examined.

(f) The special agent should endeavor to plan the joint investigation with the cooperating officer in such a manner that the cooperating officer is engaged in the joint investigation in continuous periods of time without interruptions, as much as possible, rather than spasmodically. The cooperating officer should be informed as much in advance as possible of the plans for joint activities on the case and informed as soon as possible when his/her active participation is completed.

(10) There are many policies and procedures which the special agent must consider when planning and conducting an investigation. These are found primarily in IRM 9320 through 9380. Also, knowledge of possible sources of information, techniques to discover fraud, methods of proving income, law and evidence, etc., which are discussed elsewhere in this Handbook, all come into play during the planning and conducting of investigations. The ability to properly plan and conduct an investigation comes with experience, under the guidance of senior investigators and supervisors.

(11) When the special agent has completed his/her planned inquiries, he/she should evaluate the facts and evidence in the light of these considerations.

(a) Is the purpose of the investigation met? If it appears that criminal action is warranted, is there sufficient evidence concerning all elements of the offense?

(b) Are all questions material to the offense, or relevant to the matter involved, answered (who, what, when, where, how and why?).

(c) Are all implied questions answered? This involves questions not directly material to the main facts, but which are pertinent to a complete understanding of the case. For example, a witness' statement indicates that he/she paid the taxpayer $50,000 but no evidence of the means of payment has been developed. Implied questions may also arise when unusual transactions are discovered but no explanation developed about the reason for the variation from the normal method of handling transactions.

(d) Are any further inquiries necessary?

(12) As a measure of relative success, special agents may review their cases after ultimate completion with the following questions in mind:

(a) How could the solution have been uncovered earlier?

(b) How could a concealed weakness have been unearthed before substantial investment of resources?

(c) How could a prejudicial action have been avoided?

(d) How could it have been foreseen before certain evidence was obtained that it would not be usable?

(e) How could the evidence available at one time and which subsequently became unavailable have been safeguarded?

3(10)8.2 *(1-18-80)* 9781
Control of ADP Operations

3(10)8.21 *(1-18-80)* 9781
Procedure

The Chief, Criminal Investigation Division, will notify the Service Center Director of any cases under investigation by Criminal Investigation in which control over ADP operations should be established. Form 4135, Criminal Investigation Control Notice, will be used for this purpose. (See Exhibit 300-28)

3(10)8.22 *(1-18-80)* 9781
Transaction Codes

(1) TC 910 will prevent the removal of tax filing or payment data from the Master File to the Retention Register. Such data is routinely removed relative to taxpayers whose tax module reflects no tax liability (zero balance) and no activity for a period of three years. TC 910 will permit Criminal Investigation to retain on the Master File all transactions on the file at the time the TC 910 is posted. At the time TC 910 posts, a complete transcript (entity and all tax modules) titled "INTEL—910" is generated and forwarded by the service center to district Criminal Investigation. In addition, a quarterly inventory listing will be generated and forwarded to Criminal Investigation (See IRM 9326.1:(7)). The list will provide Document Locator Numbers of all returns currently posted to the Master File relative to modules under TC 910 control. TC 910 should be useful in monitoring the filing of returns by certain taxpayers, such as racketeers and Special Enforcement Programs subjects.

(2) TC 914 will provide all of the controls described above for TC 910. In addition, TC 914 will provide the following:

(a) Prevent posting of all original input transactions addressed to the tax modules, except TC 910, 911, 912 and 019. (TC 019 is for assigning ZIP codes.) A tax *module* is a record of tax data for a taxpayer, covering only one type of tax for one tax period.

(b) Permit posting of input transactions which have been reviewed and deemed acceptable for posting. This will also allow subsequent normal processing operations to proceed. For example, if a balance due return is permitted to be posted, a first notice to the taxpayer will be generated. If a refund return is permitted to be posted, a refund check to the taxpayer will be generated.

(c) Prevent a merge of modules if one or both modules are subject to TC 914.

(d) Prevent the computerized issuance of Form 5546, Examination Return Charge-Out, and prevents establishment of record on the AIMS data base.

(e) Prevent the issuance of TDI's or the operation of delinquency check procedures on the BMF and control the issuance of outputs under the operation of the Information Returns Processing (IRP) program and the IMF Delinquency Check.

(f) Terminate any further investigation by generating a Taxpayer Delinquency Investigation (TDI) recall for all tax modules in TDI status.

(g) Terminate any further collection action by preventing subsequent issuances of TDA's. If a tax module is in TDA status, the TDA will be placed in Inactive status.

(h) At the time of posting TC 914, produce a complete National Computer Center transcript of the tax modules titled "INTEL-914."

(i) Controls on the Individual Retirement Account File (IRAF) may be input directly; however, a TC 914 Control on the IMF will automatically place a control for the same taxpayer on the IRAF. The IRAF is a separate master file wherein voluntary contributions from self-employed persons to their own retirement accounts are recorded.

(3) TC 911 will reverse TC 910. It will also allow the issuance of TDA's for modules in Notice status, subject to a seven-cycle delay (about seven weeks). When the control has been terminated, the Chief, Criminal Investigation Branch at the service center will send the original Form 4135 together with any original documents, other than service center forms, that may have been retained in the account folder to the district Criminal Investigation office which requested TC 911.

(4) TC 912 will reverse TC 914. See IRM 9326.1 for the preparation of Form 4135 for input of TC 912.

(5) TC 916 will post to the tax module identified by the Master File Transaction Code (MFT) and will establish a Criminal Investigation freeze on the tax module and will provide for a Refund Schemes freeze on the module.

(6) TC 918 will post to the entity module and will establish a Criminal Investigation freeze on the entire account. It prevents refunds, credit elect and offset outs to BMF and IRAF.

(7) TC 915 posts to the module identified by the MFT and tax period of the incoming transaction and reverses only the refund freeze portion of the TC 916 and 918.

(8) TC 917 posts to the module identified by the MFT and tax period of the incoming transaction and reverses the TC 916 on the tax module.

(9) TC 919 posts to the entity module and reverses the TC 918.

(10) Further information pertaining to controlling ADP operations is contained in IRM 9326. See also IRM 9324.3.

3(10)8.3 *(1-18-80)* 9781
Initial Inquiries In an Investigation

3(10)8.31 *(1-18-80)* 9781
General

The initial investigative activity in an investigation should involve such inspection of the taxpayer's books and records or other related inquiries as are necessary to make an early determination as to whether or not the case possesses criminal potential. These inquiries should include a check of the Examination and Criminal Investigation Divisions to determine whether there is a pending or previous examination or investigation relating to the principal.

3(10)8.32 *(1-18-80)* 9781
Interview with Taxpayer or Inspection of His/Her Books

(1) The special agent must possess the original return or returns involved, if any were filed for the pertinent period, as a prerequisite to independently interviewing a taxpayer, his/her representative, or one of his/her present employees or inspecting the taxpayer's books and records.

(2) Exceptions may be made in cases where an examination is extended to include taxable periods for which the original return is not available and the examination is based on the taxpayer's retained copy, or where such action is approved in writing by the Chief.

(3) The Chief, Criminal Investigation Division, or his/her designee, in assigning an investigation originating from a source other than a referral from Examination or Collection, may authorize the special agent to interview the taxpayer, his/her representative, or one of his/her present employees, or to inspect the taxpayer's books and records. He/she may authorize the special agent to make such inquiries independently or he/she may request the cooperation of a revenue agent or revenue officer, as appropriate, to assist in making the inquiries.

(4) The procedures outlined in (1), (2), and (3) above are limited to a taxpayer's own tax matters and have no application in an inquiry where an agent is merely securing information from another person, not under tax investigation, but who engaged in transactions with the taxpayer or has data relevant to the tax liability under inquiry.

3(10)8.33 *(8-13-81)* 9781
Information from Referring Agent/Officer

(1) It is essential that certain information be obtained by the special agent from the agent/officer of the Examination, Collection or Employee Plans and Exempt Organizations functions who initiates a fraud referral. This will help identify and resolve potential weaknesses (from a criminal standpoint) before significant time has been spent on the investigation by Criminal Investigation.

(2) Prior to Criminal Investigation accepting a fraud referral for investigation, the special agent shall obtain from the referring agent/officer information relating to occurrences in the case prior to the referral. Particular attention should be given to:

(a) Any explanations offered concerning the alleged offense;

(b) Whether returns were solicited, there were any attempts at civil settlement, or prior actions similar to the alleged offense were condoned by the IRS; and

(c) The referring agent/officer's observations about the age, health (physical and mental) and education of the taxpayer.

(3) The above information will be considered by Criminal Investigation in the referral evaluation process. If solicitation or condonation is an issue, it must be resolved before the referral is accepted for investigation.

(4) When a referral is accepted for investigation by Criminal Investigation, the special agent shall promptly meet with the referring agent/officer and determine whether a detailed memorandum is required concerning contacts with the taxpayer, the taxpayer's representative and the preparer of the taxpayer's return. If such a memorandum is needed, the following areas should be included:

(a) The date of each contact the referring agent/officer had with the taxpayer, the taxpayer's representative, and the preparer of the taxpayer's return; and

(b) A summary of what took place during each of those contacts, and in particular any explanations offered concerning the alleged offense and any action that could be construed as solicitation, condonation or an attempt at civil settlement.

(5) The memorandum will be submitted to the special agent for association with the Criminal Investigation case file.

3(10)9 *(1-18-80)* 9781
Withdrawals

3(10)9.1 *(1-18-80)* 9781
General

(1) Except under circumstances outlined in (3) below, a special agent shall withdraw from an investigation when it is determined that the case has no Criminal Investigation potential; i.e., prosecution will not be recommended. Therefore, an agent should be particularly alert to any circumstances affecting the criminal potential in a case.

(2) Early recognition of a fatal weakness to successful prosecution should substantially reduce the time spent by the special agent on cases involving only civil fraud. The special agent must adopt a positive case approach and make every reasonable effort to overcome the effect of adverse development in an investigation by obtaining all pertinent facts relating to the weakness. If sufficient evidence cannot be obtained by further investigation to overcome the identified weaknesses and the investigation is not substantially completed, the special agent should promptly initiate action to withdraw from the case. The proposal to withdraw must be based solely on the lack of Criminal Investigation potential without regard for the civil fraud aspects of the case. As long as it appears that a recommendation for prosecution may be made in the case, the special agent should not initiate a withdrawal.

(3) Subsequent to the initiation of withdrawal action by the Criminal Investigation Division, the cooperating division may request through supervisory channels that the special agent continue with the investigation. Such requests generally are made only in cases where considerable duplication of effort by other Service personnel would be required to support a recommendation for assertion of the fraud penalty. However, the special agent will not resume the investigation unless so directed by his/her supervisor. If he/she is directed to continue participation, the special agent will complete the investigation and be responsible for recommending any civil penalties in the case (except those relating to tax estimations). He/she will also be responsible for developing, documenting, evaluating, and presenting the evidence necessary to sustain the assertion of such penalties. Text 761 contains information about the procedure for civil settlement of cases.

(4) The special agent will not withdraw, or signify his/her intention to withdraw, from a case in which the investigation has been substantially completed. Generally, the investigation will be considered substantially completed if one or more of the following conditions is present in the case:

(a) all significant investigative inquiries have been made;

(b) the special agent has prepared a draft of the final report in the case;

(c) the investigation has progressed to the point where the taxpayer would normally be afforded a final interview as provided in IRM 9355;

(d) the documentary evidence in possession of the special agent with respect to the civil fraud features of the case is such that its submission to the cooperating officer would require considerable time by the cooperating officer in becoming familiar with such evidence and preparing the detailed report necessary to present that evidence.

(5) Non-prosecution and discontinued reports will contain a section relating to evidence developed during the investigation which would

tend to support a subsequent recommendation of the civil fraud penalty. (See text 638.)

(6) See also IRM 9328.1 and IRM 9633.

3(10)9.2 *(1-18-80)* 9781
Written Notification to Taxpayers When Criminal Investigation Division Discontinues an Investigation

(1) A letter will be sent to the taxpayer advising that the Criminal Investigation Division is no longer participating in the investigation and the case has been referred to Examination or Collection for completion. This procedure will be followed when:

(a) the Criminal Investigation Division has discontinued an investigation without a criminal recommendation; and

(b) the taxpayer is aware of the investigation because of a contact with the taxpayer by a special agent; or

(c) the taxpayer may be aware of the investigation because of third party contacts.

(2) The letter will be prepared by the Chief, Criminal Investigation Division for the signature of the District Director or designee and sent to the taxpayer by mail. Pattern Letter P-543, Exhibit 300-29, is a sample notification letter which should be used as a guide. Preprinted form letters will not be used.

(3) A copy of the letter will be mailed to the principal's representative (agent or attorney) if a power of attorney or tax information authorization has been filed in the case.

3(10)9.3 *(1-18-80)* 9781
Additional Indications of Fraud

Additional indications of fraud in discontinued cases, found during subsequent examination by the revenue agent or revenue officer, which he/she believes should be considered by Intelligence shall be the subject of a referral report regardless of whether or not the original investigation resulted from a referral report.

3(10)(10) *(1-18-80)* 9781
Non-prosecution Cases

(1) If at the conclusion of an investigation, the special agent believes that sufficient evidence cannot be obtained to establish a prosecution case, he/she shall discuss with his/her group manager his/her findings and proposed recommendations.

(2) See also 637 and IRM 9327.2.

3(11)0 *(1-18-80)* 9781
Calendar

Exhibit 300-17 is a 250-year calendar for general investigative use.

3(12)0 *(1-18-80)* 9781
Map

Exhibit 300-19 is a map which illustrates the Internal Revenue and Judicial District boundaries for general investigative use.

Exhibit 300-1

FORM 1180

Handbook Reference Text 334.32:(2)

Standard Form 1180
Treasurer's Memo No. 6 (Rev.)

REQUEST FOR STOP PAYMENT
(Forward to Office of Treasurer, U.S.)

1. Date of Request	2. Reason		3. Amount	4. Date of Check	5. Symbol	6. Check Number
5/9/80	☐ Non-receipt ☒ Other	☐ "x" if confirmation ☐ Lost ☐ Stolen ☐ "x" if correction	$2500.35	4/13/80	3127	23,137,850

7. Payee's Name (enter only when not identical to the claimant's name in Box 9) Kenneth and Jane M. Taxpayer 987-65-4320

8. Remarks (including identification or reference)	9. Claimant of Check and Current Address	11. (RESERVED FOR TREAS. U.S.)	
Don't issue substitute Certified Photocopy Requested Date needed by 5/13/80	S/A John Smith Internal Revenue Service Criminal Investigation Division P.O. 489 Anywhere, U.S.A. 05401	STOPPED	
		NOT PAID	REM'L AUTH'D BY
		BOND/APPL./LETTER TO	ON

10. To: TREASURER, U.S., CHECK CLAIMS DIVISION, STOP PAY BRANCH, WASHINGTON, D.C. 20226
From: Disbursing Officer

I CERTIFY that the above check description is correct and that nothing in my records indicates that the payee is not entitled to its proceeds UNLESS OTHERWISE STATED UNDER "REMARKS."

	OTHER
1208	
1133	
MISC.	

1180-116

Exhibit 300–2

The Numerical System of the American Bankers Association Index to Prefix Numbers Handbook Reference: Text 338.14 ◊

THE NUMERICAL SYSTEM
of
The American Bankers Association
Index to Prefix Numbers of Cities and States

Numbers 1 to 49 inclusive are Prefixes for Cities
Numbers 50 to 99 inclusive are Prefixes for States
Prefix Numbers 50 to 58 are Eastern States
Prefix Number 59 is Alaska, American Samoa, Guam, Hawaii, Puerto Rico, and Virgin Islands
Prefix Numbers 60 to 69 are Southeastern States
Prefix Numbers 70 to 79 are Central States
Prefix Numbers 80 to 88 are Southwestern States
Prefix Numbers 90 to 99 are Western States

Prefix Numbers of Cities in Numerical Order

1 New York, N.Y.
2 Chicago, Ill.
3 Philadelphia, Pa.
4 St. Louis, Mo.
5 Boston, Mass.
6 Cleveland, Ohio
7 Baltimore, Md.
8 Pittsburgh, Pa.
9 Detroit, Mich.
10 Buffalo, N.Y.
11 San Francisco, Calif.
12 Milwaukee, Wis.
13 Cincinnati, Ohio
14 New Orleans, La.
15 Washington, D.C.
16 Los Angeles, Calif.
17 Minneapolis, Minn.
18 Kansas City, Mo.
19 Seattle, Wash.
20 Indianapolis, Ind.
21 Louisville, Ky.
22 St. Paul, Minn.
23 Denver, Colo.
24 Portland, Ore.
25 Columbus, Ohio
26 Memphis, Tenn.
27 Omaha, Neb.
28 Spokane, Wash.
29 Albany, N.Y.
30 San Antonio, Texas
31 Salt Lake City, Utah
32 Dallas, Texas
33 Des Moines, Iowa
34 Tacoma, Wash.
35 Houston, Texas
36 St. Joseph, Mo.
37 Fort Worth, Texas
38 Savannah, Ga.
39 Oklahoma City, Okla.
40 Wichita, Kan.
41 Sioux City, Iowa
42 Pueblo, Colo.
43 Lincoln, Neb.
44 Topeka, Kan.
45 Dubuque, Iowa
46 Galveston, Texas
47 Cedar Rapids, Iowa
48 Waco, Texas
49 Muskogee, Okla.

Prefix Numbers of States in Numerical Order

50 New York
51 Connecticut
52 Maine
53 Massachusetts
54 New Hampshire
55 New Jersey
56 Ohio
57 Rhode Island
58 Vermont
59 Alaska, American Samoa, Guam, Hawaii, Puerto Rico, and Virgin Islands
60 Pennsylvania
61 Alabama
62 Delaware
63 Florida
64 Georgia
65 Maryland
66 North Carolina
67 South Carolina
68 Virginia
69 West Virginia
70 Illinois
71 Indiana
72 Iowa
73 Kentucky
74 Michigan
75 Minnesota
76 Nebraska
77 North Dakota
78 South Dakota
79 Wisconsin
80 Missouri
81 Arkansas
82 Colorado
83 Kansas
84 Louisiana
85 Mississippi
86 Oklahoma
87 Tennessee
88 Texas
89 ....
90 California
91 Arizona
92 Idaho
93 Montana
94 Nevada
95 New Mexico
96 Oregon
97 Utah
98 Washington
99 Wyoming

Exhibit 300–3

Routing Symbols of Banks that are Members of the Federal Reserve System
Handbook Reference: text 334.4:(1) ◊

ROUTING SYMBOLS (IN ITALICS) OF BANKS THAT ARE MEMBERS OF THE FEDERAL RESERVE SYSTEM

ALL BANKS IN AREA SERVED BY A FEDERAL RESERVE BANK OR BRANCH CARRY THE ROUTING SYMBOL OF THE FEDERAL RESERVE BANK OR BRANCH

FEDERAL RESERVE BANKS AND BRANCHES		
1. Federal Reserve Bank of Boston Head Office	5–1	*110*
2. Federal Reserve Bank of New York Head Office	1–120	*210*
Buffalo Branch	10–26	*220*
3. Federal Reserve Bank of Philadelphia Head Office	3–4	*310*
4. Federal Reserve Bank of Cleveland Head Office	0–1	*410*
Cincinnati Branch	13–43	*420*
Pittsburgh Branch	8–30	*430*
5. Federal Reserve Bank of Richmond Head Office	68–3	*510*
Baltimore Branch	7–27	*520*
Charlotte Branch	66–20	*530*
6. Federal Reserve Bank of Atlanta Head Office	64–14	*610*
Birmingham Branch	61–19	*620*
Jacksonville Branch	63–19	*630*
Nashville Branch	87–10	*640*
New Orleans Branch	14–21	*650*
7. Federal Reserve Bank of Chicago Head Office	2–30	*710*
Detroit Branch	9–29	*720*
8. Federal Reserve Bank of St. Louis Head Office	4–4	*810*
Little Rock Branch	81–13	*820*
Louisville Branch	21–59	*830*
Memphis Branch	26–3	*840*
9. Federal Reserve Bank of Minneapolis Head Office	17–8	*910*
Helena Branch	93–26	*920*
10. Federal Reserve Bank of Kansas City Head Office	18–4	*1010*
Denver Branch	23–19	*1020*
Okalahoma City Branch	39–24	*1030*
Omaha Branch	27–12	*1040*
11. Federal Reserve Bank of Dallas Head Office	32–3	*1110*
El Paso Branch	88–1	*1120*
Houston Branch	35–4	*1130*
San Antonio Branch	30–72	*1140*
12. Federal Reserve Bank of San Francisco Head Office	11–37	*1210*
Los Angeles Branch	16–16	*1220*
Portland Branch	24–1	*1230*
Salt Lake City Branch	31–31	*1240*
Seattle Branch	19–1	*1250*

Exhibit 300-4

U.S. Secret Service Offices and Resident Agencies
Handbook Reference 334.3:(4)(b) ◇

City	Commercial No.	F.T.S.
Aberdeen, SD	605-225-7341	782-7355
Albany, GA	912-436-0323	230-6446
Albany, NY	518-472-2884	562-2884
Albuquerque, NM	505-766-3336	474-3336
Anchorage, AK	907-274-4913	265-5200
Atlanta, GA	404-221-6111	242-6111
*Atlantic City, NJ	609-646-9306	346-0200
Austin, TX	512-397-5103	734-5103
Baltimore, MD	301-962-2200	922-2200
Birmingham, AL	205-254-1144	229-1144
Bismarck, ND	701-255-3294	783-4329
Boise, ID	208-384-1403	554-1403
Boston, MA	617-223-2728	223-2728
Buffalo, NY	716-846-4401	437-4401
Canton, OH	216-455-3026	294-4265
Charleston, SC	304-343-6181 x255	924-1255
Charlotte, NC	704-523-9583	672-6154
Chattanooga, TN	615-266-4014	852-8271
Cheyenne, WY	None	328-2380
Chicago, IL	312-353-5431	353-5431
Cincinnati, OH	513-684-3585	684-3585
Cleveland, OH	216-522-4365	293-4365
Columbia, SC	803-765-5446	677-5446
Columbus, OH	614-469-7370	943-7370
Dallas, TX	None	729-8021
Dayton, OH	513-222-2013	774-2900
Denver, CO	303-837-3027	327-3027
Des Moines, IO	515-284-4565	862-4565
Detroit, MI	313-226-6400	226-6400
El Paso, TX	915-543-7546	572-7546
Fort Worth, TX	817-334-2015	334-2015
Fresno, CA	209-487-5204	467-5204
Gettysburg, PA	717-334-7173	None
	717-334-7174	
Grand Rapids, MI	616-456-2276	372-2276
Great Falls, MT	406-452-8515	585-1343
Honolulu, HI	808-546-5637	None
Houston, TX	713-226-5791	527-5791
Indianapolis, IN	317-269-6444	331-6444
Jackson, MI	601-969-4436	490-4436
Jacksonville, FL	904-791-2777	946-2777
Kansas City, KA	816-374-5022	758-5022
Knoxville, TN	615-524-4191	854-4527
Las Vegas, NV	702-385-6446	598-6446
Little Rock, AR	501-378-6241	740-6241
Los Angeles, CA	213-688-4830	798-4830
Louisville, KY	502-582-5171	352-5171
Lubbock, TX	806-762-7347	738-7347
Madison, WI	608-252-5191	364-5191
Melville, NY	516-249-0404	665-8541
Memphis, TN	901-521-3568	22-3568
Miami, FL	305-350-5961	350-5961
Milwaukee, WI	414-291-3587	362-3587
Minneapolis, MN	612-725-2801	725-2801
Mobile, AL	205-690-2851	534-2851
Montgomery, AL	205-832-7601	534-7601
Nashville, TN	615-251-5841	852-5841
Newark, NJ	201-645-2334	341-2334
New Haven, CT	203-865-2449	643-8770
New Orleans, LA	504-589-2219	682-2219
New York, NY	212-466-4400	668-4400
Norfolk, VA	804-441-6736	939-6736
Oklahoma City, OK	405-231-4476	736-4476
Omaha, NE	402-221-4671	864-4671
Orlando, FL	305-420-6333	820-6333
Philadelphia, PA	215-597-0600	597-0600
Phoenix, AZ	602-261-3556	261-3556
Pittsburgh, PA	412-644-3384	722-3384
Portland, ME	207-774-7576	833-3493
Portland, OR	503-221-2162	423-2162
Providence, RI	401-331-6456	838-4462
Raleigh, NC	919-755-4335	672-4335
Reno, NV	702-784-5354	470-5354
Richmond, VA	804-782-2274	925-2274
Riverside, CA	714-787-1350	796-1350
Roanoke, VA	703-982-6208	937-6208
Rochester, NY	716-263-6830	473-6830
Sacramento, CA	916-440-2413	448-2413
St. Louis, MO	314-425-4238	279-4238
Salt Lake City, UT	801-524-5910	588-5910
San Antonio, TX	512-229-6175	730-6175
San Diego, CA	714-293-5640	895-5640
San Francisco, CA	415-556-6800	556-6800
San Juan, PR	809-753-4539	753-4539
Santa Barbara, CA	805-967-3583	960-7708
Savannah, GA	912-234-0241	248-4401
Scranton, PA	717-346-5781	592-8333
Seattle, WA	206-442-5495	399-5495
Shreveport, LA	318-226-5299	493-5299
Spokane, WA	509-456-2532	439-2532
Springfield, IL	217-525-4033	955-4033
Springfield, MO	417-881-4688	754-2723
Syracuse, NY	315-423-5338	950-5338
Tampa, FL	813-228-2636	826-2636
Toledo, OH	419-259-6434	625-6434
Tucson, AZ	602-792-6823	762-6823
Tulsa, OK	918-581-7272	736-7272
Washington, DC	202-634-5100	634-5100
West Palm Beach, FL	305-659-0184	820-7696
White Plains, NY	914-682-8181	656-9734
Wichita, KA	316-267-1452	752-6694
Wilmington, DE	302-571-6188	487-6188

Exhibit 300-5

Form 5228
Handbook Reference: Text 342.133:(4)

Form **5228** (April 1974)
Department of the Treasury
Internal Revenue Service

Waiver of Right to Remain Silent and of Right to Advice of Counsel

Statement of Rights

Before we ask you any questions, it is my duty to advise you of your rights.

You have the right to remain silent.

Anything you say can be used against you in court, or other proceedings.

You have the right to consult an attorney before making any statement or answering any question, and you may have him present with you during questioning.

You may have an attorney appointed by the U.S. Magistrate or the court to represent you if you cannot afford or otherwise obtain one.

If you decide to answer questions now with or without a lawyer, you still have the right to stop the questioning at any time, or to stop the questioning for the purpose of consulting a lawyer.

However --

You may waive the right to advice of counsel and your right to remain silent, and you may answer questions or make a statement without consulting a lawyer if you so desire.

Waiver

I have had the above statements of my rights read and explained to me and fully understanding these rights I waive them freely and voluntarily, without threat or intimidation and without any promise of reward or immunity. I was taken into custody at ____________ *(time)*, on ____________ *(date)*, and have signed this document at ____________ *(time)*, on ____________ *(date)*.

____
(Name)

Witnesses:

____
(Name)

____
(Name)

Form **5228** (4-74)

Exhibit 300-6

Suggested Outline for Questioning Person Who Prepared Returns, If Other Than Taxpayer
Handbook Reference: text 346.32

◊

(This is not intended to be inclusive)

1. Occupation and qualifications of preparer
   A. Education
   B. Experience
   C. Enrolled

II. Description of all books and records in detail
   A. Primary records
      1. Cash receipts and disbursements book
      2. Journals: sales, purchases, cash
      3. Invoices and other original documents
   B. Secondary Records
      1. Ledgers: general and subsidiary
      2. Trial balance books, and records of financial statements
   C. Extent of witness' audit of books and records

III. Source of all information on returns
   A. Books and records (tie in with return)
   B. No records (obtain information in detailed form)
   C. Oral information
   D. Records and books of other third parties

IV. Items not shown on boooks or records (including income, assets, etc.)

V. Instructions and data received from taxpayer and any other persons

VI. Information as to whether returns were explained to taxpayer, and to what extent

VII. Copies of workpapers used in preparation of returns and copies of returns
   A. Tie in with return
   B. Supporting data
   C. Arrange to inspect the workpapers and copies of returns

VIII. Conversations regarding tax matters with:
   A. Taxpayer
   B. Taxpayer's agent or other persons

IX. Details about witness' and taxpayer's knowledge concerning the signing and filing of each return, including
   A. Identification of each return prepared by witness
   B. Where each return was prepared.
   C. Where each return was signed

Exhibit 300-7

Form 2311
Handbook Reference: Text 346.52

Affidavit

United States of America **Southern**) ss
Judicial, District of **Florida**)

I, **David J. Clark**, state that:

I reside at **1742 Alpencress Drive, North Miami, Florida**.

I am currently employed as a real estate salesman for the Cedar Realty Co., Inc., 1429 79th St. N.W., Miami, Florida. I have been employed in this capacity since 1963. In early March, 1974 I was introduced to Lawrence Elder of Tiffin, Ohio by a mutual acquaintance at a dinner meeting in Coral Gables, Florida. On March 17,

I have given Special Agent Joseph Smith the "settlement sheet" and the "offer to purchase" relative to the sale of the previously mentioned property and have received a receipt for them.

I have read the foregoing statement consisting of **2** pages, each of which I have signed. I fully understand this statement and it is true, accurate and complete to the best of my knowledge and belief. I made the corrections shown and placed my initials opposite each.

I made this statement freely and voluntarily without any threats or rewards, or promises of reward having been made to me in return for it.

/s/ David J. Clark
(Signature of affiant)

Subscribed and sworn to before me this **12** day of **February**, 19**77**, at **1429 79th St. N.W. Miami, Florida**

/s/ Joseph Smith
(Signature)

Special Agent
(Title)
Internal Revenue Service

____
(Signature of witness, if any)

Department of the Treasury - Internal Revenue Service — Form **2311** (Rev. 9-76)

NOTE: If needed, use bond or lined paper as continuation sheets. When practicable, have each paragraph in the statement contain information relating to one topic only. If applicable (see Handbook Subsection 242.13), use the following statement.

"I fully understand that I have the right under the United States Constitution to decline to make any statements, answer any questions, or present any data or evidence which may tend to incriminate me and I am aware that anything I say or any evidence I present may be used against me. I also understand that I have the right to counsel."

Exhibit 300-8

Suggested Format for Statement
Handbook Reference: text 346.53 ◊

SUGGESTED FORMAT FOR STATEMENT

In re: Name and address of subject

Time: Date and hour of interview

Place: Location of interview

On________ 19—, I, Special Agent ________ questioned Mr. ________ about ________.

Mr. ________ stated ________ ________ ________ ________.

. . . .

Note: If feasible, the subject should be requested to examine and sign it. If he refuses, the following legend will be inserted at the end of the statement when applicable. "This statement was read by Mr. ________ (the subject), on ________ 19— who stated that it was true and correct, but refused to be placed under oath or to sign it.

____________________	____________________
Date and Time	Special Agent Internal Revenue Service
____________________	____________________
Date and Time	Witness
____________________	____________________
Date and Time	Witness

Exhibit 300-9

Suggested Format for Question and Answer Statement
Handbook Reference: text 346.541 ◊

SUGGESTED FORMAT FOR QUESTION AND ANSWER STATEMENT

Testimony of John J. Jones, 115 South Street, Chester, Pennsylvania 19013, given in the office of the Criminal Investigation Division, Internal Revenue Service Room ________, United States Courthouse, 401 N. Broad Street, Philadelphia, Pennsylvania, at 9:30 a.m., on Tuesday, September 7, 19 ________, about his Federal income tax.

Present: Mr. John J. Jones, Taxpayer
Adam Adams, Attorney
John Smith, Special Agent
Alexander White, Revenue Agent
Evelyn Green, Reporter

(Questions were asked by Special Agent Smith and answers were given by Mr. Jones unless otherwise specified).

(Mr. Jones, this interview is being recorded, as we agreed, by means of the tape recorder on your left).

1. Q. Mr. Jones, you were requested to appear at this office to answer questions concerning your Federal income tax for the years 19— to 19—, inclusive. First, I advise you that under the Fifth Amendment to the Constitution of the United States I cannot compel you to answer any questions or to submit any information if such answers or information might tend to incriminate you in any way. I also advise you that anything you say and any documents you submit may be used against you in any criminal proceeding which may be undertaken. Do you fully understand this? (If the taxpayer requests clarification, either as to his rights or the purpose of the investigation, the special agent will give such explanation as is necessary to clarify the matter. If the taxpayer appears without an attorney, the special agent will advise him that he may, if he wishes, seek the counsel of an attorney before responding to questions).

2. Q. Please stand and raise your hand. Do you, John J. Jones, solemnly swear that the answers you are about to give to the questions asked will be the truth, so help you God? (The special agent will stand while administering the oath).

270. Q. Mr. Jones, have I, or has any other Federal agent, threatened or intimidated you in any manner?
A. No.

271. Q. Have I, or any other Federal agent, offered you any rewards, or promises of reward or immunity, in return for this statement?
A. No.

272. Q. Have you given this statement freely and voluntarily?
A. Yes.

273. Q. Is there anything further you care to add for the record?
A. No.
(After this statement has been transcribed, you will be given an opportunity to read it, correct any typographical errors, and sign it.)

United States of America)
Eastern Judicial District of) SS
Pennsylvania)

I have carefully read the foregoing statement consisting of pages 1 to ________, inclusive, which is a correct transcript of my answers to the questions asked me on the ________ day of ________, 19—, at the offices of the Criminal Investigation Division, Internal Revenue Service, Philadelphia, Pennsylvania, relative to my Federal income tax. I hereby certify that the foregoing answers are true and correct, that I have made the corrections shown and have placed my initials opposite each correction, and that I have initialed each page of the statement.

Exhibit 300-9 Cont.

Suggested Format for Question and Answer Statement ◊

____

Subscribed and sworn to before me at ________ m, this ________ day of ________ 19___, at ____

____

____

Special Agent

________ ________, Reporter, do hereby certify that I took the foregoing statement of ________ ________ in shorthand, personally transcribed it from my shorthand pages, and initialed each page.

/s/ ____________________________

Exhibit 300–10

Example of Memorandum of Interview
Handbook Reference: text 346.55

◊

EXAMPLE OF MEMORANDUM OF INTERVIEW

In re: Name and address of subject(s) being investigated

Date and time of interview: Tuesday, July 19 ________

________ a.m. to ________ p.m.

Place: Location of interview

Present: ________ ________ *(Taxpayer, witness, etc.)*

________ ________ Internal Revenue Agent

________ ________ Special Agent

Interview conducted by Special Agent ________________

....

Note: All pertinent information relating to the interview should be in the memorandum in some logical manner, either in order of topics discussed, importance, chronological, or any other appropriate order.

....

________________ Date and Time	________________ Special Agent
________________ Place	________________ Internal Revenue Agent
________________ Date and Time	________________

* When applicable

If pertinent the following may be included:

I (prepared) (dictated) this memorandum on ________, 19—, after refreshing my memory from notes made during and immediately after the interview with the taxpayer.

____
Special Agent

I certify that this memorandum has recorded in it a summary of all pertinent matters discussed with the taxpayer on ________ 19—

____
Internal Revenue Agent

Exhibit 300-11

Example of Informal Notes
Handbook Reference: text 346.56 ◊

EXAMPLE OF INFORMAL NOTES

On Wednesday July-19-at 10:00 a.m., I questioned Tom Brown of 1124 Euclid Street N.W., Washington, D.C., 20017 in his office, 117 Elm Street, Washington, D.C., about his purchase of a 19— Station Wagon from Smith Motors Inc. He stated that he purchased the Station Wagon, bearing serial number 1173945, for $3,250.00 from Joseph Smith, President of Smith Motors, and that he gave Mr. Smith his personal check number 117, dated ________ 19—— for $3,250.00. He agreed to submit an affidavit relating to his purchase. Internal Revenue Agent King, of Baltimore, Maryland, witnessed the interview which was concluded at 10:47 a.m.

/S/ William Penn
Special Agent

Exhibit 300-12

Form 2725
Handbook Reference: Text 342.12:(9)

FORM 2725
(REV. DEC. 1970)

DEPARTMENT OF THE TREASURY - INTERNAL REVENUE SERVICE
DOCUMENT RECEIPT

1. DOCUMENTS SUBMITTED IN RE:
Harrison Sales Co., Inc. 718 Rand Street, Houston, Texas 77015

2. DISTRICT	3. DATE
Southern District of Texas	August 6, 19__
4. SUBMITTED BY	5. PLACE OF SUBMISSION
Mr. J. C. Harrison, President	Harrison Sales Co., Inc. Houston, Texas

6. I ACKNOWLEDGE RECEIPT OF THE FOLLOWING DOCUMENTS SUBMITTED IN AN OFFICIAL MATTER:

Forty-two customers' files for the years 19__, 19__, and 19__ containing the following data:

(1) The customer's accounts receivable account cards reflecting installment payments on these sales.
(2) Retained copies of the customer's invoices on charge sales made in the years 19__, 19__, and 19__.
(3) Delivery receipts on these sales.

NO. CONTINUATION SHEETS ATTACHED: None

7A. RECEIVED BY (Signature)	7B. ADDRESS
Norman A Stone	210 Federal Building Houston, Texas
7C. TITLE	7D. PHONE NO.
Special Agent	PI 8-8386
8A. ACCOMPANIED BY (Signature)	8B. TITLE
/s/ Joseph Howe	Internal Revenue Agent

9. Acknowledgment of return of documents

	10A. DATE RETURNED	10B. PLACE AT WHICH RETURNED
The above documents were returned to me as indicated at right ⟶	8/21/__	Harrison Sales Co., Inc.
		10C. NAME OF PERSON RETURNING DOCUMENTS
		Special Agent Norman A. Stone

11. SIGNATURE OF PERSON TO WHOM DOCUMENTS WERE RETURNED
JC Harrison, President

FORM **2725 (Part 1)** (REV. 12-70)

Exhibit 300-12 Cont. (1)

Form 2725 (Reverse)

HISTORY AND CUSTODY OF DOCUMENTS

12. HOW DOCUMENTS WERE OBTAINED *(Check one)*

☐ BY CONSENT *(Note any significant comments of the principal or third-party witness and any unusual circumstances which occurred)*

☒ BY LEGAL PROCESS *(Describe)* Mr. J. C. Harrison failed to comply with a summons served upon him on July 18, 19__. A court order directing compliance was issued in the U.S. District Court, Southern District of Texas, on August 5, 19__.

13. RELATIONSHIP BETWEEN DOCUMENTS AND PERSON SUBMITTING THEM

Mr. J. C. Harrison is custodian of the records for the Harrison Sales Co., Inc.

14A. WERE MANUAL TRANSCRIPTS OR FACSIMILE COPIES MADE OF ANY OF THE DOCUMENTS EITHER IN WHOLE OR IN PART?

☒ YES ☐ NO

14B. Documents Copied	Manner of Reproduction
1. All customers' accounts receivable cards	Photostated
2. All retained copies of invoices	Photostated
3. Delivery receipts (Receipt number, customer name, and	
date of delivery)	Transcribed

15. HAVE ALL COPIES BEEN COMPARED WITH THE ORIGINAL DOCUMENTS AND IDENTIFIED?

☒ YES ☐ NO *(Mention reason for any exceptions)*

16. WERE THE ORIGINAL DOCUMENTS DESCRIBED HEREIN UNDER YOUR CONTROL OR SUPERVISION AT ALL TIMES PRIOR TO THEIR RETURN TO THE PRINCIPAL, THIRD-PARTY WITNESS, OR REPRESENTATIVE?

☒ YES ☐ NO *(Set forth circumstances of any transfer in control)*

17. DID THE PRINCIPAL, THIRD-PARTY WITNESS, OR A REPRESENTATIVE REQUEST ACCESS TO THE DOCUMENTS DURING YOUR CUSTODY?

☒ YES *(What action was taken?)* ☐ NO

Mr. F. J. Black, an attorney and representative of the Harrison Sales Co., Inc., examined the records in my presence on August 10, 19__.

18A. SIGNATURE	18B. TITLE
Norman A. Stone	Special Agent

FORM **2725 (Part 2)** (REV. 12-70)

Exhibit 300-12 Cont. (2)

General Instructions for Form 2725

◊

(1) Indicate the full name and address, including the street number, city and State of the principal whose tax liability or other alleged violation is being investigated.

(2) The Internal Revenue or the Judicial District having jurisdiction over the matter under investigation should appear after the word "District".

(3) Insert the date on which the document receipt was executed by the issuing officer. This date should correspond with the date the documents were actually submitted by the principal, third-party witness, or a representative.

(4) Set forth the full name of the individual from whom the documents were received. If the records were obtained from the principal, his/her name should appear in this space as well as in the space provided for the subject (Item 1). If the documents were received from an officer or employee of a corporation, his/her full name and title should be shown. List the name of the corporation involved and its location, where applicable, as the place of submission.

(5) Designate the actual address where the documents were obtained. If the records were delivered, note the place of delivery in this space.

(6) Itemize the documents in sufficient detail so that the identity of the books, records, or other data may be ascertained at all times. A separate sheet of paper prepared in duplicate may be used as a continuation sheet where the items are numerous. The continuation sheets should be clearly identified and associated with the document receipt form.

(7) The officer receiving the documents shall sign the receipt and enter his/her address, official title, and phone number in the space provided.

(8) If the person receiving the documents is accompanied by another officer, the accompanying officer should sign the document receipt and enter his/her official title.

(9) An acknowledgement shall be obtained on the original copy of the receipt form showing the return of the documents.

(10) The principal, third-party witness, or a representative should fill in the date the documents were returned, the address at which the items were returned, and the full name and title of the person returning the records.

(11) Whenever conveniently possible the documents should be returned to the principal, third-party witness, or the respective representative who originally submitted the items. His/Her signature should be obtained acknowledging the return of the records. If that person is not available, the acknowledgment may be executed by a clearly authorized employee, representative, or replacement. When the officer is unable to obtain the original of the document receipt which he/she issued, the acknowledgment should be solicited on the retained copy in his/her possession. The agent or other officer should exercise special care to prevent the disclosure of any information appearing in the history and custody of documents section whenever the acknowledgment is obtained on the retained copy of the document receipt. Each piecemeal return of records may be accomplished by preparing a document receipt form showing the items returned, and obtaining the acknowledgment. Items 7A through 8B should be left blank in such instances. If the person to whom the receipt was issued refuses to execute an acknowledgment for any reason, cross out the words "to me" and complete items 10A through 10C.

(12) Show the manner in which the documents were obtained by checking one of the squares and comment briefly regarding any unusual circumstances or remarks occurring at the time the records were submitted on a voluntary basis. A principal may give the reason for his/her voluntary action at this time or make other statements relating to the completeness or incompleteness of the documents. If there are extended conversations relating to the records, it will suffice to refer to a memorandum of such discussions. Where the records were secured by means of a summons or other legal process, an account of the action should be shown. A typical situation may be as follows: "I issued a summons for the documents on November 3, 19—".

Exhibit 300-12 Cont. (3)

General Instructions for Form 2725

◊

(13) Note whether the person submitting the records prepared the documents, holds the documents as custodian, owns the documents, or has some other basis for possessing them.

(14) Indicate whether all or any parts of the documents were copied for possible future use, and follow with a list of documents copied and the manner of reproduction. An example would be: Bank statements—Photostated: Cancelled checks—Columnar analysis prepared; Patient account cards—Transcribed all cards and photostated representative group; Disbursement records—Summaries prepared.

(15) Check whether manual transcripts or facsimile copies were compared with original documents and identified. Set forth the reason for any exceptions.

(16) The person receiving the documents should exercise adequate care to safeguard the items in his/her custody and any transfer of control should be outlined in this section. The administrative procedure of securing photostats or other reproductions of documents should not be construed as a loss or transfer of control. However, the transfer of a case to another agent, the transfer of documents to the jurisdiction of the court, or any analogous situation should be explained.

(17) Any requests for access to or the return of documents by the principal, third-party witness, or a representative should be outlined briefly.

(18) The person having knowledge of the history and custody of the documents should sign the statement and enter his/her official title.

Form M-2060

Department of the Treasury **Internal Revenue Service**	Order No. 4 (Rev. 9)	
Delegation Order	Date of issue June 27,1979	Effective Date June 27, 1979
Subject	Authority to Issue Summonses, to Administer Oaths and Certify, and to Perform Other Functions	

1(a). The authorities granted to the Commissioner of Internal Revenue by 26 CFR 301.7602-1(b), 301.7603-1, 301.7604-1, 301.7605-1(a) and the authorities contained in Section 7609 of the Internal Revenue Code of 1954 and vested in the Commissioner of Internal Revenue Service by Treasury Department Order No. 150-37, dated March 17, 1955, to issue summonses; to set the time and place for appearance; to serve summonses; to take testimony under oath of the person summoned; to receive and examine books, papers, records or other data produced in compliance with the summons; to enforce summonses; to apply for court orders approving the service of John Doe Summonses issued under Section 7609(f) of the Internal Revenue Code; and to apply for court orders suspending the notice requirements in the case of summonses issued under Section 7609(g) of the Internal Revenue Code, are delegated to the officers and employees of the Internal Revenue Service specified in paragraphs 1(b), 1(c), and 1(d) of this Order and subject to the limitations stated in paragraphs 1(b), 1(c), 1(d), and 6 of this Order.

(b). The authorities to issue summonses and to perform the other functions related thereto specified in paragraphs 1(a) of this Order, are delegated to all District Directors, the Director of International Operations, and the following officers and employees, provided that the authority to issue a summons in which the proper name or names of the taxpayer or taxpayers is not identified because unknown or unidentifiable (hereinafter called a "John Doe" summons) may be exercised only by said officers and employees and by them only after obtaining preissuance legal review by Regional Counsel, Deputy Regional Counsel (General Litigation) or District Counsel, or the Director, General Litigation Division in the case of Inspection.

(1) Inspection: Assistant Commissioner and Director, Internal Security Division.

(2) District Criminal Investigation: Chief of Division, except this authority in streamlined districts is limited to the District Director.

(3) International Operations: Chiefs of Divisions.

(4) District Collection Activity: Chief of Division, except this authority in streamlined districts is limited to the District Director.

Form M-2060 (Rev. 8-56)

Exhibit 300-13 Cont. (1)

Form M-2060

◊

(5) District Examination: Chief of Division, except this authority in streamlined districts is limited to the District Director.

(6) District Employee Plans and Exempt Organizations: Chief of Division.

(c) The authorities to issue summonses except "John Doe" summonses, and to perform other functions related thereto specified in paragraph 1(a) of this Order, are delegated to the following officers and employees:

(1) Inspection: Regional Inspectors and Assistant Regional Inspectors (Internal Security) and Chief, Investigations Branch.

(2) District Criminal Investigation: Assistant Chief of Division; Chiefs of Branches; and Group Managers.

(3) International Operations: Assistant Director; Chiefs of Branches; Case Managers; and Group Managers.

(4) District Collection Activity; Assistant Chief of Division; Chiefs of Collection Section; Chiefs of Field Branches and Office Branches; Chiefs, Special Procedures Staffs; Chiefs, Technical and Office Compliance Branches and Groups and Group Managers.

(5) District Examination: Chiefs of Branches, Case Managers, Group Managers and, in streamlined districts, Chiefs, Examination Section.

(6) District Employee Plans and Exempt Organizations: Group Managers.

(d) The authority to issue summonses except "John Doe" summonses and to perform the other functions related thereto specified in paragraph 1(a) of this Order is delegated to the following officers and employees except that in the instance of a summons to a third party witness, the issuing officer's case manager, group manager, or any supervisory official above that level, has in advance personally authorized the issuance of the summons. Such authorization shall be manifested by the signature of the authorizing officer on the face of the original and all copies of the summons or by a statement on the face of the original and all copies of the summons, signed by the issuing officer, that he/she had prior authorization to issue said summons and stating the name and title of the authorizing official and the date of authorization.

(1) International Operations: Internal Revenue Agents; Attorneys, Estate Tax; Estate Tax Examiners; Special Agents; Revenue Service and Assistant Revenue Service Representatives; Tax Auditors; and Revenue Officers, GS-9 and above.

(2) District Criminal Investigation: Special Agents.

(3) District Collection: Revenue Officers, GS-9 and above.

(4) District Examination: Internal Revenue Agents; Tax Auditors; Attorneys, Estate Tax; and Estate Tax Examiners.

(5) District Employee Plans and Exempt Organizations: Internal Revenue Agents; Tax Law Specialists; and Tax Auditors.

(e) Each of the officers and employees referred to in paragraphs 1(b), 1(c), and 1(d) of this Order may serve a summons whether it is issued by him/her or another official.

(f) Revenue Officers and Revenue Representatives who are assigned to the District Collection Activity and to International Operations may serve any summons issued by the officers and employees referred to in paragraphs 1(b), 1(c) and 1(d) of this Order.

2. Each of the officers and employees referred to in paragraphs 1(b), 1(c) and 1(d) of this Order authorized to issue summonses, is delegated the authority under 26 CFR 201.7602-1(b) to designate any other officer or employee of the Internal Revenue Service referred to in paragraph 4(b) of this Order, as the individual before whom a person summoned pursuant to Section 7602 of the Internal Revenue Code shall appear. Any such other office or employee of the Internal Revenue Service when so designated in a summons is authorized to take testimony under oath of the person summoned and to receive and examine books, papers, records or other data produced in compliance with the summons.

3. Internal Security Inspectors are delegated the authority under 26 CFR 301.7603-1 to serve summonses issued in accordance with this Order by any of the officers and employees of the Inspection Service referred to in paragraphs 1(b)(1) and 1(c)(1) of this Order even though Internal Security Inspectors do not have the authority to issue summonses.

Exhibit 300-13 Cont. (2)

Form M-2060 ◊

4(a). The authorities granted to the Commissioner of Internal Revenue by 26 CFR 301.7602-1(a), and 301.7605-1(a) to examine books, papers, records or other data, to take testimony under oath and to set the time and place of examination are delegated to the officers and employees of the Internal Revenue Service specified in paragraphs 4(b), 4(c), and 4(d) of this Order and subject to the limitations stated in paragraphs 4(c) and 6 of this Order.

(b) General Designations.

(1) Inspection: Assistant Commissioner; Director, Internal Security Division; Director, Internal Audit Division; Regional Inspectors; Internal Auditors; and Internal Security Inspectors.

(2) District Criminal Investigation: Chief and Assistant Chief of Division; Chiefs of Branches; Group Managers; and Special Agents.

(3) International Operations: Director; Assistant Director; Chiefs of Divisions and Branches; Special Agents; Case Managers; Group Managers; Internal Revenue Agents; Attorneys, Extate Tax; Estate Tax Examiners; Revenue Service and Assistant Revenue Service Representatives; Tax Auditors; and Revenue Officers.

(4) District Collection Activity: Chief and Assistant Chief of Division; Chiefs of Field Branches and Office Branches; Chiefs, Special Procedures Staffs; Chiefs, Technical and Office Compliance Branches; Chiefs, Collection Section; Chiefs, Technical and Office Compliance Branches and Groups; Group Managers and Revenue Officers.

(5) District Examination: Chief of Division; Chiefs of Examination Sections; Chiefs of Examination Branches; Case Managers; Group Managers; Internal Revenue Agents; Tax Auditors; Attorneys, Estate Tax; and Estate Tax Examiners.

(6) District Employee Plans and Exempt Organizations: Chief of Division; Chief, Examination Branch; Chief, Technical Staff; Group Managers; Internal Revenue Agents; Tax Law Specialists; and Tax Auditors.

(7) Service Center: Chief, Compliance Division; Chief, Examination Branch; Chief, Collection Branch; Chief, Criminal Investigation Branch; Revenue Agents; Tax Auditors; Tax Examiners in the Correspondence and Processing function; and Special Agents.

(c) District Directors, Service Center Directors, Regional Inspectors, the Chief of Investigation Branch, and the Director of International Operations may redelegate the authority under 4(a) of this Order to Law Clerks (Estate Tax), aides or trainees, respectively, for the positions of Revenue Agent, Tax Auditor, Tax Examiner in the Service Center Correspondence and Processing function, Tax Law Specialists, Revenue Officer, Internal Auditor, Internal Security Inspector, Attorney (Estate Tax) and Special Agent, provided that each such Law Clerk (Estate Tax), aide or trainee shall exercise said authority only under the direct supervision, respectively, as applicable of a Revenue Agent, Tax Auditor, Tax Examiner in the Service Center Correspondence and Processing function, Tax Law Specialist, Revenue Officer, Special Agent, Internal Auditor, Internal Security Inspector or Attorney (Estate Tax).

(d) District Directors may redelegate the authority under 4(a) of this Order to Revenue Representatives and Office Collection Representatives.

5. Under the authority granted to the Commissioner of Internal Revenue by 26 CFR 301.7622-1, the officers and employees of the Internal Revenue Service referred to in paragraphs 1(b), 1(c), 1(d), and 4(b) and 4(c) of this Order are designated to administer oaths and affirmations and to certify to such papers as may be necessary under the internal revenue laws and regulations *except* that the authority to certify shall not be construed as applying to those papers or documents the certification of which is authorized by separate order or directive. Revenue Representatives and Office Collection Representatives referred to in paragraph 4(d) of this Order are not designated to administer oaths or to perform the other functions mentioned in this paragraph, except that Revenue Representatives are authorized to certify the method and manner of service, and the method and manner of giving notice, when performing the functions and duties contained in paragraph 1(f) of this order.

6. The authority delegated herein may not be redelegated except as provided in paragraphs 4(c) and 4(d).

7. This Order supersedes Delegation Order No. 4 (Rev. 8), issued April 16, 1979.

/s/ Jerome Kurtz
Commissioner

Exhibit 300-14

Form 2039

(Rev. 11-78) **Summons**

Department of the Treasury
Internal Revenue Service

In the matter of the tax liability of Harrison Sales Co., Inc. 718 Rand Street Houston, Texas 77015 ← (1)

Internal Revenue District of Austin, Texas ← (2) Periods 19—, 19—, and 19—. ← (3)

The Commissioner of Internal Revenue
To Mr. J.C. Harrison, as President of Harrison Sales, Co., Inc. ← (4)

At 718 Rand Street, Houston, Texas 77015 ← (5)

You are hereby summoned and required to appear before Norman A. Stone ← (6), an officer of the Internal Revenue Service, to give testimony relating to the tax liability or the collection of the tax liability of the person identified above for the periods shown and to bring with you and produce for examination the following books, records, papers, and other data:

The following records of Harrison Sales Co., Inc.
Customer's files for the years 19__, 19__, and 19__ containing the following data:

(1) Retained copy of customer's invoices on charge sales made in the years 19__, 19__, and 19__. ← (7)
(2) Delivery receipts on these sales.
(3) Customer's accounts receivable account cards reflecting installment payments made on these sales.

Customer's account cards for accounts to whom sales were made in 19__, 19__, and 19__ on which current payments are still being made are excepted from the requirement for production at the time and place shown, provided that access to such of these records as is required will be granted at a mutually appointed time at the company's office, to be agreed upon at this appearance.

Business address and telephone number of Internal Revenue Service officer named above:
Suite 250, 2525 North Loop W., Houston, Texas #713-527-4681 ← (8)

Place and time for appearance:
at 210 Federal Land Bank Building, 430 Lamar Ave., Houston, Texas ← (9)

on the 29th day of July, 19— at 10:00 o'clock A M. (10)

Issued under authority of the Internal Revenue Code this 18th day of July, 19 ___ (11)

Norman A. Stone ← (12) → Special Agent
Signature of Issuing Officer — Title

Benjamin Morrison ← (13) → Group Manager
Signature of Approving Officer (if applicable) — Title

Original to be kept by IRS — **Form 2039 (Rev. 11-78)**

Part A — To be given to person summoned — **Form 2039-A (Rev. 11-78)**

Part C — To be given to noticee — **Form 2039-C (Rev. 11-**

Form 2039

Certificate of Service of Summons and Notice

(Pursuant to section 7603, Internal Revenue Code)

I certify that I served the summons shown on the front of this form on: (14)

Date	Time
July 18, 19__	10:15 A.M.

How Summons Was Served

(15) ☒ I handed an attested copy of the summons to the person to whom it was directed.

718 Rand Street, Houston, Texas (16)

☐ I left an attested copy of the summons at the last and usual place of abode of the person to whom it was directed. I left the copy with the following person (if any). (17)

(18)

Signature	Title
Norman A. Stone	Special Agent

This certificate is made to show compliance with section 7609, Internal Revenue Code. This certificate applies only to summonses served on third-party recordkeepers and not to summonses served on other third parties or any officer or employee of the person to whose liability the summons relates nor to summonses in aid of collection, to determine the identity of a person having a numbered account or similar arrangement, or to determine whether or not records of the business transactions or affairs of an identified person have been made or kept.

I certify that, within 3 days of serving the summons, I gave notice (Form 2039-D) to the person named below on the date and in the manner indicated. (19)

Date of Giving Notice: ____________ Time: ____________

Name of Noticee: ____________ (20)

Address of Noticee (if mailed): ____________

How Notice Was Given (21)

☐ I gave notice by certified or registered mail to the last known address of the noticee.

☐ In the absence of a last known address of the noticee, I left the notice with the person summoned.

☐ I gave notice by handing it to the noticee.

☐ I left the notice at the last and usual place of abode of the noticee. I left the copy with the following person (if any).

(22) ☒ No notice is required.

(23)

Signature	Title
Norman A. Stone	Special Agent

Form 2039 (Rev. 11-78)

Exhibit 300-14 Cont. (2)

Form 2039-A

Sec. 7602. Examination of books and witnesses

For the purpose of ascertaining the correctness of any return, making a return where none has been made, determining the liability of any person for any internal revenue tax or the liability at law or in equity of any transferee or fiduciary of any person in respect of any internal revenue tax, or collecting any such liability, the Secretary is authorized—

(1) To examine any books, papers, records, or other data which may be relevant or material to such inquiry;

(2) To summon the person liable for tax or required to perform the act, or any officer or employee of such person, or any person having possession, custody, or care of books of account containing entries relating to the business of the person liable for tax or required to perform the act, or any other person the Secretary may deem proper, to appear before the Secretary at a time and place named in the summons and to produce such books, papers, records, or other data, and to give such testimony, under oath, as may be relevant or material to such inquiry; and

(3) To take such testimony of the person concerned, under oath, as may be relevant or material to such inquiry.

• • •

Authority to examine books and witnesses is also provided under sec. 6420(e)(2)—Gasoline used on farms; sec. 6421(f)(2)—Gasoline used for certain nonhighway purposes or by local transit systems; sec. 6424(d)(2)—Lubricating oil not used in highway motor vehicles; and sec. 6427(f)(2)—Fuels not used for taxable purposes.

• • •

Sec. 7605. Time and place of examination

(a) Time and Place.—The time and place of examination pursuant to the provisions of section 6420(e)(2), 6421(f)(2), 6424(d)(2), 6427(f)(2), or 7602 shall be such time and place as may be fixed by the Secretary, and as are reasonable under the circumstances. In the case of a summons under authority of paragraph (2) of section 7602, or under the corresponding authority of section 6420(e)(2), 6421(f)(2), 6424(d)(2), or 6427(f)(2) the date fixed for appearance before the Secretary, shall not be less than 10 days from the date of the summons.

• • •

Sec. 7603. Service of summons

A summons issued under section 6420(e)(2), 6421(f)(2), 6424(d)(2), 6427(f)(2), or 7602 shall be served by the Secretary, by an attested copy delivered in hand to the person to whom it is directed, or left at his last and usual place of abode; and the certificate of service signed by the person serving the summons shall be evidence of the facts it states on the hearing of an application for the enforcement of the summons. When the summons requires the production of books, papers, records, or other data, it shall be sufficient if such books, papers, records, or other data are described with reasonable certainty.

• • •

Sec. 7609. Special procedures for summonses issued to third-party recordkeepers

Special provisions relating to the issuance of a summons to a third-party recordkeeper are contained in section 7609.

Sec. 7604. Enforcement of summons

(a) Jurisdiction of district court.—If any person is summoned under the internal revenue laws to appear, to testify, or to produce books, papers, records, or other data, the United States district court for the district in which such person resides or is found shall have jurisdiction by appropriate process to compel such attendance, testimony, or production of books, papers, records, or other data.

(b) Enforcement.—Whenever any person summoned under section 6420(e)(2), 6421(f)(2), 6424(d)(2), 6427(f)(2), or 7602 neglects or refuses to obey such summons, or to produce books, papers, records, or other data, or to give testimony, as required, the Secretary may apply to the judge of the district court or to a United States commissioner[1] for the district within which the person so summoned resides or is found for an attachment against him as for a contempt. It shall be the duty of the judge or commissioner[1] to hear the application, and, if satisfactory proof is made to issue an attachment, directed to some proper officer, for the arrest of such person, and upon his being brought before him to proceed to a hearing of the case; and upon such hearing the judge or the United States commissioner[1] shall have power to make such order as he shall deem proper, not inconsistent with the law for the punishment of contempts, to enforce obedience to the requirements of the summons and to punish such person for his default or disobedience.

[1] Or United States magistrate, pursuant to P.L. 90-578.

• • •

Sec. 7610. Fees and costs for witnesses

(a) In General.—The Secretary shall by regulations establish the rates and conditions under which payment may be made of—

(1) fees and mileage to persons who are summoned to appear before the Secretary, and

(2) reimbursement for such costs that are reasonably necessary which have been directly incurred in searching for, reproducing, or transporting books, papers, records, or other data required to be produced by summons.

(b) Exceptions.—No payment may be made under paragraph (2) of subsection (a) if—

(1) the person with respect to whose liability the summons is issued has a proprietary interest in the books, papers, records or other data required to be produced, or

(2) the person summoned is the person with respect to whose liability the summons is issued or an officer, employee, agent, accountant, or attorney of such person who, at the time the summons is served, is acting as such.

(c) Summons to which section applies.—This section applies with respect to any summons authorized under section 6420(e)(2), 6421(f)(2), 6424(d)(2), 6427(f)(2), or 7602.

Sec. 7210. Failure to obey summons

Any person who, being duly summoned to appear to testify, or to appear and produce books, accounts, records, memoranda, or other papers, as required under sections 6420(e)(2), 6421(f)(2), 6424(d)(2), 6427(f)(2), 7602, 7603, and 7604(b), neglects to appear or to produce such books, accounts, records, memoranda, or other papers, shall, upon conviction thereof, be fined not more than $1,000, or imprisoned not more than 1 year, or both, together with costs of prosecution.

Form 2039-A (Rev. 11-78)

Exhibit 300-14 Cont. (3)

Form 2039-B

NOTICE TO THIRD-PARTY RECIPIENT OF IRS SUMMONS

As a third-party recipient of a summons, you may be entitled to receive payment for certain costs directly incurred which are reasonably necessary to search for, reproduce or transport records in order to comply with a summons.

This payment is made only at the rates established by the Internal Revenue Service to certain persons served with a summons to produce records or information in which the taxpayer does not have an ownership interest. The taxpayer to whose liability the summons relates and the taxpayer's officer, employee, agent, accountant, or attorney are not entitled to this payment. No payment will be made for any costs which you have charged or billed to other persons.

The rate for search costs is $5 an hour or fraction of an hour and is limited to the total amount of personnel time spent in locating and retrieving documents, or information requested by the summons. Specific salaries of such persons may not be included in search costs. In addition, search costs do not include salaries, fees, or similar costs for analysis of material or for managerial or legal advice, expertise, research, or time spent for any of these activities. If itemized separately, search costs may include the actual cost of extracting information stored by computer in the format in which it is normally produced, based on computer time and necessary supplies; however, personnel time for computer search may be paid for only at the Internal Revenue Service rate specified above.

The rate for reproduction costs for making copies or duplicates of summoned documents, transcripts, and other similar material is 10 cents for each page. Photographs, films, and other materials are reimbursed at cost.

The rate for transportation costs is the same as the actual cost necessary to transport personnel to locate and retrieve summoned records or information, or costs incurred solely by the need to transport the summoned material to the place of examination.

In addition to payment for search, reproduction, and transportation costs, persons who appear before an Internal Revenue Service officer in response to a summons may request payment for authorized witness fees and mileage fees. You may make this request by contacting the Internal Revenue Service officer or by claiming these costs separately on the itemized bill or invoice as explained below.

Instructions For Requesting Payment

After the summons is served, you should keep an accurate record of personnel search time, computer costs, number of reproductions made, and transportation costs. When you are notified that the summons has been satisfactorily complied with, you may submit an itemized bill or invoice to the Internal Revenue Service officer before whom you were summoned to appear, either in person or by mail to the address furnished by the Internal Revenue Service officer. Please write on the itemized bill or invoice the name of the taxpayer to whose liability the summons relates.

If you have any questions about the payment, please contact the Internal Revenue Service officer before whom you were summoned to appear.

Anyone submitting false claims for payment is subject to possible criminal prosecution.

Part B —To be given to person summoned **Form 2039-B (Rev. 11-78)**

Exhibit 300-14 Cont. (4)

Form 2039-D

Tax Liability of:

Tax Periods:

Date of Notice:

To:

Address:

Enclosed is a copy of a summons served by the IRS to examine records or to request testimony relating to records which have been made or kept of your business transactions or affairs by the person summoned. If you object to the examination of these records, you may stay (prevent) examination of the records until a summons enforcement proceeding is commenced in court. Compliance with the summons will be stayed if, within 14 days from the date of this notice, you advise the person summoned, in writing, not to comply with the summons, and you send a copy of that notice by certified or registered mail to the Internal Revenue Service at the address shown on the summons. The copy should be sent to the attention of the Internal Revenue Service officer before whom the summoned person is to appear.

The Internal Revenue Service may begin an action to enforce the summons in the United States District Court. In such case you will be notified and you have the right to intervene and present your objections before the court whether or not you have previously objected to examination of the records or the taking of testimony. The court will decide whether or not the person summoned should be required to comply with the summons request. A stay of compliance with the summons or intervention by the taxpayer (or by an agent, nominee or other person acting under the direction or control of the taxpayer) will suspend the running of the statute of limitations for civil liability or for criminal prosecution for offenses under the tax laws for the tax periods to which the summons relates. The suspension is in effect while any proceeding and appeals related to the enforcement of the summons are pending.

The relevant provisions of the law are printed on the back of this notice. If you have any questions regarding this matter, please contact the Internal Revenue Service officer before whom the person summoned is to appear. The officer's name and telephone number are shown on the summons.

Part D —To be given to noticee **Form 2039-D (Rev. 11-78)**

Form 2039-D

Sec. 7609. Special procedures for third-party summonses.

(a) Notice —

(1) In General.—If—

(A) any summons described in subsection (c) is served on any person who is a third-party recordkeeper, and

(B) the summons requires the production of any portion of records made or kept of the business transactions or affairs of any person (other than the person summoned) who is identified in the description of the records contained in the summons, then notice of the summons shall be given to any person so identified within 3 days of the day on which such service is made, but no later than the 14th day before the day fixed in the summons as the day upon which such records are to be examined. Such notice shall be accompanied by a copy of the summons which has been served and shall contain directions for staying compliance with the summons under subsection (b)(2).

(2) Sufficiency of notice.—Such notice shall be sufficient if, on or before such third day, such notice is served in the manner provided in section 7603 (relating to service of summons) upon the person entitled to notice, or is mailed by certified or registered mail to the last known address of such person, or, in the absence of a last known address, is left with the person summoned. If such notice is mailed, it shall be sufficient if mailed to the last known address of the person entitled to notice or, in the case of notice to the Secretary under section 6903 of the existence of a fiduciary relationship, to the last known address of the fiduciary of such person, even if such person or fiduciary is then deceased, under a legal disability, or no longer in existence.

(3) Third-party recordkeeper defined.—For purposes of this subsection, the term "third-party recordkeeper" means—

(A) any mutual savings bank, cooperative bank, domestic building and loan association, or other savings institution chartered and supervised as a savings and loan or similar association under Federal or State law, any bank (as defined in section 581), or any credit union (within the meaning of section 501(c)(14)(A));

(B) any consumer reporting agency (as defined under section 603(d) of the Fair Credit Reporting Act (15 U. S. C. 1681a(f)));

(C) any person extending credit through the use of credit cards or similar devices,

(D) any broker (as defined in section 3(a)(4) of the Securities Exchange Act of 1934 (15 U S. C. 78c(a)(4))),

(E) any attorney, and

(F) any accountant.

(4) Exceptions.—Paragraph (1) shall not apply to any summons—

(A) served on the person with respect to whose liability the summons is issued, or any officer or employee of such person,

(B) to determine whether or not records of the business transactions or affairs of an identified person have been made or kept, or

(C) described in subsection (f).

(5) Nature of summons —Any summons to which this subsection applies (and any summons in aid of collection described in subsection (c)(2)(B)) shall identify the taxpayer to whom the summons relates or the other person to whom the records pertain and shall provide such other information as will enable the persons summoned to locate the records required under the summons.

(b) Right to intervene; Right to Stay Compliance.—

(1) Intervention.—Notwithstanding any other law or rule of law, any person who is entitled to notice of a summons under subsection (a) shall have the right to intervene in any proceeding with respect to the enforcement of such summons under section 7604.

(2) Right to stay compliance.—Notwithstanding any other law or rule of law, any person who is entitled to notice of a summons under subsection (a) shall have the right to stay compliance with the summons if, not later than the 14th day after the day such notice is given in the manner provided in subsection (a)(2)—

(A) notice in writing is given to the person summoned not to comply with the summons, and

(B) a copy of such notice to comply with the summons is mailed by registered or certified mail to such person and to such office as the Secretary may direct in the notice referred to in subsection (a)(1).

(c) Summons to Which Section Applies.—

(1) In general.—Except as provided in paragraph (2), a summons is described in this subsection if it is issued under paragraph (2) of section 7602 or under section 6420(e)(2), 6421(f)(2), 6424(d)(2), or 6427(f)(2) and requires the production of records.

(2) Exceptions.—A summons shall not be treated as described in this subsection if—

(A) it is solely to determine the identity of any person having a numbered account (or similar arrangement) with a bank or other institution described in subsection (a)(3)(A), or

(B) it is in aid of the collection of—

(i) the liability of any person against whom an assessment has been made or judgment rendered, or

(ii) the liability at law or in equity of any transferee or fiduciary of any person referred to in clause (i).

(3) Records; certain related testimony.—For purposes of this section—

(A) the term "records" includes books, papers, or other data, and

(B) a summons requiring the giving of testimony relating to records shall be treated as a summons requiring the production of such records.

(d) Restriction on Examination of Records.—No examination of any records required to be produced under a summons as to which notice is required under subsection (a) may be made—

(1) before the expiration of the 14-day period allowed for the notice not to comply under subsection (b)(2), or

(2) when the requirements of subsection (b)(2) have been met except in accordance with an order issued by a court of competent jurisdiction authorizing examination of such records or with the consent of the person staying compliance.

(e) Suspension of Statute of Limitations.—If any person takes any action as provided in subsection (b) and such person is the person with respect to whose liability the summons is issued (or is the agent, nominee, or other person acting under the direction or control of such person), then the running of any period of limitations under section 6501 (relating to the assessment and collection of tax) or under section 6531 (relating to criminal prosecutions) with respect to such person shall be suspended for the period during which a proceeding, and appeals therein, with respect to the enforcement of such summons is pending.

(f) Additional Requirement in the Case of a John Doe Summons.—Any summons described in subsection (c) which does not identify the person with respect to whose liability the summons is issued may be served only after a court proceeding in which the Secretary establishes that—

(1) the summons relates to the investigation of a particular person or ascertainable group or class of persons.

(2) there is a reasonable basis for believing that such person or group or class of persons may fail or may have failed to comply with any provision of any internal revenue law, and

(3) the information sought to be obtained from the examination of the records (and the identity of the person or persons with respect to whose liability the summons is issued) is not readily available from other sources.

(g) Special Exception for Certain Summonses.—In the case of any summons described in subsection (c), the provisions of subsections (a)(1) and (b) shall not apply if, upon petition by the Secretary, the court determines, on the basis of the facts and circumstances alleged, that there is reasonable cause to believe the giving of notice may lead to attempts to conceal, destroy, or alter records relevant to the examination, to prevent the communication of information from other persons through intimidation, bribery or collusion or to flee to avoid prosecution, testifying, or production of records.

(h) Jurisdiction of District Court.—

(1) The United States district court for the district within which the person to be summoned resides or is found shall have jurisdiction to hear and determine proceedings brought under subsections (f) or (g). The determinations required to be made under subsections (f) and (g) shall be made ex parte and shall be made solely upon the petition and supporting affidavits. An order denying the petition shall be deemed a final order which may be appealed.

(2) Except as to cases the court considers of greater importance, a proceeding brought for the enforcement of any summons, or a proceeding under this section, and appeals, take precedence on the docket over all cases and shall be assigned for hearing and decided at the earliest practicable date.

Form 2039-D (Rev. 11-78)

Exhibit 300-14 Cont. (6)

Instructions for Completing Form 2039

◊

(1) Insert the name and address, including street number, city and state of the taxpayer whose tax liability is being investigated. If returns are under investigation and bear different addresses, or if the taxpayer during the periods resided at several addresses, and his present address is still another place, show all of the addresses known. It is also important that only the name of the taxpayer appears in this item. Under certain circumstances in an investigation of related taxpayers, it is appropriate to list the names of all taxpayers assigned for investigation in the caption of the summons where the summons is directed to a witness having information concerning said taxpayers. Whether or not more than one summons should be used in each case will depend upon the facts of the case. If the liability is corporate, the name of an individual should not be shown in this item even though the individuals may be the summoned party, own substantially all the stock of the corporation, and/or be the only corporate officer. If the liability is that of an individual, the name of a corporation or other individual should likewise not appear even though the individual liability may stem from corporate affairs, as in the case of a 100-percent penalty assessment. When the liability relates to a business carried on under a trade name or by a partnership, the item should include both the name of the business and the name(s) of the individual(s) involved.

(2) Insert the city designation of the Internal Revenue district in which the returns were filed or should have been filed or the district where the assessment for collection is outstanding. For example, "Internal Revenue District of Los Angeles." If returns under investigation were filed in various districts, show the name of each district.

(3) Insert the calendar years, fiscal years, quarterly or monthly periods involved in the investigation.

(4) Insert the correct name of the person summoned or the name by which he/she is customarily known. It is immaterial whether that is his/her true and legal name. When the appearance is sought of more than one person, even though they are husband and wife, separate summonses, each directed to one individual, should be served. If it is desired to obtain testimony or records from a person in his/her capacity as trustee, receiver, custodian, corporate or public official, his/her title or official status, including the name of the corporation or other entity with respect to which the witness acts in such capacity, should be added to his/her name. Where a summons is for corporate records, it may be directed to a corporate officer and the corporation, i.e. "Mr. X, as president of XYZ Corporation and the XYZ Corporation." The latter description is preferable where records of a corporation or entity are summoned. However, there may be instances in which the personal testimony of a specific corporate officer is desired. It is also acceptable to issue a summons to a corporation only, for production of corporate records, in which event service must be made on a corporate officer or corporate employee probably authorized by the corporation to accept service on behalf of the corporation. The agent's supervisor should be consulted if there is any problem. The exact corporate name should be used.

(5) Insert the correct address of the person summoned which may be either the street and number of a place of business, the place of residence, or the location of the place where the person is found.

(6) Insert the name of the officer before whom the summoned witness is to appear and give testimony and/or produce records. If the officer authorized to issue a summons desires the person summoned to appear before another employee, the name of that employee will be inserted.

(7) When the summons requires the production of books, records, papers, or other data, it is important that they be properly designated and described with reasonable certainty, that is, that they be specified with sufficient precision for their identification. The description of records should specify the period of time covered by the records. If the witness is not required to produce books, records, papers, or other data, the phrase "and to bring with you and produce for examination the following books, records, papers, and other data" may be stricken.

(8) Insert the business address and telephone number of the IRS officer before whom the summoned party is to appear.

Exhibit 300-14 Cont. (7)

Instructions for Completing Form 2039

◊

(9) Insert the place for the witness' appearance. Show the complete address including the room number of the building at which the person is required to appear. The place of appearance shall be one reasonable under the circumstances of the case.

(10) Insert the date and time the witness is to appear. IRC 7605 provides that the date and time fixed for the appearance shall be such as are reasonable under the circumstances and shall not be less than 11 calendar days from the date of the summons, which for this purpose means the date on which the summons is legally served. If the summons is one requiring notice under IRC 7609, 17 days generally (but in no event more than 20 days) will be allowed from the date of service of the summons to the date for compliance, to ensure sufficient time for the notices of issuance of the summons and staying of compliance to be given. In computing the period, the day of service should not be counted but the day of appearance should be counted. Strict compliance with this provision is necessary in the preparation and issuance of a summons in order to enable the enforcement of obedience to its requirements if the person refuses to comply. The date set for appearance of the person summoned shall be on a workday and not on Sunday or a legal holiday. If a witness indicates a willingness to comply with the requirements of the summons by the delivery of books or records for immediate examination or on a date earlier than that required by statute, the time for his/her appearance should, nevertheless, be inserted in compliance with the statute. This will not preclude the officer, if aggreeable to the person summoned, from making an earlier or immediate examination of the records or the earlier taking of testimony, except if the summons is one requiring notice under IRC 7609. In that event, see IRM 9368.42 for the conditions under which early examination may be made.

(11) Insert the date the summons is signed by the issuing officer. This date is not to be considered as the "date of summons" in setting the date for appearance pursuant to IRC 7605. (See Item 10 above.)

(12) The authorized issuing officer will manually sign the summons in the space labeled "Signature of Issuing Officer" and insert his/her official title in the space labeled "Title."

(13) If authorization for issuance of the summons is required by Delegation Order No. 4, as revised, the officer designated to authorize the issuance of the summons will manually sign the summons in the space labeled "Signature of Approving Officer" and insert his/her official title in the space labeled "Title." If the authorization was oral, the issuing officer will insert and sign a statement of the face of the original and all copies of the summons that he/she had prior authorization to issue the summons, and indicate the name and title of the approving officer and the date of approval. In addition, the special agent shall prepare a record of the oral authorization as soon as is practicable; submit the record, for approval, to the official who gave the oral authorization; and associate the document with the retained copy of the summons.

(14) Insert the date and the time of day on which the summons was served.

(15) Show the manner in which the summons was served by checking one of the squares provided.

(16) Insert the address of the place or the location where the attested copy of the summons was delivered to the person summoned.

(17) If the summons is served by leaving an attested copy with a person at the last and usual place of abode of the party summoned, the name and address of the person to whom it is handed will be entered. If the summons is merely left at the witness' last and usual place of abode, only the address will be entered, and the phrase "I left the copy with the following person (if any)" shall be stricken.

(18) The officer serving the summons will sign the certificate of service of summons in the space provided for "Signature" and enter his/her official title in the space designated "Title."

(19)-(21) These items will be completed, as described below, only if notice is required under IRC 7609.

(19) Insert the date and time the notice was placed in the mail or delivered personally.

(20) Insert the name of the noticee and, if the notice is mailed, the address of the noticee.

(21) Show the manner in which notice was given by checking one of the squares provided. If notice is given by leaving the notice with a person at the last and usual place of abode of the noticee, the name and address of the person to whom it was handed will be entered. If the notice is merely left at the noticee's last and usual place of abode, only the address will be entered and the phrase "I left the copy with the following person (if any)" shall be stricken.

(22) Check this square if no notice is required.

(23) The officer serving the summons will sign the certificate of notice in the space provided for "Signature" and enter his/her official title in the space designated "Title."

Exhibit 300-15

Pattern Declaration ◊

Handbook Reference: Text 36(10).33

IN THE UNITED STATES DISTRICT COURT FOR THE
_____________ DISTRICT OF _____________

UNITED STATES OF AMERICA)
and (*enter name*), Special Agent)
of the Internal Revenue Service)
)
Petitioners)
)
)
)
)
)
Respondent(s))

DECLARATION

(*Name of Special Agent*), a petitioner herein, declares:

1. I am a duly commissioned Special Agent employed in the Criminal Investigation Division of the Office of the (District Director of Internal Revenue) (Director of International Operations) at *(address of office where assigned)*.

2. In my capacity as a Special Agent, I am conducting an investigation (into the tax liability of) (for the collection of the tax liability of) (name of taxpayer) for the (year(s) ________) (taxable period(s) ________).

3. In furtherance of the above investigation and in accordance with Section 7602 of Title 26, U.S.C., I issued on (*date*) an administrative summons, Internal Revenue Service Form 2039 to *(name of summoned person)*, (to give testimony) (and) (to produce for examination books, papers, records, or other data as described in said summons).

The summons is attached to the Petition as Exhibit *(leave blank)*.

(Next page is 9781-218.1)

Exhibit 300-15 Cont. (1)

◊

Pattern Declaration

Handbook Reference: Text 36(10).33

(To be used when the Special Agent executing the declaration did not perform the relevant activity)

4. I have been advised by *(specify title and name of person serving summons)* that on *(date)*, in accordance with Section 7603 of Title 26, U.S.C., (s)he served an attested copy of the Internal Revenue Service summons described in Paragraph 3 above on the respondent, *(name of summoned person)* by *(specify manner of service)*. This is further evidenced in the certificate of service on the reverse side of the summons.

5. On *(date)*, the notice required by Section 7609(a) of Title 26, U.S.C., was served by *(specify title and name of person serving notice)*, on *(specify person(s) entitled to notice)*, by *(specify manner of service, i.e., personal; left at last and usual place of abode; sent by registered or certified mail; or left with the person summoned)*. I have been apprised of this by *(specify title and name of person serving notice)* and it is further evidenced in the certificate of service of notice on the reverse side of the summons.

6. I have been informed by *(specify title and name of person designated as the individual before whom the summoned party was to appear)*, that on *(date)*, the respondent, *(name of summoned person), (did not appear in response to the summons) (appeared but refused to comply with the summons by producing the books, records and other documents demanded in the summons or by giving testimony as to the matters requested in said summons) (failed to appear because notice not to appear had been given in accordance with section 7609(b)(2) of Title 26, U.S.C.)*. The respondent's refusal to comply with the summons continues to the date of this declaration.

(To be used when the Special Agent executing the declaration did perform the relevant activity)

4. In accordance with section 7603 of Title 26, U.S.C., on *(date)*, I served an attested copy of the Internal Revenue Service summons described in Paragraph 3 above on the respondent, *(name of summoned person)*, by *(specify manner of service)*, as evidenced in the certificate of service on the reverse side of the summons.

5. On *(date)*, I served the notice required by Section 7609(a) of Title 26, U.S.C., on (specify person(s) entitled to notice), by *(specify manner of service, i.e., personal; left at last and usual place of abode, sent by registered or certified mail; or left with the person summoned)*, as evidenced in the certificate of service of notice on the reverse side of the summons.

6. On *(date)*, the respondent, *(name of summoned person), (did not appear in response to the summons) (appeared but refused to comply with the summons by producing the books, records and other documents demanded in the summons or by giving testimony as to matters requested in said summons) (failed to appear because notice not to appear had been given in accordance with section 7609(b)(2) of Title 26, U.S.C.)*. The respondent's refusal to comply with the summons continues to the date of this declaration.

7. The books, papers, records or other data sought by the summons are not already in the possession of the Internal Revenue Service (except as follows): (specify any summoned materials that have been obtained since the summons was served. Also, where the summons seeks Wage Tax Statements (W-2), Forms 1099, or other items which the Service technically may have in its possession, the paragraph should be modified to include a statement to the effect that these items are not readily accessible or retrievable without undue administrative burden or expense, together with an explanation thereof.)

8. All administrative steps required by the Internal Revenue Code for issuance of a summons have been taken.

9. It is necessary (to obtain the testimony) (and) (to examine the books, papers, records, or other data) sought by the summons in order (to properly investigate) (to collect) the federal tax liability of (name of taxpayer) for the (year(s) ________) (for taxable period(s) ________). The Internal Revenue Service has not made any recommendation for criminal prosecution to the Department of Justice.

I declare under penalty of perjury that the foregoing is true and correct.

Executed this ________ day of ________, 19 ________.

____
(Name of Person Seeking Enforcement)
Special Agent

Exhibit 300-15 Cont. (2)

Pattern Declaration ◊

Handbook Reference: Text 36(10).33

Instructions For Preparing Summons Declaration

The Department of Justice has the option to request separate declarations where more than one special agent is involved in issuance, service, or designation as the party before whom the summoned party is to appear. Paragraph 3, 4, 5, and 6 should be modified as appropriate when separate declarations are required.

Paragraph 5 should only be used when a summons is directed to a third-party recordkeeper as defined in IRC 7609(c).

Paragraph 7 is a general provision. However, in the event the Service does have some of the summoned material at the time of the enforcement proceeding, those materials should be excepted.

(Next page is 9781-219)

Exhibit 300-16

Pattern Letter P-549

WAIVER

To:
Address: Date:

Under Section 7602 of the Internal Revenue Code, the Internal Revenue Service has the authority to examine books and records and take testimony. If a summons is issued to a person who keeps or maintains records related to my business transactions or affairs, I understand that I am entitled to be notified and have the right to stay (prevent) compliance and intervene under Section 7609 of the Code.

Being fully aware of the authority of the Internal Revenue Service and my rights under the law, upon the issuance of a summons, I waive my rights and request that you furnish the Service the following records of my business transactions or affairs:

Name:

Address:

Signature **Date**

Exhibit 300-17

Calendar's—1800 to 2050
Handbook Reference: text 3(11)0

DIRECTIONS FOR USE

Look for the year you want in the index at left. The number opposite each year is the number of the calendar to use for that year.

I N D E X

Year	No.	Year	No.	Year	No.	Year	No.	Year	No.	Year	No.	Year	No.	Year	No.	Year	No.
1800	4	1828	10	1856	10	1884	10	1912	9	1940	9	1968	9	1996	9	2024	9
1901	5	1829	5	1857	5	1885	5	1913	4	1941	4	1969	4	1997	4	2025	4
1802	6	1830	6	1858	6	1886	6	1914	5	1942	5	1970	5	1998	5	2026	5
1803	7	1831	7	1859	7	1887	7	1915	6	1943	6	1971	6	1999	6	2027	6
1804	8	1832	8	1860	8	1888	8	1916	14	1944	14	1972	14	2000	14	2028	14
1805	3	1833	3	1861	3	1889	3	1917	2	1945	2	1973	2	2001	2	2029	2
1806	4	1834	4	1862	4	1890	4	1918	3	1946	3	1974	3	2002	3	2030	3
1807	5	1835	5	1863	5	1891	5	1919	4	1947	4	1975	4	2003	4	2031	4
1808	13	1836	13	1864	13	1892	13	1920	12	1948	12	1976	12	2004	12	2032	12
1809	1	1837	1	1865	1	1893	1	1921	7	1949	7	1977	7	2005	7	2033	7
1810	2	1838	2	1866	2	1894	2	1922	1	1950	1	1978	1	2006	1	2034	1
1811	3	1839	3	1867	3	1895	3	1923	2	1951	2	1979	2	2007	2	2035	2
1812	11	1840	11	1868	11	1896	11	1924	10	1952	10	1980	10	2008	10	2036	10
1813	6	1841	6	1869	6	1897	6	1925	5	1953	5	1981	5	2009	5	2037	5
1814	7	1842	7	1870	7	1898	7	1926	6	1954	6	1982	6	2010	6	2038	6
1815	1	1843	1	1871	1	1899	1	1927	7	1955	7	1983	7	2011	7	2039	7
1816	9	1844	9	1872	9	1900	2	1928	8	1956	8	1984	8	2012	8	2040	8
1817	4	1845	4	1873	4	1901	3	1929	3	1957	3	1985	3	2013	3	2041	3
1818	5	1846	5	1874	5	1902	4	1930	4	1958	4	1986	4	2014	4	2042	4
1819	6	1847	6	1875	6	1903	5	1931	5	1959	5	1987	5	2015	5	2043	5
1820	14	1848	14	1876	14	1904	13	1932	13	1960	13	1988	13	2016	13	2044	13
1821	2	1849	2	1877	2	1905	1	1933	1	1961	1	1989	1	2017	1	2045	1
1822	3	1850	3	1878	3	1906	2	1934	2	1962	2	1990	2	2018	2	2046	2
1823	4	1851	4	1879	4	1907	3	1935	3	1963	3	1991	3	2019	3	2047	3
1824	12	1852	12	1880	12	1908	11	1936	11	1964	11	1992	11	2020	11	2048	11
1825	7	1853	7	1881	7	1909	6	1937	6	1965	6	1993	6	2021	6	2049	6
1826	1	1854	1	1882	1	1910	7	1938	7	1966	7	1994	7	2022	7	2050	7
1827	2	1855	2	1883	2	1911	1	1939	1	1967	1	1995	1	2023	1	[illegible]	

1

2

3

4

5

6

Exhibit 300-17 Cont.

Calendars 1800 to 2050

7

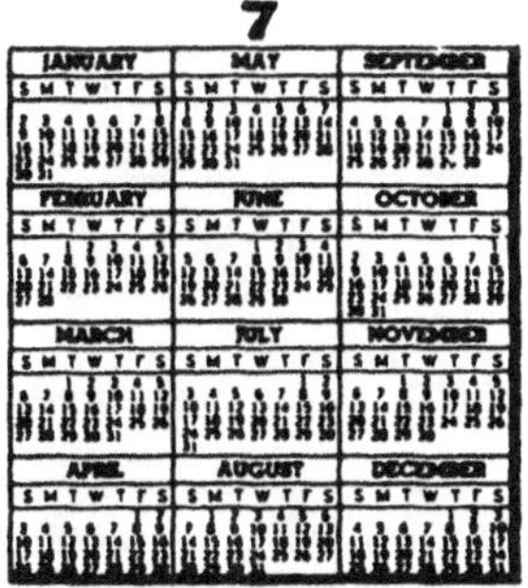

8

9

10

11

12

13

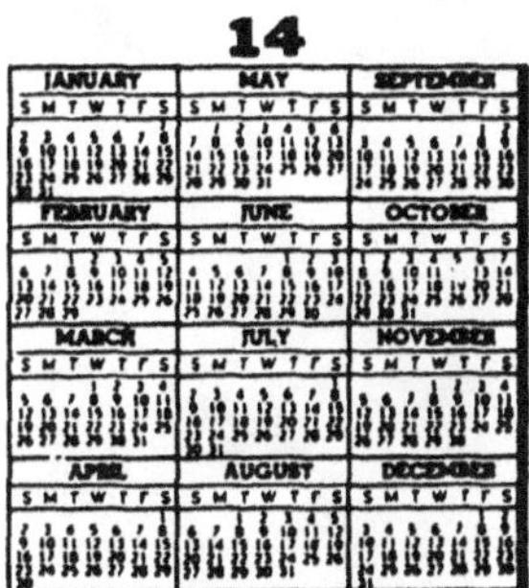

14

Exhibit 300–18

Waiver of Privilege and Authorization for Release of Medical Information
Handbook Reference: text 344.7:(2) ◊

WAIVER OF PRIVILEGE AND AUTHORIZATION
FOR RELEASE OF DIAGNOSTIC
AND TREATMENT INFORMATION

Date

To: ______________________________

____

I hereby waive any and all patient-psychotherapist privilege I may have, and authorize you to release to Special Agent of the Internal Revenue Service all information you may possess relating to the diagnosis and treatment of my mental and emotional condition.

(Signed) ______________________________

Address ______________________________

Witness: ______________________________

Address: ______________________________

Exhibit 300–19

Map of IRS and Judicial District Boundaries

Handbook Reference: text 3(12)0

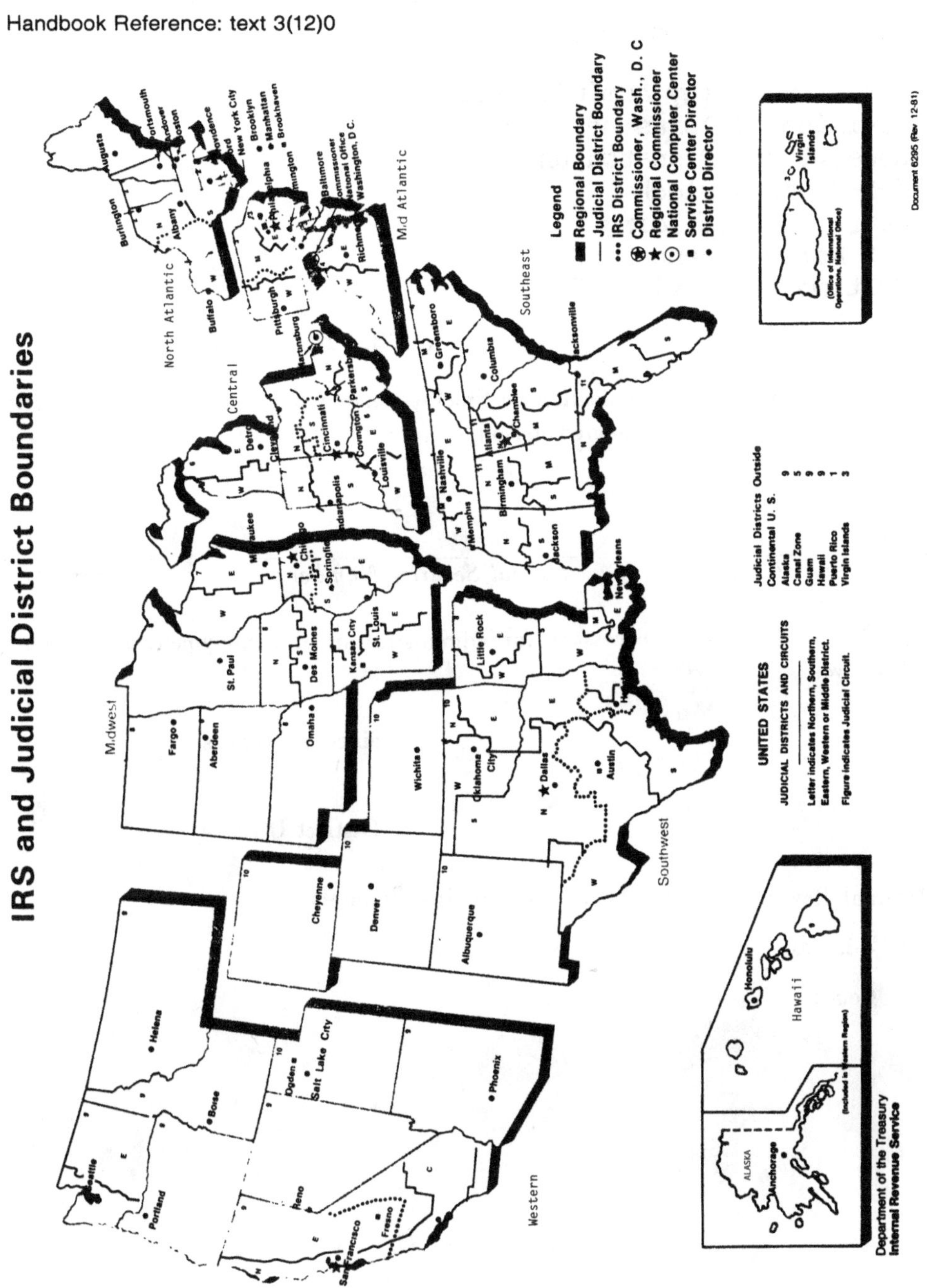

Exhibit 300-20

Memorandum Format for Request of Information From Social Security Administration
Handbook Reference: text 333.2:(2)(d)

To: Social Security Administration
Division of Adjustment Operations
Receipt and Dispatch Unit
4-N-7 South Block
Metro West Building
300 North Greene Street
Baltimore, Maryland 21201

Date:

IRS-CRITICAL CASE

Please furnish an itemization by Employer name and address of the quarterly wages earned for the indicated period(s) for:

_______________ _______________ _______________
(Taxpayer's Name) *(Social Security Number)* *(Year(s))*

This information is necessary for administration of employment and income tax laws.

Sincerely Yours,

District Director

Internal Revenue Service District Originating Request:

Address:

Code:

Exhibit 300-21

List of Payment Centers of the Social Security Administration
Handbook Reference: text 333.2:(2)(h) ◊

First Three Digits of Social Security Account Number	Payment Center
001-134	Social Security Administration Payment Center 96-05 Horace Harding Expressway Flushing New York 11368
135-222 232-236 577-584	Social Security Administration Payment Center 401 North Broad Street Philadelphia Pennsylvania 19108
223-231 237-267 400-428 587	Social Security Administration Payment Center 2225 Third Avenue, North Birmingham Alabama 35285
268-302 316-399 700 Series	Social Security Administration Payment Center 165 North Canal Street Chicago Illinois 60606
501-504 516-524 526-576 586	Social Security Administration Payment Center Post Office Box 100 San Francisco California 94101
303-315 429-500 505-515 525 585	Social Security Administration Payment Center Federal Office Building 601 East 12th Street Kansas City Missouri 64106

Exhibit 300-24

Form 2275

1 SOCIAL SECURITY OR E I NUMBER: 000-00-0000
2 FORM NO: 1040
3 TAX PERIOD: 1975
3A DISTRICT CODE: 00
4 DOCUMENT LOCATOR NUMBER AND PROCESSING YEAR
5 NAME AND ADDRESS OF TAXPAYER (Please print)
John F. Doe
Any Street
Your Town, State 00000
6 RENUMBERED DOCUMENT LOCATOR NUMBER AND PROCESSING YEAR
7 OTHER NUMBER
8 ASSESSMENT NUMBER
9. ENCODER NUMBER
10 FED TAX DEPOSIT NO (TUS)

ADJUSTMENT CONTROL NUMBER

11 REQUESTED BY
A SERVICE CENTER OR OTHER LOCATION ("X" proper box)
☐ ANDOVER ☐ CINCINNATI ☐ OGDEN
☐ ATLANTA ☐ FRESNO ☒ PHILADELPHIA
☐ AUSTIN ☐ KANSAS CITY
☐ BROOKHAVEN ☐ MEMPHIS
OTHER (Specify) National OFFICE
B DIVISION: Criminal Investigation
C BRANCH: Operations
D SECTION
E UNIT
F. GROUP
G STOP NO
H NAME OF ORIGINATOR: BJ. Peterson
I PHONE NO: 123-4567

12 APPROVAL SIGNATURE: Ira Martin
13 DATE: 3-23-77
14 DOCUMENT ☐ CHARGED TO ☐ RECHARGE TO DATE
A OFFICE LOCATION (Specify)
B DIVISION
C BRANCH
D SECTION
E UNIT
F GROUP
G STOP NO
H NAME
I PHONE NO

15 INFORMATION REQUESTED ("X" proper box)
A ☒ ORIGINAL DOCUMENT
B ☐ MICROFILM TRANSCRIPT
C ☐ OTHER (Specify in Item 22)
D. ☐ PHOTOCOPY
1 ☐ PUBLIC USE (Specify portion in Item 22)
2 ☐ INTERNAL USE
a ☐ COMPLETE DOCUMENT
b ☐ PORTION (Specify in Item 22)

16 TYPE OF REQUEST ("X" proper box)
A ☒ INITIAL
B ☐ SECOND
1. ☐ NO RECORD OF DOCUMENT
2 ☐ NO RESPONSE TO INITIAL REQUEST

17 SOURCE
A EXAMINATION PICK-UP
1 ☐ NOL
2 ☐ RELATED
3. ☐ OTHER
B ☐ REFERENCE AND INFORMATION
C. FOR ASSOCIATION WITH RETURN IN AUDIT DIVISION UNDER THE NAME OF

18. ACTION
SECTION A MICROFILM
A. ☐ REQUEST FILLED
B. ☐ NO RECORD OF DLN
C ☐ OTHER (Explain)
CYCLE NUMBER
DATE
SECTION B · FILES
A. ☐ REQUEST FILLED
B. ☐ NO RECORD OF DLN
C. ☐ DOCUMENT MISSING FROM BLOCK
D. ☐ OTHER (Explain)

19 DOCUMENT RETAINED IN ("X" proper box and indicate location)
A. ☐ SERVICE CENTER
B. ☐ DISTRICT OFFICE
C. ☐ FEDERAL RECORDS CENTER
D ☐ OTHER

20. FEDERAL RECORDS CENTER REFERENCE	A ACCESSION NO	B. FRC CONTAINER NO.	C. SHELF LIST NO

21. ☐ **REFILE** IN LOCATION INDICATED IN ITEM 19.

22. REMARKS

FORM 2275 (REV. 6-73)

RECORDS REQUEST, CHARGE AND RECHARGE

DEPARTMENT OF THE TREASURY
INTERNAL REVENUE SERVICE

Exhibit 300-24 Cont. (1)

Form 2275 DO-MW

1. SOCIAL SECURITY OR E.I. NUMBER: 000-00-0000
2. FORM NO.: 1040
3. TAX PERIOD: 1975
4. DOCUMENT LOCATOR NUMBER AND PROCESSING YEAR
5. NAME AND ADDRESS OF TAXPAYER *(Please print)*

John F. Doe
Any Street
Your Town, State 00000

6. RENUMBERED DOCUMENT LOCATOR NUMBER AND PROCESSING YEAR
7. OTHER NUMBER
8. ASSESSMENT NUMBER
9. ENCODER NUMBER
10. FED. TAX DEPOSIT NO. *(TUS)*

ADJUSTMENT CONTROL NUMBER ________

11. REQUESTED BY

A. DISTRICT OFFICE LOCATION *("X" proper box)*

☒ CHICAGO, 36 ☐ ST. LOUIS, 43 ☐ MILWAUKEE, 39
☐ ST. PAUL, 41 ☐ SPRINGFIELD, 37 ☐ DES MOINES, 42
☐ OMAHA, 47 ☐ ABERDEEN, 46 ☐ FARGO, 45

SUBORDINATE OFFICE *(Specify)*: Rock Island

B. DIVISION: Criminal Investigation
C. BRANCH
D. SECTION
E. UNIT
F. GROUP
G. STOP NO.
H. NAME OF ORIGINATOR: S. Vicca
I. PHONE NO.: 1234567

12. APPROVAL SIGNATURE: Richard Francis
13. DATE: 3-23-77

14. DOCUMENT ☐ CHARGED TO: ☐ RECHARGE TO: DATE

A. OFFICE LOCATION *(Specify)*
B. DIVISION
C. BRANCH
D. SECTION
E. UNIT
F. GROUP
G. STOP NO.
H. NAME
I. PHONE NO.

15. INFORMATION REQUESTED *("X" proper box)*

A. ☐ ORIGINAL DOCUMENT
B. ☐ OTHER *(Specify in Item 22.)*
C. ☐ PHOTOCOPY
 1. ☐ PUBLIC USE *(Specify portion in Item 22.)*
 2. ☐ INTERNAL USE
  a. ☐ COMPLETE DOCUMENT
  b ☐ PORTION *(Specify in Item 22.)*

16. TYPE OF REQUEST *("X" proper box)*

A. ☐ INITIAL
B. ☐ SECOND
 1. ☐ NO RECORD OF DOCUMENT.
 2. ☐ NO RESPONSE TO INITIAL REQUEST.

17. SOURCE

A. EXAMINATION PICK-UP
 1. ☐ NOL
 2. ☐ RELATED
 3. ☐ OTHER ________
B. ☐ REFERENCE AND INFORMATION

C. FOR ASSOCIATION WITH RETURN IN AUDIT DIVISION UNDER THE NAME OF:

18. ACTION *(To be completed by Research or Files Personnel) ("X" proper box)*

A. ☐ REQUEST FILLED
B. ☐ NO RECORD OF DOCUMENT
 1. CYCLE NUMBER ________
 2. DATE ________
C. ☐ DOCUMENT MISSING FROM BLOCK
D. ☐ OTHER *(Explain)*

19. DOCUMENT RETAINED IN *("X" proper box and indicate location)*

A. ☐ SERVICE CENTER ________
B. ☐ DISTRICT OFFICE ________
C. ☐ FEDERAL RECORDS CENTER ________
D. ☐ OTHER ________

20. FEDERAL RECORDS CENTER REFERENCE	A. ACCESSION NO.	B. FRC CONTAINER NO.	C. SHELF LIST NO.

21. ☐ REFILE IN LOCATION INDICATED IN ITEM 19.

22. REMARKS

DEPARTMENT OF THE TREASURY
INTERNAL REVENUE SERVICE

RECORDS REQUEST, CHARGE AND RECHARGE

FORM 2275 DO-MW (4-69)

Exhibit 300–24 Cont. (2)

Instructions for Form 2275 and 2275 DO

Instructions for Completing Forms 2275 and 2275 DO—Records Request Charge and Recharge

Self-explanatory items and items to be filled in by files personnel are not listed.

Item 2. For example "1040", "941", etc.

Item 3. Show the period of time covered by the return or document being requested.

Item 4. Always show the latest Document Locator Number, if known, including the processing year (14th digit).

Item 5. If S.S. or E.I. Number given in Item 1, show name of taxpayer only. If Item 1 is not filled in, show complete name and address of the taxpayer.

Item 8. Show identification numbers assigned returns prior to ADP and other documents of a non-ADP nature.

Item 9. If available, show the IRS identification number (encoder number) on the back of the taxpayer's remittance, which will assist in locating full-paid returns that have not been processed.

Item 11A. Form 2275 If the originator is located in other than a Service Center, type or print originating office (Western Regional Office, National Office, etc.) after "Other (Specify)." When this form is used by district offices as back-up stock, enter the originating district office in the "Other (Specify)" space.

Item 11A. Form 2275 DO Place an "X" in the box that designates the originating district office. Print or type subordinate office locations (physically located outside of a District Headquarters Office) in the space provided.

Items 11B through G Fill in these items to the extent applicable.

Item 11H and I Give full name and telephone number.

Item 12. Immediate or first line supervisor will enter his signature of approval if organizationally prescribed.

Item 13. Enter the date the requisition is forwarded.

Item 15B. Place an "X" in this box to request miscellaneous data or documents and specify exactly what is desired immediately below if there is room or in Item 22 if more space is needed.

Item 16B. Place an "X" in this box when the initial requisition has not been satisfied. Place an "X" in sub-block 1. or 2. to explain why the second request is being initiated.

Item 19. Either the preparer or unit responsible for routing the requisition will place an "X" in the appropriate box and enter the location of the files storage point.

Item 22. Use this item to specify what is being requested in Item 15, "Information Requested." Conserve space, since this item is also used by files personnel to provide the requester with pertinent data.

GUIDELINES FOR RECHARGE REQUESTS FOR ORIGINAL DOCUMENTS

Item 14. Place an "X" in the "RECHARGE TO:" box. Show the date the document was recharged.

Item 14A. Show the office and location of the new user. (Example: District Office, Seattle)

Items 14B through G Fill in these items to the extent applicable.

Items 14H and I Give full name and telephone number of the person to whom the document is being recharged (the new user).

Exhibit 300-25

Form 4338

Information or Certified Transcript Request
(DO NOT use this form for IMF. See reverse for instructions.)

Transcript DLN

Taxpayer's EIN or SSN: EIN: 00-0000000

Taxpayer's Full Name and Address *(Underline Name Control)*
N.E Twitchell Inc.
1234 Any Street
Northern, VA 22003

Description
X Regular Certified *(to be used only to satisfy legal requirements)* ☐ Supplement ☐ Under Seal

Number of copies | Date required

Reason for request

ADP
(Master File - Computer Transcript)

"X"	Type of Transcript Requested	Code	MFT	Period Ending
	Specific Module *(A specific return for a specific period)*	990		
	Open Module *(All return periods which have debit or credit balance)*	991	59 or 69	If specific or class of tax transcript requested and M.F.T. not known, complete the following:
X	**Complete** *(All return periods for a taxpayer regardless of balance)*	992	59 or 69	Place "X" in Appropriate Box
	Class of Tax *(All return periods for a taxpayer within the Specified MFT)*	992		☐ BMF ☐ RMF
	Entity *(All names lines and transactions posted to the entity section)*	993	59 or 69	Form Number:

Non-ADP
(Manually Processed)

"X"	Information Requested	Form Number	Taxable Period(s)	DLN and Account Numbers
	Transcript			
	Photo Copy of Unit Ledger Card			
	All Outstanding Balances			

District or Service Center where Return(s) are Filed

Return or Document in Possession of Requester
☐ Yes ☐ No
(See Item 3 on reverse.)

Give any business names, aliases, names used previously, other addresses, or other information that may assist in locating the account if a taxpayer's EIN/SSN or complete name are not known.

Requester

Name and Address: Robert L. Harley, P.O. Box 1382, Northern, VA 22003

Title: Special Agent

Date: 11/19/79

Phone Number: 372-2412

Form **4338** (Rev. 7-76) *Use prior issue first* Department of the Treasury - Internal Revenue Service

Exhibit 300-25 Cont. (1)

Instructions for Form 4338

◊

GENERAL INFORMATION

1. Prepare separate request forms for ADP and Non-ADP accounts. For ADP Account Transcripts, use separate request forms for BMF and RMF information.

2. Form 4303, Computer Transcript, is generated for accounts from BMF. CP Notice Transcript will come out for RMF accounts. Form 4340 is used to provide requested information on Non-ADP accounts.

3. Do not use Transcript DLN block at top of request form.

4. Use the following format to list taxpayer's EIN: NN–NNNNNNN; Use the following format to list taxpayer's SSN: NNN–NN–NNNN.

5. Complete the blocks for Number of Copies, Date Required, and Reason for Request **only** if a certified transcript is required.

6. Use separate Forms 4338 to request Specific transcripts for multiple tax periods. Request Class of Tax or Complete transcripts if more than three tax periods are required.

7. Complete MFT block or indicate either BMF or RMF and Form Number when a Specific or Class of Tax transcript is requested only. For RMF use 59 for F. 706, 709; use 69 for F. 11, 11B, 11C, 730, 2290, & 4638. Line thru "59 or 69" on all BMF requests.

8. For Non-ADP requests, if the following Returns or Documents are in the Possession of the Requester, attach photocopies as indicated to the request form:

(1) Return—Photocopy of front page

(2) Amended Return—Photocopy of front page

(3) Estimated Tax Documents—Photocopy of document

(4) Tentative return attached to corporation return—Photocopy of front page

(5) Form 899 or 4340—Photocopy of transcript

9. For Non-ADP requests, forward Form 4338 to the Service Center for the District Office where the return was filed.

CERTIFIED TRANSCRIPTS

1. Request certified transcripts only when formal certification is necessary to satisfy legal requirements.

2. For ADP Accounts, if time does not permit obtaining a computer transcript (Form 4303), Form 4340 will be prepared and certified from IDRS data if available. Otherwise use microfilm data.

3. The Special Procedures Section or Appellate Division will always specify what documents are needed, how many copies are required, and what is to be certified.

4. Requests for certified transcripts, especially for Non-ADP returns, require additional research and processing time and should be made at the earliest practical date to insure receiving completed transcripts when needed.

CERTIFIED SUPPLEMENTAL TRANSCRIPTS

1. Request a supplemental transcript, if needed, to cover the period of time after an original request and certification has been acted on.

2. Attach a copy of the prior transcript to the supplemental request.

Exhibit 300-25 Cont. (2)

Preparation of Requests ◊

Preparation of Requests

In addition to the instructions appearing on the reverse side of Form 4338, all requests for transcripts should contain the following information:

(1) Employer Identification or Social Security Number of taxpayer. (EI Number for BMF requests, SSN for IMF requests.)

(2) Name of taxpayer. This should be exact as possible. For ADP requests it should be shown on the directory or any notices, TDA's or other computer output. In the event the above sources are not available, information to complete the request may be obtained from the return or other available sources.

(3) Transcript requested (designate by an "X"). Note: If the request is for Certified, Supplemental or Under Seal, list the number of copies required, the date the transcript must be received by the requester and the reason for the request.

(4) ADP Requests—The type of transcript requested (Specific, Open, Complete, Entity or Tax Class). Indicate by an "X" the type of transcript requested. Complete the MFT block for "SPECIFIC MODULE" and "CLASS OF TAX." MFT is the Master File tax account, a two-digit number which identifies the type of tax as follows:

MFT	*Tax Class*	*Master File Account*	*Form Number and Type of Tax*
01	1	BMF	941 Withholding and FICA
30	2	IMF	1040A, 1040 Individual Income
02	3	BMF	1120 Corporation Income
03	4	BMF	720 Excise
09	7	BMF	CT-1 Railway Retirement
10	8	BMF	940 FUTA
—	9	BMF	All types of BMF tax

(5) For "SPECIFIC MODULE" Transcript the return form number and the period ending date must be shown. A separate transcript request should be submitted for each module record needed.

(6) In order to facilitate service center contact with the Intelligence Division "requester" the telephone number, including area code of the requester (normally the special agent assigned the case), will be included in the location or address block (bottom line) of Form 4338.

Exhibit 300-25 Cont. (3)

Form 4338-A

IMF Information or Certified Transcript Request
(Prepare in duplicate. See instructions below.)

Transcript DLN

Requester

Name and Address	Title	
William Gerard P.O. Box 10049 Yorktown, MD	Special Agent	
	Date: 10-31-77	Phone Number: 924-2435

Identification of Transcript

Taxpayer's SSN: 157-00-9255

Taxpayer's Full Name and Address *(Underline Name Control)*

John F. Doe
2230 Pine Street
Warren, MD 19212

Description

[X] Regular [ ] Supplemental [ ] Under Seal
[ ] Certified *(to be used only to satisfy legal requirements)*

Number of copies | Date required

Reason for request

Master File - Computer Transcript

"X"	Type of Transcript Requested	Code	Period Ending
X	**Specific Module** *(A specific return for a specific period)*	990	7612 - 1040
	Open Module (All return periods which have debit or credit balance)	991	
	Complete *(All return periods for a taxpayer regardless of balance)*	992	
	Entity *(All name lines and transactions posted to the entity section)*	993	

Give any business names, aliases, names used previously, other addresses, or other information that may assist in locating the account if a taxpayer's SSN or complete name are not known.

XYZ Co.
2230 Pine Street
Warren, MD 19212

Instructions

General	1. Form 4303, Computer Transcript, is generated for accounts from IMF. 2. Do not use Transcript DLN block at top of request form. 3. Use the following format to list taxpayer's SSN: NNN-NN-NNNN.	4. Complete the blocks for Number of Copies, Date Required, and Reason for Request *only* if a certified transcript is required. 5. Use separate Forms 4338-A to request specific transcripts for multiple tax periods. Request complete transcripts if more than three tax periods are required.
Certified Transcripts	1. If time does not permit obtaining a computer transcript *(Form 4303)*, Form 4340, Certificate of Assessments and Payments, will be prepared and certified from IDRS data, if available. Otherwise, use microfilm data. 2. The Special Procedures Section or Appellate Division will always specify what documents are	needed, how many copies are required, and what is to be certified. 3. Requests for certified transcripts, especially for non-ADP returns, require additional research and processing time and should be made at the earliest practical date to ensure receiving completed transcripts when needed.
Certified Supplemental Transcripts	1. Request a supplemental transcript, if needed, to cover the period of time after an original request and certification has been acted on.	2. Attach a copy of the prior transcript to the supplemental request.

Form **4338-A** (7-76) ☆ U.S. G.P.O. 1976-621 742/6590 Department of the Treasury - Internal Revenue Service

Exhibit 300-26

Form 4303

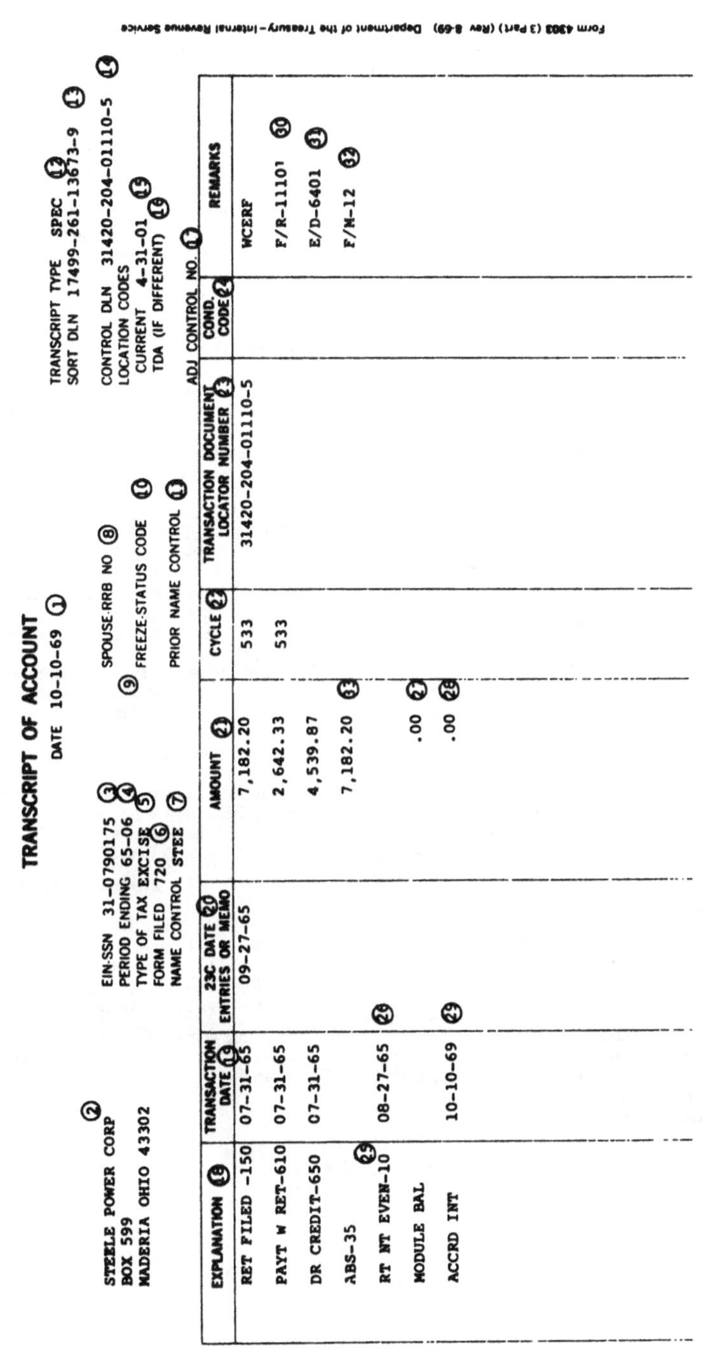

Form 4303 (3 Part) (Rev 8-69) Department of the Treasury - Internal Revenue Service

TRANSCRIPT OF ACCOUNT

DATE 10-10-69 (1)

TRANSCRIPT TYPE SPEC (12)
SORT DLN 17499-261-13673-9 (13)

STEELE POWER CORP (2)
BOX 599
MADERIA OHIO 43302

EIN-SSN 31-0790175 (3)
PERIOD ENDING 65-06 (4)
TYPE OF TAX EXCISE (5)
FORM FILED 720 (6)
NAME CONTROL STEE (7)

SPOUSE-RRB NO (8)
(9) FREEZE-STATUS CODE (10)
PRIOR NAME CONTROL (11)

CONTROL DLN 31420-204-01110-5 (14)
LOCATION CODES
CURRENT 4-31-01 (15)
TDA (IF DIFFERENT) (16)
ADJ CONTROL NO. (17)

EXPLANATION (18)	TRANSACTION DATE (19)	23C DATE (20) ENTRIES OR MEMO	AMOUNT (21)	CYCLE (22)	TRANSACTION DOCUMENT LOCATOR NUMBER (23)	COND. CODE (24)	REMARKS
RET FILED -150	07-31-65	09-27-65	7,182.20	533	31420-204-01110-5		WCERF
PAYT W RET-610	07-31-65		2,642.33	533			F/R-11101 (30)
DR CREDIT-650	07-31-65		4,539.87				E/D-6401 (31)
ABS-35			7,182.20 (33)				F/M-12 (32)
RT NT EVEN-10 (25)	08-27-65	(26)					
MODULE BAL			.00 (27)				
ACCRD INT	10-10-69	(29)	.00 (28)				

Exhibit 300–26 Cont. (1)

Description of Form 4303

Description of Form 4303—Computer Transcripts

(1) One modular record is printed per transcript page. If a module requires more than one page, additional pages are printed with identifying information from the heading repeated.
(2) Transactions are printed in their order of posting to the Master File.
(3) When a transaction reflects a secondary amount (such as Withholding Tax on an Income Tax Return) the secondary amount is shown as a separate transaction. The DLN for the secondary amount is *not* shown. Therefore, a transaction lacking a DLN can be recognized as being part of the preceding primary transaction.

Explanation of Contents of Transcript of Account, Form 4303

① Date: Corresponding to NCC cycle in which the transcript is produced.

② Name and Address: Taxpayer's name and current address—on IMF modules the name shown is the name as given on the tax module, *NOT* the entity module. For example, if Alice Wills files her return for 1966 and changes her name to Alice Hays in 1969 the entity name is Alice Hays; but, the name shown on the 1966 transcript is Alice Wills.

③ EIN/SSN:
(1) An asterisk following an SSN indicates an invalid number.
(2) Invalid SSN release—IMF only —R printed if condition is present.
(3) Scrambled SSN—IMF only—S printed if condition is present.

④ Period Ending: Year and month in which the period covered by each module ended.

⑤ Type of Tax: Income, WT-FICA, Excise, RR-Ret., FUTA or blank.

⑥ Form Filed: 1040A, 1040, 941, 1120, 720, CT-1 or 940. "NONE" if no return filed on IMF.

⑦ Name Control: Of the *Entity* module.

⑧ Spouse or RRB No.: On IMF modules, spouse's SSN if present. On BMF modules, Railroad Board Number of present.

⑨ and ⑩ Freeze Codes: Alphabetic codes indicating up to three freeze or status conditions present in a module. For example: (TC 914), Intelligence control.

⑪ Prior Name Control: Present only if different from current name control.

⑫ Transcript Type: Transcript title. For example, "SPECIFIC," "COMPLETE," ETC.

⑬ Sort DLN: On requested transcripts, is the DLN of transcript request; on generated transcripts, is the DLN specified by extraction criteria.

⑭ Control DLN: Tax module control DLN.

⑮ Location Codes (current): Shown as R (Region), DD (District) and AA (Area office).

⑯ Location Codes (TDA): Present if different from current location codes. Printed in the same format as current location code.

⑰ Adjustment Control Number.

⑱ Transaction Explanation: Abbreviations for each transaction followed by the actual transaction code. For example, PAYT W RET - 610. Refer to ADP Handbook 370-725 for complete explanation of each transaction.

⑲ Transaction Date—Received date of returns, credits and credit reversals; transfer date for account transfer in or out; transaction date for transactions without money fields; special interest computation date for TC 294, 298, 304 and 308 and 23C date for machine-generated transactions.

⑳ 23C Date: Assessment date for transactions, usually a Friday.

㉑ Transaction Amount—Amount of each transaction: Credits are indicated by a minus (—) sign.

㉒ Cycle Posted: Cycle of the posted transaction printed in the format YY-WW.

㉓ Transaction DLN:DLN of the transaction. Not printed for "Secondary Amount" Transactions. Replaced by TUS (Treasurer U.S.) number if present on FTD payments. TUS numbers are printed in the format XXX97-XXXXXXXX-XX.

㉔ Condition Codes—BMF only: printed next to return if present–1, 2, 3 and A-Z.

㉕ Status Explanation: Abbreviations for module status followed by status code. For example, 1st Notice–21.

㉖ Status Date: Pertaining to module status explanation (25) above.

㉗ Module Balance: Tax module balance after posting, including tax, penalty and unpaid assessed interest.

㉘ Accrued Interest: Amount of unassessed interest for the module.

㉙ Accrued Interest Date: Date to which accrued interest is computed.

㉚ Filing Requirements—BMF only: The presence of a filing requirement will be indicated by "1." No filing requirement will be shown as "0." The format of these print lines will be as follows:

Example F/R W C E R F
1 1 1 0 1

W—941 Filing Requirement
C—1120 Filing Requirement
E—720 Filing Requirement
R—CT-1 Filing Requirement
F—940 Filing Requirement

In the example above a filing requirement exists for "W" (Form 941), "C" (Form 1120), "E" (Form 720) and "F" (Form 940).

Exhibit 300-26 Cont. (2)

Description of Form 4303

(31) Establishment Period—BMF only: Year and month entity established on Master File.

(32) Fiscal Month—BMF only: Month in which taxpayer's year ends.

(33) Abstract Amount—BMF only: Printed only for Form 720 tax modules following posted transactions. ABSTRACT-NN is printed explanation in column followed by abstract amount.

Exhibit 300-27

Form 4340

Certificate of Assessments and Payments

Name of Taxpayer	Address (Number, street, city, and state)	EIN or SSN
John F. Doe	Any Street, Your Town, State 00000	000-00-0000

Date (a)	Explanation of Transactions (b)	Assessment (Abatement) (c)	Credit (Credit Reversal) (d)	Balance (e)	DLN or Account No. (f)	23 C Date (g)	Period Ending (h)
9/15/65	Estimated Tax		200,000.00		582345678		6512
12/15/65	Estimated Tax		200,000.00				
3/15/66	Tentative Payment		250,000.00				6512
6/15/66	Part-Paid Return	1,000,000.00	250,000.00	100,000.00		6/30/66	6512
6/30/66	First Notice						
7/15/66	Payment		50,000.00	50,000.00			
8/3/66	Lien Filed						
8/15/66	Payment		45,000.00	5,000.00			
9/15/66	Estimated Tax		300,000.00				6612
12/15/66	Estimated Tax		300,000.00				
3/15/67	Full-Paid Return	962,453.22	362,453.22	-0-		3/30/67	6612

I certify that the foregoing transcript of the taxpayer named above in respect to the taxes specified is a true and complete transcript for the period stated, and all assessments, penalties, interests, abatements, credits, refunds, and advance or unidentified payment relating thereto as disclosed by the records of this office as of the date of this certification are shown therein

Signature of Director	Location	Date

Form **4340** (Rev. 7-74) *Use all prior issues* U.S. G.P.O. 1976-621 747/6535 Department of the Treasury - Internal Revenue Service

Exhibit 300-28

Form 4135

Criminal Investigation Control Notice

To: Director Philadelphia Service Center
Attn: Chief, Criminal Investigation Branch (1)

From: Chief, Criminal Investigation Division (2)
P. O. Box 1382
Northern, VA 12345
(City, State, ZIP Code)

On Master Files marked with "X" (4)

		For (5) X Individual ☐ Spouse
X	IMF	
X	BMF	
	RMF	
	IRAF	

Initiate control indicated by item marked "X" (one only) (3) (13)

	TC910	CID Account Hold	Retain all periods on Master File.
	TC911	Reverse TC910	
X	TC914	CID Module Freeze	Active Criminal Investigation
	TC914	TC914 Update	Enter Changes only to Freeze
	TC912	Reverse TC914	

Initiate control indicated by item marked "X" (one only)

	TC915	Refund Release	Partial Reverse of TC916/918
	TC916	QRP Module Freeze	QRP Criminal Investigation
	TC917	Reverse TC916	
	TC918	QRP Entity Freeze	QRP Criminal Investigation
	TC919	Reverse TC918	

Taxpayer Identification

Complete if control on one of following (check one): ☒ IMF ☐ IRAF ☐ RMF (SSN) (6)

Individual SSN 4 5 6 3 8 8 7 1 9 — Spouse SSN

Taxpayer's name (Last, First, Middle)
Louis, Sarah

Address (Number, Street, City, State, ZIP Code)
3912 Ann St., Northern, VA 12345

Complete if control on one of following (check one): ☒ BMF ☐ RMF (EIN) (7)

Employer's Identification No. 1 8 9 0 1 2 6 4 3

Business name
Twitchell Farms

Business address (Number, Street, City, State, ZIP Code)
2170 Charlotte St., Northern, VA 12345

Complete for failure-to-file case, if known (8)
☐ Known non-filer

Complete if account currently under control (9)
Old level of control: ☐ TC-910 ☐ TC-914 ☐ TC-916 ☐ TC-918

☒ See below for Special instructions

Special Instructions—Criminal Investigation Division/Branch

Remarks: (10)

On BMF - only interested in 1120's for years 1975 to 1979, inclusive. Post all other BMF transactions to MF.

On IMF - only interested in 1040's for years 1975 to 1979, inclusive. Post any ES returns and payments received.

Assessment of Delinquency Penalty should be suppressed.

Chief, Criminal Investigation Division/Branch (Signature)	Date
(11) s/Richard Williamson	3/7/80 (12)

Form **4135** (Rev. 4-79) Department of the Treasury - Internal Revenue Service

Exhibit 300-28 Cont.

Instructions for Form 4135

Form 4135—Criminal Investigation Control Notice

1. Listed below are the instructions for completing Form 4135. For each numbered instruction below, a corresponding circled number appears on Exhibit 300-28 to indicate which item on the Form 4135 the instruction relates to.

To be completed by District Criminal Investigation:

1 Service Center responsible for servicing District Criminal Investigation Office

2 Address of District Criminal Investigation Office initiating control

3 Level of control requested

4 Master File(s) on which account(s) is located

a. Control over IMF and BMF accounts for the same taxpayer can be requested on one form

5 Account control on the IMF:

a. Control over single person's account (or modules within the account) is indicated by marking the Individual block

b. If failure to file case and it is not known whether separate or joint returns may be filed, check both the Individual and the Spouse blocks. This will also control joint returns filed

6 SSN, name and address of accounts to be controlled on the IMF, IRAF, or RMF (SSN) (check the correct block(s)). If there is more than one file checked and there are different TINs, indicate the TIN and its respective Master File in the Special Remarks section on back of form

7 EIN, business name and address of BMF or RMF (EIN) accounts to be controlled. Follow instructions in 6, above, for different TINs

8 Indicates taxpayer has not previously filed a return

9 Current level of control, if any

10 Indicates special control conditions

a. Tax years to be controlled (must be entered if TC 914 control is requested)

b. Different TINs with respective Master Files in cases mentioned in 6, above

11 Signature of Chief, or authorized delegate, Criminal Investigation Division, requesting control

12 Date

13 Special closeout procedures

◇

Exhibit 300-29

Pattern Letter P-543 ◊

Person to Contact:
Contact Telephone Number:

Salutation

You are no longer the subject of a criminal investigation by the Criminal Investigation Division regarding your Federal tax liabilities for (year(s)). However, this does not preclude reentry by the Criminal Investigation Division into the investigation.

The matter is presently in the (Examination) (Collection/Collection and Taxpayer Service) Division for further consideration.

If you have any questions, please contact the person whose name and telephone number are shown above.

Sincerely yours,
Space for signature
District Director

(Next page is 9781-245)

Exhibit 300-30

Treasury Department Order No. 246 (Revision 1) ◊

Responsibilities for Oversight of Foreign Intelligence Activities Under Executive Order 12036

By virtue of the authority vested in me as Secretary of the Treasury, including the authority vested in me by Reorganization Plan No. 26 of 1950, and pursuant to Executive Order 12036, it is ordered as follows:

1. The Inspector General established by Treasury Department Order No. 256 shall assume for the Treasury Department the duties and responsibilities established under Executive Order 12036 (hereinafter Executive Order) for Inspectors General within the Intelligence Community.

2. The General Counsel shall assume for the Treasury Department the duties and responsibilities established under the Executive Order for General Counsels within the Intelligence Community.

3. The Inspector General shall inform in writing all employees in the Office of the Assistant Secretary for International Affairs (OASIA) and in the Office of Intelligence Support of the restrictions on intelligence activities contained in Section 2 of the Executive Order and obtain a written acknowledgment from each such employee that he has read the materials provided by the Inspector General. Heads of inspection services of Treasury Department Bureaus shall provide a copy of Section 2 of the Executive Order to each employee within their bureau.

4. Treasury Department employees shall report in confidence to the Inspector General, the General Counsel, or the head of the inspection service of their bureau any matters which they feel raise questions of propriety or legality under the Executive Order.

5. The Inspector General shall review at appropriate intervals any foreign intelligence activities of the Treasury Department to determine whether any such activities raise questions of propriety under the Executive Order. Any questions arising from this review as to the legality of such activities shall be referred by the Inspector General to the General Counsel. In connection with the activities of the OASIA representatives stationed overseas, the Inspector General shall seek to make appropriate arrangements with the State Department to provide for adequate inspection while avoiding duplication of inspection activities by the State and Treasury Departments.

Exhibit 300-30 Cont.

Treasury Department Order No. 246 (Revision 1) ◊

6. The inspection service within a bureau shall review at appropriate intervals the activities of the bureau in its relations with U.S. foreign intelligence agencies to determine whether such activities raise questions of legality or propriety. Any questions of legality or propriety arising from this review shall be referred to the Inspector General who shall report to the General Counsel any illegal activities. The procedures established by Treasury Department Order No. 240 (Revision 1), which provides for coordination and review of support arrangements between the Treasury Department and U.S. foreign intelligence agencies, shall remain in full force and effect.

7. Treasury Department employees shall cooperate with the Inspector General, the General Counsel, and the inspection service within their bureau and shall make available all necessary data to allow those official to perform their duties and responsibilities under this Order.

8. Treasury Department Order No. 246 is rescinded, effective this date.

/s/ W. Michael Blumenthal
Secretary of the Treasury

Date: July 18, 1978

United States Foreign Intelligence Activities ◊

United States Foreign
Intelligence Activities

Executive Order 12036. January 24, 1978

UNITED STATES INTELLIGENCE ACTIVITIES

By virtue of the authority vested in me by the Constitution and statutes of the United States of America including the National Security Act of 1947, as amended, and as President of the United States of America, in order to provide for the organization and control of United States foreign intelligence activities, it is hereby ordered as follows:

TABLE OF CONTENTS

SECTION 2

RESTRICTIONS ON INTELLIGENCE ACTIVITIES

2-1. *Adherence to Law.*

2-101. *Purpose.* Information about the capabilities, intentions and activities of foreign powers, organizations, or persons and their agents is essential to informed decision-making in the areas of national defense and foreign relations. The measures employed to acquire such information should be responsive to legitimate governmental needs and must be conducted in a manner that preserves and respects established concepts of privacy and civil liberties.

2-202. *Principles of Interpretation.* Sections 2-201 through 2-309 set forth limitations which, in addition to other applicable laws, are intended to achieve the proper balance between protection of individual rights and acquisition of essential information. Those sections do not authorize any activity not authorized by sections 1-101 through 1-1503 and do not provide any exemption from any other law.

2-2. *Restrictions on Certain Collection Techniques.*

2-201. *General Provisions.*

(a) The activities described in Sections 2-202 through 2-208 shall be undertaken only as permitted by this Order and by procedures established by the head of the agency concerned and approved by the Attorney General. Those procedures shall protect constitutional rights and privacy, ensure that information is gathered by the least intrusive means possible, and limit use of such information to lawful governmental purposes.

(b) Activities described in sections 2-202 through 2-205 for which a warrant would be required if undertaken for law enforcement rather than intelligence purposes shall not be undertaken against a United States person without a judicial warrant, unless the President has authorized the type of activity involved and the Attorney General has both approved the particular activity and determined that there is probable cause to believe that the United States person is an agent of a foreign power.

2-202. *Electronic Surveillance.* The CIA may not engage in any electronic surveillance within the United States. No agency within the Intelligence Community shall engage in any electronic surveillance directed against a United States person abroad or designed to intercept a communication sent from, or intended for receipt within, the United States except as permitted by the procedures established pursuant to section 2-201. Training of personnel by agencies in the Intelligence Community in the use of electronic communications equipment, testing by such agencies of such equipment, and the use of measures to determine the existence and capability of electronic surveillance equipment being used unlawfully shall not be prohibited and shall also be governed by such procedures. Such activities shall be limited in scope and duration to those necessary to carry out the training, testing or countermeasures purpose. No information derived from communications intercepted in the course of such training, testing or use of counter-measures may be retained or used for any other purpose.

United States Foreign Intelligence Activities ◊

2-203. *Television Cameras and Other Monitoring.* No agency within the Intelligence Community shall use any electronic or mechanical device surreptitiously and continuously to monitor any person within the United States, or any United States person abroad, except as permitted by the procedures established pursuant to Section 2-201.

2-204. *Physical Searches.* No agency within the Intelligence Community except the FBI may conduct any unconsented physical searches within the United States. All such searches conducted by the FBI, as well as all such searches conducted by any agency within the Intelligence Community outside the United States and directed against United States persons, shall be undertaken only as permitted by procedures established pursuant to Section 2-201.

2-205. *Mail Surveillance.* No agency within the Intelligence Community shall open mail or examine envelopes in United States postal channels, except in accordance with applicable statutes and regulations. No agency within the Intelligence Community shall open mail of a United States person abroad except as permitted by procedures established pursuant to Section 2-201.

2-206. *Physical Surveillance.* The FBI may conduct physical surveillance directed against United States persons or others only in the course of a lawful investigation. Other agencies within the Intelligence Community may not undertake any physical surveillance directed against a United States person unless:

(a) The surveillance is conducted outside the United States and the person being surveilled is reasonably believed to be acting on behalf of a foreign power, engaging in international terrorist activities, or engaging in narcotics production or trafficking;

(b) The surveillance is conducted solely for the purpose of identifying a person who is in contact with someone who is the subject of a foreign intelligence or counterintelligence investigation; or

(c) That person is being surveilled for the purpose of protecting foreign intelligence and counterintelligence sources and methods from unauthorized disclosure or is the subject of a lawful counterintelligence, personnel, physical or communications security investigation.

(d) No surveillance under paragraph (c) of this section may be conducted within the United States unless the person being surveilled is a present employee, intelligence agency contractor or employee of such a contractor, or is a military person employed by a non-intelligence element of a military service. Outside the United States such surveillance may also be conducted against a former employee, intelligence agency contractor or employee of a contractor or a civilian person employed by a non-intelligence element of an agency within the Intelligence Community. A person who is in contact with such a present or former employee or contractor may also be surveilled, but only to the extent necessary to identify that person.

2-207. *Undisclosed Participation in Domestic Organizations.* No employees may join, or otherwise participate in, any organization within the United States on behalf of any agency within the Intelligence Community without disclosing their intelligence affiliation to appropriate officials of the organization, except as permitted by procedures established pursuant to Section 2-201. Such procedures shall provide for disclosure of such affiliation in all cases unless the agency head or a designee approved by the Attorney General finds that non-disclosure is essential to achieving lawful purposes, and that finding is subject to review by the Attorney General. Those procedures shall further limit undisclosed participation to cases where:

(a) The participation is undertaken on behalf of the FBI in the course of a lawful investigation;

(b) The organization concerned is composed primarily of individuals who are not United States persons and is reasonably believed to be acting on behalf of a foreign power; or

(c) The participation is strictly limited in its nature, scope and duration to that necessary for other lawful purposes relating to foreign intelligence and is a type of participation approved by the Attorney General and set forth in a public document. No such participation may be undertaken for the purpose of influencing the activity of the organization or its members.

Exhibit 300-31 Cont. (2)

United States Foreign Intelligence Activities ◊

2-208. *Collection of Nonpublicly Available Information.* No agency within the Intelligence Community may collect, disseminate or store information concerning the activities of United States persons that is not available publicly, unless it does so with their consent or as permitted by procedures established pursuant to Section 2-201. Those procedures shall limit collection, storage or dissemination to the following types of information:

(a) Information concerning corporations or other commercial organizations or activities that constitutes foreign intelligence or counterintelligence;

(b) Information arising out of a lawful counterintelligence or personnel, physical or communications security investigation;

(c) Information concerning present or former employees, present or former intelligence agency contractors or their present or former employees or applicants for any such employment or contracting, which is needed to protect foreign intelligence or counterintelligence sources or methods from unauthorized disclosure;

(d) Information needed solely to identify individuals in contact with those persons described in paragraph (c) of this section or with someone who is the subject of a lawful foreign intelligence or counterintelligence investigation;

(e) Information concerning persons who are reasonably believed to be potential sources or contacts, but only for the purpose of determining the suitability or credibility of such persons;

(f) Information constituting foreign intelligence or counterintelligence gathered abroad or from electronic surveillance conducted in compliance with Section 2-202 or from cooperating sources in the United States;

(g) Information about a person who is reasonably believed to be acting on behalf of a foreign power, engaging in international terrorist activities or narcotics production or trafficking, or endangering the safety of a person protected by the United States Secret Service or the Department of State;

(h) Information acquired by overhead reconnaissance not directed at specific United States persons;

(i) Information concerning United States persons abroad that is obtained in response to requests from the Department of State for support of its consular responsibilities relating to the welfare of those persons;

(j) Information collected, received, disseminated or stored by the FBI and necessary to fulfill its lawful investigative responsibilities; or

(k) Information concerning persons or activities that pose a clear threat to any facility or personnel of an agency within the Intelligence Community. Such information may be retained only by the agency threatened and, if appropriate, by the United States Secret Service and the FBI.

2-3. *Additional Restrictions and Limitations.*

2-301. *Tax Information.* No agency within the Intelligence Community shall examine tax returns or tax information except as permitted by applicable law.

2-302. *Restrictions on Experimentation.* No agency within the Intelligence Community shall sponsor, contract for, or conduct research on human subjects except in accordance with guidelines issued by the Department of Health, Education and Welfare. The subject's informed consent shall be documented as required by those guidelines.

2-303. *Restrictions on Contracting.* No agency within the Intelligence Community shall enter into a contract or arrangement for the provision of goods or services with private companies or institutions in the United States unless the agency sponsorship is known to the appropriate officials of the company or institution. In the case of any company or institution other than an academic institution, intelligence agency sponsorship may be concealed where it is determined, pursuant to procedures approved by the Attorney General, that such concealment is necessary to maintain essential cover or proprietary arrangements for authorized intelligence purposes.

2-304. *Restrictions on Personnel Assigned to Other Agencies.* An employee detailed to another agency within the federal government shall be responsible to the host agency and shall not report to the parent agency on the affairs of the host agency unless so directed by the host agency. The head of the host agency, and any successor, shall be informed of the employee's relationship with the parent agency.

United States Foreign Intelligence Activities

◊

2-305. *Prohibition on Assassination.* No person employed by or acting on behalf of the United States Government shall engage in, or conspire to engage in, assassination.

2-306. *Restrictions on Special Activities.* No component of the United States Government except an agency within the Intelligence Community may conduct any special activity. No such agency except the CIA (or the military services in wartime) may conduct any special activity unless the President determines, with the SCC's advice, that another agency is more likely to achieve a particular objective.

2-307. *Restrictions on Indirect Participation in Prohibited Activities.* No agency of the Intelligence Community shall request or otherwise encourage, directly or indirectly, any person, organization, or government agency to undertake activities forbidden by this Order or by applicable law.

2-308. *Restrictions on Assistance to Law Enforcement Authorities.* Agencies within the Intelligence Community other than the FBI shall not, except as expressly authorized by law:

(a) Provide services, equipment, personnel or facilities to the Law Enforcement Assistance Administration (or its successor agencies) or to state or local police organizations of the United States; or

(b) Participate in or fund any law enforcement activity within the United States.

2-309. *Permissible Assistance to Law Enforcement Authorities.* The restrictions in Section 2-308 shall not preclude:

(a) Cooperation with appropriate law enforcement agencies for the purpose of protecting the personnel and facilities of any agency within the Intelligence Community;

(b) Participation in law enforcement activities, in accordance with law and this Order, to investigate or prevent clandestine intelligence activities by foreign powers, international narcotics production and trafficking, or international terrorist activities; or

(c) Provision of specialized equipment, technical knowledge, or assistance of expert personnel for use by any department or agency or, when lives are endangered, to support local law enforcement agencies. Provision of assistance by expert personnel shall be governed by procedures approved by the Attorney General.

2-310. *Permissible Dissemination and Storage of Information.* Nothing in Sections 2-201 through 2-309 of this Order shall prohibit:

(a) Dissemination to appropriate law enforcement agencies of information which indicates involvement in activities that may violate federal, state, local or foreign laws;

(b) Storage of information required by law to be retained;

(c) Dissemination of information covered by Section 2-208(a)-(j) to agencies within the Intelligence Community or entities of cooperating foreign governments; or

(d) Lawful storage or dissemination of information solely for administrative purposes not related to intelligence or security.

/s/ Jimmy Carter

The White House,
January 24, 1978.

[Filed with the Office of the Federal Register, 11:12 a.m., January 25, 1978]

(Next page is 9781-255)

Tax Cases (Evidence and Procedure)

410 *(1-18-80)* 9781
Law and Elements of Offenses

411 *(1-18-80)* 9781
Civil and Criminal Sanctions Distinguished

(1) The Internal Revenue Code provides civil and criminal sanctions for violations of the internal revenue laws. (See IRM 9221.)

(2) The civil sanctions, generally assessed as additions to the tax and also referred to as ad valorem penalties, are covered in Chapter 68 of the Code. Some of these penalties are: the delinquency penalty (not exceeding 25 percent) for failure to file a return or a timely return [26 IRC 6651]; the 5 percent negligence penalty for negligence or intentional disregard of rules and regulations (without intent to defraud) [26 IRC 6653(a)]; and the 50 percent fraud penalty on an underpayment any part of which is due to fraud [26 IRC 6653(b)]; but the fraud and delinquency penalties cannot be asserted with respect to the same underpayment. [26 IRC 6653(d)] Handbook text 252 to 252.5 contain other information covering ad valorem penalties.

(3) The criminal sanctions, generally involving imprisonment and fines, are covered in Chapter 75 of the Code. In addition, some of the criminal sanctions in Title 18, and Title 31 United States Code, also apply to internal revenue matters. See text 221 to 222.(33) for the criminal penalties under the Internal Revenue Code and Title 18, and Title 31 USC.

(4) Both civil and criminal sanctions may be imposed for the same offense. Although criminal sanctions provide punishment for offenses, the fraud penalty is a remedial civil sanction to safeguard and protect the revenue and to reimburse the Government for the heavy expense of investigation and loss resulting from the taxpayer's fraud. [*Helvering v. Mitchell*]

(5) Acquittal in a criminal case is not decisive of the civil fraud issue. [*Helvering v. Mitchell*] However, a criminal conviction for income tax evasion does decide the fraud issue and the taxpayer is collaterally estopped from raising it in the civil proceedings. [*Tomlinson v. Lefkowitz*, In re Amos, *Jerome H. Moore v. U.S.*] The relationship between civil and criminininal cases is also discussed in text 762:(3).

(6) The burden and measure of proof differs in civil and criminal cases. In the latter, the Government must prove every facet of the offense and show guilt beyond a reasonable doubt. In civil cases, the Commissioner's determination of the deficiency is presumptively correct and the burden is placed on the taxpayer to overcome this presumption. When fraud is alleged the Government has the burden of establishing such fraud by clear and convincing evidence. Text 323.6 contains further information on the burden of proof.

(7) The tax computation in a particular case may differ for civil and criminal purposes since the evidence relating to certain of the income adjustments may not meet the criteria of proof necessary in a criminal case although it may be adequate for the civil case. There also may be adjustments of a controversial or off-setting nature which are allowed in the criminal tax computation to remove controversial issues from the criminal action, as well as additional adjustments or disallowances of a minor, technical, and non-fraudulent nature which are considered solely for civil purposes.

(8) The civil liability and the ad valorem penalties are generally assessed against the taxpayer, whereas *any person* who partakes in the commission of an offense is subject to the criminal sanctions of the law. For example, any person who willfully attempts to evade or defeat any tax or the payment thereof, even though it is not his/her own tax liability, could be charged with this offense. Thus, A can be charged with evading B's tax; a spouse can be charged with evading the other spouse's tax; and corporate officers in addition to the corporation can be charged with evading the corporation's tax. [*U.S. v. Troy, U.S. v. Augustine*] Participation in the commission of an offense includes the failure of a person to perform a required act. A *person* is defined in IRC 7343 as follows:

> "The term 'person' as used in this chapter includes an officer or employee of a corporation, or a member or employee of a partnership, who as such officer, employee, or member is under a duty to perform the act in respect of which the violation occurs."

(9) Further information on parties to criminal offenses is set forth in 322.3.

412 *(1-18-80)* 9781
Avoidance Distinguished From Evasion

Avoidance of taxes is not a criminal offense. Any attempt to reduce, avoid, minimize, or alleviate taxes by legitimate means is permissible. The distinction between avoidance and evasion is fine yet definite. One who avoids tax does not conceal or misrepresent. He shapes events to reduce or eliminate tax liability and, upon the happening of the events, makes a complete disclosure. Evasion on the other hand involves deceit, subterfuge, camouflage, concealment, some attempt to color or obscure events, or making things seem other than they are. For example, the creation of a bona fide partnership to reduce the tax liability of a business by dividing the income among several individual partners is tax avoidance. However, the facts of a particular case may show that an alleged partnership was not in fact established and that one or more of the alleged partners secretly returned his/her share of the profits to the real owner of the business, who in turn did not report this income. This would be an instance of attempted evasion.

413 *(1-18-80)* 9781
Attempted Evasion of Tax or Payment Thereof (IRC 7201)

413.1 *(1-18-80)* 9781
Statutory Provisions

The willful attempt in any manner to evade or defeat any tax and the willful attempt in any manner to evade or defeat the payment of any tax constitute criminal offenses. The statutory provisions covering these offenses are set forth in IRC 7201 and are quoted in full in text 221.2 and IRM 9212.

413.2 *(9-8-80)* 9781
Elements of the Offenses

(1) *The elements of the offense of willfully attempting in any manner to evade or defeat any tax are:* Additional tax due and owing; an attempt in any manner to evade or defeat any tax; and willfulness.

(a) *Additional tax due and owing*—The Government must establish that at the time the offense was committed an additional tax was due and owing; that the taxpayer "owed more tax than he reported." [*U.S. v. Schenck; Gleckman v. U.S.; Tinkoff v. U.S.*] However, it is not necessary to prove evasion of the full amount alleged in the indictment. It would be sufficient to show that a substantial amount of the tax was evaded [*U.S. v. Schenck; Tinkoff v. U.S.*], and this need not be measured in terms of gross and net income or by any particular percentage of the tax shown to be due and payable. [*U.S. v. Nunan*] Carryback losses are technically no legal impediment to prosecution for years in which they eliminate the tax liability. [*Willingham v. U.S.*] However, the probability of conviction could be lessened where it is shown that a tax deficiency does not exist by operation of law. Likewise, the acceptance by Government agents of agreement Form 870 (Waiver of Restrictions on Assessment and Collection of Deficiency in Tax and Acceptance of Overassessment) does not bar prosecution. [*Clark v. U.S.*] However, experience has demonstrated that attempts to pursue both the criminal and the civil aspects of a case concurrently may jeopardize the successful completion of the criminal case. As a result, Policy Statement P-4-84 provides, among other things, that the consequences of civil enforcement actions on matters involved in the criminal investigation and prosecution case should be carefully weighed. See IRM 9324.3 for further instructions on balancing the civil and criminal aspects of investigations.

(b) *Attempt to evade or defeat any tax.*

1 The substance of the offense under IRC 7201 is the term "*attempt* in any manner." Attempt does not mean that one whose efforts are successful cannot commit the crime of willful *attempt*. The crime is complete when the attempt is made and nothing is added to its criminality by success or consummation, as would be the case with respect to attempted murder. It has been held that "attempts cover both successful and unsuccessful endeavors or efforts" and that "a willful attempt to evade or defeat an income tax includes successful, as well as futile endeavors." [*O'Brien v. U.S.*] As the courts have stated, "The real character of the offense lies, not in the failure to file a return or in the filing of a false return, but rather in the attempt" to evade any tax. [*Emmich v. U.S.*] The statute does not define attempt, nor does it limit or define the means or methods by which the attempt to evade or defeat any tax may be accomplished. However, it has been judicially determined that *the term "attempt" implies some affirmative action or the commission of some overt act.* [*Spies v. U.S.*] The actual filing of a false or fraudulent return is not requisite for the commission of the offense [*U.S. v. Albanese*] though the filing of such a return is the usual attempt to evade or defeat the tax. [*Myres v. U.S.; Guzik v. U.S.*] A false statement made to Treasury agents for the purpose of concealing unreported income has also been judicially determined to be an attempt to evade or defeat the tax. [*U.S. v. Beacon Brass Co; Canton v. U.S.*]

2 The willful omission of a duty or the willful failure to perform a duty imposed by statute does not per se constitute an attempt to evade or defeat. However, a willful omission or failure (such as a willful failure to make and file a return) when coupled with affirmative acts or conduct from which an attempt may be inferred would constitute an attempt. In the case of Spies v. United States [*Spies v. U.S.*], the Supreme Court gave certain illustrations from which acts or conduct the attempt to evade or defeat any tax may be inferred; such as keeping a double set of books [*Noro v. U.S.*]; making false entries, alterations, invoices, or documents [*U.S. v. Lange; Gariepy v. U.S.*]; destruction of books or records [*Yoffe v. U.S.; Gariepy v. U.S.*]; concealment of assets or covering up sources of income [*Gendelman v. U.S.*]; handling of one's affairs to avoid making the records usual in transactions of the kind [*Gleckmman v. U.S.; U.S. v. Hornstein*]; and any conduct, the likely effect of which would be to mislead or to conceal; in other words, *in any manner.* Text 423:(2) contains a list of the more common tax evasion schemes.

3 It is well settled that a separate offense may be committed with respect to each year. Therefore, an attempt for one year is a separate offense from an attempt for a different year. [*U.S. v. Stoehr*]

4 There may also be more than one violation in one year resulting from the same acts such as the willful attempt to evade the payment of tax and the willful attempt to evade tax. [U.S. v. Bardin] *Likewise there may be charged a willful attempt to evade tax and a willful failure to file a return for the same year.* [*U.S. v. Kafes*]

(c) *Willfulness*—The attempt in any manner to evade or defeat any tax must be willful, and willfulness has been defined as an act or conduct done with a bad or evil purpose. [*U.S. v. Murdock*] Mere understatement of income and the filing of an incorrect return does not in itself constitute willful attempted tax evasion. [*Holland v. U.S.*] The offense is made out when conduct such as exemplified in the Spies case (supra) is present. Text 41(11) contains a further discussion of willfulness.

(2) *The elements of the offense of willfully attempting in any manner to evade or defeat the payment of any tax are:* A tax due and owing; an attempt to evade or defeat the *payment* of any tax; and willfulness.

(a) *A tax due and owing*—The Government must establish that a tax is due and owing at the time the offense is committed. This amount need not be any additional tax or deficiency but could *be the amount of tax shown on the original return which had not been paid.*

(b) *Attempt to evade or defeat the payment of any tax*—The mere failure or willful failure to pay any tax does not constitute an attempt to evade or defeat the payment of any tax. The comments set out in (1)(b) above with respect to attempts also apply to this offense. The attempt implies some affirmative action or the commission of some overt act. Examples of such action or conduct relating to the attempted evasion of the payment of the tax are found in the Giglio case. [*U.S. v. Giglio*] These are concealing assets; reporting income through others; misappropriating, converting, and diverting corporate assets; together with filing late returns, failing to withhold taxes as required by law, filing false declarations of estimated taxes, and filing false tentative corporate returns.

(c) *Willfulness*—The comments set forth in (1)(c) above and in 41(11) on willfulness apply equally to this offense. Courts have held that disbursement of available funds to creditors other than the Government [*Wilson v. U.S.*], or to corporate stockholders [*U.S. v. Jannuzzio*] is not of itself an attempt to evade or defeat payment of taxes.

(3) *Venue and Statute of Limitations*—Venue for these offenses lies in the judicial district in which the return is filed or other overt acts are committed. A further discussion of this subject is in 727. The statutory period of limitations for these offenses is six years. A more complete discussion of this subject is in 419.

414 *(1-18-80)* 9781
Failure to Collect, Account For, and Pay Over Tax

414.1 *(1-18-80)* 9781
Willful Failure to Collect, Account For, and Pay Over Tax (IRC 7202)

414.11 *(1-18-80)* 9781
Statutory Provisions

It is a criminal offense if any person required to collect, account for, and pay over any tax willfully fails to collect or truthfully account for and pay over such tax. The statutory provisions covering this violation are set forth in full in 221.3. Information showing the applicable civil penalty is set forth in 252.5.

414.12 *(1-18-80)* 9781
Elements of Offense

(1) The elements of a criminal violation under this Code section are:

(a) One or both of the following:

1 A duty to collect any tax.

2 A duty to account for and pay over any tax.

(b) One or both of the following:

1 Failure to collect any tax.

2 Failure to truthfully account for and pay over any tax.

(c) Willfulness. (The subject of willfulness is covered in 41(11).)

(2) Venue lies in the judicial district where the act should have been performed [*U.S. v. Commerford*] and a three-year period of limitations is applicable to this offense, which is a felony. Further information concerning the statute of limitations is contained in 419.

(3) Section 406.603, Code of Federal Regulations, states, "The return shall be signed and verified by. . . . (2) the President, Vice-President, or other principal officer, if the employer is a corporation." However, considerable difficulty has been encountered in determining the "person" charged with the duty of collecting, accounting for and paying over taxes, especially in cases involving small corporations where the precise duties of the officers are not clearly defined or rigidly carried out. For example, in the case of U.S. v. Fago, it was determined that although the president of the corporation was the dominating force in the management of the firm, the fact that there were other officers who signed some returns and engaged in financial activities on behalf of the coporation made it doubtful whether the president was the officer under a duty to perform the required acts, and the indictment was dismissed. On the other hand, there is a reported decision [*Wilson v. U.S.*] which holds that the term "person" includes a chief executive officer of a corporation who possesses the authority to determine how corporate funds should be expended. Accordingly, it is imperative to ascertain the various activities and responsibilities of all officers of a corporation before recommending prosecution against any one of them as the "person" defined in IRC 7343.

(4) Willfulness under this Code section refers to motive or purpose and includes some element of an evil motive and want of justification in view of all the financial circumstances of the taxpayer. It is not enough merely to prove that the acts were knowingly and intentionally committed. [*Paddock v. Siemoneit*] For example, a successful prosecution under this section was based upon the following facts: The taxpayer filed timely employment tax returns but habitually failed to pay the amount of tax shown to be due thereon. He willingly signed agreements for partial payments, made the first payment, and then ignored further requests for payments. When his bank accounts were levied upon, he closed the accountnts and made arrangements with his customers to receive future payments in cash. All his assets were then transferred to the names of others. His only defense was that he used the money withheld from his employees to meet current operating expenses. An analysis of his bank accounts and records of personal expenditures showed that, contrary to his contentions, a profit was realized from the business in all years and funds were available to pay the taxes shown on the returns.

(5) Violations under this section usually involve failure to truthfully account for and pay over withholding, social security, and excise taxes with the exception of wagering excise taxes. Failure to file returns would involve violations of IRC 7203 (text 415) and filing false and fraudulent returns would constitute violations under IRC 7201 (text 413).

(6) Willful failure to truthfully account for and pay over is considered to be an inseparable dual obligation. [Chief Counsel memo, 5-8-64, CC:E-172.] Failure to pay, even though an accounting is made in the sense of a return filed, leaves the duty as a whole unfulfilled.

414.2 *(1-18-80)* 9781
Failure to Collect and Account For Certain Collected Taxes (Nonwillful Violation) (IRC 7215)

414.21 *(1-18-80)* 9781
Statutory Provisions

It is a criminal offense to fail, after due notice [26 USC 7512], to collect and deposit, in a special trust account for the United States, employment, withholding, and certain excise taxes [Employment Taxes imposed by Subtitle C and Miscellaneous Excise Taxes imposed by Chapter 33 which pertain to Communications and Transportation of persons by air—See text 453.2.] and to keep the funds in the account until payment over to the United States. The statutory provisions covering this violation are set forth in full in text 221.(12).

414.22 *(1-18-80)* 9781
Elements of Offense

(1) The elements of a criminal violation under this Code section are:

(a) One or more of the following:

1 A duty to collect employment taxes or certain miscellaneous excise taxes.

2 A duty to account for and pay over employment taxes or certain miscellanous excise taxes.

(b) One or more of the following:

1 Failure to collect employment taxes or certain miscellaneous excise taxes.

2 Failure to truthfully account for and pay over employment taxes or certain miscellaneous excise taxes.

(c) Notice, delivered in hand, instructing the taxpayer to collect and deposit employment taxes or certain miscellaneous excise taxes in a separate bank account designated as a special fund in trust for the United States and to keep the taxes so collected in the account until payment over to the United States.

(d) One or more of the following with respect to taxes *collectible after the receipt of notice:*

1 Failure to collect employment taxes or certain excise taxes;

2 Failure to deposit employment taxes or certain excise taxes in a special trust account for the United States;

3 Failure to keep the collected taxes in a special trust account until payment over to the United States.

(e) One or more of the following:

1 Absence of information showing that the person had reasonable doubt as to whether the law required the collection of the tax, or that he/she had reasonable doubt that he/she was the one who was required by law to collect the tax;

2 Absence of information showing that the failure to collect, deposit and to keep the tax in a separate account was due to circumstances beyond the control of the taxpayer.

(2) Venue lies in the judicial district where the act should have been performed [*U.S. v. Commerford*] and a three-year period of limitations [26 USC 6531] is applicable to this offense, which is a misdemeanor. Further information concerning statute of limitations is contained in 419.

(3) In the case of a corporation, partnership or trust, notice delivered in hand to an officer, partner, or trustee is deemed to be notice delivered in hand to the corporation, partnership, or trust and to all officers, partners, trustees and employees thereof.

(4) A lack of funds immediately after the payment of wages (whether or not resulting from the payment of wages) is not considered a circumstance beyond a person's control. For example, if an employer received the required notice and had gross payroll requirements of $1,000 with respect to which he/she was required to withhold $100 of income tax and if he/she had on hand only $900 and paid out the entire amount in wages, withholding nothing, the fact that the net wages due equaled that amount would not relieve him/her of the penalty imposed by this Code section. [Senate Committee on Finance Report (No. 1182, 85th Congress) (Jan. 23, 1958) 3 U.S. Cong. News '58, Page 255.]

(5) Circumstances causing a lack of funds after the payment of wages (but not immediately after) which are considered beyond a taxpayer's control include: theft, embezzlement, or destruction of the business by fire, flood, or other casualty, occurring within the period before which the person was required to deposit the funds; or the failure of the bank in which the person deposited the funds prior to transferring them to the Government's trust account. A lack of funds due to the payment of creditors would not be considered such a circumstance. [*U.S. v. Plotkin*]

(6) Procedures to be used in Trust Fund Cases (IRC 7512 and 7215) are contained in IRM 9340.

415 *(1-18-80)* 9781
Willful Failure to File Returns, Supply Information, or Pay Tax (IRC 7203)

415.1 *(1-18-80)* 9781
Statutory Provisions

The willful failure to make any return (other than a declaration of estimated tax); or to pay any estimated tax or tax; or to keep records; or to supply information, at the time or times required by law or regulation, constitutes a criminal offense. Any one of the above violations is a separate offense. The statutory provisions covering these offenses are set forth in IRC 7203 and are quoted in full in 221.4.

415.2 *(1-18-80)* 9781
Elements of the Offenses

415.21 *(1-18-80)* 9781
Willful Failure to Make a Return

(1) This offense applies to the willful failure to make any type of required return, except declarations of estimated tax. The following elements of the offense must be established to sustain a conviction: the person was under a duty, as required by law or regulations, to make a return for the year or period involved; he/she failed to file a return for such year or period at the time required by law or regulation; and the failure to file such return was willful. [*U.S. v. McCormick*]

(a) *A duty to make a return*—The general requirements for making a return are set forth in IRC 6012 to 6046. Persons liable under IRC 7203 include those described in IRC 7343, quoted in 411:(8). In corporate cases the person responsible for filing corporate returns may be any of several officials and it will be a matter of fact to be developed by competent evidence as to which one has the duty. This evidence may be proof of signing past Federal returns or any state returns, or it may be in the corporate by-laws or minutes of directors' meetings. [*U.S. v. Fago*] A further discussion of this point is contained in 414.12:(3).

(b) *Failure to make a return when due.*

1 The Government must establish that a return was due within the time provided by law or regulations and that there was a failure to file such return within such time. The time within which a return must be filed has been held to be the date set out in the Code or under regulations prescribed by the Secretary plus that last date covered in any extension of time granted by the Secretary or the Secretary's delegate. [*U.S. v. Habig; Haskell v. U.S.*] The date when a return is due under the Code or regulations varies, depending upon the type of tax involved or the type of return required to be filed. Thus, individual income tax returns, self-employment tax returns, and partnership returns made on the basis of the calendar year shall be filed on or before the 15th day of April following the close of the calendar year; or, if made on a fiscal year basis, the return shall be filed on the 15th day of the 4th month following the close of the fiscal year. [26 USC 6072(a)] Corporate returns for calendar years are due on the 15th day of March; or, if on a fiscal year basis, returns are due on the 15th day of the 3d month following the close of the fiscal year. [26 USC 6072(b)] IRC 6075 relates to the time for filing estate and gift tax returns, and IRC 6071 and the regulations promulgated thereunder to the time for filing excise tax returns and other forms of returns required under the particular type of tax involved.

2 In addition to showing that a return was due, the Government must establish that the person did not file a required return on the due date. Usually this is accomplished by proving that the defendant did not file a return in the district of his/her legal residence or principal place of business [*Haskell v. U.S.*] or service center.

(c) *The failure to file a return was willful*—The Government must establish willfulness in the failure to file a return. However, as distinguished from willfulness in a tax evasion case, the Government need not prove a tax evasion motive. Willfulness connotes something "done with a bad purpose, or done without justifiable excuse, or done stubbornly or obstinately or perversely, or with bad motive." [*U.S. v. Cirillo*] As applied to this offense willful means voluntary, purposeful, deliberate, and intentional, as distinguished from accidental, inadvertent, or negligent; and the only bad purpose or bad motive which the Government must prove is the deliberate intention not to file returns, which such person knew ought to have been filed, so that the Government would not know the extent of his/her liability. [*Yarborough v. U.S.; U.S. v. DiSilvestro*] Although an additional tax due is not an essential element of the offense, willfulness is difficult to establish without proof of a substantial tax liability.

415.22 *(1-18-80)* 9781
Willful Failure to Pay Tax

(1) This offense applies to the willful failure to pay any type of tax, including estimated taxes. The elements of this offense are that the person was under a duty to pay a tax which was due and owing; that he/she failed to pay such tax at the time or times required by law or regulations; and that the failure to pay was willful. The mere failure to pay the tax is not a crime; it must be willful. Some evil motive or bad purpose must be shown. The Supreme Court stated:

> "In view of our traditional aversion to imprisonment for debt, we would not without the clearest manifestion of Congressional intent assume that mere knowing and intentional default in payment of a tax, where there had been no willful failure to disclose the liability, is intended to constitute a criminal offense of any degree. We would expect willfulness in such a case to include some element of evil motive and want of justification in view of all the financial circumstances of the taxpayer." [*Spies v. U.S.*]

(2) Repeated failure to pay taxes coupled with large expenditures for luxuries when taxes were owing may be evidence of willfulness within the meaning of the statute. [*U.S. v. Frank Palmero*]

415.23 *(1-18-80)* 9781
Willful Failure to Supply Information

This offense applies to the willful failure to supply information at the time or times required by law or regulations. The elements of this offense are that the person was under a duty to supply the information; that he/she failed to supply such information at the time required by law or regulations; and that the failure to supply such information was willful. The willfulness required to be shown under this offense would be the deliberate and intentional withholding and failing to supply the required information with the evil and bad purpose of concealing income, property, or other required or requested information. [*U.S. v. Murdock*] For example, the intentional and deliberate failure and refusal to furnish a schedule of the partnership assets and liabilities as required on the partnership return, was held to be willful. Disclosure of such information revealed considerable cash on hand. [*Pappas v. U.S.*]

415.24 *(1-18-80)* 9781
Willful Failure to Keep Records

(1) This offense applies to the willful failure to keep records. The elements of this offense are that the person was under a duty to keep records; that he/she failed to keep such records; and that the failure to keep records was willful. The general requirement to keep records is provided for in IRC 6001. However, the types of records kept by various individuals are not alike, and neither the statute nor the regulations defines minimum standards for specific transactions or for types of business. For example, a showing that his returns were prepared from third-party records (banks, brokers, employers) may obviate the necessity for a taxpayer to keep records. IRM 4297 provides for the service of a notice, Letter to Taxpayer Regarding Inadequate Records (Form 7020 or 7021), and the procedure to be followed where taxpayers have failed to maintain proper records. The deliberate, intentional, and utter disregard of this notice with evil intent and a bad purpose may be deemed a circumstance from which willfulness may be inferred. Willfulness will also be inferred if the concealment motive plays any part of the failure to keep records. However, an important factor in the probability of conviction in these cases may be a substantial deficiency attributable to the failure to keep records. See IRM 9552.

(2) Specific record keeping requirements involving wagering taxes are covered in 461.3.

415.3 *(1-18-80)* 9781
Venue and Statute of Limitations

Venue for the above offenses lies in the judicial district in which the required acts should have been performed. Text 727 contains a further discussion of venue. The statutory period of limitations for willful failure to file returns (other than information returns) or to pay tax is six years. A three-year period of limitations applies to willful failure to file information returns such as partnership returns, and to willful failure to keep records or supply information. Text 419 contains further information on the statute of limitations.

416 *(1-18-80)* 9781
Fraudulent Statement or Failure to Make Statement to Employees (IRC 7204)

416.1 *(1-18-80)* 9781
Statutory Provisions

It is a criminal offense to willfully furnish an employee a false or fraudulent wage withholding receipt or to willfully fail to furnish a receipt in the appropriate manner or at the appropriate time. The statutory provisions covering this violation are set forth in full in 221.5. Information showing the applicable civil penalty is set forth in Exhibit 200-2.

416.2 *(1-18-80)* 9781
Elements of Offense

(1) The elements of a criminal violation under this Code section are:

(a) A duty to deduct employment tax or to withhold income tax [26 USC 3102(a), 3402(a)];

(b) A duty to timely furnish to the employee a written statement showing specified information concerning the deductions [26 USC 6051];

(c) Furnishing a false or fraudulent statement to an employee, or the failure to furnish a statement to an employee at the required time and in the required manner;

(d) Willfulness. (The subject of willfulness is covered in 41(11).)

(2) Venue lies in the judicial district where the employer was required to perform [*U.S. v. Anderson; U.S. v. Commerford*] and a three-year period of limitations is applicable to this offense [26 USC 6531] which is a misdemeanor. Further information concerning statute of limitations is contained in 419.

(3) A successful prosecution under this Code section was based upon the following facts. In order to attract and hold scarce workers, a taxpayer put into effect a scheme whereby actual weekly wages paid were recorded on regular weekly payroll sheets, the sum total of which was deducted for income tax purposes. Individual payroll sheets were also maintained for most of the employees, but the amounts of gross wages shown on the sheets were understated to accommodate the employees so that they would not have to report their entire wages for income tax purposes. The tax withheld from the wages was based upon the understated figure. In some instances individual payroll sheets were not maintained for employees. At the end of the year the employees whose names were shown on individual payroll sheets were furnished false and fraudulent withholding statements, Forms W-2, based upon the false payroll sheets and the employees whose names did not appear on payroll sheets did not at any time receive withholding statements. The failure to furnish withholding statements to some employees and the furnishing of false and fraudulent statements to other employees constitute separate violations under this Code section.

417 *(1-18-80)* 9781
Fraudulent Withholding Exemption Certificate or Failure to Supply Information (IRC 7205)

417.1 *(9-8-80)* 9781
Statutory Provisions

An employee who willfully supplies false or fraudulent information, in connection with his/her withholding exemption status, to his/her employer, or who willfully fails to supply information which would require an increase in the tax to be withheld, commits a criminal offense. The statutory provisions covering this violation are quoted in full in 221.6. IRC 6682 is the civil penalty applicable to this offense.

417.2 *(1-18-80)* 9781
Elements of Offense

(1) The elements of a criminal violation under this Code section are:

(a) A duty to supply information to employer [26 USC 3402(f)(2)];

(b) Furnishing false or fraudulent information or failure to supply information which would require an increase in tax to be withheld;

(c) Willfulness. (The subject of willfulness is covered in 41(11).)

(2) Venue lies in the judicial district where the offense has been committed. A three-year period of limitations is applicable [26 USC 6531], and the offense is a misdemeanor. In a case which involves furnishing false or fraudulent information, the offense is committed and the period of limitations begins the date the document is filed. No known reported case has stated whether willful failure to supply information to an employer is a continuing offense for purposes of determining the date from which the period of limitations is to run. The safe practice is to assume that it is not continuing, and that the offense is committed and statute begins to run on the date when it becomes a duty for the employee to supply information, which he/she willfully fails to do. However, if all other facts indicate that prosecution should be recommended for this offense, the continuing offense theory may be employed. Further information concerning the statute of limitations is contained in 419.

(3) The employee is required to notify his employer within ten days of a change in his withholding exemption status which would require an increase in tax to be withheld.

(4) There is no penalty for failing to file an original certificate (Form W-4) or for failure to supply information which would require a decrease in tax to be withheld, and a certificate is not considered false or fraudulent if it contains information showing fewer exemptions than the employee is entitled to claim.

418 *(1-18-80)* 9781
False and Fraudulent Statements

418.1 *(1-18-80)* 9781
False or Fraudulent Return, Statement, or Other Document Made Under Penalty of Perjury (IRC 7206(1))

418.11 *(1-18-80)* 9781
Statutory Provisions

A person who willfully makes and subscribes, under penalty of perjury, any return, statement, or other document which he/she does not believe to be true and correct, as to every material matter, commits a criminal offense. The statutory provisions covering this violation are set forth in full in 221.7.

418.12 *(2-15-80)* 9781
Elements of Offense

(1) The elements of a criminal violation under this Code section are:

(a) Making and subscribing a return, statement or other document under penalty of perjury;

(b) Knowledge that it is not true and correct as to every material matter;

(c) Willfulness. (The subject of willfulness is covered in 41(11).)

(2) Venue may lie in the judicial district in which the document is prepared, signed or filed. There has been little litigation of the venue issue. In the majority of cases, prosecution is had in the district in which the return is subscribed. A court has limited venue to that district. [*U.S. v. Wyman*] Other cases have considered the place or date of *filing* the return to be determinative and not the place or date of *signing*, on the theory that the document is not a return until filed. [*U.S. v. Horowitz*] Section 3237 of Title 18, United States Code, which is captioned "Offenses begun in one district and completed in another," provides that any offense involving the use of mails is a continuing offense and may be prosecuted in any district in which the offense was begun, continued, or completed. In specifically providing that IRC 7206(1) prosecutions may be transferred to the district of residency, this statute tends to support a position that the offense may be prosecuted where the return is made, subscribed, or filed.

(3) A six-year period of limitations is applicable to this offense, which is a felony. Further information covering statute of limitations is contained in 419.

(4) This Code section imposes the penalty of perjury upon a person who willfully falsifies a return as to a material matter, whether or not his/her purpose was to evade or defeat the payment of taxes. [*Siravo v. U.S.; Hoover v. U.S.; Schepps v. U.S.; Gaunt v. U.S.*] Prosecution is appropriate when the Government is able to prove falsity of a partnership return, the issue being falsity rather than evasion. [*Goldbaum v. U.S.*] The test of materiality is whether the false statement was material to the contents of the return. It is not necessary that the government actually rely on the statement. It is sufficient that it be made with the intention of inducing such reliance. [*Genstil v. U.S.; U.S. v. Rayor*] Although the offense is complete upon signing the statement or document, prosecutions under this Code section should involve only false returns or statements presented to or filed with the Internal Revenue Service. This sanction is appropriate when it is possible to prove falsity of a return but difficult to establish evasion of an ascertainable amount of tax, or, when the falsification results in a relatively small amount of tax evaded in relationship to the total tax liability.

(5) If an individual files a false and fraudulent return, it is possible for him/her to incur criminal liability for attempting to defeat and evade the payment of tax and for making a false and fraudulent statement under the penalty of perjury even though both offenses relate to the same return and the making of the false statement is an incidental step in the consummation of the completed offense of attempting to defeat and evade taxes. [*Gaunt v. U.S.*]

418.2 *(1-18-80)* 9781

Aid or Assistance in Preparation or Presentation of False or Fraudulent Return, Affidavit, Claim or Other Document (IRC 7206(2))

418.21 *(1-18-80)* 9781

Statutory Provisions

Any person who willfully aids or assists or procures, counsels, or advises in the preparation or presentation under, or in connection with any matter arising under, the internal revenue laws, of a false or fraudulent return, affidavit, claim or other document, commits a criminal offense under this Code section, whether or not such falsity or fraud is with the knowledge or consent of the person authorized or required to present such return, affidavit, claim or other document. The statutory provisions covering this violation are set forth in full in 221.7:(2).

418.22 *(1-18-80)* 9781

Elements of Offense

(1) The elements of a criminal violation under this Code section are:

(a) Aid, assist, counsel, advise or procure the preparation or presentation of a false or fraudulent document;

(b) A matter under, or in connection with any material matter arising under, the internal revenue laws;

(c) Willfulness. (The subject of willfulness is discussed in 41(11).)

(2) Venue lies in the judicial district where the criminal acts were committed, or if the acts were committed in one district and the return was filed in another district, venue lies in either district. The period of limitations applicable to this offense, which is a felony, is six years. Further information concerning the statute of limitations is contained in 419.

(3) The false document must be filed with the Internal Revenue Service in order for the crime to be complete but pecuniary loss to the Government is not necessary. Any impairment of its governmental function is sufficient. [*Butzman v. U.S.; U.S. v. Potsada*]

(4) The crime is complete on the submission of the false document notwithstanding the fact that had he filed a different and truthful document the defendant or his principal might have been entitled to equivalent relief or benefit. [*Butzman v. U.S.; U.S. v. Potsada*]

(5) Generally, income tax returns or partnership information returns are involved but any document required or authorized to be filed can give rise to this offense.

(6) If two partners execute a false partnership return and file it, they may each commit a criminal offense, but if there is evidence that only one of the partners willfully aided, assisted, procured, counseled or advised the preparation or the presentation of such return, then only he/she could be held liable for this offense. [*U.S. v. Wyman*]

(7) The aiding and assisting in the preparation of a false return, and the subscribing of a false return are two separate offenses. [*U.S. v. Wyman*] A defendant can, therefore, be prosecuted under IRC 7206(1) for subscribing a false return and under this Code section for aiding and assisting in the preparation of the same false return.

(8) It is sufficient to establish that the defendant willfully and knowingly prepared false and fraudulent income tax returns for another although the fraud involved was without the knowledge and consent of the person required to make the return. [*U.S. v. Kelley; U.S. v. Borgis*] For example, in the case of U.S. v. Herskovitz, et al., the defendants, who conducted a "refund factory," interviewed taxpayers for ten or fifteen minutes and obtained information which was written on worksheets. Signed blank income tax returns were then obtained from the taxpayers and they were told the amounts of the refunds allegedly due, but they were not furnished any of the details relative to the deductions to be claimed on the returns, which were prepared at later dates. At the trial the clients testified that they did not furnish the defendants the information relating to deductions shown on their completed returns and that the information was placed on the returns without their knowledge or consent. On the other hand, if the taxpayers who testify against the defendant are shown to have had knowledge that their returns were false, resulting in fraud penalties or successful prosecutions, for evasion, the defendant is entitled to have the court caution the jury to weigh accomplice testimony carefully. [*Hull v. U.S.*]

(9) In all race track payoff cases IRC 7206(2) should be used either as the primary statutory provision or, at least, as a supplement to 18 USC 1001, when prosecuting either the "ten percenter" or the true winner. [Chief Counsel's Memorandum 7-31-67, CC:E-MA 1589; see Int. Digest, 11-67, p. 41.]

418.3 *(12-7-81)* 9781
Fraudulent Returns, Statements, or Other Documents (IRC 7207)

(1) It is a criminal offense to willfully deliver or disclose to the Secretary or the Secretary's delegate any list, return, account, statement, or other document known to be fraudulent or to be false as to any material matter. The statutory provisions covering this violation are set forth in 221.8.

(2) As of September 28, 1976, the Department of Justice has modified its long-standing policy of not authorizing prosecution under Section 7207. The current policy allows for use of Section 7207 in cases commonly referred to as altered-document-type cases whenever the computed tax deficiencies are such as to be considered *de minimis* in relation to the circumstances of the particular case under consideration and the means and methods utilized in committing the offense are commensurate with charging a misdemeanor rather than a felony. The policy otherwise remains unchanged in that Section 7207 is neither suitable nor appropriate in tax cases other than the altered-document-type case. This modification is strictly limited to cases arising out of presentation of false or altered documents by taxpayers in response to requests for substantiation of claimed deductions during the course of examination activity.

418.4 *(1-18-80)* 9781
False Statements of Entries Generally (Section 1001, Title 18)

418.41 *(1-18-80)* 9781
Statutory Provisions

In connection with any matter within the jurisdiction of any department or agency of the United States, it is a criminal offense to willfully falsify, conceal or cover up by trick, scheme, or device a material fact or to make any false, fictitious, or fraudulent statements or representations or to make or use any false writing or document knowing the same to contain any false, fictitious or fraudulent statement or entry. The statutory provisions covering this violation are set forth in 222.(15).

418.42 *(1-18-80)* 9781
Elements of Offense

(1) The elements of a criminal violation under this USC section are:

(a) A matter within the jurisdiction of a department or agency of the United States;

(b) One or more of the following:

1 Falsification or concealment by trick, scheme or device, of a material fact;

2 The making of false, fictitious or fraudulent statements or representations;

3 The making or using of any false writing or document;

(c) Knowledge of the falsity by the party charged;

(d) Willfulness. (The subject of willfulness is covered in 41(11).)

(2) Venue lies in the judicial district where the concealment of fact occurred, the false statement was communicated, or the false writing was made or used. A five-year period of limitations is applicable to this offense, which is a felony. Further information concerning statutes of limitations is in 419.

(3) The term "jurisdiction" means the power to deal with a subject matter and the term "department" includes the United States Treasury Department. [5 USC 1]

(4) It is not necessary that the statement be required to be made by some regulation or law. [*Cohen v. U.S.*] For example, a taxpayer could commit a violation under this USC section by voluntarily furnishing a false and fraudulent net worth statement during an official investigation of his/her income tax liability, provided all other necessary elements of the offense were present.

(5) The weight of authority requires proof of materiality in any prosecution under this USC section. [*Poonian v. U.S.; U.S. v. Zambito; Gonzales v. U.S.*] However, some jurisdictions do not require it in prosecutions for making false statements or submitting false documents, as opposed to falsifying, concealing or covering up material facts by trick, scheme or device. [*U.S. v. Silver*] The argument for this distinction is that the statute has two parts, of which the first, relating to falsification or concealment by trick, scheme or device, includes the word "material," whereas the second, relating to false statements, does not. [*U.S. v. Silver*] However, it must be borne in mind even in the jurisdictions making this distinction, that it is difficult to prove willfulness of false statements unless they are material. [Chief Counsel Memorandum, 11-8-62, CC:E-235 (I.D. Digest, 12-62, p. 23.]

(6) The violation may involve formal or informal records, forms and instruments, and even oral statements. [*Neely v. U.S.*] It is not essential that the statements be under oath, and the

perjury corroboration rule does not apply. [*Neely v. U.S.; U.S. v. McCue*]

(7) It is possible for a defendant to be charged with a violation under this USC section and also to be charged with an attempt to defeat or evade the payment of tax [26 USC 7201] in connection with the same return. [*Gaunt v. U.S.*]

(8) Knowledge cannot be imputed to a corporate officer merely because the officer appears to be active in corporate affairs. [*Freidus v. U.S.*]

(9) The statute is concerned with false statements which might impede the exercise of Federal authority. [*U.S. v. Leviton*] Pecuniary loss to the Government is not necessary. Any impairment of administration of its governmental functions is sufficient and the commission of the crime is not dependent upon the success of the intended fraud. [*Butzman v. U.S.*] However, mere negative, exculpatory "no" answers in a question and answer interview are held not to pervert the investigative function, and are not considered statements within the meaning of this statute. [*Paternostro v. U.S.; U.S. v. Stark*] Prosecution may lie under this statute, as well as under 18 USC 1503 (obstruction of justice), against persons summoned to produce records in their possession, who falsely state that the records have been stolen from them, and conspire together to conceal them. [*U.S. v. Curcio*]

418.5 *(1-18-80)* 9781
False, Fictitious, or Fraudulent Claims (Section 287, Title 18)

418.51 *(1-18-80)* 9781
Statutory Provisions

It is a criminal offense to make or present a claim upon or against the United States, or any department or agency thereof, knowing such claim to be false, fictitious or fraudulent. The statutory provisions covering this violation are set forth in 222.(10).

418.52 *(1-18-80)* 9781
Elements of Offense

(1) The elements of a criminal violation under this USC section are:

(a) Making or presenting a claim upon or against the United States;

(b) Knowledge that the claim is false, fictitious or fraudulent.

(2) Venue lies in the judicial district where the false claim is presented or filed to where it is to be acted upon. [*Fuller v. U.S.*] A five-year period of limitations is applicable to this offense, which is a felony. Further information concerning statute of limitations will be found in 419.

(3) The term "false" means unfounded or unjust; "fictitious" means not real; and "fraudulent" means wrong or deceitful. These terms have no special legal significance in their use in this statute but are to be taken in their ordinary and well understood sense. [*U.S. v. Bittinger*]

(4) Fraud within this USC section includes any conduct calculated to obstruct or impair the efficiency of the United States and to destroy the value of its operations. [*U.S. v. Gottfried*] Actual pecuniary loss to the Government is not an essential element of this offense.

(5) Whether the claim is false, fictitious, or fraudulent must be determined in view of all of the facts and circumstances surrounding it and it is not essential that the bill, voucher, or other things used as the basis for the claim should in and of itself contain fraudulent or fictitious statements or entries. [*Dimmick v. U.S.*] For example, an income tax return, correct on its face, would still constitute a false claim if the taxpayer filing the return knew that the refund shown to be due had already been paid as the result of the filing of a prior return.

(6) An income tax return claiming a refund of withheld taxes represents a false claim in spite of the fact that the amount claimed represents an overpayment of withholding taxes resulting from a fraud perpetrated on the employer. For example, if an individual arranges with a paymaster to defraud an employer by having the individual's name entered on a payroll without performing any work or receiving any wages and withholding tax is then paid to the Government based on the amount of the alleged wages, the filing of a final income tax return by the phantom employee, showing the alleged wages and claiming a refund of the withheld tax, constitutes the filing of a false claim under this USC section. [*U.S. v. Mandile*]

(7) This USC section is particularly appropriate in instances where a false claim for refund has been filed. It is only necessary to prove that the defendant made a claim for refund taxes against the Government and that he/she knew that he/she was not entitled to receive it. [*U.S. v. Mandile*]

418.6 *(1-18-80)* 9781
Removal or Concealment with Intent to Defraud (IRC 7206(4))

418.61 *(1-18-80)* 9781
Statutory Provisions

Any person who removes, deposits, or conceals property upon which any tax is or shall be imposed, or upon which levy is authorized by IRC 6331, with intent to evade or defeat the assessment or collection of any tax, commits a criminal offense under this Code section. The statutory provisions covering this violation are set forth in text 221.7.

418.62 *(1-18-80)* 9781
Elements of Offense

(1) The elements of a criminal violation under this Code section are:

(a) Tax imposed on the property, or

(b) Property upon which tax is imposed or levy is authorized;

(c) Removal or concealment

(d) With intent to evade or defeat assessment or collection of any tax.

(2) "Concealment" under this Code section does not mean merely to secrete or hide away, but includes also "to prevent the discovery or to withhold knowledge of." Thus, it is not necessary for the Government to prove a physical removal, concealment or transfer from one place to another. A violation of this Code section may be committed by making false book entries indicating transfer of property rights. [*U.S. v. Bregman*]

(3) It is probable that the period of limitations for this offense is six years. However, since this has not been determined by case law, prosecution should be instituted within three years, to avoid unnecessary controversy.

419 *(1-18-80)* 9781
Statute of Limitations

419.1 *(1-18-80)* 9781
Introduction

Statutes of limitation are founded upon the liberal theory that prosecutions should not be allowed to ferment endlessly in the files of the Government to explode only after witnesses and proof necessary to the protection of the accused have by sheer lapse of time passed beyond availability. They amount to legislative restraints on the executive power to punish wrongdoers, which grant malefactors complete immunity from prosecution after stated periods of time. Text 241 through 243 contain information showing the specific statutory provisions [26 USC 6531] relating to the time limit within which prosecutions may be instituted against persons charged with violations of the internal revenue laws and the applicable sections of the United States Criminal Code.

419.2 *(1-18-80)* 9781
Statute of Limitations Statutory Provisions

419.21 *(1-18-80)* 9781
Statute of Limitations on Criminal Violations

(1) The Internal Revenue Code provides a three-year limitation period for criminal violations with the exception of the following described offenses investigated by the Criminal Investigation Division, which fall within a six-year limitation period:

(a) Those Code sections in which defrauding or attempting to defraud the United States is an ingredient of the offense.

(b) 7201—Willfully attempting in any manner to evade or defeat any tax or the payment thereof.

(c) 7206(2)—Willfully aiding, assisting, counseling, procuring or advising the preparation or presentation of a false return or other document.

(d) 7203 (in part)—Willfully failing to timely pay any tax or make any return (other than declaration of estimated tax, partnership returns or other information returns).

(e) 7206 (1)—Willfully making and subscribing a false return under penalty of perjury.

(f) 7207—Willfully delivering or disclosing to the Secretary a fraudulent return, statement or other document.

(g) 7212(a)—Corruptly or forcibly attempting to interfere with the administration of the internal revenue laws.

(h) 371, Title 18—Conspiracy in connection with an attempt to defeat or evade any tax or the payment thereof.

(2) The limitation period under the United States Criminal Code is generally five years for offenses other than capital. [18 USC 3282]

419.22 *(1-18-80)* 9781
Statute of Limitations on Civil Assessments

(1) Generally, taxes must be assessed within three years after they become due. However, IRC 6501 provides that a six-year limitation peri-

od is applicable where an amount in excess of 25 percent of gross income has been omitted from the return, and that there is no limitation on assessment when:

(a) A false or fraudulent return has been filed with intent to evade tax;

(b) No return has been filed; or—

(c) There has been a willful attempt to defeat or evade a tax (other than income, estate and gift taxes).

419.23 *(1-18-80)* 9781
Consents

(1) Extension of the statutory period of limitation upon assessment of the tax will be requested of a taxpayer only in a case involving unusual circumstances and where the taxpayer has been contacted previously, except where compelling reasons exist. However, if it is determined by the special agent and approved by the Chief, Criminal Investigation Division, by reason of the discovery of indications of a tax deficiency, that an extension of the statutory period is warranted pursuant to this policy regarding a tax return in the custody of Criminal Investigation, and further, if the tax involved is one for which the statutory period of limitations may be extended, the special agent who has the actual custody of the return shall, after receiving the concurrence of his/her group manager, request the extension. The Request for Execution of Consent Extending Statutory Period which is Letter 907(DO), formerly Form L-64, will be used for this purpose. (See IRM 9325.2 and policy statement P-4-79.)

(2) In joint investigations wherein the administrative file has not been forwarded in connection with the referral of the criminal case to District Counsel and there is danger of an early expiration of the statutory period for assessment, the cooperating revenue agent will, through the Chief, Examination Division, timely advise Criminal Investigation that he/she proposes to solicit consents extending the statutory period for assessment. Normally, the solicitation of such a consent does not prejudice a criminal case, and unless Criminal Investigation requests otherwise, within ten workdays following the date the cooperating revenue agent submits his/her notification of intention to solicit a consent, the cooperating revenue agent will endeavor to obtain the consent.

(3) Except in unusual circumstances, consents in these cases shall be solicited by letter, rather than by personal contact, using Letter 907(DO). Any subsequent inquiry, whether oral or written, received from the taxpayer or his/her representative concerning consents in such cases will be referred to the Chief, Criminal Investigation Division, for reply. Where personal contact is necessary to obtain the consent, either because of the time element involved or for some other compelling reason, such contact should be made jointly by the special agent and the cooperating officer.

(4) The revenue agent will, through the Chief, Examination Division, inform the Chief, Criminal Investigation Division, of the results of the efforts to obtain the consent(s). If the revenue agent is unable to obtain a consent(s), he/she will prepare a memorandum, with the supporting reasons, to the District Counsel recommending that a statutory notice be issued. The memorandum will be prepared for the signature of the District Director or Director of International Operations and cleared through the Chiefs, Examination and Criminal Investigation Divisions. In clearing this memorandum, the Chief, Criminal Investigation Division should follow the procedures in IRM 9325.2:(5).

(5) In making the determination of whether a statutory notice should be issued, the District Director or Director of International Operations, will be guided by the following procedures.

(a) A statutory notice will be issued in all cases where such action is appropriate to protect the assessment of civil liability and it appears unlikely the criminal prosecution will be recommended.

(b) If it appears likely that criminal prosecution will be recommended, a statutory notice normally will not be issued if either of the following situations exist.

1 The facts and circumstances are deemed such as to warrant the assertion of the fraud penalty, providing there is sufficient probative evidence available to sustain the Commissioner's burden of proof in establishing fraud relating to the particular tax period, thus permitting the assessment of the tax at any time.

2 The issuance of the statutory notice would imperil successful criminal investigation or prosecution. In this respect, peril to the criminal aspects of the case may result from inconsistent theories between the civil and criminal cases, the disclosure of the details of evidence or sources thereof, including the identity of particular witnesses, or other factors which reasonably could be expected to lead to the destruction of evidence, efforts by the taxpayer to tamper with or discredit testimony of documentary evidence to be relied upon in support of the potential criminal case.

(c) Jeopardy assessments will not be made if such action would imperil successful criminal investigation or prosecution. However, if collection of civil liability in the case is in jeopardy, such as in situations described in IRM 9329, and a jeopardy assessment is recommended, care should be taken to avoid unnecessary disclosures in the deficiency letter and in any accompanying statement that would imperil successful criminal investigation of prosecution.

(d) Consideration should also be given to the fact that if a statutory notice is issued and the taxpayer appeals to the United States Tax Court, the Government may lose control over the facts which it will be required to reveal to the taxpayer, either in the answer or at the trial of the civil case ahead of the criminal case.

(6) IRM 9325.2:(3) through 9325.5 contains further information on the issuance of statutory notices.

419.3 *(1-18-80)* 9781

Construction of Statute of Limitations Provisions

(1) *Interpretation generally*—"The statute (of limitations) is not a statute of process to be scantily and grudgingly applied, but an amnesty, declaring that after a certain time oblivion shall be cast over the offense." [Wharton, Criminal Procedure, 415 (10th Ed. 1918] In other words, the statute is liberally interpreted in favor of the accused.

(2) *Toll*—To toll the statute of limitations means to show facts which remove its bar of the action. [Black's Law Dictionary] Thus, to toll the statute is to suspend the running of the statute for a period of time. The tolling of the statute of limitations should not be confused with the expiration date of the period of limitations.

(3) *Running of the statute*—The limitation period begins to run from the day on which the offense is committed. The day following is the first of the period. [Rule 45, Federal Rules of Criminal Procedure; 18 USC; *Pendergast v. U.S.*] For example, if a false and fraudulent income tax return is filed on April 20, 1971, the period of limitations begins to run on April 21, 1971, and, provided there are no circumstances to toll the statute, it will operate to bar prosecution on April 21, 1977.

(4) *Willful failure to perform*—Offenses relating to the willful failure to perform certain acts are not complete until the failure becomes willful. [*Arnold v. U.S.*] Usually it is possible to prove that willfulness was present on the date the return was due. An exception would be a situation where an individual failed to pay his/her tax on the due date and continued in this failure until three months later, at which time he/she stated that he/she was not going to pay the tax because he/she did not want the Government to spend his/her money. Under such circumstances, the statute may be interpreted as running from the date the individual made the latter statement. [*Capone v. U.S.*]

(5) *Continuing offense*—In the case of instantaneous crimes, the statute of limitations begins to run with the consummation of the crime whereas in the case of a continuing offense, such as conspiracy, the statute of limitations does not begin to run until the criminal conduct ceases.

(6) *Attempt to defeat and evade*—Violations involving willful attempts to defeat and evade taxes are complete on the date of the occurrence alleged as a means of attempted evasion. Usually, the filing of the return marks the climax of the willful attempt and the period of limitations begins to run from the filing date or the due date. However, an attempt to evade tax, or attempt to evade payment, may occur at a later date. A false statement by a taxpayer during a conference several months after a return was filed was determined to be a willful attempt to evade tax for which the period of limitations began on the date of the false statement. [*U.S. v. The Beacon Brass Co., Inc.*] False statements made in 1955, 1956, and 1957 in offers to compromise tax liabilities for 1941 through 1946 constituted willful attempt to evade payment, on which the periods of limitation began when the statements were made. [*U.S. v. Mousley*]

(7) *Conspiracy*—The crucial question in determining whether the period of limitations has run in a conspiracy charge "is the scope of the

conspiratorial agreement, for it is that which determines both the duration of the conspiracy, and whether the act relied on as an overt act may properly be regarded as in furtherance of the conspiracy." [*Grunewald v. U.S.; Forman v. U.S.*] For example, if the central objective of a conspiracy was to protect taxpayers from tax evasion prosecutions on which the statute of limitations did not bar prosecution until 1980 and if nonprosecution rulings were obtained in 1977 as an installment of what the conspirators aimed to accomplish, then the period of limitations on the conspiracy would not begin to run until 1980 when the objective of the conspiracy was entirely accomplished. If the conspiracy is limited to an attempt to defeat and evade taxes by filing a false and fraudulent return, the conspiracy ends at the time the return is filed and the statute of limitations begins to run from that date. [*U.S. v. Rosenblum, et al.*]

(8) *Statutory filing date*—IRC 6531 states, among other things, "For the purpose of determining the periods of limitation on criminal prosecutions, the rules of Section 6513 shall be applicable." The pertinent portion of IRC 6513 provides that ". . . any return filed thereof shall be considered as filed on such last day." This language from IRC 6513 has been judicially approved, on the theory that Congress has the right to legislate concerning periods of limitations. [*U.S. v. Black*] In order to avoid controversial issues, a conservative approach would be to measure the limitation period from the date on which the return was actually filed or the last overt act was committed. The statutory filing date should be used when the conservative approach would bar prosecution.

(9) *Extension of time*—Under the Internal Revenue Code of 1954, where an extension is granted and the return is thereafter filed, the statute of limitations begins to run from the date of filing. [*U.S. v. Habig*]

419.4 *(1-18-80)* 9781
Tolling of the Statute of Limitations

(1) IRC 6531 provides:

(a) That the statute of limitations will be inoperative during the time an offender is outside the United States or is a fugitive from justice; and

(b) That where a complaint is instituted before a Commissioner of the United States within the limitation period, the time is extended until nine months after date of the making of the complaint.

(2) *Absence from the United States*—Taxpayer absence from the United States tolls the statute of limitations for that period regardless of the reason for the absence.

(3) *Fugitive from justice*—"The essential characteristic of fleeing from justice is leaving one's residence or usual place of abode or resort, or concealing one's self, with the intent to avoid punishment." [*Brouse v. U.S.*] A flight to escape an anticipated prosecution is sufficient and it does not have to be made after an indictment has been brought. [*Streep v. U.S.*] The intent is indispensable and thus the withdrawal or concealment must be voluntary. [*U.S. v. Hewecker*] Moreover, if one voluntarily flees with the requisite intent, he/she cannot later successfully contend that his/her absence was prolonged against his/her will and that the statute should have commenced running again when he/she would have returned had he/she been free to do so. [*McGowen v. U.S.*] The character of the original flight colors the absence so as to render the defendant a fugitive from justice throughout the period of absence.

(4) *Complaint*—The extension applies if the complaint filed with the Magistrate contains probable cause that an offense has been committed and that the defendant committed it. The defendant must be given notice by service of a court summons or an arrest warrant. A preliminary hearing is held within reasonable time unless waived by the defendant or superseded by indictment. If the complaint does not support a finding of probable cause, the tolling of the statute of limitations is invalidated. This provision relates to situations in which the Government cannot obtain an indictment within the normal limitation period because of the grand jury schedule and is not intended to provide the Government additional time to conduct its investigation. [*Jaben v. U.S.*]

(5) Further discussion of complaints is in 721.

41(10) *(1-18-80)* 9781
Conspiracy (Section 371, Title 18)

does not create a new conspiracy. [*U.S. v. Marino; Hagen v. U.S.*] Conversely, if one or more of the conspirators withdraw, such withdrawal neither creates a new conspiracy nor changes the status of the remaining members. [*Graham Johnson v. U.S.; Craig v. U.S.*] A person may become a conspirator by joining in an existing agreement or by knowing of its existence and committing an overt act in furtherance thereof. [*Craig v. U.S.; U.S. v. Olmstead*] After joining, a co-conspirator becomes responsible for all acts and all statements of all participants which are committed in connection with the plan and common object of the conspiracy [*Connelly v. U.S.*] whether done before or after he/she joins the conspiracy. [*Baker v. U.S.; Coates v. U.S.*] A conspirator may withdraw by an affirmative and effective act that disavows or defeats the purposes of the conspiracy. [*Blue v. U.S.; U.S. v. Christian W. Beck*] He/she is not liable for the subsequent acts of his/her former associates and the statute of limitations commences to run, as to him/her, upon his/her withdrawal. [*Hyde v. U.S.; Eldredge v. U.S.*] A conspirator may avoid guilt completely by withdrawing prior to the commission of the first overt act that furthers the conspiracy. [*Marino v. U.S.*] When only two persons are charged with conspiracy and there is no evidence implicating anyone else, acquittal or reversal as to one is acquittal or reversal as to the other. [*U.S. v. Fox*] However, if the indictment charges two named conspirators and persons unknown as co-conspirators, and there is evidence to support the charge that one of the two defendants conspired with the unknown persons, that defendant's convictions may stand in spite of the fact that the other named defendant is acquitted. [*Pomerantz v. U.S.; U.S. v. Gordon*] The rule that acquittal of all alleged conspirators except one results in acquittal of all applies only to acquittals on the merits. [*U.S. v. Fox*] Thus, if the charge against one of two conspirators is dismissed as the result of a nolle prosequi, it would not affect the case against the other since a nolle prosequi does not amount to a dismissal on the merits. All acts and statements in furtherance of the conspiracy may be introduced in evidence against the conspirators on trial regardless of whether the person who committed such act or made such statement is on trial. [*Lewis v. U.S.*] A person's involvement in a conspiracy cannot be established through his/her alleged co-conspirator's acts or declarations done or made in his/her absence without proof from another source of his/her connection with the conspiracy. [*Glasser v. U.S.; U.S. v. Wortman*] A corporation can be a conspirator with other corporations, or with natural persons including its own officers, employees or stockholders. It is responsible for the acts of its agents which are performed within the scope of their authority. [*Old Monastery Company v. U.S.*] Partners may be prosecuted for conspiracy to defraud the Government of income taxes by making false and fraudulent partnership and individual returns. [*Lisansky v. U.S.*] A husband and wife may be found guilty of conspiracy, being considered separate persons under the conspiracy statute. [*U.S. v. Dege*] All conspirators need not be defendants. Should the prosecution require the testimony of one of the conspirators to prove the conspiracy, he/she could be named in the indictment as a co-conspirator even though he/she is not named as a defendant. [*U.S. v. Gordon*]

41(10).43 *(1-18-80)* 9781
Nature of Conspiracy Agreement

Conspirators usually do not put their agreements into writing nor do they make public their plans. Hence, a conspiracy is rarely susceptible of proof by direct evidence and must usually be deducted from the conduct of the parties and the attending circumstances. [*Cruz v. U.S.; Telman v. U.S.*] It is sufficient to show that the minds of the parties met in an understanding way so as to bring about an intelligent and deliberate agreement to do the act or acts charged, although such an agreement is not manifested by any formal words. [*Telman v. U.S.*] It is not necessary that each conspirator know or see the others [*Blumenthal v. U.S.; Martin v. U.S.*], but it is necessary to prove that each person charged in the conspiracy knew of the agreement and had a corrupt motive or evil intent. [*Cruz v. U.S.*] The conspiracy is distinct from the crime contemplated and one may be convicted of both the completed crime and the conspiracy, even though the completed crime was alleged as the overt act necessary to convict for conspiracy. [*Pinkerton v. U.S.*] After the central purpose of a conspiracy has been attained, a subsidiary agreement to conceal may not be implied from circumstantial evidence showing merely that the conspiracy was kept secret and that the conspirators took care to cover up their crime in order to escape detection and punishment. [*Grunewald v. U.S.; Forman v. U.S.; Krulewitch v. U.S.; Lutwak v. U.S.*]

41(10).44 *(1-18-80)* 9781
Overt Act in Conspiracy

An overt act is any act or statement designed to advance, aid, or assist in accomplishing the object of the conspiracy agreement. It need not be a violation of the law within itself and may be as innocent as calling at the office of the District Director of Internal Revenue in order to obtain a blank claim form. It is not necessary that each conspirator commit an overt act [*Braverman v. U.S.; U.S. v. Donald Johnson*] and, therefore, a party to a conspiracy agreement may become guilty of conspiracy without any knowledge that a co-conspirator actually committed an overt act. [*Brock v. Hudspeth*] Preparing, signing, and filing a false return are appropriate overt acts in a conspiracy to attempt to defeat and evade the payment of tax by filing a false and fraudulent return.

41(10).45 *(1-18-80)* 9781
Defraud in Conspiracy

The word "defraud" as used in this USC section is broad enough to include anything which interferes with or hampers the United States in the successful prosecution of any policy, as well as the ordinary common law meaning of the word. [*U.S. v. Slater*] For example, a conspiracy to cause Government officers to neglect their duties would be a conspiracy to defraud the United States of their honest and effective services.

41(10).46 *(1-18-80)* 9781
Duration of Conspiracy

(1) Conspiracy is a continuing crime [*Ryan v. U.S.*] first complete upon the performance of the first overt act in furtherance of the conspiracy agreement, and it continues until the completion of the last overt act, including the division of the fruits of the crime, if any. The terminal date of the conspiratorial relationship is particularly important in settling problems relating to the admissibility of evidence, prosecution of later joining conspirators, and the running of the period of limitations. In determining the termination date, it is necessary to consider carefully the terms of the agreement. The Supreme Court has stated that:

> "... the crucial question in determining whether the statute of limitations has run is the scope of the conspiratorial agreement, for it is that which determines both the duration of the conspiracy and whether the act relied on as an overt act may properly be regarded as in furtherance of the conspiracy." [*Grunewald v. U.S.*]

(2) If the conspiracy involves an attempt to defeat and evade the payment of income tax by filing a false and fraudulent income tax return, the conspiracy ordinarily terminates at the time the return is filed. [*U.S. v. Rosenblum*] However, a conspiracy to evade taxes by making false statements to conceal unreported income was held to continue through the making of such statements. [*Forman v. U.S.*]

41(11) *(1-18-80)* 9781
Willfulness

41(11).1 *(1-18-80)* 9781
Definition of Willfulness

(1) Willfulness is an essential element of proof with respect to most criminal violations investigated by special agents. The term "willful" however, is not defined by statute; thus for its definition we must rely on precedent established by court decisions. In commenting on this statutory omission the Supreme Court in Spies v. U.S. stated that:

> "Congress did not define or limit the methods by which a willful attempt to defeat and evade might be accomplished and perhaps did not define lest its efforts to do so result in some unexpected limitation. Nor would we by definition constrict the scope of the Congressional provision that it may be accomplished 'in any manner'."

(2) Willfulness has been interpreted in many ways with respect to the various statutes. It may mean one thing in civil cases and quite another thing in criminal prosecutions.

(a) Usually, where civil penalties are involved, willfulness means actions "knowingly," "consciously," or "intentionally" taken. A voluntary course of action as distinguished from accidental would seem to satisfy the civil requirements. [*Paddock v. Siemoneit; Wilson v. U.S.*]

(b) When used in criminal revenue statutes, the word "willful" generally means an act done with a bad purpose; without justifiable excuse; stubbornly, obstinately, perversely. As stated by the Supreme Court in U.S. v. Murdock:

> "The word is also employed to characterize a thing done without ground for believing it is lawful ... or conduct marked by careless disregard whether or not one has the right so to act. ... "This court has held that where directions as to the method of conducting a business are embodied in a revenue act to prevent loss of taxes, and the act declares a willful failure to observe the directions a penal offense, an evil motive is a constituent element of the crime.
>
> * * * * *
>
> "Congress did not intend that a person, by reason of a bona fide misunderstanding as to his liability for the tax, as to his duty to make a return, or as to the adequacy of the rec-

ords he maintained, should become a criminal by his mere failure to measure up to the prescribed standard of conduct."

(3) Knowledge, specific intent, and bad purpose are necessary elements of criminal willfulness. They are to be distinguished from motive, which is the reason or inducement for committing an act. For example, an individual may deliberately understate his income in order to have sufficient funds to support invalid parents. While his motive may be admirable, he had a specific intent to evade payment of his income taxes. It has been stated that:

> "Motive is not an essential element of a crime. The most laudable motive is no defense where the act committed is a crime in contemplation of law. . . . Proof as to motive may be of assistance in throwing light on the intent with which the act was committed. . . ." [*Kobey v. U.S.*]

(4) The Supreme Court in the Spies case enunciated the same principle in a different fashion. The court stated:

> "If the tax-evasion motive plays any part in such conduct the offense may be made out even though the conduct may also serve other purposes such as concealment of other crime."

41(11).2 *(1-18-80)* 9781
Proof of Willfulness

(1) Willfulness is a state of mind which is rarely susceptible of direct proof. It involves a mental process which is usually proved through circumstantial evidence. [*Paschen v. U.S.*] Direct evidence of willfulness can only be accomplished through an admission or a confession.

(2) In the Spies case, supra, the court enumerated certain conduct which may create inferences of willful attempted evasion of income taxes:

> "by way of illustration, and not by way of limitation, we would think affirmative willful attempt may be inferred from conduct such as keeping a double set of books, making false entries or alterations, or false invoices or documents, destruction of books or records, concealment of assets or covering up sources of income, handling of one's affairs to avoid making the records usual in transactions of the kind, and *any conduct, the likely effect of which would be to mislead or to conceal.*" (Italics supplied.)

(3) Frequently, circumstantial evidence of willfulness will consist of acts *subsequent* to the filing of a false income tax return. For example, attempted bribery of a revenue agent during an investigation [*Barcott v. U.S.*]; visits to undisclosed safe deposit boxes after having been questioned about assets [*Barcott v. U.S.*]; making false statements [*U.S. v. Beacon Brass Co.*]; withholding records during the investigation [*U.S. v. Glascott*] and influencing the testimony of prospective witnesses. [*Myers v. Comm.*]

(4) Furthermore, in proving willfulness, evidence of other similar offenses and like conduct at time proximate to the offense charged may be admitted. [*Weiss v. U.S.*] This type of evidence does not prove the particular crime charged but tends to show a continuity of unlawful intent and is an exception to the general rule that evidence of another crime unconnected with the one on trial is inadmissible. Cases contain numerous instances of this principle. For example, admitted into evidence was testimony concerning the failure to file returns in prior years [*Ayash v. U.S.; U.S. v. Gannon; U.S. v. Merle Long*]; also the filing of a fraudulent return for a prior year [*Hoyer v. U.S.; Morrison v. U.S.*]; and the failure to supply information for many prior years. [*Pappas v. U.S.*]

(5) The determination of willfulness of a criminal act is the function of the jury under proper instructions from the court. [*Morissette v. U.S.*] Usually, the jury will be told that direct proof of willful or wrongful intent or knowledge is not necessary; that it is not possible to look into a man's mind to see what went on; that intent can only be determined from all the facts and circumstances; that intent and knowledge may be inferred from various acts. [*U.S. v. Swidler*] The instruction may include the comment that the jury may consider the taxpayer's refusal to produce books and records for inspection by the Internal Revenue Service. [*Louis C. Smith v. U.S.; Beard v. U.S.; Olson v. U.S.*] However, it has been held improper for a judge to instruct the jury that it may consider attempts to impede in determining intent, where a corporate officer-taxpayer has resisted, on purely technical rather than self-incrimination grounds, the legality of a summons served on his/her corporation. Unsuccessful resistance does not create any different connotation than successful resistance. [*U.S. v. Grant Foster*]

(6) It is error to instruct the jury that every citizen is presumed to know the law, and that ignorance of the law is no excuse or justification for its violation. Guilty knowledge of the consequences of the act done is the essence of the offense, and evidence which may support or detract from such guilty knowledge is admissible. [*Haigler v. U.S.*]

41(11).3 *(1-18-80)* 9781
Defenses Bearing upon Willfulness

41(11).31 *(1-18-80)* 9781
Defenses of Willfulness

(1) *Advice of counsel* [*U.S. v. Phillips*], *accountant* [*Samish v. U.S.*], *or Government agent* [*Benetti v. U.S.*], if relied upon by the defendant, may be a valid defense to a willful violation. However, if it can be shown that the defendant did not act in good faith upon such advice by not following it [*Barrow v. U.S.*], or that he/she did not fully inform the advisor of all the facts [*U.S. v. McCormick; Clark v. U.S.*], or that he/she sought advice from one not qualified to give it [*Pottash Bros. v. Comm.*], or from one who he/she had reason to believe was not qualified, the defense is vitiated. An attempt by the defendant to shift responsibility for a fraudulent return to the person who made out the return or kept the books can be met with proof, direct or circumstantial, that the defendant knew or should have known the return was false. [*Lurding v. U.S.*] Such proof may take the form of testimony by bookkeepers or other office help about the defendant's knowledge of the book entries or lack of entries.

(2) *Disclosures, amended returns, and payments of tax* after the filing of fraudulent returns may have probative value in establishing the state of mind at the time of the alleged criminal acts. [*Heindel v. U.S.*] Most courts have regarded the prompt filing of amended returns and payment of delinquent tax as admissible evidence to show lack of willfulness. [*Heindel v. U.S.; Berkovitz v. U.S.; U.S. v. Stoehr*] However, evidence that such disclosure and delinquent payment was prompted by a fraud investigation could serve as an incriminating admission of the defendant's culpability. [*Emmich v. U.S.*] Accordingly, intensive investigation of the circumstances attending the preparation and filing of amended returns in such instances is imperative.

(3) *Cooperation* of the taxpayer at the start of the investigation is sometimes claimed to be indicative of innocence. The contention is that he/she willfully defrauded the revenue he/she would continue to conceal the truth from the investigators. This defense is rarely persuasive if the facts and circumstances attending the commission of the alleged offense create an inference of willfulness. [*U.S. v. Swidler*] Subsequent cooperation during the investigation may only serve to mitigate the penalty.

(4) *Lack of education and business experience* are used as defenses to criminal intent. Ignorance of internal revenue requirements and unfamiliarity with business practices may be urged as the reasons for alleged violations. Taxpayers faced with conclusive evidence of substantial amounts of unreported income will frequently claim that it resulted from mistake caused by their *lowly* educational background or inexperience in financial affairs. For example, a successful shoe manufacturer may claim that he/she is an expert shoe fabricator but that he/she can hardly read or write, while a prominent physician may contend that he/she was never good at figures and was too busy caring for the ill to keep accurate records of his/her earnings. These defenses may be argued to the jury, but their effect would depend, as in the case of cooperation, upon all the facts and circumstances surrounding the commission of the offense. [*Fischer v. U.S.; U.S. v. Glascott*]

(5) *Poor health, good character, and integrity* are also resorted to as exculpatory factors. Whether the mental and physical condition of the defendant at the time of the alleged offense was such as to deprive him/her of his/her sense of reason is one more fact to be determined by the jury. The defense is made that willfulness cannot be present when the defendant did not know what he/she was doing or was so incapacitated as to be unable to attend to his/her financial affairs properly. [*Collins v. Comm.; U.S. v. Glascott*] Closely connected with this defense is the claim that the defendant was a person of good character and integrity and could not reasonably have intended to defraud the United States. The courts have held that the jury may consider good reputation in itself sufficient to raise a reasonable doubt of the defendant's guilt. [*U.S. v. Wicoff*]

(6) The defendant may utilize any other defense which might have a bearing on willfulness. The validity of the contention is determined by the jury. All defenses are usually rebutted with evidence of specific acts which create an inference of intentional violation.

41(11).32 *(1-18-80)* 9781
Entrapment

(1) Entrapment may be used as a defense against the allegation of willfulness, if a Government agent induces a person to commit a crime he/she would not otherwise have committed. To constitute entrapment it must be shown that the agent originated and implanted the intent in the mind of the violator. If the agent merely offers the opportunity for a person to commit a crime the person already intended, or if a per-

son already engaged in the violation is simply awaiting an opportunity to continue with it, which the agent furnishes, there is no entrapment. [*Sorrels v. U.S.; Sherman v. U.S.; Gorin v. U.S.*]

(2) Government undercover agents or informants may present themselves to violators in disguise, as long as the disguise does not motivate an otherwise innocent person to commit a crime. It is not entrapment to use an informant or decoy to obtain evidence of the commission of a crime, even though the informant participates in the violation, so long as the crime is not instigated by the Government agent. [*U.S. v. Roett; Papadakis v. U.S.*] However, a contingent fee arrangement for an informant to produce evidence against a particular person, of a crime not yet committed, is improper unless the agent has prior certain knowledge that the person is already engaged in illegal activity, and specifically instructs the informant not to induce commission of the offense, but merely to offer opportunity to continue with it. [*Williamson v. U.S.*]

(3) If a person offers a Government agent a bribe, which the agent has not solicited, it is not improper to set a trap to apprehend the bribe offeror. [*Lopez v. U.S.; U.S. v. Kabot; Todisco v. U.S.*]

(4) When a principal unjustifiably claims entrapment, evidence should be obtained of his/her past record, including his/her reputation for committing similar acts, to combat his/her claim.

(5) A defense of entrapment is rarely raised where the alleged violation consists of filing a fraudulent return, since the violation would usually occur before an investigation has been initiated.

41(11).33 *(1-18-80)* 9781
Embezzled Funds and Other Illegally Obtained Income

(1) In the past some taxpayers have successfully met allegations of understated income with the defense that it was not income because it constituted embezzled funds. The theory for nontaxability of such funds was: absence of a claim of right to the alleged gain; and a definite unconditional obligation to repay. [*Wilcox v. Commissioner*] This theory was under constant attack almost from the time that the landmark Wilcox case was decided. Courts weakened the theory by including as taxable income, money acquired by swindling or through fraudulent representations [*Rollinger v. U.S.*], extortion [*Rutkin v. U.S.*], kickbacks [*U.S. v. Wyss; Berra v. U.S.*] or larceny. [*U.S. v. Iozia*] In holding the proceeds of extortion taxable, the Supreme Court said, "An unlawful gain, as well as a lawful one, constitutes taxable income when its recipient has such control over it that, as a practical matter, he derives readily realizable economic value from it." [*Rutkin v. U.S.*] Lower courts confronted with embezzlement-like situations went to great lengths to distinguish their facts from Wilcox, using the reasoning plainly stated in Rutkin: "We limit that case (Wilcox) to its facts."

(2) Finally, confronted squarely in an income tax evasion case with taxability of embezzled funds, the Supreme Court on May 15, 1961, on the authority of Rutkin, reversed Wilcox, using this language: "We believe that Wilcox was wrongly decided. . . . Thus, we believe that we should now correct the error and the confusion resulting from it, certainly if we do so in a manner that will not prejudice those who might have relied on it." [*James v. U.S.*]

(3) Although reversing Wilcox and making embezzled funds taxable, the James opinion reversed the defendant's conviction, on the theory that willfulness could not be proved because he might have relied on Wilcox in failing to include embezzled funds in gross income. The same theory has since been followed in a Court of Appeals case. [*Beck v. U.S.*]

420 *(1-18-80)* 9781
Methods of Proving Income

421 *(1-18-80)* 9781
Introduction

(1) In order to establish a criminal offense under IRC 7201, the special agent must develop evidence to prove a substantial amount of additional tax due and willful attempt to evade it. To prove the first element of the offense, it is necessary to establish that the correct taxable income is in excess of that reported.

(2) Taxable income may be established by the direct or indirect approach. The former consists of the specific item method which involves proof of transactions (sales, expenses, etc.) affecting taxable income. The latter approach relies upon circumstantial proof of income by use of such methods as net worth, expenditures, and bank deposits. Usually, taxable income can be established with less difficulty by the direct approach and for this reason it should be used whenever possible.

(3) Taxpayers, almost without exception, report their income by the specific item or specific transaction method; that is, the computations which are reflected in their income tax returns are based upon the sum total of the transactions they engaged in during the taxable period. Most taxpayers maintain books and records in which these various transactions are recorded as they occur. In a specific transactions case, the Government endeavors to prove that the transactions in which the taxpayer engaged during the year were not completely or accurately reflected in his/her income tax return, with the result that his/her income tax liability was understated, and that such result was willful.

(4) In numerous cases the courts have approved the use of the following indirect methods of determining income: net worth [*Holland v. U.S.*]; expenditures [*U.S. v. William R. Johnson*]; and bank deposits. [*Gleckman v. U.S.*] Although these methods are considered circumstantial proof of taxable income, the courts have approved them for use in determining taxable income for criminal prosecution on the theory that proof of unexpended funds or property in the hands of a taxpayer may establish a prima facie understatement of income requiring a taxpayer to overcome the logical inference drawn from the provable facts. In one income tax case [*Jelaza v. U.S.*], the Government employed all three methods—net worth, expenditures, and bank deposits—to show corrected income. With respect to the establishment of a prima facie case by such evidence, the Court stated:

> "In these (and other similar) cases, the Courts have been careful to point out that findings of fraud have been sustained if, but only if, the taxpayer has offered no explanation, or no adequate explanation, of the discrepancies between (on the one hand) expenditures and/or bank deposits and/or increases in net worth and (on the other hand) the amount of income reported by the taxpayer."

(5) Another indirect method of proof is percentage mark-up. (Intell. Digest, Oct.-Nov.-Dec. 1975, p. 9) This method is sometimes used to corroborate other methods used in criminal cases and has been used as the method of proof in civil cases.

422 *(1-18-80)* 9781

Distinguishing Between Accounting Systems, Accounting Methods, and Methods of Proving Income

(1) For many years there has been much confusion regarding the synonymous use of the terms "accounting system," "accounting methods," and "methods of proving or determining income." It is not unusual to hear reference made to the net worth and expenditures method as a method of accounting when in fact it is a method of proving income by circumstantial or indirect evidence. [*Holland v. U.S.*]

(2) There are two *basic* accounting *systems*, the *single* entry and the *double* entry system, but there are *various methods of accounting*, such as cash, accrual, hybrid, installment, and long-term or completed contract methods. The usual *methods of determining or proving income* are specific item, net worth, expenditures, bank deposits, and percentage methods.

(3) Taxable income must be computed, for purposes of criminal prosecution, under the accounting method by which the taxpayer regularly computes his income. The reason for this is given in Morrison v. U.S.:

> "In this criminal proceeding it was necessary to establish not only that the tax liabilities here were understated, but that the understatement was attributable, at least in part, to the fact that the taxpayer's returns were not honestly prepared. Proof of the latter fact could only be accomplished by adopting and consistently applying the taxpayer's own method of accounting."

(4) If no method of accounting has been regularly employed or if the method employed does not clearly reflect income, the computation shall be made in accordance with such method as, in the opinion of the Commissioner, does clearly reflect income. [26 USC 446]

423 *(12-7-81)* 9781

Specific Item Method of Proving Income

423.1 *(12-7-81)* 9781

General

(1) In a specific item case, the Government tries to prove that the specific transactions in which the taxpayer engaged during the year were not completely or accurately reflected in his/her income tax return, with the result that his/her income tax liability was understated, and that such understatement was willfully made. This method offers the most direct method of proving unreported income. It is easier

than other methods to present in court and is readily understood by jurors.

(2) Omitted income, fictitious deductions, false exemptions, or false tax credits in their broadest concept are the means whereby taxes may be evaded.

(3) Omitted income results from failure to report any of the numerous items of taxable income expressed and implied in the Internal Revenue Code. In the examination of merchant taxpayers the item of omitted income most frequently encountered is sales revenue and, in the case of individuals, omitted income is usually in the form of salaries, dividends, commissions, gains from the sale of property, and/or fees.

(4) Often a deduction which is considered fraudulent takes the guise of a fictitious purchase of merchandise or a fictitious expense. However, it could be any fictitious deduction or exemption fraudulently claimed as allowable under the authority of the Internal Revenue Code.

423.2 *(12-7-81)* 9781
Unreported Income from Certificates of Deposit

(1) There are two types of certificates of deposit. First, a standard certificate of deposit that pays interest at intervals throughout the term of the note, often quarterly. The interest may be withdrawn without penalty although the underlying principal may not be withdrawn without incurring a substantial penalty. Financial institutions will issue Forms 1099 INT to the depositor reflecting the interest earned. The second type is known as an original issue discount certificate in which the interest is payable only at the note's maturity. Pursuant to I.R.C. Section 1232(a)(3), the Service requires holders of this type of certificate of deposit to report the interest earned on the note pro rata throughout its term.

(2) The position of the Criminal Tax Division is that the Criminal Investigation Division should not recommend prosecution of criminal cases based upon failure to report interest from original issue discount certificates before the certificates of deposit mature, unless unusual circumstances warrant prosecution. In these cases, a willfulness problem usually arises from the taxpayer's lack of actual possession, use, and enjoyment of the interest during the holding period. No similar problems should be present in cases involving the standard certificates of deposit when the interest is made available to the taxpayer.

(3) In order to properly identify the type of certificates of deposit, the final report must exhibit copies of the 1099's and copies of the underlying contracts of the certificates. In addition, the report should discuss exhaustively the issue of willfulness. For example, the investigation should determine whether the principal and interest on a matured certificate was rolled-over into a new certificate of deposit, whether premature withdrawal of the principal is subject to penalties, and whether or not there was a premature redemption.

424 *(1-18-80)* 9781
Net Worth Method of Proving Income

424.1 *(1-18-80)* 9781
Introduction

Next to the specific item method, the net worth method is probably the most frequently used way of proving taxable income in civil and criminal income tax cases. There is nothing complex in the theory of the method. It involves a determination of the taxpayer's net worth (assets less liabilities) at the beginning and end of a taxable year, computing the increase or decrease in net worth, and then adjusting this amount for nondeductible and nontaxable items. The amount resulting from application of this theory is taxable income. By comparing it with income reported, the special agent may determine whether taxable income has been correctly reported.

424.2 *(1-18-80)* 9781
Authority for Net Worth Method

There is no statutory provision defining the net worth method and specifically authorizing its use by the Commissioner. However, in numerous cases courts have approved the use of this method. Perhaps the leading case in this respect is Holland v. United States handed down in 1954 by the Supreme Court along with three companion cases, [*Smith v. U.S.; Friedberg v. U.S.; U.S. v. Calderon*] wherein is outlined the broad principles governing the trial and review of cases based on the net worth method of proving income. With reference to the use of the net worth technique, the court stated that:

(Next page is 9781-278.1)

"To protect the revenue from those who do not 'render true accounts,' the Government must be free to use all legal evidence available to it in determining whether the story told by the taxpayer's books accurately reflect his financial history."

424.3 *(1-18-80)* 9781

When and How Net Worth Method Used

(1) The net worth method is most often used when one or more of the following conditions prevail:

(a) Taxpayer maintains no books and records.

(b) Taxpayer's books and records are not available.

(c) Taxpayer's books and records are inadequate.

(d) Taxpayer withholds books and records.

(2) The fact that the taxpayer's books and records accurately reflect the figures on his return does not prevent the use of the net worth theory of proof. The Government can look beyond the "self serving declarations" in the taxpayer's books and records and use any evidence available to contravene their accuracy. [*Holland v. U.S.*]

(3) In addition to being used as a primary method of proving taxable income in civil and criminal income tax cases, the net worth method can be used:

(a) To corroborate other methods of proving income.

(b) To test-check accuracy of reported taxable income.

424.4 *(1-18-80)* 9781

Establishing the Starting Point

(1) In the Holland case the Supreme Court said that an essential condition in a net worth determination of income is the establishment, "with reasonable certainty," of an opening net worth, to serve as a starting point from which to calculate future increases in the taxpayer's net worth. The wisdom of this statement is apparent since an inaccurate beginning net worth will affect the accuracy of the determination of income subsequent to the base point. For instance, if a taxpayer's beginning net worth is understated, taxable income for the period under consideration will be overstated.

(Next page is 9781-279)

(2) Proof of visible assets and liabilities comprising beginning net worth is usually easily established by such means as bank records; county real estate records; brokerage records; Bureau of Public Debt records; Federal and state income, inheritance, and gift tax returns and records; and books and records of the taxpayer. To establish a firm starting point, it is necessary to show that the defendant had no large sum of cash for which credit was not given. This is usually done by offering evidence which negates the existence of a cash hoard, for example:

(a) Written or oral admissions of the taxpayer to the investigating officers concerning net worth. [*U.S. v. Calderon*] Examples are: signed net worth statement, oral statement as to cash on hand.

(b) Failure by defendant to file returns for years prior to indictment period. [*Smith v. U.S.*]

(c) Returns filed by the taxpayer for years prior to prosecution years reflecting income reported that is inconsistent with existence of a cash hoard. [*Smith v. U.S.*] This would also apply to copies retained by the taxpayer. The taxpayer's filing record and copies of available income tax returns should be furnished for at least five (5) preceding and all years subsequent to the starting point to furnish additional support to the starting point. (See IRM 9327.1(4)) and text 424.4:(2)(h)

(d) Low earnings for years prior to prosecution years as shown by records of the Social Security Administration and former employers.

(e) Net worth as established by books and records of the taxpayer. [*U.S. v. Chapman*]

(f) Certificate of Assessments and Payments showing tax assessed for years prior to the prosecution period. [*Vloutis v. U.S.*] With this information and tables showing tax rates and the amount allowed for exemptions and dependents, it *may* be possible to calculate income reported by a taxpayer for the years in question. The certificate will not show amount of withholding, capital gains or nontaxable income.

(g) Financial statement presented for credit or other purposes at a time prior to or during prosecution period. [*Friedberg v. U.S.*] Banks, loan companies, bonding companies, and the Internal Revenue Service (offers in compromise) are some of the better sources from which to obtain this type of document.

(h) Bankruptcy prior to prosecution periods. [*U.S. v. Vassallo*] Special Agents may use the public record of a bankruptcy as a starting point for net worth purposes. However, Section 7(a)(10) of the Bankruptcy Act 11, USCA 525(a)(10) as amended by title 11 of the Organized Crime Control Act of 1970, P.L. 91-452, provides that no testimony or evidence which is directly or indirectly derived from testimony given by a bankrupt during bankruptcy proceedings may be offered in evidence against him in any criminal proceedings.

(i) Prior indebtedness, compromise of overdue debts, avoidance of bankruptcy. [*Holland v. U.S.*]

(j) Installment buying. [*Barcott v. U.S.*]

(k) History of prior low earnings and expenditures, and checks returned for insufficient funds. [*McFee v. U.S.*]

(l) Loss of furniture and business because of financial reasons. [*Holland v. U.S.*]

424.5 *(1-18-80)* 9781

Taxable Source of Income

(1) In order for income to be taxable, it must come from a taxable source. [*Commissioner v. Glenshaw Glass Co.*] In the Holland case, the Supreme Court said: "Increase in net worth, standing alone, can not be assumed to be attributable to currently taxable income. But proof of a likely source, from which the jury could reasonably find that the net worth increases sprang, is sufficient. . . ."

(2) On the basis of the Holland decision, it appeared to many that proof of a likely source was necessary in every net worth case. This was clarified by U.S. v. Massei in which the Supreme Court said: "In Holland we held that proof of a likely source was 'sufficient' to convict in a net worth case where the Government did not negative all the possible non-taxable sources of the alleged net worth increases. This was not intended to imply that proof of a likely source was necessary in every case. On the contrary, should all possible sources of nontaxable income be negatived, there would be no necessity for proof of a likely source."

(3) In view of the two decisions cited above, it appears that the Government must either prove a likely source of taxable income, or negate all nontaxable sources of income. In cases where the Government resorts to the latter type of proof, it is even more important than otherwise to establish a firm starting point, particularly with reference to cash on hand.

(4) Proof of a likely taxable source of income has been found sufficient in a number of criminal income tax cases by:

(a) Showing that defendant did not report certain income on his tax returns. [*U.S. v. Chapman*]

(b) Showing that defendant did not report certain income for years prior to indictment period. [*U.S. v. Skidmore*]

(c) Comparison of business operations and profits of defendant for indictment years with profits or prior operations for a comparable period. In the Holland case the Supreme Court pointed out that the business of the defendant, a hotel, apparently increased during the years in question, whereas the reported profits fell to approximately one quarter of the amount declared by the previous management in a comparable period.

(d) Effectively contradicting defendant's assertions as to nontaxable sources. In *United States v. Adonis,* the salaried defendant had asserted in a prior unrelated judicial proceeding that the $44,000 he used to purchase a house had come from loans and gifts. The Government proved that the alleged donor was supported by her family, that the supposed creditors were dummies or of such financial condition as to imply that they had no available assets to loan. The court considered the conduct of the defendant "an effort to conceal . . . the real sources of taxable gain."

(e) Opportunities of defendant to receive graft. In *United States* v. *Bryan Ford,* the taxpayer was a policeman and a member of the vice squad. The Court held that evidence admitted to show opportunity to receive graft, not the actual receipt of graft, was sufficient to show a possible source of income. (The Supreme Court remanded the case to the District Court to vacate judgment and dismiss the indictment on account of the death of the taxpayer.) However, in *Fred M. Ford* v. *United States,* the court said: "The evidence sufficiently disclosed that in the defendant's office of Chief of Police, he had opportunities of receiving income from graft, payoffs or other illegal sources. There can, of course, be no presumption that the defendant was guilty of such gross misconduct as to be the recipient of such ill gotten gains. The presumption is to the contrary . . . the testimony of this woman as to payoffs with which the defendant was not shown to be connected was both erroneous and highly prejudicial." Upon retrial, a conviction was sustained after the same witness testified that the defendant had acknowledged the receipt of graft payments.

(f) The character of the business has the capacity to produce income in amounts determined by the net worth method. [*Costello v. U.S.*]

(5) A likely source is established in net worth cases by showing that the source reported by the taxpayer had the potential to produce income substantially in excess of that reported.

(6) Negating nontaxable sources of income may be accomplished by proving nonreceipt of loans, gifts, and inheritances by taxpayer's admissions, Federal gift tax returns filed by alleged donor, or probate records of deceased relatives' estates. If the taxpayer advances a specific explanation of the sources of funds expended, the Government does not have to pursue possible nontaxable sources when the one given is proven false. [*Feichtmeir v. U.S.*]

424.6 *(1-18-80)* 9781
Corroboration of Extra-Judicial Admissions

(1) During the course of many income tax investigations involving the net worth method of proof, the taxpayer will make admissions which the Government will use in evidence against him/her during trial of the case. Admissions may relate to all facets of a case, although in many instances they pertain to the starting point, items of living expenses, source of income, and willfulness.

(2) Admissions after the commission of the crime must be corroborated, if they embrace an element vital to the Government case. [*Daniel Smith v. U.S.*]

(3) The degree and types of corroboration, along with other aspects of the subject of admissions, are discussed in 345.

424.7 *(1-18-80)* 9781
Investigation of Leads

When a taxpayer offers leads or information during a net worth investigation which, if true, would establish his/her innocence, the special agent must investigate the leads if they are reasonably susceptible of being checked. [*Holland v. U.S.*] This also applies if a taxpayer offers leads or information after completion of an investigation, but within a sufficient time before trial. [*U.S. v. Vardine*] If the Government fails during the trial of the case to show an investigation into the validity of the data furnished, the trial judge may consider the information as true and the Government's case insufficient to go to the jury. Most leads refer to cash hoards, gifts, inheritances, and loans. These are well known to the special agent and should be checked during normal routine of the investigation. The courts have held that the Government does not have to investigate leads which are not within the category of reasonable verification. [*Mighell v. U.S.; Louis Smith v. U.S.; U.S. v. Bryan Ford*] This is a question of judgment and in the final analysis, is always a matter for the court to determine.

424.8 *(1-18-80)* 9781
Summaries Prepared by Government Agents

(1) During a trial of an income tax case involving use of the net worth method of proving taxable income there may be admitted in evidence certain exhibits variously referred to as schedules or summaries. Strictly speaking these exhibits are not evidence, but are admitted as summaries of other evidence in the case only for the assistance and convenience of the jury in considering the evidence which they purport to summarize. The admissibility and use of summaries are discussed in 353.

(2) The summary which the special agent should become most familiar with is the one showing the computation of taxable income, an example of which is set forth in Exhibit 400-1.

(3) During trials the net worth computation also has been shown by other means, such as blackboards and charts.

(4) Perhaps the most difficult phase of preparing a net worth statement or summary for use in a criminal case is in making adjustments to the net worth increases and decreases for the nondeductible and nontaxable items. The most frequently encountered adjustments involving individual taxpayers and the way of handling them are as follows:

(a) Add to net worth increases or decreases:

1 Personal living expenses. (See 424.8:(6)(b).)

2 Federal income tax payments.

3 Nondeductible portion of capital loss.

4 Losses on sale of personal assets.

5 Gifts made.

6 Life insurance premiums.

(b) Deduct from net worth increases or decreases:

1 50% of the excess of net long-term capital gain over net short-term capital loss. [If a capital loss carryover is involved, the amount allowed in determining capital gain or loss must be deducted in the net worth computation.]

2 Gifts received.

3 Inheritances.

4 Nontaxable pensions.

5 Veteran's benefits.

6 Dividend exclusions.

7 Tax exempt interest.

8 Proceeds from life insurance.

9 Errors in taxpayer's records (in his favor). [This adjustment relates to honest mathematical and bookkeeping errors found in books and records of the taxpayer which tend to account for part of understated income.]

10 Gains on sale of personal residence (assuming funds are to be invested within the statutory period).

11 Net operating loss carryback and carry-forward. In criminal income tax cases there is judicial authority to ignore net operating loss carrybacks. (See 413.2:(1) and (2).)

12 *Allowed* capital loss carry-over (Item 1).

13 50 percent of net long-term capital gain when there is both a net long-term capital gain and a net short-term capital gain (Item 1).

14 Income tax refunds.

(c) No adjustment is necessary to net worth increase or decrease for:

1 Net short-term capital gain (Item 1).

2 Deductible portion of net short-term capital loss (Item 1).

3 Deductible portion of net short-term capital loss.

4 Excess of net short-term capital gain over net long-term capital loss (Item 1).

(5) The net worth statement may reflect taxable income by whichever method of account-

ing (cash, accrual, etc.) is appropriate. Reflecting a certain accounting method in the net worth computation is accomplished by including certain accounts in the net worth statement and omitting others. For instance, where it is desired to compute income of a physician on the cash basis, patient accounts receivable and business accounts payable at the beginning and end of each year would be omitted. If the accrual method were used, these accounts would be included in the net worth computation.

(6) In preparing a net worth statement or summary for use in a criminal case, the special agent should see that:

(a) It follows the taxpayer's method of accounting. In Scanlon v. United States, the defendant, who reported his income on the cash basis, contended that the Government's proof of net worth did not include the liabilities of his enterprise. The appeals court held that it was proper to exclude accounts payable (and accounts receivable) since to include them would not accurately reflect defendant's income.

(b) The cost of assets and actual amounts of liabilities are used. The value (such as market, reproduction, and the like) of these two items is not considered. Normally, unless the taxpayer agrees to the estimated amount, estimated nondeductible expenditures are eliminated from the net worth computation, although in some cases it has appeared proper to include some minimum estimated living expense figures.

(c) Good accounting principles are followed. For example, bank balances should be adjusted (reconciled) for outstanding checks and cash (deposits) in transit.

(d) Technical adjustments that increase income have been eliminated (for example, unintentional errors or omissions relating to capitalized expenses, depreciation, revaluation of the basis of property, and changing inventory basis; or doubtful items such as unidentifiable commingled funds).

424.9 *(1-18-80)* 9781

Common Defenses in Net Worth Cases

(1) *Lack of Willfulness*—Defense counsel usually contends that there is no evidence of willfulness. This contention may be overcome by evidence outlined in 41(11).

(2) *Cash on hand.*

(a) To support this allegation, the taxpayer usually alleges that he/she had a large amount of cash on hand which the Government has not considered in the beginning net worth. The taxpayer also may allege that cash balances are wrong for years subsequent to the base year. In all cases where the net worth method is the primary method of proving income, the special agent should anticipate this defense and attempt to get evidence to negate it. *Admissions of the taxpayer are most effective to pin down the cash amount, and should be obtained at the initial interview or early in the investigation.* The line of questioning should be directed toward developing:

1 The amount of cash on hand (undeposited currency and coin) at the starting point and at the end of each prosecution year.

2 The amount of cash on hand at the date of the interview. (This data is sometimes useful in computing cash on hand for earlier years.)

3 The source of cash referred to in 1 and 2 above.

4 Where the cash was kept.

5 Who knew about the cash.

6 Whether anyone ever counted it.

7 When and on what was any cash spent.

8 Whether any record is available with respect to the alleged cash on hand.

9 The denominations of the cash on hand.

(b) In most cases the spouse should also be questioned about cash on hand as well as other matters. In order to avoid any misunderstanding by the taxpayer, it is suggested that the meaning of cash on hand be explained prior to discussing the matter. The taxpayer (and spouse) also should be questioned regarding financial history from the time he/she was first gainfully employed—employers, salary, etc. This information will serve in many cases to check the accuracy of the taxpayer's statements about cash on hand.

(c) In addition to admissions, evidence used to establish the starting point will most often be sufficient to refute the defense of cash on hand.

(3) *Failure to Adjust for Nontaxable Income*—The usual sources of nontaxable income claimed by the taxpayer are gifts, loans, and inheritances. Negating evidence of the type described in 424.5 will most often be sufficient to overcome these claims.

(4) *Inventories Overstated*—In some net worth cases the Government has relied upon inventory figures shown by the taxpayer's returns as prima facie evidence to establish the values of this asset in the net worth computation. In some of those cases it was alleged that the taxpayer, either through ignorance or for other reasons reported inventory at retail value instead of at cost or some other value. (In a net worth computation where the inventory used exceeds cost and is larger at the end of the prosecution period than the beginning, income will be overstated.) To resolve this, the investigating officers should try to corroborate the inventory figures shown on the taxpayer's returns by admissions of the taxpayer, statements of employees who took the inventory, copies of inventory records, etc.

(5) *Holding Funds or Other Assets as Nominee*—In certain cases the taxpayer has falsely claimed that he/she was holding, as nominee of some individual, funds or other assets which the Government had included in the net worth computation of income. Interviewing the taxpayer about this matter in the early stages of the investigation is one suggested solution.

(6) *Net Operating Loss Carry-forward*—This defense is usually predicated on a net worth computation of taxable income made by the taxpayer's accountant for years prior to the starting point which will show an operating loss. Defense strategy is to carry the loss forward to the prosecution years and reduce the alleged tax deficiency as much as possible. The key to resolving this is to make a net worth determination of income for several years prior to the prosecution period and then on the basis of this computation either:

(a) Allow the carry-forward loss or

(b) Show the incorrectness of the accountants' determination.

(7) *False Loans*—The objective of this defense is to reduce taxable income by claiming nonexistent loans, usually from friends or relatives of the taxpayer. Often this defense may be overcome by showing that the alleged lender was financially unable to lend the amount claimed. *The matter of loans should always be covered during the initial interview with the taxpayer.*

(8) *Jointly Held Assets of the Taxpayer and Spouse*—In some cases the taxpayer and spouse may report income on separate returns, but assets they acquired are held in joint title. If the jointly held assets are included in the net worth computation, the claim may be made that they were acquired with income of the spouse. Usually this defense can be overcome by tracing the invested funds to the taxpayer and by showing the disposition of the spouse's income. Cases may be encountered where funds of the taxpayer and spouse are so intermingled that it is not possible to trace the invested or applied funds to either party. In such cases the net worth computation may be made by including assets, liabilities, and other pertinent items of both and deducting the taxable income of the spouse to arrive at the taxable income of the one to be charged.

425 *(1-18-80)* 9781
Expenditures Method of Proving Income

425.1 *(1-18-80)* 9781
Introduction

(1) The expenditures method is, in theory, closely related to, if not identical with, the net worth method of proving income. The method is based on the theory that if the taxpayer's expenditures during a given year exceed reported income, and the source of such expenditures is unexplained, it may be inferred that such expenditures represent unreported income. One court noted the similarity of the net worth and the expenditures methods by the following statement:

> "... The two computations are merely accounting variations of the same basic method, the expenditure theory being an outgrowth of the net worth method. ..." [*McFee v. U.S.*]

(2) The similarity is further indicated by the fact that the same items or accounts used in determining taxable income by the net worth method are also considered when the expenditures method is employed.

425.2 *(1-18-80)* 9781
Authority for Using Expenditures Method

Like the net worth method, there is no statutory provision expressly authorizing use of the expenditures method by the Commissioner. There are, however, many cases in which the courts have approved the use of this method. [*U.S. v. Wm. R. Johnson* is the leading expenditures method case.]

425.3 *(1-18-80)* 9781
When and How Expenditures Method Used

(1) The statements made in discussing the net worth method with regard to when and how that method is used are equally applicable to the expenditures method. In cases where the taxpayer has several assets (and liabilities) whose cost bases remain the same throughout the prosecution period, the expenditures method may be preferred over the net worth method because a more brief presentation can be made of the computation of taxable income. This is true because assets and liabilities which do not change during the prosecution period may be omitted from the expenditures statement. The expenditures method probably is used most often in cases where the taxpayer spends income on lavish living and has little, if any, net worth.

(2) In an expenditures case it is always desirable and usually necessary to prepare a complete net worth statement which may be required to rebut a defense that the funds used came from the conversion of some asset not considered in the expenditures computation. With rare exceptions, the Department of Justice prefers the net worth method. Therefore in submitting an expenditures case the special agent should consider the desirability of also including in the report proof of taxable income by the net worth method. If both methods are shown, the trial attorney can make the final decision as to which will be the best method to present the case.

425.4 *(1-18-80)* 9781
Establishing the Starting Point

In employing either the expenditures method or the net worth method, the Government must determine with reasonable certainty the taxpayer's beginning net worth. [*McFee v. U.S.*] The approach to this matter is the same irrespective of which method is used. For additional information see 424.4, which relates to establishing the starting point in net worth cases.

425.5 *(1-18-80)* 9781
Taxable Source of Income—Corroboration of Extra-Judicial Admissions—Investigation of Leads

Text 424.5, 424.6, and 424.7 relating to net worth are applicable to these three topics.

425.6 *(1-18-80)* 9781
Expenditures Summaries Prepared by Government Agents

(1) Exhibit 400-2 is an expenditures statement which may be used to summarize the evidence relating to the computation of taxable income.

(2) An approach which has been found helpful in the preparation of an expenditures statement is as follows:

(a) First, prepare a net worth statement.

(b) Next, determine the amount of increase or decrease in each asset and liability appearing on the net worth statement in each taxable year. For instance, if the beginning and ending bank balances for a taxable year were $4,500 and $150, respectively, it would be determined that this asset has decreased by $4,350. The amounts so determined and the amounts appearing as adjustments to net worth increases or decreases are then posted to the expenditures statement.

(3) For guidance in posting to the appropriate section of the aforementioned statement, the following information is offered:

(a) Money spent or applied on nondeductible items:

1 Increase in assets.

2 Decrease in liabilities.

3 Nondeductible items (living expenses, income tax payments, and the like).

(b) Nontaxable sources:

1 Decrease in assets.

2 Increase in liabilities.

3 Nontaxable items (gifts, inheritances, and the like received by taxpayer).

425.7 *(1-18-80)* 9781
Defenses in Expenditures Method Cases

Defenses discussed in 424.9 regarding the net worth method of determining income are equally applicable to the expenditures method.

426 *(1-18-80)* 9781
Bank Deposits Method of Proving Income

426.1 *(1-18-80)* 9781
Formula For Bank Deposits Method

426.11 *(1-18-80)* 9781
Introduction

The bank deposits method is another means of proving income by indirect or circumstantial evidence. By this method, taxable income is proved through analysis of deposits in all bank accounts; canceled checks; and currency transactions of the taxpayer. Very often it will be found that the taxpayer has made cash payments from currency receipts not deposited. Such cash receipts or cash expenditures must be taken into account in computing additional gross income. If the taxpayer reported income on the accrual basis, adjustments should be made in the bank deposits method to reflect accrued income and expenses. The usual formula for determining taxable income by the bank deposits method of a taxpayer, whose only source of income is from a business operation, is as follows:

Line No.	
1. Total deposits	$ ______
2. Add: Payments made in cash	$ ______
3. Subtotal	$ ______
4. Less: Nonincome deposits and items	$ ______
5. Total receipts	$ ______
6. Less: Business expenses and costs	$ ______
7. Net income from business	$ ______
8. Less: Deductions and exemptions	$ ______
9. Taxable Income	$ ______

426.12 *(1-18-80)* 9781
Total Deposits

(1) Total deposits of a taxpayer (line 1, formula, text 426.11) consist of not only amounts deposited to all bank accounts maintained or controlled by him/her, but also deposits made to accounts in savings and loan companies, investment trusts, brokerage houses, etc. Since some taxpayers have bank accounts in fictitious names or under special titles such as "Special Account No. 1," "Trustee Account," "Trading Account," etc., the special agent should inquire about this during the investigation. If a taxpayer lists checks on a deposit and deducts therefrom an amount to be paid to him/her in cash, only the net amount of the deposit should be used in computing total deposits.

(2) The deposits involved in the Gleckman case, one of the leading bank deposits cases, were for the most part derived from wholly unidentified sources. The usual case is one in which a number of specific omitted sales are traced to the bank accounts, but other deposits remain unidentified. The fact that some suppressed sales are traced to the bank accounts obviously strengthens the Government's case immeasurably and lends credence to the allegation that the unidentified deposits also represent omitted income.

426.13 *(1-18-80)* 9781
Payments Made in Cash

All provable payments made in cash (line 2, formula, text 426.11), including business expenses, personal expenses, investments, etc., should be added to total bank deposits. Since adjustments will be made in the section below for nonincome deposits and items, it is immaterial whether the cash used was derived from a taxable or nontaxable source.

426.14 *(1-18-80)* 9781
Nonincome Deposits and Items

Generally all nontaxable income received by a taxpayer will be deducted as a nonincome deposit or item in the bank deposit computation. Examples of nonincome deposits and items are proceeds of loans, redeposits, gifts, and inheritances. (For other examples see Exhibits 400-3 and 400-5.) Failure to eliminate any nonincome deposit or item would result in an overstatement of income and might be damaging to a criminal case.

426.15 *(1-18-80)* 9781
Business Expenses and Costs

(1) All business expenses and costs which are found to be deductible must be allowed, whether paid by check or in cash (line 6, formula, text 426.11). Where an analysis of the checks or other evidence of the disbursements leaves some doubt about the deductibility of some of the disbursements, it is preferable for the prosecution case to allow all except those items definitely provable as being nondeductible, such as personal expenses, investments, and gifts. Whether or not canceled checks are available for analysis and classification, every effort should be made to arrive at all items constituting allowable expense that might have been

paid from the bank accounts, or from undeposited cash. The allowable depreciation on all known depreciable assets must be deducted as in any other type of case.

(2) Frequently it will be realized that the taxpayer must have paid out funds for expenses obviously incurred, but for which no checks or evidences of specific cash disbursements have been found. In such instances the amount claimed therefore by the taxpayer (or if not claimed, a reasonable amount) should be allowed in line 6 (formula, text 426.11), and a corresponding amount of additional income should be added in line 2.

426.16 *(1-18-80)* 9781
Deductions and Exemptions

All allowable personal deductions, itemized or standard, and exemptions (line 8, formula, text 426.11) must be deducted from net business income in order to arrive at taxable income.

426.2 *(1-18-80)* 9781
Use of Bank Deposits Method

Bank deposits have been a factor in the determination of the additional taxable income involved in many criminal tax cases and may be used if no books or records of the taxpayer are available; if the taxpayer invokes constitutional privilege and will not allow an examination of books and records; if the taxpayer's records are not complete and do not adequately reflect his/her correct taxable income; or if the taxpayer uses the bank deposits method in preparing his/her tax return. However, the courts have held that there is no necessity to disprove the accuracy of the taxpayer's books and records as a prerequisite to the use of the bank deposits method. [*Bostwick v. U.S.; Canton v. U.S.*].

426.3 *(1-18-80)* 9781
Authority For Bank Deposits Method

There is no statutory provision defining the bank deposits method of proving income and specifically authorizing its use by the Commissioner. There are numerous reported criminal cases [*Gleckman v. U.S.; Stinnett v. U.S.; U.S. v. Venuto; Kirsch v. U.S.; Buttermore v. U.S. Oliver v. U.S.; Capone v. U.S.*] in which bank deposits have been a factor in the determination of the additional taxable income involved.

426.4 *(1-18-80)* 9781
Proof of Taxable Income in Bank Deposits Case

(1) The bank deposits theory assumes that under certain circumstances proof of deposits is substantial evidence of taxable receipts. The circumstances are the existence of a business or calling of a lucrative nature and proof that during the prosecution years the taxpayer made periodic deposits to accounts in his/her own name or accounts over which he/she exercised dominion and control. The Government must establish that the deposits reflect *income* which is *current*. This may be accomplished by showing that the taxpayer was engaged in an income-producing business, that he/she made periodic deposits to his/her bank account, that the deposits have been analyzed to eliminate nonincome items such as loans or gifts, and income items which may be duplications of amounts actually accounted for and reported or, amounts which have been earned in prior years. The analysis may indicate that certain withdrawals from the bank account represent business expenditures. If these were not claimed by the taxpayer as deductions, they will nevertheless be allowed for prosecution purposes.

(2) In *Gleckman v. U.S.*, the Government proved that in each of the indictment years, 1929 and 1930, the taxpayer had gross deposits (minus certain nontaxable items) exceeding $90,000. There was evidence that he was engaged in illegal liquor transactions. There was also testimony that in each of the indictment years the taxpayer had expended substantial amounts of money. The taxpayer claimed that his bank deposit slips were erroneously admitted in evidence because the Government did not prove that they reflected specific amounts of taxable income. Hence, it was argued, it was improper for the Government's expert witnesses to testify that there was additional tax owing, based on consideration of the deposits as income. The Court of Appeals overruled this contention, employing the now classic language:

> ". . . if it be shown that a man has a business or calling of a lucrative nature and is constantly, day by day and month by month, receiving moneys and depositing them to his account and checking against them for his own uses, there is most potent testimony that he has income, and, if the amount exceeds exemptions and deductions, that the income is taxable. . . .
>
> "The bank deposits and large items of receipts by Mr. Gleckman do not, therefore, stand entirely alone as the sole proof of the existence of a tax due from him, but they are identified with business carried on by him and so, are sufficiently shown to be of a taxable nature."

(3) By way of contrast, occasional or irregular deposits are not necessarily ruled out; they may, if properly analyzed, be considered as income. Also, bank deposits proof alone will suffice to support a conviction, and it is not a mere form of corroboration for other kinds of evidence.

(4) In *Stinnett v. U.S.*, the defendant argued that under the *Gleckman* case the bank deposits theory required not only a showing of periodic bank deposits but some further corroboration (in Gleckman there was a corroborative net worth analysis). The Government, however, contended that the net worth proof in Gleckman did not add to or detract from the bank deposits rule and that proof of periodic bank deposits and of an income producing business alone warranted a finding that the deposits reflected current business receipts. The Stinnett opinion refers to the existence of corroborative evidence in the record (Stinnett's purchase of bonds and cashier's checks in amounts exceeding reported net income for certain years). Although there was corroboration, the court stated that "a gross discrepancy between bank deposits and gross receipts without any adequate explanation by the taxpayer is . . . sufficient in itself to take the case to the jury. . . ." This would appear to indicate that corroboration of bank deposits proof is not a legal requirement in a tax evasion prosecution.

(5) In *U.S. v. Venuto*, there was evidence that the defendant had regularly and currently deposited in four Philadelphia banks the receipts of his slaughterhouse, meat store, and rentals, and that expenses were paid by checks drawn on the accounts. Government agents testified that they had reconstructed the defendant's income by analyzing his bank accounts and disbursements. They determined that the bank deposits constituted business receipts, except for some $18,000 of nonincome items for the period from 1942 through 1945. For each year the nonincome items were deducted from the respective annual deposits. The balance was considered gross business receipts from which the actual purchases (stipulated by defendant) were deducted. The defendant was given full credit for the expense deductions claimed on his returns. The defendant testified that his sole source of income was from the meat businesses and rental of properties and that all receipts from those enterprises went into the bank accounts. A new trial was ordered because the defendant had been deprived at trial of his constitutional right to consult with counsel. The Third Circuit, however, made it clear that it considered the bank deposits evidence legally sufficient:

> "Suffice it to say that this record contains evidence from which a jury could conclude beyond a reasonable doubt that during the prosecution years defendant had businesses of a lucrative nature, that he made periodic deposits in, and withdrawals from, bank accounts, that the difference between such deposits and withdrawals reflected current income, and that there was a substantial understatement in reporting income. Such proof meets the requirement of the so-called bank deposit method of reconstructing a taxpayer's income picture, and would be legally sufficient to support a verdict finding that there was a substantial tax deficiency for each of the prosecution years, which defendant knowingly and willfully attempted to defeat and evade."

426.5 *(1-18-80)* 9781

Defenses in Bank Deposits Case

(1) The chief defense contentions in bank deposits cases (other than lack of criminal intent) are: that the spasmodic nature or unconventional amounts of the deposits indicate that prior accumulated funds, not current receipts, are involved; that the deposits reflect, in whole or in substantial part, nonincome items, income items attributable to other years, or duplication of current income items already accounted for by the taxpayer.

(2) In *Kirsch v. U.S.*, a conviction based chiefly on bank deposits evidence was reversed because the Government's own testimony showed that the deposits could not be identified as income. The court quoted the *Gleckman* case, "that the bare fact standing alone, that a man has deposited a sum of money in a bank would not prove that he owed income tax on the amount." The assumption of the Government's expert witness that the deposits in this case represented income was:

> ". . . not only without evidentiary support even from permissible inference from proven facts, but was definitely disproved by the Government's own evidence. It is one thing for . . . (the Government's witness) to say in effect, as was done in the Gleckman case, that he had exercised all of the means he reasonably could to determine how much of a bank account was income, had eliminated all that he could determine was not income, and was therefore assuming for the purpose of calculating taxes due that the remainder was income, and quite another and different thing to say in effect, as was done in this case—My evidence shows that all of these deposits were not income, but I do not know how much was not, I have made no effort to find out. So I am assuming that all are income and am casting the burden on the defendant to show, if he can, how much is not, or suffer the consequences. The latter procedure cannot be approved."

(3) In *Buttermore v. U.S.*, the defendant asserted that the Government agents had failed to make reasonable determination concerning the sources of certain unidentified deposits and that a reasonable investigation of the facts would have disclosed that many of the deposits did not constitute taxable income. The defendant relied upon the *Kirsch* decision but the court held that what constitutes a reasonable effort to establish the facts, and what facts and circumstances will constitute a proper foundation for an assumption that deposits represent income, must be left to a considerable extent to the discretion of the trial court.

(4) The proof concerning what cash a taxpayer had on hand at the beginning of the taxable year in question is relevant to the bank deposits method of proof of income. If the deposits or expenditures came from funds accumulated in prior years, obviously they do not represent current income. However, if all the requirements set forth in text 426.4:(1) are met, the lack of proof of the amount of cash on hand would not be fatal to the case.

426.6 *(1-18-80)* 9781
Schedules and Summaries in Bank Deposits Case

(1) The schedules and summaries in Exhibits 400-3 through 400-6 are illustrative of those which may be submitted during trials where the bank deposits method of proving income is used. Exhibit 400-3 shows the computation of taxable income of John and Mary Roe. The computation of this same income by the net worth method was previously shown in Exhibit 400-1. Comparison and study of these two schedules will be beneficial since many times in criminal tax cases taxable income will be evidenced before the court by two methods of proof, one tending to corroborate the other.

(2) Exhibit 400-4 shows a computation which may be used to determine the amount of currency disbursements to be added to total deposits. (See line 2, payments made in cash, 426.11.)

(3) Exhibit 400-5 is a summary analysis of disbursements made by check and by currency. This schedule should be studied together with the net worth statement and the bank deposits schedule.

(4) The analysis of deposits is the vital part of a bank deposits case and too much importance cannot be placed upon its accuracy. Exhibit 400-6 is illustrative of a schedule which may be used to show the results of this analysis.

427 *(1-18-80)* 9781
Other Methods

427.1 *(1-18-80)* 9781
Percentage Method

427.11 *(1-18-80)* 9781
Use of Percentage Method

The percentage method is not a prime method of proof and by itself would be of very little value in criminal cases. However, there have been cases in which taxes and penalties based on this kind of circumstantial evidence have been sustained by the tax court. The percentage method is very useful for test checking; for corroborating the results obtained by some other means of proof such as specific item, net worth, expenditures, and bank deposits; and for evaluating allegations from informants regarding unreported profits or income of others.

427.12 *(1-18-80)* 9781
Application of Percentage Method

(1) This method is a computation whereby determinations are made by the use of percentages or ratios considered typical of the business under investigation. By reference to similar businesses or situations, percentage computations are secured to determine sales, cost of sales, gross profit, or even net profit. Likewise, by the use of some known base and the typical percentage applicable, individual items of income or expense may be determined.

(2) These percentages may be externally derived or they may in some instances be internally derived from the taxpayer's accounts for other periods or from an analysis of subsidiary records; however, many percentages may be secured from the examination of the taxpayer's records even though only part of the records are available. Gross profit percentages may be determined by comparing purchase invoices with sales invoices, price lists, and other similar data. Also other years not covered by the investigation or portions of years under investigation may indicate typical percentages applicable to the entire year or years under current investigation.

427.13 *(1-18-80)* 9781
Limitations on Percentage Method

(1) Although the percentage method may be a useful method of determining or verifying income, especially when the books and records are inadequate, the special agent should make sure that the comparisons are made with situations that are similar to those under investigation. Some of the factors to be considered are as follows:

(a) *Type of merchandise handled*—In order that a proper comparison may be made, the businesses must be dealing in the same type of merchandise or service. Comparison of the gross profit of a restaurant with that of a grocery store would be of little value and should not be used.

(b) *Size of operation*—In many instances gross profit, cost of doing business, and net profit percentage on sales will vary according to the size of a business. This is especially true with respect to expense items and the net profit as compared with sales. The percentage of net profit to sales of a large department store might vary considerably from the small independently owned general store.

(c) *Locality*—Mark-ups and costs of operations will normally vary with the size of the city or the location of the businesses in the locality. As an example, a small business in a community of 5,000 may use newspapers as a means of advertising, whereas a business doing the same volume in a city of 500,000 will normally find the cost prohibitive and confine advertising to some other medium.

(d) *Period covered*—Since gross profit ratios and expense ratios will tend to vary year by year with economic conditions, the comparison should normally be made with similar periods covered by the investigation.

(e) *General merchandising policy*—Comparison should not be made between businesses having different merchandising policies. Some businesses may work on large volume with small mark-up, offering the customer little service; others may operate on the reverse policy. In situations of this kind, comparisons should be made only with those businesses having similar merchandising policies.

427.14 *(1-18-80)* 9781
Examples of Percentage Method

(1) The following examples are illustrative of the percentage method of computation. The percentages used are arbitrary and are not necessarily applicable to the businesses mentioned.

(a) Gross Profit on Sales:

Retail sporting goods store:	
Net sales (determined from books or by other means)	$50,000
Gross profit percentage	28.6%
Gross profit as computed	$14,300

(b) Sales on Cost of Sales:

Bar and tavern:	
Cost of liquor	$20,000
Cost of beer	15,000
Cost of food (determined from books or by other means)	5,000
	40,000
Cost of sales—liquor	331/3%
Cost of sales—beer	662/3%
Cost of sales—food	50%
Sale of liquor	$60,000
Sale of beer	22,500
Sale of food	10,000
Total sales as computed	92,500

(c) Net Profit on Sales:

Filling Station:	
Net sales (determined from books or by other means)	$30,000
Net profit percentage	8%
Net profit as computed	$2,400

(d) Miscellaneous Ratios:

Waitress:	
Sales by restaurant	$30,000
Number of waitresses employed	3
Percentage of tips received	10%
Average sales handled by waitress	$10,000
Income from tips as computed	$1,000

427.2 *(1-18-80)* 9781
Unit and Volume Methods

(1) In many instances the determination or verification of gross receipts may be computed by applying price and profit figures to the known or ascertainable quantity of business done by the taxpayer. This method is feasible when the special agent can ascertain the number of units handled by the taxpayer and also when the price or profit charged per unit is known. The number of units sold or quantity of business done by the taxpayer may be determined in certain instances from the taxpayer's books, since the records may be adequate with respect to cost of goods sold or expenses, but inadequate as to sales.

(2) There may be a regulatory body to which the taxpayer reports units of production or service. A funeral director is required to report each burial to the city or town where such burial takes place. A garment manufacturer with union employees buys union labels to be sewed into the garments manufactured. A taxpayer may also be required to report his production and payroll to a trade association allied with the labor union. There are also instances where the royalty paid for leased machinery is based upon the units of production. A piecework system of wages for production workers might also give an accurate measure of units produced.

(3) The use of this method lends itself to those businesses in which only a few types of items are handled or there is little variation in the type of service performed, with the charges made by the taxpayer for the merchandise or

services being relatively the same throughout the taxable period.

(4) The following example is illustrative of the unit and volume method of computation:

Volume of Merchandise (manufacturer):	
Number of machines manufactured	92
Average sales price	$1,100
Computed total sales	$101,200
Sales reported	$93,500
Omitted sales	$7,700

430 *(1-18-80)* 9781
Refund Cases

431 *(1-18-80)* 9781
Introduction

(1) Fraudulent refund cases fall within two distinct major groups, namely—

(a) *Multiple claims for refund,* involving that group of claims made on Federal income tax returns supported by withholding statements (Forms W-2) which are completely fabricated and false. They are filed either by one person individually or by two or more persons in collusion with one another with intent to defraud the Government. There is generally no authenticity whatsoever to the returns and the supporting documents.

(b) *Return preparers (unscrupulous)*—This group of claims involves Federal income tax returns prepared by unscrupulous return preparers who claim excessive deductions and/or exemptions on returns prepared for clients. Their benefit derives either from developing a large clientele through having established a reputation for saving client's money, from exorbitant fees charged on the basis of the large refunds obtained, or both. The clients may or may not have had knowledge of the excessive deductions claimed. On occasion the return preparer has caused the refund check to be mailed to his/her office, and, through having possession of the check, has exacted an exorbitant fee, or has forged the endorsement and negotiated the check without the client's knowledge.

(2) The investigative techniques employed in these two groups of cases are distinctly different. In the multiple claims for refund cases, the investigation is directed toward—

(a) Determining whether the returns and supporting documents are fabricated and fictitious; and

(b) Ascertaining who is responsible for their preparation and filing.

(3) The special agent may be called upon to make a forthwith arrest of the person or persons involved in the violation upon the establishment of "probable cause." Therefore the special agent usually, with authority of the Chief, Criminal Investigation Division, consults closely with the United States attorney's office.

(a) Cases involving arrests by special agents will ordinarily be forwarded direct to the United States Attorney by the Chief.

(b) *Violations of Section 287, Title 18, USC, involving multiple fictitious tax returns claiming fraudulent refunds*—Authorization for direct referral of this type of case relates only to multiple fictitious tax returns. It does not apply to the situation where the taxpayer files multiple income tax returns reporting in each return a part of the income which the taxpayer did in fact receive, claiming fraudulent refund of tax thereon. For example, an individual may receive withholding statements, Forms W-2, from more than one employer during the year, and file an income tax return for each such withholding statement, claiming refunds thereon. Such a case is included in the category of a multiple return case involving offenses other than violations of Section 287, Title 18, USC, and would not be referred directly to the United States Attorney but would be processed through normal channels. Cases in which there is a question as to the proper method of referral should be forwarded to District Counsel for advice.

(4) In the cases involving unscrupulous return preparers, the returns are of authentic origin but are fraudulent because of the excessive deductions and/or exemptions claimed. The investigation of these cases is directed toward determining the responsibility for the overstatement of the deductions and/or exemptions claimed; and toward establishing whether such overstatements were made with corrupt intent.

432 *(1-18-80)* 9781
Investigation of Multiple Claims For Refund

(1) Cases in this group originate in a variety of ways such as:

(a) The service center may forward information indicating that multiple returns have been filed by the same taxpayer.

(b) Returns indicating false claims for refunds may be discovered upon receipt by Collection Division and forwarded to the Chief, Criminal Investigation Division.

(c) A postman may notice numerous Government checks being delivered to certain addresses or observe some individual showing unusual interest in the mail delivered to such addresses.

(d) Someone either in the U.S. Postal Service or in the Internal Revenue may notice an excessive number of mail-forwarding requests.

(e) An audit may disclose no address or taxpayer as listed, a nonexistent employer, or apparent excessive deductions claimed.

(f) A violator may, in the presence of an informant, boast about how much he/she received in refunds.

(g) Through an inspection of the undeliverable Forms 1040A and 1040 mailed for current use or an analysis of the returns currently being filed, a special agent or some other Internal Revenue Service employee may detect a pattern of sameness pervading a group of returns which will lead to the discovery of a fraudulent operation.

(2) The special agent should understand the provisions of Section 287, Title 18, U.S. Code (text 222.(10) and 418.5), and be prepared to coordinate his/her activities in an investigation of an alleged violation thereof with any investigations being conducted by the Secret Service, the U.S. Postal Service, and any other services, departments, or agencies of the Government. It is not unusual for a violator of this section of the law to be involved in violations of other Federal statutes, within the investigative jurisdiction of such other services, departments and agencies. The Secret Service is particularly interested in knowing of a violation of the counterfeiting and forgery statutes (text 334.7). The Postal Service is interested in knowing of any use of the mails to defraud the Federal Government. The assistance of the United States attorney's office may be sought in obtaining an arrest warrant and/or search warrant. Therefore, several services, departments, and agencies may participate in a coordinated surveillance and in locating and apprehending a violator. Local authorities also have been of considerable assistance in this respect.

(3) A violation of Section 287, Title 18, occurs upon the filing of a fabricated Federal income tax return whereon a false representation is made that the tax has been overpaid and there is a claim made for a refund of the overpayment (See 418.5).

(4) Multiple filing may be confined to a single Internal Revenue district or it may extend to many districts. The name used on a fraudulent return may be either an alias, a fictitious name, or a variation of the violator's name. The address usually used is that of a hotel, a motel, a rooming-house, a post office box number, or general delivery. Street numbers have been used on occasion. There is usually attached to the returns a fabricated and false Form W-2 (sometimes handwritten) showing the name of a fictitious employer, a fictitious amount of salary received, and a fictitious amount of tax withheld. The name of the employer shown may or may not be an existent firm or person. If the name is that of an existent firm or person, an out-of-state address is frequently shown. Usually the only income reported on the fictitious return is salary under $5,000 from one employer; Form 1040A is used more often than Form 1040; and, if the violator is acquainted with the Service's prerefund audit procedures, the amount claimed for dependents and/or other deductions will be such as to keep the claimed refund within a certain amount. This is done to eliminate the possibility of detection by a prerefund audit. Early detection of this type of violation enables the Government to intercept promptly the fictitious returns and forestall the issuance and delivery of refund checks to fraudulent claimants. Some of the characteristic features of multiple fraudulent returns which will lead to their detection as fictitious are listed below:

(a) A substantial refund is claimed solely on the basis of the number of exemptions listed. These are questionable as to why the taxpayer did not claim more exemptions on Form W-4 for withholding tax purposes.

(b) An unrealistic amount shown as tax withheld.

(c) Absence of, or unrealistic social security information shown. Unless an exempt occupation, such as Government employment, is involved, a social security number should be shown and the correct amount of social security deduction listed. Social Security numbers should appear 000-00-0000. They always begin with a number 0 to 5 or 7—never begin with a 6, 8, or a 9. Prior to January 1966, the middle two digits had to be odd if the number was under ten (01, 03, 05, 07 or 09) and even for higher numbers (10, 12, 14, etc.). Presently, as each area exhausts their sequence of numbers in the odd and even categories, they will start using the even numbers under ten then the odd numbers above ten. The first three digits of the social security number identify the area of issuance. A list of numbers and their assigned areas of issuance are shown in Exhibit 400-7. The percent and maximum amount withheld should agree with the law for the year involved.

(d) Absence of, or an unrealistic Employer's Identification Number shown on Form W-2. These should always appear 00-0000000 with the first two digits being the code number of the Internal Revenue district. For example, a Tennessee employer's number should ordinarily begin 62- and the following 7 digits should be within the limits of the numbers assigned thus far.

(e) Unusual delivery instructions such as different addresses being shown on Form W-2 and the tax return, a boulevard address for small towns unlikely to use such terms, or taxpayer's use of Post Office Box, General Delivery, and mail forwarding services as a mailing address.

(f) Similarity of information, format, or writing on several returns. Frequently, cases involving numerous returns being filed by one person can be detected by his/her continued use of similar names as to taxpayers, employers, exemptions, and types of deductions claimed; or similarity in the arrangement of the information and the printing, handwriting or typewriting appearing on the returns.

(g) Undeliverable refund checks resulting from violator's miscalculations of intentional design. In instances where the violator plans to receive the refund check at an address other than the one listed on the return, the scheme is usually to file a change of address with the Postal Service prior to delivery of the check, or recover the check after it has been returned to the Internal Revenue Service by providing forwarding instructions. Undeliverable refund checks frequently include those the violator failed to intercept because of improper timing of change of address instructions to the postal authorities or the failure of postal employees to observe such instructions. Those refund checks retrieved by the violator after they have been returned to the Internal Revenue Service leave a trail of forwarding instructions and a record of the wrong address initially listed.

(5) The investigation is not ended upon the detection of the fraudulent filing. It will be the responsibility of a special agent to identify and locate the violators without causing their flight and sacrificing the case. The agent should know the techniques of surveillance (see 381), since he/she probably will have to conduct a surveillance in an effort to identify and locate the violators. Since it may also become his/her duty to make an arrest, or a search, or file a complaint, the agent should understand the meaning of "Probable Cause" and be acquainted with Handbook text 390, 383.2, and 721 relating to arrests, searches, and complaints, respectively.

(6) The utilization of the Department of the Treasury and other crime laboratories may be necessary in handwriting and typewriting comparisons. The National Fraudulent Check and Anonymous Letter files maintained by the FBI are particularly useful in this connection. The special agent should be acquainted with the procedure prescribed in 356.7. The disposition and attitude of the United States attorney's office toward the prosecution of the case in the event the special agent makes the arrest should also be ascertained.

(7) For the purpose of identifying the violators, their handwriting, and their typewriting sufficiently to tie them in with returns filed, the special agent should:

(a) Obtain copies of any refund check which may have been cashed; have any necessary handwriting analyses made of the endorsements; and follow through with appropriate inquiries. Such inquiries will probably lead to the identification of the negotiator of the checks by disclosing the name of the person or firm who either cashed or deposited them.

(b) Examine all records that may be in the files of the various post offices where the boxes are rented and obtain copies of any papers or documents on which a specimen of the renter's handwriting appears. Inquire into the references given by the renter upon applying for a box and determine in the case of fake references how the renter arranged to intercept and reply to the postal authorities' inquiry. The special agent should also obtain any available printed and typewritten specimens, together with the handwriting specimens, and have an expert compare them with any handwriting, printing, and typewriting on the tax returns filed, endorsements on refund checks and forwarding instructions, to determine whether they are the same.

(c) Prior and subsequent years' returns should be requisitioned.

(8) The special agent will ascertain if there are any existent employers whose names correspond with those shown on Forms W-2 and tax returns filed. If there are, determine whether they have, or have had, on their payrolls persons of the names shown on the returns, and continue with any pertinent inquiries suggested by the facts disclosed. The records of the State Unemployment Compensation office, which records FUTA tax information on employers and their insured employees, are particularly useful in quickly determining if there is in existence in the particular state, such an employer, employee, or social security number as listed. This state office can usually supply by telephone all information shown on the application for the social security number involved.

(9) The special agent may ask the postmaster or postal inspector for a description of the renter of each box involved and, with the postmaster's knowledge and cooperation, arrange a surveillance of the box.

(10) The special agent should also decide in advance whether he/she should make a forthwith arrest of the person opening the box and picking up the check, or should delay the arrest and shadow this person in an effort to determine what disposition will be made of the check. This decision will hinge largely on what evidence the agent has that the person opening the box is actually the violator, and what evidence the agent has at that time to establish probable cause. These are details which the agent should work out in advance in collaboration with the Chief, Criminal Investigation Division or immediate supervisor with the advice of the United States attorney's office. The agent should be sure of his/her ground before attempting to effect an arrest. Upon making the arrest, this agent will make such searches of the person, automobile, and residence as are lawful (383) with the object of seizing any equipment and records used in the commission of the violation. The prisoners should be escorted without unnecessary delay before the nearest United States Magistrate or other nearby officer empowered to commit Federal prisoners (383.(10)). The special agent will also interview the person or persons arrested. A stenographic transcript of their statements is desirable but not always practicable to obtain. If stenographic services cannot be used, the special agent should make a contemporaneous memorandum of any admissions or statements made by the suspect, or if this is not practicable, a memorandum should be made as soon after the interview as possible.

(11) See IRM 9625 for information regarding direct referral of multiple filer cases.

433 *(1-18-80)* 9781
Investigation of Multiple Fraudulent Returns Prepared by Unscrupulous Return Preparers

(1) Cases in this group originate from a variety of sources, such as:

(a) Letters of complaint from the public and information from informants concerning returns preparers.

(b) Complaints from ethical practitioners and professional societies.

(c) Screening of returns by service center personnel.

(d) Identification of suspect preparers by Criminal Investigation Division and other IRS personnel.

(2) The returns in this group of cases are usually of authentic origin but are fraudulent because of overstated deductions and/or exemptions claimed. Some of the most flagrant violations have been committed by unscrupulous return preparers who have an illiterate, trusting clientele. Occasionally it has been established that a preparer has conspired with the taxpayer to file a false and fraudulent return. IRC 7206(2) (see 221.7:(2) and 418.2) is usually used in the prosecution of the preparer in the former cases; and either this section or Section 371, Title 18, is used in the latter type of case, although these are not necessarily the only statutes that may be invoked in the prosecution of these cases. Section 371, Title 18, is the conspiracy state and the techniques of investigation of conspiracy cases are set forth in text 41(10).

(3) Multiple refund cases involving unscrupulous preparers are developed by patient and painstaking interviews of a representative number of the clientele to ascertain who is responsible for the fraudulent returns. The facts can often be obtained more expeditiously and with less alarm by a preliminary informal interview of each client whose return is under investigation, than by an immediate formal interview. If the preliminary interview discloses information or records which are material to the establishment of the facts of the case, the client's testimony can be obtained later, under oath. It is some-

times advisable to have a cooperating officer accompany the special agent during interviews to complete the tax examination of the witnesses' affairs, including the execution of agreement forms and collection of additional tax due. In an effort to quickly evaluate allegations, consideration should be given to deployment of a special agent in an undercover status. The investigator, possessing the necessary employment papers, such as a fictitious Form W-2, can frequently have a return prepared and learn the practitioner's modus operandi as well as obtain admissible evidence. A special agent was successfully used in an undercover role during which the preparer listed fictitious exemptions and deductions on a return prepared for the agent. [*U.S. v. Blount.*] On the other hand, records seized during a search incident to an arrest, based on a complaint that an accountant overstated deductions on a return prepared for an undercover agent, were ordered returned and suppressed as evidence. The court held that a valid search was limited to the means by which the accountant prepared the return for the agent and any wide ranging search for unconnected material or seizure of such material was unreasonable. [*U.S. v. Cohen.*]

(4) The investigation should be directed toward establishing whether the fraud on the return is attributable to the preparer, the client, or both. An interview should therefore be designed to ascertain:

(a) The name of the person who recommended the preparer and the identity of others known to have used his/her services, thus expanding the area of investigation. It is advisable to obtain prior years' returns filed by the client to ensure that all those prepared by the particular preparer are found, and more importantly, for comparison purposes where the prior year return was prepared by someone else;

(b) What information and records the client furnished the preparer for use in the preparation of the return;

(c) Any memorandum the preparer may have made of information furnished, together with a description of the memorandum;

(d) Any discussion between the preparer and client regarding the amount of deductions and exemptions to be claimed;

(e) Any suggestions the preparer made that more deductions should be claimed, with a full explanation;

(f) Whether each deduction claimed is in the same amount that was furnished the preparer by the client. Obtain any relevant documents concerning amount claimed, and also a statement from the client regarding the amounts he/she was entitled to deduct. If the amount claimed is greater than that which the client is able to support or than that which was furnished the preparer, obtain the client's explanation;

(g) Whether client knew that an excessive amount had been claimed and if so, why he/she permitted it; and if he/she did not know, how it escaped him/her.

(h) The circumstances of the client's signing the return, and whether it was affixed to the return before or after the return was completed. If the client signed the return in blank, why? If the return was completed before the client affixed a signature to it, what sort of review did the client make of the contents and how could the excessive deductions have escaped his/her notice?

(i) Whether the client knew that a refund was claimed;

(j) How the client justified in his/her own mind that he/she had a refund coming in the light of his/her income and allowable deductions;

(k) The client's literacy;

(l) The amount of the preparer's fee and whether the amount charged was based on the amount of refund obtained;

(m) Where the refund check was to be mailed. If to the preparer's address, why;

(n) Whether the client cashed the refund check;

(o) Obtain an explanation of the circumstances of the cashing. Find out whether it was cashed by the preparer, whether he/she extracted his/her fee from the proceeds, and whether the possession of the check was used as a means of coercing the payment of an exorbitant fee;

(p) Whether the preparer endorsed the client's name to the check. If so, what authorization had the client given the preparer to do so.

(5) The questions listed above are given merely as a suggested outline for use in an interview of this nature. Other pertinent questions may arise as the interview proceeds. The preparer should be similarly interviewed if he/she will submit voluntarily to such an interview. If possible, obtain from the preparer copies of:

(a) Any memorandums that he/she or his/her employees may have made at the time of interviews with the clients;

(b) Any memorandums, documents, and data furnished the preparer by the client for use in preparing his/her return;

(c) Any lists of fees charged, list of clients, retained copies of returns filed, or other pertinent material that the preparer may have in his/her files.

(6) The preparer's employees should be interviewed to establish the procedure followed in the preparation of a return for a client from the time the client entered the preparer's office until the completion, signing, and filing of the return. They should be interviewed further as indicated by the outline or questions set forth above for use in interviewing clients to ascertain what other pertinent information they may have.

(7) In investigating multiple fraudulent returns prepared by unscrupulous returns preparers, those pattern return cases most susceptible to development for successful criminal prosecution of a practitioner are the cases involving returns on which the entire deductions or excesses claimed are completely without basis; a representative number of the clientele testify that the deductions were taken entirely without their knowledge; and the surrounding conditions, circumstances and conduct of the practitioner tend to corroborate their testimony. The special agent should be careful not to make an issue for criminal prosecution of those deductions the legitimacy of which might be considered arguable or debatable. Furthermore, he/she should keep in mind that the clients may be as culpable as the practitioner since they also stood to benefit. Therefore, the special agent in his/her investigation should be concerned with recognizing and resolving these issues as much as possible.

(8) There is another group of cases in which the unscrupulous preparer accepts the tax payment from the client when preparing his/her tax return, but does not file the return or pay the tax. In these cases, the preparer cannot be charged with violation of IRC 7203; however, IRC 7201 has been tried in several instances. In one case tried under IRC 7201, [*U.S. v. Mesheski.*] the court held that such acts involve only the crime of embezzlement under state law, and do not come within the definition of attempt to evade or defeat tax. Other courts have disagreed with that conclusion, and found that the defendant intended to cheat not only his/her clients by embezzling their money but also the Government by evading the clients' taxes. [*U.S. v. Charles L. O. Edwards.*]

440 *(1–18–80)* 9781
Employee Plans/Exempt Organizations (EP/EO) Cases

441 *(1–18–80)* 9781
Introduction

(1) The Tax Reform Act of 1969, and the Employee Retirement Income Security Act (ERISA) of 1974, reflect national concern that abuses or fraudulent practices and self dealings in the employee plans and exempt organizations areas are jeopardizing both employee pensions and the collection of tax revenues. The large amounts of money involved in employee plan trust funds and tax exempt organizations provide both a temptation and an opportunity for fraud.

(2) The traditional criminal and civil provisions of the Internal Revenue Code will apply to the violations in the Employee Plan and Exempt Organization area. The only significant difference may be that instead of a tax deficiency, the element of damage to the Government may be established by showing a tax benefit, such as making income non-taxable or contributions tax-deductible.

442 *(1–18–80)* 9781
Scope of The Law

(1) The Employee Retirement Income Security Act of 1974 (ERISA) has made sweeping changes in the way private employee plans are administered. While the Department of Labor (DOL) is primarily responsible for ERISA enforcement, the Internal Revenue Service has significant involvement since qualified employee plans receive favored tax treatment via the deduction of the contribution by the employer, tax exemption for the related trust, and the deferral of income by the employee. These tax advantages can be used in criminal cases to meet the requirements that a tax be due and owing as described in IRC Section 7201 (Attempt to evade or defeat tax) and that damage inures to the government as described in IRC Section 7206 (Fraudulent or False Statement).

(2) The Tax Reform Act of 1969 established new and more stringent requirements for recognition as an exempt organization, expanded information reporting and annual reports, im-

posed a new series of excise taxes, and placed substantial restrictions on the permissible activities of an exempt organization. It also provided penalties for repeated and willful violations of the various prohibitions and enumerated in the Act.

(3) IRC 6033 requires that every exempt organization, with some exceptions, file an annual return stating specifically the items of gross income receipts and disbursements and such other information as may be prescribed by the Secretary or appropriate delegate. In addition, IRC 6011 requires the filing of certain taxable returns by exempt organizations. These information reports and returns are used to determine whether the submitting organization continues to qualify for favored tax treatment and to report any taxes for which it may be liable. Like the application forms, these reports and returns are subscribed under the penalty of perjury. If an organization ceases to qualify under the provisions of IRC 501 or 521 for which exemption was granted, its exempt status will be revoked.

443 *(1-18-80)* 9781
Criminal Provisions

(1) IRC 7206(1) (Declaration under penalties of perjury), is the criminal provision which will probably be the most useful in the employee plans and exempt organizations area. This section makes it a felony for anyone to willfully subscribe to a return or other document made subject to penalties of perjury which is not believed to be true and correct as to every material matter. This provision also applies to documents other than tax returns and a *prima facie* violation of IRC 7206(1) can be proven even in the absence of a probable tax deficiency. All of the forms filed with the IRS in connection with employee plans and exempt organizations contain a declaration that they are made subject to the penalties of perjury. Additionally, the declaration includes a statement that supporting documents are certified as being true and correct and this certification is subject to the same penalty. Thus, filing an application for a determination letter containing false statements or submitting falsified documents in support of such an application or submitting a falsified annual return for an employee plan and exempt organizations would give rise to a potential IRC 7206(1) prosecution if the falsifications are shown to be willful and material.

(2) Filing of a false application for a determination letter, annual return or registration statement can also be an act leading to tax evasion proscribed by IRC 7201 (Attempt to Evade or Defeat Tax). To prove tax evasion, the Government must show a tax deficiency, affirmative acts to evade assessment or payment of tax, and willfulness.

(3) Willful failure to file annual returns, registration statements, or actuarial statements can be a criminal violation of IRC 7203 (Willful Failure to File Return, supply information, or pay tax).

444 *(1-18-80)* 9781
Fraudulent Schemes and Devices

(1) Some of the more common fraudulent schemes and devices used in employee plans and exempt organizations cases are set forth as follows:

(a) Backdating of applications and related documents.

(b) Diversion of funds by officials of exempt organizations or by trustees of employee plans.

(c) Payment of improper expenses of exempt organization and trust officials.

(d) Loans of trust funds disguised as purchases or allowable deductions.

(e) Intentional failure to keep financial records.

(f) Double set of books.

(g) Disguising taxable receipts (interest and dividends) as non-taxable receipts.

(h) Making false statements on applications.

(i) Providing false receipts to donors by exempt organizations.

(j) Willful and intentional failure to exercise plan amendments agreed to during review of the determination letter application.

445 *(1-18-80)* 9781
Tax Protest-Type Cases

445.1 *(1-18-80)* 9781
Introduction

(1) A tax protester is a person who employs one or more illegal schemes that affect the payment of taxes.

(2) The following are schemes used by illegal tax protesters:

(a) *Constitutional Basis*—Refusal to include tax return information on Form 1040/1040A because of violation of Constitutional rights. In lieu of information required on Form 1040/1040A, the illegal tax protester either show "-0-," "none," "Object," or a Fifth Amendment annotation in all of the blanks or will include a broad general statement regarding his/her constitutional rights (including 4th Amendment and 16th Amendment). This is commonly referred to as a Porth/Daly type return.

(b) *Fair Market Value*—Reducing gross income because of declining value of dollar. The gross income is listed on the face of the return and there is a large adjustment to income which makes adjusted gross income small enough for standard deduction to eliminate taxable income. The adjustment to gross income is on Schedule D, Schedule of Capital Gains and Losses, or Form 2106, Statement of Employee Business Expenses, for Form 1040.

(c) *Gold/Silver Standard*—Any return with a statement that only gold or silver currency can be taxed.

(d) *Blank Form 1040/1040A*—These generally fall into two categories. In one category the individual files a return with only a name and address, and possibly signature, and Form(s) W-2 is attached. This scheme is usually verified upon correspondence with the taxpayer. In the second category the individual files a return similar to the Porth-type return, i.e., the lines contain "object," "Fifth Amendment," etc., with the exception that Form(s) W-2 is attached. In both instances the return could or could not list marital status and/or exemptions.

(e) *Non-Payment Protest*—Non-Payment or underpayment of tax based upon some type of protest statement written or attached to the return.

(f) *Protest Adjust*—This is similar to Non-Payment Protest, in that the return contains specific unallowable items (e.g., deductions, exclusions, etc.) identified to some type of protest.

(g) *Mail Order Ministries*—Individual receives income from non-religious sources and declares that it is non-taxable because of "vow of poverty." This scheme also involves returns where the individual includes all or substantially all of gross income as a contribution deduction on Schedule A of Form 1040. Some individuals will complete Form 1040 and then take an unusually large contribution deduction on Schedule A of Form 1040, normally 50 percent or more of adjusted gross income.

(h) *Protester Letters and Cards*—The receipt of letters and cards (without tax return) protesting the use of taxes for war, defense and/or other government spending policies, and *indicating that this will effect their reporting and payment of taxes.*

(i) *Family Estate Trust*—The trusts are filed on Forms 1041. Terms such as "family," "equity pure," "prime," or "constitutional" are used in the title of the trust. Income is from "wages" or "Contract" sources and deductions are for personal living expenses, such as housing, medical, auto, child care, interest or taxes. Generally, an individual will establish a trust, give his/her wages or other income to the trust and the trust pays for the expenses of the individual. The expenses claimed as administrative expenses of the trust, resulting in the individual paying no tax and the trust paying little or no taxes.

(j) *W4—Excessive Overstatement of Allowances*—This scheme is usually employed in conjunction with one of the other schemes mentioned above. The claiming of excessive allowances is usually directed towards eliminating of withholding of Federal taxes from wages.

(k) *Forms 843 and Amended Returns*—Some individuals are filing Form 843 Claims and/or Amended Form 1040 (1040X) returns to obtain a total refund on all taxes paid in prior years, even though returns have not been filed for the prior years.

445.2 *(1-18-80)* 9781
Background

(1) Some so-called tax protesters are making speeches and offering seminars around the country at which serious misrepresentations about the tax laws are being presented to the public as fact.

(2) Generally these protesters are counseling taxpayers not to comply with the Federal

income tax return filing statutes on the ground that they violate a person's constitutional rights under the Fifth Amendment. As early as 1927, the Supreme Court of the United States held in *United States v. Sullivan,* that a taxpayer could not refuse to file a Federal income tax return because of the Fifth Amendment privilege against self-incrimination.

(3) Further, the requirement that a taxpayer include information on the tax return concerning income does not, by itself, violate the self-incrimination clause of the Fifth Amendment as the court noted in *United States v. Daly.* This case, as well as others, represents an extension of the holding in *Sullivan* that a taxpayer must do more than file a blank tax return or tax return with little or no information.

(4) Illegal protesters also assert that various provisions of the Internal Revenue laws violate the due process clause of the Fifth Amendment. Generally they claim that the graduated income tax scale and the fact that certain deductions or benefits allowed by the Internal Revenue Code are available to some and not to others deny those latter persons their Constitutional rights. The protesters also assert that some of the statutory collection procedures violate the due process clause. However, in *Swallow v. United States,* the court held, "It is now well settled that the income tax laws are not unconstitutional under the due process clause of the Fifth Amendment. . . ."

(5) Federal Courts have held in numerous cases that there is no Constitutional right to refuse to pay income taxes in whole or part on religious or moral grounds or because the funds are used for government programs that the taxpayer opposes. For example, in *Autenrieth v. Cullen,* the court said, "The fact that some persons may object, on religious grounds, to some of the things that the government does is not a basis upon which they can claim a constitutional right not to pay a part of the tax."

(6) Some illegal protesters have offered an argument that income in the form of currency or checks is not subject to tax on the grounds that currency is now worthless since the United States is no longer on a gold or silver standard. They also argue that Federal Reserve notes are only accounts receivable and thus are not subject to tax. However, the law taxes "income from whatever source derived," and income may be in many forms, including currency, goods and services. In *United States v. Daly,* the court, referring to the gold and silver argument, stated, "This contention is clearly frivolous." The court arrived at a similar conclusion in *United States v. Wangrud.* The Tax Court in *Hatfield v. Commissioner,* which involved a Fifth Amendment return, dismissed an argument that Federal Reserve notes should not be taxed since they constitute accounts receivable.

(7) Some illegal protesters have promoted noncompliance through tax schemes involving family estate trusts, while others have offered assignments of all income to newly created organizations purporting to be churches, religious orders, or other religious organizations in which the organization acts only as a nominee receiving the assigned income which is then used to pay the donor's living expenses.

(8) Under the family estate plan the individual is advised to assign assets and income from current employment to the trust. The promoters then advise that, in exchange, the creator of the trust may receive "compensation" as an officer, trustee or director, as well as certain "fringe benefits," such as "pension rights," "tax-free use of a residence," and "educational endowments" for children.

(a) According to the promoters, once the creator's income is shifted to the trust, the trust is supposedly taxed only on undistributed new income. The promoters misrepresent that substantially all living expenses of the grantor and his or her family may be deducted on the trust's fiduciary income tax return as business expenses and that the balance might then be distributed to the creator's family or to a separate "non-profit" educational trust leaving little or no taxable income to be reported.

(b) Several IRS rulings have been published adverse to these schemes, and IRS challenges to these trusts have been upheld in various court cases.

(c) One of the most basic principles of taxation is that income is taxed to the taxpayer earning it. In other words, a person cannot escape the liability to report and pay tax on income of such person that is assigned to another person or entity. Thus, the United States Tax Court has rejected taxpayers' arguments that assigning to family trusts all compensation for services of the creator relieved the creator of reporting and paying tax on such compensation.

(9) While the "church" or "religious order" plans vary in certain aspects, a common scheme calls for an individual taxpayer to obtain minister's credentials and a church or religious order charter by mail for a fee. No profession of adherence to a creed, dogma, or moral code may or may not be required and duties of fiduciary responsibilities may or may not be undertaken in order to receive and administer these charters or credentials. The individual sets up an organization that purports to be a church, religious order, or other religious organization. The plan then calls for the individual to take a "vow of poverty" and to assign the individual's assets—house, car, savings account, etc.—and the income earned from current employment to the new organization. The income assigned is expended for housing, food, clothing, personal transportation and other living expenses incurred by the individual, and for his or her occasional "spiritual retreats" to traditional vacation areas. Typically, the solicitations conclude that a vow of poverty can make a person rich.

(a) Such representations are misleading and plans of the type described will not produce the tax benefits claimed by their promoters. The tax law affords significant benefits to churches and other religious organizations and to individuals who make gifts or contributions to qualified organizations. The law requires, however, that religious organizations qualifying for certain tax benefits actually be operated for religious purposes and that they not be operated for private purposes.

(b) Under a recently published IRS ruling and established principles of tax law, such an assignment of income whether by an individual claiming to be under a vow of poverty, or otherwise, will not prevent the individual from being taxed on such income. Moreover, when the organization to which income is assigned is not actually organized and operated for religious purposes, the assigned income will not be deductible by the taxpayer. In any event, contributions to an organization are not deductible when made in the expectation of receiving some commensurate benefit in return.

445.3 *(1-18-80)* 9781
Criminal Investigation Division Procedures In Tax Protester-Type Cases

(1) Each protest return received from the Chief, CID will be immediately assigned for evaluation. This evaluation will be completed within 15 working days from the date of receipt. To assist in evaluation of the criminal potential of protest cases, the Chief, CID may assign the item to a special agent for limited inquiries, as defined in IRM 9311.2:(3). Also, if necessary for proper evaluation, the Chief may authorize individual information gathering. When unusual legal questions exist, the Chief is encouraged to contact District Counsel for advice.

(2) If the case is selected for investigation, the district will submit a Form 4135 (Criminal Investigation Control Notice) to the service center to establish a TC 914 Control.

(3) Cases selected for investigation will be designated as priority cases and investigated as expeditiously as possible. To ensure that illegal tax protester cases are investigated as quickly as possible, the Chief, Criminal Investigation Division should consider devoting additional resources to these cases and/or establishing teams of special agents to work these cases.

(4) In selecting cases for investigation, consideration should be given to the potential impact and/or deterrent effect a successful prosecution case will generate. Experience in this area has indicated that cases involving leaders and/or flagrant non-compliance situations achieve the best results. (See Policy Statement P-9-3.)

(5) Any surveillance activities conducted in conjunction with illegal tax protester cases and/or information gathering projects will conform to the guidelines contained in IRM 9383.6.

(a) Surveillance activities at tax protest meetings will be limited to attendance at those meetings for the purpose of obtaining information concerning new techniques being advocated in the so-called tax protest movement. Special agents who attend these meetings will not identify individuals who attend the meetings unless the individuals openly admit that they:

1 have committed or intend to commit a tax violation; or

2 advocate that others commit violations of the tax laws; or

3 advocate the use of threat and/or assault tactics in dealing with Service personnel.

(b) The attendance at tax protest meetings is to be distinguished from peaceful demonstrations directed towards some sort of tax protest. In this regard, Service personnel will be guided by Treasury Department policy which directs that no information should be collected on peaceful demonstrations which involve the exercise of First Amendment rights without contacting the office of the Assistant Secretary (Enforcement and Operations). In such situations, the Chief, Criminal Investigation Division, with the concurrence of the District Director, and ARC, Criminal Investigation will notify the Director, Criminal Investigation Division, who will contact the Assistant Secretary (Enforcement and Operations).

(6) Any district information gathering projects must be authorized in accordance with Manual instructions. (See IRM 9391.9.)

(7) Guidelines and procedures regarding the use of informants are found at IRM 9373.

(8) Guidelines concerning the use of confidential expenditures are found at IRM 9372.

(9) Since some so-called tax protesters advocate the use of force in dealing with Service personnel, the special agent assigned the investigation should consider having all contacts with the taxpayer made at the district office or the post of duty nearest the taxpayer. If it is determined that this could jeopardize successful completion of the investigation, the special agent's group manager will be consulted prior to contact with the taxpayer. Also, special agents should recognize that many third-parties may also be illegal tax protest advocates. Extreme care and discretion should be exercised prior to making contacts that could fall into this category.

(10) Cases involving illegal tax protesters have been associated with the following violations:

(a) Title 26 U.S.C.

1 Section 7201—Attempt to Evade or Defeat Tax;

2 Section 7203—Willful Failure to File Return, Supply Information or Pay Tax;

3 Section 7202—Willful Failure to Collect or Pay over Tax;

4 Section 7205—Fraudulent Withholding Exemption Certificate or Failure to Supply Information;

5 Section 7206—Fraud and False Statements; and

6 Section 7212—Attempts to Interfere with Administration of Internal Revenue Laws.

(b) Title 18 U.S.C.

1 Section 2—Principals;

2 Section 287—False, Fictitious or Fraudulent Claims;

3 Section 371—Conspiracy to Commit Offense or to Defraud United States;

4 Section 1001—Statement or Entries Generally; and

5 Section 1503—Influencing or Injuring Officer, Juror or Witness Generally.

450 *(1-18-80)* 9781
Excise Taxes

451 *(1-18-80)* 9781
Definition and Purposes

(1) *Definition.*—An excise tax is a duty or impost levied upon the manufacture, sale, or consumption of commodities within the country, and upon certain occupations.

(2) *Purposes.*—A few excise taxes are merely regulatory and some are imposed for both regulatory and revenue purposes. Most excise taxes, however, are levied exclusively for the purpose of revenue.

452 *(1-18-80)* 9781
Excise and Income Taxes Distinguished

452.1 *(1-18-80)* 9781
Base

Income taxes are based on net income or net profits, and are graduated. Excise taxes are not graduated, and they can be based upon any of the following factors: selling price of merchandise or facilities; services sold or used; number, weight, or volume of units sold; and nature of occupation.

452.2 *(1-18-80)* 9781
Tax Period

Certain excise tax returns are required to be filed on either a fiscal-year or calendar-year basis. In general, excise tax returns are filed on a calendar quarter-year basis. Income tax returns are required to be filed on either a fiscal-year or calendar-year basis.

452.3 *(1-18-80)* 9781
Additional Taxes and Penalties

Assessments of additional or delinquent excise taxes are referred to as "additional taxes." In income tax cases, such assessments are known as "deficiencies." There are many types of civil penalties specifically applicable to excise tax cases. Civil penalties in income tax cases are limited to three types: delinquency, negligence, and fraud.

452.4 *(1-18-80)* 9781
Court Appeals

Income tax cases may be appealed to the Tax Court of the United States without prepayment of the taxes, but excise tax cases cannot be appealed to the Tax Court. All court appeals by excise tax litigants must be made to either the U.S. Court of Claims or to the U.S. District Court, and then only upon prepayment of the taxes.

453 *(1-18-80)* 9781
Excise Tax Reduction Bill of 1965

453.1 *(1-18-80)* 9781
Statutory Provisions

The Excise Tax Reduction Bill of 1965 (P.L. 89-44) and the Comprehensive Drug Abuse Prevention and Control Act of 1970 (P.L. 91-513) lowered or removed most of the Federal excise taxes.

453.2 *(1-18-80)* 9781
Excise Taxes Remaining in Effect

(1) The following remaining excise taxes are of interest to the Criminal Investigation Division.

(a) Retailers' excise taxes: diesel fuel and special motor fuels.

(b) Manufacturers' excise taxes: truck parts and accessories, trucks, trailers, tires and inner tubes, gasoline and lubricating oil (used in motor vehicles).

(c) Miscellaneous excise taxes: air transportation of persons, foreign insurance policies, wagering-occupational and gross wagers, coin-operated gaming devices, (expires June 30, 1980), highway vehicle usage, and local and long-distance telephone service.

(2) Excise tax regulations under IRC 4481 expired October 1, 1972 and new regulations were not effective until March 2, 1976. Consult District Counsel prior to conducting investigations of possible violations relating to interim periods.

453.3 *(1-18-80)* 9781
Occupations Subject to Tax

Various occupations are subject to special (occupational) taxes. Many of these taxes are regulatory in nature. Those of chief interest to the Criminal Investigation Division relate to persons engaged in wagering (see 460) and those who maintain coin-operated gaming devices on their premises. The tax on coin-operated gaming devices will no longer be in effect after June 30, 1980.

454 *(9-8-80)* 9781
(Reserved)

455 *(1-18-80)* 9781
Civil Penalties and Jeopardy Assessments

455.1 *(1-18-80)* 9781
Civil Penalties

455.11 *(1-18-80)* 9781
Delinquency Penalty (IRC 6651(a))

An ad valorem delinquency penalty of 5 percent a month may be asserted when an excise tax return is filed delinquently without reasonable cause, or when a taxpayer fails to file a return without fraudulent intent. The penalty, limited to 25 percent, is imposed on the net amount due. It is not imposed, however, if the 50 percent civil fraud penalty is assessed under IRC 6653(b). (See 250.)

455.12 *(1-18-80)* 9781
Fraud Penalty Applicable to Returns (IRC 6653(b))

A 50 percent civil fraud penalty may be imposed under IRC 6653(b) on the underpaid excise tax on "non-collected taxes," such as, manufacturers' or retailers' taxes. The test for the application of the fraud penalty in an excise tax case is the same as it is for any other type of fraud penalty case: the Government must prove that a willful fraudulent act was committed. With respect to excise taxes, the 50 percent civil fraud penalty applies to "noncollected taxes" only. "Collected taxes" levied on the purchaser or user, such as transportation and withholding taxes are subject to the 100 percent penalty, under IRC 6672.

455.13 *(1-18-80)* 9781
Fraud Penalty Applicable to Documentary Stamps (IRC 6653(e))

A 50 percent civil fraud penalty may be asserted under IRC 6653(e) against anyone who willfully fails to pay or attempts to evade or defeat any tax imposed by means of a stamp, coupon, ticket, book, or other device.

455.14 *(1-18-80)* 9781
One Hundred Percent Penalty (IRC 6672)

A 100 percent penalty may be imposed on any person required to collect, truthfully, account for and pay over any tax who willfully evades, or fails to collect or account for and pay over such tax. This relates to *"collected" and "withheld"* taxes only and serves merely as a device whereby the collecting agent is made liable for the unpaid portion of the tax. The penalty under this IRC section is limited to this amount and is not in addition to it. [*Chief Counsel Memorandum, 6/11/64, CC:CL-2284.*]

455.15 *(1-18-80)* 9781
Other Civil Penalties

In addition to the general civil penalties previously mentioned, the 1954 Code provides for various penalties applicable to specific types of excise taxes. Such penalties are included in those enumerated in 252.

455.2 *(1-18-80)* 9781
Jeopardy Assessment in Excise Tax Cases

IRC 6862 provides that when the collection of the excise tax is deemed in jeopardy, it may be immediately assessed.

456 *(1-18-80)* 9781
Criminal Penalties for Excise Tax Violations

Criminal Penalties for most violations of excise taxes are imposed by the same 1954 Code sections as related to income taxes, which, in general, cover offenses such as willful failure to file a return, pay tax, supply information, or keep records; willful failure to account for, collect and pay over a particular tax; and willful attempts to defeat the tax in any manner. The 1954 Code also provides specific penalties which have a limited application to the various excise taxes. (The various criminal penalties are enumerated in 221.) For example, IRC 7215 and 7512, which relate to Offenses With Respect to Collected Taxes, cover noncompliance with an official notice to collect and deposit "trust fund" taxes.

457 *(1-18-80)* 9781
Excise Tax Investigations

457.1 *(1-18-80)* 9781

Origin of Excise Tax Cases

(1) Excise tax returns, unlike those for income taxes, do not admit to ready analysis to determine the possible existence of tax violations. The information contained in quarterly excise tax returns on Form 720 is limited to the kind of tax, the gross tax, the credit for overpaid tax in prior returns, and the net tax due. Hence, excise tax investigations which relate to false or fraudulent returns usually result from referrals following field audit of taxpayers' books and records. As violations applicable to excise taxes often occur simultaneously with income tax offenses, field audits conducted by the Examination Division in income tax matters often disclose violations with respect to excise taxes. Therefore, referrals in such cases often relate to both excise and income tax violations. Investigations of offenses involving willful failure to file excise tax returns, or willful failure to collect and pay over excise tax, are usually based upon referrals from the Collection or Examination Division.

(2) Some excise tax investigations result from information furnished by informants.

(3) Excise tax violations also are disclosed through surveys conducted by the Criminal Investigation Division, and by information obtained by special agents during their investigation of income tax offenses. As most excise tax offenses are committed in conjunction with income tax violations, investigation of both types of cases usually arise from the same sources.

457.2 *(1-18-80)* 9781

Techniques of Excise and Income Tax Investigations Compared

Although the criminal penalties for most violations of the excise taxes are imposed by the same 1954 Code sections as relate to income taxes, the nature of the evidence to sustain prosecution of excise tax cases differs in many respects from that required in income tax cases. Excise tax is based on specifically enumerated articles or services, whereas income tax is based strictly on income. For this reason, the established methods of determination of income in income tax cases may be inadequate to sustain criminal prosecution for evasion of the excise tax on specifically enumerated articles or services. Under certain circumstances the specific item method of proving income may be effectively used in excise tax cases, especially if an adequate breakdown of records in maintained by the taxpayer. Furthermore, any other method of proving income may be used if the circumstances are such that the evidence thus developed will serve to establish or buttress proof of violation of the excise tax on the specifically enumerated articles or services involved. In general, the investigative techniques applicable to income tax cases may be used in excise tax investigations.

460 *(1-18-80)* 9781

Wagering Tax

461 *(1-18-80)* 9781

Law Relating to Wagering Tax

461.1 *(1-18-80)* 9781

Excise Tax on Wagering

461.11 *(1-18-80)* 9781

Statutory Provisions

IRC 4401 imposes a 2 percent excise tax on wagers. This tax is distinct from the $500 annual occupational tax imposed by IRC 4411 although every person who is liable for the excise tax is also liable for the occupational tax.

461.12 *(1-18-80)* 9781

Definitions of Wagering Terms

461.121 *(1-18-80)* 9781

Wager

The term wager means any wager with respect to a sports event or a contest placed with a person engaged in the business of accepting such wagers; any wager placed in a wagering pool with respect to a sports event or a contest, if such pool is conducted for profit; and any wager placed in a lottery conducted for profit.

461.122 *(1-18-80)* 9781

Lottery

(1) The term lottery includes the numbers game, policy, and similar types of wagering. The term does not include:

(a) any game of a type in which usually

1 the wagers are placed,

2 the winners are determined, and

3 the distribution of prizes or other property is made in the presence of all persons placing wagers in such game, and

(b) any drawing conducted by an organization exempt from tax under IRC 501 and 521, if no part of the net proceeds derived from such drawing inures to the benefit of any private shareholder or individual.

461.13 *(1-18-80)* 9781
Amount of Wager

In determining the amount of any wager, all charges incident to the placing of such wager shall be included; except that if the taxpayer establishes, in accordance with regulations prescribed by the Secretary or his delegate, that an amount equal to the tax has been collected as a separate charge from the person placing such wager, the amount so collected shall be excluded.

461.14 *(1-18-80)* 9781
Persons Liable for Wagering Excise Tax

(1) Each person who is engaged in the business of accepting wagers shall be liable for and shall pay the tax on all wagers placed with him. Each person who conducts any wagers, pool or lottery shall be liable for and shall pay the tax on all wagers placed in such pool or lottery.

(2) A person is engaged in the business of accepting wagers if he makes it a practice to accept wagers with respect to which he assumes the risk of profit or loss depending upon the outcome of the event or the contest with respect to which the wager is accepted. It is not intended that to be engaged in the business of accepting wagers a person must be either so engaged to the exclusion of all other activities or even primarily so engaged. Thus, for example, an individual may be primarily engaged in business as a salesman, and also for the purpose of the tax be engaged in the business of accepting wagers. The courts have ruled that a single transaction without additional evidence so indicating does not constitute engaging in the business. However, a single wagering transaction made under circumstances that indicate that it is made in the ususal course of business may make the person liable for the special tax. The chance for successful prosecution is better where there is evidence that the person accepted several wagers and competent witnesses are available to testify as to the passage of money and its acceptance as wagers.

(3) The 2 percent excise tax is applicable to the acceptor of wagers (principal), while the $500 special tax applies to both the acceptor and the receiver of wages (agent). In addition, under IRC 4401(c), any person who as agent for a principal is liable under IRC 4411 for the special $500 tax and who fails to disclose his principal, becomes liable himself for the excise tax imposed by IRC 4401.

461.15 *(1-18-80)* 9781
Exclusions From Wagering Excise Tax

(1) No 2 percent excise tax shall be imposed on:

(a) any wager placed with, or any wager placed in a wagering pool conducted by, a pari-mutuel wagering enterprise licensed under State law, and

(b) any wager placed in a coin-operated device with respect to which an occupational tax is imposed by IRC 4461.

461.16 *(1-18-80)* 9781
Territorial Extent of Wagering Excise Tax

(1) The tax imposed by IRC 4401 shall apply only to wagers which are:

(a) accepted in the United States, or

(b) placed by a person who is in the United States

1 with a person who is a citizen or resident of the United States, or

2 in a wagering pool or lottery conducted by a person who is a citizen or resident of the United States.

461.2 *(1-18-80)* 9781
Wagering Occupational Tax

461.21 *(1-18-80)* 9781
Statutory Provisions

(1) IRC 4411 imposes a special tax of $500 per year to be paid by each person who is liable for tax under IRC 4401, or who is engaged in receiving wagers for or on behalf of any person so liable. The application of IRC 4411 may be illustrated by the following examples:

(a) A, who is engaged in the business of accepting horse race bets, employs ten persons to receive on his behalf wagers which are transmitted by telephone. A also employs a secretary and a bookkeeper. A and each of the ten persons who receive wagers by telephone on behalf of A are liable for special tax. The secretary and bookkeeper are not liable for the special tax unless they also receive wagers for A.

(b) B operates a numbers game and has an arrangement with ten persons, who are employed in various capacities, such as bootblacks, elevator operators, news dealers, etc., to receive wagers from the public on his behalf. B also employs C to collect from the ten persons referred to the wagers received by them on B's behalf and to deliver such wagers to B. C performs no other services for B. B and the ten persons who receive wagers on his behalf are liable for the special tax. C is not liable for the special tax since he is not engaged in receiving wagers for B.

461.22 *(1-18-80)* 9781

Registration

IRC 4412 provides that each person required to pay a special tax under IRC 4411 shall register with the District Director in charge of the Internal Revenue District where the wagering business is conducted. Form 11C is used for the registration and requires: The name and place of residence of taxpayer; if he is liable for the 2 percent excise tax, each place of business where the activity which makes him so liable is carried on, and the name and place of residence of each person who is engaged in receiving wagers for him or on his behalf; if he is engaged in receiving wagers for or on behalf of any person subject to the 2 percent excise tax, the name and place of residence of each such person. In the event a firm or company conducts the wagering business, the names and places of residence of the several persons constituting the firm or company shall be registered.

461.3 *(1-18-80)* 9781

Record Requirements

Every person required to pay the excise tax imposed by IRC 4401, shall keep a daily record showing the gross amount of all wagers on which he is liable in addition to all other records required pursuant to IRC 6001. An agent or employee who received wagers for or on behalf of another person shall keep a daily record of bets received, commissions retained, and amount turned over to his principal. The records required to be maintained by principal and agent shall at all times be open for inspection by revenue officers, and they shall be maintained for a period of at least three years from the date the wager was received.

461.4 *(1-18-80)* 9781

Payment of Special Tax Before Engaging in Wagering Business

IRC 4901 requires that the special tax imposed by IRC 4411 be paid before an individual or firm engages in accepting wagers. The special tax is computed as of the first day of July in each year, or the first day that wagers are accepted. In the former case the special tax shall be computed for one year, i.e., $500 and in the latter case it shall be prorated from the first day of the month in which wagers were accepted, to and including the 30th day of June following.

461.5 *(1-18-80)* 9781

Wagering Excise Tax Returns

Monthly returns of the 2 percent excise tax on wagers must be filed on Form 730. The taxes are due and payable to the District Director, without notice from the director, on or before the last day of the month following that for which it is made.

461.6 *(1-18-80)* 9781

Criminal Violations for Wagering Taxes

(1) Willful attempt to evade or defeat the payment of wagering tax, willful failure to file return or supply information, and failure to pay special wagering tax incur the penalties prescribed in IRC 7201, 7203, and 7262 respectively. Collateral violations, such as filing false claims, conspiracy, and false statements, may also incur penalties prescribed by sections 287, 371, and 1001 of Title 18, U.S. Criminal Code.

(2) Congress repealed IRC 6107 which allowed for public inspection of certain tax records and has enacted IRC 4424. IRC 4424 was intended to remove any constitutional problems regarding enforcement of the wagering taxes resulting from improper disclosure of wagering tax information.

462 *(1-18-80)* 9781
Elements of Wagering Tax Violations

462.1 *(1-18-80)* 9781
General

The elements of a wagering tax violation subject to the criminal sanctions of IRC 7203 are: The wagering activity must be subject to the wagering tax laws (IRC 4421); failure of the person to register and pay the special tax before accepting the wager and/or failure of the person to file wagering excise tax returns and pay tax; and evidence to prove that the person willfully failed to comply with the law. In addition to proving the above elements the Government must prove affirmative acts which indicate a willful intent to evade or defeat the tax in order to sustain a violation of IRC 7201. No proof of willfulness is required for a violation under IRC 7262, which provides a $1,000 to $5,000 fine for doing an act which makes a person liable for the special tax without having paid such tax.

462.2 *(1-18-80)* 9781
Wagering Tax Enforcement

(1) Primary enforcement efforts in the wagering tax area shall be aimed at the independent initiation and development of criminal cases against major operators and financiers and in other situations involving wide-spread noncompliance. Service efforts will strive to promote balanced enforcement with respect to investigations of wagering occupational, wagering excise and income tax violations on identified subjects. (See Policy Statement P-9-472 and IRM 9420.

(2) Generally, a major wagering operation is one comprised of five or more individuals who conduct, finance, manage, supervise, direct or own all or a part of a gambling business and:

(a) has a daily gross of over $2000, or

(b) conducts business at more than one location, or

(c) actively handles lay-off bets; or

(d) a principal of the operation is notorious or powerful with respect to local criminal activity.

(3) Cases not meeting the criteria may be investigated and recommended for prosecution only if they are associated with and submitted for prosecution simultaneously as a package with the case(s) meeting the criteria.

463 *(1-18-80)* 9781
Investigative Techniques

(1) Violations of criminal statutes by IRS personnel are prohibited. However, under certain circumstances, investigative techniques used by special agents in the performance of their official duties, which would appear to violate a state or local criminal statute, do not actually constitute a violation. One such technique may be the placing of a bet by a special agent, using a temporary identity, to obtain evidence relating to a wagering tax investigation. Whether a particular investigative technique constitutes a violation of a statute depends upon the justifiability of the use of the investigative technique under the circumstances. Among the factors to be considered in determining justifiability are: the realistic availability of alternative investigative techniques, including timing, cost and staffing considerations; the degree of actual harm that such conduct is likely to cause; the efforts of the agent to minimize such harm; and the potential benefits for society from such conduct. Of course, no technique to secure evidence can be deemed justifiable and is, therefore, impermissible if it involved a violation of the person or property of any individual. Under no circumstances can agents employ such techniques as illegal threats or assaults against any persons, breaking and entry into another's premises without a search warrant, the unauthorized taking of papers or other property, or the unauthorized overhearing of conversations. In order to protect IRS personnel and to assure that IRS personnel act within the law, District Counsel should be consulted if doubt exists as to how the law applies to a particular situation.

(2) Investigations of wagering tax violations usually require surveillance of violators and localities to obtain probable cause for issuance of search warrants. (See IRM 9383.6.)

(3) Special agents shall only be used in a penetration type undercover capacity after having received training in the technique. This will provide for consistency in approach and avoid possible violations of law which could occur by using untrained agents in undercover activities. The Assistant Regional Commissioner (Criminal Investigation) will make arrangements through the Director, Criminal Investigation Division, Attn:CP:CI:O for interregional use of trained undercover agents. (See IRM 9389.(11)).

(4) Special agents may place wagers and participate as customers to obtain evidence of wagering activities. Such assumption of a temporary identity for this nonpenetrating type activity will be carried out in accordance with current guidelines on surveillance. Paid informants may be used when appropriate. Expenditures for the placing of wagers and payments of informants will be designated "Confidential Expenditures". (See IRM 9372.)

(5) Special agents will at all times conform to the Department of Justice guidelines on monitoring of private conversations. Mechanical, electronic, or other devices will be used only in accordance with policy statement P-9-35 and the procedures set forth in IRM 9388 and 9389.

464 *(1-18-80)* 9781
Venue in Wagering Investigations

Text 727 covers the question of venue as it pertains to IRC 7201 and 7203, and the comments made in 727 are applicable to wagering tax cases. Violation of IRC 7262, which provides a maximum penalty of $5,000 for not paying the special tax imposed by IRC 4411, is committed in the judicial district where the wager was accepted. Therefore, venue lies in the judicial district where the wager was accepted without regard to the location of the District Directors' office.

465 *(1-18-80)* 9781
Statute of Limitations on Wagering Taxes

The statute of limitations with regard to both excise and occupational wagering taxes (IRC 7201 or 7203) begins to run on the day following the last overt act and ends six years from that date.

466 *(1-18-80)* 9781
Civil Penalties on Wagering Taxes

The 50 percent civil fraud penalty provided by IRC 6653(b), is applicable to both the excise and the occupational wagering taxes. Application of the 50 percent penalty precludes imposing the 25 percent delinquency penalty. Since this is not a "collected tax," IRC 6653(e) is not applicable.

Exhibit 400-1

Net Worth Statement
Handbook Reference: Text 424.8

◊

NET WORTH STATEMENT
John and Mary Roe
Dayton, Ohio

ASSETS	12/31/—	12/31/—	12/31/—
1. Cash—First National Bank	$ 4,500.00	$ 150.00	$ 2,500.00
2. Cash on hand	25.00	25.00	25.00
3. Inventory, Liquor Store	4,800.00	13,000.00	29,000.00
4. U.S. Savings Bonds	-0-	3,750.00	-0-
5. Note Receivable, Frank Roe	-0-	-0-	300.00
6. Note Receivable, Roger Jones	-0-	-0-	16,000.00
7. Accounts Receivable, Doc's Market	-0-	1,600.00	-0-
8. Lot on Dayton Road	1,000.00	1,000.00	1,000.00
9. Ohio Tourist Camp	12,000.00	12,000.00	12,000.00
10. Residence, 1100 Vine Street	2,800.00	2,800.00	-0-
11. 30 Acre Farm, East Dayton	-0-	7,400.00	7,400.00
12. 150 Acre Farm, North Dayton	-0-	-0-	7,000.00
13. Equipment—Liquor Store	800.00	800.00	800.00
14. Ace Automobile	2,800.00	2,800.00	2,800.00
15. Farm Truck	-0-	-0-	800.00
16. Farm Equipment	-0-	1,250.00	2,250.00
17. Livestock on Farm	-0-	900.00	1,300.00
Total Assets	$28,725.00	$47,475.00	$83,175.00
LIABILITIES			
18. First Federal Savings & Loan Assn.	$ 2,400.00	$ 1,800.00	$ -0-
19. First National Bank	2,900.00	2,700.00	-0-
20. Depreciation Reserve	2,500.00	3,200.00	4,300.00
Total Liabilities	$ 7,800.00	$ 7,700.00	$ 4,300.00
NET WORTH	$20,925.00	$39,775.00	$78,875.00
Less: Net Worth of Prior Year		20,925.00	39,775.00
Increase in Net Worth		$18,850.00	$39,100.00
ADJUSTMENTS			
Add:			
21. Living Expenses		$ 2,500.00	$ 2,500.00
22. Life Insurance Premium		300.00	500.00
23. Federal Income Taxes Paid		750.00	900.00
Less:			
24. Long-Term Capital Gain on Sale of Residence (50%)		-0-	(500.00)
25. Inheritance		-0-	(10,000.00)
Adjusted Gross Income		$22,400.00	$32,500.00
Less: Standard Deduction		1,000.00	1,000.00
Balance		$21,400.00	$31,500.00
Less: Exemptions (4)		2,400.00	2,400.00
Taxable Income		$19,000.00	$29,100.00
Less: Taxable Income Reported		6,100.00	6,400.00
Taxable Income Not Reported		$12,900.00	$22,700.00

Exhibit 400-2

Expenditures Statement
Handbook Reference: Text 425.6

EXPENDITURES STATEMENT
John and Mary Roe
Dayton, Ohio

Item No.	Money Spent or Applied on Nondeductible Items	19—	19—
1.	Cash—First National Bank (increase)	-0-	$ 2,350.00
3.	Inventories	$ 8,200.00	16,000.00
4.	U. S. Savings Bonds	3,750.00	-0-
5.	Note Receivable, Frank Roe	-0-	300.00
6.	Note Receivable, Roger Jones	-0-	16,000.00
7.	Accounts Receivable, Doc's Market	1,600.00	-0-
11.	30 Acre Farm, East Dayton	7,400.00	-0-
12.	150 Acre Farm, North Dayton	-0-	7,000.00
15.	Farm Truck	-0-	800.00
16.	Farm Equipment	1,250.00	1,000.00
17.	Livestock on Farm	900.00	400.00
	Payments on Loan:		
18.	First Federal Savings & Loan Assn.	600.00	1,800.00
19.	First National Bank	200.00	2,700.00
21.	Living Expense	2,500.00	2,500.00
22.	Life Insurance Premium	300.00	500.00
23.	Federal Income Taxes Paid	750.00	900.00
	TOTAL:	$27,450.00	$52,250,000
	Nontaxable Sources of Funds		
1.	Cash—First National Bank (decrease)	$4,350.00	-0-
4.	U. S. Saving Bonds	-0-	$3,750.00
7.	Accounts Receivable, Doc's Market	-0-	1,600.00
10.	Sale of Residence, 1100 Vine Street (cost)	-0-	2,800.00
20.	Depreciation reserve	700.00	1,100.00
24.	Capital Gain on Sale of Residence, 1100 Vine Street (50%)	-0-	500.00
25.	Inheritance	-0-	10,000.00
	TOTAL:	$5,050.00	$19,750.00
	Adjusted Gross Income	$22,400.00	$32,500.00
	Less: Standard Deduction	1,000.00	1,000.00
	Balance	$21,400.00	$31,500.00
	Less: Exemptions (4)	2,400.00	2,400.00
	Taxable Income	$19,000.00	$29,100.00
	Less: Taxable Income Reported	6,100.00	6,400.00
	Taxable Income Not Reported	$12,900.00	$22,700.00

Exhibit 400-3

◊

Schedule A
Handbook Reference: Text 426.6

SCHEDULE—A

COMPUTATION OF TAXABLE INCOME BY BANK DEPOSITS METHOD

John and Mary Roe

Dayton, Ohio

For the Year Ended December 31, 19—

Total Deposits—First National Bank		$163,015.00
Currency Disbursements (see schedule B)		2,900.00
Subtotal		$165,915.00
Less: Nonincome Deposits and Items:		
(1) U.S. Savings Bonds Redeemed	$ 3,750.00	
(2) Notes Receivable, Doc's Market Collected	1,600.00	
(3) Sale of Residence at 1100 Vine St.	3,800.00	
(4) Inheritance	10,000.00	19,150.00
Gross Receipts from Business		$146,765.00
Less: Cost of Goods Sold:		
Inventory 1-1—	$ 13,000.00	
Purchases -19—	124,000.00	
Goods Available for Sale	$137,000.00	
Less—Inventory 12-31—	29,000.00	
Cost of Goods Sold		108,000.00
Gross Profit from Business		$ 38,765.00
Less: Business Expenses		
Interest	$ 150.00	
Salaries	4,200.00	
Rent	1,200.00	
Material and Supplies	115.00	
Depreciation	1,100.00	
Total Business Expense		6,765.00
Net Profit from Business		$ 32,000.00
Add: Long-Term Capital Gain on Sale of Residence (50%)		500.00
Adjusted Gross Income		$ 32,500.00
Less: Standard Deduction		1,000.00
Balance		$ 31,500.00
Less: Exemptions (4)		2,400.00
Taxable Income		$ 29,100.00
Less: Taxable Income Reported		6,400.00
Taxable Income not Reported		$ 22,700.00

Schedule B
Handbook Reference: Text 426.6

◊

SCHEDULE—B

COMPUTATION OF CURRENCY DISBURSEMENTS

John and Mary Roe

Dayton, Ohio

For the Year Ended December 31, 19—

Purchases		$124,000.00
Interest		150.00
Salaries		4,200.00
Rent		1,200.00
Materials & Supplies		115.00
Loan to Frank Roe		300.00
Loan to Roger Jones		16,000.00
Purchase 134 Acre Farm, North Dayton		7,000.00
Purchase Farm Truck		800.00
Purchase Farm Equipment		1,000.00
Purchase of Livestock		400.00
Payments on Loan—First Federal Savings & Loan		1,800.00
Payments on Loan—First National Bank		2,700.00
Living Expense		2,500.00
Life Insurance Premiums		500.00
Federal Income Taxes Paid		900.00
Total Disbursements		$163,565.00
Bank Balance 1-1—	$ 150.00	
Total Deposits	163,015.00	
Funds Available to Spend	$163,165.00	
Bank Balance 12-31—	2,500.00	
Bank Disbursements		160,665.00
Currency Disbursements		$ 2,900.00

Note: This computation may be made when canceled checks are incomplete or not available from which to make an analysis as shown in Exhibit 300–5. Data necessary to make such a computation is usually obtainable from income tax returns of the taxpayer and third-party sources.

Exhibit 400-5

Summary—Analysis of Checks and Currency Disbursements
Handbook Reference: Text 426.6

SUMMARY—ANALYSIS OF CHECKS AND CURRENCY DISBURSEMENTS

John and Mary Roe, Dayton, Ohio
For The Year Ended December 31, 19—

Disbursements for Business Expenses:

Accounts	Check	Currency	Total
Purchases	$123,465	$535	$124,000
Interest	100	50	150
Salaries	4,000	200	4,200
Rent	1,200		1,200
Materials		115	115
Total	$128,765	$900	*$129,665

Disbursements for Net Worth Items:

Accounts	Check	Currency	Total
Loan to Frank Roe	$ 300		$ 300
Loan to Roger Jones	16,000		16,000
Purchase of 134 Acre Farm, North Dayton	6,000	$1,000	7,000
Purchase of Farm Truck	800		800
Purchase of Farm Equipment	1,000		1,000
Purchase of Livestock	400		400
Payments on Loan, First Federal Savings	1,800		1,800
Payments on Loan, First National Bank	2,700		2,700
Living Expense	1,500	1,000	2,500
Life Insurance Premiums	500		500
Federal Income Taxes Paid	900		900
Total	$ 31,900	$2,000	$ 33,900
Total Disbursements, Business Expenses and Net Worth Items	$160,665	$2,900	$163,565

* The business expenses of $129,665 are the same as amounts claimed on Form 1040.

Exhibit 400-6

Analysis of Deposits to Checking Account
Handbook Reference: Text 426.6 ◊

John and Mary Roe
First National Bank of Dayton, Ohio

Date	Total Deposit	Gross Receipts Deposited: Currency	Checks: Identified	Checks: Unidentified	Loans, Transfers, etc.	Report Exhibit No.	Source
19—							
1-3	$2,400	$100					Unidentified
					$1,600	6	Loan—Doc's Market
			$500			7	Sale to Social Club
			$100			8	Sale to John Smith
				$100			Unidentified
1-4	$1,200	$400					Unidentified
			$800			9	Sale to Frank Lee
1-5	$10,500	$200					Unidentified
					$10,000	10	Inheritance
			$300			11	Sale to John Smith
1-6	$3,750				$3,750	12	U. S. Savings Bonds Redeemed
Bal. of Year	$145,165	$40,300	$72,300	$28,765	$3,800		
Total	$163,015	$41,000	$74,000	$28,865	$19,150		

Exhibit 400-7

List of First Three Digits of Social Security Numbers (SSN) and their Assigned Areas of Issuance 

LIST OF FIRST THREE DIGITS OF SOCIAL SECURITY NUMBERS (SSN)
AND THEIR ASSIGNED AREAS OF ISSUANCE

Number(s)	Area	Number(s)	Area
001–003	New Hampshire	449–467	Texas
004–007	Maine	468–477	Minnesota
008–009	Vermont	478–485	Iowa
010–034	Massachusetts	486–500	Missouri
035–039	Rhode Island	501–502	North Dakota
040–049	Connecticut	503–504	South Dakota
050–134	New York	505–508	Nebraska
135–158	New Jersey	509–515	Kansas
159–211	Pennsylvania	516–517	Montana
212–220	Maryland	518–519	Idaho
221–222	Delaware	520	Wyoming
223–231	Virginia	521–524	Colorado
232–236	West Virginia	525,585	New Mexico
(1) 232,237–246	North Carolina	526–527	Arizona
247–251	South Carolina	528–529	Utah
252–260	Georgia	530	Nevada
261–267	Florida	531–539	Washington
268–302	Ohio	540–544	Oregon
303–317	Indiana	545–573	California
318–361	Illinois	574	Alaska
362–386	Michigan	575–576	Hawaii
387–399	Wisconsin	577–579	District of Columbia
400–407	Kentucky	580	Virgin Islands
408–415	Tennessee	(2) 580–584	Puerto Rico
416–424	Alabama	586	Guam
425–428,587	Mississippi	(3) 586	American Samoa
429–432	Arkansas	(3) 586	Philippine Islands
433–439	Louisiana	700–729	Railroad Retirement Board
440–448	Oklahoma		

(1) Area 232: Number 30 (middle 2 digits of SSN) allocated to N. Carolina by transfer from W. Virginia.

(2) Area 580: Numbers 01–18 (middle 2 digits of SSN) allocated to the Virgin Islands; number 20 and above allocated to Puerto Rico.

(3) Area 586: Numbers 01–18 (middle 2 digits of SSN) allocated to Guam; numbers 20–28 allocated to American Samoa; numbers 30–58 reserved for possible future allocation to other Pacific possessions or trust territories; numbers 60–78 allocated during initial registration of armed service personnel for assignment to those who were natives of the Phillippine Islands; number 80 and above not allocated.

(Next page is 9781-325)

Procedures and Techniques in Other Investigations

510 *(1-18-80)* 9781
Interference, Forcible Rescue of Seized Property

511 *(1-18-80)* 9781
Interference Cases

511.1 *(1-18-80)* 9781
Corrupt or Forcible Interference (IRC 7212(a))

(1) The text of the law under this section is set forth in text 221.(10).

(2) The elements essential to constitute an offense under this section are:

(a) Corruptly, or by force or by threats of force (including any threatening letter or communication)

1 Endeavors to intimidate or impede an offical acting in an official capacity under this title, OR

2 Endeavors to impede or obstruct the due administration of this title.

(3) This section provides for the punishment of threats or threatening acts against agents of the Internal Revenue Service or any other officer or employee of the United States or members of the families of such persons on account of the performance by such agents or officers or employees of their official duties.

(4) Although in the Conference Committee's Report (House and Senate) it is stated that "this section will also punish the corrupt solicitation of an Internal Revenue Employee," the section of the law itself does not literally embody the word "solicitation." However, it appears that the broad phrase "in any other way CORRUPTLY . . . obstructs or impedes" would include not only solicitation, but other acts of a similar nature. The Committee's Report also states that:

> "Subsection (a) of Section 7212 is broader than Section 111, Title 18 of the United States Code relating to persons assaulting, resisting or impeding certain officers or employees of the United States while engaged in the performance of their official duties, in that 7212(a) covers force or threats of force (including any threatening letter or communication) or corrupt solicitation. Threats of force have been defined as meaning threats of bodily harm to the officer or employee of the United States or members of the families of such persons, on account of the performance by such agents or officers or employees of their official duties."

(5) CORRUPTLY characterizes an attempt to influence any official in his/her official capacity under this title by any improper inducement. For example, an offer of a bribe or a passing of a bribe to an Internal Revenue employee for the purpose of influencing him/her in the performance of his/her official duties is corrupt interference with the administration of Federal laws.

511.2 *(1-18-80)* 9781
Assault, Resisting or Impeding Certain Officers or Employees (18 USC 111)

The text of this statute is in text 222.5. Although there is some overlapping between it and IRC 7212(a), the latter is broader because it includes use of force or threats of bodily harm to the officer or employee of the United States acting in an official capacity under the Internal Revenue laws, or any member of his/her family. A mere threat of force under IRC 7212(a) may be chargeable only as a misdemeanor, even if the threat consists of pointing a rifle at the agent. On the other hand, 18 USC 111, which makes it an offense to assault, resist, oppose, impede, intimidate, or interfere with officers or employees designated under 18 USC 1114 (including Internal Revenue Service employees), provides a much more severe punishment when the act is committed with a deadly or dangerous weapon. Furthermore, cases under 18 USC 111 have not required proof of knowledge of the official capacity of the person assaulted. [*U.S. v. Lombardozzi.*]

511.3 *(1-18-80)* 9781
Investigative Responsibility

(1) The Inspection Service has primary jurisdiction for investigation of all threats, assaults, and forcible interference against IRS personnel. All reports of assaults, threats or forcible interference against Service employees must go either directly or through appropriate supervisory channels to the Inspection Service. The Criminal Investigation Division will assist Inspection in urgent or emergency situations. The Regional Inspector will evaluate the situation and when, in the view of the Regional Inspector, the deployment of Inspection personnel does not meet the urgency required, the Regional Inspector may request assistance from Criminal Investigation to conduct the investigation of the alleged threat, assault or other forcible in-

terference. Inspection will be provided with a copy of the investigative report.

(2) In emergency forcible interference situations, where an employee is in imminent danger of physical harm and Internal Security Inspectors are not readily available, Criminal Investigation will respond immediately. As soon as possible the Regional Inspector will be notified so that the appropriate investigation can be conducted or completed by Criminal Investigation or Inspection.

(3) If forcible interference takes place during an armed escort assignment, or during an arrest or raid in connection with a matter pending before the Criminal Investigation Division, Criminal Investigation will conduct the necessary investigation. The Regional Inspector shall be notified by the Chief at the earliest opportunity and provided with a copy of the investigative report.

511.4 *(1-18-80)* 9781
Investigation of Interference Cases

(1) Interference cases may arise quite suddenly in Federal tax proceedings, such as during a seizure or some other enforcement, levy, or collection activity. Ordinarily the information causing this type of investigation comes direct to the Chief, who, thereafter, because of the hazard involved to the investigating officer as well as the peril in which the enforcement system of the Service is placed in a violation of this nature, keeps abreast of the developments of the investigation. This is necessary because every action taken has to be planned with utmost circumspection. However, prompt action is of the essence.

(2) It must be established that the assaulted or threatened officer was engaged in the performance of official duties when the assault or threats occurred and, at least, if prosecution is intended under IRC 7212(a), that the assault or threats were intended to impede or obstruct the performance of those duties. If the assault or threat is in connection with official duties, it is immaterial whether the act occurred during the agent's official working hours. The investigating special agent should promptly:

(a) Examine the file relating to the assignment of the case, and obtain from it copies of all records and data pertaining to the date and circumstances of the assignment;

(b) Obtain from the assaulted or threatened officer a sworn statement concerning whether he/she was engaged in the performance of official duties in pursuance of such assignment when the assault or threats occurred;

(c) Ascertain if there had been any prior ill will or altercation between the assailant and the Government officer, and if so find out the nature of it;

(d) Obtain from the assaulted or threatened officer, as well as from any other persons who witnessed either the assault or the menacing gestures or heard any threats of force, sworn testimony of knowledge of the incidents and circumstances leading up to and accompanying the assault or threats of force. This sworn testimony should include:

1 A recital of any conversation that took place and any threatening language that was used.

2 A description of the assault, any menacing gestures, and any weapons or instruments used. The investigating special agent should also, if possible, obtain possession of such instruments or weapons and get the names and addresses of witnesses who can identify them.

(e) Consider the advisability of interviewing the person who allegedly made the threat or assault.

(3) A diagram of the premises where an assault, menacing gestures, and threatening language occurred has been used advantageously to orient the witnesses while taking their testimony.

(4) For reasons stated above, it is intended that the investigating special agent will daily keep his/her Chief and/or immediate supervisor apprised of the developments, and that together they will determine what further investigation is required or what further action should be taken.

(5) Exhibit 600-11 of this Handbook illustrates the type of investigation that may be required when a member of an IRS employee's family receives a threat through the mails.

511.5 *(1-18-80)* 9781
Assault or Resistance to Search or Service of Process (18 USC 1501; 18 USC 2231)

Both of these statutes concern assaults upon, resistance to, and interference with persons serving or executing legal process, or making searches and seizures. The text of Section 1501 appears in 222.(19), and the text of Section 2231 is found in 222.(31). Section 1501, which carries a lighter penalty, includes nonforcible acts of obstruction, but requires knowledge that the person impeded was an officer engaged in serving or executing process. Section 2231 is restricted to forcible interference with searches and seizures, or service and execution of search warrants. It would normally appear that if the activity involved is a search, with or without warrant, and force is alleged, prosecution might better be recommended under Section 2231 because of the more severe punishment provided, particularly if a deadly or dangerous weapon is used. On the other hand, if the alleged willful interference involves some legal process other than a search warrant or if there has been no showing of force, prosecution would lie only under Section 1501. No case has yet determined if interference with service of a Commissioner's summons is a violation of Section 1501.

511.6 *(1-18-80)* 9781
Obstruction of Criminal Investigations (18 USC 1510)

This statute provides criminal sanctions against anyone who attempts to prevent the transmission of information regarding a violation to a criminal investigator or who injures any person or his/her property because of giving of such information. The text is set forth in 222.(21).

512 *(1-18-80)* 9781
Forcible Rescue of Seized Property

512.1 *(1-18-80)* 9781
Elements of Forcible Rescue Cases

512.11 *(1-18-80)* 9781
Forcible Rescue (IRC 7212(b))

(1) The essential elements of this offense are:

(a) That there is a forcible rescue or attempt to forcibly rescue.

(b) That the property is under valid seizure under Title 26.

(2) The text of this statute is set forth in 221.(10).

512.12 *(1-18-80)* 9781
Rescue of Seized Property (18 USC 2233)

(1) The essential elements of the offense under the Criminal Code (18 USC 2233) are:

(a) That there is a forcible rescue or dispossession or an attempt to forcibly rescue or dispossess;

(b) That the property has been taken, detained, or seized under the authority of a revenue law of the United States, or by any person authorized to make searches and seizures.

(2) The text of this statute is set forth in 222.(33).

(3) Prosecution recommendation may be made under this section if:

(a) There has been a seizure, levy, or other taking which is sufficient to put the retaker on notice that the prooperty is under process of seizure for taxes;

(b) There is a retaking by physical force, stealth, or in any other manner which indicates a willful defiance of the legal process.

512.2 *(1-18-80)* 9781
Investigation of Forcible Rescue Cases

(1) Cases interpreting forcible rescue under both IRC 7212(b) and 18 USC 2233 permit prosecution for rescuing or dispossessing, or attempting to rescue or dispossess property of which the Government has taken legal possession, against a stranger as well as a former owner. [Chief Counsel memo, 3/9/60, CC:En:SAK-A-63868.]

(2) By present practice, determination of whether an alleged forcible rescue is to be investigated by the Criminal Investigation Division or the Federal Bureau of Investigation depends on whether the property was taken before or after it was adjudicated Government property. Before undertaking an investigation, the special agent should first determine if it is one to be handled by the Criminal Investigation Division, as prescribed in IRM 9123:(3), as follows:

"The Criminal Investigation Division has the responsibility for investigating cases involving forcible rescue or dispossession of property seized under the Internal Revenue laws, except property seized by the Bureau of Alcohol, Tobacco and Firearms. However, cases involving theft of Government property are within the responsibilities of the Federal Bureau of Investigation, including seized property which has been adjudicated as Government property and seized property which has been turned over to the United States Marshal in a libel proceeding."

(3) Upon determining that it is a case within the Criminal Investigation jurisdiction the special agent should promptly establish whether the property was under valid seizure under the Internal Revenue Code when rescued, and whether it was forcibly rescued or there was an attempt to forcibly rescue it.

(4) To be a basis for a forcible rescue case under 18 USC 2233 or IRC 7212, the taking by the Government must have been made with at least some semblance of authority, i.e., the seizure must be valid on its face. [*Cooper v. U.S.*] It should be shown that the person retaking the property had knowledge of the seizure or of the fact that the property is in the possession of the Government. [Chief Counsel memo, 3/9/60, CC:En:SAK-A-63868.] A seizure valid on its face will generally support a rescue conviction even if the seizure could be invalidated by court proceedings. It is no defense that the person retaking claims to be the real owner and that the property was seized by mistake. A person's remedy is judicial, not self-help. [*U.S. v. Scolnick*]

(5) "Forcible" does not necessarily mean actual violence to the person of an officer. It includes "threatening language, or conduct calculated and intended to intimidate prudent, cautious, and ordinarily brave men and make them desist from the performance of official duty from well-grounded apprehension of serious bodily harm." [*U.S. v. Wm. Ford*] It has been held that a forcible rescue, under IRC 7212(b), includes the use of force against property, such as the breaking of a bank window, the removal of the Service's seal on a safe deposit box, and the removal of the box and its contents from the bank. [*U.S. v. Scolnick*]

(6) The procedure in investigating to determine whether the property has been validly seized, and whether there has been a forcible rescue or attempt to forcibly rescue, should be as follows:

(a) *Validity of Seizure.*

1 Examine the file relating to the seizure and obtain therefrom certified copies of all the documents giving legal basis to the seizure;

2 Interview under oath all officers, employees, and other persons having any knowledge of the circumstances leading up to and including the seizure, concerning all facts pertinent to the accomplishment of the seizure; and

3 Establish that a notice of seizure was attached to the property.

(b) *Forcible Rescue of the Seized Property.*—Interview under oath those officers, employees, and other persons who may have witnessed the forcible rescue regarding the circumstances leading up to and including the forcible rescue, with a recital of any threatening language as well as a description of any menacing gestures, instruments, or weapons used. The special agent should try to obtain any instruments or weapons used by the assailant and get the names and addresses of witnesses who can identify them. An effort should also be made to establish what knowledge the defendant had that the property was under seizure when the forcible rescue was committed or attempted.

520 *(1-18-80)* 9781
Offer of Bribe (18 USC 201)

521 *(1-18-80)* 9781
Reference

The text of the law under this section is set forth in 222.6.

522 *(1-18-80)* 9781
Elements of Offer of Bribe

The principal elements of the offense described in this section are: Promising, offering, or giving of a thing of value to an officer or an employee or a person acting for or on behalf of the United States for the purpose of influencing his/her official conduct [*Kemler v. U.S.*]; corrupt intent of the promisor, offeror, or giver to influence such officer, employee, or person in the discharge of his/her duties [*Kemler v. U.S.*]; and knowledge by the person making the promise, offer, or gift of the official function of the person to whom the promises, offer, or gift is made. [*Bradshaw v. U.S.*] To "offer" and to "give" bribes are distinct crimes even when part of a single transaction. The test of whether a single transaction includes distinct offenses of offering and of giving a bribe is whether separate acts have been committed with requisite criminal intent. [*U.S. v. Michelson*] The statute is violated when a bribe is given or an offer to bribe is made regardless of the occasion therefor, provided the acceptor or offeree of the bribe is a person of the sort described in the statute. [*Kemler v. U.S.*]

523 *(1-18-80)* 9781
Jurisdiction in Offer of Bribe

(1) The jurisdiction of the Criminal Investigation Division in offer of bribe cases is prescribed in IRM 9123:(1) as follows:

> "Except in raid or arrest cases, charges of attempted bribery of Internal Revenue employees will be investigated by Inspection. The Criminal Investigation Division has the responsibility for investigating attempted bribery which occurs during a raid or an arrest in connection with any matter pending before the Criminal Investigation Division. In such instances a written report of the attempted bribery will be furnished to Inspection for information purposes. Cases involving alleged solicitation of gratuities by Service employees, and extortion or bribes received by employees are within the jurisdiction of Inspection and the Federal Bureau of Investigation. However, when there has been an allegation of an acceptance of a bribe, the Criminal Investigation Division may cooperate in a joint investigation with Inspection by inquiring into possible attempted evasion of income tax on the amount of bribe received and possible tax violations which the alleged bribe was made to conceal."

(2) In any case, except raid and arrest cases, when a special agent is offered a bribe, or has reasonable grounds for believing that such an offer will be made, he/she should follow the procedures as set forth in IRM 9142.2.

524 *(1-18-80)* 9781
Investigation of Offer of Bribe

(1) If a bribe offer occurs during a raid or an arrest, the statements of the officers with respect to what is said should be reduced to sworn testimony. It is essential to establish beyond any question, from the words and conduct of the offeror, that his/her intent was that of offering a bribe to a Government officer. The officers should, therefore, be able to testify fully and with absolute certainty about the conduct of the parties, their conversations, and any transactions that take place.

(2) If during a raid the bribe offer is made by someone other than the person under arrest, the individual making the offer should also be placed under arrest and charged with offer of a bribe. If the offer is made by someone already under arrest additional charges for offering the bribe should be placed against him/her. If money has been handed to the Government officer, he/she should be careful to make a list of the serial numbers and denominations in the presence of at least one other Government officer and note any other distinguishing features. The officer should then put the money in an envelope or in some other suitable container and seal it in such manner that he/she can later identify the seal and that it will have to be broken to get at the contents. Thereupon the container shall be delivered by the officer for safekeeping to the district office cashier or cashier's representative. The container shall be held by the cashier or cashier's representative in safe custody in its exact state of condition on delivery. The special agent should exercise due care in issuing instructions relative to the conditions of custody so that the chain of evidence will be preserved.

(3) This technique of investigation requires the greatest expertness and discretion to obviate a defense of entrapment. The Government officer should be extremely circumspect about what he says and does after the offer of bribe has been made.

530 *(1-18-80)* 9781
Perjury

531 *(1-18-80)* 9781
Reference

The text of 18 USC 1621, relating to perjury, is set forth in 222.(22).

532 *(1-18-80)* 9781
Elements of Perjury

(1) *Oath.*

(a) The oath must be solemnly administered by a duly authorized officer. It is immaterial in what form the oath is given if the party at the time professes such form to be binding on his/her conscience. However, a special agent, when administering an oath, should follow the language in Section 1621 as a guide and call upon the witness to testify truly. The special agent's demeanor should be such as to impress upon the witness the solemnity of the oath and the need for telling the truth.

(b) In order to constitute perjury under the laws of the United States, the officer administering the oath must be authorized so to do by the laws of the United States. The source of a special agent's authority to administer an oath is stated in 346.2 and Exhibit 300-13. Notaries public can administer oaths and take affidavits on which perjury can be predicated in Federal courts only in cases and to the extent authorized by Federal statutes.

(2) *False statement.*—In order to constitute perjury, the matter sworn to must be a material matter that the deponent knows or believes to be false. [*State v. Doto*] The essence of perjury is the false assertion of knowledge or belief, rather than the truth or falsity of the statement itself. Thus, perjury may be committed as to a statement which is true in fact, if the deponent falsely asserts it to be true to his/her knowledge or belief, when he/she really believes it to be false or lacks any knowledge of its truth or falsity. It is equally as perjurious for a person to knowingly and corruptly to swear that he/she is ignorant of a fact of which he/she is actually aware [*People v. Moretti*] as it is to swear that he/she knows something to be a fact when he/she is actually ignorant of it.

(3) *Materiality.*

(a) Any statement which is relevant to the matter under investigation is sufficiently material to form the basis of a perjury charge. The question of materiality is one of law for the court. [*Breckanstin v. U.S.; U.S. v. Moran*] The test of materiality is whether the false statement can influence, impede, or dissuade the tribunal or the Government officer. [*Boehm v. U.S.*] Materiality is not a matter of degree. It is sufficient if the false statement is collaterally, remotely, corroboratively, or circumstantially material or has a legitimate tendency to prove or disprove a fact in the chain of evidence. [*U.S. v. Weiler*]

(b) A special agent's principal consideration in determining whether a false statement given in the course of an official investigation is material and perjurious is: can the statement affect the investigation?

(4) *Willfulness, Knowledge, and Intent.*—In order to constitute perjury, the false statement must be made with criminal intent, that is, it must be made with intent to deceive, and must be willfully, deliberately, knowingly and corruptly false. [*Breckanstin v. U.S.*] The subject of willfulness is discussed in 41(11). The crime of perjury in an affidavit is complete when the oath is taken with the necessary intent, but it is immaterial and irrelevant that the false affidavit is never used. [*Steinberg v. U.S.*]

(5) To convict of perjury the prosecution must produce testimony of more direct and positive type than is required to justify a verdict of guilty in other offenses. [*Hart v. U.S.; Allen v. U.S.*]

533 *(1-18-80)* 9781
Establishing Elements of Perjury

(1) *Establishing Authority to Administer Oath.*—Since the burden of proof is on the prosecution to establish the false swearing before an officer or tribunal having authority to administer the oath, the prosecution must adduce sufficient evidence to establish such authority. The Government shall therefore be prepared to present as evidence the required copies of those instruments or the official record establishing the authority of the officer administering the oath. The fact that the oath was administered must be proved beyond a reasonable doubt.

(2) *Establishing That a Statement Was Made.*—The prosecution must show beyond a reasonable doubt that the accused made the statement assigned as perjury. The special agent shall therefore obtain authenticated copies of the record of proceedings wherein the alleged statement was made, or be prepared to produce:

(a) the document embodying the perjurious statement;

(b) the officer who administered the oath in connection therewith; and

(c) any witnesses who were present when the document was signed.

(3) *Establishing Falsity of Statement.*

(a) The burden of proof is upon the prosecution to establish that the deponent knew or believed that the statement to which he/she testified was false. This must be established by testimony of two witnesses, or by one witness and written documents of strong corroborating circumstances proved by independent testimony of witnesses. [*Phair v. U.S.; Allen v. U.S.*]

(b) The mere fact that a prior statement was inconsistent with a later statement does not satisfy the elements of perjury. [*U.S. v. Letchos*] The prosecution must adduce sufficient evidence of the circumstances under which each statement was made for the jury to determine if one of them was false. Mere showing that the accused later denied the truth of an earlier statement is insufficient, even if the denial is established by testimony of more than one witness. There must still be strong, clear evidence to establish the falsity of the earlier statement. [*Phair v. U.S.; Allen v. U.S.*]

(c) There can be no conviction for perjury if the defense can show that the statements or answers are literally accurate, technically responsive, and legally truthful. [*J. Robt. Smith v. U.S.*] Mere showing of rash or reckless statements under oath will not support a charge of perjury, since the willful intent to mislead or deceive is lacking. [*U.S. v. Edwards*] However, proof that a person gave testimony under oath in reckless disregard of its truth or falsity would be equivalent proof that he/she have testimony with knowledge of its falsity.

(d) The special agent in the interview of the witness must be sure that the questions put to the witness are specific and couched in terms which are understandable to such witness, and that the answers thereto are specific, since the proof must be of a specific false statement or statements. [*Galanos v. U.S.*] Questions put to the witness must search for the truth. [*U.S. v. Slutsky*] If it appears that the witness is tending to deviate from the truth, the special agent may remind him/her that he/she is testifying under oath. This should not be done in a threatening manner, but rather in the spirit of emphasizing the gravity of the situation and the importance of the witness' telling the truth. The entire proceedings should be recorded.

(4) *Establishment of Materiality.*—The special agent should be prepared to adduce testimony and/or other competent evidence concerning the purpose of information sought from the witness and the place it takes in the chain of evidence sufficient to convince the court of its materiality. The materiality of the false testimony may be shown by the record of the proceedings in which it was given or by other competent evidence. [*U.S. v. Weber; U.S. v. Moran*]

534 *(1-18-80)* 9781

False Declarations Before Grand Jury or Court

The text of 18 U.S.C. 1623, relating to false declarations under oath before a grand jury or court, is set forth in 222.(24). Passed as part of the Omnibus Crime Bill of 1970, the offense requires proof that the defendant knowingly made two or more declarations which are inconsistent to the degree that one of them is necessarily false. The Government need not specify which declaration is false if each declaration was material to the point in issue and each statement was made within the statute of limitations period for this offense. It is not necessary that proof be made by any particular number of witnesses or by documentary or other type of evidence.

540 *(1-18-80)* 9781

Criminal Enforcement of International Boycott Provisions of the Internal Revenue Code (IRC 999).

(1) The text of the law specifying criminal penalties is IRC 999(f). This section provides that any person who willfully fails to make an international boycott report shall, in addition to other penalties provided by law, be guilty of a misdemeanor, the penalty for which is imprisonment up to one year and/or a fine up to $25,000.

(2) The term "person" is defined to include "an officer or employee of a corporation, or a member or employee of a partnership, who as such officer, employee, or member is under a duty to perform the act in respect of which the violation occurs." (IRC 999(f), 6671(b).) Prosecutions, especially of individuals, may be complicated by difficulties in ascertaining which officer, employee or member is under the duty to make the international boycott report.

(3) Insofar as IRC 999(f) is concerned, there are two elements: the requirement that an international boycott report be filed and the requirement that the failure to file such a report be wilful.

(4) Whether or not a report is required is a technical matter, discussion of which should be reserved for pre-referral conferences in respect of specific cases. Suffice it to say that there is an abundance of complexities in IRC 999 which taxpayers will undoubtedly raise as a defense to any proposed prosecution.

(5) The term "wilful" is believed to mean the voluntary, intentional violation of a known legal duty. (U.S. v Bishop and U.S. v Pomponio). There is nothing to indicate that Congress intended a more restrictive standard to apply in the context of IRC 999(f), i.e., there is no requirement that a specific intent (or evil motive) be established.

(6) A failure to make (file) a report will not be a willful failure if the taxpayer had no knowledge of a boycott operation *unless the taxpayer's failure to have knowledge is so negligent as to constitute a reckless disregard of the requirements of the law.*

(7) A prima facie case under IRC 999(f), without reference to any deficiency, can be estab-

lished. In fact, the question of deficiency is technically irrelevant and should theoretically be inadmissible at trial. Nevertheless, the reasonable probability of conviction would be significantly increased if the willful failure to file was coupled with a revenue effect.

(8) It is conceivable that the failure to file an international boycott report under IRC 999(a)(1) could also result in a violation of IRC 7201, IRC 7203, or IRC 7206(1). It would generally be preferable to recommend under IRC 999(f) rather than under IRC 7203.

550 *(1-18-80)* 9781
Special Investigation

551 *(1-18-80)* 9781
Offers in Compromise

551.1 *(1-18-80)* 9781
Reference

The text of the laws relating to compromise is set forth in IRC 7121, 7122, 7123, and 7206(5). Compromise procedures are discussed in IRM 9262 and 9541 and IRM 5700, Offers in Compromise.

551.2 *(1-18-80)* 9781
Criminal Investigation Division Responsibility

(1) The Criminal Investigation Division is concerned with the following types of offers in compromise:

(a) alleged fraudulent offers;

(b) offers involving cases that were jointly investigated by the Criminal Investigation Division with the Examination or Collection Division and in which the criminal aspects have been disposed of; and

(c) offers made while criminal proceedings are pending.

551.3 *(1-18-80)* 9781
Alleged Fraudulent Offers

(1) This type of case is referred either by the Examination Division or by the Collection Division upon discovery of indications of the falsity of material statements made in, or in connection with any offer in compromise.

(2) The text of the law under IRC 7206 relating to criminal penalties for concealment of property, false statements, or falsifying and destroying records in connection with any compromise, or offer of compromise is stated in Paragraph (5)(A) and (B) (See 221.7).

(3) The principal offenses are the willful:

(a) concealment from any officer or employee of the United States of any property belonging to the estate of a taxpayer or any other person liable in respect to the tax;

(b) receiving, withholding, destruction, mutilation or falsification of any book, document, or record of the taxpayer or any other person liable in respect of the tax; and

(c) making a false statement relating to the estate or financial condition of the taxpayer or other person liable in respect of the tax.

551.4 *(1-18-80)* 9781
Offers in Closed Cases

(1) Offers involving cases that were jointly investigated with the Examination or Collection Division and in which the criminal aspects have been disposed of will be examined by the Examination Division. After completion of such examination, the Chief, Examination Division (or District Director in streamlined districts) will refer the entire file to the Chief, Criminal Investigation Division, for concurrence or comment when *all* the following conditions exist:

(a) The merits of the ad valorem fraud or negligence penalty are involved.

(b) The case is one in which the special agent has recommended the assertion of such a penalty in the final report in the case.

(c) The Examination Division contemplates recommending acceptance of the offer.

(2) This does not include cases in which the sole issue presented by the offer in compromise is the ability to pay. (See IRM 5700, Offers in Compromise.)

551.5 *(1-18-80)* 9781
Offers in Pending Criminal Proceedings Cases

Investigations of offers in pending criminal proceedings cases result from requests made by the Chief Counsel or District Counsel for examination or investigation of a taxpayer's financial status in connection with an offer in compromise submitted in a case in which criminal proceedings are pending either in Counsel's office, in the Department of Justice, or with the United States Attorney. Any such investigation shall be conducted jointly by the Criminal Investigation and Examination Divisions. (See IRM 9262.4.)

551.6 *(1-18-80)* 9781
Investigation of Offers in Compromise

The special agent should acquaint himself/herself with the contents of the sections of the 1954 Code especially those cited at text 551.1 and the pertinent sections of IRM 5700, Offers in Compromise.

551.7 *(1-18-80)* 9781
Alleged Fraudulent Offers

(1) The Criminal Investigation Division shall investigate, report, and process such cases in the same manner as other tax fraud cases. (See IRM 9262.2).

(2) Cases of concealment entail the unearthing of all assets belonging to the taxpayer or to any other person liable in respect of the tax. The matter of establishing willfulness and intent is accomplished in the same manner as in other tax fraud cases using techniques set forth in 41(11).

(3) Cases involving the receiving, withholding, destruction, mutilation, or falsification of any book, document, or record are investigated similarly to any other tax fraud case. The special agent will assemble documentary or oral evidence to establish the commission of the act and that the act was committed willfully, with intent to defraud the Government.

(4) The techniques to be applied in the investigation of false statements are similar to those used in the investigation of violations of 18 USC 1001 and 1621 "False Statements" and "Perjury," respectively.

551.8 *(1-18-80)* 9781
Investigating Offers in Closed Cases

Investigation of cases in which the three conditions listed in 551.4 are present are usually limited to the discovery of additional facts relating to the propriety of asserting the fraud or negligence penalty. However, district officials will not remove civil penalties for any periods for which the taxpayer has been indicted or for which a Criminal Information has been filed. Civil penalties for years on which conviction was not obtained will be considered in the light of all available evidence in the same manner as the civil penalties in nonprosecution cases. (See IRM 9358.) The special agent should be extremely careful not to reverse recommendations for the addition of the fraud or negligence penalty unless he discovers additional facts or information that would warrant and logically support a change in his recommendation.

551.9 *(1-18-80)* 9781
Offers in Criminal Proceedings Cases

Investigations of this type will be centered primarily on the determination of the accuracy of the accompanying financial statements and any other sworn statements submitted therewith. The reasons for any inaccuracies that are found will have to be ascertained and the techniques mentioned in 551.7 may be used to determine willfullness and intent in connection therewith. Cases of this type often challenge the ingenuity and resourcefulness of the agent in efforts to uncover concealed property. The agent should closely examine statements of financial conditions and be watchful for possible sources for the collection of taxes. Every clue which could possibly lead to the disclosure of concealed assets or to property transferred without consideration should be investigated diligently and the results should be included in the investigator's report on the case. (See IRM 5700, Offers in Compromise.)

552 *(1-18-80)* 9781
Jeopardy Assessments

552.1 *(1-18-80)* 9781
References

The text of the law relating to jeopardy assessments is set forth in IRC 6861, 6862, and 6863 and IRM 9263, 9329, and 9634.3.

552.2 *(1-18-80)* 9781
Criminal Investigation Division Responsibility

The Criminal Investigation Division is responsible for recommending jeopardy or termination assessments in cases under active consideration by Criminal Investigation and in cases under joint active consideration with Examination or Collection. In other instances, special agents should be alert for information indicating the possible existence of jeopardy situations and should report such information by memorandum to the affected division. Recommendations should be prepared on Forms 2644 (Recommendation for Jeopardy/Termination Assessment) and 2645 (List of Property Belonging to Taxpayer). See IRM 9634.3. Recommendations will be referred for concurrence or comment to the Chief, Collection Division; to the Chief, Examination Division; to the Chief, Special Procedures Staff; and, if time permits, to District Counsel prior to referral to the District Director for personal approval.

552.3 *(1-18-80)* 9781
Jeopardy Situations

(1) A jeopardy assessment is recommended when it appears that collection of tax will be endangered if regular assessment and collection procedures are followed.

(2) In determining whether a jeopardy assessment may be made at least one of the following three conditions must exist:

(a) The taxpayer is, or appears to be, designing quickly to depart from the United States or to conceal himself/herself.

(b) The taxpayer is, or appears to be, designing quickly to place property beyond the reach of the Government by removing it from the United States, concealing it, dissipating it, or transferring it to other persons.

(c) The taxpayer's financial solvency is or appears to be imperiled. However, the taxpayer should not be considered to be insolvent by virtue of the accrual of the proposed deficiencies of tax, penalty, and interest.

(3) The jeopardy assessment procedure is a drastic exception to the normally accepted method of assessment and collection of taxes and should not be used as an additional penalty or for any other improper purpose. It should be used sparingly and care should be taken to avoid excessive and unreasonable assessments. It should be limited to amounts which reasonably can be expected to protect the Government and must be personally approved by the District Director.

(4) Notwithstanding the existence of one or more of the above-cited conditions, in any case which might cause serious inconvenience to the general public, a jeopardy or termination assessment should not be made without prior notification to the appropriate Regional Commissioner. If necessary, the Regional Commissioner will notify the Deputy Commissioner. Examples of such cases include banks, newspapers, insurance companies, hospitals and public utility companies.

(5) Jeopardy assessment will be withheld in potential criminal tax cases to the extent necessary to avoid imperiling successful investigation or prosecution of such cases. On the other hand, when such action is warranted in those cases, it must be taken whenever it is feasible to do so. The District Director is responsible for this practice when jeopardy assessment recommendations are submitted to him/her for approval. See Policy Statement P-4-84.

552.4 *(1-18-80)* 9781
Investigation of Jeopardy Assessment Cases

(1) Upon the receipt or discovery of information indicating the presence of any one of the three jeopardy situations enumerated in 552.3:(2), the special agent should obtain all available facts and evidence which will either establish or refute the existence of a jeopardy situation. Promptness and discretion is of the essence in this type of investigation, since it could work to the serious disadvantage of the Government if the taxpayer should discover that such an investigation or inquiry is being made. Surveillance may be necessary in some cases.

(2) The special agent should make every effort to locate all assets belonging to the taxpayer and list them in the report recommending a jeopardy assessment. However, to avoid unnecessary expenses and embarrassment to the Government through levying upon property in which, although title stands in taxpayer's name, his/her actual equity has no marketable value, the special agent should endeavor to ascertain if practicable, the nature and conditions of any existent liens and encumbrances on the assets. The agent should include this information in the report, together with any other information that should be considered in determining the advisability of making a jeopardy assessment.

(3) The mere levy of a jeopardy assessment, in the absence of a showing by a defendant that the defense of the criminal case was thereby hampered, was insufficient to preclude trial of an indictment for tax evasion. [*Summers v. U.S.; O'Connor, Kenneth A. v. U.S.*] On the other hand, a motion to postpone a criminal trial until conclusion of civil proceedings in Tax Court was granted on the theory that freezing the defendant's assets might prevent the retaining of counsel and accountants to help defend a net worth tax case and thus depriving the defendant of a fair trial. [*U.S. v. Brodson*]

553 *(1-18-80)* 9781
Termination Assessments

553.1 *(1-18-80)* 9781
References

The text of the law relating to termination assessments is set forth in IRC 6851. Manual references are in IRM 9263, 9329, and 9634.3.

553.2 *(1-18-80)* 9781
Introduction

(1) Another type of immediate assessment action is the termination assessment of income tax under IRC 6851. It may be made only on income tax liabilities. It specifically applies when the taxable year of a taxpayer has not ended, or when the taxable year has ended but the due date for filing the return, or the due date as extended, has not arrived.

(2) Criminal Investigation Division responsibility for termination assessments is stated in Text 552.2. Termination assessments may be made only if at least one of the three conditions found in Text 552.3 exists.

553.3 *(1-18-80)* 9781
Requirements

(1) Termination assessments must be used sparingly and care taken to avoid excessive and unreasonable assessments. They should be limited to amounts which reasonably can be expected to equal the ultimate tax liability.

(2) The District Director or, for cases in International Operations, the Director, OIO, must approve termination and jeopardy assessments.

(3) An assessment made as a result of termination of taxable period must be based on a reasonable computation of tax liability. An assessment equal to the amount of money or other valuable property held by a person at the time of arrest is not considered a reasonable computation unless supported by other facts.

(4) The basis used in arriving at adjusted gross income in terminations of taxable periods will be stated. The computation will be determined using an acceptable legal basis such as a source and application of funds statement or a net worth computation. The following information illustrates the types of items that may have to be considered in order to arrive at an adjusted gross income computation:

(a) Cost of living expenses should include professional estimates by a narcotics agent (or other expert) as to the "Cost of Habit" for a narcotics addict.

(b) Estimates of income from the sale of narcotics should be supported, if possible, by testimony from a narcotics agent (or other expert) who may have knowledge of the subject's activities.

(c) Estimates of income from illegal gambling, including "gross take" and "payoffs" may be supported by testimony of law enforcement officers who are familiar with the gambler's operations. Efforts should be made to obtain similar testimony in cases involving other illegal activities.

(d) The taxpayer should be interviewed, if feasible, preferably before assessment is made, in order to afford him/her an opportunity to explain questioned assets, liabilities, income or expenses, filing history, etc. Such an interview may also be of value in revealing previously unknown assets, liabilities, income or expenses.

(e) Efforts should be made to locate and examine books and records, if any, of the taxpayer to the extent possible in the available time.

560 *(8-1-80)* 9781
Crimes Under Title 31, United States Code

(1) The provisions of Title 31, United States Code, that are cited and summarized below provide for the punishment of crimes committed in contravention of Financial Recordkeeping and Reporting requirements of Treasury Regulations, 31 CFR Part 103.

(2) General Provisions of Treasury Regulations, 31 CFR Part 103 *Regulations Section(s).*

(a) 103.22, 103.25(a) and 103.26. When any person engages in a currency transaction of more than $10,000 with a financial institution, the financial institution must report the identity of the person or persons involved and file a report on a Currency Transaction Report, Form 4789, containing certain details of the transaction within 15 days.

(b) 103.23(a), 103.23(b) and 103.25(c). Any person transporting or causing transportation of more than $5,000 of currency or certain monetary instruments at any one time, into or out of the United States, must file a report with the U.S. Customs Service on a Report of International Transportation of Currency or Monetary Instruments, Form 4790, at the time of departure, mailing or shipping.

(c) 103.24 and 103.32. A person must indicate on his/her income tax return whether or not he/she has any interest in or authority over a foreign financial account.

(d) The Criminal Investigation Division has investigative jurisdiction for enforcement of (a) and (c) above. The U.S. Customs Service enforces (b).

(3) *Criminal Penalties under Title 31, United States Code*

(a) For each willful violation of these regulations, a fine of up to $1,000 and/or imprisonment for not more than one year (except for recordkeeping violations by insured banks and savings and loan associations).

(b) For each violation of the recordkeeping requirements, a fine of up to $10,000 and/or imprisonment of not more than five years if the violation is committed in connection with the violation of a Federal law punishable by imprisonment for more than one year.

(c) For each false statement or representation in any report required by these regulations, a fine of not more than $10,000 and/or imprisonment of not more than five years.

(d) For each violation of the reporting requirements, a fine of up to $500,000 and/or imprisonment of not more than five years if the violation is committed in furtherance of the commission of any other violation of Federal law or committed as part of a pattern of illegal activity and which involves more than $100,000 in a twelve-month period.

(4) See also IRM 9214.

610 *(1-18-80)* 9781
Purpose and Importance of Reports

The result of all the work done by a special agent, together with conclusions and recommendations, is finally expressed in a written report. The purpose of a report is to present in suitable form all the pertinent facts relating to a matter in order that appropriate action may be taken. To have value, a report must be so written that the reader comprehends the full significance of its contents, is convinced of its thoroughness, and is willing to take action based on the facts set forth. A report constitutes a measure of a special agent's ability and worth. It is an official document and may not be furnished to any person outside the Service without proper authorization. In a criminal case, a report ultimately serves as the basis for the preparation and presentation of the case for trial.

620 *(1-18-80)* 9781
Planning and Writing Reports

621 *(1-18-80)* 9781
Essentials of a Good Report

621.1 *(1-18-80)* 9781
Introduction

It is not an easy matter to write a report which will convey to the mind of the reader with accuracy and clearness the essential facts disclosed as the result of an investigation. Report writing is an art which requires study, practice, and persistent effort. Since the art of report writing admits of no hard and fast rules applicable to all cases at all times, it must be based primarily on the broad ground of experience and common sense. The essentials of a good report are fairness, accuracy, completeness, uniformity, conciseness, and logical presentation.

621.2 *(1-18-80)* 9781
Fairness

Reporting the facts with fairness is as important as procuring them with impartiality. A special agent should always be an unbiased factfinder, not a partisan to a particular cause of action. An agent should report all material facts and evidence in such manner that they speak for themselves and require little or no explanation of their significance. Any distortion of the significance of evidence reacts against the report writer and materially diminishes the value of the report. The taxpayer's explanation should be presented fairly. When a special agent quotes, he/she should quote exactly, if possible, or, if it is not possible, he/she should say so. Hearsay, and rumors, properly identified as such, may be included in the report, but only if relevant and material to the matter being discussed. Reports should reflect an impersonal attitude and should contain no offensive remarks regarding the taxpayer.

621.3 *(1-18-80)* 9781
Accuracy

(1) Reports are the basis for administrative and legal actions of the utmost importance, including the assessment of substantial amounts of tax and penalties and criminal action which may result in imprisonment. Accuracy in every particular, therefore, is essential. Facts must be reported with exactness. The report writer should aim to present the facts in such manner that he/she will not have to state opinions and conclusions except in the portion of the report provided for that purpose. The distinction between fact and opinion should be clearly shown when it is necessary to explain the theory of cases based largely on circumstantial evidence. Avoid using statements such as: "The taxpayer could give no plausible explanation." That is a conclusion, and others may find that the explanation is plausible. State what the taxpayer said and let the evidence show whether the statement is worthy of belief. Avoid the phrase "conclusively proved." Do not allow conclusions to surpass the evidence. A conservative statement that is consistent with the facts is stronger than an exaggeration. Exaggerations tend to raise doubt against all the evidence presented in the report. Inaccuracies, carelessness in detail, errors in computation, and incorrect dates materially affect the value of a report. Discrimination in the choice of words, punctuation which clarifies the meaning, and a correct application of the rules of grammar are essential to accurate reports. Errors in those essentials have an unfavorable effect on the mind of the reader.

(2) Avoid using slang and technical terms including those used in accounting. However, in some instances slang terms may be necessary

for clarity in reporting the results of investigations, particularly those involving taxpayers in illegal pursuits. In such instances the meaning of the term should be explained when it is first used in the report. For example, it may be advantageous in a report concerning a numbers lottery to describe the nature of operation, including the slang terms used therein, before presenting evidence of the violation. If numerous slang or technical terms are necessary, it may be advisable to prepare a glossary.

621.4 *(1-18-80)* 9781
Completeness

(1) A special agent should present the material in a report from the viewpoint of a reader having no knowledge of the case. The agent must exercise good judgment in selecting the facts that are material to the matter and take care that nothing essential to a complete understanding of the case will be omitted. Every statement of material fact bearing on the proof of the allegation of violation should be documented to the extent necessary and possible to establish its truth and accuracy, and the source of the evidence should be reported.

(2) Likewise, explanations of taxpayers and important *facts* developed by the investigation that point to weaknesses in the case should not be omitted. Subsequent disclosure of facts indicating weaknesses that were known to the report writer reflects unfavorably on him/her. Moreover, any weaknesses in a case should be made known before action is taken relative to criminal prosecution or settlement of the civil liability in order to prevent surprise in the course of conferences or legal actions and to give reviewers an opportunity to suggest means of overcoming the weak points. However, speculation and conjecture of agents concerning possible defense theories have no place in a factual report. The reader primarily is interested in knowing what happened and how the events can be proved. The difficulties met by the special agent in securing the information, or in the ingenuity used in making the investigation, are of no interest. The writer should always remember that the report is about a violation or other obscured situation and not about the investigation. However, where certain pertinent evidence was not obtained, the special agent should state the avenues of inquiry pursued in attempting to procure the evidence in order that no doubts may arise in the reader's mind regarding whether the investigation was thorough. Important matters in exhibits generally should be narrated briefly in the report unless the exhibit is adequately described in an appendix and does not require any further explanation. The use of an appendix is discussed in 625. Finally, in order to ensure completeness, the report should be read and revised as often as necessary before it is submitted for review. A special agent should strive to submit a report in final form for initial review. The agent should not rely upon reviewers to complete the report by resolving the difficulties encountered in the investigation.

621.5 *(1-18-80)* 9781
Uniformity

Reports should be as uniform as possible for each type of case investigated by the Criminal Investigation Division. A special agent in one division should report the results of an investigation in the same sequence as a special agent in another division who has conducted an investigation of the same type. In order to promote uniformity, outlines for the various types of cases are furnished in IRM 9500; and 630 contains suggestions and sample reports for guides in report writing.

621.6 *(1-18-80)* 9781
Conciseness

(1) Conciseness suggests the removal of all that is elaborate or not essential. If a report contains a mass of irrelevant data, the important matters will not be clear to the reader. There is force in brevity. When you have something to say, say it in as few words as you can. The rule of conciseness applies to individual sentence construction as well as to the whole report. Repetition and unnecessarily lengthy descriptions of documents should be avoided. It is not necessary to copy into the report entire statements, letters, and exhibits when concise reference to the principal points and brief explanation will suffice. Tabulations and schedules in the form of appendices to the report frequently may be used to reduce narrative and emphasize important facts relative to matters such as summaries of net worth or omitted sales and analyses of bank accounts.

(2) A special agent should not indulge in attempts to wit or sarcasm; neither should he/she refer to himself/herself as the "undersigned," the "writer," or "your agent". Do not hesitate to state "the taxpayer informed *me*," or "The taxpayer gave *me* (documents or books)," if that information is material. However, in view of the necessity for maintaining an impersonal attitude, the personal pronouns "I" and "we" should be used sparingly. Avoid superfluous statements such as: "the following report is submitted," or "as the result of investigation, I have to report as follows." The phrase "This case relates to an investigation of an alleged evasion of income tax by ________ " may be better stated as, "This report relates to the alleged evasion of income tax by ________." The statement "Attached hereto as Exhibit 6 is a sworn affidavit of John Jones wherein he testified . . ." contains unnecessary words. Merely say, "John Jones stated (Exhibit 6, affidavit) that . . ." Avoid trite phrases and superlatives, and the word "very" only on rare occasions. Use of the active voice promotes conciseness and accuracy in writing. It is also more forceful. For example, the statement, "Information obtained from Mr. Witness disclosed that the proceeds of the sale were given by him to the taxpayer on May 14, 19——" may be reduced in length and made more forceful by revision to, "Mr. Witness said that he gave the proceeds of the sale to the taxpayer on May 14, 19——." Use of the active voice also will eliminate the possibility that the report writer will omit stating who gave the proceeds to the taxpayer.

621.7 *(1-18-80)* 9781
Logical Presentation

(1) A report otherwise well written may lose its effectiveness for want of logical arrangement. A mass of data thrown promiscuously into the report is an imposition on the reader and an adverse reflection upon the writer. Effective presentation is largely dependent upon adherence to the principles of style, namely: unity, coherence, and emphasis.

(2) *The principal of unity* requires adherence to the single main idea or proposition and exclusion of all matter that does not tend to prove that idea or proposition. Each sentence, paragraph, and division should help to establish the main point of the report.

(3) *Coherence* is defined as sticking together. This principle counsels logical sequence of thought. No one is likely to achieve coherence by chance or inspiration. It demands careful planning, critical review, and frequent revision by the report writer. Words, phrases, and clauses should be so placed in a sentence that their relationship is clear and the meaning of the sentence is obvious. Sentences should be so arranged that the progress of thought is clear and continuous from beginning to end. Each paragraph must bear an unmistakable relation to the whole composition, especially to the paragraph immediately preceding it. The most common fault in the presentation of evidence is the failure to show precisely what part it plays in the whole argument. This failure is sometimes due to the fact that secondary matters are not properly subordinate to the principal facts. Much evidence has only a casual connection with the main proposition, but the connection must be made evident. If the bearing of the evidence is not felt at the point where it is presented, it usually is not felt at all. Each violation, event, or circumstance, and all facts in support thereof, should be narrated in full before passing on to the next feature of the report. Phrases and sentences which merely introduce an exhibit may interrupt the rea reader's train of thought. In many instances that difficulty may be avoided by parenthetical insertion of exhibit numbers during discussion of the contents of the exhibit. Insofar as possible, references to other sections of the report should be avoided because the arrangement of the report will show,the relationship between the various facts and events.

(4) *Emphasis* requires careful placement of words, phrases, and sentences for the purpose of calling attention to the important facts. If the writer does not emphasize the more significant information the reader will not retain the essential facts. important words or phrases should be placed in important positions—usually at the beginning of a clause or sentence, or at the end. The same rule applies to the arrangement of sentences within a paragraph. A new topic or idea should be the subject of a new paragraph. A sentence or short passage requiring special emphasis may be paragraphed separately. Important matters can be emphasized by using concrete terms and terse sentences, by numbering and indenting a series of important and related facts, and by using schedules and tabulations. The last mentioned technique is particularly valuable in showing comparisons.

622 *(1-18-80)* 9781
Planning the Report

(1) Before starting to write a report, the special agent should have in mind a definite outline of the arrangement in which the facts and evidence may be presented in the most effective manner. The best arrangement rarely is the order in which the facts were developed during the investigation. A good general plan is to state the problem, present the results of the investigation, and set forth the conclusions and recommendations. The outlines in the IRM 9512.2 and Handbook Exhibit 600-3 are guides for uniform arrangement of data in the report. Details under the various headings should be arranged in paragraphs each confined to a particular topic. Special agents may use the method of assembling the facts and evidence into a coherent and logical presentation which he/she finds most effective. Keep in mind the witness who will produce, identify, and/or testify about each item of evidence. The use of either an outline or an arrangement based on appendices and exhibits is suggested to assist in assembling material for the report.

(a) In using the former method, prepare an outline of the topics or events considered essential to proof of the violation, or, with respect to reports not relating to violations, to accomplishment of the purpose of the report. List under each topic the pertinent facts and evidence. New agents may find it helpful to list the evidence in detail. The amount of detail can be reduced with the acquisition of experience and facility in writing reports. When the outline is finished, study it and make any revisions necessary to ensure compliance with the principles of completeness, conciseness, unity, coherence, and emphasis. Since each topic ordinarily will be the subject of a paragraph, the special agent can direct his/her attention to the writing of each paragraph on the basis of the topical outline.

(b) In lieu of an outline, effective presentation can be accomplished by arranging appendices, exhibits, and workpapers in logical order based on the above-mentioned principles of good writing, and discussing each fact and event in that order. Consideration also should be given to the order desirable for presentation of the evidence in court.

(2) One of the first steps in making ready to write a report regarding a fraud case is to prepare the summaries of income, tax, penalties, and adjustments. In cases based on specific items, the criminal items should be segregated from the civil items. The civil items are technical adjustments based upon: mere clerical errors; mistaken ideas relative to some regulation or requirement of the Internal Revenue Service; adverse decisions on controversial questions; erroneous legal or accounting advice on which the taxpayer honestly relied; and items which the taxpayer is unable to substantiate. The civil items could also include unreported income and other adjustments which pertain to a year or years for which prosecution is not being recommended. When appropriate, technical adjustments should be grouped into summary topics. With respect to criminal cases, the special agent should determine before beginning the report which criminal items are to be proposed for use in the criminal proceedings, and whether there are any technical adjustments favoring the taxpayer that should be offset against the additional income.

623 *(1-18-80)* 9781
Reports on Related Cases

(1) As a general rule, a separate report shall be written for each case. However, if the facts and events concerning two or more related taxpayers or case classifications are the same or are intermingled, the results of the related investigations shall be set forth in the report regarding the principal violator or classification. For example, when an investigation discloses evidence of tax evasion by a corporation and its principal officers, the report on the president of the corporation may serve as the focal point for assembling and presenting the facts and evidence regarding all taxpayers involved including the corporation. Similarly, violations of the excise and occupational taxes on wagering involving one taxpayer or several closely related taxpayers should be discussed in one report. Regional guidelines will be followed in all cases in which there is any uncertainty as to the need for separate reports.

(2) Notations shall be made on the index cards pertaining to the related cases to show the number of the case file containing the report, and a cross-reference sheet shall be placed in each of the related case files.

(3) When consolidating two or more defendants in one report, consideration should be given to ensuring that a sound basis for a joint trial exists. The absence of evidence of a conspiracy to violate tax laws, lack of a common violation to be charged, problems of venue, or other factors may indicate that the defendants are entitled to separate trials. If so, separate reports should be written with duplication of exhibits where appropriate.

624 *(1-18-80)* 9781
Format of Reports

624.1 *(1-18-80)* 9781
Address

(1) Reports shall be addressed as follows:
District Director, Internal Revenue Service
Attention: Chief, Criminal Investigation Division
Name of District (city and state)

(2) The address of the originating office will be shown on the first page of each report.

(3) See IRM 9267.5:(1) regarding the addressing of grand jury reports.

624.2 *(1-18-80)* 9781
Subject

The subject of the report consists of the name, the current address, and the taxpayer identification number of the principal person or legal entity in whose name the case was concerned. The address will consist of the street address, city and state where an individual resides or a corporation has its principal office. If the facts and evidence concerning related cases are included in one report, the subjects of the related cases, properly identified as such, shall be shown below the subject of the principal case. Related cases not discussed in the report will be mentioned in the introduction but will not be included in the subject heading. It is not necessary that the subject include the type of violation or the years involved, since that information is set forth in the opening paragraph of the report and the general classification of the violation is indicated by the case number. Text 624.4 and the sample reports contain suggested forms for presenting the subject of a report. The name and current address (including street address, city, state and zip code) of the taxpayer's representative should be listed below the subject.

624.3 *(1-18-80)* 9781
Case Number and Designation

In order to provide uniformity, the case number should be typed a single space below the subject on the first page of all reports and intra-Service communications relative to numbered cases. The case number also should be typed in the upper left corner of each succeeding page of a report. When a report covers more than one person or classification, only the number relating to the principal violator will appear on the succeeding pages. A designation indicating the nature of the report should be placed on the initial page immediately under the case number. Reports should bear a designation of "Final" for those closing a case, and "Supplemental" for those submitted after the case is closed. The designations "Parole," "Jeopardy Assessment," "Inadequate Records," "Arrest," "Legal Action," "Claim for Reward," and "Special Investigation" should be used where appropriate. The types of reports included in the terms "Special Investigation" and "Legal Action" are set forth in IRM 9500. Correspondence relating to collateral inquiries should bear the designation "Collateral Request" or "Collateral Reply" below the case number.

624.4 *(1-18-80)* 9781
Sample Subjects and Designations

(1) Assume that an investigation disclosed evidence of tax evasion by a corporation and two of its officers, and that the evidence is to be presented in the report relative to the president, who is the principal violator. The subject should be shown as follows:

In re: I.M. BIG SSN: 000-00-0000
1010 Blank Street
Chicago, Illinois 60647
36730321B
Final
Related Cases:
JOHN R. MINUTE SSN: 000-00-0000
4321 South Quincy Street
Chicago, Illinois 60635
36730296E
BIG CORPORATION, INC. EIN: 00-0000000
4354 North State Street
Chicago, Illinois 60632
36730325B

(2) Assume that an investigation disclosed evidence of tax evasion by three individuals who reside and conduct business as a partnership in Boston, Massachusetts, and that John Doe, the partner who is responsible for maintenance of the records, is the principal violator.

The subject of the report should be shown as follows:

In re: JOHN DOE SSN: 000-00-0000
4533 High Street
Boston, Massachusetts 02135
04730322C
Final

Related Cases:
JAMES ROE SSN: 000-00-0000
8346 Main Street
Boston, Massachusetts 02164
04730324D

JOSEPH MOE SSN: 000-00-0000
2538 Elm Street
Boston, Massachusetts 02134
04730326F

(3) The name and address of the taxpayer's representative should be shown as follows:

Representative:
C. W. LAW, Attorney
100 Ewe Street
Chicago, Illinois 60651

624.5 *(1-18-80)* 9781
Approval Stamps

Approval stamps should be placed on the signature page of a report, thus providing a uniform location for information regarding approvals and improving the appearance of the first page of the report.

624.6 *(1-18-80)* 9781
Assembly of a Report

(1) A report should be assembled in the following manner, although it is recognized that all reports will not include each of the listed parts:

(a) Table of Contents.

(b) Body of Report.

(c) List of Exhibits.

(d) List of Witnesses.

(e) Appendices.

(f) Exhibits.

(2) The page number shall be in the center at the bottom of each page, preceded and followed by a hyphen, i.e., -6-.

624.7 *(1-18-80)* 9781
Identification of Principals, Witnesses, Etc.

The names of individuals, corporations, partnerships, and other business and taxable entities will be typed in capital letters when and wherever used in reports of investigations as well as in correspondence between Criminal Investigation Division offices relating to investigations. (See IRM 9512.)

625 *(1-18-80)* 9781
Appendices and Exhibits

625.1 *(11-10-81)* 9781
General

(1) In cases involving a detailed computation of net worth, bank deposits, or expenditures, or numerous fraudulent items, clarity in reporting may best be accomplished by presenting the details in appendices and including in the body of the report only brief summaries thereof, together with a general discussion of the related evidence. Narrative in the report may be reduced by including on the appendix, in addition to the pertinent figures, a brief description of each item, a reference to exhibits containing the documents supporting each item, and the name of any witness who will produce documents and testify regarding each item. It is not necessary to discuss in the body of the report each item on the appendix. However, the report shall contain a description of the appendix; a brief summary or restatement of totals, if such is applicable; and an explanation of any significant particulars or details that are not made evident by inspection of the appendix. Since appendices are essential to a complete understanding of any case wherein they are used, they shall be typed or reproduced in sufficient quantities for inclusion with each copy of the report. With respect to cases involving the tabulation of numerous items which can be assembled into groups, a clear and concise presentation may require placing on the basic appendix only the total amount for each group and tabulating the items comprising the group on supporting appendices or schedules. For example, in a net worth case embracing numerous bank accounts and holdings of stocks and real estate, the computation of net worth on the basic appendix should show the aggregate cost or other value of the bank accounts, the stocks, and the real estate, and the various items included in each total should be set forth on separate appendices or schedules. Samples of appendices are provided in Exhibits 600-2 through 600-6.

(2) Exhibits are an essential part of a report. They may consist of originals or copies of statements and documents, such as affidavits, transcripts of interviews, contemporaneous memorandums, canceled checks, invoices, bank records, books of account, and transcripts or analyses of accounts and records and related workpapers. It generally is not feasible to provide extra copies of exhibits consisting of checks, invoices, bank records, account books, long detailed transcripts, and similar documents. However, the copy of the report which is retained at the office having responsibility for the conduct of the investigation should include a copy of each exhibit if such is available. The latter suggestion particularly applies to affidavits, memorandums or transcripts of interviews, and workpapers.

(3) The body of the report should contain reference to the exhibits and appendices, and the appendices should contain reference to exhibits which consist of supporting documents. Such reference may be to individual exhibits or groups of related exhibits. For example, the report may state: "Appendix A is a summary of the unreported receipts from sales, and Exhibits 8 through 25 are copies of documents in support thereof, including canceled checks, invoices and affidavits." Important matters in exhibits generally should be explained in the report. However, in many instances documents, such as invoices, checks, and bills of lading require only a brief description. If a document of that nature is adequately described on an appendix, no further explanation may be necessary. When mentioning or referring to a document that is submitted as an exhibit, including the written statement of a witness, insert the exhibit number in parentheses immediately following the reference. In most instances it is unnecessary to state that the document is submitted as Exhibit 1. An exhibit is underlined the first time (only) it is mentioned in the report so the reader will know when he/she sees an exhibit number whether it is being discussed for the first time or has previously been referred to.

(4) It is suggested in 622 that the special agent, before beginning a report, arrange the proposed appendices and exhibits in the order of planned presentation of facts and evidence, and that he/she prepare the report by discussing the appendices and exhibits in that order. In many instances the agent will find it necessary to rearrange those documents for more effective presentation. When the report is completed, the exhibits should be assembled in the order in which they are originally mentioned in the report, and they should be numbered for easy reference. If a number of documents such as canceled checks are included in one exhibit, give each document a sub-exhibit number. For example, if Exhibit 11 consists of 16 canceled checks, the checks should be numbered from 11-1 to 11-16. Each exhibit should be examined to determine whether it is properly identified. The source of the exhibit should be shown, especially if it consists of a transcript or summary. If the exhibits are numerous they should be bound separately from the report. Index tabs may be used to facilitate reference.

(5) The report should include a list of exhibits containing the number and a description of each exhibit. The content and arrangement of a list of exhibits is illustrated in the sample report on a specific item case (Exhibit 600-2). It is suggested that a copy of the list of exhibits be mounted immediately under the cover sheet for the exhibit file itself. This will eliminate having to use the special agent's report as the index.

(6) The appendices should be attached as part of the report and should be listed in the table of contents. Pre-lettered tab dividers (Documents 6654-A through F) should be used, if available, to identify appendices. If there are more than six appendices, the additional letters (G, H, etc.) should be typed on the reverse (blank) side of the dividers.

(7) Where the statement of a witness or subject is lengthy it may be helpful to prepare a synopsis of the important answers and attach this as a cover sheet to the exhibit. The summary should be quite brief, desirably not more than one line for each point, and should be referenced to appropriate question or page and line numbers.

625.2 *(1-18-80)* 9781
Exhibits—Supplemental Reports

Exhibits submitted with original and supplemental reports should be numbered in continuous sequence. This procedure is desirable in order to clearly identify which exhibits were submitted with each report. Thus, if the last exhibit to the special agent's final report is numbered

51, the first exhibit with the supplemental report will be numbered 52.

625.3 *(1-18-80)* 9781
Documents Submitted with Collateral Reports

Documents submitted with a collateral report should not be marked as exhibits, because they may later be submitted with the special agent's final report at which time they will be assigned a number. If only a few documents are transmitted as enclosures with a collateral report, it usually is unnecessary to assign any numbers to them. However, if, for reasons such as the volume of documents to be transmitted, it is desirable to identify the enclosures by number, such identification should be made either by attaching a paper tag to the document or by enclosing the document in a marked envelope.

626 *(8-11-80)* 9781
List of Witnesses

(1) The list of witnesses is an essential part of a report on a criminal case. It is especially important to the United States Attorney and to any agent who assists in the preparation of the case for trial, particularly in instances where the special agent who had conducted the investigation and had written the report is not available. The list of witnesses frequently is used by the United States Attorney as the basis for issuing subpoenas.

(2) The witnesses may be listed in alphabetical order, in the order in which they are mentioned in the report, or in the probable order of their appearance in the trial. If the latter procedure is used, consideration should be given to an arrangement which will provide for the introduction of documents required in the testimony of subsequent witnesses. The name, address, telephone number, and title or other identification of each witness should be set forth, together with a reference to any exhibit or appendix that is pertinent to his/her testimony and to the records and other evidence he/she may be expected to produce or identify. The use of such references will eliminate the need for a summary of each witness's probable testimony as part of the list of witnesses.

(3) However, the list of witnesses should include a summary of the testimony of the special agent, cooperating officer, and other key witnesses. This description should be a brief outline or statement concerning all matters about which the witness can be expected to testify. If those matters are set forth in exhibits consisting of workpapers or records of interviews, such as memorandums, transcripts, and affidavits, a brief identification together with reference to the appropriate exhibit numbers, is sufficient. If reference is made to a detailed transcript of an interview, the numbers of the specific pages or answers that contain important statements of the taxpayer or the witness should be referenced. Reference also should be made to appendices that contain descriptions of evidence that will be presented by a special agent. For example, assuming that Appendix A is a net worth statement and that the special agent's testimony is required to establish the cost of certain assets, the description of the special agent's testimony in the list of witnesses should include a statement that he/she can testify regarding the cost of the properties at Columbus, Ohio, and the automobile (Appendix A, items 4, 6, and 10). The sample report on a specific item case (Exhibit 600-2) contains a sample list of witnesses, which provides an illustration of the procedure for describing the testimony of key witnesses.

(4) In some instances it may be necessary to list one witness who will produce and identify certain records and another who will testify relative thereto. Listing the name of a person who can be expected to appear as a witness is preferable to showing only the name of a corporation, bank, or other organization, especially where an individual has custody of records or has an intimate knowledge of the records and transactions involved. In cases where evidence is available to rebut a probable defense, it may be advisable to list the witnesses who will testify in the event that the principal presents the anticipated defense. Witnesses of that nature should be identified as rebuttal witnesses.

(5) The special agent may prepare the list of witnesses as the report is written. The use of appendices containing names of witnesses and the procedure of capitalizing names of witnesses, as explained in 624.7, will assist in the preparation of a complete list of witnesses. When the report has been written, the special agent should review the facts and evidence to determine whether a witness has been listed for each item of evidence.

627 *(1-18-80)* 9781
Table of Contents

A table of contents showing subject matter and page numbers should be submitted with any report exceeding ten pages. It should be designed to provide quick reference to important features of the case, and the amount of detail will be determined by the length of the report and the circumstances of the case. Any appendices to the report should be listed in the table of contents.

630 *(1-18-80)* 9781
Types of Final Reports

631 *(1-18-80)* 9781
Introduction

(1) This text of the Handbook is concerned with reports on investigations relating to fraud and miscellaneous criminal law violations. The following suggestions and samples are provided, not as inflexible rules which must be followed in all reports, but as guides to assist special agents in writing reports within the general framework of the outlines in IRM 9500.

(2) Whenever a prosecution recommendation is contemplated, the special agent should discuss findings and proposed recommendations with the immediate supervisor prior to preparing the final report. The agent should obtain the supervisor's opinion as to the sufficiency of the investigation conducted. In writing the report, the special agent is responsible for using clear and correct language, for its mathematical accuracy, for proper descriptions of each exhibit and for presenting all material facts in an impartial manner. An experienced special agent is expected to attain report writing proficiency which will permit him/her to submit prosecution reports in final typed form to the supervisor for review and processing. In non-prosecution cases the special agent is expected to submit the report in final typed form.

(3) Final prosecution reports in the Criminal Investigation Division are presented in either the narrative format or the optional format styles of report writing.

(4) Text 633 through 633.7 discuss the recommended outline, format, and content of the narrative report. Exhibit 600-2 presents a sample specific item case written in the narrative format.

(5) Exhibit 600-3 shows a comparison between the narrative and optional format reports.

(6) Text 634 through 634.(10) discuss the recommended outline, format and content of the optional report. Exhibit 600-4 presents a sample specific item case written in the optional format.

(7) Exhibit 600-5 presents a sample net worth case written in the narrative format; and Exhibit 600-6 presents a sample Bank Deposits case written in the narrative format.

632 *(1-18-80)* 9781
Outline for Final Reports on Prosecution Cases

(1) Introduction.

(2) Summary of Cooperating Officer's Findings.

(3) History of Taxpayer.

(4) Evidence.

(5) Explanation and Defense.

(6) Facts Relating to Intent.

(7) Conclusions and Recommendations.

633 *(1-18-80)* 9781
Tax Fraud Cases (Prosecution)

633.1 *(1-18-80)* 9781
Introduction

(1) The introduction to the report should contain a brief mention or discussion of any of the following matters that are pertinent to the case:

(a) Type of violation.

(b) Tax periods involved in the investigation.

(c) Name and address (city and state) of taxpayer.

(d) Business or vocation of the taxpayer.

(e) *Origin of the case.*—The origin may be: regular examination, confidential source, claim for refund, or special program. Do not use the term "routine audit." If significant, state how the Criminal Investigation Division acquired jurisdiction. The special agent should not in any part of the report identify an informant by name, occupation, or relationship. If an investigation resulted from an informant's communication, merely state that the information was obtained from a confidential source. (See IRM 9373.3:(8) and P-1-190.)

(f) *Names and titles of cooperating officers.*—The term "cooperating officer" does not include special agents. The report should be signed by all special agents who significantly participated in the investigation exclusive of collateral inquiries. If it is anticipated that a special agent, including one who conducted a collateral inquiry, will be called as a witness, that matter should be covered in the evidence section and in the list of witnesses.

(g) *Date the taxpayer was first notified that his/her returns were under examination by the Internal Revenue Service.*—Brief description as to when, by whom, and how the taxpayer was notified. This information is particularly important if the taxpayer raises a defense of voluntary disclosure. The date the taxpayer was first contacted by a special agent should also appear in the introduction of the report. The report should contain a statement concerning whether the special agent explained his/her function to the taxpayer and advised the taxpayer of his/her Constitutional rights under existing guidelines.

(h) *Notice of reexamination.*—If the investigation includes tax periods previously examined, mention that a notice of reexamination was issued to the taxpayer. (See IRM 9324.4)

(i) *Representative of taxpayer.*—State the names and addresses of current representatives of the taxpayer, and whether they are enrolled. Indicate whether powers of attorney have been filed. Include as exhibits copies of the latest powers. (See IRM 9359.2)

(j) *Related cases.*—Mention any related cases not discussed in this report, such as cases involving attempted bribery or impeding an officer. Include a brief statement concerning the status of any related case currently under investigation by the Criminal Investigation Division.

(k) Statement that prosecution is recommended for designated years.

(l) Brief description of the method used in the evasion or other violation. Mention the method of determining the income for use in criminal proceedings if other than specific item. If the income for civil purposes is computed on a different basis, mention that fact.

(m) *Periods of Limitations.*—Present in tabular form information relative to the dates on which prosecution will be barred for the tax periods included in the recommendation for criminal proceedings and the dates on which the period of limitations on assessment of tax will expire. Include in the tabulation, when appropriate, information concerning any extensions of the period for assessment of tax. Discuss briefly any unusual circumstances that extend the period of limitation on prosecution, such as the taxpayer's being a fugitive from justice or absence from the United States.

(n) *Venue.*—Mention the judicial district in which the returns were filed. If venue might lie in more than one judicial district, mention the districts involved and briefly state the basis on which each might have jurisdiction. The facts and evidence relative to the matter of venue should be discussed in the section of the report relating to evidence. See IRM 932(10).

633.2 *(1-18-80)* 9781
Summary of Cooperating Officer's Findings

(1) This section of the report concerns the civil liability except for cases wherein the income proposed for use in criminal proceedings is the same as that involved in the civil case. If the income for both purposes is the same, mention that fact. Consideration should be given to any of the following matters which are pertinent to the case:

(a) Reference to the cooperating officer's report, a copy of which should be submitted as an exhibit. Do not repeat details included in that report.

(b) Tabulation of the income and tax reported, if any, and the income, tax and penalties proposed as a result of the investigation. This includes all additional taxes and penalties of other taxpayers which directly result from the case, such as victims of "tax experts," involved corporations, partners and spouses, if not assigned for investigation of their separate tax liabilities. If the report relates to more than one taxpayer, there should be a separate tabulation for each. Lengthy tabulations may be set forth on an appendix to the report. Exhibit 600-1 contains sample forms of tabulation.

(c) The computation of income for criminal proceedings should be reconciled with the determination of income shown by the internal revenue agent's report. In some cases, it is sufficient to point out the differences by means of a brief narrative statement; in others, the summary may be presented as an appendix (Exhibit 600-1). Unless the technical adjustments have an unusual significance, the special agent should merely mention in the report that such adjustments are explained in the internal revenue agent's report. Details of the criminal computation should be reserved for the section relating to evidence. In some cases on net worth, expenditures, or bank deposits, adjustments should be made to account for technical and nonfraudulent increases in reported income.

(d) The block adjustment method sets forth in tabular form the items of income and expenses as shown by the tax return, the criminal and civil adjustments, the corrected income for criminal purposes and the corrected income shown in the revenue agent's report. This method may be used (if appropriate) in cases involving numerous adjustments affecting both the criminal and civil computations if this would provide a clearer presentation than a summary of only the adjustments. The block adjustment method ordinarily lends itself more to specific item type of cases and usually only for years recommended for prosecution Items of income and expenses that are not changed by any adjustment should be grouped together by categories and explained in a footnote. The use of this method, which requires a separate schedule for each tax year involved, will in most instances supplement appendices rather than replace them. However, in cases involving several tax periods, a simultaneous presentation of the evidence for all periods shall be used if a separate discussion of the evidence for each year will result in duplication. An example of a block adjustment method of summarizing income and adjustments is illustrated in Exhibit 600-1 as an alternative method of presenting Appendix A.

(e) Gross income means all income from whatever source derived, including (but not limited to) the following items [*26 USC 61*]:

1 Compensations for services, including fees, commissions, and similar items.

2 Gross income derived from business (use gross profit).

3 Gains derived from dealings in property (use gain before the 50 percent deduction).

4 Interest.

5 Rents (use gross rents).

6 Royalties.

7 Dividends (after exclusion).

8 Alimony and separate maintenance payments.

9 Annuities.

10 Income from life insurance and endowment contracts.

11 Pensions.

12 Income from discharge of indebtedness.

13 Distributive share of partnership gross income (separately calculate the distributive share of partnership business profit and distributive share of partnership gross rents, etc.).

14 Income in respect to a decedent.

15 Income from an interest in an estate or trust.

(f) Gross income figures are used by U.S. Attorneys in complaints, informations, and indictments filed against taxpayers in willful failure to file income tax cases. Therefore, if the special agent's report involves the alleged willful failure to file income tax returns, and if the case is based on specific items or bank deposits, the gross income in each prosecution year should be shown in the Summary of Cooperating Officer's Findings. The amount of gross income is generally determinable in such cases and should be included in this section (Exhibit 600-6). If the special agent uses the net worth method of proof in a failure to file case, adjusted gross income or taxable income would be used rather than gross income.

(g) Discuss briefly any significant action taken by either the Government or the taxpayer with respect to the civil liability, including the filing of delinquent or amended returns. Set forth the facts concerning any assessments and resulting payments or collections, or any voluntary payments for the years involved in the investigation. Tabulate the taxes and penalties assessed if they are different from those proposed in the cooperating officer's report. Discuss any unusual circumstances and mention any anticipated action of significance, such as the imminence of proceedings before the Tax Court. If no action has been taken concerning the civil liability, mention that fact.

633.3 *(1-18-80)* 9781
History of Taxpayer

(1) In narrating the history of the taxpayer, the special agent should identify the sources of information and should include information relative to any of the following matters that are pertinent to the case, with particular emphasis on the criminal period:

(a) Individual.

1 Personal information.

a Name and alias.

b Age, citizenship, physical and mental health.

c Location of residence (city and state) during years involved.

d Marital status and number of dependents.

e Education.

f Military service.

g Reputation and criminal record.

h A copy of the taxpayer's criminal record should be submitted with the report as an exhibit to support the narrative.

2 Financial information.

a Business addresses during the years involved.

b Sources of income.

c Taxpayer's connection with business emphasizing responsibility and participation in the income producing and accounting phases.

d General familiarity with books of account.

e Knowledge of tax matters.

(b) Partnership or corporation.

1 Name and address.

2 Nature of business.

3 Date formed or date and place of incorporation.

4 Partnership—names of partners and terms of partnership agreement. Corporation—names and titles of all officers during the taxable periods, and shares of stock owned by each if essential to case.

5 Corporation—names of officers in active control and particular duties or responsibilities of each.

6 Statement concerning whether the business is still in operation.

(2) If facts and circumstances relative to the history of the taxpayer constitute part of the evidence of the violation, they should be included in the section of the report concerning the evidence for use in criminal proceedings. This procedure is particularly applicable to cases in which evidence of the taxpayer's financial history in prior years establishes or corroborates the starting point for a net worth or similar computation, and to cases in which willful intent may be inferred from actions of the taxpayer during prior years. Care should be exercised to avoid unnecessary repetition. If facts concerning the history of the taxpayer are included in the evidence section of the report, a brief mention thereof in the history section, together with reference to the part of the report containing the information, is sufficient.

633.4 *(1-18-80)* 9781
Evidence

633.41 *(1-18-80)* 9781
Evidence in Support of Civil Penalties

(1) This part of the report should set out the facts and evidence to support any civil penalties recommended by the special agent. Separation of the evidence proposed for use in the criminal proceeding from that relating specifically to the civil penalties will be helpful not only to United States Attorneys and others who are primarily concerned with the criminal phase of the case, but also to attorneys who are concerned with the civil aspects of the case. This part of the report should contain a discussion of the nature and extent of the evidence available to support recommended civil penalties. Evidence which pertains to both the criminal phase and recommended civil penalties should be covered in the part of the report concerning evidence for use in the criminal proceeding, with a reference thereto being included in this part of the report. This part of the report would also cover evidence available in support of civil penalties recommended with respect to tax periods or taxpayers not included in the recommendation for prosecution. Documentary evidence should be mentioned in the report and retained for subsequent use in connection with the civil settlement.

(2) Evidence to support the civil fraud penalty in a willful failure to file case or with respect to tax periods not included in the prosecution recommendation should be clearly set forth, including a summary of the facts relating to the requisite fraudulent intent. Such evidence should be of the type which will establish that some part of the underpayment of tax is due to fraud. Although it is sufficient to refer to other parts of the report which cover such material, the portions of the report concerning intent and the evidence for use in the criminal case usually do not contain such information concerning taxpayers or tax periods not included in the prosecution recommendation. Furthermore, the facts and evidence to support a criminal charge of a willful failure to file a return are not necessarily sufficient to establish the specific fraudulent intent required to sustain the civil fraud penalty since a criminal charge of willful failure to file may be established without proof of such fraudulent intent. Some, but not all, of the indications of fraud which should be supported by evidence mentioned in this section of the report, where applicable, are such affirmative acts as keeping a double set of books, making false entries or alterations, or false invoices or documents, destruction of books or records, concealment of assets or covering up sources of income, handling of one's affairs to avoid making the records usual in transactions of the kind and any conduct, the likely effect of which would be to mislead or to conceal.

633.42 *(1-14-82)* 9781
Evidence for Use in Criminal Proceedings

(1) This section is concerned with the evidence which is anticipated to be used as the Government's criminal case. Every substantial fact should be documented. The evidence should include not only proof of additional income but also any available proof pertaining to the disposition of funds and any related evidence of intent. It also should include any admissions of the taxpayer.

(2) Since venue might lie in more than one district, the special agent should determine the following facts during the investigation and document them in the evidence section.

(a) Residence and principal business address at the time the alleged offense was committed.

(b) Place where records were maintained, where the returns were prepared, and where the returns were signed.

(c) Location of the post office, if the return was mailed, or the Internal Revenue Service office if delivered.

(d) Other pertinent evidence which might aid in establishing venue outside the judicial district in which the District Director's office is located or which might assist in resolving questions arising from defendant's motion for a change in venue. See IRM 932(10).

(3) Any evidence of intent that is closely related to evidence regarding the filing and preparation of returns, the maintenance of books and records, and the receipt or disposition of income should be presented with the discussion of those topics. The facts relating to intent will then be repeated in concise outline form in the section of the report provided for that purpose.

(4) In order to make the evidence section adaptable to use in a criminal trial, the special agent may introduce such evidence in the order proposed for presentation in court insofar as that procedure is consistent with coherence and continuity in the report. This suggestion applies not only to the order of introducing witnesses but also to the form of presenting the testimony of each witness. For example, in narrating the information furnished by a witness, state the name, address (city and state), and title or other identification of the witness, and the name of any organization which he/she may represent. Mention the evidence which he/she may be expected to produce and the pertinent information which he/she has furnished. In most instances it is preferable to discuss the complete testimony of a witness at one point in the report rather than to present part under one topic and part under another. For example, if a witness furnishes information relating to both evidence of the receipt of income and evidence of intent, his/her complete testimony generally should be discussed in connection with the receipt of income. This suggestion, however, should not prevent the special agent from discussing part of the information furnished by a witness under one topic and part under another when that presentation promotes clarity, coherence, and emphasis in the report. In some instances it will be necessary to set forth, either before or after introducing a witness' proposed testimony, sufficient background information to show its relevancy.

(5) This part of the report should include any *facts* indicating weaknesses in the evidence and the reliability of witnesses. It will not, however, contain any conclusions. Avoid using the words "proves," "seems," "appears."

(6) The following matters, if pertinent to the case, should be considered in this part of the report, but the order of presentation should be varied with the facts of the particular case. Topic headings should be used when appropriate, but in many instances the evidence may not be adaptable to segregation into topics.

(a) *Information regarding the filing of returns.*

1 This topic concerns the returns for the tax periods involved in the recommendation for prosecution and any other returns which constitute a part of the evidence. In failure to file cases it is essential to establish that the taxpayer knew the requirement to file income tax returns. Copies of available income tax returns preceding the first recommended prosecution year should be furnished unless it has been established that the taxpayer has never filed a return. Copies of returns filed after the periods for which prosecution was recommended should also be furnished.

2 The record of filing original and amended returns may be set forth in a schedule with the following headings:

Tax Period
Serial No.
Date Filed
Exhibit No.

3 One photostat of each return should be submitted as an exhibit.

4 Introduce the exhibit containing a certificate of assessments and payments (Form 4340, for non-ADP returns) or a computer transcript (Form 4303, for ADP returns) for whatever current and prior tax periods are pertinent to the criminal phase of the case.

5 Present facts regarding the identification of the returns including the signature, sources and amounts of income reported, deductions claimed, and any other significant matters. This may involve merely a statement that the taxpayer in the presence of the named officers identified this data.

6 Set forth any pertinent evidence concerning who filed the returns of the tax periods for which prosecution is proposed; when those returns were filed; and how, i.e., mailed, or filed at an office of the Internal Revenue Service.

7 If no returns were filed, mention that fact and introduce the exhibit containing the certification of the District Director or other appropriate Internal Revenue Service representative. Include any admissions of the taxpayer that returns were not filed.

8 Include as exhibits all requests for Extensions (of time to file). Set forth the pertinent evidence concerning the Request for Extensions including date filed, place filed, reason for requesting extension, date to which extension granted, and reasons, if any, when extension was denied.

(b) *Evidence regarding preparation of returns.*

1 Introduce the statement of the person who prepared the alleged fraudulent returns. Whenever possible submit as an exhibit a copy of that person's affidavit or a transcript of his/her testimony under oath. The information which should be obtained from this witness is set forth in Exhibit 300-5.

2 Include any pertinent statements by the taxpayer.

(c) *Description of books and records of taxpayer.*

1 Describe the taxpayer's books and records and their relationship to the tax returns. Insert all evidence which bears on the taxpayer's knowledge of and responsibility for the recordkeeping process. Statements under oath or affidavits should be included from bookkeepers, accountants or other persons involved in keeping the taxpayer's records.

2 Discuss the circumstances under which access to the records was obtained with particular emphasis on any unusual circumstances, such as discovery of records subsequent to the taxpayer's denial of their existence or the refusal to produce all or part of the records. Mention what records of the taxpayer were examined, and state who reconciled the books and records with the returns. Submit as an exhibit a memorandum of the cooperating officer or the special agent relative to this.

3 In net worth, bank deposits, and expenditures cases, it is particularly important that available evidence showing lack of records, or their incompleteness or inadequacy be submitted. Present pertinent details concerning any oral or written notice given the taxpayer regarding his inadequate records.

(d) *Theory of proof to be followed,* or the type of case to be presented, i.e., specific item, net worth, bank deposits, expenditures, or a combination thereof. Any *facts* showing a pattern or scheme of evasion may be narrated at this point. Such facts also relate to intent and in some cases it may be preferable to cover them in connection with that matter. In net worth and similar cases the evidence of sources of income may be introduced at this point, or in some cases it may be more effectively presented in connection with other evidence. Mention other methods of determining income which may be used as corroboration of the method recommended for use in criminal proceedings. Complete presentation of the alternative method(s), which may consist of one or more of those listed above or a percentage mark-up computation, may be set forth in a subsequent part of the evidence section if the special agent believes that detailed presentation will make the report more conclusive.

(e) *In net worth, expenditure, and bank deposit cases, the evidence corroborating the starting point* may be presented here, preparatory to the introduction of evidence relating to the prosecution period. In some instances it may be preferable to reverse that order of presentation. The net income should be established for such number of prior to subsequent years as may be required to support the starting point. The taxpayer's filing record and copies of available income tax returns should be furnished for *at least* five years immediately preceding the starting point and for all years between that point and the first prosecution year. If any of the required returns are not available, a certification of the District Director relative to the amounts of tax paid should be submitted, together with photostats or transcripts of any available taxpayer's retained copies of pertinent returns. If the taxpayer's income in years for which the returns are unavailable cannot be determined from other sources, the maximum net income which might have been reported on the missing returns may be computed on the basis of the tax paid. Since statements of assessments and payments do not include amount withheld from salaries or wages, such method of computing estimated income may not be feasible unless records such as those of employers or the Social Security Administration can be utilized to reconstruct the amounts of salaries or wages received.

(f) *Tabulation of corrected income.*—This topic comprehends a summary of the items which are proposed for use in criminal proceedings and a comparison of corrected income with reported income. It may relate to specific items of omitted income and overstated expense, or to a summary of a computation based on net worth, bank deposits, or expenditures. Suggested forms of presentation are furnished in the sample reports.

1 In computing corrected income involving a self-employed individual who earns self-employment income as defined in IRC 1402(a), (b), and (c) include in the computations for criminal purposes the corrected self-employment tax figures whenever the original fraudulent return reflects an amount of self-employment tax. Further, in a criminal case involving multiple fraudulent returns, the corrected self-employment tax figures should be computed for each return where self-employment tax would be applicable if self-employment taxes are reported on any of the fraudulent returns. Criminal computations will continue to exclude self-employment tax figures in failure to file cases or in cases where none of the fraudulent returns reflect a self-employment tax figure.

2 The Criminal Section of the Tax Division, Department of Justice, has requested that income averaging computations be prepared and forwarded to the Department of Justice in all cases where applicable and base year data is ascertainable, regardless of whether an income averaging election was made by the taxpayer. Pertinent returns should be requisitioned for base periods at the outset of all income tax investigations. As appropriate, requests should be made for information of base period data to the taxpayer or the taxpayer's return preparer at the initial interviews. Where applicable, the determination of income averaging may be most effectively accomplished through the use of an appendix to the Special Agent's Report.

3 Base period data should be computed as follows:

a In those instances involving a return filed for a pre-prosecution base period, base period data will be obtained from such filed return. Base period data as reported on a filed return will be adjusted only when such adjustments are in the taxpayer's favor or, if in favor of the government, are subject to proof beyond a reasonable doubt as constituting income additional to that reported.

b Base period data is not to be computed by reconstructing the amount of taxable income reported on the basis of tax liability reflected per Service records (other than tax returns), such resulting figure being unacceptably susceptible to inaccuracy due to the variables involved.

(g) *Evidence of income.*—With reference to cases involving several tax periods, a simultaneous presentation of the evidence for all periods shall be used if a separate discussion of the evidence for each year (specific adjustments, net worth items, bank deposits) will result in duplication. The first item should be discussed for all years involved before the evidence relative to the next item is presented. Pertinent facts relating to occurrences in the investigation prior to its status as a joint investigation should be furnished. Those facts include statements made by the taxpayer to, or in the presence of, the cooperating officer, and the latter's memorandums concerning those matters should be submitted as exhibits. The evidence in specific item cases should establish the receipt, omission, and intent relating to each understatement of income and the overstatement and intent relating to each false deduction or expense. Consideration also should be given to any relevant evidence regarding the disposition of funds, which may consist of evidence showing increases in net worth or proof of the disposition of specific amounts. In net worth and similar cases, furnish any available evidence of specific items of omitted income, and if possible, show how they are reflected in the increased net worth.

(h) *Evidence of any collateral violation,* i.e., false statements or documents and other violations included in the same case classification as the principal violation. The special agent should not recommend alternative or multiple criminal charges without a sound basis. In most instances collateral violations such as conspiracy and false statements require additional evidence which should be separately presented to support each specific charge.

(i) Unreported interest from certificates of deposit—If the specific item omitted is interest from a certificate of deposit, see Text 423.2 for information that is required in the final report.

633.5 *(1-18-80)* 9781
Explanation and Defense

(1) In this part of the report the special agent shall set forth explanations of the taxpayer, *facts* regarding his/her attitude toward the investigation, facts indicating his/her defense, and rebuttal evidence. If any of those matters have been discussed in detail in a previous part of the report, this section should contain only a brief summary of, or reference to, the preceding discussion.

(2) Admissions of the taxpayer relative to the receipt of income or to intent in the matter should be presented with the other facts concerning those topics, even though such admissions were made in connection with his/her explanation.

(3) The taxpayer's explanation and *facts* developed during the investigation may indicate a probable defense. Since this section of the report shall include only facts and evidence, any conclusions regarding the taxpayer's explanation and defense will be reserved for the section provided for that purpose. The special agent should not engage in speculation or conjecture about possible defenses in the report.

(4) If a District Criminal Investigation Conference (see Text 342.4) was held at the completion of the investigation to discuss with the taxpayer the criminal features of the case, set forth the results thereof and submit as an exhibit a transcript or memorandum of the proceedings. Admissions made by the taxpayer during the conference should be included with the evidence of the receipt of income or the facts relating to intent, as appropriate. In that event, it may be advisable to introduce the exhibits pertaining to the conference at the point where that occurrence is first mentioned.

(5) Introduce any available evidence to controvert the probable defenses, including a discussion of the efforts made to verify the assertions of the taxpayer.

(6) Present the *facts* relating to the extent that the taxpayer and his/her representatives were cooperative or uncooperative during the investigation.

633.6 *(1-18-80)* 9781
Facts Relating to Intent

This section of the report will contain an outline or succinct summary of the evidence of intent presented in preceding sections of the report, together with a discussion of any additional evidence of intent.

633.7 *(1-18-80)* 9781
Conclusions and Recommendations

(1) The special agent shall identify the features of the case on which a recommendation for criminal prosecution is based and shall present an appraisal of the related facts and evidence. In making this appraisal, the agent should consider the facts set out in the evidence section, including those indicative of defenses and the reliability of witnesses. He/she also may comment, if pertinent, on the factual significance of any item of evidence, and on any unusual circumstances in the case. The special agent shall state his/her conclusions regarding whether the available evidence of any violation disclosed through the investigation is sufficient to establish a successful prosecution. Attention should be given in this section of the report to the flagrancy of the violation and any evidence of a non-cooperative or hostile attitude on the part of the taxpayer.

(2) The special agent shall make specific recommendations concerning the institution of criminal proceedings, including the particular penal sections of law and tax periods involved in each recommendation.

(3) Specific recommendations also shall be made respecting the assertion of any appropriate civil penalties within the jurisdiction of the Criminal Investigation Division. If the case involves tax periods for which prosecution is not recommended, the special agent shall identify the evidence relied upon for the penalty recommendations relating to such periods, and shall set forth the reasons for recommending against prosecution.

633.8 *(1-18-80)* 9781
Sample Reports, Tax Fraud Cases

(1) The sample reports illustrate the format of reports and methods of presenting and arranging facts, evidence, and conclusions. Although in practice the organization of material in each report will depend upon the particular facts and circumstances of the case, the samples can be used as guidelines for effective presentation. The sample reports concern hypothetical situations and are not designed to provide either qualitative or quantitative standards for evaluating the sufficiency of evidence. Since lists of exhibits and witnesses usually are similar in format, samples thereof are included with only the first sample report. Likewise, samples of only one appendix are provided in cases involving two or more appendices that would be similar in content and arrangement. To illustrate a technique that may be used to facilitate reference to the probable testimony of witnesses and to assist in the preparation of the list of witnesses, the surname of the taxpayer and of each prospective witness is typed in capital letters in the sections of the sample reports relating to evidence, explanation of the taxpayer, and intent. Likewise, pertinent business names appear in capital letters. One sample report also follows the practice of underscoring exhibits when initially introduced.

(2) *Specific Item Case.*—Exhibit 600-2 is a sample report on a specific item case in which prosecution is recommended. The body of the report contains a summary of the total unreported receipts from each customer with references to several appendices, each showing a tabulation of the unreported payments from one customer, descriptions of the supporting evidence, references to pertinent exhibits, and the name of the witness who will produce the documents and testify relative thereto. A sample of one such appendix is provided. In the body of the report, discussion of items appearing on the appendices is confined to evidence that is not adequately described on an appendix and matters that require elaboration. The sample report contains a summary showing the disposition of proceeds from unreported sales, followed by a discussion of the exhibits relative thereto. Such detailed discussion of the exhibits relating to the disposition of funds is not necessary in all cases. For example, in instances where such exhibits are adequately described by their title, further discussion may be unnecessary.

(3) *Sample Appendices (Specific Item Case).*—Exhibit 600-2 contains sample appendices showing methods of presenting the evidence of unreported sales in a prosecution case based on specific items.

(a) Appendix A provides a concise summary of the facts and evidence relating to the receipt of income which, if used as a basis for preparation of the narrative report, will assist the special agent in making a concise and coherent presentation. If the evidence is adequately described on the appendix, it is unnecessary to repeat that information in the body of the report. However, if the brief description in the appendix does not clearly explain the facts and evidence, the matter should be discussed in the body of the report. Exhibit 600-2—Cont. (12) is an alternate method of presenting Appendix A in block adjustments. The alternate method shows the amounts reported on the tax return, the adjustments, corrected for criminal purposes, other adjustments for civil purposes, and corrected for civil proceedings per the Revenue Agent's Report. The facts and evidence pertaining to disposition of the funds from the unreported sales may be set forth in a form similar to Appendix B. A copy of each appendix will be submitted with each copy of the report.

(b) The information to be included on an appendix and the arrangement thereof will vary according to the facts of the particular case. In many cases it is not necessary or desirable to include information relating to the reported income, and in instances where few columns are required, it may be feasible to combine the schedules regarding the receipt of income and the disposition of funds.

(4) *Net Worth Case.*—Exhibit 600-5 is a sample report on a net worth case involving a recommendation of prosecution with respect to three of the five years included in the investigation. It is assumed in the sample that the case resulted from the receipt of an informant's communication and that the investigation disclosed fraudulent returns filed for the years involved. The body of the report contains a summary of the computation of net worth and expenditures and the details are set forth on appendices. The summary which appears in the body of the report should contain a tabulation of the major classifications of assets and liabilities that show changes sufficient to have a material effect on income. The remaining amounts should be grouped under the classifications of "other assets" or "other liabilities." In the summary of the income computation in Exhibit 600-5, the corrected net income is determined by adding nondeductible expenditures to the increases in net worth. A separate item should be inserted in the summary whenever it is necessary to make adjustments for nontaxable income or unallowable deductions, such as gifts, the nontaxable portion of capital gains, or unallowable losses. Because of the number of columns involved, the detailed computations of net worth are presented on two separate appendices: one (Appendix A) relating to the period from the starting point to the first year included in the criminal case, and the other (Appendix B) concerning the years involved in the recommendation for prosecution. Appendix B contains a description of the evidence for each item, references to pertinent exhibits, and the names of witnesses for each item. Appendix A contains similar information for each item not continued on Appendix B, but in instances where an item appears on both appendices, the former shows, in lieu of a description of the evidence, a reference to the number of the item on Appendix B. In instances where one document constitutes evidence relative to a number of net worth items, repetition may be avoided by placing a notation "see Note 1" in the column headed "Description of Evidence" and describing the document in a footnote. If any classification of assets or liabilities is comprised of numerous items, the basic appendix usually should show only the total amount for the particular classification with reference to a subsidiary appendix containing the detailed tabulation of such items. For example, in a case involving numerous bank accounts, the basic appendix will show the aggregate amount on deposit in all the accounts at the end of each period, and the balances in the individual accounts will be tabulated on supporting appendices.

(5) *Bank Deposits Case.*—Exhibit 600-6 is a sample report on a bank deposit case, in which it is assumed that the taxpayer operated a retail drug store and that the bulk of receipts from sales are in the form of cash. It also is assumed that business expenses were paid by checks and that the canceled checks were available during the investigation. The computation of income on the basis of bank deposits and cash expenditures is presented on Appendix A, with a brief summary thereof in the body of the report. In order to simplify the basic computation of income, only the total amounts of payments in cash, nonincome items and deposits, purchases, and operating expenses are shown on that appendix and the detailed information concerning those items is set forth on subsidiary appendices. In more complicated cases, it might be advisable to use separate appendices or schedules for the particulars of other items. It is assumed in the report that the evidence concerning deposits of customers' checks will be shown on Appendix A-1. Since the format of that appendix is adequately described in the body of the report, a sample is not provided. Although the sample report may be used as a guideline in preparing reports on bank deposit cases, the form and content of the report and appendices will vary according to the facts and circumstances of the case.

634 *(1-18-80)* 9781
Final Reports on Prosecution Cases (Optional Format)

634.1 *(1-18-80)* 9781
Introduction

(1) The optional format report was implemented on June 2, 1972, amended on July 19, 1973, and developed in its present form on March 14, 1975 as a result of constructive suggestions from District, Regional and National Office personnel. The ARC (Criminal Investigation) may authorize the use of the optional format report on either a regional or district basis.

(2) The optional format report is a witness oriented rather than an exhibit oriented report, for example: Witnesses are numbered chronologically as they are introduced—W1, W2, W3, and so forth. Each exhibit pertaining to a given witness is likewise numbered chronologically. For example, the exhibits relating to witness number 3 would be designated as W3-1, W3-2, and W3-3. This form of a witness-exhibit referencing system eliminates the need for separate witness and exhibit lists as both lists are combined in one. No disassembly or reassembly of witness-exhibits is required for pretrial or trial use. The optional report requires less introductory narrative concerning the individual witness and exhibits. However, the pertinent facts and circumstances of the case should be thoroughly discussed in the narrative and fully documented with appropriate witness-exhibit references. Exhibit references should be underlined and explained the first time they are mentioned in the report in order to facilitate review and pretrial use of the report. Subsequent references to the exhibit should not be underlined or explained. For example: "The results of the civil examination (*W4-2, Revenue Agent's Report*) are as follows. . . . The civil adjustments (W4-2) are reconciled to the criminal adjustments in Appendix A."

(3) The optional report has a standard format, but additional sub-headings may be used to add clarity to the report and facilitate review. (See 634.2, Outline for Final Reports on Prosecution Cases-Optional Format and Exhibit 600-4). Additional sub-headings should be used liberally to highlight any significant issues.

(4) The optional report makes maximum use of appendices and eliminates the need for a detailed explanation of each of the supporting exhibits and minor details of the case. Each of the appendices should contain complete references to all relevant testimony and documentary evidence. Furthermore, each appendix should be referenced to all corroborative evidence.

(5) The optional format report contains details of the revenue agent's recommendations and a reconciliation of the civil and criminal adjustments. A copy of the Revenue Agent's Report should be included as an exhibit to the Special Agent's Report. The Special Agent's Report should state where the evidence in support of the fraud penalty is maintained.

634.2 *(1-18-80)* 9781
Format For Final Reports in Prosecution Cases (Optional Format)

(1) Introduction
(2) History of taxpayer
(3) Evidence of income
  (a) Theory of the case
  (b) Books and records
  (c) Preparation and filing of returns
  (d) Reconciliation of books and records to tax return (if applicable)
    1 Reported Income
    2 Reported Expenses
  (e) Explanation of appendix items (if applicable) or
  (f) Evidence for use in criminal proceedings
  (g) Additional deductions (if applicable)
  (h) Corrected taxable income and tax (if applicable)
(4) Corroborative proof (if applicable)
(5) Evidence of intent
(6) Explanation and defense of taxpayer
(7) Conclusions and recommendations

634.3 *(1-18-80)* 9781
Introduction

(1) The introduction to the report should contain the principal's social security number or employer's identification number. Both numbers should be added where applicable. In addition, this section should make maximum use of the following subheadings and brief statements of fact as opposed to extensive narrative.
  (a) Name and address of the Taxpayer
  (b) Name and address of Representative
  (c) Type of Report
  (d) Type of Case and Prosecution Years
  (e) Recommended Charges

(f) Investigating Agents
(g) Related cases
(h) Method of proof
(i) Method of Evasion
(j) Returns Filed and Statutes of Limitation
(k) Venue
(l) Source of Case
(m) Initial Contact with Taxpayer and Date of Referral
(n) Constitutional Advice
(o) Power of Attorney
(p) Revenue Agent's Recommendations
(q) Reconciliation of Civil and Criminal Adjustments
(r) Civil Actions

(2) The narrative relating to "Returns Filed and Statutes of Limitation" should include filing information (with pertinent exhibits) of periods subsequent to those for which prosecution was recommended.

(3) The narrative relating to "Venue" should include not only where venue may lie but also what evidence supports the conclusions. Evidence of venue should be fully documented as set forth in IRM 932(10).

(4) The narrative relating to "Initial Contact With Taxpayer and Data of Referral" should state not only who contacted the principal but also, when, where, how, and why. If the case was referred to the Criminal Investigation Division from either Examination, Collection, or the Service Center, the referral date should be included. If the case was not referred from within the IRS, this section should be entitled "Initial Contact with Taxpayer."

(5) The narrative relating to "Constitutional Advice" should state when, where, and by whom the advice was given; who was present; and statements made by the principal as to his/her understanding of his/her rights. (See IRM 9384.2.)

(6) The narrative relating to the revenue agent's recommendations should schedule the corrected taxable income and tax for use in civil proceedings. A copy of the Revenue Agent's Report should be included as a witness-exhibit reference. Samples of the scheduling of corrected taxable income and tax are set forth in Exhibits 600-1, 600-2, and 600-4.

(a) If applicable, any differences between the criminal and civil adjustments should be reconciled and explained either in this section, an exhibit or an appendix. A suggested format for reconciling the return to the civil and criminal adjustments is set forth in Appendix A-2, Exhibit 600-4—Cont. (20).

(b) The report should state where the evidence in support of the fraud penalty is being maintained. When recommending the Civil Fraud Penalty in willful failure to file cases and/or with respect to tax periods not included in the prosecution recommendation, consideration should be given to including in the report the facts and evidence used to support the Civil Fraud Penalty (see Text 252.3). This may be accomplished by creating a separate heading or sub-section in the optional report. (See subsection 634.1:(3).)

(7) All significant civil actions instituted either by or against the taxpayer should be fully explained. This applies whether the actions are for prior years, prosecution years, subsequent years, or relative to a different type of tax.

634.4 *(1-18-80)* 9781

History of Taxpayer

(1) This section remains the same as in the narrative format report, except that maximum use is made of subheadings and brief statements of fact. In addition, this section should make maximum use of the following subheadings and brief statements of fact as opposed to extensive narrative:

(a) Full Name
(b) Aliases, Business Names
(c) Date and Place of Birth
(d) Physical and Mental Health
(e) Marital Status and Spouse's Name
(f) Dependents
(g) Place of Residence During Years Involved
(h) Education
(i) Military Service
(j) Reputation in the Community
(k) Criminal Actions (a copy of the criminal record should be submitted as an exhibit with the report)
(l) Business Address During Years Involved
(m) Business History
(n) Sources of Income
(o) Other Pertinent Data

634.5 *(1-18-80)* 9781
Evidence of Income

(1) The "*Theory of the Case*" section is designed primarily to present an overview or brief synopsis of the case. This section should avoid conclusions and adhere to a capsule presentation of the facts and evidence developed during the investigation. The synopsis need not be documented but must be based upon facts proven elsewhere in the report. The report should mention whether the principal is a cash or accrual basis taxpayer and the basis used to determine the unreported income for use in criminal proceedings. This section should also set forth the method(s) of proof used. If an indirect method of proving income is used, an explanation should be given as to why the method was selected.

(2) The "*Books and Records*" section should contain a brief description of the principal's records as opposed to a mere listing of the records. This section is not intended to be an exhaustive analysis of the recordkeeping system but should relate enough information to familiarize the reader with the records and how they are used to record the principal's income and expenses. The recordkeeping responsibilities and detailed office procedures should be explained under the "Explanation of Appendix Items" section. The "Books and Records" section should include information as to when, how, and from whom the records were obtained and their disposition, that is, whether or not the records were copied, compared, certified, and returned to the principal.

(3) The "*Preparation and Filing of Returns*" section should contain all details surrounding the preparation and filing of the principal's returns. Particular emphasis should be placed upon who was responsible for each facet of the preparation, signing, and filing the return. The scope of the evidence presented in this section is basically the same as in the narrative format report; however, it has been given a separate section to emphasize the basic importance of this aspect of the investigation.

(4) The "*Reconciliation of the Books and Records to Tax Returns*" section should summarize the major income and expense categories as well as deductions and show the agreement with amounts reported on the tax return. If applicable, those items which are not in agreement should be explained. This section should make reference to either the summary schedule exhibit or appendix which shows the detailed reconciliation. If a reconciliation is not possible or necessary, a statement to that effect should be included in this section.

(5) The "*Explanation of Appendix Items*" section is one of the more significant sections of the report. The evidence in support of the violation should be set forth in full detail in this section. Although extensive narration of each appendix item and exhibit is not necessary with a well planned appendix, sufficient detail must be presented to fully explain the facts and circumstances of the case. Subheadings may be used liberally to clarify this section. The first part of this section should set out a schedule of the specific categories and items of unreported income or a summary of the net worth, bank deposit, or expenditure schedules, whichever is applicable. This section should explain each appendix: what it is; how the data on the appendix is derived; what analyses were made; what evidence is used; and what the appendix shows. Only those individual appendix items which are not self-explanatory need be explained. If appendices are not used in presenting the case, the heading "*Explanation of Appendix Items*" may be replaced with the heading "*Evidence for Use in Criminal Proceedings.*"

(6) The "*Additional Deductions*" section should not only summarize but also explain any additional deductions or adjustments determined during the investigation. This heading should be deleted if there are no additional deductions or adjustments.

(7) The final subsection under the major section "*Evidence of Income*" is "*Corrected Taxable Income and Tax.*" This section sets forth the computation of corrected taxable income and tax for use in criminal proceedings. If the

case in chief is presented by an indirect method of proof, this section need only show the corrected tax computation if taxable income is shown on the appendices. Include as tax for criminal purposes corrected self-employment tax figures whenever the original fraudulent return reflects an amount of self-employment tax. Exclude self-employment tax figures in failure to file cases or in cases where none of the fraudulent returns involved reflect a self-employment tax figure. Income averaging computations should be prepared in all cases where appropriate. (See Text 633.42:(6)(f).)

634.6 *(1-18-80)* 9781
Corroborative Proof

If no corroborative proof is used, this section should be deleted from the report. If the primary method of proof is corroborated by another method of proof, the heading "*Corroborative Proof*" should be centered on the page as a major subheading after the "*Corrected Taxable Income and Tax*" section and before the "*Evidence of Intent*" section. The "*Corroborative Proof*" section should set forth the details of the corroborative proof used in the case. In a combined net worth/specific item case, the evidence for the method supporting the government's case in chief would be set forth under the "*Explanation of Appendix Items*" section and evidence of the corroborative method would be set forth under the "*Corroborative Proof*" section.

634.7 *(1-18-80)* 9781
Evidence of Intent

The "*Evidence of Intent*" section remains basically the same in content as in the narrative format report. This important section of the report should contain brief, concise statements of the evidence of intent presented in the preceding sections of the report, together with a discussion of any additional evidence of intent. Generally, if an item is presented in the "*Evidence of Intent*" section, it should be fully developed in prior sections of the report.

634.8 *(1-18-80)* 9781
Explanation and Defense of Taxpayer

The "*Explanation and Defense of Taxpayer*" section of the report remains basically the same as in the narrative format report except this section now follows the "*Evidence of Intent*" section so that evidence not previously covered in the report can be introduced.

634.9 *(1-18-80)* 9781
Conclusions and Recommendations

(1) The special agent should identify the features of the case on which the recommendation for criminal prosecution is based and shall present an appraisal of the related facts and circumstances of the case. The special agent shall comment on the flagrancy of the violation and any evidence of a hostile attitude on the part of the taxpayer.

(2) The special agent shall make specific recommendations concerning the institution of criminal proceedings, including the particular penal sections of law and tax period involved in each recommendation.

(3) Special recommendations should be made relative to the assertion of any appropriate civil sanctions within the jurisdiction of the Criminal Investigation Division, including the particular sections of law and the tax period involved in the recommendation.

(4) If the case involves tax periods for which prosecution is not recommended, the special agent should identify the evidence relied upon to support the penalty recommendations relating to such periods and set forth the reasons for recommending against prosecution. In addition, the report should indicate where the evidence in support of the civil sanctions is being maintained.

634.(10) *(8-11-80)* 9781
Witness-Exhibit Files

(1) A separate witness file should be established for each witness developed during the investigation. The witness file should include the applicable testimony. Documents relating to each witness file can then be reviewed for relevancy and each item therein arranged in a logical sequence.

(2) In assembling the witness files, each witness file and each evidentiary item contained in each witness file will be numbered.

(3) The documents in the files should be secured within each file and all files then attached together in a manageable package with fasteners or by other methods.

(4) A separate cover sheet should be prepared for each witness file. The witness cover sheet should contain the following information: case number; name and title of witness; name and title of employers, if applicable; home or business address and telephone number where witness can be located in the event of trial; pertinent facts bearing on the credibility of the witness, including any known criminal record; a concise summary of the witness' testimony, including any known criminal record; a concise summary of the witness' testimony when a lengthy or complicated statement is involved. General statements need not be documented, but specific statements should have references (Witness-Exhibit) to the relevant document. The witness number and total number of exhibits should be listed on the cover sheet.

635 *(1-18-80)* 9781
Reports on Wagering Tax and Coin-operated Gaming Device (COGD) and Seizure Cases

635.1 *(1-18-80)* 9781
Introduction

(1) In preparing reports on wagering tax and coin operated gaming device cases the special agent should follow the outline for reports on tax fraud cases shown in 633, with the elimination of any section that is not necessary to a complete presentation of the facts. The flagrancy of the violation, the importance of the violator, and whether the case was adopted from local police authorities or developed through independent investigation by Criminal Investigation should be covered in the report. An optional short form report has been developed for use in wagering tax and coin-operated gaming device cases. To the extent possible the short form report should be utilized in these cases.

(2) The excise tax on coin-operated gaming devices is repealed, effective for years beginning after June 30, 1980.

(3) Exhibit 600-8 is an affidavit for search warrant; Exhibit 600-8 Cont. (1) is a search warrant; and 600-8 Cont. (2) is the return of the search warrant. The sample affidavit, search warrant, and return concern a hypothetical situation and are not designed to provide qualitative or quantitative standards to be used in every case. As far as possible, the samples contain information that the courts have recognized as valid and necessary for the issuance of a legal search warrant.

635.2 *(1-18-80)* 9781
Reports in Wagering Cases

(1) A final report will be submitted by special agents at the conclusion of each investigation in accordance with IRM 9512.1.

(2) When a special agent makes an arrest in a wagering occupational tax case, he/she will prepare an Arrest Report, Form 1327A, which will be furnished by the Chief, Criminal Investigation Division to the United States Attorney by the close of business on the next business day following the arrest. Arrest reports will be processed in accordance with IRM 9447.8.

(3) Final reports containing recommendations for prosecutions will be forwarded by the Chief, Criminal Investigation Division to District Counsel for review. The Chief, Criminal Investigation Division will comment in the transmittal memorandum that the criteria in IRM 9421 were met. In those instances where a package of cases is being recommended for prosecution and not all the cases met the criteria, the Chief will identify in the transmittal memorandum those cases which met the criteria. However, wagering occupational cases involving arrests which do not include recommendations for prosecution of other tax violations will be referred directly to the United States Attorney. In cases where an arrest was made for a wagering occupational violation and the investigation also gathered sufficient evidence of a wagering excise tax violation to warrant a recommendation for prosecution, District Counsel will be provided with a report concerning the excise tax portion of the case only. District Counsel will refer wagering cases (except COGD cases) directly to the United States Attorney.

(4) If the United States Attorney later decides to prosecute a wagering tax defendant for a substantive gambling violation, he may need to prove that none of the information used at trial is tainted by the tax disclosure. Where this is not possible, the prosecution of non-tax violations may be precluded. To avoid this potential interference with non-tax gambling investigations and prosecutions, all information controlled by IRC 4424 (See Chapter (26)00 of the "New" IRM 1272, Disclosure of Official Information Handbook) which is forwarded to the United States Attorney will have the following statement on the cover sheet of each report:

"THIS DOCUMENT CONTAINS WAGERING INFORMATION WHICH UNDER IRC SEC-

TIONS 4424 AND 6103 MAY BE DISCLOSED ONLY FOR THE ADMINISTRATION AND CRIMINAL ENFORCEMENT OF THE INTERNAL REVENUE CODE. IT MAY NOT BE USED FOR INTELLIGENCE OR PROSECUTORIAL PURPOSES FOR GAMBLING OFFENSES SET FORTH IN TITLE 18, U.S.C., OR ANY OTHER PURPOSE."

(5) When state or local court actions of any type have been initiated or concluded against the subject of a wagering investigation at the time a final report containing a recommendation for prosecution is written, the facts relating to such court action should be incorporated in the final report. If the court action takes place after the report has been submitted, a supplemental report containing significant details concerning the matter will be submitted.

635.3 *(1-18-80)* 9781
Seizure Report, Form 4008

(1) Form 4008 will be used to report seizures of all personal property, regardless of whether the property is subject to judicial forfeiture or administrative forfeiture. Adoption of a form report as a substitute for the narrative report is not meant to encourage brevity of reported information. Because the information contained in the seizure report constitutes the basis for forfeiture action, it must be accurate and complete. Furthermore, the information and evidence is needed to process and answer such legal actions as Petitions for Remission and Mitigation of Forfeiture, Claim and Cost Bonds, and Offers in Compromise. A seizure report should not be abbreviated simply because the seized property is valued at $2,500 or less and may be subject to administrative forfeiture since the property, regardless of the value, may later become subject to judicial forfeiture by the filing of a claim and cost bond. (See IRM 9455.7)

(2) Form 4008 is a seven part snap-out assembly. Item instructions are included with the sample seizure report (Exhibit 600-9).

(3) The following documents, if prepared, should be attached to the original copy of the seizure report:

(a) Form 181, Inventory Record of Seized Vessel, Vehicle or Aircraft.

(b) Form 226-A, Appraisement List.

(c) Copy of Affidavit for Search Warrant.

(d) Copy of Search Warrant and Return of Search Warrant.

(e) Form SF-1034, Public Voucher for Purchases and Services Other Than Personal.

(f) Form 141-A, Special Moneys Report.

(4) The case identification number shall be noted on all copies of inventory records, appraisal forms, tags, receipts, and other documents relating to a particular seizure. A separate report shall be prepared covering all property seized at the time from each premises on which a seizure is made, regardless of ownership, although details of ownership shall be covered in the report.

635.4 *(1-18-80)* 9781
Report of Investigation Relating to Petition for Remission or Mitigation of Forfeiture

Exhibit 600-10 contains the format and instructions for a special agent's report of an investigation relating to petition for remission or mitigation of forfeiture. The format and instructions shall be followed insofar as applicable. (See IRM 9458.5)

636 *(1-18-80)* 9781
Miscellaneous Criminal Law Violations

The general outline provided in 632 should be used in preparing reports on miscellaneous criminal violations in which fraud is not the prime factor. The section relating to summary of the cooperating officer's findings is not applicable to these cases, and other parts of the outline may be eliminated or modified according to the circumstances of the case. Exhibit 600-11 is a sample report relative to a miscellaneous criminal violation.

637 *(1-18-80)* 9781
Reports on Nonprosecution Cases

(1) Reports on investigations in which prosecution is not recommended shall be similar to, but less detailed than, those pertaining to criminal cases. Since in completed investigations the special agent is responsible for any recommendations concerning civil penalties other than those relating to tax estimations, he/she shall identify and summarize the facts and evidence upon which the recommendation is based. The investigative procedures followed shall be described or outlined in enough detail to enable supervisory and reviewing officials to determine whether the investigation was sufficiently exhaustive to have uncovered any existing evidence of fraud. Particular attention shall be given to setting forth the specific reasons for recommending against criminal proceedings. (See IRM 9521 and 9327.2)

(2) *Fraud penalty.*—Since in cases involving the ad valorem addition to the tax for civil fraud the burden of proving fraud is on the Government, care must be exercised to ensure that there is sufficient evidence to sustain that burden. Cases should be documented to the extent necessary to establish clear and convincing proof of the violation.

(a) With respect to nonprosecution cases wherein an agreement was not obtained from the taxpayer, available documents material to the matter of fraud should be submitted as exhibits. In the body of the report maximum use should be made of the technique of summarization. In many instances narrative may be reduced by the use of appendices containing brief descriptions of the evidence.

(b) In reports on cases in which the taxpayer has agreed to the assertion of the fraud penalty, emphasis should be placed on an explanation of the specific reasons for the conclusion that prosecution is not warranted. The facts and circumstances on which the assertion of the penalty is based should be set forth, but discussion of specific items of evidence and submission of exhibits usually is unnecessary. However, because of the possibility that a taxpayer who had executed an agreement might subsequently file a suit for refund, the files of the Criminal Investigation Division should contain all available documents relating to evidence on which the penalties are based. To illustrate the suggested procedure regarding agreed cases, assume that a part of the facts disclosed by an investigation concerned a taxpayer's failure to report 18 checks received in payment for sales to a corporation, and that the special agent obtained an affidavit from an officer of the corporation, together with photostats of the pertinent canceled checks and invoices. The taxpayer's receipt of that income may be covered in the report by a statement that "During the year 19—, __________ received 18 checks aggregating $5,283 from the A.B.C. Corporation, Baltimore, Maryland, in payment for sales of machinery." Although the affidavit and the photostats will not be submitted as exhibits, they will be retained in the files of the Criminal Investigation Division.

638 *(1-18-80)* 9781
Reports on Discontinued Investigation

(1) Reports of withdrawal from investigations will specify the basis for the investigation, the extent of the investigation, the results obtained, the reason for recommending discontinuance of the investigation and a recommendation as to disposition to be made of the case (close to files or refer to Examination or Collection Divison). The special agent will not make a recommendation concerning civil penalties in discontinued investigations. Exhibit 600-12 is a sample report on a discontinued investigation.

(2) Any documentary evidence to support the assertion of civil fraud penalty will be included with the final report.

(3) Special agents should not use language which may discourage subsequent developments of the fraud issue. For example, if a case is closed due to a lack of prosecution potential, that is, age, health, education, de minimis etc., no conclusion should be drawn concerning the lack of intent by the taxpayer to commit fraud unless there are other facts and circumstances present which make the statement proper.

(4) In those instances where an investigation has been terminated or a referral declined by a memorandum, a statement should be made in the report to the effect that nothing was discussed or occurred in the case which precludes the assertion of the civil fraud penalty.

(5) In joint investigations the withdrawal report should contain a statement that the cooperating officer's Group Manager has been advised of the proposed withdrawal action and concurs with it. See 3(10)9.

639 *(5-9-80)* 9781
Collateral Reports

(1) A sample report of a collateral request and one of a reply are illustrated in Exhibits 600-13 and 600-14. Collateral requests should contain only sufficient information to advise the receiving office of the essential facts of the case. Collateral replies should not restate information that was requested or action that was required but should begin by answering the request in the first paragraph. Ending paragraphs such as, "It is recommended that this report be forwarded to," should be omitted as this information can be included in the heading of the report as shown in Exhibit 600-14. Collateral replies shall include the number of hours charged to the collateral investigation by each agent assigned.

(2) Exhibits 600-13—Cont. and 600-14—Cont. contain optional formats for placement of the approval legend on collateral requests and replies.

(3) IRM 9264 sets forth procedures to be followed in collateral requests and in obtaining information from the National Office and other sources. Reference to a Directory of Post Offices (formerly Postal Guide) to identify the county in which a particular municipality is located, and then to IRM 1119 (Listing of Internal Revenue Regions, Districts, and Service Centers, with Background History) or to one of the tax services to identify the specific district in which the country is located, will facilitate proper direction of collateral requests.

(4) See 625.3 for treatment of documents submitted with collateral reports.

640 *(1-18-80)* 9781
Chronological Worksheet

Special agents may be required to maintain Criminal Investigation Division chronological worksheet, Form 4365, to record the sources, dates of origin and other facts and circumstances involved in obtaining leads and evidence in investigations. Completed chronological worksheets relating to investigations should be maintained as a permanent part of the district case file. Exhibit 600-15 is a sample chronological worksheet.

650 *(1-18-80)* 9781
Legal Action Reports

651 *(1-18-80)* 9781
General

(1) Current information concerning the movement and disposition of criminal cases is provided regional and National Office officials through the prompt submission by special agents of Forms 1327 (Report of Legal Action) (Report Symbol NO-CP:1-19). Form 1327 will be prepared or updated and mailed on the same day the reported action takes place. Air mail will be used when the delivery date will be materially advanced. Legal actions, especially those involving matters significant to tax administration or cases of national importance will be reported by the Chief, Criminal Investigation Division, to the regional and National offices by telephone or telegram and promptly confirmed by submission of Form 1327. Instructions for preparing Form 1327 are set forth in Exhibit 600-16.

(2) Care should be taken to ensure that any remarks or conclusions that are critical of officials or employees of any department or agency of the Government are adequately supported by the facts in the case.

(3) Form 1327 is also utilized to furnish data for statistical operations reports. The disposition of all cases forwarded to the U.S. Attorney will be reported, including those closed without court action. A Form 1327 reporting a "no true bill" will not be considered as closing a case unless the report specifically so states, inasmuch as many such cases are resubmitted or submitted to a subsequent grand jury. If a case is held open for further consideration, after the return of a "no true bill," and it is later decided to take no further action, a Form 1327 reporting the decision and closing the case should be submitted. Forms 1327 reporting closing actions, such as sentences, dismissals, and acquittals returned by the U.S. Attorney, will state the methods of evasion presented in the last proceeding related to the criminal violations alleged.

(4) Form 4930, Criminal Investigation Case/Project Record (Turnaround), should be prepared in accordance with Exhibit 400-3 of IRM 9570, Case Management and Time Reporting System Handbook, when a pertinent legal action occurs.

652 *(10-3-80)* 9781
Procedures

(1) Federal Rules of Criminal Procedure prohibit the disclosure of an indictment before it is returned in open court. Generally a Form 1327, Report of Legal Action (Report Symbol NO-CP:CI-19), on an indictment will be submitted at the time the grand jury makes its report to the court. However, where it is anticipated that the grand jury's report to the court will be delayed, as in the secret or sealed indictments, a Form 1327 will be promptly submitted showing that the case was presented to the grand jury, and that a supplemental Form 1327 will be mailed at the time the grand jury returns its report in open court.

(2) The Form 1327 will be updated each time court action takes place. Routine and special distribution requirements for Form 1327 are contained in IRM 9531.2:(2) through 9531.2:(6).

653 *(1-18-80)* 9781
No True Bill Cases

When a grand jury fails to return a true bill, Form 1327 will be prepared by the special agent assigned to the case indicating whether the agents were able to present all the facts to the grand jury, and whether the facts or other circumstances point out the desirability of obtaining supplemental information to strengthen the case. The report will comment upon appearance before the grand jury of the defendant or any defense witnesses, and upon any other relevant matters. It should contain the special agent's conclusion as to the probable reason for the grand jury's action and the special agent's views concerning resubmission of the case to the same or subsequent grand jury.

654 *(1-18-80)* 9781
Cases in Which a Conviction is Not Obtained

(1) In every case which a United States Attorney declines to prosecute, or which is dismissed before or during trial, or in which the jury is unable to reach a verdict, or which results in a verdict of not guilty, Form 1327 will include a narrative of the circumstances which, in the special agent's opinion, resulted in the action taken. In a tried case, a transcript of pertinent remarks and decision of the judge should accompany the report.

(2) The special agent will not seek out any of the jurors in a tried case for the purpose of soliciting information to be incorporated in the Form 1327 unless approved in advance by the National Office. However, the special agent should include any pertinent information proffered to him/her by jurors acting on their own initiative or submitted by them to other Government representatives.

655 *(1-18-80)* 9781
Cases Containing Unique or Important Matters of Law

Unique, important, or unusual matters of law arising in any case, regardless of its outcome, will be reported on Form 1327. This information is particularly desired in cases which will not ordinarily be reported in any legal or tax service. Copies of the court's decisions or remarks may be transmitted with the Form 1327.

656 *(1-18-80)* 9781
Reporting Arrests

(1) The special agent shall immediately report to his/her Group Manager any arrests that he/she makes. The Group Manager shall immediately report such information to the Chief. Such notification may be by wire or telephone.

(2) When it is necessary to make an arrest prior to consulting the United States Attorney, he/she shall be notified promptly of the arrest, advised fully of the facts in the case, and requested to represent the Government in the preliminary examination before the United States magistrate.

(3) In addition to the reporting procedure in (1) and (2) above, the special agent will prepare a Form 1327-A, Arrest Report (see Exhibit 600-7), before the close of the next business day following the arrest. The form will be submitted in the original and six copies and, upon approval by the Chief, the following distribution will be made:

(a) original to appropriate U.S. Attorney.

(b) two copies to Director, Criminal Investigation Division, Attention: CP:I:O.

(c) one copy to Chief Counsel, IRS, Attention: Director, Criminal Tax Division.

(d) one copy to ARC (Criminal Investigation).

(e) one copy to District Counsel.

(f) one copy to Chief's file.

(g) Also see IRM 9531.2.

(4) If the arresting agent believes valid reasons exist for opposing release of the prisoner on personal bond, these reasons will be brought to the attention of the United States Attorney prior to the bail hearing. The U.S. Attorney may request that the agent prepare Bail Reform Act Form No. 1, AO-201, for use at the hearing. The form is available at the Clerk's Office for each U.S. District Court. The original will be furnished to the U.S. Attorney and a duplicate will be retained in the Criminal Investigation case file.

660 *(1-18-80)* 9781
Claim for Reward Reports

(1) In any case where the special agent participated to conclusion and in which it is known that a claim for reward has been or will be filed, the special agent will prepare a separate claim for reward report. It will be made in an original and two copies and will be clearly labeled "Official Use Only." Upon conclusion of an investigation where prosecution is not recommended the special agent will prepare a claim for reward report as soon as he/she is in a position to make a final recommendation concerning the percentage of reward, if any, to which the informant is entitled. In prosecution cases preparation of the report may be deferred pending disposition of the criminal aspects of the case.

(2) In a prosecution case, if the claim for reward report is prepared before the disposition of the criminal aspects, it will be forwarded to the Chief for approval, after which the report will be retained in a suspense file until the criminal aspects of the case have been disposed of. At that time, the report will be reviewed by the special agent, updated if necessary to include further developments affecting the claim, and forwarded by the Chief, to the Chief, Examination Division, Attention: Informants Claims Examiner, for processing.

(3) The report will contain a consideration of the applicable factors stated as the Service criteria for allowance or rejection of informant's claims for reward, as detailed in IRM 9300. In addition, it will include the following.

(a) Name and address of informant.

(b) Name, case number, and address of the taxpayer, nature of the informant's relationship with the taxpayer and manner in which the information was obtained by the informant.

(c) A statement as to whether the information caused the investigation and whether any of the years involved had been examined previously, including the results of any such prior examination.

(d) A statement as to the value of the information furnished in relation to the facts developed by the investigation, specifying which adjustments were brought about by the information and the amount of taxes and penalties recommended as a result of those adjustments, if known.

(e) A statement regarding the extent of any assistance rendered by the informant during the course of the investigation and any additional information which may be pertinent, such as prosecution of the taxpayer.

(f) A recommendation by the special agent as to whether the informant is entitled to a reward, and if so, the percentage of the total recovery to which the informant is entitled. See IRM 9371 for the basis for computing rewards.

(g) The cooperating officer, if any, shall indicate his/her concurrence or nonconcurrence with the special agent's recommendation by signing a statement to that effect near the bottom of the last page of the original and all copies of the report. If the cooperating officer does not agree with the recommendation of the special agent as to the allowability of a reward or the percentage determined as appropriate, the cooperating officer will prepare and forward to the Informants Claims Examiner a separate report setting forth the reasons for his/her nonagreement.

670 *(1-18-80)* 9781
Supplemental Reports

(1) Supplemental reports add to or clarify information contained in a final report previously submitted on the same subject. A supplemental report may be initiated by a special agent to transmit information gathered since submission of the final report, or may be submitted in response to requests for information or clarification from the District Counsel or other offices processing or reviewing final reports.

(2) See 625.2 for information concerning the procedure in numbering exhibits for Supplemental Reports. Also see IRM 9357 relative to Supplemental Investigations.

680 *(1-18-80)* 9781
Grand Jury Investigation Reports

A report, similar in content to a special agent's final report, should be prepared and addressed to the attorney for the Government upon the conclusion of the grand jury investigation. The report, whether with or without prosecution recommendation, is to be transmitted to designated District Counsel attorneys. Prior to transmitting the report to the District Counsel attorneys who will review the report, those attorneys and necessary secretarial personnel will be identified and a written request from the Government attorney naming such individuals to assist him/her will be obtained. Documents governed by the secrecy provisions of Rule 6(e) should be bound in exhibit folders separate from all other documents and clearly identified so as to facilitate subsequent identification of the source of documents. Copies of the report will not be supplied to the District Director or to any persons not specifically authorized by the attorney for the Government as his/her assistants. (see IRM 9267.5)

690 *(1-18-80)* 9781
Reporting Derogatory Information Relating to Enrolled Persons, Attorneys, and Certified Public Accountants

691 *(1-18-80)* 9781
General

(1) Special agents who have reason to believe that an enrolled person or an attorney or certified public accountant has violated any provisions of the laws or regulations governing practices before the IRS, or receives information to that effect, shall make a written report which shall be immediately forwarded by the Chief, Criminal Investigation Division, through the District Director, to the Director of Practice, Department of Treasury, Washington D.C. 20220. Derogatory information coming to the attention of regional Criminal Investigation personnel should be reported in writing through the ARC (Criminal Investigation) to the Regional Commissioner for reference to the Director of Practice. The written report forwarded to the Director of Practice shall include sufficient detailed information, including any documentation or exhibits to substantiate the information regarding each specific violation to enable the Director of Practice to fully understand the basis of the alleged violation. If the information also involves allegations of employee misconduct or an attempt to corrupt an employee, Criminal Investigation personnel are required to report the matter directly to Inspection rather than through channels to the Director of Practice.

(2) If an enrolled person, attorney or certified public accountant becomes the subject of a Criminal Investigation Division investigation, Inspection and the Director of Practice will be notified, in writing, by the Chief, Criminal Investigation Division, through the District Director. If the investigation does not result in prosecution, a copy of the special agent's report will be forwarded, through the District Director, to the Director of Practice, together with such documentation or exhibits obtained during the investigation to substantiate the information regarding each specific violation to enable the Director of Practice to fully understand the basis of the alleged violation.

(3) In prosecution cases, and whenever an enrolled person, attorney or certified public accountant becomes the subject of a Report of Legal Action, Form 1327, an extra copy of Form 1327 will be prepared and forwarded by the Chief, Criminal Investigation Division, through the District Director, to the Director of Practice for his/her information and files. If the legal action does not result in a conviction, at such time as the criminal features of the case are disposed of, a copy of the special agent's report will be forwarded by the Chief, through the District Director, to the Director of Practice. If the subject is convicted, after sentencing, a copy of the judgment and commitment order, together with a copy of the special agent's report, will be forwarded by the Chief, through the District Director, to the Director of Practice.

(4) Because disciplinary proceedings cannot be instituted against attorneys and certified public accountants unless they are engaged in actual practice before the Service, reports of violations by such persons should contain a statement regarding their recent appearances before the Service together with a copy of declarations filed pursuant to Section 10.3 of Treasury Department Circular 230.

692 *(1-18-80)* 9781
Procedure for Reporting Derogatory Information Concerning Unenrolled Preparers of Tax Returns

(1) As set forth in current procedures, unenrolled preparers of tax returns to be eligible to represent the taxpayers must adhere to the same standards of professional conduct as enrolled persons. The successful policing of compliance with these standards depends to a great extent upon the vigilance of IRS employees in reporting instances where violations occur.

(2) Any special agent who has reason to believe that an unenrolled preparer's conduct or practices have been or are such as to render the preparer ineligible to represent taxpayers shall immediately communicate such information, through appropriate supervisory channels, to the District Director. If the information concerning the preparer also involves information or allegations of employee misconduct, or an attempt by the preparer to corrupt an employee, the matter should be reported to Inspection in the same manner as set out in IRM 9558.1. Inspection will be notified, through the District Director, whether an investigation is approved that involves an unenrolled preparer of tax returns.

(3) The District Director will determine from the pertinent facts in each case whether the unenrolled preparer is eligible or ineligible to appear as a taxpayer's representative. (An unenrolled preparer is not eligible to represent taxpayers under investigation by the Criminal Investigation Division. However, such preparer is not precluded from appearing solely in the role of a witness.) Where the District Director determines, either before or after the preparer has been recognized, that the preparer's conduct or practices have been or are such as to render the preparer ineligible to appear as a taxpayer's representative, the District Director, in accordance with the procedures in IRM 4053.3:(2), shall so inform the preparer in writing, except under the circumstances related in (4) below. A copy of the District Director's final determination of ineligibility will be transmitted to the Director, Examination Division, for the Director, Examination Division's information in the event the unenrolled preparer may claim to be aggrieved and communicates with the Director, Examination Division. It should be observed that prohibited solicitation and advertising by the preparer are included as specific grounds for revocation of eligibility.

(4) If the Criminal Investigation Division is conducting a criminal investigation of an unenrolled preparer, or if a criminal case involving the preparer is pending at any level, the District Director will not take any action toward declaring such person ineligible to represent taxpayers in the District Director's district under the provisions of (3) above without first consulting the division or office having control of the criminal case. Accordingly the Chief, Criminal Investigation Division, will, upon request, furnish the District Director an opinion as to whether the issuance of a notice of proposed determination of ineligibility to a preparer who is under criminal investigation would in any way prejudice the criminal case. Likewise, the Chief will obtain for the District Director through usual channels the views of the District Counsel or the Department of Justice appropriate, if a criminal case against the preparer is pending at one of those levels. The Chief should obtain the views of the United States Attorney by direct communication when the criminal case against the preparer is pending with that official. The issuance of a notice of proposed determination of ineligibility to an unenrolled preparer because of advertising, solicitation or other course of conduct not related to the pending criminal case may not be prejudicial to the criminal case. However, when a criminal case involving an unenrolled preparer is under investigation or pending, a proposed notice to such preparer must be considered on its merits by the office then having jurisdiction of the criminal case. No action will be taken that would jeopardize a pending criminal case.

(Next page is 9781-377)

Federal Court Procedures and Related Matters

710 *(1-18-80)* 9781
Law Governing Federal Courts

(1) Since the general police power is still lodged in the several states, Federal prosecution is limited to the areas prescribed by Federal statute. Thus, Federal crimes are exclusively statutory crimes. A fundamental consideration never to be lost sight of is that the jurisdiction of all courts of the United States is limited by the Constitution. The district courts and Courts of Appeals have been established by Congress under the authority of the Constitution. The district courts of the United States have general jurisdiction of all offenses against the laws of the United States. The criminal and civil statutes which special agents are normally concerned with are set forth in Chapter 200, and the statutory periods of limitations on institution of criminal proceedings are in 240.

(2) Under the provisions of an act of Congress on June 29, 1940, the Supreme Court prescribed "Rules of Criminal Procedure for the District Courts of the United States." These procedural rules, as amended, became law on November 21, 1946, and are published in full as a separate volume of Title 18, USC. As stated in Rule 1, the rules govern the procedure in the courts of the United States and before United States Magistrates in criminal proceedings. They are "intended to provide for the just determination of every criminal proceeding" and "shall be construed to secure simplicity in procedure, fairness in administration and the elimination of unjustifiable expense and delay" (Rule 2).

720 *(1-18-80)* 9781
Federal Rules of Criminal Procedure (Pre-Trial)

721 *(1-18-80)* 9781
Complaint (Rule 3)

(1) A complaint is a sworn written statement made before a United States Magistrate or, if not reasonably available, other person empowered to commit persons charged with offenses against the United States. [U.S. Judge, chancellor, judge of Supreme or Superior Court, chief or first judge of common pleas, mayor of a city, justice of the peace, or other magistrate of any State where the offender may be found. (18 USC 3041)] It should set forth the substantial and material features of the offense charged and should be worded substantially in the statutory language of the offense. It must be sworn to positively and not merely aver information and belief, and should be based upon the complainant's personal knowledge or supported by other proof. [*U.S. v. Langsdale; Giordenello v. U.S.*] Usually the special agent signs the complaint.

(2) The filing of a complaint before a United States Magistrate prior to the expirration of the statute of limitations will extend the period nine months from the date filed in internal revenue cases. [26 USC 6531] Exhibit 700-1 is a sample complaint. The Supreme Court held that a complaint using this format contained sufficient probable cause and was valid since it directly indicated that the defendant committed the crime charged, and it disclosed the source of the directly incriminating information. [*Jaben v. U.S.*] *Complaints are also discussed in Subsection 319.4:(3).*

722 *(1-18-80)* 9781
Warrant or Summons Upon Complaint (Rule 4)

(1) If it appears from the complaint, or from an affidavit or affidavits filed with the complaint, that there is probable cause to believe that a defendant has committed an offense, the magistrate will issue a warrant for his/her arrest to any officer authorized by law to execute it. Upon the request of the attorney for the Government the magistrate will issue a court summons (instead of a warrant) requiring the defendant to appear before the magistrate at a stated time and place to answer the complaint. If the defendant fails to appear in response to the summons, a warrant shall be issued. A warrant is executed by arrest of the defendant. More than one warrant or summons may be issued on the same complaint in order to facilitate service and return where several defendants are named in the same complaint. Physical delivery of the warrant to the officer is not necessary to the timely institution of the complaint. The officer need not have physical possession of the warrant in order to arrest lawfully, but upon request must show it to the defendant as soon as possible. A warrant for arrest in a criminal case is effective anywhere in the United States.

(2) Text 383 through 396 set out information relative to special agents' activities in connection with search warrants and arrests.

723 *(1-18-80)* 9781
Preliminary Examination (Rule 5)

(1) At the initial appearance of the arrested person, the judge or magistrate shall fix a date for the preliminary examination to determine whether there is probable cause to believe that an offense has been committed and that the arrested person has committed it. The examination shall be held within a reasonable time after the initial appearance, but in any event not later than—

(a) Ten days after the date of the initial appearance if the arrested person is held in custody without any provision for release, or is held in custody for failure to meet the conditions of release imposed, or is released from custody only during specified hours of the day; or

(b) Twenty days after the initial appearance if the arrested person is released from custody under any condition other than a condition described in (a) above.

(2) With the arrested person's consent, the date fixed for the preliminary examination may be later than that prescribed by (1) above, or may be continued one or more times from the date initially fixed. Without the arrested person's consent, dates later than that prescribed by (1) above, or continuances may be fixed only by an order of a judge of the appropriate United States district court after a finding that extraordinary circumstances exist, and that the delay of the preliminary hearing is indispensable to the interests of justice.

(3) Failure to comply with the above provisions shall result in the discharge of the arrested person from custody or from the requirement of bail or any other condition of release, without prejudice, however, to the institution of further criminal proceedings against him/her relative to the charge upon which he/she was arrested.

(4) No preliminary examination is required nor shall an arrested person be released in accordance with (3) above if, at any time after the initial appearance before the judge or magistrate and prior to the date fixed for the preliminary examination pursuant to (1) and (2) above, indictment is returned, or, in appropriate cases, an information is filed in a United States court against such person.

(5) At the preliminary hearing, the accused may cross-examine witnesses against him/her and may introduce evidence in his/her own behalf. The accused is not required to plead at this time. If the magistrate concludes from the evidence that there is probable cause to believe the accused has committed an offense, or if the accused waives preliminary examination, the magistrate shall forthwith hold the accused to answer in the district court; otherwise the magistrate shall discharge him/her. This would not prevent subsequent indictment of the accused on the same charge.

(6) Subject to the control of the United States Attorney, agents are authorized to conduct the prosecution at the committal trial for the purpose of having the offenders held for action of the grand jury. This will ordinarily be done only when the attorney for the Government is not available. [IRC 5557]

724 *(1-18-80)* 9781
The Grand Jury (Rule 6)

(1) The grand jury consists of 16 to 23 members summoned by order of the court. They serve until discharged by the court, but not longer than 18 months. An indictment may be found only upon concurrence of 12 or more jurors. Otherwise, a "no bill" is returned. The court may direct that an indictment be kept secret until the defendant is in custody or has given bail. In that event the clerk seals the indictment and no person may disclose the finding of the indictment except when necessary for the issuance and execution of a warrant or summons. [Rule 6(e), FRCP]

(2) Grand jury proceedings are kept secret to: prevent the escape of those whose indictment may be contemplated; ensure freedom to the grand jury in its deliberations by protecting its members from annoyance and undue influence; prevent subornation of perjury or tampering with witnesses; and protect the reputations of persons investigated but not indicted. Accordingly, while it is in session, the only persons who may be present are attorneys for the Government, the witness under examination, a stenographer or operator of a recording device, and interpreters when needed. An indictment may be dismissed upon a showing that an unauthorized person was present during the proceedings. No person other than the jurors may be present while the grand jury is deliberating or voting. [Rule 6(d), FRCP]

(3) Disclosure of matters occurring before the grand jury may be made to those Government personnel deemed necessary by a Government attorney to assist in the performance of his/her duty to enforce Federal criminal law. With the consent of the Government attorney, agents of the Service may examine documents and records which are before the grand jury, inspect its minutes, and assist in the investigation of possible criminal tax violations. An intentional violation of Rule 6 may be punished as a contempt of court.

(4) Federal rules do not impose any obligation of secrecy upon witnesses [Rule 6(e), FRCP, Note of Advisory Committee], although some Federal jurisdictions require an oath of secrecy.

(5) A grand jury is not obliged to grant a request from a prospective defendant to appear before it as a witness. However, Justice Department procedures provide that where no burden upon the grand jury or delay of its proceedings is involved, reasonable requests of a prospective defendant to personally testify before the grand jury are to be given favorable consideration. This may be done provided that such witness explicitly waives his/her privilege against self-incrimination, is represented by counsel or voluntarily and knowingly appears without counsel, and consents to full examination under oath.

(6) After the grand jury's functions have ended, a trial court may order disclosure of its minutes to the defendant if he/she shows a "particularized need" to support an attack upon the indictment, to impeach a witness or refresh his recollection, or, in a perjury prosecution, to inspect his/her own grand jury testimony.

(7) Under 18 USC 3331, a special grand jury may be convened for a period of up to thirty-six months. Although such grand jury can inquire into all offenses against the criminal laws of the United States, its main activities are related to organized crime, and misconduct and misfeasance in office involving organized criminal activity by an appointed public officer or employee.

725 *(1-18-80)* 9781
Indictment and Information

725.1 *(1-18-80)* 9781
Definitions of Indictment and Information

(1) An indictment (Exhibit 700-2) is an accusation in writing found and presented by a grand jury to the court in which it is impaneled charging that the person named therein has done some act, or been guilty of some omission, which, by law, is a criminal offense.

(2) An information (Exhibit 700-3) is an accusation in writing against a person named therein for some criminal offense and is filed with the court by a competent officer on his/her oath of office.

725.2 *(1-18-80)* 9781
Indictment and Information Distinguished (Rules 7a and 7b)

(1) In criminal tax cases, an indictment is returned by the grand jury and presented to the court by the foreman of the grand jury. An information is filed with the court by the United States Attorney.

(2) Misdemeanors may be prosecuted by either indictment or information; felonies must be prosecuted by indictment, unless waived by the defendant in open court. If indictment is waived, a felony may be prosecuted by information. As here used a felony is an offense which may be punished by imprisonment of more than one year; a misdemeanor is any other offense. [18 USC 1]

(3) The court may permit an information to be amended at any time before verdict or finding if no additional or different offense is charged and if substantial rights of the defendant are not prejudiced. [Rule 7(e), FRCP]

725.3 *(1-18-80)* 9781
Bill of Particulars (Rule 7f)

(1) A bill of particulars is a written statement of the specific charges against which the defendant must defend. It is designed to aid the defendant in properly answering the allegations and in preparing for trial by informing him/her of the particular transactions in question in order to avoid surprise at the trial and to protect him/her against a second prosecution for the same offense. It need not set forth all the evidence to be used in support of the charges. Generally, the granting of a bill of particulars is within the discretion of the trial judge.

(2) Where it is granted, the Government is faced with the problem of complying with the order of the court without, at the same time, disclosing so much of the Government's evidence as to jeopardize successful prosecution. Generally, information concerning the nature and source of income allegedly understated and the manner in which the returns are claimed to be false and fraudulent will be allowed by the court, but not the evidence by which the Government will attempt to prove the charges set forth in the indictment.

(3) With simplified forms of indictments and informations now approved, the bill of particulars is especially important because, although not technically a part of the indictment, the Government's proof is limited by statements in the bill. However, the Government has the right to amend its bill of particulars "at any time subject to such conditions as justice requires."[Rule 7(f), FRCP.]

725.4 *(1-18-80)* 9781
Joinder of Offenses and Defendants (Rule 8)

(1) Two or more offenses (felonies or misdemeanors or both) may be charged in the same indictment or information in a separate count for each offense, if they are of similar character or are based on the same act or transaction or on two or more acts or transactions constituting parts of a common scheme or plan. For example, separate counts of an indictment may charge conspiracy to defraud and income tax evasion.

(2) Two or more defendants may be charged in the same indictment or information if they participated in the same transaction or series thereof constituting an offense. They may be charged in one or more counts together or separately and all need not be charged in each count. This applies in cases involving equal partners whose knowledge of unreported partnership income can be established by the same evidence.

726 *(1-18-80)* 9781
Arraignment and Preparation for Trial

726.1 *(1-18-80)* 9781
Arraignment (Rule 10)

An arraignment consists of calling a defendant before a judge, reading the indictment to him/her or informing him/her of the charge, calling on him/her to state whether he/she is guilty or not guilty, and entering his/her plea. The defendant will be given a copy of the indictment or information before he/she is called upon to plead.

726.2 *(1-18-80)* 9781
Pleas (Rule 11)

(1) A defendant may plead not guilty, guilty or, with the consent of the court, nolo contendere (no contest). The court may refuse to accept a plea of guilty, and shall not accept such plea or a plea of nolo contendere without first addressing the defendant personally and determining that the plea is made voluntarily with understanding of the nature of the charge and the consequences of the plea. If a defendant refuses to plead or if the court refuses to accept a plea of guilty or if a defendant corporation fails to appear, the court shall enter a plea of not guilty. The court shall not enter a judgment upon a plea of guilty unless it is satisfied that there is factual basis for the plea.

(2) If a not guilty plea is entered, the court proceeds by setting a date for trial.

(3) If the defendant pleads guilty or nolo contendere at arraignment, the procedural steps prior to and during trial as prescribed in Rule 12 through Rule 31 do not apply and the court proceeds to hear the facts preliminary to imposing sentence. Some courts do not permit persons other than attorneys who are officers of the court to address the court—in such instances the Government attorney will present the facts for the Government. However, many courts are informed of the facts by the investigating special agent or other representative of the Criminal Investigation Division. The role of the special agent in this regard is especially important since his/her oral presentation of facts in open court forms the only supporting basis of the offenses charged in the information or indictment. Text 73(13).2 discusses the procedures prescribed in Rule 32 with respect to pre-sentence report by the Court's probation officer, sentencing, and judgment.

(4) A plea of nolo contendere subjects the defendant to the same punishment as a plea of guilty, but does not admit the charges. It cannot be used against him/her as an admission in any civil suit for the same act.

726.3 *(1-18-80)* 9781
Motions Raising Defenses and Objections (Rule 12)

All defenses and objections raised before trial are by motion (e.g., motion for bill of particulars, for discovery and inspection, to suppress, etc.) and are limited to those capable of determination without the trial of the general issues. Defenses or objections based on defects in the institution of the prosecution or in the indictment or information (except lack of jurisdiction of the court or failure to charge an offense) *must* be raised before trial or they are waived, unless the court is shown cause to grant relief from the waiver.

726.4 *(4-15-81)* 9781
Depositions (Rule 15)

(1) Whenever, due to exceptional circumstances of the case, it is in the interest of justice that the testimony of a prospective witness of a party be taken and preserved for use at trial, the court may upon motion of such party and notice to the parties order that his/her testimony be taken by deposition and that any designated documents or tangible objects, not privileged, be produced at the same time and place.

(2) The usual practice is for the deposition to be taken before a magistrate appointed by the court with counsel for both sides examining and cross-examining the witness under oath. At the trial a part or all of the deposition, so far as admissible under the rules of evidence, may be used as evidence if the witness is unavailable, as defined by Rule 804(a) of the Federal Rules of Evidence, or the witness gives testimony at the trial or hearing inconsistent with his/her deposition. The Government as well as the defense, may read into evidence any relevant part of the deposition not offered by the other party.

(3) Under 18 USC 3503, whenever it is in the interest of justice that the testimony of a prospective witness of a party be taken and preserved, the court at any time after filing of an information or indictment may upon motion of such party and notice to the parties order that the testimony of such witness be taken and that any book, paper, document, record, recording or other material not privileged be produced at the same time and place. A motion by the Government to obtain an order under this section shall contain certification by the Attorney General or the Attorney General's designee that the legal proceeding is against a person who is believed to have participated in an organized crime activity. The deposition may be used if the witness is unavailable or for impeachment purposes when the witness testifies.

726.5 *(4-15-81)* 9781
Discover and Inspection and Subpoenas for Production of Documentary Evidence (Rules 16 and 17(c))

(1) Pre-trial opportunities for the Government and the defense to examine documentary and real evidence within the opposing party's possession, custody or control are afforded by Rule 16 which provides "that, upon motion of the defendant, the court may order the Government's attorney to permit the defendant to inspect and copy or photograph any relevant:

(a) Written or recorded statements or confessions made by the defendant;

(b) Results or reports of physical or mental examinations and of scientific tests or experiments made in connection with the case;

(c) Recorded testimony of the defendant before a grand jury, or

(d) Books, papers, documents, tangible objects, buildings or places, or copies or portions thereof, upon a showing of materiality to the preparation of the defense and that the request is reasonable.

(2) Except as to the items in (b), this rule does not authorize the discovery or inspection of reports, memoranda, or other internal Government documents made by Government agents in connection with the investigation or defense of the case, or of statements made by Government witnesses (other than the defendant) to agents of the Government except as provided in 18 USC 3500." (See 737.82.) "If the court grants relief under (b) or (d), it may, upon motion of the Government, condition its order by requiring that the defendant permit the Government to inspect and copy or photograph scientific or medical reports, books, papers, documents, tangible objects, or copies of portions thereof, which the defendant intends to produce at the trial, upon a showing of materiality to the presentation of the government's case and that the request is reasonable. Except as to scientific or medical reports, this does not authorize the discovery or inspection of reports, memoranda, or other internal defense documents made by the defendants or his attorneys

or agents in connection with the investigation or defense of the case, or of statements made by the defendant, or by Government or defense witnesses, or by prospective Government or defense witnesses, to the defendant, his agents or attorneys. If, subsequent to compliance with an order issued pursuant to Rule 16, and prior to or during trial, a party discovers additional material previously requested or ordered which is subject to discovery or inspection, he shall promptly notify the other party or his attorney or the court of the existence of the additional material."

(3) Rule 17(c) provides a means by which the Government or a defendant can, by subpoena duces tecum, prior to trial, compel production of evidentiary material (books, papers, documents, or other objects). The court may on motion quash or modify the subpoena if compliance would be unreasonable or oppressive. It may also on motion let the Government or defendant inspect the material before trial. In some circumstances, a court may, under this rule, allow a defendant to subpoena a transcript of his statement made to Government agents, to be used, for instance, to impeach a Government witness' testimony about its contents.

(4) It has been held that the defendant is not entitled under these rules to inspect documents such as: agent's reports, which are not ordinarily admissible [*U.S. v. Iozia*] (although a report may be material for cross-examination, and may be inspected if the agent uses it to refresh his/her recollection) [*Montgomery v. U.S.* See also 18 USC 3500]; and agents' "work products," consisting of workpapers and summaries [*Schneider v. U.S.*], statements of third parties made to the investigating agents [*U.S. v. Anthony M. Palermo*], confidential information such as names of informers and sources of information received from them, unless the evidentiary value of such may fairly be considered "essential to the defense". [*U.S. v. Schneiderman*]

(5) The amount of information the Government or the defendant can obtain through the discovery procedure of Rule 16 and the subpoena process of Rule 17(c) depends upon the ruling of the district judge. Some, following the liberal policy indicated by the Supreme Court in the Bowman Diary case, have held that broad discovery procedures expedite a trial and are necessary to better safeguard the rights of defendants. [*U.S. v. Raymond A. O'Connor*] Others have held that due to its heavy burden of proof the Government should not be required to disclose its case to the defendant, and that the rules should be strictly construed. [*U.S. v. Iozia*]

726.6 *(1-18-80)* 9781

Motions to Suppress Evidence and for Return of Property (Rule 41(e))

(1) A motion may be made for the return of unlawfully seized property and to suppress for use as evidence anything so obtained. The motion shall be made before trial unless opportunity for it did not exist or the defendant was not aware of the grounds for the motion, but the court, in its discretion may entertain the motion at the trial. The motion may also be made before an indictment is returned.

(2) This motion may be made either in the district where the property was seized or where the trial is to be held.

(3) The grounds for the motion are that the property was illegally seized without warrant, or the warrant is insufficient on its face, or the property seized is not that described in the warrant, or there was not probable cause for the issuance of the warrant, or the warrant was illegally executed. (See 383.3.)

(4) Under this rule motions have been made seeking the suppression of private books, records, papers, statements or any other documents or evidence obtained as leads or clues therefrom on the ground that they were obtained in violation of the defendant's constitutional rights. Some instances in which such motions have been granted are:

(a) Adopting items seized by city police following an agreement between them and special agents to cooperate in investigating gaming cases. [*U.S. v. Silbert*]

(b) Failure of affidavit to set forth sufficient facts or chain of circumstances to show the existence of probable cause in support of a search warrant. [*U.S. v. Lassoff*]

(c) Deceiving taxpayer into believing his/her books were to be used for civil purposes only when one of the purposes of the investigation was to obtain evidence of his/her criminal wrongdoing with internal revenue employees. [*U.S. v. Wheeler*]

(d) Practice of subterfuge by special agent who remained in the background without disclosinng to taxpayer his assignment to the case, while directing the revenue agent to obtain extensive information of incriminatory nature from taxpayer's records. [*U.S. v. Lipschitz*]

(e) Examining contents of a taxpayer's filing cabinet including certain records, invoices and papers without his knowledge or consent. [*U.S. v. Guerrina*]

726.7 *(1-18-80)* 9781
Other Matters Before Trial

The court may order multiple indictments or informations to be tried together if they could have been joined in a single indictment or information (Rule 13). However, if it appears that a defendant or the Government is prejudiced by a joinder of offenses or defendants or trials, the court may order separate trials of courts, grant a severance of defendants, or provide whatever other relief justice requires (Rule 14).

727 *(5-9-80)* 9781
Venue

(1) Venue is the place in which a case is brought to trial; it does not relate to jurisdiction, which means the authority by which a court can take cognizance of and decide a case. Proceedings are undertaken in the district in which the offense is committed. The court shall fix the place of trial within the district with due regard to the convenience of the defendant and the witnesses. Exceptions to the general rule are:

(a) In a judicial district consisting of two or more divisions the arraignment may be had, a plea entered, the trial conducted or sentence imposed in any division if the defendant consents (Rule 19).

(b) The case may be transferred from the district where prosecution is pending or where the arrest warrant was issued to the district where the defendant was arrested or is held if the defendant states, in writing, that he/she wishes to plead guilty or nolo contendere, to waive trial in the district in which indicted or in which the arrest warrant was issued, and to consent to the disposition of the case in the district in which he/she was arrested or is held. The United States Attorney for each district must agree (Rule 20).

(c) The court upon motion of the defendant will transfer the proceeding to another district if satisfied that there exists so great a prejudice against the defendant that he/she cannot obtain a fair and impartial trial in the district where the prosecution is pending (Rule 21(a)), or if it appears that for the convenience of the parties and witnesses, and in the interest of justice, the proceeding should be transferred (Rule 21(b)).

(d) If an offense described in IRC 7201 or 7206(1), (2) or (5) involves use of the mails, and if prosecution is begun in a judicial district other than the one in which the defendant resides, he/she may elect to be tried in the district in which he/she was residing at the time alleged offense was committed; provided he/she files a motion in the district in which the prosecution was begun within 20 days after arraignment. (Section 3237 (G), Title 18 USC)

(2) Venue in failure to file cases lies in the judicial district of the internal revenue district where the returns were required to be filed. [*Yarborough v. U.S.*] For example, venue of a failure to file case involving a Miami taxpayer would lie in the Middle Judicial District of Florida since the District Director's office is located in Jacksonville. An individual taxpayer is required to file his/her return in the internal revenue district where he/she resides or his/her principal place of business is located. [Sec. 6091(b)(1), IRC] If he/she resides in one revenue district and has his/her principal place of business in another, he/she may be tried, for failure to file a return, in the judicial district of either revenue district. [*U.S. v. Commerford*] Where direct filing with the service center has been instituted, an option to hand carry returns to the District Director's office has been authorized in the Service regulations. This provision establishes venue in the judicial district where the District Director's office is located as well as in the judicial district where the service center is located. Where a defendant resides in a revenue district located in one judicial district, and has his/her principal place of business in a revenue district located in a second judicial district, and is required to file his/her return at a service center located in still another judicial district, venue may lie in any of the three judicial districts. A regulation authorizing the filing of a return at a permanent post of duty became effective on July 1, 1977 and applies to all returns which were required to be filed on or after this date.

(3) In tax evasion cases where the crime is alleged to have been committed by the filing of a false and fraudulent return, venue lies in the collection and judicial district where the return is filed [*U.S. v. Warring*], unless the defendant makes the election discussed in (1)(d) above. If a return is prepared, signed, and deposited in the mail in one judicial district and filed in another, venue may be fixed in the former district if the

indictment charges attempted evasion by preparation, signing or depositing a fraudulent return in the mail in a particular judicial district. [*U.S. v. Albanese*] A taxpayer was properly indicted in the district where the accountant prepared the return from information sent to him by the taxpayer. [*U.S. v. Harold Gross*] Although the tax evasion was not yet complete when the return was prepared, because it had not yet been filed, the court held that the offense occurs not only where the return is signed, mailed, and filed, but in every district where the taxpayer has committed acts that are part of the evasion. Where an indictment charges attempted tax evasion by maintaining false records, trial may be held in the judicial district in which the records were maintained. [*Beaty v. U.S.*]

(4) If the crime is that of aiding or assisting in, or procuring, counseling, or advising preparation, or presentation of false and fraudulent returns, the case can be tried in the judicial district where the specified acts were committed. [*U.S. v. Kelley*] If the acts took place in one judicial district and the document was filed in another, venue may lie in the district of filing. [*Newton v. U.S.*] For willfully making and subscribing a document known not to be true, see 418.12.

(5) Service Policy provides that it is preferable for deterrent purposes that venue be established in the judicial district of the taxpayer's place of residence or place of business, rather than in the judicial district of the District Director, unless compelling reasons exist. Hence, the special agent should strive to gather evidence to establish venue at the taxpayer's residence or place of business whenever there is a choice in venue for a trial for tax violations.

730 *(1–18–80)* 9781
Trials and Related Federal Rules of Criminal Procedure

731 *(1–18–80)* 9781
Trial by Jury or by Court

731.1 *(1–18–80)* 9781
Provisions of the Constitution

The Constitution of the United States provides in part: "The trial of all Crimes, except in Cases of Impeachment, shall be by jury. . . ." and "In all criminal prosecutions, the accused shall enjoy the right to a speedy and public trial, by an impartial jury. . ."

731.2 *(1–18–80)* 9781
Provisions of Federal Rules (Rule 23)

Trial will be by jury unless the defendant waives a jury trial in writing with the approval of the court and consent of the Government. [*Singer v. U.S.*] Juries consist of 12 persons, but prior to verdict the parties may stipulate in writing with the approval of the court that the jury shall consist of any number less than 12. If a jury trial is waived, the court decides the case on the basis of the competent, relevant evidence presented, determining the facts and applying the law involved.

731.3 *(4–15–81)* 9781
Trial by United States Magistrates

Title 18 U.S.C. 3401 provides that a United States magistrate, when specially designated to exercise such jurisdiction by the district court or courts he/she serves, shall have the jurisdiction to try persons accused of, and sentence persons convicted of, misdemeanors committed in that judicial district. A defendant must consent in writing to trial by magistrate, the consent specially waiving trial, judgement and sentencing by a judge of the district court.

732 *(1–18–80)* 9781
Trial Jurors (Rule 24)

Statutory law determines the manner in which the trial jurors are selected. [62 Stat. 951, 28 USC 1861–1865] The rule prescribes the examination of the petit jury, but the manner of questioning prospective jurors is discretionary with the court. Usually the court conducts the examination and then permits the defendant (or his/her attorney) and the attorney for the Government to supplement the examination by further inquiry as deemed proper. Any juror will be excused for cause if he/she admittedly is unable to render a verdict on the evidence alone and on the law as the court charges. In addition to challenges for cause, the defendant is given 10 peremptory (without cause) challenges and the Government 6 in felonies; each has 3 peremptory challenges in misdemeanors. If there is more than one defendant, the court may allow the defendants additional peremptory challenges to be exercised separately or jointly. The court may direct that not more than 6 jurors in addition to the regular jury be called as alternate jurors. They sit with the regular jurors and replace, in the order in which they are selected, any who become unable to perform their duties prior to the time the jury retires to consider its verdict. If the regular jury remains intact the alternates are dismissed following the court's instructions in the case. Each side is entitled to 1 additional peremptory challenge if 1 or 2 alternate jurors are to be impaneled, 2 additional peremptory challenges if 3 or 4 alternate jurors are to be impaneled, and 3 peremptory challenges if 5 or 6 alternate jurors are to be impaneled, to be used only with respect to such alternates.

733 *(1-18-80)* 9781
Disability of Judge (Rule 25)

This rule provides for the replacement of the presiding judge if by reason of absence from the district, death, sickness or other disability the judge is unable to perform his/her duties after a verdict or finding of guilt or during the trial.

734 *(1-18-80)* 9781
Evidence (Rule 26)

In all trials the testimony of witnesses is taken orally in open court, unless otherwise provided by law or these rules. The admissibility of evidence is governed by the Federal Rules of Evidence. This is a comprehensive code of evidence intended to govern the admissibility of proof in all trials before the Federal courts. Information about the admission of testimony and documentary evidence is set forth in 320, 340 and 350.

735 *(1-18-80)* 9781
Opening Statements

The prosecution opens; the defense follows. An opening statement primarily is to advise the jury what each party intends to prove. In some districts no opening statement is made. The defense may decline to make an opening statement or defer opening until the completion of the Government's case. Usually the prosecution will explain each count of the indictment and then outline the evidence to support it. Generally, where defense counsel elects to make an opening statement at the outset, he/she will explain to the jury that the defendant need prove nothing, that the defendant's plea of not guilty is a denial of all the charges, and that the jury should keep an open mind until the entire case is presented.

736 *(1-18-80)* 9781
Presentation of Case

The Government goes first in presenting proof of the offenses charged. It does this by questioning witnesses and introducing documentary evidence. Upon conclusion of the direct examination of each witness by the United States Attorney, the witness is turned over to the defense counsel for cross-examination, if desired. After cross-examination the Government has the opportunity for redirect examination as to matters brought out on the cross-examination. Upon the conclusion of the Government's case the prosecution rests and the defendant then has the burden of going forward with the evidence. The prosecution may cross-examine defense witnesses, and after the defendant rests, may offer proof in rebuttal.

737 *(1-18-80)* 9781
Witnesses

737.1 *(1-18-80)* 9781
Definition

A witness is a person who can testify as to what he/she knows from having heard, seen, or otherwise observed.

737.2 *(1-18-80)* 9781
Competence

(1) The judge rather than the jury determines the competency of a witness to testify. A witness will ordinarily be presumed to have the mental capacity to testify. That capacity may be challenged in situations involving: infants—the trial judge should decide if the child is sufficiently mature to make an intelligent statement of what he/she saw, heard, or observed; mental derangement—an insane person usually will be permitted to testify if he/she understands the obligations of an oath and the consequences of lying, and can tell an intelligent story of what he/she saw take place; and intoxication—the test as to a witness on the stand is whether he/she is capable of making an intelligent and truthful statement.

(2) In a Federal criminal case, a husband and wife are competent to testify for each other, but not against each other without the consent of both, except where one spouse has committed

some offense against the other, or the case involves polygamy or some other crime detrimental to the marital relationship. Generally, divorce removes the incompentency of husband and wife to testify against each other, except as to confidential communications made by one to the other during marriage. (See also 344.4 and 344.9.)

(3) A convicted perjurer may testify and the jury must determine credibility. A Federal officer (even one who is a witness in the case) may be permitted to sit in the courtroom during the trial, to advise the United States Attorney. A defendant in the criminal case is a competent witness and his/her testimony must be judged in the same way as that of any other witness, with due regard for his/her personal interest in the outcome of the case.

737.3 *(1-18-80)* 9781
Credibility

(1) The jury (or judge if a jury is waived), determines the weight and credibility of a witness' testimony. A witness is presumed to tell the truth. Credibility is judged by whether the witness had the capacity or opportunity to observe or be familiar with the subject matter of his/her testimony and to remember it. Among the matters affecting credibility are the witness' interest, bias, prejudice, demeanor on the stand, prior inconsistent statements, prior mental derangement, intoxication at the time of the transaction to which he/she testifies, and prior convictions of a felony or a crime involving moral turpitude. If a witness gives contradictory testimony the jury may accept the portion it believes and reject the remainder. It may reject the witness' entire testimony if he/she has testified falsely as to a material point.

(2) If neither party will vouch for a witness the court may call and question such witness and allow both sides the right of cross-examination and impeachment.

737.4 *(1-18-80)* 9781
Impeachment

737.41 *(1-18-80)* 9781
Impeachment of Opposing Witness

(1) The principal purpose of impeachment is to lessen the likelihood that the court or jury will believe the witness' story. A witness may be impeached by bringing out on cross-examination or through other witnesses facts:

(a) Proving that the witness made a statement out of court (it could be before a grand jury) that is inconsistent with his/her testimony on the witness stand provided it is relevant to the case and a foundation is laid by inquiring of the witness on cross-examination whether he/she did or did not make such a statement to a certain named person at a certain named time and place.

(b) Showing bias, such as family relationship, friendship, gratitude, obligation, employment, hatred, injured feelings and the like [Wigmore on Evidence, sec. 948–953], interest growing out of the relationship between the witness and the cause of action, e.g.; partner, creditor, or corruption, such as acceptance of a bribe to testify, or expression of willingness to give false testimony. [Wigmore, sec. 956–965]

(c) Establishing insanity or drunkenness at the time of the events testified to, or while on the stand, or in the interval between the two if it was of such a degree as to affect the witness' mental faculties. [Wigmore, sec. 931–933)

(d) Showing a bad reputation for truth and veracity in the community in which the witness resides [Wigmore, sec. 920–923] or

(e) Proving through cross-examination that the witness has been convicted of a specific crime, or putting into evidence a record of his/her conviction. Evidence of his/her arrest not admissible. The test to be applied is whether the conviction inquired about tends to prove a lack of character with respect to the witness' credibility.

(2) In certain instances an impeached witness may be rehabilitated. If testimony as to his/her bad character for veracity has been given, testimony of his/her reputation for good character in that respect may be offered. [Wigmore, sec. 1105] If a witness has been impeached by showing that he/she made a prior statement inconsistent with his/her testimony on the stand, it may be shown that he/she made prior statements consistent with his/her testimony in certain situations. For example, the story of the witness may be assailed as a recent fabrication or evidence may be offered showing a cause for his/her bias. If so, it may be shown that the witness made a statement similar to his/her testimony on the stand before he/she had any reason to fabricate [Wigmore, sec. 1129] or prior to the occasion for bias. [Wigmore, sec. 1128]

(3) When a defendant takes the stand in his/her own defense he/she is subject to impeachment like any other witness. The law does not presume that a defendant is of good character; it merely prevents the prosecution from going into the matter during the original presentation of its case. When the defendant takes the stand, he/she does so not only as a person accused of a crime, but also as a witness. As an accused, his/her character is not subject to attack unless he/she opens the question by offering evidence of his/her good character. Such evidence is to be considered by the jury on the issue of his/her guilt or innocence. Thus, if the defense offers evidence of good character (by testimony of the defendant or other witnesses) the prosecution can introduce evidence as to his/her bad character to be considered by the jury on the same issue. As a witness, his/her position is different and the prosecution can offer evidence of his/her bad character for consideration not upon his/her guilt or innocence but upon his/her credibility as a witness. [Wigmore, secs. 890, 891]

737.42 *(1-18-80)* 9781
Impeachment by a Party of His Own Witness

(1) A rule of law exists in many jurisdictions that a party will not be allowed to impeach a witness he/she has called because by putting the witness on the stand the party has guaranteed his/her credibility. However, the prosecution may impeach a Government witness: whom it is under a legal obligation to call; who has testified before a grand jury; or whom the court compels it to call, if in each instance it was surprised or prejudiced by his/her testimony. Most courts now permit impeachment for self-contradiction particularly if the party calling the witness has been surprised by variances from the latter's previous attitude and statements. The impeaching matter must be limited to the point of surprise and should not go beyond removing damage caused by surprise.

(2) The latitude allowed the prosecution in examining a hostile witness is wholly within the discretion of the trial judge. Questions may be in the nature of cross-examination and the witness may be asked if he/she made contradictory statements at other times. The United States Attorney may read prior inconsistent statements which the witness has given Government agents and ask him/her to verify the truth of such prior statements.

737.5 *(1-18-80)* 9781
Recall

The matter of recalling a witness for further testimony is ordinarily within the discretion of the trial judge.

737.6 *(1-18-80)* 9781
Refreshing Memory or Recollection

737.61 *(1-18-80)* 9781
Introduction

A witness may not be able to recall a fact about which he/she is called to testify. If so, that fact can be put into evidence in either of two ways, described as "past recollection recorded" or "present recollection revived."

737.62 *(1-18-80)* 9781
Past Recollection Recorded

A witness may not be able to state directly facts from present memory, but may be willing to swear that the contents of a memorandum which he/she or another prepared setting forth such facts, are true. On his/her so testifying the memorandum may be introduced into evidence as a record of his/her past recollection. The memorandum must have been made fairly contemporaneously with the facts or events recorded while the details were fresh in the memory of the witness. If it was written by another, the witness must testify that he/she read it at the time it was written and that it is true.

737.63 *(1-18-80)* 9781
Present Recollection Revived

A witness whose memory suddenly fails when asked about a certain fact may be able to refresh his/her memory by reference to some relevant paper. It may be a letter, book, memorandum, or anything counsel thinks will awaken his/her independent recollection of the fact sought to be established. The writing must, on request, be shown to opposing counsel for use on cross-examination to test the witness' actual memory, but is not admissible in evidence, unless independently admissible. [Wigmore on Evidence, sec. 758-765.]

737.7 *(1-18-80)* 9781
Specific Witnesses

737.71 *(1-18-80)* 9781
Expert Witness (Rule 28)

(1) An expert witness is one who has acquired ability to deduce correct inferences from hypothetically stated facts, or from facts involving scientific or technical knowledge. The trial judge determines whether his/her qualifications are sufficient. The court may appoint expert witnesses agreed upon by the parties or may select the expert itself. The expert advises the parties of his/her findings and may be called to testify by the court or by either party. He/she may also be cross-examined. The expert witness' testimony must be based upon facts personally perceived by or known to him/her or made known to him/her at the trial. The parties also may call expert witnesses of their own selection.

(2) In tax cases, expert witnesses may be used to testify concerning various matters such as handwriting comparison, accounting and bookkeeping matters, methods of operating a lottery and computation of income tax liability.

737.72 *(1-18-80)* 9781
Special Agent

(1) Testifying in court is one of the most important duties that a special agent may be called upon to perform. The agent's testimony concerning admissions of the taxpayer may be vital in establishing willfulness. He/she may also be required to testify about: the examination of the taxpayer's books, records, and tax returns; analyses or transcripts made of various book accounts, invoices, bank deposits, and canceled checks; specific amounts of income not entered in the taxpayer's records or reported in his/her tax returns; particular deductions of expenses for which no substantiation was offered or found during the investigation; statements made by the taxpayer explaining entries on the records or concerning unrecorded transactions; computations of unreported income established by evidence in the record; and the tax deficiencies based upon a hypothetical question. The agent may also be required to describe the records maintained by the taxpayer and explain in detail the extent to which he/she examined them, the procedures followed, and the facts discovered. (See 750, "Assisting United States Attorney.")

(2) The special agent as a witness must be thoroughly prepared and clear on the facts; present a neat, businesslike appearance; and testify in a natural, frank and forthright manner with a respectful attitude toward the court and jury. He/she is frequently subject to rigorous and lengthy cross-examination. The agent must then preserve an even, courteous demeanor and refrain from any display of anger, hostility, or evasiveness. Some rules of conduct for the special agent or other internal revenue official on the stand are:

(a) Listen to the question carefully and answer truthfully.

(b) Answer the question only. *Do not volunteer.* It may seriously affect the United States Attorney's strategy.

(c) Do not answer a question you do not understand. Tell the questioner that you do not understand.

(d) If an objection to a question is raised by either counsel, wait to answer until the court rules. Otherwise, a mistrial may result.

(e) Wait until the question is completed before attempting to answer.

(f) Anticipate the unexpected.

(g) Direct your answers to the jury but do not ignore the judge.

(h) Speak clearly and loudly enough to be heard by the juror farthest removed from the witness stand.

(i) Refrain from any demonstration of personal feelings.

737.73 *(1-18-80)* 9781
Revenue Agent

In a tax trial, the revenue agent is often used by the Government as the expert witness to establish the computations of deficiencies as set forth in the indictment or information. The revenue agent may also testify respecting various matters set forth in 737.72.

737.8 *(1-18-80)* 9781
Cross-Examination

737.81 *(1-18-80)* 9781

General Rules

(1) When a witness has finished his/her direct examination, the opponent has the right to cross-examine him/her. The purpose of cross-examination is to test the truth of the statements made by the witness. This is done by questions designed to: amplify the story given on direct examination so as to place the facts in a different light; establish additional facts in the cross-examining party's favor; discredit the witness' testimony by showing that testimony on direct examination was contrary to circumstances, probabilities, and other evidence in the case; and discredit the witness by showing bias, interest, corruption, or specific acts of misconduct. In view of such purposes, the courts allow a wide latitude on cross-examination and the cross-examiner may ask leading questions. Another method often used is to question the witness in such a manner as to obtain apparent inconsistent statements by going over the same ground covered in the direct examination.

(2) The general rule in Federal courts with respect to witnesses other than defendants, is that questions asked on cross-examination must pertain to matters brought out on direct examination. The rule is liberally construed and where the direct examination opens a general subject, the cross-examiner may go into any phase of that subject. If the cross-examiner wishes to obtain from the witness evidence on subjects not opened on direct examination, he/she must call the witness as his/her own witness and subject him/her to direct examination on such matters.

737.82 *(1-18-80)* 9781

Demands for Production of Statements and Reports of Witness

(1) Title 18, USC 3500 provides that after a witness has testified on direct examination the defendant may inspect any pre-trial statements of the witness relating to the subject matter about which he/she has testified. If the Government claims that the prior statement is not relevant, it is to be inspected by the trial court *in camera* (in private) so that the portion not relating to the subject matter of the witness' testimony can be excised before delivery to the defendant. If the Government refuses to comply with the production order the judge has discretion either to strike the testimony of the witness or to declare a mistrial.

(2) The term "statement" is defined in 18 USC 3500 as follows:

"(1) A written statement made by said witness and signed or otherwise adopted or approved by him;

"(2) A stenographic, mechanical, electrical, or other recording, or a transcription thereof, which is substantially a verbatim recital of an oral statement made by said witness and recorded contemporaneously with the making of such oral statement; or

"(3) a statement, however taken or recorded, or a transcription thereof, if any, made by said witness to a grand jury."

(3) A statement which is not substantially verbatim and has not been recorded contemporaneously does not have to be produced. A written statement made by a witness and signed or otherwise adopted or approved by him/her may be inspected by the defense whether or not it is contemporaneous with the interview to which it relates. An agent's interview report based upon notes read back to and approved by the witness is considered adopted by the witness and producible although the notes themselves have been destroyed. A summary of an oral statement made to a special agent which is not substantially verbatim does not have to be produced. The Supreme Court has outlined the reason for this rule:

"It is clear that Congress was concerned that only those statements which could properly be called the witness' own words should be made available to the defense for purposes of impeachment. It was important that the statement could fairly be deemed to reflect fully and without distortion what had been said to the government agent. Distortion can be a product of selectivity as well as the conscious or inadvertent infusion of the recorder's opinions or impressions. It is clear from the continuous congressional emphasis on 'substantially verbatim recital,' and 'continuous narrative statements made by the witness recorded verbatim or nearly so . . .' that the legislation was designed to eliminate the danger of distortion and misrepresentation inherent in a report which merely selects portions, albeit accurately, from a lengthy oral recital. Quoting out of context is one of the most frequent and powerful modes of misquotation. We think it consistent with this legislative history, and with the generally restrictive terms of the statutory provision, to require that summaries of an oral statement which evidence substantial selection of material, or which were prepared after the interview without the aid of complete notes, and hence rest on the memory of the agent, not to be produced. Neither, of course, are statements which contain the agent's interpretations or impression." [*Anthony M. Palermo v. U.S.*]

(4) Where a Government agent interviewed a witness and recorded in his/her notebook a substantially verbatim statement in the witness' presence, the defense was entitled to production of relevant portions of the notebook as well as an exact typewritten copy of the statement which has been made from the agent's notes, but was not entitled to the agent's report. [*U.S.*

v. Papworth] When the agent is a witness, his/her report has been held to be a statement made by him/her, subject to defense inspection at the discretion of the court. [*U.S. v. Sheer*] Inspection is limited to the report alone, and does not include exhibits prepared from third party witness interviews, nor signed statements of the witnesses. [Ayash v. U.S.]

(5) In view of the substantial discretionary authority of a trial judge to permit defense inspection of reports, the special agent should avoid speculation about weaknesses of a case, and expressions indicating prejudice or dislike of a taxpayer in memorandums or reports. This should not preclude complete reporting of every material fact which tends to establish or disprove the alleged violation, and is essential to a thorough understanding of the case.

(6) In view of the use of pre-trial statements for impeachment purposes, a statement of a prospective Government witness containing information inconsistent with his/her prior statement should clearly set forth an explanation of the reasons for the inconsistencies.

737.9 *(1-18-80)* 9781
Redirect Examination

Following cross-examination the party calling the witness may ask him/her further questions respecting matters brought out on cross-examination. This is permitted to obtain the witness' explanation of the meaning of answers in the cross-examination, to clarify any apparent inconsistencies in his/her statements, or to rehabilitate him/her in the eyes of the jury if his/her character has been attacked.

738 *(1-18-80)* 9781
Stipulations

(1) A stipulation is an agreement between the prosecuting attorney and defense counsel respecting certain facts in the case. The purpose of a stipulation is to expedite the progress of the trial by eliminating the necessity of introducing evidence to prove undisputed facts. For example, the defense may admit the receipt of income, the acquisition of certain assets, the making of specified expenditures, or even the source and amount of income and the tax deficiency alleged. This would relieve the Government of the burden of producing evidence in court as proof of such matters and would leave willfulness as the only real issue to be proved. Since willfulness is usually inferred from the manner in which transactions are handled, and presenting a number of witnesses before a jury dramatizes the defendant's knowledge thereof, the Government exercises great care in agreeing to stipulations in cases involving willfulness.

(2) Stipulations are generally made in writing, such as agreements prior to trial; however, they may be stated orally in open court and recorded by the court reporter during the trial.

739 *(1-18-80)* 9781
Motion for Judgment of Acquittal (Rule 29)

(1) After the evidence on either side is closed, the court on motion of a defendant, or on its own motion, shall order the entry of a judgment of acquittal of one or more offenses charged if the evidence is insufficient to sustain a conviction. The motion may be made orally or in writing. In some circuits the motion will be denied if the trial judge determines that the evidence, taken in the light most favorable to the Government, tends to show that the defendant is guilty beyond a reasonable doubt. In others it will be denied if the evidence is enough to send the case to the jury in a civil action. (See also 323.6.)

(2) If the motion for acquittal is made by the defense upon the conclusion of the Government's case and the motion is denied, the defendant may proceed by introducing evidence in his/her own behalf. This waives any objection to the denial. The defendant may renew his/her motion for judgment of acquittal after both sides rest. A failure to do so may foreclose any right on appeal to question the sufficiency of the evidence to sustain the conviction.

(3) The trial court may reserve decision on this motion, submit the case to the jury, and decide it either before the verdict, after it, or after the jury is discharged without reaching a verdict.

73(10) *(1-18-80)* 9781
Rebuttal

After the defense rests, the prosecution may offer proof in rebuttal to explain, counteract, or disprove the defendant's evidence. For example, after a defendant testified that he/she made substantial payments to a deceased brother-in-law for services rendered, the Government put into evidence the brother-in-law's tax return, which did not include any such amount, in order to discredit the defendant. [*Barshop v. U.S.*]

73(11) *(1-18-80)* 9781
Instructions to the Jury (Rule 30)

(1) Either party or both may file with the court written instructions regarding the law to be given the jury. The court will inform counsel of its proposed action on the requests before their arguments to the jury. It is sufficient if the substance of the requested instructions is given. Normally, the defense opens summation (final argument to the jury) and the Government follows, although some courts allow the Government to open, the defendant to follow, and the Government to close.

(2) The court then charges the jury as to the law. Objection, if any, to the charge or omissions therefrom must be made before the jury retires to consider its verdict. Failure to request special instructions or to make specific objections to the charge before the jury retires constitutes a waiver on the point on appeal unless, under Rule 52(b), there are "plain errors or defects affecting substantial rights. . ."

73(12) *(1-18-80)* 9781
Verdict (Rule 31)

(1) The conclusion of the jurors is the verdict. It must be returned to the judge in open court, and to convict or acquit it must be unanimous. Where there is more than one defendant, the jury may return a verdict or verdicts with respect to a defendant or defendants as to whom it is agreed. If the jury cannot agree regarding any defendant, he/she may be tried again.

(2) Where the indictment contains more than one count, each count is considered as if it were a separate indictment, so that acquittal on one or more counts will not generally be considered inconsistent with conviction on others.

(3) The defendant may be found guilty of an offense necessarily included in the offense charged, or of an attempt to commit either the offense charged or an offense necessarily included therein if the attempt constitutes an offense. The Supreme Court has indicated in this connection that, where some of the elements of the crime charged themselves constitute a lesser crime, the defendant, if the evidence justifies it, is entitled to an instruction which would permit the jury to return a verdict of guilty of the lesser offense. However, where the facts necessary to prove the crime charged are identical with those required to prove the lesser offense, the defendant is not entitled to an instruction which would permit the jury to make a choice between the two crimes in returning its verdict.

(4) The trial court will poll the jury at the request of either the Government or the defense or upon its own motion in order to be certain the verdict is unanimous. If upon poll there is not unanimous concurrence, the jury may be directed to retire for further deliberations or may be discharged.

73(13) *(1-18-80)* 9781
Judgment (Rules 32 Through 35)

73(13).1 *(1-18-80)* 9781
Definition

A judgment of conviction sets forth the plea, the verdict or findings, and the adjudication and sentence. It must be signed by the judge and entered by the clerk.

73(13).2 *(1-18-80)* 9781
Presentence Investigation

In order to help the court impose sentence or grant probation, the probation service of the court may make a presentence investigation and report. The investigation and report are concerned with any prior criminal record of the defendant and personal background, individual characteristics, financial condition, and any circumstances which may have affected his/her behavior. In this connection, the probation officer will usually consult with the special agent on the case for information about the defendant's cooperation (or lack of it) during the investigation, the defendant's mental and physical history, whether he/she has made any payments on the tax deficiencies involved in the criminal case, other tax obligations due the government, and data regarding any other matters which might be helpful to the court in imposing sentence or granting probation. The court before imposing sentence may disclose to the defendant or his/her counsel all or part of the material contained in the report of the presentence investigation and afford an opportunity to the defendant or his/her counsel to comment thereon. Any material disclosed to the defendant or his/her counsel shall also be disclosed to the attorney for the Government (Rule 32).

73(13).3 *(1-18-80)* 9781
Withdrawal of Plea of Guilty

A motion to withdraw a plea of guilty or of nolo contendere may be made only before sentence is imposed or imposition of sentence is suspended; but to correct manifest injustice, the court after sentence may set aside the judgment of conviction and permit the defendant to withdraw his/her plea.

73(13).4 *(1-18-80)* 9781
Sentence

The sentence must be imposed without unreasonable delay and, pending sentence, the court may commit the defendant or continue or alter the bail. Before sentencing, the court will give the defendant an opportunity to make a statement in his/her own behalf and to present information in mitigation of his/her punishment. Within the limits set out in the criminal statute involved, the court has a wide discretion in determining sentence and it will rarely be upset by reviewing court. Although within the discretion of the trial court, consecutive sentences in tax cases where there has been a conviction on more than one count are seldom imposed. The court must arrest (withhold) judgment if the indictment or information does not charge an offense or if the court did not have jurisdiction of the offense charged. An illegal sentence may be corrected by the court at any time; however, definite time limitations are fixed for a reduction of sentence.

73(13).5 *(1-18-80)* 9781
Probation

After conviction of an offense not punishable by death or life imprisonment, the court may suspend sentence and place the defendant on probation. [18 USC 3651] A condition of probation may be that the defendant pay or make every effort to pay the tax ultimately determined. Failure to comply with the terms of probation may result in its revocation and imposition of sentence. The period of probation, together with any extension thereof, cannot exceed five years. [18 USC 3651] Since civil tax proceedings usually do not begin until the criminal features are closed, the condition of probation that the defendant pay the tax ultimately determined becomes inoperative in any case if the ultimate determination occurs more than five years after the date of sentence. [18 USC 3651] If the probation period is less than five years and the final determination of tax is not made during such period, that condition of probation will become inoperative unless the court modifies its order.

73(14) *(1-18-80)* 9781
Right of Appeal (Rule 37)

(1) An appeal by a defendant may be taken within 10 days after entry of the judgment or order appealed from, but if a motion for a new trial or an arrest of judgment has been made within the 10-day period an appeal from a judgment of conviction may be taken within 10 days after entry of the order denying the motion. When authorized by statute the Government may take an appeal in a criminal case within thirty days after entry of judgment. [See Title 18 USC sec. 3731 about Appeals by the United States from decisions based upon invalidity or construction of statutes, dismissing informations and indictments, and arresting judgments of conviction.]

(2) Appeal from the decisions of the Federal district courts is heard in the Court of Appeals for the appropriate circuit, except for certain statutory exceptions which permit the Government to appeal direct to the Supreme Court.

740 *(1-18-80)* 9781
Compromise of Criminal Tax Cases

(1) The Secretary of the Treasury or the Secretary's delegate may compromise any civil or criminal tax case prior to referral to the Department of Justice. [26 USC 7122(a).] The Secretary has delegated this authority to the Commissioner of Internal Revenue. [Sec. 601, 203 C.F.R.] (See IRM 5700, Offers in Compromise.) Strict compliance with the statutory provisions is required to effect a compromise. Accordingly, attempted settlement by subordinate Service officials will not bar criminal prosecution. A valid compromise is as complete a discharge from prosecution as an acquittal by a jury.

(2) The Criminal Investigation Division makes investigations of offers in compromise in cases in which criminal proceedings are pending only as specifically requested by the Chief Counsel or Regional Counsel. (See IRM 9262.4.)

(3) After referral of a case to the Department of Justice, authority to compromise rests with the Attorney General.

(4) Tender of tax or actual payment thereof prior to a verdict or plea of guilty is not a bar to criminal prosecution.

750 *(1-18-80)* 9781

Assisting the United States Attorney

751 *(1-18-80)* 9781

Planning for Presentation to Grand Jury and for Trial

(1) Prior to the presentation of a case before a grand jury, the special agent may be requested by the United States Attorney to review the case with him/her so that the latter may evaluate its merits, weaknesses, and particular problems. The special agent may assist in the preparation of the indictment form and may testify at length before the grand jury concerning the investigation. An indictment based solely on his/her testimony is valid even though he/she has no personal knowledge of the transactions on which his/her computations are based.

(2) The special agent will frequently be asked to aid in the preparation of a trial brief or trial book. A sheet (copy for U.S. Attorney and for each person who will assist in the trial) should be prepared for each witness showing his/her name and address, business or occupation; expected testimony, list and description of documents, if any, which he/she will produce or identify, location of the records or documents if not in the custody of the witness; and data of a derogatory nature including criminal record, pertinent to his/her reliability or credibility. Because of the Jencks Act (Section 3500, Title 18, U.S. Code), it is also advisable to list any documents such as question and answer statements, affidavits, or memorandums of interview obtained from the witness or prepared by the agent. (See 737.82.) The witness sheets may be placed in a looseleaf note book in the order in which the witnesses are expected to testify. If many are involved it is helpful for reference purposes to assign each a number and prepare a list of witnesses arranged and numbered in the same order as the witness sheets.

(3) Usually a folder should be prepared for each witness, bearing his/her name and number. Any documents, such as memorandums, affidavits, or question and answer statements relating to a witness should be placed in his/her folder. Documents obtained from a witness prior to trial which are to be offered as evidence and copies to be substituted when originals are withdrawn, and charts or schedules prepared to show the theory of the case or computation of unreported income should also be put in the appropriate witness folder.

(4) The special agent should study his/her notes and reports to refresh his/her memory concerning the general phases of the investigation and conferences with the taxpayer. The agent should arrange his/her notes, memorandums, workpapers, etc., to which he/she may have to refer while testifying, in an order which will provide for quick reference at the time of trial. He/she should also arrange to have copies of all statements, memorandums and reports that have any bearing on his/her testimony for presentation to the court if such data is requested by the defense under 18 USC 3500.

(5) The special agent may (with the approval of the United States Attorney) reinterview witnesses immediately before the trial begins to ascertain whether they have brought subpoenaed documents or physical evidence; recall their previous statements (it may be advisable for them to read transcripts of prior statements); and can identify the defendant and time and place of occurrence, if pertinent. The special agent should report any anticipated difficulties with the witnesses to the United States Attorney, who might decide against using a hostile witness or one thought to be unreliable.

(6) Assistance may also be given the United States Attorney in the formulation of the Government's answers to various pretrial motions, such as motions to suppress evidence, for a bill of particulars, for discovery and inspection, etc.

752 *(1-18-80)* 9781

Trial

752.1 *(1-18-80)* 9781
Responsibility and Conduct of Special Agent at Trial

(1) During the trial, the special agent ordinarily may be present at the counsel table with the United States Attorney and should give him/her any assistance he/she can. This may include maintaining all Government exhibits in proper order for ready reference and presentation; keeping a list of both Government and defense exhibits as they are introduced; and checking to ensure that Government witnesses are present and ready to testify. (See also 737.72.) The special agent should conduct himself/herself circumspectly when in the courtroom, showing respect for the judicial authority.

(2) The special agent may be called upon to prepare charts or schedules showing the taxpayer's sources of income, correct taxable income, or the related tax liability. The charts or schedules may reflect summaries of specific items, net worth increases, expenditures in excess of available resources shown on tax returns, or other transactions that lend themselves to visual presentation. In some instances such summaries have been formally introduced in evidence, in others they have been exhibited to the jury, and then, at the end of the case, used by the jury during deliberations. [*Beaty v. U.S.*, but see *Steele v. U.S.*] The need for charts, the type of charts, and the method of preparation will be affected by such considerations as the complexity of the case, the attitude of the court toward visual aids, the preferences of the United States Attorney, and available facilities. Hand drawn charts or schedules have been effectively used by special agents in the past. However, if commercial or government photocopy facilities are available in the area where the District Court is located, the charts may be drawn in small scale or typed on ordinary bond paper, and then enlarged by a photocopy process at a nominal cost. Advance arrangements for this service should be made to avoid delays during the trial. The special agent must base all charts and schedules upon evidence in the trial record. He/she must also be able to testify that he/she prepared the chart or that it was prepared under his/her supervision. If a special agent uses a bar graph, line graph or similar exhibit for trial purposes, he/she should show the unit of measurement on the chart.

(3) The special agent should listen carefully to all testimony, making notes from which he/she may alert the United States Attorney, at the appropriate time, as to any false, misleading or erroneous statements. The agent may also assist in preparing questions to be asked defense witnesses on cross-examination.

(4) The special agent should avoid any direct contact with the defendant at the trial in order to eliminate the possibility of any embarrassing or compromising situations arising. Likewise his/her association with defense counsel should be only in open court and with the knowledge and consent of the United States Attorney.

(5) The court will usually instruct the jury against any contact with the attorneys or witnesses in the case. Any attempts by the special agent to associate with a member or members of the jury may cause a mistrial.

(6) During the trial and after a verdict has been rendered in the case, the special agent should refrain from any demonstration of personal feelings in the matter.

(7) The special agent should not seek out any of the jurors in a tried case in which a conviction is not obtained for the purpose of soliciting information to be incorporated in the narrative report required by IRM 9533 unless approved in advance by the National Office. However, the report should include any information provided him/her by jurors acting on their own initiative or submitted by them to other Government representatives or third parties.

752.2 *(1-18-80)* 9781
Separation of Witnesses

(1) Some courts on their own motion or on request of either counsel will bar from the courtroom all witnesses except the one on the stand. This involves "(a) preventing the prospective witnesses from consulting each other, (b) preventing them from hearing a testifying witness, and (c) preventing them from consulting a witness who has left the stand; the last including consultation between witnesses who have left the stand, since they may be prospective witnesses." [Wigmore on Evidence (3d ed.) sec. 1840.] If the order of exclusion is knowingly disobeyed, the court may in its discretion disqualify the witness. [Wigmore, sec. 1842.]

(2) If this rule is invoked, the court may at the request of the United States attorney make an exception permitting necessary Service representatives to remain in the courtroom to assist in the trial.

760 *(1-18-80)* 9781
Case Settlement

761 *(1-18-80)* 9781
Internal Revenue Service (Joint Investigations)

(1) Information which may have a substantial effect on the civil settlement of a case may be developed after a special agent's report has been submitted. For example, this may occur while assisting counsel in preparing for trial or during trial for the criminal offense. Such information may consist of admissions of liability or relate to the existence of additional records or witnesses which may have an important bearing on the determination of the civil liability. In these instances, a special agent should obtain copies of any exhibits introduced during the trial which contain information not uncovered during the investigation and which may have a significant bearing on the civil liability. Procedures for the processing of this information are contained in IRM 9536.

(2) Civil settlement may also be effected in criminal cases prior to final disposition of the criminal features. Before imposition of sentence, after acceptance of a plea of guilty or conviction upon trial, the court may desire to know the final determination of the defendant's total tax liabilities as an element for its consideration in fixing sentence. Likewise, the defendant may wish to attempt to mitigate sentence by paying or arranging to pay his/her tax liabilities before sentence is passed.

(3) Since jurisdiction in criminal tax cases lies with the Department of Justice, action to effect civil settlement in the circumstances described in (2) above should be initiated by the United States Attorney. He/she will arrange, through the Department of Justice and the Chief Counsel (Criminal Tax Division), for civil settlement proceedings in the appropriate District Director's office. When instructed by the Chief, Criminal Investigation Division, the special agent who participated in the joint investigation will consult with and assist the Examination representative in the civil settlement negotiations.

(4) The civil fraud penalty may not be removed by an Appeals Office except upon the recommendation or concurrence of counsel in the following instances. These include where a civil fraud penalty is recommended in connection with a tax year or period, or is related or affects such year or period, for which the criminal prosecution against a taxpayer (or a related taxpayer involving the same transaction) has been recommended to the Department of Justice for willful attempt to evade or defeat tax, or for willful failure to file a return. Where there has been a criminal conviction under IRC 7201, 7203, 7206(1) or 7207, the concurrence of counsel is required for any settlement that would reduce the amounts of any criminal fraud item.

762 *(1-18-80)* 9781
United States Tax Court

(1) The Tax Reform Act of 1969 changed the name of the Tax Court of the United States to the United States Tax Court and established it as a court of record under Article I, Section 8, Clause 9, of the Constitution. It is now part of the Judicial Branch of Government. In addition to the powers it already possesses, the Court has been given the power to punish contempt of its authority, and to enforce its decisions by issuing any writ, etc., which a District Court of the United States can issue. [IRC 7441-7456.]

(2) In a Tax Court trial evidence is admitted and excluded much as it would be in a civil nonjury trial in the United States District Court. In general, the Commissioner's determination of deficiency is presumed to be correct. [Rule 32, Tax Court Rules of Practice.] However, if the fraud penalty is asserted, the burden is upon the Commissioner to prove fraud with intent to evade tax. [IRC 7454(a).] The evidence in that respect must be "clear and convincing"; not "beyond a reasonable doubt" as in a criminal case, but more than a mere preponderance. The failure of the Commissioner to prevail on the fraud issue does not relieve the taxpayer of the burden of overcoming the prima facie correctness of the determination of the deficiencies unless the assessment was not made within the applicable period of limitations.

(3) Record of the disposition of the criminal case against a taxpayer is admissible in the Tax Court on the issue of fraud. Despite an acquittal in a criminal case, the same evidence may be sufficient to prove fraud in the civil cases. A conviction for attempted tax evasion in the district court is conclusive in Tax Court proceedings as to the fraud issue. A guilty plea in a criminal case will be received by the Tax Court as an admission to be given weight according to the circumstances. Without any explanation of the circumstances, it is sufficient to establish

fraud. However, such a plea in a failure to file case may constitute only a willful omission and passive neglect to perform a statutory duty and not render the taxpayer liable for the fraud penalty.

(4) The Commissioner is not barred from assessing the 50 percent fraud penalty by: the taxpayer's filing correct amended returns and paying additional taxes due after filing fraudulent returns; or the death of the taxpayer, since the penalty is for an offense against property rights and not personal rights.

(5) The responsibility during investigation for the development of evidence to sustain the ad valorem additions to the tax (except those concerning tax estimations) rests upon the special agent. Consequently, upon the trial of a Tax Court case where the fraud penalty is at issue, the special agent is often a principal witness for the Government.

(6) It is the duty of the special agent, in the preparation for trial and the presentation of the case in Tax Court, to consult with and assist the attorney assigned to the matter by the Regional Counsel.

770 *(1-18-80)* 9781

Citation of Cases

Exhibit 700-4, Table of Cases, is an alphabetical listing of court cases cited in this Handbook.

(Next page is 9781-505)

Exhibit 700-1

Complaint
Handbook Reference: 721:(2) ◊

IN THE DISTRICT COURT OF THE UNITED STATES
FOR THE ________ DISTRICT OF ________

UNITED STATES OF AMERICA)
)
—against—) COMPLAINT
)
)
________________________________)

Complaint for Violation of Section 7201,
Internal Revenue Code of 1954

Before ________ ________, United States Magistrate, ________ ________, ________ ________.

The undersigned complainant, being duly sworn, states:

That he/she is a Special Agent (or Revenue Agent) of the Internal Revenue Service and, in the performance of the duties imposed on him/her by law, he/she has conducted an investigation of the Federal income tax liability of ________ ________ for the calendar year 19——, by examining the said taxpayer's tax return for the year 19—— and other years; (by examination and audit of the said taxpayer's business and financial books and records;) (by identifying and interviewing third parties with whom the said taxpayer did business;) (by consulting public and private records reflecting the said taxpayer's income;) (and by interviewing third persons having knowledge of the said taxpayer's financial condition).

That based on the aforesaid investigation, the complainant has personal knowledge that on or about the ________ day of ________, 19——, at ________, ________, in the ________ District of ________, ________ (who during the calendar year 19—— was married) did willfully and knowingly attempt to evade and defeat a large part of the income tax due and owing by said taxpayer (and spouse) to the United States of America for the calendar year 19——, by filing and causing to be filed with the Director of Internal Revenue at ________, ________, a false and fraudulent (joint) income tax return (on behalf of said taxpayer and spouse), wherein he/she (it was) stated that his/her (their) taxable (or adjusted gross) income for the said calendar year 19—— was $________, and that the amount of tax due and owing thereon was the sum of $________, when in fact his/her (their joint) taxable (or adjusted gross) income for the said calendar year was the sum of $________, upon which said taxable income he/she owed (there was owing) to the United States of America an income tax of $________.

____
Here type: Title of subscribing Internal
Revenue Service Officer

Sworn to before me and subscribed in my presence, this —— day of ———, 19——.

____
United States Magistrate

The bracketed descriptions of the kinds of investigations conducted by the subscribing agent may all be used if they correctly reflect the facts. Otherwise, the inapposite description should, of course, be deleted. When appropriate, the description of a different investigative course should be added or substituted based on the facts.

This form is adaptable for use in connection with situations where either an individual or a joint tax return has been filed. The bracketed portions in the second paragraph relate to a joint tax return and should be deleted if an individual return is involved.

Exhibit 700-2

Indictment
Handbook Reference: 725.1 ◊

INDICTMENT

IN THE DISTRICT COURT OF THE UNITED STATES
FOR THE ________ DISTRICT OF ________

UNITED STATES OF AMERICA	)	No. ________ ________
—against—	)	(26 United States Code
________________________	)	Section 7201)

The grand jury charges:

That on or about the ________ day of ________, 19——, in the ________ District of ________, ________, late of ________, did willfully and knowingly attempt to evade and defeat a large part of the income tax due and owing by him/her in the United States of America for the calendar year 19——, by filing and causing to be filed with the Director of Internal Revenue for the ________, Internal Revenue District of ________, at ________, a false and fraudulent income tax return wherein he/she stated that his/her taxable income for said calendar year was the sum of $ ________ and that the amount of tax due and owing thereon was the sum of $ ________, whereas, as he/she then and there well knew, his/her taxable income for the said calendar year was the sum of $ ________, upon which said net income he/she owed to the United States of America an income tax of $ ________.

In violation of Section 7201, Internal Revenue Code; 26 U.S.C., Section 7201.

A True Bill.

____
Foreman

____
United States Attorney

Exhibit 700-3

Information
Handbook Reference: 725.1 ◊

INFORMATION

IN THE DISTRICT COURT OF THE UNITED STATES
FOR THE ________ DISTRICT OF ________

UNITED STATES OF AMERICA) No. ________ ________ ________
—against—) (26 United States Code
) Section 7203)

____

The United States Attorney charges:

That during the calendar year 19——, ________, who was a resident of the City of ________, State of ________, had and received a gross income of $ ________; that by reason of such income he/she was required by law, after the close of the calendar year 19——, and on or before April 15, 19——, to make an income tax return to the Director of Internal Revenue for the ________ Internal Revenue District of ________, stating specifically the items of his/her gross income and any deductions and credits to which he/she was entitled; that well knowing all of the foregoing facts, he/she did willfully and knowingly fail to make said income tax return to the said Director of Internal Revenue, or to any other proper officer of the United States.

In violation of Section 7203, Internal Revenue Code; 26 U.S.C., Section 7203.

Exhibit 700-4

Table of Cases ◊

A

Handbook Section	Case Name and Citation
424.5	Adonis, U.S. v., 221 F 2d 717 (CA-3), 55-1 USTC 9310.
383.5	Aguilar v. Texas, 378 U.S. 108, 84 S. Ct. 1509 (1964).
323.4	Alaska v. American Can Co., 358 U.S. 224, 79 S. Ct. 274 (1958).
413.2, 727	Albanese, U.S. v., 224 F 2d 879 (CA-2), 55-1 USTC 9494, cert. denied 350 U.S. 845.
383.(12)	Alioto v. U.S., 216 F. Supp. 48, 63-1 USTC 9552 (E.D. Wis.).
433, 532, 533	Allen v. U.S., 194 F 2d 664 (CA-4).
323.4	American Can Co., Alaska, v.
411	Amos, In re, (CA-4), 66-1 USTC 9130.
383.3	Amos v. U.S., 255 U.S. 313, 41 S. Ct. 266 (1921).
416.2	Anderson, U.S. v., 328 U.S. 699.
356.3	Angelo, U.S. v., 153 F 2d 247 (CA-3).
383.3	Antonelli Fireworks Co., U.S. v., 155 F 2d 631 (CA-2, 1946).
419.3	Arnold v. U.S., 75 F 2d 144 (CA-9), 35-1 USTC 9086.
344.4	Ashby, U.S. v., 245 F 2d 684 (CA-5), 57-2 USTC 9743.
411	Augustine, U.S. v., 188 F 2d 359 (CA-3), 51-1 USTC 9247.
343.31	Austin-Bagley Corp., U.S. v., 31 F 2d 229 (CA-2, 1929).
445.2	Autenrieth v. Cullen, 418 F 2d 586 (1969), cert. denied, 397 U.S. 1036 (1970).
323.6	Avery v. Comm'r, 1 USTC 254 (CA-5).
41(11).2, 737.82	Ayash v. U.S., 352 F 2d 1009 (CA-10), 65-2 USTC 9739.

B

Handbook Section	Case Name and Citation
342.16	Backer v. Comm'r, 275 F 2d 141 (CA-5), 60-1 USTC 9285.
344.2	Baird v. Koerner, 279 F 2d 623 (CA-9), 60-2 USTC 9527.
41(10).42	Baker v. U.S., 21 F 2d 903 (CA-4), cert. denied 276 U.S. 621.
342.15	Ballantyne v. U.S., 237 F 2d 657 (CA-5), 56-2 USTC 9959.
344.2	Banks v. U.S., 204 F 2d 666 (CA-8, 1953).
41(11).2, 424.4	Barcott v. U.S., 169 F 2d 929 (CA-9), 48-2 USTC 9377.
413.2	Bardin v. U.S., 224 F 2d 255 (CA-7), 55-1 USTC 9488, cert. denied 350 U.S. 383, 76 S. Ct. 134.
41(11).31	Barrow v. U.S., 171 F 2d 286 (CA-5), 49-1 USTC 9112.
73(10)	Barshop v. U.S., 191 F 2d 286 (CA-5), 51-2 USTC 9425, cert. denied 342 U.S. 920, 72 S. Ct. 367.
41(10).3	Bayer, U.S. v., 331 U.S. 532, 67 S. Ct. 1394.
413.2, 419.3, 41(11).2	Beacon Brass Co. v. U.S., 344 U.S. 43, 73 S. Ct. 77, 52-2 USTC 9528.
383.6	Beal v. U.S., 79 F 2d 135.
323.5, 342.12, 41(11).2	Beard v. U.S., 222 F 2d 84 (CA-4), 55-1 USTC 9400, cert. denied 350 U.S. 846, 76 S. Ct. 48.
353.24, 727, 752.1	Beaty v. U.S., 213 F 2d 712 (CA-4), 54-2 USTC 9466, cert. denied 348 U.S. 905, 75 S. Ct. 312.
322.3	Beauchamp v. U.S., 154 F 2d 413 (CA-6, 1946), cert. denied 329 U.S. 723, 67 S. Ct. 66, rehearing denied 329 U.S. 826.
41(10).42	Beck, C. W., U.S. v., 118 F 2d 178 (CA-7, 1941), cert. denied 313 U.S. 587, 61 S. Ct. 1121.
353.24	Beck, Dave, U.S. v., 59-2 USTC 9786.
41(11).33	Beck, Dave, v. U.S., 298 F 2d 622 (CA-9), 62-1 USTC 9227.
532	Beckanstin v. U.S., 232 F 2d 1 (CA-5).
36(10).4	Becker, U.S. v., 58-1 USTC 9403, aff'd 58-2 USTC 9885 (CA-2).
323.5	Bender, U.S. v., 218 F 2d 869 (CA-7), 55-1 USTC 9142.
323.4, 41(11).31	Benetti v. U.S., 97 F 2d 263 (CA-9), 38-2 USTC 9358.

Exhibit 700-4 Cont. (1)

Table of Cases

◊

Handbook Section	Case Name and Citation
343.2	Benjamin, U.S. v., 120 F 2d 521 (CA-2).
323.7	Beno, U.S. v., 324 F 2d 582 (CA-2, 1963).
41(11).31	Berkovitz v. U.S., 213 F 2d 468 (CA-5), 54-1 USTC 9425.
41(11).33	Berra v. U.S., 221 F 2d 590 (CA-8).
418.52	Bittinger, U.S. v., 21 Int. Rev. Rec. 342, 24 Fed. Cases No. 14,599, (W.D. Mo., 1875).
419.3	Black, U.S. v., 216 F. Supp. 645 (W.D. Mo.), 63-2 USTC 9564.
243.2, 244.4, 343.2, 344.4	Blau v. U.S., 340 U.S. 159.
383.3	Block, Joseph Harry, U.S. v., 202 F. Supp. 705 (S.D. N.Y., 1962).
433	Blount, U.S. v., 339 F 2d 331, 64-2 USTC 9863.
41(10).42	Blue v. U.S., 138 F 2d 351 (CA-6, 1943), cert. denied 332 U.S. 736, 64 S. Ct. 1046.
41(10).43	Blumenthal v. U.S., 332 U.S. 539.
532	Boehm v. U.S., 123 F 2d 791 (CA-8), cert. denied 315 U.S. 800, rehearing denied 315 U.S. 828, 62 S. Ct. 794.
367.41	Bolich v. Rubel, 67 F 2d 894 (CA-2), 3 USTC 1184.
367.2	Boren v. Tucker, 239 F 2d 767 (CA-9), 57-1 USTC 9246.
418.22	Borgis, U.S. v., 182 F 2d 274 (CA-7), 50-1 USTC 9330.
426.2	Bostwick v. U.S., 218 F 2d 790 (CA-5), 55-1 USTC 9170.
323.5	Botany Mills v. U.S., 278 U.S. 282.
367.35	Boudreaux, U.S. v., 328 F. Supp. 154, 71-2 USTC 9635 (E.D. La., 1972).
344.2	Boughner, Tillotson v.
344.3	Bouscher, U.S. v., 316 F 2d 451 (CA-8), 63-1 USTC 9424.
344.3	Bowman v. U.S., 236 F. Supp. 548 (M.D. Pa.), 65-1 USTC 9134.
341.31, 342.12, 342.2:(1)	Boyd v. U.S., 116 U.S. 616, 6 S. Ct. 524 (1886).
522	Bradshaw v. U.S., 15 F 2d 970 (CA-9).
	Bratton v. U.S., 73 F 2d 795 (CA-10).
41(10).44	Braverman v. U.S., 317 U.S. 49, 42-2 USTC 9731.
418.62	Bregman, U.S. v., 306 F 2d 653 (CA-3), 62-2 USTC 9589.
41(10).41	Britton, U.S. v., 108 U.S. 199.
41(10).44	Brock v. Hudspeth, 111 F 2d 447 (CA-10).
552.4	Brodson, U.S. v., 155 F. Supp. 407 (E.D. Wis.).
36(10).3, 36(10).31, 36(10).32	Brody v. U.S., 243 F 2d 378 (CA-1), 57-1 USTC 9606, cert. denied 345 U.S. 923, 77 S. Ct. 1384.
383.5	Brooks v. U.S., 303 F 2d 851 (CA-6), cert. denied 371 U.S. 889, 83 S. Ct. 184.
419.4	Brouse v. U.S., 68 F 2d 294 (CA-1, 1933).
367.54	Brownson v. U.S., 32 F 2d 844 (CA-8), 1 USTC 394.
367.51	Brunwasser v. Pittsburgh National Bank (W.D. Pa.), 64-2 USTC 9871.
345.23	Bruton v. U.S., 391 U.S. 123, 88 S. Ct. 1620 (1968).
323.6	Budd v. Comm'r, 43 F 2d 509 (CA-3), 2 USTC 570.
341.31, 367.422	Burdeau v. McDowell, 256 U.S. 465, 41 S. Ct. 574 (1920).
426.3, 426.5	Buttermore v. U.S., 180 F 2d 853 (CA-6), 50-1 USTC 9228.
418.22, 418.42	Butzman v. U.S., 205 F 2d 343 (CA-6), 53-2 USTC 9450.
	C
345.152, 424.2, 424.4	Calderon, U.S. v., 348 U.S. 160, 75 S. Ct. 186, 54-2 USTC 9712.
383.3	California, Stoner v.
352.3	Canister Co. v. U.S., 70 F. Supp. 904, 108 Ct. Cl. 558, cert. denied 332 U.S. 830, 68 S. Ct. 207.
413.2, 426.2	Canton v. U.S., 226 F 2d 313 (CA-8), 55-2 USTC 9705.

Table of Cases ◊

Handbook Section	Case Name and Citation
367.51, 36(10).31	Caplin, Reisman v.
419.3, 426.3	Capone v. U.S., 51 F 2d 609 (CA-7), 2 USTC 786, cert. denied 248 U.S. 669.
344.2	Carliner, Wasserman and, In re.
342.31	Carolene Products Co. v. U.S., 140 F 2d 61 (CA-4, 1944).
367.4	Carroll, App. of, 149 F. Supp. 634, aff'd 246 F 2d 762, 57-2 USTC 9819 (CA-2), cert. denied 355 U.S. 857, 78 S. Ct. 85.
383.3, 383.92	Chapman, Elmer, v. U.S., 365 U.S. 610, 81 S. Ct. 776 (1961).
424.4, 424.5	Chapman, Samuel, U.S. v., 168 F 2d 997 (CA-7), 48-1 USTC 9312, cert. denied 335 U.S. 853, 69 S. Ct. 82.
383.5	Chin Kay v. U.S., 311 F 2d 317 (CA-9), 1962).
367.421	Chin Lim Mow, U.S. v., 12 F.R.D. 433 (N.D. Cal.).
415.21	Cirillo, U.S. v., 251 F 2d 638 (CA-3), 58-1 USTC 9164.
353.21	Clainos v. U.S., 163 F 2d 593 (CA-Dist. of Col.).
344.2	Clark, G. A., v. U.S., 289 U.S. 1, 53 S. Ct. 465 (1933).
413.2, 41(11).31	Clark, J., v. U.S., 211 F 2d 100 (CA-8), 54-1 USTC 9291.
383.3, 383.5, 383.93	Clay, Will P. v. U.S., 239 F 2d 196, 57-2 USTC 9800.
41(10).42	Coates v. U.S., 59 F 2d 173 (CA-9).
418.42	Cohen v. U.S., 201 F 2d 386 (CA-9), 53-1 USTC 9165.
433	Cohen, U.S. v., 231 F. Supp. 171 (S.D. N.Y., 1964).
344.3	Cohen, U.S. v., 388 F 2d 464 (CA-9), 68-1 USTC 9140.
41(11).31	Collins v. Comm'r, 7 BTA 913.
344.2	Colton v. U.S., 306 F 2d 633 (CA-2), 62-2 USTC 9658, cert. denied 371 U.S. 951, 83 S. Ct. 505.
414.12, 414.22, 416.2, 727	Commerford, U.S. v., 64 F 2d 28 (CA-2, 1933).
353.24	Conford v. U.S., 336 F 2d 285 (CA-10), 64-2 USTC 9752.
344.9	Conforti v. U.S., 200 F 2d 365 (CA-7).
41(10).42	Connelly v. U.S., 249 F 2d 576, 57-2 USTC 10,029, cert. denied 356 U.S. 921, pet. for rehearing den. 356 U.S. 964.
367.521	Cooley v. Bergin, 27 F 2d 930 (CA-1), 1 USTC 321.
512.2	Cooper v. U.S., 299 Fed. 483 (CA-3).
424.5	Costello, U.S. v., 221 F 2d 668 (CA-2), 55-1 USTC 9342.
353.21	Cotter, U.S. v., 60 F 2d 689 (CA-2).
367.421	Couch v. U.S., 409 U.S. 322, 73-1 USTC 9159.
41(10).42	Craig v. U.S., 81 F 2d 816 (CA-8), cert. denied 298 U.S. 690.
41(10).43	Cruz v. U.S., 106 F 2d 828 (CA-10).
342.32, 367.51, 367.54, 418.42	Curcio v. U.S., 279 F 2d 681 (CA-2), 60-2 USTC 9514.
322.3	Currier Lumber Co., Inc., U.S. v., 166 F 2d 346 (CA-1), 48-1 USTC 9191.
	D
367.36	D.I. Distributing Co., In re, 240 F. Supp. 672 64-2 USTC 9814.
223.4	Dandridge, App. of, 186 F. Supp. 276 (D.C.N.J., 1960).
322.3	Daniels v. U.S., 17 F 2d 339, cert. denied 274 U.S. 744, 47 S. Ct. 591.
445.2	Daly, U.S. v., 481 F 2d 98, Cert. denied, 414 U.S. 1064 (1973).
445.2	Daly, U.S. v., 481 U.S. 1064 (1973).
344.3	Deck v. U.S., 339 F 2d 739 (CA-D.C.), 64-2 USTC 9581, cert. denied 379 U.S. 967, 85 S. Ct. 660.
41(10).42	Dege, U.S. v., 364 U.S. 51, 80 S. Ct. 1589.
356.3	Desimone v. U.S., 227 F 2d 864 (CA-9).
41(10).2	Diehl v. U.S., 98 F 2d 545 (CA-8).
418.52	Dimmick v. U.S., 116 F 825 (CA-9, 1902).
415.21	DiSilvestro, U.S. v., 147 F. Supp. 300 (E.D. Pa.), 57-1 USTC 9424.

Exhibit 700-4 Cont. (3)

Table of Cases

◊

Handbook Section	Case Name and Citation
362, 367.51	Donaldson v. U.S., 400 U.S. 517, 71-1 USTC 9173.
532	Doto, State v., 16 N.J. 397, 109 Atl 2d 9, cert. denied 349 U.S. 912.
353.24	Doyle, U.S. v., 234 F 2d 788 (CA-7), 56-1 USTC 9553.
383.3, 383.6	Draper v. U.S., 358 U.S. 307, 79 S. Ct. 329.
353.22	Duffin v. People, 107, Ill. 113.
	E
367.36	Edmond, U.S. v., 355 F. Supp. 435, 73-1 USTC 9170 (W.D. Okla., 1972).
533	Edwards, U.S. v., 43 F 67 (Circuit Court, S.D., Ala.).
433	Edwards, Charles L. O., U.S. v., 230 F. Supp. 881 (D.C. Ore.), 64-2 USTC 9739, rev. on other grounds, 67-1 USTC 9356 (CA-9).
353.24	Eggleton v. U.S., 227 F 2d 493 (CA-6), 56-1 USTC 9108, cert. denied 352 U.S. 826, 77 S. Ct. 38.
383.91	Eisner, U.S. v., 297 F 2d 595 (CA-6, 1962).
41(10).42	Eldredge v. U.S., 62 F 2d 449 (CA-10, 1932).
367.53	Electric & Music Industries, Ltd., In re, 155 F. Supp. 892, aff'd 249 F 2d 308 (CA-2).
341.31	Elkins v. U.S., 364 U.S. 206, 80 S. Ct. 1437 (1960).
413.2, 41(11).31	Emmich v. U.S., 298 F 5 (CA-6), 1924 CCH 3481.
342.15	Emspak v. U.S., 349 U.S. 190.
342.133	Escobedo v. Illinois, 378 U.S. 478, 84 S. Ct. 1758 (1964).
356.4	Euge, U.S. v., 587 F 2d 25.
	F
414.12, 415.21	Fago, U.S. v., 58-2 USTC 9820.
41(10).3	Falcone v. U.S., 109 F 2d 579, 581 (CA-2).
342.12, 344.2, 344.3, 361, 367.421, 367.54, 36(10).31, 36(10).33	Falsone v. U.S., 205 F 2d 734 (CA-5), 53-2 USTC 9467, cert. denied on other grounds 346 U.S. 864, 74 S. Ct. 103.
424.5	Feichtmeir v. U.S., 389 F 2d 498 (CA-9), 68-1 USTC 9217.
352.3	Fidelity Trust Co. v. Mayhugh, 268 F 712 (CA-5).
343.4, 367.31, 367.5, 367.52	First Natl. Bank of Mobile v. U.S., 160 F 2d 532 (CA-5), 47-1 USTC 9168, 9203, modifying and affirming 67 F. Supp. 616 (S.D. Ala.), 47-1 USTC 9149.
367.522	First Natl. City Bank of N.Y. v. IRS, 271 F 2d 616 (CA-2), 59-2 USTC 9755, cert. denied 361 U.S. 948, 80 S. Ct. 589.
344.3	Fisher v. U.S., 425 U.S. 391 (1976.)
41(11).31	Fischer v. U.S., 212 F 2d 441 (CA-10), 54-1 USTC 9370.
384.2	Five Coin-Operated Gaming Devices, U.S. v., 154 F. Supp. 731 (D.C. Md.), 57-2 USTC 10,017.
352.3	Fogel v. U.S., 162 F 2d 54 (CA-5).
424.5, 424.7	Ford, Bryan, U.S. v., 237 F 2d 57 (CA-2), 56-2 USTC 9823.
424.5	Ford, Fred v. U.S., 210 F 2d 313 (CA-5), 54-1 USTC 9233.
512.2	Ford, Wm., U.S. v., 33 Fed. 861 (W.D. N.C.).
419.3, 41(10).43, 41(10).46	Forman v. U.S., 361 U.S. 416, 60-1 USTC 9287.
367.51, 41(11).2	Foster, Grant, v. U.S., 309 F 2d 8 (CA-4), 62-2 USTC 9775.
341.31	Four Thousand One Hundred Seventy One Dollars in U.S. Currency, U.S. v., 200 F. Supp. 28 (N.D. Ill., 1961).
41(10).42	Fox, U.S. v., 130 F 2d 56 (CA-3), cert. denied 317 U.S. 666 (1942).
344.9	Fraser v. U.S., 245 F 2d 139 (CA-6), cert. denied 324 U.S. 849, 65 S. Ct. 684.
341.31	Fraternal Order of Eagles v. U.S., 57 F 2d 93 (CA-3, 1932).
418.42	Freidus v. U.S., 223 F 2d 598 (CA-D.C., 1955).

Exhibit 700-4 Cont. (4)

Table of Cases

◊

Handbook Section	Case Name and Citation
424.2, 424.4	Friedberg v. U.S., 348 U.S. 142, 75 S. Ct. 138, 54-2 USTC 9713.
367.422	Fuller, In re, 262 U.S. 91, 43 S. Ct. 496.
342.31, 342.32, 418.52	Fuller v. U.S., 110 F 2d 815 (CA-9).
367.422	Fuller v. U.S., 31 F 2d 747 (CA-2), cert. denied 280 U.S. 556, 50 S. Ct. 17.
	G
533	Galanos v. U.S., 49 F 2d 889 (CA-6).
41(11).2	Gannon, U.S. v., 244 F 2d 541 (CA-2), 57-2 USTC 9701.
413.2	Gariepy v. U.S., 220 F 2d 252 (CA-6), 55-1 USTC 9267, cert. denied 350 U.S. 825.
418.12, 418.42	Gaunt v. U.S., 184 F 2d 284 (CA-1), 50-2 USTC 9412.
413.2	Gendelman v. U.S., 191 F 2d 993 (CA-9), 51-2 USTC 9474.
418.12	Genstil v. U.S., 326 F 2d 243 (CA-1), 64-1 USTC 9187, cert. denied 377 U.S. 916, 84 S. Ct. 1179.
384.52	Gerth v. U.S., 132 F. Supp. 894 (D.C. Cal.).
413.2	Giglio, U.S. v., 232 F 2d 589 (CA-2), 56-1 USTC 9484.
721	Giordenello v. U.S., 357 U.S. 480.
	Gladden v. Self, 55-1 USTC 9227 (E.D. Ark.), aff'd 224 F 2d 282 (CA-8).
41(11).2, 41(11).31	Glascott, U.S. v., 216 F 2d 487 (CA-7), 54-2 USTC 9652.
41(10).42	Glasser v. U.S., 315 U.S. 60, 62 S. Ct. 457 (1942).
413.2, 421, 426.3, 426.4	Gleckman v. U.S., 80 F 2d 394 (CA-8), 35-2 USTC 9645.
424.5	Glenshaw Glass Co., Comm'r. v., 348 U.S. 426, 75 S. Ct. 473, 55-1 USTC 9308.
418.12	Goldbaum v. U.S., 204 F 2d 74 (CA-9), 53-1 USTC 9342.
341.31	Goldberg, Morris C., U.S. v., 330 F 2d 30 (CA-3), 64-1 USTC 9316, cert. denied 377 U.S. 953, 84 S. Ct. 1630.
36(10).32	Goldfine v. U.S., 268 F 2d 941, 59-2 USTC 9598 (CA-1).
345.23	Goldsmith, Warren, U.S. v., 277 F 2d 335 (CA-D.C.), cert. denied 364 U.S. 863, 81 S. Ct. 106.
36(10).32	Goldstein, U.S. v., 105 F 2d 150 (CA-2).
418.42	Gonzales, v. U.S., 286 F 2d 118 (CA-10, 1960), cert. denied 365 U.S. 878, 81 S. Ct. 1028.
343.2	Goodman, U.S. v., 289 F 2d 256 (CA-4), 61-1 USTC 9373, cert. granted, judgment vacated, and case remanded on issue of fact 368 U.S. 14, 82, St. Ct. 127 (1961).
41(10).42	Gordon, U.S. v., 242 F 2d 122 (CA-3), 57-1 USTC 9443, cert. denied 354 U.S. 921.
41(11).32	Gorin v. U.S., 313 F 2d 641 (CA-1), 63-1 USTC 9295, cert. denied 374 U.S. 829, 83 S. Ct. 1870.
418.52	Gottfried, U.S. v., 165 F 2d 360 (CA-2, 1948).
383.3	Gouied v. U.S., 255 U.S. 298, 41 S. Ct. 261 (1921).
367.53	Grand Jury Subpoena Duces Tecum, In re, 72 F. Supp. 1013 (S.D. N.Y.).
342.31	Grant, Walter B., v. U.S., 227 U.S. 74, 33 S. Ct. 190 (1913).
322.3	Gray v. U.S., 260 F 2d 483 (CA-D.C., 1958).
345.23	Gray v. U.S., 9 F 2d 337 (CA-9).
346.55	Greco, U.S. v., 298 F 2d 247, cert. denied 369 U.S. 820, 82 S. Ct. 831.
342.11, 343.2, 727	Gross, Harold, U.S. v., 276 F 2d 816 (CA-2), 60-1 USTC 9401.
343.2, 419.3, 41(10).3, 41(10).43, 41(10).46	Grunewald v. U.S., 353 U.S. 391, 57-1 USTC 9693.
341.31, 342.15, 726.6	Guerrina, U.S. v., 112 F. Supp. 126 (E.D. Pa.), 53-1 USTC 9369.

Exhibit 700-4 Cont. (5)

Table of Cases

◊

Handbook Section	Case Name and Citation
413.2	Guzik v. U.S., 54 F 2d 618 (CA-7).
	H
415.21, 419.3	Habig, U.S. v., 390 U.S. 222 (1968), 88 S. Ct. 926.
41(10).42	Hagen v. U.S., 268 F 344 (CA-9).
323.5, 41(11).2	Haigler v. U.S., 172 F 2d 986 (CA-10), 49-1 USTC 9171.
41(10).41	Halbrook, U.S. v., 36 F. Supp. 345 (E.D. N.Y.).
342.31	Hale v. Henkel, 201 U.S. 43, 26 S. Ct. 370 (1906).
356.3	Hardy v. U.S., 199 F 2d 704 (CA-8).
532	Hart v. U.S., 131 F 2d 59 (CA-9).
345.23	Hartsell v. U.S., 72 F 2d 569 (CA-8).
415.21	Haskell v. U.S., 241 F 2d 790 (CA-10), 57-1 USTC 9553, cert. denied 354 U.S. 921, 77 S. Ct. 1379.
343.5	Hav, U.S. v., 376 F. Supp. 264 (D. Col. 1974).
342.132	Heffner, U.S. v., 420 F 2d 809 (CA-4), 70-1 USTC 9152.
41(11).31	Heindel v. U.S., 150 F 2d 493 (CA-6), 45-2 USTC 9372.
411	Helvering v. Mitchell, 303 U.S. 391, 38-1 USTC 9152.
418.22	Herskovitz, U.S. v., 209 F 2d 881 (CA-2), 54-1 USTC 9182.
419.4	Hewecker, U.S. v., 79 F 59 (S.D. N.Y., 1896).
341.31	Hoffa v. U.S., 385 U.S. 293, 87 S. Ct. 408 (1966).
353.21	Hoffman v. Palmer, 129 F 2d 976 (CA-2), aff'd 318 U.S. 109, 63 S. Ct. 477, rehearing denied 318 U.S. 800, 63 S. Ct. 757.
343.2	Hoffman v. U.S., 341 U.S. 479.
353.24, 413.2, 421, 422, 424.2, 424.3, 424.4, 424.5, 424.7	Holland, U.S. v., 348 U.S. 121, 54-2 USTC 9714.
345.23	Holt v. U.S., 280 F 2d 273 (CA-8).
418.12	Hoover v. U.S., 358 F 2d 87 (CA-5) 66-1 USTC 9343, cert. denied 385 U.S. 822.
345.151, 413.2	Hornstein, U.S. v., 176 F 2d 217 (CA-7), 49-2 USTC 9326.
418.12	Horowitz, U.S. v., 247 F. Supp. 412 (N.D. Ill.), 66-1 USTC 9112.
367.421	House, In re, 144 F. Supp. 95 (N.D. Cal.), 56-2 USTC 9780.
41(11).2	Hoyer v. U.S., 223 F 2d 134 (CA-8), 55-1 USTC 9518.
343.4, 367.31, 367.33, 367.51	Hubner v. Tucker, 245 F 2d 35 (CA-9), 57-1 USTC 9362.
41(10).44	Hudspeth, Brock v.
418.22	Hull v. U.S., 324 F 2d 817 (CA-5), 63-2 USTC 9821.
41(10).42	Hyde v. U.S., 226 U.S. 347, 32 S. Ct. 793 (1911).
	I
41(11).33, 726.5	Iozia, U.S. v., 13 F.R.D. 335 (S.D. N.Y.).
367.53	International Commodities Corp. v. I.R.S., 224 F 2d 882 (CA-2), 55-1 USTC 9526.
367.31, 367.41	International Corp. Co., In re, 5 F. Supp. 608 (S.D. N.Y.), 4 USTC 1225.
	J
419.4, 721	Jaben v. U.S., 381 U.S. 214, 65-1 USTC 9408.
41(11).33	James v. U.S., 366 U.S. 213, 81 S. Ct. 1052.
413.2	Jannuzzio, U.S. v., 184 F. Supp. 460 (D.C. Del.), 60-2 USTC 9512.
383.3, 384.2	Jeffers, U.S. v., 342 U.S. 48, 72 S. Ct. 93 (1951).
421	Jelaza v. U.S., 179 F 2d 202 (CA-4), 50-1 USTC 9149.

Table of Cases ◊

Handbook Section	Case Name and Citation
41(10).44	Johnson, Donald, U.S. v., 165 F 2d 42 (CA-3), cert. denied 332 U.S. 852.
41(10).42	Johnson, Graham, v. U.S., 62 F 2d 32 (CA-9).
322.3, 321, 425.2	Johnson, Wm. R., U.S. v., 319 U.S. 503, 63 S. Ct. 1233, 43-1 USTC 9470.
383.3, 383.5	Jones, Cecil, v. U.S., 362 U.S. 257, 80 S. Ct. 725 (1960).
344.4	Jones, Nelson, E., U.S. v., unreported opinion, No. 31442R (S.D. Cal.) 1948.
383.(12)	Joseph, U.S. v., 174 F. Supp. 539 (E.D. Pa., 1960), aff'd 278 F 2d 504, cert. denied 364 U.S. 823.
344.2, 344.3	Judson, U.S. v., 322 F 2d 460 (CA-9), 63-2 USTC 9658.
	K
41(11).32	Kabot, U.S. v., 295 F 2d 848 (CA-2), 61-2 USTC 9746, cert. denied 369 U.S. 803, 82 S. Ct. 641.
413.2	Kafes, U.S. v., 214 F 2d 887 (CA-3), 54-2 USTC 9492.
342.11	Kastigar v. U.S., 406 U.S. 441, 92 S. Ct. 2478 (1972).
341.33	Katz v. U.S., 389 U.S. 347 (1967), 88 S. Ct. 507.
418.22, 727	Kelley, U.S. v., 105 F 2d 912 (CA-2), 39-2 USTC 9621.
522	Kemler v. U.S., 133 F 2d 235 (CA-1).
367.31	Kenefick, Pacific Mills v.
383.5	King v. U.S., 282 F 2nd 398 (CA-4).
426.3, 426.5	Kirsch v. U.S., 174 F 2d 595 (CA-8), 49-1 USTC 9274.
352.3	Klein v. U.S., 176 F 2d 184 (CA-8).
323.4	Knapp-Monarch Co., App. of, 296 F 2d 230 (Ct. of Customs & Patent Appeals, 1961).
41(11).1	Kobey v. U.S., 208 F 2d 583 (CA-9), 54-1 USTC 9106.
344.2	Koerner, Baird v.
344.2	Kovel, U.S. v., 296 F 2d 918 (CA-2), 62-1 USTC 911.
41(10).43	Krulewitch v. U.S., 336 U.S. 440.
367.523	Kyle, U.S. v., 21 R.F.D. 163 (E.D., N.Y.).
	L
323.4	Lamar v. Micou, 114 U.S. 218, 5 S. Ct. 857 (1885).
342.12	Landy v. U.S., 283 F 2d 303 (CA-5), 60-2 USTC 9765, cert. denied 365 U.S. 845, 81 S. Ct. 805.
413.2	Lange, U.S. v., 161 F 2d 699 (CA-7), 47-1 USTC 9249.
721	Langsdale, U.S. v., 115 F. Supp. 489 (W.D. Mo.).
367.2	LaSalle National Bank, U.S. v.
726.6	Lassoff, U.S. v., 51-1 USTC 9639 (E.D. Ky.).
341.31	Lassoff v. Gray, (W.D. Ky.), 62-2 USTC 15,421, 15,431.
342.2, 342.31, 342.32	Lawn, U.S. v., 115 F. Supp. 674 (S.D. N.Y.), 53-1 USTC 9288.
345.14	Leach & Co. v. Pierson, 275 U.S. 120, 48 S. Ct. 57.
342.132	Leahey, U.S. v., 434 F 2d 7 (CA-1), 70-2 USTC 9636.
343.5	Leal, U.S. v., 509 F. 2d 122 (9th Cir. 1975).
322.3	Legatos v. U.S., 222 F 2d 678 (CA-9), 55-1 USTC 9443.
322.3	Lester, U.S. v., 363 F 2d 68 (CA-6, 1966).
533	Letchos, U.S. v., 316 F 2d 481 (CA-7), 63-1 USTC 9451, cert. denied 375 U.S. 824, 84 S. Ct. 65.
384.2	Leveson, U.S. v., 262 F 2d 659 (CA-5), 59-1 USTC 15,212.
418.42	Leviton, U.S. v., 193 F 2d 848 (CA-2, 1951).
41(10).42	Lewis, Al, v. U.S., 11 F 2d 745 (CA-6).
342.15	Lipshitz, U.S. v., 132 F. Supp. 519 (E.D. N.Y.), 55-2 USTC 9540.

Exhibit 700-4 Cont. (7)

Table of Cases ◊

Handbook Section	Case Name and Citation
323.6, 342.15, 353.22, 353.3, 41(10).42	Lisansky v. U.S., 31 F 2d 846 (CA-4), cert. denied 279 U.S. 873.
323.6	Littlefield, U.S. v., 56-2 USTC 10,083 (S.D. Fla.).
367.31, 367.51, 36(10).33	Local 174, etc. v. U.S., 240 F 2d 387 (CA-9), 56-1 USTC 9136.
511.2	Lombardozzi, U.S. v., 335 F 2d 414 (CA-2, 1964), cert. denied 379 U.S. 914, 85 S. CT. 261.
343.2, 41(11).2	Long, Merle, U.S. v., 58-2 USTC 9621 (CA-3).
41(11).32	Lopez v. U.S., 373 U.S. 427, 83 S. Ct. 1381 (1963).
41(11).31	Lurding v. U.S., 179 F 2d 419 (CA-6), 50-1 USTC 9159.
383.3	Lustig v. U.S., 338 U.S. 74, 69 S. Ct. 1372 (1949).
344.3	Lustman v. Comm'r., 332 F 2d 253 (CA-3), 63-2 USTC 9677.
41(10).43	Lutwak v. U.S., 344 U.S. 604.
	Mc
342.11	McCarthy v. Arndstein, 266 U.S. 34, 45 S. Ct. 16 (1924).
415.21, 41(11).31	McCormick, U.S. v., 67 F 2d 867 (CA-2), 3 USTC 1187, cert. denied, 291 U.S. 662.
418.42	McCue, U.S. v., 301 F 2d 452 (CA-2), 62-1 USTC 9359, cert. denied, 370 U.S. 939, 82 S. Ct. 1586.
352.3	McDonald, C., v. U.S., 89 F 2d 128 (CA-8).
344.2	McDonald, Thomas G., U.S. v., 313 F 2d 832 (CA-2), 63-1 USTC 9313.
344.2, 424.4, 425.1, 425.4	McFee v. U.S., 206 F 2d 872 (CA-9), 53-2 USTC 9549.
419.4	McGowen v. U.S., 105 F 2d 791 (CA-D.C.), (1944).
352.3	McKnight v. U.S., 115 Fed. 972 (CA-6).
323.5	McKenna v. U.S., 232 F 2d 431 (CA-8), 56-1 USTC 9492.
345.23	McNabb v. U.S., 318 U.S. 332, 63 S. Ct. 608, rehearing denied, 319 U.S. 784, 63 S. Ct. 1322.
	M
342.11, 343.2	Malloy v. Hogan, 378 U.S. 1, 84 S. Ct. 1489 (1964).
418.52	Mandile, U.S. v., 119 F. Supp. 266 (E.D. N.Y.), 54-1 USTC 9277.
367.33	Mangone, Philip Co., v. U.S., 54 F 2d 168, 73 S. Ct. Cls. 239.
353.21	Manton, U.S. v., 107 F 2d 834 (CA-2).
383.3	Mapp v. Ohio, 367 U.S. 643, 81 S. Ct. 1684 (1961).
41(10).41, 41(10).42	Marino v. U.S., 91 F 2d 691 (CA-9).
424.5	Massei, U.S. v. 355 U.S. 595, 78 S. Ct. 495, 58-1 USTC 9326.
345.16	Massiah v. U.S., 377 U.S. 201, 84 S. Ct. 1199 (1964).
342.133	Mathis v. U.S., 391 U.S. 1, 88 S. Ct. 1503, 68-1 USTC 9357.
352.3	Mayhugh, Fidelity Trust Co., v.
383.5	Merritt, Regina v. U.S., 249 F 2d 19 (CA-6), 57-2 USTC 10,000.
433	Mesheski, U.S. v., 286 F 2d 345 (CA-7), 61-1 USTC 9233.
522	Michelson, U.S. v., 165 F 2d 732 (CA-2), 335 U.S. 469, 69 S. Ct. 213.
323.4	Micou, Lamar v.
424.7	Mighell v. U.S., 223 F 2d 731 (CA-10), 56-2 USTC 9630, cert. denied 352 U.S. 832, 77 S. Ct. 47.
367.31	Miles v. United Founders Corp., 5 F. Supp. 413 (D.C. N.J.), 3 USTC 1061.
367.523, 367.53	Minas De Artemisa, Securities & Exchange Commission v.
383.94	Minker, U.S. v., 312 F 2d 632 (CA-3), 63-1 USTC 15,458, cert. denied 372 U.S. 953, 83 S. Ct. 952.
242.133	Miranda v. Arizona, 384 U.S. 436, 86 S. Ct. 1602 (1966).
345.23	Mitchell, James, U.S. v., 332 U.S. 65, 64 S. Ct. 896.
344.4, 344.9	Mitchell, William, U.S. v., 137 F 2d 1006 (CA-2).

Exhibit 700-4 Cont. (8)

Table of Cases

◊

Handbook Section	Case Name and Citation
343.4, 367.521	Mobile, First National Bank of, U.S. v.
726.5	Montgomery, J. R. v. U.S., 203 F 2d 887 (CA-5), 53-1 USTC 9336.
411	Moore, Jerome H. v. U.S., (CA-4), 66-1 USTC 9131.
532, 533	Moran, U.S. v., 194 F 2d 623 (CA-2), cert. denied 343 U.S. 965.
532	Moretti, People v., 349 Ill. App. 67, 109 N.E. 2d 915.
41(11).2	Morrissette v. U.S., 342 U.S. 246.
41(11).2, 422:(3)	Morrison v. U.S., 270 F 2d 1 (CA-4), 59-2 USTC 9657.
419.3	Mousley, U.S. v., 194 F. Supp. 119 (E.D. Pa.), 61-2 USTC 9515.
344.5	Mullen v. U.S., 263 F 2d 275 (CA-D.C.).
36(10).4, 413.2, 415.23, 41(11).1	Murdock, U.S. v., 290 U.S. 389, 3 USTC 1194.
342.11, 343.2	Murphy v. N.Y. Waterfront Comm., 378 U.S. 52, 84 S. Ct. 1594 (1964).
356.3	Murray v. U.S., 247 F 874 (CA-4).
323.5, 342.12, 413.2	Myres v. U.S., 174 F 2d 329 (CA-8), 49-1 USTC 9275, cert. denied 338 U.S. 849.
	N
418.42	Neely v. U.S., 300 F 2d 67 (CA-9), 62-1 USTC 9297.
727	Newton v. U.S., 162 F 2d 795 (CA-4), 47-2 USTC 9353, cert. denied 333 U.S. 848, 68 S. Ct. 650.
342.15	Nicola v. U.S., 72 F 2d 680 (CA-3), 4 USTC 1331.
367.422, 413.2	Noro v. U.S., 148 F 2d 696 (CA-5), 45-1 USTC 9272, cert. denied 326 U.S. 720.
413.2	Nunan, U.S. v., 236 F 2d 576 (CA-2), 56-2 USTC 9876, cert. denied 353 U.S. 912.
	O
413.2	O'Brien v. U.S., 51 F 2d 193 (CA-7), 1931 CCH 9474 cert. denied 284 U.S. 673, 52 S. Ct. 129.
343.2	O'Connell v. U.S., 40 F 2d 201 (CA-2).
552.4	O'Connor, Kenneth A., v., U.S., 203 F 2d 301 (CA-4), 53-1 USTC 9324.
726.5	O'Connor, Raymond A., U.S. v., 237 F 2d 466 (CA-2), 56-2 USTC 9956.
352.3	O'Donnell v. U.S., 91 F 2d 14 (CA-9), cert. granted, U.S. v. O'Donnell, 302 U.S. 677, 58 S. Ct. 146, rev. on other grounds, 303 U.S. 501, 58 S. Ct. 708.
41(10).42	Old Monastery Company v. U.S., 147 F 2d 905.
344.2, 344.9, 245.152	Olender v. U.S., 210 F 2d 795 (CA-9), 54-1 USTC 9254.
426.3	Oliver v. U.S., 54 F 2d 48 (CA-7), cert. denied 285 U.S. 545, 52 S. Ct. 395.
41(10).42	Olmstead, U.S. v., 5 F 22d 712.
323.5, 342.12, 41(11).2	Olson v. U.S., 191 F 2d 985 (CA-8), 51-2 USTC 9468.
342.2, 367.54	Onassis, U.S. v., 125 F. Supp. 190 (D.C. Dist. of Col., 1954).
384.2	One 1953 Glider Trailer, U.S. v., 120 F. Supp. 504 (E.D. N.C., 1954).
384.2	One 1953 Oldsmobile Sedan, U.S. v., 132 F. Supp. 14 (W.D. Ark.), 55-1 USTC 9510.
384.2	One 1958 Plymouth Sedan v. Pa., 380 U.S. 693, 85 S. Ct. 1246 (1965).
384.2	One Thousand Fifty Eight Dollars in Currency, U.S. v., 323 F 2d 211 (CA-3), 63-2 USTC 15, 526.

Exhibit 700-4 Cont. (9)

Table of Cases

◊

Handbook Section	Case Name and Citation
	P
367.31	Pacific Mills v. Kenefick, 99 F 2d 188 (CA-1), 38-2 USTC 9510.
414.12, 41(11).1	Paddock v. Siemoneit, 49-1 USTC 9202.
323.6	Paddock v. U.S., 280 F 2d 563 (CA-2), 60-2 USTC 9571.
726.5	Palermo, Anthony, U.S. v., 21 F.R.D. 11 (S.D. N.Y.), 57-2 USTC 9911.
346.55, 737.82	Palermo, Anthony, v. U.S., 360 U.S. 343, 79 S. Ct. 1217, 59-2 USTC 9532.
415.22	Palermo, Frank, U.S. v., 152 F. Supp. 825 (E.D. Pa.), 58-1 USTC 9137, rev'd in part 58-2 USTC 9850.
41(11).32	Papadakis v. U.S., 208 F 2d 944 (CA-9), 54-1 USTC 9137.
415.23, 41(11).2	Pappas v. U.S., 216 F 2d 515 (CA-10), 54-2 USTC 9637.
346.55, 737.82	Papworth, U.S. v., 156 F. Supp. 842 (N.D. Tex., 1957).
41(11).2	Paschen v. U.S., 70 F 2d 491 (CA-7).
418.42	Paternostro v. U.S., 311 F 2d 298 (CA-5), 62-2 USTC 9808.
36(10).31	Patterson, U.S. v., 219 F 2d 659 (CA-2), 55-1 USTC 9189.
419.3	Pendergast v. U.S., 317 U.S. 412.
344.4	Pereira v. U.S., 202 F 2d 830 (CA-5).
367.422	Perlman v. U.S., 247 U.S. 7, 38 S. Ct. 417.
533	Phair v. U.S., 60 F 2d 953 (CA-3).
41(11).31	Phillips, U.S. v., 217 F 2d 435 (CA-7), 54-2 USTC 9707.
41(10).43	Pinkerton v. U.S., 328 U.S. 640.
367.51	Pittsburgh Nat'l Bank, Brunwasser, v.
414.22	Plotkin, U.S. v., 239 F. Supp. 129 (E.D. Wis.), 65-1 USTC 9441.
342.32, 36(10).32	Pollock, U.S. v., 201 F. Supp. 542 (W.D. Ark.), 62-1 USTC 9231.
344.2, 367.54	Pollock v. U.S., 202 F 2d 281 (CA-5), 53-1 USTC 9229.
41(10).42	Pomerantz v. U.S., 51 F 2d 911 (CA-3).
540	Pomponio, U.S.v., 429 U.S. 10(1976).
323.4	Porter v. Sunshine Packing Co., 81 F. Supp. 566 (W.D. Pa., 1948).
344.7	Portomene v. U.S., 221 F 2d 582 (CA-5).
418.22	Potsada, U.S. v., 206 F. Supp. 792 (N.D. Cal.), 62-2 USTC 12, 117.
41(11).31	Pottash Bros. v. Comm'r, 50 F 2d 317 (CA-DC 1931).
367.32	Powell, Max, U.S. v., 379 U.S. 48, 85 S. Ct. 248 (1964).
383.3	Pugliese, U.S. v., 153 F 2d 497 (CA-2, 1945).
	Q
342.15	Quinn v. U.S., 349 U.S. 155.
343.5	Quong, U.S. v., 303 F 2d 409 (6th Cir. 1062).
	R
418.12	Rayor, U.S. v., 204 F. Supp. 486 (S.D. Cal.), 62-2 USTC 9607.
36(10).32	Reicher, In re, 159 F. Supp. 161 (S.D. N.Y.), 58-1 USTC 9324.
323.6	Reis v. Comm'r, 1 TC 9, 142 F 2d 900 (CA-6), 44-1 USTC 9347.
367.2, 367.51, 36(10).3, 36(10).32	Reisman v. Caplin, 375 U.S. 440, 84 S. Ct. 508, 64-1 USTC 9202.
352.3	Reyburn, U.S. v., 31 U.S. (6 Peters) 352.
342.31	Richardson, U.S. v., 469 F 2d 349 (CA-10), 72-2 USTC 9765.
352.3	Riggs v. Tayloe, 9 Wheaton (U.S.) 483.
356.3	Rinker v. U.S., 151 F 755 (CA-8).
367.522	Rivera, In re, 79 F. Supp. 510 (S.D. N.Y.), 48-2 USTC 9340.
323.6	Rodd v. Fahs, 56-2 USTC 9696 (S.D. Fla.).
41(11).32	Roett, U.S. v., 172 F 2d 379 (CA-3, 1949), cert. denied 336 U.S. 960, 69 S. Ct. 889.
356.3	Rogers v. Ritter, 12 Wallace (79 U.S.) 317.
342.15	Rogers v. U.S., 340 U.S. 367.

Table of Cases ◊

Handbook Section	Case Name and Citation
41(11).33	Rollinger v. U.S., 208 F 2d 109 (CA-8).
419.3, 41(10).46	Rosenblum, et al., U.S., v., 176 F 2d 321 (CA-7), 49-1 USTC 9314.
332.23, 344.8	Roviari v. U.S., 353 U.S. 53, 77 S. Ct. 623 (1957).
367.4	Rubel, Bolich v.
332.23, 344.8, 383.5	Rugendorf v. U.S., 376 U.S. 528, 84 S. Ct. 825 (1964).
384.52	Rush v. U.S., 256 F 2d 862 (CA-10).
323.4	Russell, U.S. v., 146 F. Supp. 102 (S.D. N.Y., 1955).
41(11).33	Rutkin v. U.S., 343 U.S. 130, 72 S. Ct. 571, 52-1 USTC 9260.
367.32	Ryan, Bayard Edward, v. U.S., 216 F 13 (CA-7), cert. denied 232 U.S. 726.
41(10).46	Ryan v. U.S., 216 F 13 (CA-7), cert. denied 232 U.S. 726.
383.3	Rykowski, U.S. v., 267 F 2d 866 (S.D. Ohio, 1920).
	S
41(11).31	Samish v. U.S., 223 F 2d 358 (CA-9), 55-1 USTC 9499.
36(10).31	Sauber v. Whetstone, 199 F 2d 520 (CA-7), 52-2 USTC 9497, cert. denied 344 U.S. 928, 73 S. Ct. 496.
383.5	Sawyer, U.S. v., 213 F. Supp. 38 (E.D. Pa., 1963).
424.8	Scanlon v. U.S., 223 F 2d 382 (CA-1), 55-1 USTC 9508.
353.24, 413.2	Schenck v. U.S., 126 F 2d 702 (CA-2), 42-1 USTC 9363, cert. denied 316 U.S. 705.
418.12	Schepps v. U.S., 395 F 2d 749 (CA-5), 68-2 USTC 9523.
332.23, 344.8	Scher v. U.S., 305 U.S. 251, 59 S. Ct. 174 (1938).
353.21	Schmeller v. U.S., 143 F 2d 544 (CA-6).
726.5	Schneider v. U.S., 192 F 2d 498 (CA-9), cert. denied 343 U.S. 914, 72 S. Ct. 646.
332.23, 726.5	Schneiderman, U.S. v., 104 F. Supp. 405 (S.D. Cal.).
344.2	Schulze v. Rayunec, 350 F 2d 666 (CA-7), 65-2 USTC 9549, cert. denied. Boughner v. Schulze, 382 U.S. 919, 86 S. Ct. 293.
36(10).3, 36(10).32	Schwartz, Comm'r v., 247 F 2d 70 (CA-D.C.), 57-1 USTC 9622.
367.421	Schwimmer v. U.S., 232 F 2d 855 (CA-8), 56-2 USTC 9711, cert. denied 352 U.S. 833, 77 S. Ct. 48.
512.2	Scolnick, U.S. v., 392 F 2d 320 (CA-3), 68-2 USTC 9466.
367.523, 367.53	Securities & Exchange Commission v. Minas De Artemisa, 150 F 2d 215 (CA-9).
332.23	Segurola v. U.S., 16 F 2d 563 (CA-1).
352.3	Sellmayer Packing Co. v. Comm'r 146 F 2d 707 (CA-4).
383.3	Sergio, U.S. v., 21 F. Supp. 533 (E.D. N.Y., 1937).
383.3	Sferas, U.S. v., 210 F 2d 69 (CA-7, 1954).
737.82	Sheer, U.S. v., 278 F 2d 65 (CA-7), 60-1 USTC 15,299.
41(11).32	Sherman v. U.S., 356 U.S. 369, 78 S. Ct. 819 (1958).
726.6	Silbert, U.S. v., 150 F. Supp. 456 (D.C. Md.), 57-2 USTC 9799.
418.42	Silver, U.S. v., 235 F 2d 375 (CA-2, 1956), cert. denied 352 U.S. 880, 77 S. Ct. 102.
342.2	Silverstein, In re U.S. v., 314 F 2d 789, 63-1 USTC 9346.
731.2	Singer v. U.S., 380 U.S. 24, 85 S. Ct. 783 (1965).
418.12	Siravo v. U.S., 377 F 2d 469 (CA-1), 67-1 USTC 9446.
424.5	Skidmore, U.S. v., 123 F 2d 604 (CA-7), 41-2 USTC 9716, cert. denied 315 U.S. 800, 62 S. Ct. 626.
41(10).45	Slater, U.S. v., 278 F 266 (E.D. Pa.).
533	Slutzky, U.S. v., 79 F 2d 504 (CA-3).
345.152, 345.24, 424.2, 424.4, 424.6	Smith, Dan'l, v. U.S., 348 U.S. 147, 75 S. Ct. 194, 54-2 USTC 9715.
342.11, 342.15	Smith, George, v. U.S., 337 S. Ct. 1000 (1949).

Exhibit 700-4 Cont. (11)

◊

Table of Cases

Handbook Section	Case Name and Citation
533	Smith, J. Robt., v. U.S., 169 F 2d 118 (CA-6).
323.5, 342.12, 41(11).2, 424.7	Smith, Louis C., v. U.S., 236 F 2d 260 (CA-8), 56-2 USTC 9380, cert. denied 352 U.S. 909, 77 S. Ct. 148.
41(11).32	Sorrels v. United States, 287 U.S. 435, 53 S. Ct. 210 (1932).
345.23	Spano v. N.Y., 360 U.S. 315, 79 S. Ct. 1202.
413.2, 415.22, 41(11).1	Spies v. U.S., 317 U.S. 492, 63 S. Ct. 56, 43-1 USTC 9243.
418.42	Stark, U.S. v., 131 F. Supp. 190 (D.C. Md., 1955).
345.151	Stayback, U.S. v., 212 F 2d 313 (CA-3), 54-1 USTC 9345.
353.24, 752.1	Steele v. U.S., 222 F 2d 628 (CA-5), 55-1 USTC 9438.
383.3	Stein v. U.S., 166 F 2d 851 (CA-9, 1948).
532	Steinberg v. U.S., 14 F 2d 564 (CA-2).
367.4	Stiles, U.S. v., 56 F. Supp. 881 (D.C. Ark.) 44-2 USTC 9485.
426.3, 426.4	Stinnett v. U.S., 173 F 2d 129 (CA-4), 49-1 USTC 9217, cert. denied 337 U.S. 957, 69 S. Ct. 1531.
413.2, 41(11).3	Stoehr, U.S. v., 196 F 2d 276 (CA-3), 52-1 USTC 9299, affirming 100 F. Supp. 143 (D.C. Pa.), 52-1 USTC 9119.
383.93	Stoffey, U.S. v., 279 F 2d 924, 60-2 USTC 15,303.
383.3	Stoner v. California, 376 U.S. 483, 84 S. Ct. 889 (1964).
419.4	Streep v. U.S., 160 U.S. 128.
367.422	Stroud v. U.S., 251 U.S. 15, 40 S. Ct. 50.
367.54	Subpoena Duces Tecum, In re, 81 F. Supp. 418 (N.D. Calif., 1948).
439.2	Sullivan, U.S. v., 27 U.S. 259 (1927).
552.4	Summers v. U.S., 250 F 2d 132 (CA-9).
323.6	Sunderland, U.S. v., 56-2 USTC 9651 (D.C. Colo.).
323.4	Sunshine Packing Co., Porter v.
383.3	Sutherland v. U.S., 92 F 2d 305.
41(11).2, 41(11).3	Swidler v. U.S., 55-1 USTC 9319 (E.D. Pa.), aff'd 220 F 2d 351 (CA-3), 55-1 USTC 9320, cert. denied 346 U.S. 915.
439.2	Swallow, U.S. v., 325 F 2d 97 (1963) cert. denied, 377 U.S. 951 (1964).
	T
344.2	Tellier, U.S. v., 255 F 2d 441 (CA-2, 1958).
41(10).43	Telman v. U.S., 67 F 2d 716 (CA-10), cert. denied 292 U.S. 650.
342.31	Theodore Acctg. Service, P.A., U.S. v., 72-2 USTC 9690 (D.C. S.C.).
367.2, 367.5, 371	Third Northwestern National Bank, U.S. v., 102 F. Supp. 879 (D.C. Minn.), 52-1 USTC 9302.
41(10).42	Thomas, U.S. v., 52 F. Supp. 571 (Wash., 1953).
344.2	Tillotson v. Boughner, 350 F 2d 663 (CA-7), 65-2 USTC 9548.
413.2	Tinkoff v. U.S., 86 F 2d 868 (CA-7), 36-2 USTC 9487.
41(11).32	Todisco v. U.S., 298 F 2d 208 (CA-9), 61-2 USTC 9749, cert. denied 368 U.S. 989, 82 S. Ct. 602.
411	Tomlinson v. Lefkowitz, 334 F 2d 262 (CA-5), 64-2 USTC 9623.
344.5	Totten v. U.S., 92 U.S. 105.
411	Troy, U.S. v., 293 U.S. 58, 35-1 USTC 9002.
344.4	Trammel, U.S. v., 445 U.S.—(1980).
383.3, 384.2	Trupiano v. U.S., 334 U.S. 699, 68 S. Ct. 1229.
341.33:(19)	Tijerina, U.S. v., 412 U.S. 661 (10th Cir. 1969).
	U
366	United Distillers Products Corp., U.S. v., 156 F 2d 872 (CA-2), 46-2 USTC 9327.
367.31	United Founders Corp., Miles v.
345.23	Upshaw v. U.S., 335 U.S. 410, 69 S. Ct. 176.

Exhibit 700-4 Cont. (12)

Table of Cases

◊

Handbook Section	Case Name and Citation
	V
342.12, 342.15	Vadner, U.S. v., 119 F. Supp. 330 (E.D. Pa.), 54-1 USTC 9173.
424.7	Vardine, U.S. v., 305 F 2d 60 (CA-2), 62-2 USTC 9624.
424.4	Vassallo, U.S. v., 181 F 2d 1006 (CA-3), 50-1 USTC 9320.
344.2	Vehicular Parking Ltd., U.S. v., 52 F. Supp. 751 (D.C. Del., 1943).
367.2	Venn v. U.S., 400 F 2d 207 (CA-5), 68-2 USTC 9518.
383.5	Ventresca, U.S. v., 380 U.S. 102, 85 S. Ct. 741 (1965).
426.3, 426.4	Venuto, U.S. v., 182 F 2d 519 (CA-3), 50-1 USTC 9333.
383.3	Villano v. U.S., 310 F 2d 680 (CA-10, 1962).
345.23	Vita, U.S. v., 294 F 2d 524 (CA-2).
353.32, 424.4	Vloutis v. U.S., 219 F 2d 782 (CA-5), 55-1 USTC 9262.
322.3	Von Patzoll v. U.S., 163 F. 2d 216 (CA-10), cert. denied 332 U.S. 809, 68 S. Ct. 110.
	W
439.2	Wangrud, U.S. v., 533 F 2d 495 (1976).
341.31	Walder v. U.S., 347 U.S. 62, 74 S. Ct. 354 (1954).
41(10).3	Waldin v. U.S., 149 F. Supp. 912 (E.D. Pa.), 57-1 USTC 9672.
727	Warring, U.S. v., 121 F. Supp. 546 (D.C. Md.), 54-2 USTC 9433.
345.151	Warszower v. U.S., 312 U.S. 342, 61 S. Ct. 603.
383.4	Washington v. U.S., 202 F 2d 214, U.S. App. D.C., cert. denied 345 U.S. 956, 73 S. Ct. 938.
344.2	Wasserman and Carliner, In re, 198 F. Supp. 564 (DC-D.C.), 61-2 USTC 9730.
533	Weber, U.S. v., 197 F 2d 237 (CA-2), cert. denied 344 U.S. 834, 73 S. Ct. 42.
341.31	Weeks v. U.S., 232 U.S. 383, 34 S. Ct. 341 (1914).
532	Weiler, U.S. v., 143 F 2d 204 (CA-3), Rev. on other grounds 323 U.S. 606, 65 S. Ct. 548.
41(11).2	Weiss v. U.S., 122 F 2d 675 (CA-5).
323.5	Welch v. Helvering, 290 U.S. 111.
726.6	Wheeler, U.S. v., 149 F. Supp. 445 (W.D. Pa.), 57-2 USTC 9752, Reversed on other grounds 256 F 2d 745, 58-2 USTC 9626 (CA-3).
342.2, 367.54	White, Jasper, U.S. v., 322 U.S. 694, 64 S. Ct. 1248 (1944).
41(11).31	Wicoff, U.S. v., 187 F 2d 886 (CA-7, 1951).
41(11).33	Wilcox v. Comm'r., 327 U.S. 404, 66 S. Ct. 546.
345.23	Williams v. U.S., 273 F 2d 798 (CA-9).
41(11).32	Williamson v. U.S., 311 F 2d 441 (CA-5, 1962).
413.2	Willingham v. U.S., 289 F 2d 283 (CA-5), 61-1 USTC 9401.
344.2	Willis, U.S., 145 F. Supp. 365 (M.D. Ga., 1955).
413.2, 414.12, 41(11).1	Wilson, Arthur, v. U.S., 250 F 2d 312 (CA-9), 57-2 USTC 10,040, petition for rehearing denied 264 F 2d 74, 58-1 USTC 9463.
342.31	Wilson, C. C., v. U.S., 221 U.S. 361, 31 S. Ct. 538 (1911).
344.9	Winfree, U.S. v., 59-1 USTC 9323 (E.D. Pa.).
356.3	Woitte v. U.S., 19 F 2d 506 (CA-9).
344.4	Wolfle v. U.S., 291 U.S. 7, 54 S. Ct. 279.
345.23	Wong Sun v. U.S., 371 U.S. 471, 83 S. Ct. 407 (1963).
323.6	Wood v. Comm'r, 245 F 2d 888 (CA-5), 57-2 USTC 9790.
41(10).42	Wortman, U.S. v., 326 F 2d 717 (CA-7), 64-1 USTC 9201.
418.12, 418.22	Wyman, U.S. v., 125 F. Supp. 276 (W.D. Mo.), 52-2 USTC 9564.
41(11).33	Wyss, U.S. v., 239 F 2d 658 (CA-7).

Exhibit 700-4 Cont. (13)

Table of Cases

◊

Handbook Section	Case Name and Citation
	Y
415.21, 727	Yarborough v. U.S., 230 F 2d 56 (CA-4), 56-1 USTC 9295, cert. denied 351 U.S. 969, 76 S. Ct. 1034.
344.4	Yoder v. U.S., 80 F 2d 665 (CA-10).
413.2	Yoffe v. U.S., 153 F 2d 570 (CA-1), 46-1 USTC 9171.
342.15	Young, Watson A., U.S. v., 215 F. Supp. 202 (E.D. Mich.), 63-1 USTC 9483.
	Z
353.23	Zacher v. U.S., 227 F 2d 219 (CA-8), 55-2 USTC 9745.
418.42	Zambito, U.S. v., 315 F 2d 266 (CA-4, 1963), cert. denied 373 U.S. 924, 83 S. Ct. 1524.
353.22	Zap v. U.S., 328 U.S. 624, 66 S. Ct. 1277.
367.33, 367.51, 367.54	Zimmerman v. Wilson, 105 F 2d 583 (CA-3), 39-2 USTC 9540.

www.ingramcontent.com/pod-product-compliance
Lightning Source LLC
Chambersburg PA
CBHW082129210326
41599CB00031B/5917